Brief Contents

Part I: The Nature of the Phenomena

Part II: Deceptive Behavior

Part III: Lie Detection

Part IV: Lying and Deception for the Masses

SECOND EDITION

lying AND deception *in* HUMAN INTERACTION

MARK L. KNAPP | MATTHEW S. MCGLONE | DARRIN J. GRIFFIN | WILLIAM EARNEST
UNIVERSITY OF TEXAS–AUSTIN | UNIVERSITY OF TEXAS–AUSTIN | UNIVERSITY OF ALABAMA | ST. EDWARD'S UNIVERSITY

Kendall Hunt
publishing company

Book Team

Chairman and Chief Executive Officer Mark C. Falb
President and Chief Operating Officer Chad M. Chandlee
Vice President, Higher Education David L. Tart
Director of Publishing Partnerships Paul B. Carty
Senior Developmental Coordinator Angela Willenbring
Vice President, Operations Timothy J. Beitzel
Senior Production Editor Sheri Hosek
Permissions Editor Melisa Seegmiller
Cover Designer Suzanne Millius

Cover image © Shutterstock.com

Kendall Hunt
publishing company

www.kendallhunt.com
Send all inquiries to:
4050 Westmark Drive
Dubuque, IA 52004-1840

Copyright © 2016 by Kendall Hunt Publishing Company
Copyright © 2008 Pearson Education, Inc.

This book was previously published by: Pearson Education, Inc.

ISBN 978-1-4652-8459-4

All rights reserved. No part of this publication may be reproduced,
stored in a retrieval system, or transmitted, in any form or by any means,
electronic, mechanical, photocopying, recording, or otherwise,
without the prior written permission of the copyright owner.

Printed in the United States of America

Contents

Part II: Deceptive Behavior 71

Preface

In 1997, the first author of this book offered a graduate course that surveyed lying and deception in human interaction at the University of Texas at Austin. The content of that course was very similar to the content of this book. The success of that course led to a similar course for undergraduates which, by 2001, enrolled so many students that it had to be taught in an auditorium seating 300 students. The students represented a cross section of academic disciplines across campus. Based on the interest in this subject, Dr. Knapp wrote the first edition of this book in 2008.

Dr. Earnest was a teaching assistant the first time Dr. Knapp offered the lying and deception course to undergraduates. Now he teaches his own lying and deception course at St. Edwards University in Austin, Texas. Dr. Griffin took Dr. Knapp's course as an undergraduate and as a graduate student served as a teaching assistant for the course. Subsequently, Dr. Griffin taught lying and deception courses at Gallaudet University, the University at Buffalo, and currently teaches Truth, Ethics, and Deception at the University of Alabama-Tuscaloosa. Following Dr. Knapp's retirement, Dr. McGlone assumed the teaching of the still very popular courses for both graduate and undergraduate students at the University of Texas at Austin.

In addition to our shared experiences in teaching lying and deception courses, each author of this book has published research articles, directed theses and dissertations, and/or published books on the subject—e.g., Hurley, Griffin, & Stefanone, 2014; Knapp, Hart, & Dennis, 1974; McGlone & Knapp, 2010. As a result of our common interests and background with one another, it seemed natural to pool our knowledge in order to develop the second edition of *Lying and Deception in Human Interaction*. While the book's primary perspective is the communication process, the accompanying concepts and references touch on many important areas of study across the humanities and social sciences. Working together on this edition has renewed our excitement for this topic that we believe is so central to the education of the students who will be tomorrow's leaders.

Why do we think this is especially valuable for students? Why should they read a book about lying and deception? To address these questions, consider the following:

1. **Issues bearing on lying and deception impact every act of communication we undertake and our evaluation and analysis of every message we process.** Communicating involves decisions about what to include, what to leave out, and how to say what we do say. "Effective speech is persuasive speech and one cannot consider the process of persuasion (or education) without weighing issues associated with deception and truth. 'Obtaining the desired response' confronts communicators with a constant parade of questions relative to truth telling, deception and every shade of gray between" (Knapp & Earnest, 2000, p. 375).

2. Studying and developing a better understanding of lying and deception should also provide citizens with cognitive and perceptual skills to better deal with con artists, Internet scams, and hoaxes. **In short, knowledge of lying and deception is a form of consumer protection.** At the same time, it serves as a chance to audit some personal values—reflecting on some of the more complex aspects of a subject we too often treat only superficially.

3. **It may sound strange but a course of study in lying and deception is also central to the primary mission of higher education—seeking truth.** One can't explore lying and deception without simultaneously raising questions about truth. Asking what we know and how we know it inevitably involves a consideration of information credibility. The fact that virtually every academic discipline has contributed research on some aspect of deception is further testimony that it is a central issue in higher education.

This book attempts to survey the subject from a variety of perspectives. It opens with three chapters that examine the nature of lying and deception, truth, and various ethical perspectives associated with truth telling and deception. In Part II, various manifestations of deceptive behavior are examined. To illustrate how human deception is just another manifestation of a process that all living organisms on the planet practice, Chapter 4 looks at the deceptive behavior of viruses, plants, and other nonhuman species. An examination of human deceptive behavior begins with the study of children, followed by chapters that focus on self-deception (Chapter 6) and the deception of others (Chapter 7). The behavior of people who make a habit of lying, "lying specialists," concludes this section. Part III covers what is perhaps the most common subject of research on deception—lie detection. Chapter 9 looks at the process of detecting deception by human observation while Chapter 10 reviews all the machines, drugs, tests, and other aids that have been employed to try to improve lie-detection accuracy. The last section of the book looks at lying and deception in the context of deceiving the masses as it occurs in political leadership, journalism, writing history, memoirs, résumés, and the manipulation of visual images.

References

Hurley, C.M., Griffin, D.J., & Stefanone, M.A. (2014). Who told you that? Uncovering the source of believed cues to deception. *International Journal of Psychological Studies, 6,* 19–32.

Knapp, M.L., & Earnest, W.J. (2000). Shall ye know the truth? Student odysseys in truth-seeking. *Communication Education, 49,* 375–386.

Knapp, M.L., Hart, R.P., & Dennis, H.S. (1974). An exploration of deception as a communication construct. *Human Communication Research, 1,* 15–29.

McGlone, M.S., & Knapp, M.L. (Eds.) (2010). *The interplay of truth and deception: New agendas in theory and research.* New York: Routledge.

About the Authors

 **Mark L. Knapp** (PhD, Pennsylvania State University) is the Jesse H. Jones Centennial Professor Emeritus in Communication and Distinguished Teaching Professor Emeritus at The University of Texas at Austin. He co-edited the *Handbook of Interpersonal Communication* and *The Interplay of Truth and Deception*. In addition to co-authoring *Lying and Deception in Human Interaction*, he co-authored *Nonverbal Communication in Human Interaction* and *Interpersonal Communication in Human Relationships*. He is the past president and fellow of the International Communication Association and past president and distinguished scholar of the National Communication Association.

 **Matthew S. McGlone** (PhD, Princeton University) is Associate Professor of Communication Studies at The University of Texas at Austin. His research and teaching focus on deception, persuasion, and stereotyping in human interaction. He co-edited *The Interplay of Truth and Deception* and *Work Pressures*. He is Associate Director of UT's Center for Health Communication and is a past chair of the National Communication Association's Communication and Social Cognition Division.

 **Darrin J. Griffin** (PhD, University at Buffalo) is Assistant Professor of Communication Studies at The University of Alabama. He teaches and researches topics involving deception and interpersonal communication. He has served as a research assistant at the Federal Bureau of Investigation Training Academy in Quantico, VA and the FBI's field office in Buffalo, NY.

 **William J. Earnest** (PhD, The University of Texas at Austin) is Assistant Professor of Communication at St. Edward's University in Austin. He is the author of *Save Our Slides: PowerPoint Design That Works*, which is now in its 3rd edition. He has taught the Lying & Deception course every year since joining the faculty of St. Edward's University in 2005. He is a former lecturer in business communication at the McCombs School of Business at the University of Texas. Before beginning his academic career, he was a business analyst, technical writer, and trainer for Electronic Data Systems in Atlanta.

Part I

The Nature of the Phenomena

The following three chapters focus on fundamental questions associated with the study of lying, deception, and communication. They establish a framework for ways of thinking about honesty and deception. Why is it important to understand lying and deception? Do lies have any distinguishing features? If a lie means a person isn't telling the truth, how do we identify truth? What ethical criteria do we associate with lies and truth telling?

Chapter 1: Perspectives on Lying and Deception

Chapter 2: Perspectives on Truth

Chapter 3: Ethical Perspectives

Chapter 1

Perspectives on Lying and Deception

In order to become somebody's ancestor, our earliest ancestors had to survive. And because the first human beings weren't the biggest or strongest species on the planet, they had to use their wits and work effectively as a team in order to survive. Outwitting one's competitors to ensure survival often meant using one's ability to mislead or deceive. But working effectively as a *team* meant building a social system based on trust, honesty, reliability, and mutual aid. This process is what world-renowned anthropologist Richard Leaky and his colleague called "reciprocal altruism" (Leaky & Lewin, 1978). While this form of social organization helped our human ancestors survive, it is also easy to see how individuals who wanted to use the process for their personal gain might be tempted to do so. As Leaky and Lewin say:

> During the course of natural selection, individuals are certain to arise who (unconsciously) try to "cheat" in the altruism game. They may produce sham moralistic aggression, sham guilt, sham sympathy, and sham gratitude in an attempt to take more than they give—a situation that could be biologically beneficial in the short term, at least...

> Just as natural selection inevitably produces would-be cheaters, it will inevitably give rise to individuals capable of detecting cheating. And so the game of bluff and double bluff begins, with the new emotions of trust and suspicion being invented. (p. 192)

"We are, perhaps, not only capable of lying but virtually incapable of not doing so... Deception and self-deception, according to this kinky view, may not be perversions so much as they are the very stuff of human intercourse."

— *Robert Solomon*

It is not hard to imagine how the ability to deceive became instrumental in the survival of evolving human beings. It is, after all, crucial to the survival of other plants, insects, fish, and animals on our planet (Mitchell, 1986; see Chapter 4). But just because natural selection may not favor a nervous system that produces ever more accurate images of the world, this doesn't mean that nature isn't interested in truthfulness, honesty, and candor. *The irony is that to reap the benefits of lying and deception, it has to be performed within a social system which values and expects truthfulness.* And it hardly seems reasonable that the ability to lie per se would be privy to natural selection. The first human lies occurred within a small social unit where people knew each other well, language was elementary in its form, and things could be easily checked. Under these conditions, liars had to be strategic. If they were, they probably lived and reproduced; if they weren't, their community probably took action against them. Lying in the face of reciprocal altruism loses its survival value if it is performed poorly, if it is directed at good detectors, if it is practiced too often, or if it is a pattern of behavior characteristic of too many members of the community. So even though nature seems to encourage lying and deception, it does not encourage just any kind; it encourages those who do it best. It's more than a little ironic: Reaping benefits from the use of lying and deception means performing them within a social system that values—even expects—truthfulness. But doing it effectively doesn't mean doing it whenever you want or lying about any topic or event you want. Bond and Robinson (1988) put it this way:

> *In conflict between predator and prey, in competitions for reproduction, deception confers a selective advantage: liars leave behind more offspring, and the progeny inherit their parents' advantage… Falsehoods are not always advantageous. Some forms of false communication lower an organism's likelihood of survival. These are not selected. Other falsehoods, though usually adaptive, sometimes backfire. Nature permits this occasional failure…(p. 296)*

A million or more years later we still live in a world where many believe it is okay to deceive our competitors and enemies in order to survive, while simultaneously trying to maintain a social system based on honesty and trust. And, not unlike those early hominids who took advantage of a trusting social system for personal gain, we have no shortage of people in today's society who, with various degrees of conscience and consciousness, do the same thing (Keyes, 2004). This, in turn, triggers the need for more (and more effective) lie detectors. In fact, Smith (2004) believes the ability to detect lies may also be subject to natural selection:

> *…in a world of liars, it is advantageous to possess a lie detector. In a treacherous social world—one rife with deceit and double-dealing—an individual who is good at detecting dishonesty will be far less likely to be exploited than less skeptical individuals. He or she will be likely to survive longer and reproduce more successfully than others, and thereby pass the deception-detecting gene on to the next generation…Those individuals blessed with superior deceptive skill, who use tactics that are so sophisticated and insidious that they fly under the radar of the average lie-detecting mind, will gain the upper hand in the struggle for survival. This hegemony will last*

*only until these ultra-deceptive tactics are confronted by individu-
als who have evolved even more powerful cognitive equipment in a
spiraling evolutionary arms race (p. 68).*

When something has been a part of the human condition for millions of years, one would think we'd be used to it or even able to accept it as a normal part of human behavior. Indeed, for certain cultural groups like the San Blas Kuna in northeastern Panama, trickery and deception do seem to be viewed as a natural part of the culture's discourse—even though there are deceptions which, in time, are revealed by the trickster (Howe & Scherzer, 1986). And false praise, insincere promises, giving reasons for hope when there is none, professing agreement in order to bypass argument, etc. are more prevalent in some cultures than others (Slackman, 2006; Pitt-Rivers, 1954). But in many cultures, particularly large and complex societies like the United States, there seems to be a long-standing, uneasy relationship with our known human tendency to misrepresent what we believe to be true. Even biblical accounts of deception are not consistent—praising it in one context while condemning or ignoring it in others (Sullivan, 2001). When we do accept falsehoods, we don't like to admit it. Noted sociologist Georg Simmel explains why we are loathe to embrace dishonesty:

> *…in very simple circumstances the lie is often more harmless in
> regard to the maintenance of the group than under more complex
> conditions…In a richer and larger cultural life, however, existence
> rests on a thousand premises which the single individual cannot
> trace and verify to their roots at all, but must take on faith. Our
> modern life is based to a much larger extent than is usually realized
> upon the faith in the honesty of the other. Examples are our econ-
> omy, which becomes more and more a credit economy, or our sci-
> ence, in which most scholars must use innumerable results of other
> scientists which they cannot examine. We base our gravest deci-
> sions on a complex system of conceptions, most of which presuppose
> the confidence that we will not be betrayed. Under modern condi-
> tions, the lie, therefore, becomes something much more devastating
> than it was earlier, something which questions the very foundations
> of our life (Wolff, 1950, p. 313).*

The knowledge that lies can, like a virus, infect our social system prompts many people to condemn deception and lying unequivocally. Deception, they argue, destroys trust and trust is the foundation of healthy social relations. But this doesn't keep these same people from engaging in various forms of deception. This "do as I say, not as I do" stance is not a recent phenomenon; writers have noted this issue since antiquity. While it may not be comforting to those who want life to be simple and clear cut, this seemingly hypocritical stance ("People shouldn't lie even though I do") may have been around as long as it has because it is a functional position for effectively maintaining our social lives.

It would be foolhardy to advocate the acceptance of lying and deception as a gen-eral social principle. Public support given to lying and deception as appropriate behavior is likely to open the floodgates on a terribly dysfunctional society. This is Bok's (1978) belief. She argues that accepting virtually any form of duplicity without severe sanctions will lead us down the path to a more general disregard for the truth and an eventual collapse of society. But even if we affirm a belief in a social system which keeps duplicity from predominating, most of us also seem to understand that duplicity is a natural and inextinguishable part of the human communicative repertoire. We can value the truth yet neither want to hear nor speak it all the time. No matter how much we believe it would be bad for us to publicly endorse lying and deception as a cultural norm, we also know we must live in a culture where we and others will sometimes mislead and lie.

Given these seemingly disjunctive beliefs, then, it is reasonable for us to enter into our daily encounters with the expectation that people will adhere to the cultural guideline of not deceiving others and will endeavor to tell us the truth as they know it. At the same time, we know we must recognize the possibility that there may be more to the truth than we are told and that certain conditions may sometimes give rise to both benign and harmful duplicity. This kind of dialogic alertness, in turn, spawns a productive kind of conversational monitoring. It also helps us maintain an ongoing evaluation of what we, and others, see as the pros and cons of various forms of deception and truth. Barnes (1994) sees this system as an effective check on destructive lies:

> ...a greater recognition that lies are not universally reprehensible, and that even our best friends tell lies, should lead us to a greater awareness of the ubiquity of lying and hence the diminution of misplaced trust. Success in malicious lying should thus become harder rather than easier. The level at which lying becomes counterproductive should become lower, not higher. Thus, we should have a dialectical process in which excessive malicious lying leads to its own negation (p. 164).

So a system in which people advocate truth telling while simultaneously recognizing that violations will occur seems preferable. Such a system is also far more productive than one in which people naively believe that everyone will always tell the truth. And it is certainly preferable to a world where deceiving others is condoned to the point that people must assume others are constantly trying to deceive them. A society that favors lying and deception would be dysfunctional; so would a society devoid of any duplicity.

Lying and Deception as Communication

Several studies have shown lies to be a common part of our daily intercourse. Turner, Edgley, & Olmstead (1975) asked 130 people to record and analyze their own statements in an important conversation in terms of honesty. Only 38.5% of the statements were labeled "completely honest." DePaulo, Kashy, Kirkendol, Wyer, and Epstein (1996) had 77 college students and 70 people from a Virginia community record all of their interactions lasting at least ten minutes over the course of one week. The average number of lies reported by the college students was two per day while people from the community averaged one a day. One student and six members of the community claimed they told no lies during their ten-minute interactions throughout the week.

In a sample of college students, 92% admitted they had lied to a romantic partner (Knox, Schacht, Holt & Turner, 1993). Surveys show that thousands of high school students admit lying to their parents and teachers (Josephson Institute of Ethics, 2002; Durham, 2000; Dubin, 1998; *Time,* 1998). When an online survey asked 3,000 adults if they'd ever engaged in any of thirteen different acts of dishonesty, 32% reported lying to their spouse about a purchase; 63% had called in sick to work when they weren't; 13% shifted the blame to a co-worker for something they did; 71% lied to friends or family to spare their feelings; and 28% lied to their spouse about their relationship with another person (Kalish, 2004). On the ubiquity of lying, Saxe (1991, p. 410) offers this reflection: "From individuals who lie to a partner about their other intimate relationships, to students (and professors) who create excuses for late papers, to salesmen and lawyers for whom deceptiveness can be a normatively sanctioned aspect of their daily work life, the lack of truthfulness is too common to be restricted to those who make headlines." In short, finding people who admit that lying and deception are common features of their everyday behavior is not difficult.

Nor is it difficult to find those who perceive lies all around them—in the media, in science reports, in history textbooks, in the rhetoric of our political leaders, etc. (Kick, 2001). Barnes (1994) cites a British journalist who labeled the 1980s as the "decade of lies" and an American journalist who observed in 1991 that "lying has reached epidemic proportions in recent years." Commenting on the last decade of the 20th century in the United States, Housman (2000) said, "Perhaps the 1990s will be known as the decade of doublespeak." In his National Book Award winning treatise *The Unwinding,* George Packer (2013) claims that the public's distrust of government and business over the last 30 years has prompted an "unwinding" of Americans' sense of community and has made lying more acceptable for people in all walks of life.

One common explanation for the ubiquitous nature of lying and deception is that we are a society in decay—that duplicity is characteristic of a moral and ethical vacuum. This argument might be more convincing were it not for the fact that the frequency of lying and deception is not a recent phenomenon nor has it been limited to societies in decay. Nyberg (1993) believes deception is so omnipresent because it is part and parcel of the way we conduct our everyday affairs. In other words, it is an inherent part of the way we communicate.

> *Truth telling is a means for accomplishing purposes. So is deception. My approach to an understanding of deception is not the usual one (top down) of focusing on the virtue of truth as a given, then finding ways to make benevolent compromises. It is rather to focus on human communication (bottom up), then to see what roles both play in furthering that process toward the achievement of worthwhile goals (pp. 53–54).*

Solomon (1996) echoes Nyberg's view when he says:

> *Deception is first of all a way of relating…to others and to oneself… Some deception is harmful and even immoral, but some of it is neither. Indeed, an extremist might argue that there is no such phenomenon as lying as such, only various ways in which we relate to*

one another as insecure social creatures surrounded and infiltrated
by an inevitably equivocal language (p.109).

From this perspective, then, lying and deception can best be understood in the context of practicing effective communication. To communicate effectively, we try to put ourselves in the position of our audience. What information does the audience or target seek? What will make them believe what I want them to believe? How are they likely to respond if I say this or that? The practical benefit of taking our audience's perspective is to produce messages that have the best chance of accomplishing what we want to accomplish. Both truth tellers and deceivers engage in the same process. Both are asking themselves, "out of all I could say, what do I want to say?" Two commonly accepted ways to define effective communication include "using all the available means of persuasion" and "obtaining desired responses." Both necessitate the selection and manipulation of information, highlighting how matters relevant to deception and truth telling are central to every message we construct.

And despite protestations to the contrary, part of being an effective communicator involves discreetly employing deception. In one study, college students were asked to engage another student in conversation with the goal of "getting to know them" while being videotaped. Some students were also told to appear likable; others were told to appear competent. After the conversation, the students watched a video and identified instances in which they had deceived the other person. Overall, both men and women who were told to appear likable and competent told significantly more lies than those who were not asked to present themselves in a particular way (Feldman, Forrest, & Happ, 2002). In another study, Feldman and his colleagues (Feldman, Tomasian & Coats, 1999) found that the more socially skilled an adolescent was, the more effective he or she was at deceiving. Keating & Heltman (1994) found children and adults who are socially powerful (i.e., leaders) were also skilled at deceiving. Riggio, Tucker, & Throckmorton (1988) found people who showed more expressiveness and social tact were more successful at deception than those who had less skill in those areas. It appears that the value of social harmony can, and often does, take precedence over the value of telling the truth. Being polite and trying not to hurt another person's feelings are commonly associated with effective communicators, but each may require telling something other than what one believes to be the *whole* truth. Consider the following polite but not-quite-honest examples from everyday life:

- "You made it yourself? I never would have guessed."
- "It's delicious, but I can't eat another bite."
- "Your hair looks just fine."
- "You don't look a day over 50."

The ability to tell a vivid, interesting, and enjoyable story may involve adding and/or subtracting some information from what one recalls happening. Highlighting one's strengths and minimizing one's weaknesses is usually considered good advice in a job interview or on a first date. Not responding with everything you know can protect one's friendships and one's private life. Delicate negotiations often hinge on decisions about what to reveal, when to reveal it, and to whom. Sometimes loved ones want us to help them perpetuate a lie, which obligates us to lie in order to succeed in preserving the relationship. When a seven-year-old child with terminal cancer asks whether he or she is going to die, effective communicators ask themselves how they can best adapt a response to this child in this situation rather than simply and directly reporting the truth as they know it. It may be hard for some to admit, but lies can help us cope with fear, tolerate stress, and gain a sense of control over uncertain or negative aspects of our lives.

Communicators who devise messages that do not match what they believe to be the truth and communicators who choose to tell what they believe to be the truth are both accountable for their choices. Deceptions which are considered effective communication in one situation may be deemed ineffective or unethical communication in another. Someone whose audience-adapted deceit is revealed and believed to serve solely to further the deceiver's self interests and/or harm others is unlikely to be considered an effective communicator by most observers. The same can be said about the choice to tell the truth in certain situations. When someone tells the truth without regard for another person's feelings, tells the truth in order to mislead somebody, or tells the truth to someone who doesn't want to hear it, they probably decrease the possibility of getting responses they want. In such cases, the communicator made poor strategic choices and ineffectively communicated even though he or she told the truth (e.g., see cartoon on p. 10).

By now it should be clear that decisions about truth telling and deception are inextricably woven into our pursuit of communicating effectively. By and large, these are conscious choices. But the very language we use to communicate also helps to explain why lying and deception are so much a part of our social world.

Truth and fiction can be accomplished using the same words. "Crime is reduced when compared with last year," is a true statement, but it does not accurately report that some of the types of crimes measured last year were not measured this year. Words are labels for things. They have no intrinsic connection to the things they denote. They are abstractions that capture some qualities of the things they stand for and inevitably omit others. Thus, when we use a word or words to represent something, we are inevitably engaging in an act of omission—a form of lying. Words are also subject to multiple meanings and interpretations so language can also facilitate, unintentionally or intentionally, lies of commission. When we say, "we had a good day," we may not mean that everything that happened to us was good. In fact, we may only be thinking about one thing that happened. Moreover, the person we say this to may interpret our words in other ways—thinking that because we said "good" instead of "great" that we had a very uneventful day or he or she may think our day was devoid of any negativity. Furthermore, referents for words are also subject to dramatic change as time passes—as was the case when, for a time, some people used the word "bad" to mean "good."

Language use by the first human beings was probably not unlike the signaling systems of other animals in their midst. A warning communicated by words was the equivalent of an alarm call used by another animal. Language was more closely linked to the tangible, audible, and visible referents associated with their everyday reality. In comparison to the way we use language today, opportunities for lying and deception were considerably more limited. As our sophistication in the use of language increased, however, language became increasingly adapted to lying and deception. As Rappaport (1979, pp. 180, 224, 226) said, "the very freedom of sign

GET FUZZY © 2004 Darby Conley. Used by permission of UNIVERSAL UCLICK. All rights reserved.

from signified that permits discourse to transcend the here and now, if it does not actually make lying possible, facilitates it enormously and may encourage it as well." He goes on to say that lies are the "bastard offspring of symbols." Campbell (2001, p. 230) echoes this sentiment when he says, "language is a dense layered medium empowered not just to reflect reality, but to transform it radically."

Conceiving of Deceiving

Up to this point the words *lying* and *deception* have been used almost interchangeably. The only clear distinction between the two terms is that deception is normally considered a superordinate term that encompasses various fraudulent, tricky, and/or misleading behavior—including lies. Beyond that, the distinctions are not as clear. For example, Hopper and Bell (1984), among others, argue that deception can be communicated in many ways, but lies are limited to *verbal* behavior. But we know that accusations of lying are sometimes heavily rooted in perceptions of *nonverbal* behavior—e.g., avoiding eye contact, shrugging one's shoulders, using a particular tone of voice, or even maintaining silence.

Dictionaries aren't particularly helpful in making useful distinctions either. Dictionaries define words by telling us how people have historically used a word, not what it "always" means. Words like *lying* and *deception* are no different. They are abstractions and can only "be" as they are perceived by specific people in specific situations.

It has been a common practice for social scientists to use some form of the following definition of lying to guide their research: "*the conscious alteration of information a person believes to be true in order to significantly change another's perceptions from what the deceiver thought they would be without the alteration*" (Knapp & Comadena, 1979). Two important problems arise with this approach. First, it defines a lie from the standpoint of what the *liar* does. This means the determination that a lie has occurred would too often require the suspected liar to be asked whether he or she had consciously altered information, whether that alteration was significantly different from what he or she believed to be true, and what he or she thought the target believed was true. Determining what a lie is by asking suspected liars about their own behavior is clearly problematic. Some people believe that if they have a good reason for telling a lie then it isn't really a lie. The perceptual worlds of liars and their targets are usually quite different (Gordon & Miller, 2000). The following examples from the liar's perspective illustrate the point: Colonel Oliver North, testifying before Congress during the Iran-Contra hearings, said: "I was not lying, Senator. I was presenting a different version of the facts." President Richard Nixon said, "I was not lying. I said things that later on seemed to be untrue." And as author Judy Blunt, who reported an event that didn't happen in her memoir, *Breaking Clean*, explained: "There is truth in every scene in the essay, but the facts are less reliable." Second, the central component of the typical social scientist's operational definition for lying is the treatment of the information communicated. While this can be a crucial component in the way we perceive lies, changing of information does not account for numerous situations where attributions of lying are made and there is no knowledge of whether any information has been altered.

Practically, lies and deception are defined by the way people perceive certain features of communicative acts in context. The extent to which these perceptions are commonly held or held by an influential person (e.g., a police officer or a judge) is the extent to which an attribution of lying will be considered accurate (see Chapter 2). If the behavior in question does not meet the criteria for a lie, it may be considered a half-truth (e.g., "This car has never been in a repair shop," *but it should have been*), an honest mistake, an evasive response, etc. Sometimes there will be considerable agreement on whether a lie has occurred and sometimes there will be little agreement. But more often than not, the extent to which we believe a person has or hasn't lied (and the degree of sanctioning deemed appropriate for such behavior) hinge on how people perceive the following five features.

Perceptions of Awareness

Did the person knowingly and consciously perform the falsehood in question? Was it planned? In most cases, lying is perceived as being done with a high degree of awareness. This is why liars, when accused of lying, will sometimes feign incompetence: "What? I said that? No. If I did, I must have been completely out of my mind. You know me. I wouldn't knowingly say anything like that." If this person's defense is believed, the attribution of lying is less likely and the desired sanctioning much less severe. Children, old people, and people we like are often given the benefit of the doubt when their awareness of what they were doing or saying is in question. We also make similar allowances for people who are experiencing stress, trauma, or a medical condition which affects their communicative behavior.

Perceptions of Altering Information

Sometimes liars will admit to their awareness of saying or doing something, but deny that they were aware that it involved false information. *Lies of commission* are lies in which the liar has altered information he or she believes to be true. When people make honest or even careless mistakes, they may present false information, but they believe it to be true. In such cases, we will often perceive the person to be misinformed, but not a liar. Of course, the difficulty for the perceiver is to assess what the speaker could reasonably be expected to know and whether he or she would be likely to manipulate information in this situation. It is not uncommon for us to be faced with communicators who say things that we believe to be untrue, are evasive, misleading, or perhaps unresponsive when we expect otherwise. Sometimes communicators seem to be inconsistent or even contradictory in what they say. Sometimes these are signs of lying and sometimes they are not. Of course a big part of the problem is knowing what information is true in order to be able to determine what represents an alteration (see Chapter 2 for a discussion of how we determine what is true).

Perceptions of Intent

Even if one determines that a message is composed of false information, this is not always the sole or most important reason for attributing deception to the message maker. A statement or behavior may be judged deceptive and be explicitly false, partly true and partly false, or even completely true. This is because the guiding motive or intent behind the message is perceived to be deceptive. The communicator's intent or motive is often the key factor in determining the existence and/or acceptability of a lie. Suppose you buy an exploding golf ball for your friend and he asks, prior to striking it with his driver, "I hope this thing won't explode when I hit it," and you say, "It's supposed to" and laugh. While you have made a true statement, the context was such that your friend thought you were kidding and later (if he survives) he may accuse you of lying—because he perceives the intent of your true statement was to mislead. True statements are also used with deceptive intent when people are caught doing something they don't want to admit doing. For example, when a drugstore employee asks a man who has just walked out of the store without paying for a candy bar whether he did, in fact, steal the candy bar, the man replies: "Sure. Even though that's my new Mercedes-Benz out there in the parking lot and I make $150,000 a year, I wasn't willing to spend a dollar for a candy bar. Ok, Sherlock, you got me. I'm your thief."

Our tendency to answer questions indirectly, hypothetically, or partially may also raise suspicions about our intent. Indirect responses, for example, imply a particular intent and run the risk of being judged deceptive if that intent is not pursued (Washburne, 1969). For example, if we ask whether you are going to go to your neighborhood bar this evening and you say, "It's a good night to celebrate," we assume you mean "yes" and will count on you being there. On the other hand, if you say, "I have to take an important test tomorrow morning," we assume you mean "no" and will not expect to see you for drinks tonight (Bowers, Elliott, & Desmond, 1977; Nofsinger, 1976). You may, of course, argue that it is not fair of us to label you a liar because you didn't explicitly say, nor did you intend for us to assume, that you would or wouldn't be at the bar that night. You may or may not be successful in your argument.

Lies of omission come in several guises, but they, too, are often evaluated on the basis of perceived intent. Whether you omit information which one might reasonably expect to be included or whether you induce or reinforce someone else's false belief by not saying anything contrary to what they are contending, you may be accused of deception because your intent was to mislead—especially if the consequences are serious (Levine, Asada, & Lindsey, 2003). Once again, the ambiguities involved often provide ample opportunities for arguing about the extent to which the intent was to mislead.

On the other hand, it is possible to present false and misleading information and *not* be overtly accused of lying or deception. This can happen when we are teasing, playing a joke, or planning a surprise for someone. The motive for any falsehoods in the pursuit of such goals is meant to be uncovered and excused because the lies were told for the target's benefit. Some situations also exempt people from attributions of lying and deception because such behavior is expected. Two examples of this are: politeness rituals ("I really had a great time tonight") and the behavior of poker players.

Part of the process of arriving at the decision that a person has a misleading or deceptive intent is asking yourself whether a person has a reason to lie—in general or to you specifically. You may consider your relationship and history with this person, their personality, and the particular demands of the topic being discussed in order to assess the likelihood a lie is being told. The reasons people lie are all basic goals of human interaction—e.g., getting something you want, maintaining a friendship, etc. Lies can be designed to serve oneself, to serve others, or a combination of both. We often think of self-serving lies as more reprehensible but some lies told to help others (e.g., lying to a friend about what another friend did) also can be judged harshly. Self-serving lies may include lies used to obtain power, influence, or relationships, as well as lies told for the purpose of protecting oneself against loss or harm—for example, avoiding punishment, enhancing one's self image, saving face, and avoiding tension (Lippard, 1988). Lies told to help others are performed for similar reasons—e.g., to help them obtain something they want, to protect them from trouble, to reassure and support them, and to help them save face.

Perceptions of the Situation

Sometimes we ask ourselves if there is anything about a particular situation that makes lying more likely? Is there any pressure to lie about this topic to this audience? Has lying occurred in similar situations before? Are the rewards for telling a lie greater than those for telling the truth? Questions like these help us form our perceptions about the circumstances within which lying may take place. Sometimes lies occur so often in a particular situation that they become well known throughout the culture, as when a sales clerk says, "This item you're looking at is the last one we have in stock and I don't anticipate we will be getting any more of them soon," or when the receptionist says, "The doctor will call you right back," or when the person who already owes you money says, "I promise to pay you back as soon as I get my next paycheck."

We expect lying to be common in espionage and during warfare. Similarly, we are not surprised to find lies occurring between people who intensely dislike or fear each other. The conditions associated with the acts of some politicians and sales representatives create a climate in which lying is more or less expected. We expect polite people may lie in the name of good manners. We don't enter a game of poker or sit down at the bargaining table with the expectation that everyone will be trying to tell the truth. Actors and other performers have our consent to lie to us as long as their role as actor and performer is clear. For example, as long as comedian Andy Kaufman was standing on stage and it was clear he was performing his act, audiences expected and accepted exaggerations and falsehoods. Deception was authorized as a vehicle for creating humor; his performances were not intended to be taken literally or personally. However, when he began heckling other performers as an audience member and when he seemed to take too seriously his wrestling matches with women, his fans weren't always sure what behavior was the real Andy Kaufman and what behavior was the performer Andy Kaufman. Not knowing whether he was *performing* made it difficult to know whether deception was occurring and whether it was appropriate in this situation or not. This uncertainty made a lot of people uneasy.

Perceptions of Effects/Consequences

If we suspect or know a lie has occurred, part of our assessment is focused on the effects or consequences of the behavior. Who was affected and in what ways? The way we answer these questions may alter the extent to which we perceive the behavior as a lie and greatly affect our perceptions of the kind of sanctioning deserved. On the one hand, we don't like or trust a person who tells us a lot of lies, but not all lies are perceived as equally harmful (Tyler et al., 2006).

We attribute less harm to (and reduce sanctions for) lies we perceive as having: benefited another person (not the liar); resulted in positive consequences; produced effects that were trivial rather than consequential; produced short rather than long term effects; affected few rather than many; occurred (along with any consequences) a long time ago; and being acknowledged (along with the consequences) by the liar.

Sometimes lies have multiple audiences with effects that are different for each audience. For example, a journalist writes a newspaper story about breast cancer. But the fact that he or she used a gripping, yet fictional, case study to make the story vivid comes to light. When this occurs, the consequences for the author and the newspaper may be perceived by various readers in very different ways (see Chapter 12 for specific cases). For some of the newspaper readers, the fictional example is viewed as a small and insignificant part of a larger story designed to bring certain information about breast cancer to the attention of the public. For them, the dishonesty of the case study is overridden by the positive effects achieved by the total story. Besides, they reason, even if this case was not true, there probably is someone, somewhere whose story is like the person in the case study. For the newspaper, however, the integrity of its reporters and the credibility of the organization are at stake. Making up any part of a story and presenting it as fact throws every other story they've ever printed into question. To the newspaper, this is a significant form of deception and the reporter must be fired in order to re-establish that the publisher values honesty.

While the preceding perceptual categories have been presented in the context of assessing the deceptive behavior of a single person, it is worth remembering that lies are jointly created as well. This means perceptions of the preceding five categories are relevant to both interactants. How are lies jointly constructed? Sometimes one interaction partner makes it easy for the other to lie by providing a fraudulent rationale for their partner's suspect behavior, to which the partner assents; sometimes one partner encourages lying by making it clear that they don't want to hear the truth; sometimes parties in a relationship will collaborate in creating and perpetuating a lie to help keep it afloat; and sometimes parties will cooperate in what both know to be a lie in order to adhere to a politeness ritual or cultural expectation.

Can we ever say that there are specific behaviors that are clearly known as lies—independent of what is perceived—or is the determination of lying and deception always dependent on perceptions of a particular act in a particular situation? Certainly there are behaviors which, based on a long history of perceptions in a variety of situations, will cause virtually everyone to say, "yes, this is an act of lying." But even then, when such behavior is placed in a particular context, the attributions of lying and the attendant sanctioning may change. So, yes, we do understand, for example, that if we tell somebody something other than what we believe to be true, we are engaging in a behavior which is usually associated with lying. But we also know that in some situations this behavior will not be perceived as a lie.

Summary

Lying and deception evolved as a part of the social system established by the earliest human beings. Those who were skilled at lying and deception profited by taking advantage of a system that valued and expected people to tell the truth. Those who were not skilled were punished. We see this same behavior in today's modern technological society. Studies show that lying and deception are both widely practiced *and* widely condemned in today's society. While we advocate truth telling, we also recognize that lying and deception will occur and that sometimes they may even be appropriate responses to a situation. As Miller (2003, p. 233) says, "Some accommodation to faking it is in order." We seem to realize that a society that favors lying and deception over truth telling would be dysfunctional, as would a society devoid of any lying and deception. Lying and deception occur with regularity in daily discourse because they are a way of obtaining the responses we desire from others, of accomplishing our goals—just like truth telling. In addition, the incomplete and abstract nature of language itself provides a ready vehicle for duplicity. Sometimes lying and deception are harmful, unethical, and immoral; sometimes they aren't.

Answering the question, "What is a lie?" or "What is deceit?" can best be done by finding out how people perceive various component parts of the transaction in question. Was the communicator aware of what he or she was doing? Did the communicator alter information he or she knew to be true? What was the intent or motive behind the communicator's message? Was there anything about this situation that would encourage lying or even authorize it? What consequences resulted from the communicator's behavior? Perceptions associated with these questions lead us to make attributions about whether lying or deception has occurred, whether it is serious or not, and to what extent it can or should be sanctioned.

Things to Think About

Identify one thing you do not want anyone to lie to you about. Why?

What is one thing you want people to lie to you about? Why?

Is there anything you are not willing to lie about? Why?

Describe three of your close relationships. Now imagine and describe how these relationships would be if all the parties shared everything each person thought or believed to be true.

Think of something other people would lie about, but you would not. Why do you think this would happen?

Describe two recent situations of deception in your life: one where omission played a crucial part; and another where a lie of commission was utilized.

References

Backbier, E., Hoogstraten, J., & Meerum Terwogt-Kouwenhoven, K. (1997). Situational determinants of the acceptability of telling lies. *Journal of Applied Social Psychology, 27,* 1048–1062.

Barnes, J.A. (1994). *A pack of lies: Towards a sociology of lying.* New York: Cambridge University Press.

Baumeister, R.F., & Vohs, K.D. (2004). Four roots of evil. In A.G. Miller (Ed.), *The social psychology of good and evil* (pp. 85–101). New York: Guilford.

Bok, S. (1983). *Lying: Moral choice in public and private life.* New York: Pantheon Books.

Bond, C.F. Jr., & Robinson, M. (1988). The evolution of deception. *Journal of Nonverbal Behavior, 12,* 295–307.

Bowers, J.W., Elliott, N.D., & Desmond, R.J. (1977). Exploiting pragmatic rules: Devious messages. *Human Communication Research, 3,* 235–242.

Campbell, J. (2001). *The liar's tale: A history of falsehood.* New York: Norton.

DePaulo, B.M. (2004). The many faces of lies. In A.G. Miller (Ed.), *The social psychology of good and evil* (pp. 303–326). New York: Guilford.

DePaulo, B.M., Kashy, D.A., Kirkendol, S.E., Wyer, M.M., & Epstein, J.A. (1996). Lying in everyday life. *Journal of Personality and Social Psychology, 70,* 979–995.

Dubin, M. (1998, November 1). Survey: More kids lying, cheating. *Austin American Statesman,* p. K15.

Durham, G. (2000, October 17). Study finds students lie and cheat, a lot. *Associated Press.*

Feldman, R.S., Forrest, J.A., & Happ, B.R. (2002). Self-presentation and verbal deception: Do self-presenters lie more? *Basic and Applied Social Psychology, 24,* 163–170.

Feldman, R.S., Tomasian, J.C., & Coats, E.J. (1999). Nonverbal deception abilities and adolescents' social competence: Adolescents with higher social skills are better liars. *Journal of Nonverbal Behavior, 23,* 237–249.

Gordon, A.K., & Miller, A.G. (2000). Perspective differences in the construal of lies: Is deception in the eye of the beholder? *Personality and Social Psychology Bulletin, 26,* 46–55.

Hopper, R., & Bell, R. A. (1984). Broadening the deception construct. *Quarterly Journal of Speech, 70,* 288–302.

Howe, J., & Scherzer, J. (1986). Friend Hairyfish and Friend Rattlesnake, or dealing with anthropologists through humor. *Man, 21,* 680–696.

Josephson Institute of Ethics (2002). *2002 report card: The ethics of American youth.* Los Angeles: Josephson Institute.

Kalish, N. (2004, January). How honest are you? *Reader's Digest,* 114–119.

Keating, C.F., & Heltman, K.R. (1994). Dominance and deception in children and adults: Are leaders the best misleaders? *Personality and Social Psychology Bulletin, 20,* 312–321.

Kick, R. (2001). *The disinformation guide to media distortion, historical whitewashes and cultural myths.* New York: The Disinformation Co., Ltd.

Knapp, M.L., & Comadena, M.E. (1979). Telling it like it isn't: A review of theory and research on deceptive communications. *Human Communication Research, 5,* 270–285.

Knox, D., Schacht, C., Holt, J., & Turner, J. (1993). Sexual lies among university students. *College Student Journal, 27,* 269–272.

Leaky, R., & Lewin, R. (1978). *People of the lake.* New York: Doubleday.

Levine, T. R., Asada, K.J.K., & Lindsey, L.L.M. (2003). The relative impact of violation type and lie severity on judgments of message deceitfulness. *Communication Research Reports, 20,* 208–218.

Lippard, P.V. (1988). Ask me no questions, I'll tell you no lies: Situational exigencies for interpersonal deception. *Western Journal of Speech Communication, 52,* 91–103.

Miller, A.G. (Ed.) (2004). *The social psychology of good and evil.* New York: Guilford.

Miller, W. I. (2003). *Faking it.* New York: Cambridge University Press.

Mitchell, R.W., & Thompson, N.S. (Eds.) (1986). *Deception: Perspectives on human and nonhuman deceit.* New York: SUNY Press.

Nofsinger, R.E., Jr. (1976). On answering questions indirectly: Some rules in the grammar of doing conversation. *Human Communication Research, 2,* 172–181.

Nyberg, D. (1993). *The varnished truth: Truth telling and deceiving in ordinary life.* Chicago: University of Chicago Press.

Packer, G. (2013). *The unwinding: An inner history of the new America.* New York: Farrar, Straus, & Giroux.

Pitt-Rivers, J.A. (1954). *The people of the Sierra.* Chicago: University of Chicago Press.

Randi, J. (1982). *Flim-flam! Psychics, ESP, unicorns, and other delusions.* Buffalo, NY: Prometheus Books.

Rappaport, R.A. (1979). *Ecology, meaning, and religion.* Richmond, CA: North Atlantic Books.

Riggio, R.E., Tucker, J., & Throckmorton, B. (1988). Social skills and deception ability. *Personality and Social Psychology Bulletin, 13,* 568–577.

Saxe, L. (1991). Lying: Thoughts of an applied social psychologist. *American Psychologist, 46,* 409–415.

Slackman, M. (2006, August 6). The fine art of hiding what you mean to say. *New York Times, Section 4,* p. 5.

Smith, D. L. (2004). *Why we lie: The evolutionary roots of deception and the unconscious mind.* New York: St. Martin's Press.

Solomon, R.C. (1996). Self, deception, and self-deception in philosophy. In R.T. Ames and W. Dissanayake (Eds.), *Self and deception: A cross-cultural philosophical enquiry* (pp. 91–121). Albany, NY: SUNY Press.

Sullivan, E. (2001). *The concise book of lying.* New York: Farrar, Straus & Giroux.

Time, November 2, 1998, p. 35.

Turner, R.E., Edgley, C., & Olmstead, G. (1975). Information control in conversations: Honesty is not always the best policy. *Kansas Journal of Sociology, 11,* 69–89.

Tyler, J.J., Feldman, R.S., & Reichert, A. (2006). The price of deceptive behavior: Disliking and lying to people who lie to us. *Journal of Experimental Social Psychology, 42,* 69–77.

Washburne, C. (1969). Retortmanship: Ways to avoid answering questions. *ETC, 26,* 69–75.

Wolff, K.H. (Ed. & trans.) (1950). *The sociology of Georg Simmel.* New York: The Free Press.

Chapter 2

Perspectives on Truth

Lies exist as they are measured against, and contrasted with, truth. A liar must say something is false that he or she believes to be true or say something is true when he or she believes it to be false. So in order to fully understand the nature of lying and deception we need to understand the nature of truth. Truth, according to Nyberg (1993), is a symbol for things we take to be certain as we go about our lives in a world brimming with uncertainties (even though we don't maintain all we believe to be true with the same degree of certainty). A belief in certainties, says Nyberg, can make us feel very good. He goes on to say:

> It is our species' absurdly exciting predicament to have the capacity for imagining more than we can know. Imagination has no limit. We can always imagine knowing more than we actually can know. The object of such imagining, in some cases, is what we call the truth. (p. 30)

So how do we determine what is certain, what is "true"?

Four Ways We Determine What Is True

According to Fernández-Armesto (1997), people throughout history have sought and understood truth in one or more of the following ways: 1) by what they feel; 2) by what they are told; 3) by what they figure out (reasoning) and 4) by what they observe. Each approach has enjoyed a special prominence during different human epochs, and they are also useful in helping us understand how people find the truths that help them survive the uncertainties of life in today's world. Any given truth may have more than one origin and sometimes we acquire the truth of something in different ways as time passes. For example, we may initially believe something because we feel it, then later reinforce that belief by reading a book by someone else who has the same belief and, in time, remember that our belief came about through reasoning.

"The man who tells you truth does not exist is asking you not to believe him. So don't."

— *Roger Scruton*

"Every man's truth is what he and others negotiate it to be."

— *F. G. Bailey*

"The truth." Dumbledore sighed. "It is a beautiful and terrible thing, and should therefore be treated with great caution."

— *J. K. Rowling*

The Truth We Feel

Sometimes we rely on our feelings as a source of truth. These are not feelings derived from touching something; they are visceral, instinctive, or intuitive responses. We "know" something is true, but the specific cause or causes of our feeling may be difficult to identify and explain. Comedian Steven Colbert called this "truthiness." When people observe and process the nonverbal behavior of others, for example, they sometimes accurately describe the messages being communicated but are unable to verbally articulate what cues they used or how they went about constructing inferences about the other person's behavior. They say their judgment was based on a "hunch" or "just a feeling I had" (Smith, Archer & Costanzo, 1991). Researchers in other areas have also shown that we do a lot of thinking that isn't fully within our consciousness (Myers, 2002). There are many potential origins of "gut-level" feelings. Among these are generalizations we make after a rapid scan of a tiny portion of the data available to us or a memory that we are unable to remember having.

The truth we feel, at least initially, is uniquely owned by the person experiencing it. Feelings which represent things that are true for us may occur in a variety of ways. They may be a source of truth for an abstract belief ("I know God exists. I have felt his power.") or something very tangible ("Avery is the sweetest girl in the world."). Feelings as a source of truth may precede or follow a thought. While considering solutions to a problem, it is not uncommon for a people to report that the feeling which accompanied a particular idea made them know it was correct.

Once a feeling is strong enough to intrude on our consciousness, to call attention to itself in the context of a specific object of judgment, Schwarz (2012) says that feelings are most likely to become an important source of truth under the following circumstances.

Affective Judgments

When the judgment at hand is affective in nature, feelings are often a reliable source of information—e.g., liking for another person or a preference. Believing that "Avery is the sweetest girl in the world" may be closely linked to one's feelings when in Avery's presence. Feelings may be associated with specific emotions or moods. Moods, unlike most emotions we feel, lack a clear referent, come about gradually, exist at a lower level of intensity, and may last for an extended period of time. But moods, like emotions, are known to have an effect on how we perceive reality too. For example, people who are experiencing a good mood tend to see positive emotions in the faces of others whereas those experiencing a bad mood tend to see negative emotions (Niedenthal, Halberstadt, Margolin, & Innes-Ker, 2000; Schiffenbauer, 1974).

Information Available

We rely on our feelings as a source of truth when there is very little information available about the object being judged. A similar condition arises when information is available, but for various reasons we are prevented from systematically using that information due to limited attentional resources.

When people are exposed to repeated information, it finds a place in their memory even though it may not be at a high level of consciousness. Then, when they are asked to evaluate new information that is similar to the repeated information, feelings of familiarity can result. Familiarity, in turn, may lead to the illusion that this information is true (Schwikert & Curran, 2014).

Complex Judgments

When we are trying to make a complex judgment which is based on isolated bits and fragments of information, feelings may be more likely to come into play as a marker of truth.

Time Constraints

Even when information is available and complex judgments are not required, time constraints or competing task demands may give preference to feelings as a way of assessing what is true. In such cases, feelings reflect a simplified heuristic strategy.

While the preceding represents various situational demands, there may also be particular individuals who are more likely to gravitate toward their feelings as basis for truth. Individuals who regularly focus and reflect on their inner feelings may grow to trust them and believe in their truth value.

Truth claims based on one's feelings, while valid and meaningful to the person experiencing them, may be difficult to explain to, or gain acceptance from, others. When truth claims are made, it is not uncommon for others to ask how we know the claim is true. Because the claimant knows his or her feelings are not likely to be a highly credible source to gain the other's acceptance of the claim, other responses may precede the eventual admission, "Well, that's just how I feel about it" or "I'm not sure…I just know it." For some truth claims, like one's belief in the existence of God, truth through feelings is granted and normally goes uncontested as an individual's truth. However, if an individual has a desire to have his or her "feeling truth" accepted by others, they are well advised to look for corroborating sources—others with similar feelings, books, experts, logic, observations, etc. Some venues, like courtrooms, are especially resistant to truth claims based solely on feelings.

The Truth We Are Told

Sometimes we rely on other people as our source of truth. This may be in the form of a face to face conversation, but people who write magazine articles, books, newspaper stories, or speak to us through television also become sources of what we believe to be true. This is truth that is firmly anchored to the reality perceived by one or more *other* people whom we choose to believe. Of course we may believe them because their perception of reality matches ours or even what we wish to be true. These sources of truth may be viewed as a designated authority figure, an expert in his or her field, someone who happens to agree with us on a particular issue or issues, and/or a person whom we trust to weigh the accuracy of information without apparent biases. For example, young children normally rely on their parents to determine what is true. As they grow older, other sources of truth may become equally or more reliable. When they become adults, they develop expectations about the credibility and honesty of sources based on social categories such as occupation. For example, a 2014 Gallup poll found that adults rate the honesty of nurses higher than doctors, police officers, clergy, or members of Congress (see Figure 2.1).

Please tell me how you would rate honesty and ethical standards of people in these different fields—very high, high, average, low or very low?

Dec. 8–11, 2014

Copyright © 2014 Gallup, Inc. All rights reserved. The content is used with permission; however, Gallup retains all rights of republication.

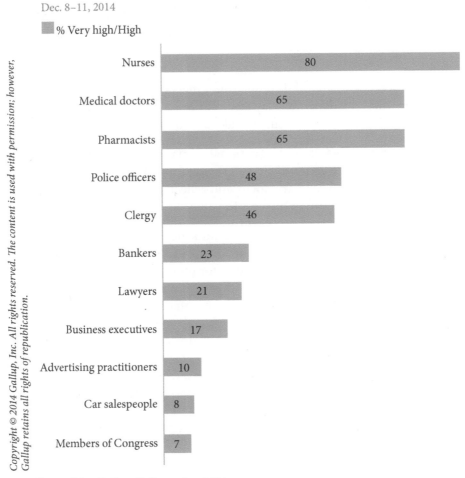

% Very high/High

Nurses	80
Medical doctors	65
Pharmacists	65
Police officers	48
Clergy	46
Bankers	23
Lawyers	21
Business executives	17
Advertising practitioners	10
Car salespeople	8
Members of Congress	7

Figure 2.1: Gallup Poll results, 2014

Compared to others, lies are least expected from our family and friends (Heyman, Luu, & Lee, 2009; Van Swol, Molhotra, & Braun, 2012). The trust we place in our friends as a source of truth is what some con artists depend on to make their scams work. For example, many victims of online "phishing" scams were lured in by an e-mail message they received from a friend or relative. In some cases, the message was forwarded to them by an acquaintance who didn't realize it was part of a scam; in others, it was sent by a scammer who hacked an acquaintance's email account and then sent messages to all the contacts listed in the address book. In both situations, scammers tricked victims into sharing financial information or downloading malicious software by exploiting the trust they invest in their social network (Wang et al., 2012). Other scammers leverage this investment not merely to gain access to new victims, but also to make old ones do their bidding. Suppose a licensed accountant convinces your friend that he or she can invest money at an extremely high interest rate. Your friend gives the accountant $100,000 and for the next four months actually gets the promised high rate of return. The accountant has not invested your friend's money at all and is paying him with money another person has given him. But as far as your friend is concerned, he is making money and wants you to share the wealth. Your friend and trusted source convinces you to invest too. Shortly thereafter, your friend stops getting his monthly payments and you never get any. The accountant has left town. Scams like this happen all the time and to everyone—the young and old, rich and poor, highly educated and less educated, the financially experienced and novices (see Chapter 8 for more on con artists and con games).

Modern society is complex and the amount of information we are expected to process on a daily basis is huge. We simply do not have the time nor energy to investigate the truth of everything we hear or see. So we take things on faith—faith that what is told to us by others is usually the truth. This tendency is known as a "truth bias" and, as noted in Chapter 9, it plays an important role in our ability to detect deceptive behavior (Levine, 2014).

A lot of what we believe is dependent on inferences we make about the credibility of others. We expect people will generally tell us the truth and we trust certain people to be the source of valid information for us. But of course, not everyone always trusts the same sources. Most people, for example, believe the United States landed astronauts on the Moon and President Barack Obama is a U.S. citizen. But there are some who don't trust these sources and maintain the government faked the moon landing and President Obama forged his birth certificate (see Chapter 13 for more on this issue.)

The truth we are told from others doesn't necessarily have to come from individuals. Sometimes we believe something is true based on the sheer number of other people who believe it. If ten people believe the color of a shirt is dark blue, you too may see it as dark blue even though you would have said it was black if someone had asked you before you knew what others had perceived. "Social proof" of this sort is a common proxy for truth in the era of social media. Facebook users commonly judge the accuracy of a story in their news feed based on the number of likes or dislikes it receives from other users. Credibility is conferred to Twitter users based on how many followers they have (MacCoun, 2012). Although social media users may believe there is "strength in numbers," computer programs that generate fake Facebook likes and phantom Twitter followers exploit the weakness of their herd mentality (Muscanell, Guadagno, & Murphy, 2014).

The Truth We Figure Out Through Reasoning

There are various ways of thinking systematically that we also use as a basis for what we believe to be true. Sometimes these decision rules are clear, formal, and well-known to others. What is true, then, is what agrees with the rules, standards, or system being used.

$$(x + y)^2 = x^2 + 2xy + y^2$$

If you believe this equation to be true, you are saying it is consistent with a system of statements in the language called algebra. If someone says, "Today is June 20th" and you reply, "That's true," you are saying you accept the same system and rules for figuring out dates. Many of the things we believe to be true are deeply ingrained in these widely accepted rules and formulas for thinking which usually go unchallenged. They are so taken for granted that people who do not accept them are labeled illogical, unable to reason, or not thinking straight. But we shouldn't forget that the truth of any claim deduced by its application to a known formula is only as strong as our faith in the truth value of the formula itself. As Fernández-Armesto (1997, p. 119) says:

> "We cannot reason our way to any conclusion except by laying down conditions in which it is foreshadowed: we cannot get to the conclusion that Socrates is mortal without saying first, 'If all men are mortal', or that spheres are round without first specifying roundness as a defining characteristic of a sphere. 'You can only find truth with logic,' as Chesterton said, 'if you have already found truth without it."

There are also ways of reasoning in which the rules are less explicit and, as a result, the reasoning and the conclusions reached can show considerable variation from person to person and society to society. For example, we use reasoning to draw conclusions about a myriad of everyday issues like the extent to which guns should be controlled and how; whether strict voter identification laws suppress voting by minorities; whether sex education classes in schools reduce teenage pregnancy; or if government surveillance of citizens' phone calls and Internet usage is necessary to prevent terrorist attacks. With issues like these people may reason differently and thereby draw different conclusions. Only information that supports one's beliefs is often the basis for reasoning. A belief in God is normally rooted in faith, but some people try to buttress their faith with what they feel is a reasoned argument to support God's existence. They reason that the world they know is so complex and inexplicable in so many ways that it could not have come about without the direction of God. However, a scientist may view this as an attempt to use reasoning to establish a scientific truth and for the scientist a scientific truth is always subject to modification or refutation—typically not the case with the reasoning to support the existence of God (Shermer, 2003). Some people also reason, incorrectly, that if a person believes in Darwin's theory of evolution that they must also be an agnostic or atheist.

Reasoning in everyday life is always subject to questionable premises, biases, and incorrect inferential short cuts (Kida, 2006). Incorrect inferences can be "reasoned" from accurate observations—e.g., a wife who heard that her husband was seen repeatedly hugging another woman may incorrectly reason her husband is having an affair; a six year old girl who has watched a number of airplanes take off is a passenger for the first time and after taking off asks, "When do we start getting smaller?" Her reasoning followed logically from the flights she had seen from the ground, but her conclusion was wrong. We also tend to discount the role of chance happenings in our life—preferring to reason that an event was caused by something. Most of us also tend to overestimate the number of deaths attributable to sensational accidents but underestimate the frequency of deaths due to diabetes, stroke, and asthma. This may be due to greater media coverage, but only a few vivid anecdotes or stories can also greatly influence our reasoning. Judging the frequency and probability of things based on how easily they come to mind or whether you have experienced them are other ways we reason our way to incorrect conclusions. Despite the fact that several hundred people reported problems with air bags in the type of car you drive, you reason this is not a problem because you haven't experienced any trouble yourself. Or you may reason that because the names of fifteen professional sports figures from your home state easily come to mind that your home state has probably produced more professional athletes than any other state (Kahneman, 2011).

In everyday conversation as well as in courtroom proceedings, we often reason incorrectly that truthfulness is always associated with consistency and deception with inconsistency. There are two pitfalls associated with this premise. First, human beings are not always highly consistent in the way they choose to report reality due to faulty memory and/or the different language choices they may make to describe a phenomena at time[1] and time[2]. Second, what may appear to be "inconsistent" to one person may be perfectly consistent to another. Consider the wife who says to her husband, "You spend too much money," and minutes later bemoans the fact that they don't ever go out and eat at nice restaurants any more. To the husband, his wife is being inconsistent since she doesn't want him to spend money, but she wants to eat out at an expensive restaurant. The wife, however, sees no contradiction. Her husband spends too much money on himself, but she approves of spending money on something both of them can enjoy.

While the preceding examples illustrate some of the troublesome aspects which may accompany truth derived from reasoning, they should not be construed as showing that reasoning is a poor way to arrive at truth. On the contrary, truth derived from reasoned thinking has served humankind well for centuries. But the examples do remind us that reasoning, like other methods of seeking truth, is subject to the frailties and shortcomings which are so much a part of being human.

The Truth We Observe

Sometimes we find truth in what we observe. Unlike the three preceding ways of arriving at something we believe to be true, this approach requires sensory contact with the object in question. The senses serve as a way of certifying the truth. When someone says, "I saw it with my own eyes so it must be true," or "I know he said it because I heard him say it," they are testifying to their reliance on their own sensory observations as a source of truth.

The observers themselves are not the only ones who believe in the truth of their sensory observations. Jurors tend to believe eyewitnesses about 80% of the time and this percentage increases if the witness shows confidence and/or includes more details in their testimony. The word of eyewitnesses has been given more credence in some court cases than fingerprint experts, polygraphs, handwriting experts, and, in at least one case, a DNA expert. The truth value of eyewitness (and earwitness) testimony in court is almost as good at getting a conviction as having the proverbial smoking gun, according to Loftus (1991, p. 13):

> *Eyewitness identification is the most damning of all evidence that can be used against a defendant. When an eyewitness points a*

finger at a defendant and says, "I saw him do it," the case is "cast-iron, brass-bound, copper-riveted, and airtight" as one prosecutor proclaimed. For how can we disbelieve the sworn testimony of eyewitnesses to a crime when the witnesses are absolutely convinced that they are telling the truth?

But research also tells us that eyewitnesses can and have been wrong. Neither the eyewitness' confident demeanor nor his or her inclusion of details has been linked to greater accuracy. In recent years, the analysis of DNA evidence has led to the release of numerous prisoners, some of whom were on death row, and most of whom were convicted solely or with the help of eyewitness testimony. Pezdek (2011) reports that of the first 292 prisoners exonerated by DNA evidence, approximately 75% were convicted based on eyewitness misidentification. What are the factors that contribute to their memory mistakes? We tend to think our eyes work like a video camera, flawlessly recording what they are directed toward. However, scientific studies tell a different story. Sometimes we do not observe large changes in objects and scenes ("change blindness") and sometimes we do not even perceive certain highly visible objects in our visual field ("inattentional blindness"). For example, drivers may fail to notice another car when trying to turn or a person may fail to see a friend in a movie theater while looking for a seat, even though the friend is waving. Our brain is constantly trying to make sense out of an environment filled with a tremendous array of changing stimuli which vary in intensity. As a result, the brain tries to create a meaningful narrative and overlooks those stimuli that don't fit the narrative being created. Simons and Chabris (1999) demonstrated this phenomenon in an experiment. People were asked to watch a one minute video in which several people were dribbling and passing a basketball and to count the number of times a pass was made from one player to another. Observers concentrated closely on the passing in order to determine the correct number of passes. During the video a person dressed in a gorilla suit walked into the middle of the players, turned toward the camera and thumped his or her chest, and walked off (see Figure 2.2). Only 50% of the observers noticed the gorilla. When we first heard of this experiment, we were skeptical of the results, but scores of our students have reacted in the same way when we gave them the same task with the same video.

Simons, D. J., & Chabris, C. F. (1999). Gorillas in our midst: Sustained inattentional blindness for dynamic events. Perception, 28, 1059-1074. Figure provided by Daniel Simons. www.dansimons.com

Figure 2.2: Inattentional blindness and the unseen gorilla

The Observer

Observations are affected by numerous long- and short-term characteristics of the observer—his or her stress level, biases/prejudices, expectations, age, gender, interest in the object of observation, motivation to observe closely, etc. (Wells, Memon, & Penrod, 2006). Examining a few of these should amply illustrate how various characteristics of the observer can affect what the observer sees and hears. Both males and females, for example, can be accurate observers, but not necessarily with the same targets. Accuracy is often linked to one's interest in and experience with the thing being observed, and the interests and experiences of males and females may differ (Davis & Loftus, 2009). Accurate facial identification of people who have a different racial background can be negatively affected by the amount of experience and exposure one has had with that race. Thus, a white woman who has had little contact and experience with Asian men may concentrate intently on the facial features of the man stealing her purse, but because she has had little exposure to Asian men and her observations were made during a time of highly negative arousal with plenty of distractions, she may not be good at distinguishing the thief from other Asian men (Scherf & Scott, 2012). Of course, too much familiarity with the object of observation may also make it difficult to accurately perceive things because we feel like we "know" the target and relax our focus our attention, thereby missing the unexpected.

Observers also have biases. One common bias stems from people's desire to perceive the world in a way that confirms their beliefs. Sometimes this "confirmation bias" motivates them to see or hear things that others do not. A UFOlogist sees a face in a picture taken by the NASA Mars rover. A devout Catholic sees the Virgin Mary on a tortilla. A paranormalist discerns the voices of dead people speaking to him in a grainy radio signal. A police offer in a crime-ridden neighborhood mistakes the cellphone a teenager is holding for a gun. In other cases, confirmation bias motivates observers to not see or hear things that others do. Sports fans don't see why the referee called a foul against the team they are cheering on, but do when their opponents do the same thing. A woman smitten with a new boyfriend is baffled when her friends tell her it's obvious that "he's just not that into you." You witness a good friend and neighbor having a tense interaction with a police officer but fail to see him making threatening gestures or hear his swearing. Bias of this sort probably occurred when the twin daughters of accused wife murderer Robert Angleton were asked to listen to a garbled tape recording of two men plotting the murder of their mother—one of whom knew many details about how to enter the victim's house. With their mother dead and their father facing a murder charge, it is not surprising that they did not hear the voice on the tape as their father's. Although the Angleton twins didn't think of their recognition failure as a choice, the consistency with which people hear and see things they want to believe and miss those they don't suggests that observations are to some degree decisions influenced by motives (Shermer, 2011).

Observers are also influenced by the extent to which they are motivated to observe something for details or not. We are rarely asked to provide the same level of detail about our experiences in daily social interaction that we would be expected to recount in a court of law. Suppose you went horseback riding last year when you were vacationing at Lake Tahoe. Some or all of the following may be things you didn't think were important to observe and remember. What was the name of the horse you rode? How many miles did you ride? What were you wearing? What color was the saddle blanket? How many other people were in your party? A familiar test of how closely we observe an object we have seen many times is the identification of the correct penny face. How accurate are you?

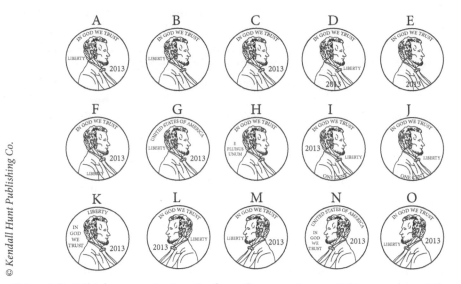

© Kendall Hunt Publishing Co.

Figure 2.3: Which penny depicts the face of an actual penny? (Answer on p. 36)

Observers also make observations during times of heightened emotions, moods, and stress. While a certain amount of stress may be optimal for accurate observations, too much or too little may adversely affect what is observed and what is remembered. Observers under high stress focus on some details but not on others. When the observer is threatened by another person with a lethal weapon, this is likely to narrow perceptions of the general situation to that of the weapon (Pezdek, 2009).

The Observation Conditions

In addition to various factors affecting the observer, there will always be certain conditions under which the observation was made which will affect what is observed. These include such things as viewing angle, lighting, distance, competing stimuli, length of time observing, etc. Photographers, film makers, and others who make their living via the visual arts know how to create a different viewer impression by varying the ways the viewer sees the presentation (Lester, 2010; Messaris, 1994, 2012;). These factors and various observer characteristics noted earlier no doubt played an important role in the different observations of 349 people who reported seeing American Airlines Flight 587 fall from the sky over New York in November, 2001.

- 52% said they saw a fire while the plane was in the air; 22% said there was no fire.
- 8% said there was an explosion.
- 22% said they saw smoke; 20% said they saw no smoke.

- 18% said the plane turned right; 18% said the plane turned left; 13% said it was wobbling, dipping, or in a side to side motion.
- 57% said they saw something separate from the airplane, but disagreed on what it was. 9% said nothing fell off the plane. ("Different Views," 2002)

Thus far we've focused on unaided human sensory perception. But observations are also made with devices which enhance and/or extend our senses. Microscopes and telescopes help us see what is prohibited by normal visual acuity and sound wave analyzers measure acoustic signals we are unable to hear. We also rely on speedometers, stethoscopes, polygraphs, and seismographs to make observations our senses cannot. These devices further add to the possibility of multiple truths, depending on the type of observation used. For example, depending on the degree of measurement precision, one might say a table length is 30 inches high, using an ordinary yard stick, or 30.019 inches with a more precise measuring instrument. Both are "true" measures, but the standard of measurement was different. Some people believe polygraphs measure lying. They don't. They measure changes in breathing, heart rate, perspiration, and blood pressure. These measures are then observed by human beings who make inferences about whether certain patterns are likely to be associated with lying (For additional information on polygraphs, see Chapter 10).

Memory

The truth of any observation we make is partly in how we perceive it and partly in how we remember our perceptions. Memory, then, is a key factor in the truth we observe. Many people believe that their memories operate like a digital camera, recording the events of their lives just as they occurred and storing them as "files" for future reference. All the details of an event are "in storage" and if not readily accessed, the use of hypnosis and other enhancement techniques can eventually recover them. Memory research, however, does not support such a view (Winter, 2012). Although our brains do record some aspects of past experiences, remembering them is a reconstructive process in which we blend the aspects we did record with information from other events we experienced in the past and our ongoing experience in the present. As a result, our memories are not precise and permanent, but rather messy and changeable.

When our memory fails us, then, it can be because we never stored the information in the first place or if we have, it has been forgotten; false memories can be implanted by our suggestibility to outside sources or through our own biases which prompt us to rewrite history based on our present beliefs (Schacter, 2001). Sometimes visual memories can be hindered simply because we try to verbally describe what we saw prior to visually identifying it. This is most likely to occur when the stimulus is complex and/or abstract and the perceiver does not have the specialized knowledge or vocabulary to adequately describe it. For example, when an eyewitness is asked to verbally describe the face of a person seen committing a crime before they are asked to identify the perpetrator's face in a photo lineup, a linguistically awkward and uncertain verbal description may create a memory which interferes with the visual memory. This is called "verbal overshadowing" (Schooler, 2013; McGlone, Kobrynowicz, & Alexander, 2005). The idea that we can and do permanently change remembered events (and create new ones) opens up the possibility that what we earnestly believe may not necessarily be what happened—not necessarily the truth. Since memories are altered in line with our own needs and interpretations, there is no reason for us to doubt them. They are beliefs that make sense to us and our sincerity in those beliefs is genuine.

Much of the information we lose or forget about an event occurs soon after our experience and then gradually continues thereafter. Some variations in this pattern will occur depending on the type of information involved, but immediately writing or talking about the event may aid in retaining details associated with it. Talking about the event, however, introduces the possibility that the remarks of the person or persons you talk to may somehow become blended into your memory of the event.

So how other people "help" us remember things may also be a part of the truth we observe. Accurate retrieval of a witness's memory of an event is critical to effective law enforcement. Letting a witness respond freely usually provides the most accurate recollections, but also the least complete version. Since our memory of an event is often incomplete and has gaps to be filled in, others can help us fill in those gaps. The "filling in" may take place immediately when you witness an event with another person and he or she turns to you and says, "Hey, what about the size of that guy's biceps?!" That may be enough to add "large biceps" to your recollection of the person you observed. Questioning subsequent to an event can also act as fillers for memory gaps. For example, the question: "Did you see *the* broken headlight?" could make a witness believe there was a broken headlight and incorporate it into his or her story. "Did you see *a* broken headlight?" or better, "Was there a broken headlight?" are less likely to imply that there was a broken headlight. The methods used in identifying a criminal from a photo lineup can also have a profound affect on memory retrieval and police departments have begun to modify their procedures. Thirty to forty per cent of the witnesses who view a photo lineup will identify one of the photos as the perpetrator of the crime even though the suspect isn't in the lineup. To offset the assumption that the suspect is there and they just need to find him/her, witnesses should be told by the administrator of the lineup that the suspect may or may not be in the lineup and that it is ok to say you don't know or aren't sure. When all the photos are shown at the same time, witnesses tend to compare the photos and select the one who most closely resembles the face they remember. Showing the photos sequentially can reduce false identifications by 10% without affecting the percentage of accurate identifications. It is also important to select a person to administer the photo lineup who does not know who the suspect is. Unconscious movements or statements like, "Be sure you look at all of the photos before you select one" (when the witness has selected someone other than the suspect known to the administrator) essentially tells the witness that his or her memory needs to be altered (Malpass, Tredoux, & McQuiston-Surrett, 2009; Wells & Olson, 2003). Once a witness has received implicit or explicit confirmation for his or her identification, it is very difficult to change their mind.

In contrast to the assumptions associated with several nationally publicized child abuse cases purported to have occurred in day care facilities in the 1980s, children are no longer uncritically accepted as totally credible sources of information (see Chapter 5). We know children engage in behavior adults would label a lie; we know children's memories are just as fallible as an adult's; and we know children may modify their memories and tell stories they think adults want them to tell. A study by the American Academy of Child Psychiatry found 36% of the charges involving children's testimony about sexual abuse in custody battles were later proved untrue. Courts in many states do not allow children under ten years of age to testify. When they do, the tests for competency are: Can the child recall and accurately report an event? Can the child distinguish lies from truth? Does the child understand the concept of one's duty to tell the truth?

Sometimes children will "lie" without prompting from adults, but most of the research in this area focuses on how children may be persuaded to tell a story by adults who have personal agendas (known or unknown to themselves). Generally, young children are more susceptible to suggestive techniques than adults, but getting a child to accept a suggestion is not always easy and may take repeated efforts over a period of time. In one study, 75 five to six year olds watched a film of a man who picked up a doll and cleaned it. After the film, an adult said to the children he thought the man was "playing with" the doll. Subsequently, the children were asked what happened and about 25% said the man in the film was playing with the doll. But when the adult kept insisting to the children that the man in the film was playing with the doll, all but two children eventually relented and agreed there was playing in the film (Goodman & Clarke-Stewart, 1991). Sometimes children can be the target of repeated interviews with leading questions which can turn a case of a candy cane being dropped into a female child's underpants into a candle which was inserted into the child's vagina. In some instances, dolls have been used during the questioning of children. Sometimes they are dolls which have realistic genitals which, given their extraordinary difference to most dolls children play with, are bound to garner special attention. However, there is little evidence to suggest that dolls add any validity to the responses of children who have been sexually abused (Ceci, Bruck, & Battin, 2000). "Coaching" children in order to influence their testimony works best when the child knows the coach and is motivated to please the coach (Lyon, Malloy, Quas, J.A., & Talwar, 2008).

While the observed truth is often given a great deal of credence in today's society, there is plenty of evidence to show that two observations of the "same" target by one individual at two (or more) different times, or by two (or more) different individuals at the same time, can be vastly different. It is relatively easy to understand how the preceding factors associated with perception and memory can affect the accuracy of other people's observations and more difficult to accept their effect on our own behavior.

Truth and Certainty

We started this chapter by saying that people seek truth because they seek certainty in their lives. But not all of the things we believe to be true are held with the same degree of certainty—the same strength of belief. Instead, we think about things in terms of their probability of being true. Those with the highest probability of being true provide us with the greatest certainty. But truth is always in process. Something we are very certain about, something that has a high probability of being true for us, may or may not remain so; something with a lower probability of being true may, in time, become more certain for us.

What is true for many individuals or an entire society is also composed of beliefs that vary in their probability of being certain. Even if 17 million people in a society composed of 317 million people believe something is true, it may still be an improbable truth for society as a whole. For example, the Gallup Poll, responded to two polls in the mid-1990s that showed 6% of the Americans polled had doubts that U.S. astronauts landed and walked on the moon by saying on their website: "Although, if taken literally, 6% translates into millions of individuals, it is not unusual to find about that many people in the typical poll agreeing with almost any question that is asked of them—so the best interpretation is that this particular conspiracy theory is not widespread." (In 2002, polls indicated 7% of the population believed Elvis may still be alive.) Of course, sometimes a belief shared by most people and which represents the prevailing truth can change. *Experts, advocates in positions of power, loud and persistent advocates who begin without a power base, new information, or conditions which change with time and make a belief more palatable, are all capable of changing societal truths.* When Copernicus first put forth the idea that the Sun, not the Earth, was at the heart of our solar system, most astronomers and natural philosophers did not believe it was true. Over a hundred years later, Galileo's support for Copernicus' ideas was denounced by leaders of the Roman Catholic church as heresy because such ideas were believed to be contrary to doctrines of that branch of Christianity. Today, the idea that the Earth, Moon, and other planets in our solar system revolve around the Sun is an astronomical truth that is not questioned by physicists. In 1930, astronomers named a celestial body Pluto, the ninth planet in our solar system; in 2006, Pluto was reclassified as a dwarf planet, thereby reducing the number of planets in our solar system from nine to eight. But even more "constant" truths like the speed of light are subject to change. Scientists whose observations of gas clouds as far away as 12 billion light years from earth have presented data indicating that there is a strong possibility that the speed of light and other universal principles of physics may change with the passage of time (Urban et al., 2013). While the preceding examples have focused on new information and observations, what is true for the general public can sometimes be changed by simply mandating that something be classified in a different way. Before 1948, the harmonica was classified as a toy. As a result, not even the most accomplished players could join a musician's union because they did not play a musical instrument. After 1948, the harmonica became a musical instrument and those who played it were considered musicians.

Telling the Truth

Up to this point we have focused on the ways people determine what they believe to be true and the degree of certainty with which those truths are held. In this section we focus on the process of talking about what we believe to be true. Two crucial decisions face a truth teller: a) what to say and b) how to say it.

At first, deciding what to say seems obvious. After all, aren't we just going to tell "the truth?" "The" truth makes it sound like there is only one thing to be said (and it is clear what that is). While we may end up saying only one thing, there may be a lot of other associated truths we don't say. We can't ever say everything about anything. So from the standpoint of the courtroom oath, we are not likely to tell "the *whole* truth" even though we can tell what we believe to be "the truth and nothing but the truth." Part of the truth teller's task, then, is to select from all that he or she believes to be true about a particular issue, that which should be said. For those who subscribe to the tenets of "radical honesty" (Blanton, 2005), this decision is an easy one because it is based more on the need to express oneself than on what the recipient should hear and what effects it might have. Adherents of radical honesty are encouraged to tell neighbors they'd rather watch TV than come over to their house for dinner; tell an employer that they left their last job because they didn't like their supervisor's attitude, or tell their spouse they look fat. From this perspective, catharsis is the motivation for telling the truth and for some people at some points in their life this may be liberating, if not costly. As Nyberg (1993, p. 17) says: "It is a great distortion to believe you are speaking the truth simply because you say what you think. It is possible to be sincere and wrong. It is also possible to be sincere, right, and dumb." This does not mean we should not try to tell the truth nor does it mean we should avoid telling the truth every time there may be costs associated with it. But when one is considering how to most effectively tell the truth, it is important to decide what parts of the truth one holds about a particular issue should be said and how those parts should be put into words.

Knowing how to put the truth into words is greatly facilitated by understanding how we determine truth in the first place. Throughout this chapter we have emphasized the potentially inexact nature of our perceptions and memory; the ongoing changes in the objects of our perceptions; the prevalent role of inferences in what we "know" to be true; that what we "know" as true can change over time; and that most, if not all, of what we know as true is based on probability rather than absolute certainty. On top of this, the language we use to describe our realities inevitably abstracts (selects some aspects and ignores others) from the referent.

If one agrees with the preceding and strives to more accurately tell the truth, then language which is more circumspect and qualified is in order. Hayakawa (1990, p.209) said: "…knowledge is power, *but effective knowledge is that which includes knowledge of the limitations of one's knowledge.*" Within this framework, truth tellers would be careful to link their telling of truths to their own perceptions ("It seems to me…" or "The way I see things…"); the perceptions of others ("I believe what the article in *The New York Times* said…"); and to anchor their claims to the here-and-now rather than imply that their claim is not subject to change over time. For example, saying "In my view, it was unethical of you to refuse to pay Bob after you said you would" provides a very different basis for interaction about the truth you perceive than, "You are an unethical person." Truth statements at lower levels of probability may be qualified with words like, "might be" or "seems to be" or "could be." Fernández-Armesto (1997, p.105) reports that "In the system of logic peculiar to the Jain philosophers of India, no statement is considered true unless it contains such qualifiers as 'perhaps' and 'as it were.'"

While being circumspect in the way you tell the truth may appropriately account for the often uncertain ways we come to know truths, it is certainly not always the best way to accomplish communicative goals. Not everyone accepts the tentative nature of truth claims—especially their own. And there are many people who fully appreciate the tentative nature of truth claims who wish it was not so and like to hear those who speak in unqualified, certain terms. (Does this mean they like liars?!) So even though you may understand and accept your truth claims as something short of certain, in some situations you may appropriately choose to act as if you had no doubts about your truth claims. Politicians who publicly acknowledge the uncertainties associated with what they believe to be true are likely to have trouble getting elected; lovers who tell their partners they aren't sure what they feel is love and that they don't always feel love may be accurate, but single. As noted in Chapter 1, effective communication may involve some forms of lying and/or deception.

Is Everyone's Truth Equally Valid?

Given what has been said up to this point, one might legitimately conclude that there is no truth apart from each person's own reality and therefore, one person's truth is just as good and just as true as another's. While some academicians embrace this idea theoretically, there does not seem to be a lot of evidence that it is widely practiced by everyday people in everyday situations. Ironically, it is not unusual for the academicians who support the idea that everyone's truth is equally valid to castigate other points of view as incorrect.

In daily life we find some areas where more truths are accepted and tolerated than others, but it is hard to think of any area where everyone's truth is treated as equally valid. In the USA, those who have found religious truth in Christianity, Buddhism, Islam, Mormonism, and Judaism may get a better sense that their truths are being treated as similarly (if not equally) valid than those who find their truth in Atheism, Wiccanism, Shamanism, or religions that sacrifice animals in their rituals. And even though the Republican and Democratic parties in the USA argue with each other and claim to stand for very different things, most would probably agree that the truths espoused by these parties are not considered commensurate with the truths espoused by other political parties in the United States such as the Tea Party, the Libertarian Party, the U.S. Socialist Party, the Green Party, and Stormfront (a white supremacist party). Are the people who say they have been abducted by aliens, taken to their space ship, examined, and released telling the truth? As they perceive it, yes. Is this truth as valid as the truth of those who do not believe our planet has been visited by a species from another planet? No, no more so than those whose religious truth denies medical help to a dying child; no more so than people who believe mental illness is caused by demonic possession; no more so than someone who won't swim in your pool because there is a pink rhino in it.

Unlike many of the preceding examples, sometimes the number of people who believe in conflicting truths is comparable (e.g., when life begins). Instead of helping to see the other's truth as equally valid, advocates on each side are likely to work even harder to make sure their truth prevails. When truths come into conflict with one another, how does one prevail? Some venues have rules of evidence and standards for truth which are tailored to their particular situation (e.g., the courtroom), but in the public sphere, the following factors often account for what is accepted as true:

- Support by many people. What is considered true is often a function of how many people believe it is true. This belief may or may not be linked to a belief in an objective reality (e.g., that there are no pink rhinos).
- Support by those who have the power to make decisions for many others.
- Support by people whose knowledge on the issue in question is respected by many others—i.e., experts.
- Repeated arguments which convincingly appeal to what many others believe is reasonable or arguments which elicit a strong emotional response from many others.
- The preference for truths linked to human survival and well-being is also a standard which may be applied.

What all this suggests is that even though we are often encouraged to treat truth as more of a journey than a destination, there are times when it may be important to at least act like you've arrived. (Is this lying?) At the same time, though, it is important to recognize that the quest for truth is an ongoing process. With this perspective, even people who advocate a particular truth will continue to seek input from a variety of sources—e.g., talking to people with different backgrounds and experiences, reading a wide spectrum of what people write, and involving themselves in a variety of life's experiences. They will also struggle to maintain the truth-seeking process by testing, analyzing, and pitting their intuition, their emotional reactions, their reasoning, their observations, and what other people tell them against one another...especially when it doesn't seem necessary.

Summary

This chapter began with the assumption that in order to properly understand lying and deception, we need to understand how people determine truth. People want certainty in their lives, which prompts them to seek truth. Four common methods for determining the truth were examined: 1) the truth we feel; 2) the truth we are told; 3) the truth we figure out through reasoning; and 4) the truth we observe. Some important factors that affect the nature of our truths, no matter how they are determined, include: 1) we don't perceive things exactly like anyone else; 2) most of what we know is based on inferences; 3) even what we know from observation is based on probabilities; 4) what we know today as true may not be known as truth tomorrow; 5) when we decide something is true, we label it (abstract some qualities and ignore others); and 6) human memory , including eyewitness observations are fallible because: not all events nor all parts of a given event are stored in the brain; that which is stored can be forgotten over time, altered by other people and events, or altered by one's own changing needs. When we tell the truth we need to determine what, out of all we know, to tell and how to tell it. Given the often tenuous nature of truth, linguistic choices which are qualified and circumspect seem appropriate, but these linguistic choices may not be helpful in accomplishing various communicative goals. While it is theoretically possible to see how the process of determining truth might mean that everyone's truth is equally valid, certain truths tend to prevail in everyday life. Particular truths prevail because they have one or more of the following: 1) many people believe it; 2) powerful people and decision-makers believe it; 3) experts believe it; 4) arguments based on reason and/ or emotion appeal to many people; and 5) the truth appeals to human survival and/ or well-being. The chapter concluded by saying that even though truth-seeking is more journey than destination, communicators may sometimes have to act as if they have reached their destination in order to get the responses they desire.

(Penny "A" depicts the face of an actual penny. This test was reprinted from: Nickerson, R.S. & Adams, M.J. (1979). Long-term memory for a common object. *Cognitive Psychology, 11,* 287–307.)

Things to Think About

Circle the degree to which you believe the following statements are true. Using the material in this chapter as a guide, explain why you believe as you do for each statement. When you are finished, talk about your answers with others who have also independently responded to these statements.

1. All persons are created equal.

   Not Very Certain It Is True   1   2   3   4   5   Very Certain It Is True

2. It will rain tomorrow.

   Not Very Certain It Is True   1   2   3   4   5   Very Certain It Is True

3. Charles Darwin developed the first theory of evolution.

   Not Very Certain It Is True   1   2   3   4   5   Very Certain It Is True

4. Lemmings are rodents that periodically commit mass suicide by marching *en masse* off high cliffs to their deaths.

   Not Very Certain It Is True   1   2   3   4   5   Very Certain It Is True

5. Lightning never strikes twice in the same place.

   Not Very Certain It Is True   1   2   3   4   5   Very Certain It Is True

6. Betsy Ross designed the first American flag.

   Not Very Certain It Is True   1   2   3   4   5   Very Certain It Is True

7. Smoking cigarettes causes lung cancer.

   Not Very Certain It Is True   1   2   3   4   5   Very Certain It Is True

8. Eight added to six is always fourteen.

   Not Very Certain It Is True   1   2   3   4   5   Very Certain It Is True

Gheorghe, The Vampire Slayer[1]

Toma Petre died. After he was buried, his brother-in-law, Gheorghe Marinescu dug him up, ripped his heart out, burned it, mixed the ashes with water, and had Toma's son, daughter-in-law, and granddaughter drink it. Why? Because Gheorge (and a number of other villagers) believed Toma was a vampire. Vampires, according to some people in Marotinu De Sus, Romania, rise from their grave at night and feed on their loved ones, draining their blood. Thus, when relatives get sick following the death of a family member, a vampire is suspected. When Gheorghe unearthed Toma, it was clear to him that Toma was a vampire. He reported that Toma was on his side with blood around his mouth even though he was originally placed in his coffin on his back without any blood present. After drinking the mixture of water and heart ashes, the members of Toma's family, some who had been sick for weeks, recovered. Costel, Toma's son, said it was a miracle and that they had been saved from a vampire (his father). When asked by a reporter how he could be sure his illness was the result of a vampire, he replied: "What other explanation is possible?"

The preceding story is about some real people who sincerely believe in the existence of vampires—that certain dead people do, in fact, rise from their coffins at night to suck blood from family members. They also believe vampires can be stopped by ripping out their hearts and burning them. To many people, this is pure superstition, has no basis in fact, and is not true. Ridiculous, they say. But many of these same people who see no truth value in vampires rising from the dead do believe it is true that a man was born to a virgin mother, walked on water, brought a dead man back to life, turned water into wine, and rose from the dead. This belief is widespread throughout the world. Why is one truth so widely accepted and not the other?

References

Austin American Statesman, "Different Views of the Same Disaster." June 9, 2002, E-1.

Begg, M., Anas, A. & Farinacci, S. (1992). Dissociation of processes in belief: Source recollection, statement familiarity, and the illusion of truth. *Journal of Experimental Psychology: General, 12,* 446–458.

Blanton, B. (2005). *Radical honesty: How to transform your life by telling the truth* (Revised Edition) New York: Dell.

Ceci, S.J., Bruck, M.. & Battin, D.B. (2000). The suggestibility of children's testimony. (pp. 169–201). In D.F. Bjorklund (Ed). *False-memory creation in children and adults: Theory, research, and implications.* Mahwah, N.J.: Erlbaum.Cutler, B.L. & Penrod, S.D. (1995). *Mistaken identification: The eyewitness, psychology, and the law.* New York: Cambridge University Press.

---

[1] Matthew Schofield, "Romanian Villagers Decry Police Investigation Into Vampire Slaying." Knight Ridder Newspapers, March 24, 2004.

Davis, D. & Loftus, E.F. (2009) Expectancies, emotion, and memory reports of visual events. In J.R. Brockmole (Ed.) *The Visual World in Memory* (pp. 178–214). New York: Psychology Press.

Eberle, P. & Eberle, S. (1993). *The abuse of innocence: The McMartin preschool trial.* Buffalo, New York: Prometheus Books.

Fernández-Armesto, F. (1997). Truth: A history and guide for the perplexed. New York: St. Martin's Press.

Goodman, G.S. & Clarke-Stewart, A. (1991). Suggestibility in children's testimony: Implications for sexual abuse investigations (pp. 92–105). In J. Doris (Ed.), *The suggestibility of children's recollections.* Washington, D.C.: American Psychological Association.

Hayakawa, S.I. & Hayakawa, A.R. (1990). Language in thought and action. 5th Ed. New York: Harcourt, Brace, Jovanovich.

Heyman, G.D., Luu, D.H., & Lee, K. (2009). Parenting by lying. *Journal of Moral Education, 38,* 353–369.

Kahneman, D. (2011). *Thinking, fast and slow.* New York: Farrar, Straus, and Giroux.

Kida, T. (2006). *Don't believe everything you think: The 6 basic mistakes we make in thinking.* Amherst, N.Y.: Prometheus Books.

Lester, P.M. (2010). The sin in sincere: Deception and cheating in the visual media. In M.S. McGlone & M.L. Knapp (Eds.), *The interplay of truth and deception* (pp. 89–103). New York: Routledge.

Levine, T.R. (2014). Truth-default theory (TDT): A theory of human deception and deception detection. *Journal of Language and Social Psychology, 33,* 378–392.

Lyon, T.D., Malloy, L.C., Quas, J.A., & Talwar, V.A. (2008). Coaching, truth induction, and young maltreated children's false allegations and false denials. *Child Development, 79,* 914–929.

Loftus, E. (1979). *Eyewitness testimony.* Harvard University Press: Cambridge, Mass.

Loftus, E. & Doyle, J.M. (1997). *Eyewitness testimony: Civil and criminal.* Charlottesville, Va.: Lexis Law Publishing.

Loftus, E. & Ketcham, K. (1991). *Witness for the defense.* New York: St. Martin's Press.

Lynn, S.J. & McConkey, K.M. (Eds.) (1998). *Truth in memory.* New York: Guilford.

MacCoun, R.J. (2012). The burden of social proof: Shared thresholds and social influence. *Psychological Review, 119,* 345–372.

MacLin, O.H., MacLin, M.K., & Malpass, R.S. (2001). Race, arousal, attention, exposure and delay: An examination of factors moderating face recognition. *Psychology, Public Policy, & Law, 7,* 134–152.

Malpass, R.S., Tredoux, C.G., & McQuiston-Surrett, D. (2009). Public policy and sequential lineups. Legal and Criminological Psychology, 14, 1–12.

McGlone, M.S., Kobrynowicz, D., & Alexander, R.B. (2005). A certain *je ne sais quoi*: Verbalization bias in evaluation. *Human Communication Research, 31,* 241–267.

Messaris, P. (1994b). *Visual literacy: Image, mind & reality.* Westview Press: Boulder, CO.

Messaris, P. (2012). Visual "literacy" in the digital age. *The Review of Communication, 12,* 101–117.

Muscanell, N.L., Guadagno, R.E., & Murphy, S. (2014). Weapons of influence misused: A social influence analysis of why people fall prey to internet scams. *Social and Personality Psychology Compass, 8,* 388–396.

Myers, D.G. (2002). *Intuition: Its powers and perils.* New Haven, CT.: Yale University Press.

Neidenthal, P., Halberstadt, J.B., Margolin, J., & Innes-Ker, A.H. (2000). Emotional state and the detection of change in facial expression of emotion. *European Journal of Social Psychology, 30,* 211–222.

Nyberg, D. (1993). *The varnished truth: Truth telling and deceiving in ordinary life.* Chicago: University of Chicago Press.

Pezdek, K. (2011). Fallible eyewitness memory and identification. In B. Cutler (Ed.), *Conviction of the innocent: Lessons from psychological research* (pp. 202–231). Washington, DC: APA Press.

Schacter, D.L. (2001). *The seven sins of memory: How the mind forgets and remembers.* Boston: Houghton-Mifflin.

Scherf, K.S., & Scott, L.S. (2012). Biases in face processing from infancy to adulthood. *Developmental Psychobiology, 54,* 643–663.

Schiffenbauer, A. (1974). Effect of observer's emotional state on judgments of emotional state of others. *Journal of Personality and Social Psychology, 30,* 31–35.

Schooler, J.W. (2013). The costs and benefits of verbally rehearsing memory for faces. In D.J. Herrmann, C. Hertzog, C. McEvoy, & P. Hertel (Eds.). *Basic and applied memory research, Volume 1: Theory in context.* New York: Psychology Press.Schwarz, N. (2012). Feelings-as-information theory. In N. Schwarz (Ed.), Handbook of theories in social psychology, Vol. 1 (pp. 289–308). Thousand Oaks, CA: Sage.

Shermer, M. (2003). *How we believe.* 2nd ed. New York: Henry Holt & Co.

Shermer, M. (2011). *The believing brain: From ghosts to gods to politics and conspiracies—how we construct beliefs and reinforce them as truths.* New York: Times Books.

Shwikert, S.R., & Curran, T. (2014). Familiarity and recollection in heuristic decision making. *Journal of Experimental Psychology: General, 143,* 2341–2365.

Simons, D.J. & Chabris, C.F. (1999). Gorillas in our midst: Sustained inattentional blindness for dynamic events. *Perception, 28,* 1059–1074.

Smith, H.J., Archer, D., & Costanzo, M. (1991). "Just a hunch": Accuracy and awareness in person perception. *Journal of Nonverbal Behavior, 15,* 3–18.

Tate, C.S., Warren, A.R., & Hess, T.M. (1992). Adults' liability for children's "lie-ability": Can adults coach children to lie successfully? In S.J. Ceci, M. D. Leichtman, & M.E. Putnick (Eds.), *Cognitive and social factors in early deception* (pp. 69–87). Mahwah, N.J.: Erlbaum.

Urban, M., Couchot, F., Sarazin, X., & Djannati-Atai, A. (2013). The quantum vacuum as the origin of the speed of light. *European Physical Journal, 67,* 58.

Van Swol, L.M., Molhotra, D., & Braun, M.T. (2012). Deception and its detection: Effects of monetary incentives on personal relationship history. *Communication Research, 39,* 217–238.

Wang, J., Herath, T., Chen, R., Vishwanath, A., & Rao, H.R. (2012). Phishing susceptibility: An investigation into the processing of a targeted spear phishing email. *IEEE Transactions on Professional Communication, 55,* 345–362.

Wells, G.L. & Olson, E.A. (2003). Eyewitness testimony. *Annual Review of Psychology, 54,* 277–295.

Wells, G.L., Memon, A., & Penrod, S.D. (2006). Eyewitness evidence: Improving its probative value. *Psychological Science in the Public Interest, 7,* 45–75.

Winter, A. (2012). *Memory: Fragments of a modern history.* Chicago, IL: University of Chicago Press.

Chapter 3

Ethical Perspectives

In the preceding chapters the point was made that effective communication (getting the response you desire) may be accomplished with behaviors associated with lying and deception. But just because lying and/or deception may help you succeed in accomplishing your communicative goals doesn't necessarily mean it is the right thing to do. Is it ever right for communicators to lie and/or deceive their fellow human beings? What standards or criteria can be used to help us determine the "rightness" or "wrongness" of lying and/or deception? These are the primary questions we explore in this chapter.

Why Concern Ourselves with Ethics?

How we feel about the propriety of lying is one of many ethical decisions we face. Almost daily, we are confronted with complex issues at work, in our family, and in other relationships that challenge us to assess our commitment to what we think is right, fair, respectful, good, responsible, etc. These values not only guide our own behavior, but serve as standards we use to evaluate the behavior of others. Giving serious thought to the values we believe should guide human conduct (ours included) is intrinsically important to each of us personally and to all of us collectively and should be an ongoing subject of personal reflection.

Some people, however, believe we should be especially attuned to ethical issues today because they believe we are living in an era of moral decay, with an abundance of lying as only one manifestation of it. Scott Raeker, President of the Josephson Institute of Ethics, concluded that the U.S. is "in a moral recession" from observing "a continual parade of headline-grabbing incidents of

> "The greatest violation of a human being's duty to himself regarded merely as a moral being is the contrary of truthfulness, lying."
>
> — *Immanuel Kant*

> "We are not angels, but we may at times be better versions of ourselves."
>
> — *Erwin Hargrove*

dishonest and unethical behavior from political leaders, business executives, and prominent athletes" (Raeker, 2014). He attributes the recession in part to a widespread belief that many are getting ahead by cheating and not being caught so one needs to play the game like everybody else or risk getting left behind economically and professionally. In a 2014 Gallup poll, approximately 2 in 3 respondents reported believing that most members of Congress and most businesses are dishonest and corrupt.

There are plenty of well-publicized examples used by those who see this society on the brink of moral bankruptcy. There have been award-winning journalists, historians, and novelists who have plagiarized or made up facts to fit their stories (see Chapter 12). The abandonment of business ethics for greed and selfishness is exemplified by Bernie Madoff's billion dollar Ponzi scheme and scandals involving Enron (accounting fraud), FIFA (taking bribes), News International (wiretapping), and Walmart (making bribes). Corrupt practices in major banks (Bank of America, Citigroup, JPMorgan Chase, etc.) triggered the worst recession of modern times in 2008. Politicians, elected officials, and others representing our federal government have regularly lied to the American people over the last forty years (Nixon about Watergate; Reagan about the Iran-Contra affair; Clinton about his affair with Monica Lewinsky; Bush and Cheney about WMDs in Iraq; Obama about NSA's warrantless wiretapping, etc.) Widespread cynicism is further fueled by the low frequency with which white collar liars are punished. Despite public outrage over their transgressions, few are ever fired or prosecuted (see Chapter 11). Stevenson and Wolfers (2011) argue that the perceived absence of repercussions for Congressional and corporate deceivers has produced a "historic sharp decline in the confidence the American public has in their government, financial, and business sectors, and to a lesser extent their media and courts." National Book Award winner George Packer (2014) claims that the public's distrust of government and business has prompted an "unwinding" of Americans' sense of community, which in turn makes lying and deception more acceptable for people in all walks of life.

Furthermore, national surveys of middle and high school students show that the young people of America also admit to a lot of lying, cheating, and stealing. Consider the findings of a recent survey of 23,000 high school students about the frequency with which they behave unethically (Josephson Institute, 2012). Lying was the focus of several questions: 1) 76% of the students said they had lied about something significant once or more; 55% said they had lied to a teacher once or more; 52% said they had cheated on a test and 74% said they had copied someone else's homework. Despite the many students who admitted cheating, stealing, and lying during the preceding year, about 81% agreed with the statement, "When it comes to doing what is right, I am better than most people I know."

Table 3.1 Deceptive Behavior Frequency Reported by
High School Students

Have You Done These Things?	Never	Only Once	Twice or More
Lied to parent about something significant	24%	28%	48%
Lied to a teacher about something significant	45%	26%	29%
Copied an Internet document for an assignment	68%	16%	16%
Cheated during a test at school	49%	24%	28%
Copied someone else's homework	25%	23%	51%
Stole something from a parent or relative	82%	10%	8%
Stole something from a friend	86%	9%	5%
Stole something from a store	80%	11%	9%

While many people are convinced that we are currently facing an ethical crisis, others aren't so sure. Historically, they point out, behaviors like lying, stealing, and cheating have always existed and it isn't clear whether things are really worse now. Illbruck (2013) attributes many current anxieties about the state of society to collective memory failure caused by the "unenlightened disease" we call nostalgia. According to the Judeo-Christian-Islamic tradition, lying has plagued the affairs of humans as long as they have existed. God is alleged to have expelled the original people, Adam and Eve, after she was tricked by a serpent into eating fruit from a forbidden tree and coaxed him to do it too. Following "the Fall," the prophets Moses, Jesus, and Mohammed are all reported to have criticized the prevalence of deceit in human society and recommended honesty and faith as the way return to God's grace. Theologians of all faiths over the centuries have perenially interpreted calamities (drought, flood, famine, plague, earthquakes, etc.) as divine retribution for widespread wickedness and treachery (Denery, 2015)., In nineteenth century America, lies were certainly plentiful in transactions involving child labor, African slaves, treaties made with native Americans, etc. In the 1920s, a study of eleven thousand school children also found cheating and dishonesty to be widespread (Hartshorne & May, 1928). Making valid comparisons across eras is wrought with difficulties. Today's population is greater than previous generations; ethical transgressions are more likely to be reported and made public; if there is a perception that "everybody's doing it," this may lead to more people admitting to lying than in previous generations; and the dissemination of such information to large groups of people is more efficient than ever before, which would certainly increase public awareness.

In addition, the very same polls that seem to point to an ethical crisis contain other data which present a somewhat different picture. In the aforementioned survey of high school students, 99% said it was important for people to trust them and to be a person of good character. 98% said honesty and trust are essential in personal relationships and 86% said it was not worth it to lie and cheat because it hurts your character. More than half of the 777 teenagers in another survey said they would "not likely" lie to their boss to cover up a mistake they made at work (Deloitte & Touche USA LLP, 2005). And one study even found 85% of the adult respondents saying they had not cheated, even a little, on their taxes or expense accounts (Smiley, 2000). Findings like this last one seem to beg us to question its validity, but why shouldn't we examine all poll results more carefully? For example, what does it mean when a lot of people say they have lied? Can we assume each respondent has the same referent for lying behavior? Would all the lies reported support the argument that our society is in a state of moral decay? Is the sheer number of lies people report a sign we are living in a moral wasteland?

Opponents of the "society in moral decay" argument also point out that there are more and more institutions in place to prevent and sanction unethical behavior. Ethics courses are offered (and sometimes required) by colleges and universities worldwide, and there are more institutes and centers for the study of ethics (Harvard's Safra Center for Ethics, Princeton's Center for Human Values, The Center for Public Integrity in Washington, DC, etc.) than ever before. New discoveries in genetics, technology, and other fields also keep ethical questions on the front page and serve as encouragement for every citizen to regularly question and test his or her values. Adler (2007) believes a society is not known for its deceit, but how it deals with deceit:

> To deceive is human. There has never been, nor ever will be, an honest society. And so long as we lack the means to quantify lies or weigh hypocrisies, we have no basis for supposing any society more dishonest than any other. Rather, what distinguishes a culture is how it copes with deceit: the sorts of lies it denounces, the sorts of institutions it fashions to expose them (p. 270).

Thus, the answer to the question of whether we are collectively experiencing a moral crisis or not may be far less important than each individual recognizing that his or her world is complex and it demands that we have as clear a sense of our own values as possible. Why? Because we often don't have the luxury of thinking long and hard about something before we have to make a decision. We live in an era when complicated ethical issues face not only leaders, but everyone. It is harder and harder to get away with simply giving lip service to values and reciting moral platitudes. More and more of us are personally involved in circumstances that require us to test and possibly modify our ethical principles as we apply them to real life situations. Determining whether to tell the truth or not is especially important in this age of information. It is an age when each of us is confronted with many opportunities and channels to lie and to cover or disguise our lies. It is a time when information about others (especially respected others) who lie is readily available—as well as the extent of their punishment. Each individual, not just public figures or institutions, is capable of lying to the masses with a computer or mobile phone. It is an age when every piece of information we communicate is processed and reacted to by numerous individuals and special interest groups. It is an age that demands an ongoing reflection about the ethics of dishonesty as well as honesty.

Is It Ever Right to Lie?

The answers typically given to the question of whether it is ever right to lie can be grouped into four broad categories which range from the staunch, absolutist position that no lie is acceptable to the Machiavellian position, within which lies are not really thought of as right or wrong—just another means for accomplishing one's goals. Between these two opposite and extreme positions are two positions that, in varying degrees, look at the role circumstances play in determining the rightness or wrongness of lying. Let's look more closely at each of these answers to our question.

No, It Is Never Right to Lie

This position does not allow for any exceptions. Lying is always wrong. Good intentions and the lack of harmful effects do not matter. Even if you are lying to save your mother's life, it is still considered wrong to lie. Aside from the practitioners of "radical honesty" (Blanton, 1996) it is difficult to find people today who are willing to publicly advocate this position, but several well-known and respected thinkers in world history have taken an unyielding stand against dishonesty. St. Augustine (345–430), St. Thomas Aquinas (1225–1274), John Wesley (1703–1791) and Immanuel Kant (1724–1804) all believed it was never right to lie (Bok, 1978).

For these philosophers and theologians, the justification for believing it is never right to lie seems to rest primarily on three ideas: 1) Lies, by their very nature, disrespect humanity and, like a disease, infect the liar's personality and ruin his or

DOONESBURY © 2004 G.B. Trudeau. Reprinted with permission of UNIVERSAL UCLICK. All rights reserved.

her integrity. 2) Lying violates religious precepts. It is a sin to lie and a transgression against God's law. 3) Lying begets lying. If you lie about something, you'll be tempted to lie about it again and you'll have to tell additional lies to avoid detection. These lies, in turn, lead you to lie about other things. Eventually the recipients of your lies will want to match your lies with lies of their own which will bring about a dysfunctional society in which everybody lies all the time.

The preceding ideas used to support the absolute prohibition against any lies are seen as flawed by enough people today to prevent the widespread advocacy of this position. In fact, it has never been a policy people could follow without provisions that excused or reinterpreted some of their behavior which had all the earmarks of lying. Let's look carefully at the backbone of this belief.

Lying Disrespects Humanity & Negatively Affects One's Personality

The underlying assumption here is that lies are always harmful and telling the truth is always beneficial. But the truth can be harmful as well, even fatal. Judas Iscariot, arguably the worst villain in the New Testament, betrayed Jesus Christ by identifying him to the Roman soldiers—an act of treacherous truthtelling. A lie told to protect people from someone whose stated intent was to kill them would also seem to be respecting humanity and strengthening the liar's personality. For example, Amsterdam businessman Victor Kugler won Israel's Yad Vashem Humanitarian Medal for his efforts to conceal Anne Frank and her family from the Nazis in the early 1940s (Kardonne, 2008). The same could be said for "noble lies" that promote social harmony rather than truth which creates social discord. Difficult choices are sure to follow those who try to live by the principle that lies of any kind are always wrong and truth-telling of any kind is always right. It won't take long before a person is confronted with a situation that requires a choice between the treasured value of truth telling and another treasured value. As Nyberg (1993, pp. 198–199) says:

> Human beings live in a world of competing genuine values, and this pluralism of values is as much a part of each individual consciousness as it is of society… Such conflict of values between peoples, or within one's own moral universe, should not always lead to a forced choice of the *right one*, the *wrong one*, the only *true or false one*. Truth telling is a value that is likely to exist in conflict with many others—kindness, compassion, self-regard, privacy, survival, and so on.

Lying is a Transgression Against God's Law

Even though St. Augustine and St. Thomas Acquinas were Catholics and John Wesley was a Methodist, all were Christians and all believed the absolute prohibition against all lying was grounded in Christian teachings and scriptures. Kant was not a theologian, but his writings on moral behavior were strongly influenced by his Christian moral beliefs. But their extreme position was not and is not shared by Christians who do not find the examples of dissimulation in the Bible as making a *prima facie* case that all lies are a sin. Some instances of deceit and concealment in the Bible do not seem to have provoked the wrath of God. And while Buddhist prayers and Jewish texts also condemn lying, they also allow for exceptions (Bok, 1978). The Koran explicitly offers permission for Muslims to conceal their faith from non-believers (the "taqiya" doctrine), but only to avoid religious persecution (Stewart, 2013).

Needless to say, those who tried to follow Augustine's prohibition against all lies found themselves sinning a lot. As a result, Augustine developed a list of eight types of lies. All were considered sins, but some were greater sins than others. Later, Thomas Acquinas boiled the list down to three: 1) lies told in jest, 2) lies told to be helpful, and 3) malicious lies. Again, telling a lie in any category was considered a sin, but only malicious lies were considered a "major" sin. In short, the extremists recognized the problem of prohibiting all lies, but instead of changing the principle, they made other modifications. In Bok's (1978, p. 34) words:

> Many ways were tried to soften the prohibition, to work around it, and to allow at least a few lies. Three different paths were taken: to allow for pardoning of some lies; to claim that some deceptive statements are not falsehoods, merely misinterpreted by the listener; and finally to claim that certain falsehoods do not count as lies.

Two ancient but ingenious inventions for dealing with the lies of people who believed in not lying (but wanted to lie) were the concepts of mental reservation and equivocation. The first allowed a person to make a misleading statement to someone else (e.g., "I have never cheated on an exam…) and silently add the qualification in his or her mind to make it true (e.g., …until the one you gave last week"). As long as the person used the mental reservation, there was no lie and no sin. Equivocation took advantage of words' multiple meanings to mislead without technically lying. For example, when asked by persecutors whether a man they intended to kill passed this way, the equivocator might reply "He did not pass here" with "here" signifying the precise spot on which the speaker stands and not the other spots the man actually did walk through (Denery, 2015). These Catholic Church-approved methods and others used to make the "lying is never right" principle more compatible with normal human social behavior (within which lying regularly takes place) created controversy and only served to highlight why the complete prohibition of lying doesn't work.

If You Lie About One Thing, You'll Lie About Another

Absolutists believe that authorizing the telling of any lies will inevitably lead to more lies which, in turn, will spread throughout society, eroding the trust that holds society together and eventually destroying it. This is called the "slippery slope" argument or the "domino effect." During President Clinton's final years as President, he publicly denied having a sexual relationship with White House intern, Monica Lewinsky. His opponents raised questions based on the domino effect: How can we trust this President not to lie to the American public when he lies about having sex with a woman other than his wife? The President's supporters contended that the President's personal life was not a public matter, that most people would lie in that situation, and that lying in that situation had little to do with how the President would respond to matters affecting the health and welfare of the country. When a person lies about one thing, can we assume that lies in other areas of this person's life will naturally follow? Obviously, this can and does happen, but it would be a mistake to assume this will normally be the case. A careful analysis of the person and the factors associated with each situation where lying might occur would be a more prudent approach.

Lying, like other forms of behavior, is influenced by many personal and contextual factors. The assumption that dishonesty in one area of your life will automatically lead to dishonesty in another area ignores a host of mitigating variables. How important is it to lie about the issue at hand? Who is the target of the lie and what is your relationship to the target? What are the chances of being caught? Have you successfully lied in the past? Are lies often performed or even expected in this situation? Etc. In a massive study of eleven thousand school children ages eight to sixteen, Hartshorne and May (1928, 1971) provide some persuasive evidence of the powerful effect of context on dishonesty. Over the course of several months, these researchers gave dozens of tests designed to measure honesty to these students. Sometimes cheating was prohibited by close monitoring by test administrators, but on similar tests the monitoring was sometimes lax or students were given an answer key and allowed to grade their own tests. Student scores under all conditions were then compared. Sometimes the work students did at home was compared to similar work they did at school. In one test, students were unobtrusively observed, but asked to provide self reports of how many chin-ups they did and how far they were able to broad jump. Other tests involved spelling, arithmetic, and other subjects. These studies did not find simple, reliable patterns of honesty or dishonesty in children's behavior. The findings led these researchers to advance the "doctrine of specificity" about children's moral compass: Honesty and dishonesty are not unified traits but specific functions of life situations, and the consistency across situations is due to what those situations have in common (see also Lee, 2011). A child may cheat on a word completion test, but not on a test of his or her physical performance. On the other hand, if you gave the same test in the same way to the same group of children six months apart, the same kids were likely to cheat in the same way on both tests. Hartshorne and May concluded that the likelihood of a child practicing deceit in any given situation was partly due to factors like his or her age, intelligence, and home background and partly due to the student's response to situational demands. In short, it does not follow that if a person lies about one thing they will necessarily lie about another.

As we've seen, prohibiting all forms of lying is a moral principle that: 1) people found extremely difficult to implement in their daily life; and 2) necessitated interpretations of the general principle which essentially indicated that even though lying is always bad, sometimes it isn't as bad as at other times. This is consistent with a poll of 1000 adults in which 52% said lying was never justified but 65% of these same people said it was sometimes OK to lie to avoid hurting someone's feelings, 40% of them said it was OK to exaggerate a story to make it more interesting, and 33% said it was OK to lie about your age (Associated Press, 2006). If there are situations in which lies aren't "as bad" as other lies, could it be that lying in those situations might even be the "right" thing to do?

A man walked by a house and saw a sign that said: "Talking Dog for Sale." Intrigued and not a little skeptical, he rang the doorbell to inquire about the dog. The owner took the man to his back yard and pointed to a rather plain looking black dog lying in the yard. The man approached the dog, sat down next to it, and asked:

"You talk?"

"Sure do," the dog replied.

Trying to control his initial shock, the man continued, "So, ah, what's your story?

The dog sat up, looked directly at the man and said, "Well, I discovered my gift of talking pretty young and I wanted to help the government so I told the CIA about my gift and in no time they had me jetting around from country to country, sitting in rooms with spies and world leaders. No one figured a dog would be eavesdropping. I was one of their most valuable spies for eight years. The jetting around really exhausted me and I knew I wasn't getting any younger. I wanted to settle down. So I signed up for a job at the local airport to do some undercover security work, mostly wandering near suspicious characters and listening in. I uncovered some incredible dealings there and was awarded a batch of medals. I had a wife, a mess of puppies, and now I'm just retired."

The man was astonished. He ran into the owner's house to ask the price of the dog.

The owner said, "Ten dollars."

"What?!," said the man, "this is an extraordinary dog. Why on earth are you selling him so cheap?

"Cause he's a liar. He didn't really do any of that crap."

It Is Not Right to Lie Except as a Last Resort

Sissela Bok's book, *Lying: Moral Choice in Public and Private Life* (1978), provides an extended discussion of this position. Although Bok believes there are circumstances under which lying could be justified, she also agrees with the basic tenets of the "lying is never justified" position—i.e., that lying is generally bad for the liar and for society in general; that people today lie too often and too easily and unless something is done, the frequency of lies will continue to grow; and that the more lies that are told, the more trust is destroyed and the more dysfunctional society becomes. For Bok, lying and deception are villains who attack social life in contrast to Nyberg (1993, p. 25) who believes, "Social life without deception to keep it going is a fantasy."

Despite her philosophical kinship to the absolutists, Bok's ethical solution differs from theirs. Instead of prohibiting all lies, she says certain lies may be acceptable if they meet her stringent (if not sometimes unrealistic) tests. Her position is grounded on what she calls the "veracity principle." The veracity principle states that "truthful statements are preferable to lies in the absence of special considerations. This premise gives an initial negative weight to lies." (p.30). So, in essence, telling the truth is always favored. Bok writes as if the referents for "the truth" and "telling the truth" are clear, well-known, and not in need of dissection. According to Bok, if a person tells the truth they don't have to justify their behavior; if they decide to lie, they must pursue the following three steps in order to see if the lie can be justified.

First, no lie is permissible if the same interaction goal can be achieved with a truthful statement. She argues that this will eliminate many lies that are told too easily and without careful examination. Even if a lie saves a life, it is not acceptable if there is a way to save the life by telling the truth. In Bok's words, "If lies and truthful statements appear to achieve the same result or appear to be as desirable to the person contemplating lying the lies should be ruled out. And only where a lie is a *last resort* can one even begin to consider whether or not it is morally justified." (p.3l) Asking liars to consider truthful alternatives is admirable, but how is the prospective liar drawn to truthful alternatives?

Presumably, the availability and desirability of truthful alternatives occurs during step two in which the liar-in-waiting is expected to weigh the moral reasons for and against the anticipated lie by trying to put him or herself in the place of the deceived and all others affected by the lie. Asking colleagues and friends how they'd react is also recommended. The liar might also ask how he or she might react if the contemplated lie were told to them. What excuses are there for lying and what arguments can be raised against the lie? Excuses are designed to forgive a wrong (i.e., a lie) but Bok says most excuses will not be persuasive nor can excuses justify the telling of a lie. Only by successfully following step three do we find those lies that can be told within Bok's ethical system.

To justify a lie, the expectant liar must seek the approval of a fictional, independent audience of "reasonable people" who support a legal, religious, or some other type of moral code. The two previous steps are put to the test by asking what a public audience of reasonable people would say about the anticipated lie or lies. How reasonable a reasonable public is and whether ethical decisions should always be ruled by majority perceptions are pertinent, but unresolved, issues here. Bok wants to know how the expectant liar thinks the general public would react if the contemplated lie was told to them? This "publicity" test is designed, says Bok, to counter the bias and hasty conclusions inherent in the liar's perspective. "Only those deceptive practices which can be openly debated and consented to in advance are justifiable in a democracy," she says (p. 181). From this perspective, no one should be subjected to a lie without informed, voluntary consent. This doesn't necessarily mean you have to tell the target of your duplicity the specific lie you are going to tell—only that the target be forewarned that a lie might be told. Since most people expect enemies to lie to each other and since one might get the consent of reasonable people to lie to an enemy, lying to enemies is justified—but only when there is no truth telling alternative; there is a crisis; and there are open, lawfully declared, hostilities.

Bok's position, that lying *can* be "right," but only as a last resort and only after the liar believes that an audience of reasonable people would approve of it, begins with the premise that lying is inherently wrong and exceptions should occur infrequently and only after much reflection, discussion, and forewarning. The antithesis of this perspective views lying as functional—with it's goodness or badness being determined by how well it helps or doesn't help in accomplishing one's goals.

It Is Right to Lie When It Serves Your Purposes

From the standpoint of a moral perspective on whether it is right or wrong to tell a lie, this position is the polar opposite of those previously discussed. To some, it is an amoral perspective at best and immoral at worst. Nevertheless, it is a perspective which assumes a position on the value of telling lies and it is a perspective that has been adopted (if unofficially) by enough people during the course of world history and in today's society that it's tenets and practitioners should be part of any journey to explore ethical perspectives on lying and deception. Instead of adopting the principle that all lying is wrong and considering whether there may be any justifiable exceptions to that rule, this perspective is totally functional—from the liar's perspective. Lies and truth assume goodness or badness only as they help or hinder the liar's ability to accomplish some goal. The liar, then, is the sole moral arbiter and what is "right" is what serves the liar best.

The best known advocate of this position is Niccolò Machiavelli, an Italian statesman and political philosopher who lived 500 years ago. His book, *The Prince* (2010/1532) was designed as a leader's guide on how to effectively govern. In Chapter 18 of this book, Machiavelli argues that the prince should know how to be deceitful when it suits his purpose. However, he cautions, the prince must not appear deceitful. Instead, he must manifest mercy, honesty, humaneness, uprightness, and religiousness. By emphasizing the strategic manipulation of others for one's own benefit, Machiavelli's name is now used by many people in the United States to signify things like deceit, treachery, manipulation, and opportunism in human relations. Most people think there are certain occasions where "the end justifies the means"—e.g., lying to survive or to protect national security. Almost 2000 years ago, the Roman rhetorician Quintilian said there was "no disgrace" in "making use of vices" to accomplish your goals and speaking "the thing that is not" (Quintilian, 1922/ca.90 CE, Chapter II, xvii, 26). Quintilian assumed the goals the rhetorician sought to accomplish were noble ones and therefore warranted deception. But for the highly Machiavellian person, lying is a justified "means" to accomplish *any* particular "end" or goal. In one of his letters to a friend, Machiavelli said: "For a long time I have not said what I believed, nor do I ever believe what I say, and if indeed sometimes I do happen to tell the truth, I hide it among so many lies that it is hard to find" (Greene, 2002, p. 321). To more fully appreciate the Machiavellian belief system, examine the statements in the boxed insert on page 52, "How Machiavellian Are You?"

People who are strongly Machiavellian in their beliefs cannot afford to be very emotionally involved with others. Empathy and affective attachments only make it harder for the Machiavellian to dispassionately manipulate and deceive others for his or her own purposes. Another reason why "High Machs" are emotionally detached from others is that they don't have much respect for most people. From the perspective of the High Mach, most people are gullible, weak, easily persuaded, and not trustworthy.

How Machiavellian Are You?*

Those who subscribe to the Machiavellian belief system will agree with the following statements:

1. The best way to handle people is to tell them what they want to hear.
2. Anyone who completely trusts anyone else is asking for trouble.
3. It is hard to get ahead without cutting comers here and there.
4. It is safest to assume that all people have a vicious streak and it will come out when they are given a chance.
5. Never tell anyone the real reason you did something unless it is useful to do so.
6. It is wise to flatter important people.
7. People suffering from incurable diseases should have the choice of being put painlessly to death.
8. Most men forget more easily the death of their father than the loss of their property.
9. Generally speaking, men won't work hard unless they're forced to.
10. The biggest difference between most criminals and other people is that criminals are stupid enough to get caught.

Those who subscribe to the Machiavellian belief system will disagree with the following statements:

1. When you ask someone to do something for you, it is best to give the real reasons for wanting it rather than giving reasons that might carry more weight.
2. Honesty is the best policy in all cases.
3. One should take action only when sure it is morally right.
4. All in all, it is better to be humble and honest than important and dishonest.
5. Barnum was very wrong when he said there's a sucker born every minute.
6. It is possible to be good in all respects.
7. Most people are basically good and kind.
8. There is no excuse for lying to someone else.
9. Most people who get ahead in the world lead clean, moral lives.
10. Most men are brave.

*From Christie & Geis (1970), pp. 17–18.

Machiavelli is often portrayed as a teacher of evil. But in *The Prince*, he never urged evil for evil's sake. The proper aim of a prince, he argues, is to maintain his state and his power over it. Politics is a province where following a virtue can ruin a state and pursuing what appears to be a vice may promote security and well-being. Leaders are called upon to make difficult choices, and prudence sometimes involves recognizing the good that can be engineered from bad options.

In his national bestseller, *The 48 Laws of Power*, Greene (2002) reiterated many of Machiavelli's principles for achieving and maintaining power. He begins his book by saying that in today's world, "Everything must appear to be democratic, civilized, and fair...but if we play by those rules too strictly, if we take them too literally, we are crushed by those around us who are not so foolish" (p. xvii). "Power," he continues, "requires the ability to play with appearances. To this end you must learn to wear many masks and keep a bag full of deceptive tricks. Deception and masquerades should not be seen as ugly or immoral... Deception is a developed art of civilization and the most potent weapon in the game of power". Deception is central to most of Greene's laws, and especially evident in the following four:

> *"LAW THREE—Conceal Your Intentions*
>
> > *Keep people off balance and in the dark by never revealing the purpose behind your actions. If they have no clue what you are up to, they cannot prepare a defense (p. 16).*
>
> *LAW FOUR—Always Say Less Than Necessary*
>
> > *When you are trying to impress people with words, the more you say, the more common you appear, and the less in control... Powerful people impress and intimidate by saying less. The more you say, the more likely you are to say something foolish (p. 32).*
>
> *LAW TWELVE—Use Selective Honesty and Generosity to Disarm Your Victim*
>
> > *One sincere and honest move will cover over dozens of dishonest ones. Honest moves bring down the guard of even the most suspicious people. Once your selective honesty opens a hole in their armor, you can deceive and manipulate them at will (p. 89).*
>
> *LAW TWENTY-ONE—Play a Sucker to Catch a Sucker: Seem Dumber Than Your Mark*
>
> > *No one likes feeling stupider than the next person. The trick, then, is to make your victims feel smart—and not just smart, but smarter than you are. Once convinced of this, they will never suspect that you may have ulterior motives" (p. 156).*

Many of us have known or been affected by communicators who have adopted a Machiavellian approach to deception. Even more of us have either used, or been the recipient of one or more of the deceptive strategies in the Machiavellian's communicative arsenal. But it is important to remember that it is not the specific strategies of deception that are at issue here. Instead, it is the unwavering self-serving intent guiding these power seekers that is at the heart of an ethical judgment of their behavior. So we must ask whether we believe it is right for anyone to lie whenever it is beneficial to their own goals and purposes. Is this the standard for human conduct and character we are seeking? "Lying whenever it suits your own purposes" is not a philosophy that is adapted to virtues that value others like fairness, mutual benefits, and justice. Whatever "goodness" may be associated with lying and deception from the Machiavellian perspective is not a shared value, but an individual one. It is not the greatest good for the greatest number, but the greatest good for the liar.

The next approach combines the acceptance of some deceptive strategies with moral standards which go beyond any given individual's preferences.

Sometimes Lying Is Right, Sometimes It Isn't

From this perspective, the extent to which lying is morally right or wrong is largely determined by taking into account the special circumstances of a particular situation within which the lie occurred. Ethical judgments, then, may vary depending on whether the target is a child or an adult; a stranger or a loved one; whether the lie impacts many people or a few; whether constructive or destructive intentions are perceived; whether lies are expected in this situation; whether cultural sanctions exist for this particular lie and if so, whether they are strong or weak (Seiter, Bruschke, & Bai, 2002); etc. History also teaches us that "the climate of the times" affects ethical judgments. Stories about President Clinton's extramarital sexual behavior were front page news at the turn of the 21st Century and his public denial of such behavior was considered scandalous by many Americans—including his congressional colleagues who impeached him. But most reporters who knew about the extramarital affairs of President Roosevelt in the 1930's and early 1940's and President Kennedy's affairs in the early 1960's chose not make these transgressions headline news. Given the many factors which can affect a moral judgment about lying, Nyberg (1993, p. 201) concludes that "…the idea of adjusting the principle of truth telling to fit the circumstances is a sound moral position just as surely as is adherence to the ideal of honesty itself."

It should be noted, however, that general principles which might apply to numerous situations are not excluded from this perspective, but instead of being the final moral arbiter, the appropriateness of a general principle gains its moral status within the context of a particular situation. For example, "malicious lies which hurt people are immoral" may be usefully applied to most situations, but may not be applicable to lies directed to an enemy in a declared war.

In theory, everything relevant to a given situation has the potential to influence whether a lie is morally justified or not. In practice, though, it is usually the liar's *motive or intent* and the *consequences* of the lie that get the most attention and are often weighted more heavily than other factors in determining the acceptability of the lie. In one study, the liar's motive accounted for three and a half times more of the variance in determining the acceptability of the lie than the liar's culture or the liar's relationship to the target (Seiter, Bruschke, & Bai, 2002). Needless to say, "good motives" and/or "good consequences" from the liar's perspective may not always be viewed as "good" by the target of the lie or even an outside observer. This is only one of the difficulties involved in evaluating the reasons and consequences used to justify a lie.

Motives

We often equate deception with self-serving motives—cheating on taxes to avoid payment, padding a resume to get a job interview, inflating one's salary to impress friends and first dates, etc. But people often try to justify a lie by linking it to pro-social motives. Isn't it ok to lie, they might argue, if you were trying to avoid harm, to produce benefits, to promote or preserve fairness, or to protect a larger truth (Bok, 1978)? What about lying because an authority figure (parents, boss) expected you to? Or lying in order to prevent being disloyal or breaking a confidentiality agreement? And what's wrong with a lie to someone who makes it clear they don't want to hear the truth (Johnson, 2001)? Given certain circumstances, any of the preceding reasons may be sufficient to argue the "rightness" or "wrongness" of lying. When school children falsely accuse their teachers of molestation and sexual abuse, we would expect widespread agreement that these lies are malicious and wrong (Bowles, 2000). Politeness routines in which people thank others for things they aren't all that thankful for are generally agreed to benefit social relations (McGlone & Giles, 2011).

On the other hand, situations are often more complicated and the "rightness" or "wrongness" of the lie less clear. For example, lies not uncommonly represent a choice between two desirable values so the question is not whether the liar's intent was driven by a revered or detested value, but why the liar chose revered value one over revered value two? For example, a husband has told his wife that he will never lie to her and that he will never hurt her. But circumstances lead him to believe that lying would be preferable to hurting her with the truth. What about a professor who lies to his students by telling them he is treating them all the same (fairness principle), but who secretly made an exception for a student who was, through no fault of her own, in need of some special considerations in order to keep her from being unfairly disadvantaged relative to the rest of the class (compassion principle)? What about being loyal to one friend by lying to another? On a somewhat larger scale, what about the employee of the federal government who lies about known wrongdoings of his or her colleagues for the sake of loyalty—loyalty to fellow employees and perceived loyalty to a country which might be harmed by the revelations? Lies driven by loyalty and confidentiality are often made in circumstances where loyalty to others and their right to know is sacrificed, as the following case illustrates:

> Take the case of a middle manager who has learned about an upcoming merger that will mean layoffs. Her superiors have asked her to keep this information to herself for a couple of weeks until the deal is completed. In the interim, employees may make financial commitments (home or car purchases) that they would postpone if they knew that major changes were in the works. Should she voluntarily share information about the merger despite her orders? What happens when a member of her department asks her to confirm or deny the rumor that the company is about to merge? (Johnson, 2001, p. 17)

The liar's conscious awareness of his or her motives is another potentially complicating factor in trying to assess the rightness or wrongness of a lie. In the pursuit of self-defense (avoiding tension or harm) or self-needs (getting something you want), liars may not spend a lot of time reflecting on their motives. But as soon as they are suspected of lying or discovered lying, they often work hard to find more acceptable motives for their behavior—"I thought it was an open-book test"; "I must have made a math error in my tax return"; "I meant that I drove a Porsche *once*, not that I owned one"; etc. Skilled communicators may be able to convince their targets that their lie was not designed to be self-serving, even though it may appear that way (Chance & Norton, 2011).

Consequences

English philosopher Jeremy Bentham (1748–1832) is normally credited with initiating a philosophical position called *utilitarianism* that maintained that decisions are moral to the extent that they promote happiness and immoral to the extent that they do the reverse. Within this framework, then, moral decisions about lies would be based on the consequences of telling them. Utilitarianism favors those things that benefit the most people and those outcomes in which the advantages outweigh the disadvantages. (Gorovitz, 1971; Hearn, 1971; Robinson, 1994; Smart & Williams, 1973). It would be "right" to tell a lie, then, that resulted in benefits that outweighed the problems or that benefited the most people. The benefits (or "good") achieved can be examined in the context of a particular situation or in the context of a rule believed to achieve the most good in the most situations. As a result, a utilitarian might determine that the telling of a lie in a particular situation was justified even though they simultaneously maintained the belief that lying usually causes more harm than good and should be avoided.

One widely used form of deception that is justified on utilitarian grounds is the placebo. When testing a new drug or surgical technique, medical researchers try to distinguish its direct benefit to patients' health from the psychological benefit that comes from believing that it will heal them. To do this, clinical studies are conducted in which the actual drug or surgery is administered to some patients while others receive a placebo (a pill containing sugar or gelatin instead of the active drug ingredient; "sham surgery" in which incisions are made in the skin and sewn up, but no invasive procedures are performed; etc.). Hundreds of studies in the medical research literature document "placebo effects"—cases when placebos benefit patients' health, sometimes as much as the real drug or surgery helps them (Kirsch, 2013). "Authorized deception" was used in some of these studies, in that patients were told beforehand they could receive the actual medical procedure or the placebo, but weren't told which until after their health outcomes were assessed; in other studies, the use of placebos wasn't revealed to patients until the assessment phase (Miller, Wendler, & Swartzman, 2005). Placebos in medical research are controversial, whether the deception is authorized or not. However, their use is rationalized in utilitarian terms. As Miller et al. (2005) put it, "in placebo research, participants are not deceived for their own benefit. Rather, they are deceived for the benefit of science and society in general, through the development of generalizable knowledge" (p. 262).

The goal of seeking consequences with more benefit than harm is not one many would disagree with. But consequences are not always easily determined—either before a lie is told or after it is told. When should consequences be measured? Some lies may have positive short-term effects and negative long-term effects. Who should determine what the consequences are? Liars tend to look at things from their own point of view so if a lie is helpful to them, it is likely to be viewed as doing good. In the same way, the targets of lies often find it difficult to positively evaluate the consequences of a lie once it is discovered. For example, deceptive placebos in medical research might undermine patients' trust of physicians and as a result reduce their willingness to seek future medical care.

In addition, some lies target multiple audiences, each with potentially different effects. Accurately assessing multiple effects and somehow calculating a score for the overall good and evil is not often a realistic expectation. Some lies target only one audience, but have effects on other audiences—some known, some unknown. In addition, some effects cannot be known because audiences decide not to reveal the effects. And some lies which are expected to have certain consequences have unanticipated ones. For example, lying to your mother about the seriousness of your father's hospitalized illness may keep her from the harm that worry may incur, but it also prevents her from making important decisions relevant to her husband's life and her future.

Ethical Guidelines

Throughout this chapter, we've examined several different answers to the question, "Is it ever right to lie?" While some may prefer one answer over others, none is without its problematic aspects. Such is the nature of ethics. So how should we proceed? First, we would do well to accept the premise that learning how to ethically deal with the subject of honesty and dishonesty is an ongoing process, not the acquisition of a list of unchanging, hard and fast rules that will apply to all situations. One ethicist put it this way: "As we practice resolving dilemmas we find ethics to be less a goal than a pathway, less a destination than a trip, less an inoculation than a process" (Kidder, 1995). This doesn't mean that at some point in life we might not need and find useful certain principles to effectively guide our behavior in all situations. Nor does it mean that general principles can't be of value as we make ethical decisions. They may serve us well, for example, when we don't have time to analyze various aspects of a situation.

But the idea that practicing ethical behavior is a journey rather than a destination means that if life reveals a situation in which broad principles do not seem to be useful, that we are willing to consider alternative behavior. It is not that a person taking this approach doesn't have a moral stance—only that he or she recognizes that their current stance may be improved. Because we are human beings we should not expect to live a mistake free life. But we can learn from our mistakes and, as the chapter's opening quote says, "at times be better versions of ourselves." We don't need to be good all the time to be a good person, but we need to struggle toward that goal. What follows are some tips to guide that struggle.

Tell the Truth Most of the Time

Start with goal of telling the truth *as you understand it* in most situations. This shows a recognition that it is good to tell the truth even though you may not do it all the time. It recognizes that truth-telling as a general rule serves the individual and his or her community well. It recognizes that even though we will deceive others in various ways in various situations, that lying should not be thought of as the norm. It also recognizes that telling the whole truth in certain situations may not be the most ethical thing to do (Plante, 2004, p. 51). Still this guideline asks us to give priority to what we believe to be the truth. An important personal benefit of this approach is that it helps to establish a track record, a history, an image of you as a communicator—a history and image that may serve you well if one of your lies is used to impugn your character.

Consider Alternatives to Lying

Lying isn't always something people think a lot about before they do it. Too often we quickly think things like, "Uh oh, I'm gonna get in trouble" or "I don't want to deal with this," followed by a lie. There are no doubt situations that require quick, spontaneous reactions, but we would do well to think more strategically when we face the possibility of lying. It is, after all, a communication decision. In some cases, we can anticipate situations where we might lie and we can avoid or plan accordingly for those situations.

It is also important to remember that just because you decide not to tell the truth doesn't mean you need to tell a falsehood. People in Bell and DePaulo's study (1996), for example, were asked to comment on a painting they disliked to a person they believed to be the artist who painted it. These creative individuals talked about more positive than negative features of the painting, but did not come right out and say they liked or disliked it. As DePaulo considered the possibility of reducing the number of altruistic lies she told, she reported: "I tried to figure out how to tell tactful truths instead of reassuring lies" (DePaulo, 2004, p. 319). Delaying a response, changing the subject, responding with vague, ambiguous, or equivocal messages in a confident, self-assured style are other methods people use. Listen carefully to what the other person says. They may be asking for less than you know, thereby allowing you to tell what you believe to be the truth but not the whole truth. Why is this important? Because, as Hosmer (2008) has observed, ethical decisions need not always be framed as a dichotomy—i.e., that something is either right or wrong. Instead we may think in terms of degrees—that a particular way of responding to a situation is either highly ethical, moderately ethical, slightly ethical, slightly unethical, moderately unethical, or highly unethical. Targets of lies or other observers may not be inclined to think in terms of gradations, but "not telling the truth" can be performed in different ways and may, in turn, be evaluated differently.

Lie Selectively

Another issue bearing on the question of rightness or wrongness of lying concerns what you choose to lie about. Is it about something trivial? Are you lying to save another person from harm? To make somebody feel better? Or is your lie focused on benefiting you and you alone? Is the lie potentially harmful to others—e.g., saying you are not HIV positive to your sex partner when you are? Lies that help others and serve mutual interests are normally considered less reprehensible than lies that hurt others and primarily serve the interest of the liar. Trivial lies are less reprehensible than "big" lies. Yes, these concepts may not be easy to accurately sort out, but it is important that we know that all dishonest acts are not evaluated similarly so we may want to lie selectively. Other people are always saying things we don't agree with, but much of the time we let things go. Only on selected occasions do we choose to engage another person in conflict. Ethically, we might do well to think about lying in the same way.

Consider Discovery

Seriously considering issues related to the discovery of a lie will surely affect the telling of it. Assume all your lies will be discovered—especially if someone else knows about them. Don't ever say to a friend, "Don't tell anyone" without assuming they will. What is the worst thing that is likely to happen if your lie is discovered—to you and others? Are you willing to live with those consequences? Will you admit and be accountable for your lie? How will you defend it? For some lies, the consequences of discovery will be minimal, but liars often put such issues out of their mind. As a result, liars often imagine "things will work out ok" even with lies that have huge consequences. The "bigger" the lie (the greater impact, the more important the issue, the more reprehensible the lie, the more people involved, etc.) the more the liar has at stake and the more work he or she will put into keeping the lie from being discovered. But we also know that "big" lies are often detected. This may be a result of the correspondingly greater desire to detect "big" lies, the greater guilt experienced by the teller, or both (Seiter & Brushke, 2007).

Consider the Golden Rule

Confucius, Aristotle, Jesus, Mohammed, and others said we should behave toward others as we would like them to behave toward us. Are you doing what you'd expect others to do to you if they were in your position? If the answer is yes, this doesn't, in and of itself, make your behavior ethical. You may think your target is just as unethical as you are. It does, however, mean you have taken some time to consider the other person's perspective and that may be a minimal but necessary investment for behaving ethically. Nyberg (personal correspondence) argues that a productive rephrasing of the familiar Golden Rule should be: "Do unto others as if you were the others." Practically, acting as if we were the person or persons affected by our behavior is likely to be extremely difficult in times of stress, but, as Nyberg points out, the rephrasing accomplishes two important goals: 1) it changes the "authority" for what is the right thing to do from the doer to the other; and 2) it highlights the need for empathic understanding that is not explicit in the traditional phrasing. Empathy, Nyberg believes, plays a key role in a variety of ethical and moral decisions.

There is no completely adequate way to summarize these ethical guidelines, but Nilsen (1966) may capture its essence as well as anyone when he says:

> If we approach the problem of truth telling [and lying] with benevolence and justice as our moral commitments, and then apply knowledge and reason to the best of our ability, we will begin to fulfill our obligations as human beings. (p. 34)

Ethics and Self-Deception

Do you think it's wrong to lie to yourself? Is there anything wrong, for example, in pretending that a problem doesn't exist, avoiding or ignoring unpleasant information, or telling yourself an illegal act is justified because the law that was broken is unjust? Just as there are those who believe lies directed toward other human beings are always wrong, there are those who believe lies directed toward ourselves are always wrong. Those who believe we should all be trying to develop an "authentic" self view any type of self-deception as a betrayal of that goal. This is not to say that self-understanding is not a worthy goal and one which self-deception can sometimes block (Zahavi, 2005). A general commitment to being honest with ourselves is no doubt helpful in coping with self-made obstacles to self-understanding. But it is also possible that an imperfect self-understanding may be a part of a worthy life as well-helping us maintain hope, restore self-esteem, or maintain productive relationships (see Chapter 6).

Ethics of Lie Detection

Is the act of *detecting* deception also subject to questions of right and wrong? There are two issues here. The first has to do with the decision to initiate detection. In daily social interaction we normally initiate detection only when the target is suspected of having lied—a story doesn't fit other known facts, a third person makes an accusation, etc. Law enforcement agencies, too, need to have reasons to justify detection deception through interrogation or wiretaps. Ethical behavior is breached, however, when detection is undertaken without "probable cause."

In 2013, a breach of epic proportions by the U.S. National Security Agency was exposed. Former NSA contractor Edward Snowden leaked classified documents to journalists revealing that the agency had been recording nearly every phone call placed in the United States for years. These documented contradicted assurances from President Barack Obama and senior intelligence officials to the American public that their privacy was protected from NSA's dragnet surveillance programs

(Greenwald, 2014). The agency was originally granted the power to monitor citizens' phone and e-mail communication by the USA PATRIOT Act passed by Congress in 2001 after the September 11th attacks. The name of the act is an acronym for "Uniting and Strengthening America by Providing Appropriate Tools Required to Intercept and Obstruct Terrorism." NSA officials interpreted vague wording in the act as allowing them to collect communication of all U.S. citizens to identify terrorists among them and to do so without a warrant. When the "bulk data collection" program was exposed, government officials initially denied its existence and charged Snowden, who had already fled the country, with espionage. Two years later, it was declared unlawful by the courts and was disowned by Congress and the President. In an op-ed marking the program's termination, Snowden (2015) urged Americans not to assume that their privacy had been restored. Although chastened, the NSA continues to spy on the communication of U.S. citizens for whom there is no probable cause to believe they are concealing their identities as terrorists. In Snowden's words,

> Though we have come a long way, the right to privacy—the foundation of the freedoms enshrined in the United States Bill of Rights—remains under threat.

Snowden went on to elaborate that our government has taken measures to undermine the security of the Internet in an effort to examine the private lives of its citizens. Governments around the globe are pressuring technology companies to place the interests of the government above those of their customers and take part in massive surveillance operations. Cell phone data and Internet use is being monitored and recorded by the United States government regardless of who you are and what you are doing.

The methods used to carry out the detection of deception comprise the second issue, an issue that has grown in importance since the September 11th attacks. Machines have always had a special credibility for the American public when it comes to lie detection, but the polygraph is not portable and requires training to administer and interpret. New technology has eliminated these barriers to public usage and has resulted in the sale of thousands of small, portable devices that claim to accurately measure micro-tremors in a person's voice. These consumers then surreptitiously use them to detect lying spouses, job applicants, employees, and insurance claimants, among others. Many of these devices, which range from twenty dollars to several thousand dollars, claim the ability to distinguish vocalized statements by the suspected deceiver that are false, inaccurate, uncertain, or true. Despite the lack of research supporting the validity of these devices, people continue to buy, use, and too often, trust them. A number of studies conducted by the U.S. Department of Defense concluded these devices were not a reliable method of detecting deception. They are, however, a reliable method of invading a person's privacy and in states with laws that forbid recording a person's communication without their knowledge, it is against the law. It is also illegal to use the readings from these devices as justification for denying a job applicant employment. There is, however, no restriction on using the results of devices that analyze the voice to flag certain responses by a job applicant which then become the basis for seeking additional information.

Creating Honest Citizens

No matter how difficult it is to say exactly what it means to be honest; no matter how often we are reminded that honesty can be dysfunctional sometimes; and no matter how many surveys tell us we frequently tell lies; citizens of the United States still consider honesty a prized virtue and a core characteristic of an ethical person. We want our children to be honest and we want those children to grow up to be honest citizens. Can we teach people to be honest? If we can't, it isn't because we don't try. We try to legislate honesty, we teach it at home and in our schools, and it is a standard theme in our books, movies, and television shows (Mazur & Kalbfleisch, 2003).

Legislating Honesty

Various approaches are used to formally specify the desirability of truthful behavior. We have libel laws that are designed to keep people from disseminating false information about others which would damage their reputation. The Federal Trade Commission oversees various forms of consumer protection, including the enforcement of honesty in product labeling, lending contracts, and advertising. However, the FTC division enforcing truth-in-advertising standards has a small staff and must grant accused deceivers due process of law, with the result that false ads can air for months before any legal action takes effect (Williams, 2015). But at least the public has *some* legal protection against false advertising about products. They do not when it comes to politics. There is no federal law preventing a candidate for office from making a false political claim. Not only can they legally lie, but the Federal Communication Act requires broadcasters to show their ads uncensored, even if the broadcaster finds evidence that the ad content is false. Truth-in-political-advertising laws have been enacted in 3 states but have had little practical success. Courts in Minnesota and Washington struck down their state laws as abridgements of a candidate's Constitutional right to free speech. Ohio's law has survived court challenges, but is so weak that most violators receive only a letter of reprimand, not a fine or forfeit of the office they lied to get (Jackson, 2011).

Organizations which serve various professional groups like physicians, lawyers, engineers, journalists, etc. also develop ethical codes which are designed to illustrate membership standards for right and wrong behavior. Expected behavior relative to appropriate disclosure and confidentiality are often an important part of these codes.

Educational institutions also try to legislate honesty through the use of honor codes. Even though the students themselves are often instrumental in creating these honor codes and they are printed in student handbooks, it is not unusual for students to be unfamiliar with them. The Honor Code at the University of Texas at Austin's McCombs Business School says lying is a violation of the honor code and explains:

> *Lying is any deliberate attempt to deceive another by stating an untruth, or by any direct form of communication to include the telling of a partial truth. Lying includes the use or omission of any information with the intent to deceive or mislead. Examples of lying*

include, but are not limited to, providing a false excuse for why a test was missed or presenting false information to a recruiter.

The academic honor codes at the U.S. military academies are not only well known to the students but also the American public. Cheating scandals that have occurred at these institutions have received national coverage in the press and resulted in the expulsion of numerous cadets.

People will follow laws, regulations, and codes of conduct that prescribe honest behavior if they are fairly and consistently enforced. They work best when they are well known, supported by the membership, and firmly entrenched as a part of the institutional culture. They are far less effective when they are viewed as largely symbolic and enforcement is weak and/or irregular.

Teaching Honesty

Children learn about honesty and lying from their parents, their school teachers, and their peers. One study found teenagers saying that they would be far more likely to seek ethical advice from their parents or friends than their teachers, clergy, or other sources (Deloitte & Touche USA LLP, 2005). As these children become adults, their exposure to these lessons takes the form of books, television shows, movies, the rhetoric of public leaders, and press accounts of noteworthy liars and truth tellers.

The teaching that parents do is the child's first exposure to the culture's expectations concerning lying and truth telling. Parents are usually the child's primary role models. During early childhood, it is common for parents to be emphatic about their desire for children not to lie. At the same time, however, the child is picking up clues that this prohibition against dishonesty doesn't always apply to the parents. A child may hear his or her father say to someone on the telephone that he has to stay home because one of his children is sick (and the child knows otherwise); they observe their mother telling their younger sibling that his scribbled coloring is a "beautiful" picture and later telling someone else that the "beautiful" remark was made simply because she didn't want to hurt her son's feelings. Children also take in elaborate rituals put forth by their parents which confirm the existence of the Tooth Fairy and Santa Claus; they believe their parents when they say Storks bring babies and grandpa just went on a long vacation—only to find out later that none of this was true. They also may find out that the punishment for blurting out the truth at the wrong time will elicit just as much punishment as telling a lie. As the child gets older, he or she learns that in order to win certain card games (Old Maid, Hearts) and sporting contests (soccer, basketball) deceiving one's opponent is an important skill. Once the child is old enough to be held accountable for being polite, he or she may be punished for *not* lying. So the message kids seem to get is that adults want them to be honest, but that there are times when lying and deception may be acceptable. Parents may feel comfortable throughout early childhood because their kids either don't raise the tough questions about honesty and dishonesty or they readily accept whatever assertion a parent makes in order to shut down further discussion of the topic. Later, when the child asks tough questions and they are accompanied by examples of the parent's behavior, parent teaching gets significantly more difficult and it may be time for implementing different teaching methods. Instead of portraying life's decisions as clear, uncomplicated, and bound by certain rules which will apply to every situation, parents may now want to reveal more about how they sometimes struggle with making the "right" decisions in certain situations involving honesty and how they go about trying to "do the right thing"—even though they aren't always sure if they are.

In some school districts, parents have been influential in supporting "character education" in which various values and "virtues" (including honesty) are taught. These parents believe there is a close connection between character and academic achievement. In elementary and secondary schools this may be done through the reading of stories that exemplify the behavior to be modeled. Elementary school teachers may, for example read stories like "George Washington and the Cherry Tree," "The Boy Who Cried 'Wolf,'" or tales about truthtelling in Cortlett's (2009) *E is for Ethics*. An animated television show based on stories from Bennett's *The Children's Book of Virtues* (1995) has been broadcast numerous times. At Leander Elementary School (near Austin, Texas) students are rewarded for acts that conform to any often statements that make up the school's code of ethics. These acts include honesty (e.g., "I tell the truth to myself and others.") as well as integrity, promise-keeping, loyalty, fairness, concern for others, respect for others, civic duty, pursuit of excellence and accountability. When students are observed exhibiting such behaviors, their names are announced in assembly and displayed in a display case. The school's goal is to honor each student at least once during the year. There are also times allotted for self-evaluation in which students give themselves a G (growing) or an I (need improvement) on each statement. Colleges and universities provide additional formal learning experiences in courses focused on honesty issues—in both applied (e.g., public relations, management) or theoretical (ethics) contexts.

As adults we are regularly confronted with experiences that cause us to examine and reflect on our beliefs about honesty and dishonesty. These may be personal experiences, historical milestones like Watergate or the Challenger Disaster, or they may be a part of current events. In February 2002, for example, newspapers reported that Defense Secretary Donald Rumsfeld said that a Pentagon campaign to influence global opinion would not include lies to the American public, but might employ "tactical" deception to confuse an enemy for battlefield advantage. A reader can't help but wonder exactly what that means and how he or she feels about it.

Adults also continue their learning about truth telling and deceit by reading books. Bennett's *The Book of Virtues* (1993) was on the New York Times Bestseller List for eighty-eight weeks. Berger's (2006) *Raising Kids with Character* and Josephson's *Making Ethical Decisions* (2002) and are two of many books that provide guidance to parents on how to instill honest and ethical behavior in children.

Learning by Doing

Each of the preceding sources of information makes a contribution to what we know and what we believe about honesty and deception. But it is one thing to pontificate about what is right and wrong after you read a newspaper story or see a television show and another thing to be responsible for making hard choices about honest and dishonest behavior in real life situations. Active learning is a powerful teacher. We can learn a lot about honesty by being honest and a lot about deceit by being deceptive. By being active in the affairs of our family, neighborhood, and community we increase the chances that we will face difficult challenges involving honesty and deception and we increase the chances of having meaningful (not necessarily pleasant) learning experiences. Thus, we increase the chances of being in a better position to pass on useful knowledge to others.

Hard-Wired Morality

Despite all the efforts to nurture honesty in this culture, it appears that nature may also play an important role in our moral development. This was first brought to the attention of the medical community in 1848 when Phineas Gage suffered a terrible accident in which an explosion hurled an iron bar through his eye, brain, and skull. His speech and other cognitive abilities remained in tact and he recovered his health rather quickly. But this pleasant, responsible person, who was popular with his fellow workers, turned into a social outcast. After his accident, he had no respect for social conventions, no sense of responsibility, could not be trusted to honor his commitments, and would lie and curse uncontrollably (Macmillan, 2000). More recent cases of damage to the ventromedial prefrontal cortex (PFC) of the brain in childhood also show a severe and negative effect on social and moral behavior—including the tendency to lie frequently. Neuroscientists theorize that this brain area connects emotional experience to decision making processes, such as the anxiety most people experience when they consider doing something that might harm someone else (Greene, 2013). People who incur damage to this area apparently never develop a moral compass to distinguish right from wrong and interventions are generally ineffective (Cushman, 2014).

Honesty, then, is not only something we can learn, but is also firmly grounded in neurobiology to the extent that one part of our brain seems hard-wired to specialize in internalizing norms/rules, getting along, and other social/moral functions which interface with our communicative choices which we subsequently label as lying and truth telling (Haidt, 2012).

Summary

Ethics addresses matters of right and wrong. Whether our nation is currently experiencing a moral crisis or not, it is important for citizens to regularly engage themselves and others on how they feel about the rightness and wrongness of the many faces of honesty and deceit. The bulk of this chapter focused on the right and wrong of lying to another person, but issues associated with the ethics of self-deception and lie detection were also examined.

Four answers were given to the question, "Is it ever right to lie?" The first two subscribed to the general principle that lying is, in principle, wrong. The absolutists say it is always wrong to lie and the almost-absolutists say there are rare occasions when it is right to lie but only as a last resort and only after you are satisfied that the general public would approve. These positions sharply contrast with a Machiavellian approach which views lying, not in terms of rightness or wrongness, but in terms of whether it will help a person accomplish his or her goals. The situational approach believes matters of right and wrong are best determined by examining the circumstances surrounding the telling of a lie (or the truth) to determine its degree of rightness or wrongness. Of particular importance to this approach are the communicator's intentions and the consequences of his or her message.

Some practical guidelines were proposed for ethical behavior relative to lying that included: 1) Tell the truth most of the time; 2) If you lie, lie creatively. There are many ways to lie and some are considered worse than others; 3) If you lie, lie selectively—i.e., when you feel it is absolutely necessary and it is done with "good" intentions. 4) If you lie, consider discovery—i.e., what it will mean to you if the lie is revealed; and 5) Consider the Golden Rule or whether your behavior is what you'd want from the target of your lie—given similar circumstances.

Because some lies create a lot of personal and social damage, and frequent lying poses a potential threat to a society held together by the belief that people will generally tell them the truth, we have implemented various measures to create an honest citizenry. We legislate honesty through laws, regulations, and honor codes. We also encourage the teaching of honesty by parents, schools, public leaders, books, movies, and the press. Whatever is gleaned from all these lessons about honesty and deception, is fused with what appears to be a section of the brain devoted to moral behavior.

Things to Think About

Recall a lie you told in which you had to choose between being dishonest or being one of the following: compassionate, loyal, courageous, dependable, or fair. Why did you make the decision you did? Make your story into a case study. Identify all the people and conditions involved, but don't use your own name and don't identify that you chose dishonesty over another value. Write your case as objectively as possible, providing only the necessary facts, relationships, hard choices, and circumstances leading up to the main character's decision about how to act. Conclude your case by asking, "What would you do?" Have someone you don't know read your case and identify how they think they would respond in such a situation and why. With your partner, discuss honesty, deception, and other values as they relate to your case.

This chapter spent a lot of time addressing the question of whether it was ever "right" to lie. Examine the other side of that question: Is it ever "wrong" to tell the "truth"? Make a list of as many different types of situations where you think telling the truth would be wrong. Indicate why you believe this. Exchange lists with another person and discuss your answers.

References

Adamec, P. (2009). Historical dictionary of Islam.

Adler, K. (2007). *The lie detectors: The history of an American obsession.* New York: Free Press.

Associated Press (July 11, 2006). You look great! Poll finds we frown on lying, but white lies are frequent.

Bell, K.L. & DePaulo, B.M. (1996). Liking and lying. *Basic and Applied Social Psychology, 18,* 243–266.

Bennett, W.J. (1993). *The book of virtues.* New York: Simon & Schuster.

Berger, J. (2006). *Raising kids with character.* New York: Jason Aronson, Inc.

Bok, S. (1978). *Lying: Moral choice in public and private life.* New York: Pantheon.

Bowles, S. "Misconduct reports against teachers changing classrooms." *USA Today,* March 21, 2000, p. 4A.

Blanton, B. (2005). *Radical honesty: How to transform your life by telling the truth* (Revised Edition) New York: Dell.

Callahan, D. (2004). *The cheating culture: Why more Americans are doing wrong to get ahead.* New York: Harcourt.

Chance, Z., & Norton, M.I. (2011). "I read Playboy for the articles": Justifying and rationalizing questionable preferences. In M.S. McGlone & M.L. Knapp (Eds.), *The interplay of truth and deception* (pp. 136–148). New York: Routledge.

Cortlett, I. (2009). *E is for ethics: Read-aloud stories about morals, values, and what matters most.* New York: Atria.

Cushman, F. (2014). The neural basis of morality: Not just where, but when. *Brain, 137,* 974–980.

DePaulo, B.M. (2004). The many faces of lies. In A.G. Miller (Ed.), *The social psychology of good and evil* (pp. 303–326). New York: Guilford.

Deloitte & Touche USA LLP (2005). Polling student attitudes on ethics. Retrieved 1–3–2006. http://www.deloitte.com/dtt/article/ 0,1002,sid%3D14780%26cid%3D98704,00.html

Denery, D. (2015). *The devil wins: A history of lying from the garden of Eden to the Enlightenment.* Princeton, NJ: Princeton University Press.

Durham, G. "Study finds students lie and cheat, a lot." *Associated Press,* October 17, 2000.

Gorovitz, S. (Ed.). (1971). *Utilitarianism: Text and critical essays.* Indianapolis, IN: Bobbs-Merrill.

Greene, R. (2002). *The 48 laws of power* (Revised Edition). New York: Penguin Books.

Greene, J. (2013). *Moral tribes.* New York: Penguin.

Greenwald, G. (2014). *No place to hide: Edward Snowden, the NSA, and the U.S. surveillance state.* New York: Metropolitan Books.

Haidt, J. (2012). *The righteous mind.* New York: Pantheon.

Hartshorne, H. & May, M. (1928). *Studies in the nature of character,* vol. I, *Studies in deceit.* New York: Macmillan.

Hartshorne, H. & May, M. (1971). Studies in the organization of character (pp. 190–197). In H. Munsinger (Ed)., *Readings in child development.* New York: Holt, Rinehart & Winston.

Hearn, T.K. Jr. (Ed.) (1971). *Studies in utilitarianism.* New York: Meredith.

Hosmer, L.T. (2008). *Ethics of management.* New York: McGraw-Hill.

Illbruck, H. (2012). *Nostalgia: Origins and ends of an unenlightened disease.* Evanston, IL: Northwestern University Press.

Jackson, B. (2010). Finding the weasel word in "literally true." In M.S. McGlone & M.L. Knapp (Eds.), *The interplay of truth and deception* (pp. 1–15). New York: Routledge.

Jaksa, J.A. & Pritchard, M.S. (1994). *Communication ethics: Methods for analysis.* Belmont, CA.: Wadsworth.

Johnson, C.E. (2001). *Meeting the ethical challenges of leadership.* Thousand Oaks, CA.: Sage.

Josephson, M.S. (2002). *Making ethical decisions.* Marina del Rey, CA.: Josephson Institute of Ethics.

Josephson Institute of Ethics (2012). *2012 Report card on the ethics of American youth.* Los Angeles, CA.

Kalish, N. (January, 2004). How honest are you? *Reader's Digest,* 114–119.

Kant, I. (1959). *Foundations of the metaphysics of morals.* New York: Liberal Arts Press, Bobbs-Merrill.

Kardonne, R. (2008). *Victor Kugler: The man who hid Anne Frank.* Jerusalem, Israel: Gefen Publishing House.

Keyes, R. (2004). *The post-truth era: Dishonesty and deception in contemporary life.* New York: St. Martin's Press.

Kirsch, I. (2013). The placebo effect revisited: Lessons learned to date. *Complementary Therapies in Medicine, 21,* 102–104.

Lee, K. (2013). Little liars: Development of verbal deception in children. *Child Development Perspectives, 7,* 91–96.

Machiavelli, N. (2010/1532). *The prince.* New York: Capstone.

Macmillan, M. (2000). *An odd kind of fame.* Cambridge, Mass.: MIT Press.

Mayhew, M. "To tell the truth." *Fort Worth Star Telegram,* April 4, 2002.

Mazur, M.A. & Kalbsleisch, P.J. (2003). Lying and deception detection in television families. *Communication Research Reports, 20,* 200–207.

McGlone, M.S., & Giles, H. (2011). Language and interpersonal communication. In M.L. Knapp & J.A. Daly (Eds.), *The SAGE handbook of interpersonal communication* (4th ed, pp. 201–237). Thousand Oaks, CA: Sage.

Miller, F.G., Wendler, D., & Swartzman, L.C. (2005). Deception in research on the placebo effect. *PLoS Medicine, 2,* 853–859.

Nilsen, T.R. (1966). *Ethics of speech communication.* Indianapolis: Bobbs-Merrill.

Nyberg, D. (1993). The varnished truth: Truth telling and deceiving in ordinary life. Chicago: University of Chicago Press.

Packer, G. (2014). *The unwinding: An inner history of the new America.* New York: Farrar, Straus, & Giroux.

Patterson, J. & Kim, P. (1991). *The day America told the truth: What people really believe about everything that really matters.* New York: Prentice Hall.

Plante, T.G. (2004). *Do the right thing: Living ethically in an unethical world.* Oakland, CA.: New Harbinger.

Raeker, S. (2014). *Strengthening a culture of ethics.* Presentation for the U.S. Senate Legislative Ethics Committee.

Quintilian, M.F. (1922/ca. 90 CE). *The institutio oratoria, Book I.* H.E. Butler (trans.). Cambridge, Mass.: Harvard University Press.

Robinson, W.P. (1994). Reactions to falsifications in public and interpersonal contexts. *Journal of Language and Social Psychology, 13,* 497–513.

Schaefer, C.E. & Millman, H.L. (1981). *How to help children with common problems.* New York: VanNostrand Reinhold.

Seiter, J.S., Bruschke, J. & Bai, C. (2002). The acceptability of deception as a function of perceivers' culture, deceiver's intention, and deceiver-deceived relationship. *Western Journal of Communication, 66,* 158–180.

Seiter, J.S., & Brushke, J. (2007). Deception and emotion: The effects of motivation, relationship type, and sex on expected feelings of guilt and shame following acts of deception in United States and Chinese samples. *Communication Studies, 58,* 1–16.

Smart, J.J.C. & Williams, B. (1973). *Utilitarians, for and against.* London: Cambridge University Press. Smiley, J. "The good lie." *New York Times Magazine,* May 7, 2000, 58–59.

Snowden, E. (2015, June 4). The world says no to surveillance. *New York Times.* Retrieved June 6, 2015 from http://www.nytimes.com.

Spero, R. (1980). *The duping of the American voter: Dishonesty and deception in presidential television advertising.* New York: Lippincott and Crowell.

Stevenson, B., & Wolfers, J. (2011). *Trust in public institutions over the business cycle.* Cambridge, MA: National Bureau of Economic Research.

Stewart, D.J. (2013). Taqiyah and the Islamic discipline of dissimulation. *Al-Qantara, 34,* 437–488.

US News & World Report, February 23,1987, 54.Wekesser, C. (Ed.) (1995). *Ethics: Current controversies.* San Diego, CA.: Greenhaven Press.

Williams, T. (2015). *False advertising and the Lanham Act.* New York: LEXISNEXIS.

Zahavi, D. (2005). *Subjectivity and selfhood: Investigating the first-person perspective.* Cambridge, MA: MIT Press.

Part II | Deceptive Behavior

There are many ways to deceive. The following five chapters focus on the research and writing associated with the performance of lying and deception. Manifestations of deception among various nonhuman species provide a fascinating beginning and a useful backdrop for understanding how human beings perform acts of deception. In the same way, an examination of how the developing child learns the skills needed to lie effectively is a useful antecedent to learning about adult prevaricators. Then, two types of adult behavior are examined: self-deception and interpersonal deception. This part concludes with an examination of people who make lying a featured part of their lives—namely, pathological liars and con artists.

Chapter 4

Nonhuman Deception

Evolution is a complex process involving many factors, but deception and deception detection are often an important part of natural selection (Darwin, 1993/1859). Nature tends to favor those who practice deception effectively as well as those who become effective perceivers (or deception detectors). The traits of deception and perception are both adaptive and useful in nature's often-fierce competition for survival, acquiring food and other resources, and reproducing. As Rue (1994, p.104) puts it:

> If the survival of an organism depends on its abilities to process information from the environment, then any improvements in those abilities would tend to be favored. If a fortuitous genetic mutation results in more acute sight or hearing, for example, then the organism bearing the improved trait will be better able to acquire resources and avoid danger. The trait will be adaptive and therefore will tend to be preserved in future generations.

But no matter how skilled a perceiver becomes, there will always be deceivers who manage to take advantage of any perceptual limitations existing in the perceiver. Magicians rely on their knowledge of human perceptual limitations in order to deceive their audiences. But nature often makes deception and deception detection a matter of life or death. Blue jays, for example, have developed a perceptual system which recognizes the colors and patterns of monarch butterflies which are toxic to blue jays. At the same time, however, they also avoid tasty, non-toxic butterflies that deceive them by mimicking the appearance of the monarch. But being deceived in this way is a small price for the blue jay to pay for a perceptual system that otherwise keeps it alive and flourishing. It is only when an organism's vulnerability to deception begins to outweigh the advantages of its perceptual system that a species is threatened. For example, let's assume that all sources of blue jay food disappeared from its habitat except the monarchs and their

> "The ability to deceive is one of the many abilities or characteristics that have made some animals better equipped to survive than others...The struggle for life has favored the better mimickers and bluffers..."
>
> — *Evelin Sullivan*

© Pete Oxford/Minden Pictures/Corbis

Figure 4.1: *Dynastor darius* pupa, native to Trinidad

non-toxic mimics. Given these conditions, some blue jays would have to develop a refined perceptual system which is capable of distinguishing the tasty butterflies from the toxic ones or face extinction.

If you thought that the cocoon in Figure 4.1 was a snake at first glance you are not alone. Predators of this caterpillar living in Trinidad avoid it during its pupal stage due to its similarity to a viper. There seem to be an infinite number of examples of the deceit taking place in the natural world. Given the important roles deception, deception detection, and counter-deception play in the survival of any given organism, it is not difficult to document the process in the lives of insects, fish, birds, amphibians, reptiles, and mammals. But we begin our tour of nonhuman deception by looking at the process as practiced by microscopic organisms within the human body.

Deception at the Molecular Level

Despite the best efforts of our immune system to target and destroy unwanted and harmful viruses and bacteria, many evade detection through the use of various forms of deception. Sometimes the deceptive pathogen (disease-producing organism) is relatively harmless so, as Goodenough (1991) says, it is "a lie we can live with." Nevertheless, the job of the immune system is to declare war on any alien organism that may be harmful. But this is more like guerrilla warfare and "winning" for the invader means surviving rather than killing its host. A virus is a parasite that is unable to replicate and survive without a host cell. Therefore, its goal is to find a way to survive undetected behind the enemy's lines where it can create havoc. The immune system's first job, then, is not to amass a huge army, but to develop effective detection techniques for recognizing and finding alien presences. How do pathogens use deception to evade detection and eradication by the immune system?

Mimicry

One common way pathogens use deception to enter a host cell is to resemble something specific which is regularly welcomed into the cell—such as serum proteins and hormones. The virus mimics or takes on characteristics of the useful molecules, which, in turn, gives them a free invitation to enter the cell (Yoshino & Coustau, 2011; Damian, 1989). This occurs with the rabies and Epstein-Barr viruses. Another example of mimicry involves several types of bacteria that have evolved a coating of sialic acid. This is an effective form of deception since sialic acid coating on healthy cells is used by the immune system as a means of distinguishing good cells from foreign parasites. Bacteria known to cause food poisoning rely on this type of molecular mimicry (Louwen et al, 2013).

Camouflage

Camouflage, like mimicry, is a form of concealment or disguise designed to avoid detection. With camouflage, though, pathogens try to blend into the background, to look like they "belong" rather than assuming any specific characteristics. The primary agent of the common cold, the rhinovirus, hides the host cell binding site, which enables it to connect with and ultimately infect the host, in a cleft that is too narrow for an antibody molecule to enter (Goodenough, 1991). Many viruses, bacteria, and parasites rely on camouflage to avoid detection by the immune system—and these mechanisms are the cause for a lack of vaccines for many illnesses (De Groot et al., 2014). Identifying and understanding camouflage at the molecular level is an important step toward creating cures and effective vaccines.

Illusion

The key to a good magic trick is the effective use of illusion—i.e., get the dupe to think one thing is happening when, in fact, it is not. Viruses also use this technique. The African trypanosome virus is transmitted by the tsetse fly and causes a form of sleeping sickness. This virus does not invade cells, but circulates in the person's blood—infecting his or her blood, tissues, and organs. Since the antibodies generated to fight this virus are also circulating in the person's blood, most trypanosomes are destroyed. But there are always survivors. The survivors have been able to change their identity so they are not recognized by the existing antibodies. These trypanosomes have evolved a built-in system that quickly switches the antigens against which the immune system produces antibodies. This is called antigenic variation. Each time the immune system identifies the surface glycoprotein displayed by the virus and sends out antibodies to combat it, the virus displays a new variant of the glycoprotein. The African trypanosome virus is believed to be capable of making a thousand antigenic variations. Chronic infections may be caused by viruses that are constantly able to elude the attacks of the immune system by continuing to change their identities.

Through vaccines and the natural efforts of our immune system, we annually seek to prevent an epidemic caused by the influenza virus. But the influenza virus also changes its identity. Each year the Centers for Disease Control and Prevention urges people to get flu shots designed to combat this virus. But this plea is always accompanied by the disclaimer that flu shots may not be effective in combating any *new* strains of the influenza virus which have mutated in such a way as to negate the effectiveness of antibodies and T-cells developed to fight a previous flu virus. The trick of the ever-changing virus can cause problems as we age. As adults our bodies create fewer antibodies that are used to detect new pathogens, thus making adults more susceptible to the flu than children (Kucharski, 2014). The immune system is under the impression that past experiences with the flu have created the recognition program to fight off future attacks, but new strains of the changing virus go undetected.

Plants Can Be Deceptive Too

To further illustrate the omnipresence of deception among organisms, we need look no further than the weeds, grasses, and flowers that surround us. These plants rely on deception to obtain food, reproduce, and to form symbiotic relationships, where both species survive due to their interaction with one another. The Venus flytrap is perhaps the best-known of many carnivorous plants throughout the world. To supplement the nutrients it gets from the soil and air, it has developed a flower-like structure which attracts insects. As the insect begins to explore the "flower," it might bend one of the short, stiff hairs which line the inside of the opening of the flower. The plant's mechanism is quite developed because a second hair must be touched within 20 seconds to activate the trap. Activating two of the trigger hairs will snap the plant shut, trapping the insect, and create a meal the plant has procured through deception.

Many orchid plants use food deception to appear as though they have a reward for attracting pollinators, but in these cases no food reward is provided. In addition, some orchids rely on deception as a means to reproduce (Gasket, 2011). The bee orchid, for example, uses a variety of tricks to entice male bees to attempt copulation with it (see Figure 4.2). This versatile flower has not only developed the appearance of a female bee, but it also feels and smells like her. As the male is mounting what he thinks is a female of his own species, the bee orchid attaches pollen sacks to the male bee's head. When the male bee visits another bee orchid, he completes the pollination process for the orchid. Another species of orchid attracts male wasps and the deception is successful enough to cause the wasp to ejaculate into the flower—these orchids have the highest pollination rates (Gaskett, Winnick, & Herberstein, 2008).

© John Navajo/Shutterstock.com

Figure 4.2: A bee orchid

Some plants have developed features and odors similar to feces; they accomplish their pollination goals by attracting insects looking for food or a place to lay their eggs. While something that has the odor or appearance of feces may not be appealing to humans, this is not the case for the dung beetle. The flower of the *Hydnora africana* (Bolin, Maass, Musselman, 2009) emits a dung-like odor which encourages the beetles to enter the flower. The opening to the flower has hairs developed in such a way that once the beetles enter they are trapped inside. In this case the insects are only temporary imprisoned; the flower opens up after a few days and releases the pollen-laden beetles.

But some plants are as interested in keeping other species away from them as they are in welcoming them. Through deception, passion flowers manage to negotiate a mutually advantageous, but potentially deadly, relationship with *Heliconius* butterflies. The main problem is that some passion flowers would like to use the butterflies to help in pollination, but the butterflies see the plant as a perfect place to lay their eggs. When their eggs become larvae, they eat the leaves of the plant, which can kill it. The evolved actions and reactions to this situation are quite remarkable. It begins with leaf shape. The butterflies are good at recognizing the leaf shape of plants that will provide the best nutrition for their larvae, so the young passion flower tries to make itself less desirable by varying its leaf shape as it grows. The butterflies have a keen sense of smell which is countered by unpleasant odors given off by the leaves of young passion flowers. To discourage egg laying, some passion flowers have produced structures which resemble *Heliconius* eggs. Since these female butterflies are programmed not to lay too many eggs in one place, this form of trickery may cause the butterfly to look for another site to lay its eggs (Williams & Gilbert, 1981). Even when eggs are deposited, the passion flower has a couple more tricks up its leaf. The leaves produce poisons and don't smell very inviting. If the larvae are not discouraged and eat the poisonous leaves, they develop a toxicity, which, as adults, will deter some predators. But the passion flower is also producing a nectar on its stems and leaves that attracts ants that destroy the larvae. Ironically, it is the passion flower's nectar and pollen that adult *Heliconius* butterflies feed on—an act which helps the flower pollinate.

Other plants that seek to keep out of harm's way (i.e., being eaten) have evolved an appearance that does not portend a good meal. Healthy plants that, from all outward appearances, are dead, or resemble bird droppings, or that look like rocks are examples. Plants also evolve to mimic other plants in their proximity that animals do not eat. When humans get involved there can be unpredicted outcomes. Such is the case in the history of the rye plant, which was originally a weed, but resembled and grew alongside the domesticated wheat crop. A process of artificial selection allowed the weed to become a crop because over time as farmers removed the rye weed from their crops those that resembled wheat went undetected, survived, and in time rye evolved to be so similar to wheat that it became a usable crop (Zohary, Hopf, & Weiss, 2012).

The preceding illustrations of deception as practiced by viruses and plants appropriately set the stage for examining deception among other creatures on Earth. The following model will help us understand and organize this behavior.

A Typology of Deceptive Strategies in the Nonhuman World

Rue (1994) identified three key components associated with deceptive interactions among species other than human beings. Each component, he argues, is directly adapted to the deception process.

> *I have said that deception is essentially an interactive phenomenon, and as such it requires categories of description that focus directly on the dynamics of interactions between deceivers and dupes (p. 107).*

Purpose(s) of the Deception

The primary goals for most species are to survive and reproduce. In order to do this, an organism needs to be able to find adequate food and be able to mate successfully with one or more partners. When deception is used in the pursuit of these goals, it is deemed to be *offensive*. Organisms also need to be able to resist various threats to their survival. Deception used toward this end is termed *defensive*. Obviously, surviving and reproducing can be and is accomplished in a variety of ways, but if an organism needs to be swift and isn't, needs to be strong and isn't, or needs to have protective armor and doesn't, deception is a useful alternative. Since most of the deceptive acts found in the nonhuman world are not subject to conscious processing and awareness by the deceptive organism, most references to the intended purposes or goals of deception are based on the observations of human beings and not the intentions of the organism itself. This has led some evolutionary biologists to study deception in nonhuman animals by focusing on the cost and benefits for the signaler regardless of intentionality (Searcy & Nowicki, 2005).

Effects of the Deception on the Dupe

The extent to which a deceptive act is successful is the extent to which it manages to defeat the perceptual system of the dupe (Thompson, 1986). In the communicative world of nonhuman species, this can be done in at least two ways. First, the deceptive act may mask the deceiver in ways which allow it to escape the perceptual system of the dupe completely. This effect is referred to as an *evasive* strategy. Second, the deceptive act may confuse, delude, or pervert the dupe's perceptual system so that the dupe activates inappropriate schemas toward the deceiver. In short, the deceiver manages to pervert or change the interpretation normally given by the dupe toward it. This is called a *perversive* strategy.

Means of Deception

How the deception is manifested comprises Rue's third component. This can be done by *morphology* or *behavior*. Morphology refers to the structure and form of the organism–its color, shape, appearance, size, and smell. Behavior refers to the actions taken by the organism to bring about the deception.

As noted by Rue, the components of the deceptive process can be combined in a variety of ways. An organism's coloration (morphology) may enable it to avoid the perceptual system of a predator (evasive strategy) for the dual purposes of resisting a threat (defensive) and being able to prey on other organisms that do not perceive its presence (offensive). And even though they are separate categories for purposes of understanding the process, morphology and behavior often work together in nature. For example, a moth's coloration may be indistinguishable from a leaf, but deception based on that morphology may not be effective unless the moth behaves appropriately—i.e., lands on the right leaf and remains motionless.

How many of the components of Rue's typology can you identify in the life cycle of the tiger swallowtail butterfly? Like a number of other species, the swallowtail larvae are "shit mimics." Birds looking for food are likely to mistake them for bird droppings and, needless to say, leave them alone. In the caterpillar stage, the swallowtail's green coloring helps it blend in with the leaves it feeds on. But it also has large yellow "eyespots" (not eyes) that have black "pupils" and there is a yellow and black stripe where its "neck" should be. These markings on its head look enough like a snake to keep some hungry birds at bay. In its next stage, the pupa takes on the coloring of the tree or twig to which it is attached. Once the swallowtail butterfly has emerged, it continues its deceptive ways. When its wings are upright, the tips have the appearance of a butterfly's head (see Figure 4.3). Birds that attack this image may damage the swallowtail's wing, but the attack will not be lethal. Finally, even though the tiger swallowtail is not a poisonous butterfly, some females mimic the darker, poisonous pipevine butterfly—which some predators have learned to avoid.

© Kendall Hunt Publishing Co.

Figure 4.3: A swallowtail butterfly with an imitation head on its wing tips

The following are some specific examples of how the different components in Rue's model manifest themselves in the lives of deceptive insects, fish, reptiles, amphibians, birds, and mammals.

Offensive Purpose, Evasive Strategy, Morphological Means

The coloring and shape of some insects is so much like the flowers they inhabit that they simply lie in wait until an unsuspecting victim approaches, thinking it is inspecting a flower. The last act of some insects is to search for nectar on the body of the orchid mantis in Figure 4.4.

© Thomas Marent/Minden Pictures/Corbis

Figure 4.4: An orchid mantis on a pink orchid

Offensive Purpose, Perversive Strategy, Morphological Means

Cleaner fish, as their name suggests, clean other fish by removing unwanted bacteria, parasites, and damaged tissue which they feed on. It's a good symbiotic relationship. Both fish receive benefits so the large clients of the cleaner fish are programmed not to hurt them. But some fish mimic the appearance of the cleaner fish and hang around them. Instead of cleaning, they sneak bites of flesh off of the client. Irritated, the client fish turns, ready for retaliation, but sees only what appear to be cleaner fish that the client will not harm. With experience, though, "clients" can develop ways of distinguishing cleaner fish from their mimics—which necessitates the mimics moving on to new "customers" (Wickler, 1968).

Brood parasitism is an intriguing deceptive act that many different species utilize for offloading the raising of their young onto other species. Birds are well known for this behavior; the female cuckoo bird lays her eggs in the nests of other birds. To fool the foster parents to her future children, the cuckoo's eggs are produced with almost exactly the same coloring as those of the host family that already occupies a nest (see Figure 4.5). The cuckoo puts only one egg into as many as twenty-five different nests. After about twelve days the cuckoo egg hatches and the nesting mother bird feeds it as her own. But newly hatched cuckoo birds aren't particularly interested in sharing the nest. So they push any remaining hatchlings or eggs from "their" nest, leaving themselves as the sole recipient of food from the nesting mother who obligingly, and perhaps unknowingly, feeds the cuckoo. Some birds can detect the work of a brood parasite and will push the parasitic egg from their nest or abandon the nest altogether. Hoover and Robinson (2007) found that cuckoos use a *mafia-like* strategy after laying an egg in another bird's nest. Visits to the nest allow the cuckoo to observe the status of her eggs. If a host bird has shown rejection of the cuckoo's eggs or young then she will destroy the host's nest. Perhaps this increases the chances of the host bird building a new nest—and another opportunity for the cuckoo—or it might increase compliance by host birds to raise the cuckoo's young.

Cloudsley-Thompson (1980, p. 41) reports that, in order to attract the birds it loves to eat, the African water mongoose "conceals itself in grass or other vegetation, raises its rear end, and distends the anal orifice to such an extent that it resembles a flower or ripe fruit. Unsuspecting birds are thereby lured to peck at the mongoose which adroitly turns about and immediately seizes them."

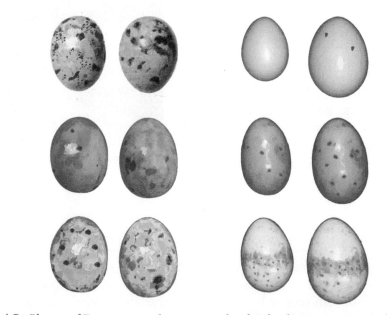

© Kendall Hunt Publishing Co.

Figure 4.5: Photos of European cuckoo eggs with other bird eggs—can you tell the difference? For example, very top left green with speckles: Cuckoo is the one on the right

Defensive Purpose, Evasive Strategy, Morphological Means

The ability to assume the coloration, textures, and even forms existing in one's habitat is a feature shared by many species. As far as predators are concerned, these animals don't exist. They are indistinguishable from the environment itself. Many amphibians (toads, frogs) and reptiles (turtles, lizards, snakes), for example, are capable of rapid color changes which conform to their surroundings. The mimic octopus is a recently discovered species (Norman & Hochberg, 2005) that takes on the shape of many other creatures, such as a poisonous flatfish swimming across the sandy bottom, and these octopuses change colors instantly to take on the appearance of seemingly any background to evade predators.

Defensive Purpose, Perversive Strategy, Morphological Means

Normally, the frilled lizard's appearance is not particularly distinctive. But when it is frightened it opens its mouth, baring its teeth. This action simultaneously causes an umbrella-like collar, with bright orange and red scales, to unfold and encircle its neck. To a predator, this display may make the frilled lizard seem like a far more formidable foe than it already is.

The "alligator bug" (or lanternfly) in the Brazilian rainforest has a long, hollow, nose-like protrusion from its head that looks very much like an alligator's head, complete with a row of formidable looking teeth (see Figure 4.6). In this environment, monkeys regularly prey on large insects like cicadas, but they tend to steer clear of the alligator bug. Anything that appears to have a lot of visible teeth or looks like an alligator or caiman (no matter how small) is likely to activate the monkey's "steer clear" program, at least initially, which provides time for the alligator bug to escape. It is a process similar to a human being who rapidly moves away from a rope, which at first glance looked like a snake (Cloudsley-Thompson, 1980).

Figure 4.6: Photo of an alligator bug

© Michael & Patricia Fogden/Corbis

The American avocets are birds that usually build their nests along the shores and nearby flat lands of sparsely vegetated lakes and sloughs. The lack of cover allows predators, looking for newborn avocets who cannot fly, to view them from a distance. Even though the newborn avocets will not learn to fly until they are about five weeks old, they develop the plumage of an adult after about two weeks—thereby giving the appearance of a full grown (and flying) adult (Sordahl, 1988).

Offensive Purpose, Evasive Strategy, Behavioral Means

Brandt and Mahsberg (2002) provide an example of this type of deception practiced by West African assassin bugs. These bugs, in order to enter an ant colony undetected, with the goal of having an ant feast, take the corpses of captured ants and glue them to their bodies. These insects' use of dust and plant parts as disguises in other contexts has also been observed.

Offensive Purpose, Perversive Strategy, Behavioral Means

Since vultures dine on dead and decaying animals, they are not perceived as a threat to small living animals. The zone-tailed hawk, however, prefers dining on animals it kills. So the hawk creates the illusion that it is a vulture by flying around in their company. As soon as the hawk sees a worthy prey, it dives out of the pack of vultures directly toward its target.

Some female fireflies (*Photuris*) obtain a needed part of their diet by giving males of another firefly species (*Photinus*) the idea that they will mate with them. The *Photuris* female sends out a coded flashing signal which is specific to the courtship ritual of the *Photinus* firefly. The signal essentially says there is a *Photinus* female who wants to have sex. When a male *Photinus* comes calling, however, he is promptly eaten by the *Photuris* female (Lloyd, 1986). By devouring the *Photinus* males, *Photuris* females (and ultimately the *Photuris* males) are able to acquire a defensive chemical in the system of the *Photinus* that they aren't able to produce themselves. The higher the concentration of this chemical in a firefly, the less desirable it is to predators like spiders and birds, so the offensive deception also plays an important defensive role in the life cycle of the *Photuris* firefly (Eisner at al., 1997).

Defensive Purpose, Evasive Strategy, Behavioral Means

The bittern is a bird with a long neck, similar to a heron or stork. It lives in aquatic areas. When it is threatened, it points its beak toward the sky and remains motionless. This act makes it look like one of the many reeds in its habitat.

Defensive Purpose, Perversive Strategy, Behavioral Means

Morris (1986) reports the following observations involving elephants at the Washington Park Zoo in Portland, Oregon. The elephants had to pull a chain to activate a shower, but the shower only lasted thirty seconds, so, in order take advantage of the full thirty seconds, one elephant had to pull the chain for another elephant who stood under the shower. During an aggressive encounter, the less-dominant elephant pulled the chain and the dominant elephant discontinued its aggression and went to the shower. In similar encounters that followed, the non-dominant elephant simply acted like it was going to pull the chain but never did. Acting like he was going to pull the chain, however, caused the dominant elephant to discontinue its aggressive actions and head for the shower area. This worked at least four times, but in the end the non-dominant elephant was beaten so badly she had to be moved to another area.

One way the eastern hognose snake (*Heterodon platyrhinos*) misleads predators is to play dead by opening its mouth, writhing as if in pain, and rolling onto its back with its mouth open and tongue hanging out. They have been known to continue playing dead and remaining limp even when they are picked up (see Figure 4.7). The term "play possum" is commonly used when a person remains quiet to avoid someone who visits his or her home uninvited or when a child feigns sleep. This colloquialism is derived from the behavior of the opossum, a night-dwelling marsupial native to North America, that when scared will feint and appear dead or sick. This uncontrolled behavior even includes the excretion of smelly anal gland fluid to add even more credence to the guise that the animal is dead.

Figure 4.7: An eastern hognose snake "playing" dead

DeWaal (1986) observed chimpanzees at the Arnhem Zoo in the Netherlands. One male chimp sustained a minor injury to his hand in a fight with another chimp, and for about a week after the fight the chimp limped—but only if he could be seen by the chimp he had been fighting with. Otherwise, he would walk normally. In this case, limping in the presence of a dominant male may have prevented further aggression.

The preceding system provides a useful way of classifying different types of nonhuman deception based on: 1) the organism's ostensible purpose, 2) the way the deception affects the dupe, and 3) the way the deception is enacted. Rue (1994) limited the means of enacting deception to morphology or behavior. Mitchell (1986; 1993) provides further detail on the way deception is enacted and, in particular, the processes driving the enacted behavior.

The Ability to Deceive: Four Levels

Table 4.1 identifies four levels of deception. Level I is primarily what we referred to as morphology in the previous section. Levels II, III, and IV all deal with behavior. With each increasing level, the deceiver exerts more control over the act of deception. Given the limited observations available for some nonhuman species, it is not always clear what "program," as Mitchell (1986) calls it, is driving the enacted deception. Behavior initially classified at level II, for example, may later be classified as level III after further observations confirm that the behavior is a result of learning. Deception in level IV is rare and scientists often disagree about whether or not a particular behavior is in fact planned or conscious; as mentioned earlier we are not able to know what a nonhuman animal is thinking—so we must make assumptions about intentionality from the situation. Interactions involving deception are often complex and involve many variables.

Table 4.1 Levels of Deception

Level	Deception Primarily Effected By	Program
I	Appearance	Always do (or look like) p
II	Coordination of Perception and Action	Do p given that q (action of target) is so
III	Learning	Do any p given that p resulted in q in the past; or avoid p if it has resulted in undesirable consequences in the past
IV	Planning	Self-programmed. Organism can program or reprogram itself based upon the past and present actions of the target and changing circumstances

(Mitchell, 1986, p. 29)

Level I

Deceptive acts at this level are not adapted by the deceiver to the target. The deceiver looks or acts in a particular way because it cannot do otherwise. Any modification of the deceiver (color, shape, pattern) or the deceiver's behavior depends largely on who the organism's natural predators choose to kill and who they avoid killing. Sometimes predators will avoid killing organisms that resemble (in appearance or behavior) other organisms that are distasteful or noxious to them. This, then, is their deception: they survive and multiply because they resemble an organism which predators have learned to avoid. In this case, survival of the fittest means survival of the look-alikes. This phenomenon is known as *mimicry*. There are at least eighteen different types of mimicry with multiple subtypes (Pasteur, 1982), but we will limit our attention to the following two types: Batesian mimicry and Müllerian mimicry.

Batesian Mimicry

From 1849 to 1860, Henry Walter Bates spent his time in the Brazilian Amazon observing and collecting thousands of insects and butterflies (O'Hara, 1995). While grouping his specimens, he noticed a striking similarity between different *families* of butterflies. He also noticed that palatable butterflies, which could easily be captured by predators due to their brightly colored wings and their slow speed in flight, were surviving quite well in areas with plenty of predators. He concluded that the palatable butterflies that most resemble the unpalatable butterflies are most likely to survive because predators mistakenly perceive them to be an unpalatable meal. This mimicry works best when the unpalatable butterflies outnumber the palatable ones. With more toxic butterflies, predators will learn the lesson that "all butterflies with these markings shouldn't be eaten" rapidly and with more assurance. This is because the predators experience mostly toxic meals from the butterflies they sample.

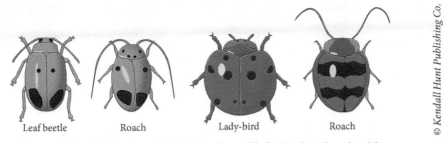

Leaf beetle   Roach   Lady-bird   Roach

Figure 4.8: Batesian mimicry: An unpalatable beetle and lady-bird with palatable mimic roaches

Batesian mimicry is not limited to butterflies or even members of the same species or family. Figure 4.8 shows mimicry of unpalatable beetles by palatable roaches. Ants and grasshoppers mimic beetles, spiders mimic ants, and harmless flies mimic poisonous wasps and bees. Mimicry is plentiful among insects, but far less common among vertebrates. One example among mammals is the visual similarity between the inoffensive aardwolf and the striped hyena. Another instance of Batesian mimicry among mammals involves the tree shrew in Borneo. Predators find the flesh of the tree shrew repulsive and tend to leave it alone. Palatable squirrels in the area have skins that look so much like the skin of the tree shrew that it is nearly impossible to tell them apart.

Müllerian Mimicry

In 1878, Fritz Müller discovered that mimicry also took place between two organisms, both of which were distasteful or noxious to predators. Wasps, bees, and butterflies show this type of mimicry. Why does this occur? What is the advantage? Müller explained it this way. Predators learn that an organism is unpalatable or harmful by killing and/or trying to kill it. Even if a species is noxious, predators may kill a number of organisms before all the predators learn the lesson that they

Monarch   Queen

Viceroy   Arizona Viceroy

Figure 4.9: Similarities of butterflies; monarch and queen butterflies show Mullerian mimicry (both unpalatable) and viceroys illustrate Batesian mimicry (both palatable)

© Kendall Hunt Publishing Co.

are to be avoided. But if the kills are spread out between the two noxious species, neither species has to sacrifice as many of their members. Figure 4.9 illustrates both Batesian and Müllerian mimicry among butterflies.

Level II

At this level the deceiver is more in control of the deceptive act than at Level I. The deceiver's deceptive act is triggered in response to a need and/or a particular behavior on the part of the target. The organism need not have learned that its deception will get a particular response, only that q (action of target) is occurring so p (deceiver's actions) occurs.

Examples of such behavior include the scare tactic of butterflies or peacocks that display eyespots on their wings in response to threat; and opossums, squirrels, birds and insects who pretend they are dead when attacked (the opossum's tongue even hangs out) in hopes that the attacker will lose interest.

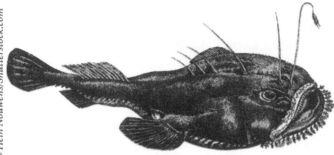

© Hein Nouwens/Shutterstock.com

Figure 4.10: One species of angler fish (there are several) showing a "lure" protruding from above the mouth

The angler fish seen in Figure 4.10 is another good example of deception at level II. In addition to an appearance that makes it appear to be part of the natural undersea environment, the angler fish species puts forth a worm-like lure just outside its mouth when in the presence of prey. When fish try to make a meal out of the dummy worm, they find out they are the dummy and the meal. Some turtles and catfish also use their tongue to enact the "come get the worm" trick.

The plover is a bird species that feigns injury in the presence of a formidable predator (e.g., a fox) in order to keep it away from its eggs or young. The birds make nests on the ground so approaching predators are led away from its eggs or young while the bird makes a distress call, limps, and drags a wing as if it were injured (Ristau, 2014a). The predator, following what it thinks is an injured bird, moves in for the kill. At that point, the bird takes flight. Feigning an injured wing is only one of many diversionary responses these birds manifest.

Fire ants have a very effective nestmate recognition system, but the myrmecophilous beetle manages to convince the ants that it is one of them (Vander Meer & Wojcik, 1982). The beetle passively acquires species-specific and colony-specific odors from its host, which give it the smell of a dues-paying member of the colony. This not only gives it permission to move about the colony unchecked, but also to feed on ants as it pleases. A parasitic mite that lives on honeybees is also able to enact this same kind of chemical mimicry to remain undetected on the bees (Kather, Drijfhout, Shemilt, & Martin, 2015). The mite acquires the host's odor to remain chemically camouflaged so that it can feed on the hemolymph (i.e., blood). As the parasite matures it shifts from adult bees to the young in the hive; the young bees smell different so the parasite is able to adjust to smell like the baby bees.

Level III

Deceptive behavior at this level can be modified or repeated by the deceiver on the basis of the actions and observations of the target. As Mitchell (1986, p. 25) says, "…deceptions at level III are based upon trial-and-error, instrumental, and/or observational learning." The deceiver's control over its deceptive actions and the extent to which the deceiver takes the target into account are both greater than at either of the two previous levels. Deceivers at this level have learned that certain actions they perform will or will not result in a particular consequence. But acting (or not acting) because it believes its behavior will have a particular effect does not mean the organism recognizes how the target is processing and interpreting the deceptive actions. So deceivers at this level are not able to take the mental perspective of the target in order to know they are behaving deceptively. This happens at level IV.

"Okay, I confess. Sometimes I wag my tail like I'm happy, but I'm really not."

Healthy dogs and chimpanzees that have received attention and comforting from humans as a result of an injury in the past will sometimes feign an injury (e.g., begin limping) in order to elicit the same human response (de Waal, 1986; Byrne & Stokes, 2003). Dogs and cats that are interested in occupying their owner's comfortable chair have also been observed to paw at the front door and, when the owner gets up to see why, the pet runs and jumps into the chair. Another version of this deception is when a household has two dogs. One is comfortably lying in a favored chair and the other dog goes to a nearby window and behaves in an alert, expectant, and focused manner. This causes the lounging dog to get up to see what is going on, thereby freeing his chair, which is promptly taken by the deceptive dog. Humans who throw a ball for a dog to retrieve will sometimes deceive the dog by going through a throwing motion while keeping the ball in their other hand. Dogs will sometimes answer that deception with deception of their own. In such cases, dogs will act like they are bringing the ball back to the thrower, but carry it away when the thrower reaches for it (Goode, 2007). Captive gorillas have been observed to act like their arm is stuck in the bars of their cage in order to lure the human attendant to them. Gorillas commonly startle people at zoos who are looking through the glass by pounding on the window. One particular gorilla found he could get a similar response from people by pretending to slam the window (Quiatt, 1984). Trainer A treated lemurs to a raisin when they accurately identified which bowl was covering it. But when their accuracy rate reached 80%, trainer B conducted the tests. When lemurs pointed to the correct bowl, trainer B would pretend to eat the raisin. This caused the lemurs to change their behavior. When lemurs pointed to the wrong bowl, they were rewarded with the raisin. Some continued to lie in order to get the reward, but others stood by and wouldn't participate. When trainer A returned, the lemurs again pointed to the correct bowl in order to get the raisin (Genty & Roeder, 2006).

© Igor Zakowski/Shutterstock.com

Just as animals learn to perform behaviors which elicit certain responses, they also learn to suppress or avoid behaviors which will elicit undesired responses. Chimpanzees, for example, learn to suppress vocal expressions of emotion in order to keep from alerting prey and to keep other chimps from knowing they have acquired some prized food (Goodall, 1986). Tanner and Byrne (1993) observed a gorilla that repeatedly inhibited its playface by placing one or both hands over its face. The exact motive was not clear, but the act of concealing the face had the effect of delaying play activity and showed that the gorilla was aware that spontaneous facial expressions affect the behavior of others. Human beings also realize the need to mask and suppress spontaneous facial expressions sometimes in order to achieve their communicative purposes (Lewis, 2011).

Level IV

Deception at level IV is not only intentional (like level III), but is intentionally deceptive. In other words, deception at level IV means that the deceiver is aware that his or her actions will be misleading to the target. This also means that the deceiver can, to some extent, understand what he or she is doing from the perspective of the other. It means that the deceiver recognizes that the target is not just a target, but also a potential deception detector and deceiver. This means the deceptive act or acts must be planned and altered if things don't go as expected. It is the kind of behavior typical of most adult human liars. Bryne and Corp (2004) found that the larger the neocortex of the brain the more often nonhuman primates will engage in deceptive tactics. In other words, larger primates rely more on trickery.

Byrne (1995) has suggested several ways nonhuman primates show us they are attributing intentions to others. Two of these are: 1) using counter-deception without any opportunity to learn such behavior by trial and error; and 2) exhibiting righteous indignation over having been deceived by another.

Counter-deception is illustrated in Menzel's (1974) account of two chimps named Belle and Rock. Belle knew a hidden location where food could be found and led other chimps to it until Rock, a dominant chimp, kept others from eating so he could have the food to himself. When Rock was not around, Belle did not hesitate to lead other chimps to the food. When he was around, she went slowly to the food and finally avoided revealing the food altogether by sitting on it. In time, Rock learned Belle was sitting on the food, waiting for him to leave, so he began pushing her away and uncovering the food. Then Belle altered her behavior by sitting near the food, but not on it. As Rock began exploring the area around Belle, Belle began to sit further and further from the food. Rock then began to monitor Belle's movements and level of agitation (higher when near food) carefully. When he determined she wasn't near the food, he acted like he was leaving the area. But he maintained his peripheral vision and as soon as Belle moved toward the food, he ran toward her. When there were two piles of food, a small one and a large one, Belle would lead everyone to the small one or to an area opposite to the food. Then she would quickly run to the large cache of food.

A male chimp named Santino at a Swedish zoo finds rocks or breaks off pieces of concrete in his enclosure to hurl at zoo visitors. He hides these projectiles in various locations prior to the arrival of any visitors and he does it in a calm, deliberate, and non-agitated manner which does not alert any of the zoo keepers. But once there are humans observing his living space, he unfurls his aggression and hurls his projectiles toward them as if to prevent a territorial intrusion (Osvath & Karvonen, 2012). The previous examples of deception among nonhuman primates illustrate both the presence of deceptive plans and an understanding of how the other might perceive and react to a particular behavior.

A study by Hare, Call, & Tomasello (2006) also supports intentional deception on the part of chimpanzees. In this experiment, chimpanzees were competing with human experimenters for food. Their behavior showed that they were well aware of what the human experimenter could see and not see. When a solid barrier wall was in place, they approached the food source from behind the wall. This indicated knowledge that the experimenter couldn't see them through the wall and they used it to hide their intentions from the experimenter. When the solid wall was replaced by one that was translucent, the chimps moved further away from the food and the experimenter and used a much more circuitous route to the food, indicating they knew the experimenter could see through the wall—thereby negating the wall's utility as an instrument of deception.

Most of the examples of counter-deception involve primates, but Bugnyar and Kotrschal (2004) provide the following example that involves a raven. Several ravens were searching for food in several film canisters which they could pry open to get to the food. When a subordinate male was successful in finding food, the dominant male took over. The subordinate male then pretended to find food in empty canisters. When the dominant male came over, the subordinate male quickly ran to places providing food. In time, the dominant male learned not to follow the subordinate male and started searching for the food canisters without depending on the actions of the subordinate male. While this experiment does involve counter-deception, the extent to which it is intentionally deceptive is not known.

Jane Goodall (1986) reports the following incident which seems to illustrate that a chimp knew it had been duped and resented it. A researcher who was working with Goodall and observing chimpanzees in their natural habitat became the object of grooming by a female chimp. Close contact between the researchers and the chimps was discouraged so he considered ways to extract himself from this situation. He did not want to push the chimp away for fear its mother, who was nearby, would see it as an act of aggression. So he looked at a bush in an alert and expectant manner, as if he had noticed something. The chimp stopped grooming in order to find out what the researcher perceived in the area of the bush. After finding nothing, the chimp returned to the researcher, hit him over the head with her hand, and ignored him the rest of the day.

Signing Apes

Since the late 1960s, researchers have taught chimpanzees, gorillas, and orangutans to communicate with gestural signs which represent words and/or ideas. Needless to say, these nonhuman primates are communicating in a way they would not use in their natural habitat. Furthermore, researchers who teach these apes to use gestural signs do not instruct them on how to use the signs deceptively. Learning signs allows them to express deceptions in novel ways.

© 2004 Phil Ramey/RameyPix/Corbis

Figure 4.11: Koko using sign language

Miles (1986) offers the following observations of deception from Chantek, an orangutan who learned to use gestures adapted from American Sign Language. Chantek used the sign for "dirty" in order to keep from doing something he didn't want to do. "Dirty" meant he had to go to the bathroom, but once there, he showed no interest in elimination. This is very similar to the level III behavior discussed earlier, where animals learn that by doing *x* they can get *y*. But Chantek also manifested more complex acts of deception. He would ask for something in order to get something very different. For example, apparently anticipating he would be denied an opportunity to play with certain tools, he asked to see a monkey (which was in the room with the tools). Once in the room, he would go directly for the tools. Still more complex behavior, similar to level IV, occurred when Chantek showed he not only realized his trainer had a certain interpretation of a sign, but that he might also discern his intention to deceive. This occurred when Chantek hid an eraser, but did more than indicate he didn't have the eraser or didn't know anything about it. Instead, he signed that he had eaten it. Despite the implausible nature of the false message, it was used in an attempt to get the trainer to acquire a new belief. Koko, another signing ape (see Figure 4.11), was asked by her handler how a sink was ripped out of a wall. Koko, in a deceptive reply not unlike one a child might use, signed "cat did it" and pointed to her pet kitten (Green, 2005).

Nonhuman Deception Detection

This chapter has presented the reader with a tremendous variety of nonhuman deceptive acts. But we shouldn't lose sight of the fact these deceptive acts aren't always successful. Sometimes the deceptive act is performed poorly or at the wrong time; sometimes a skilled detector (perceiver) sees through the deceptive act; sometimes the deceptive act works for a while, but eventually detectors catch on. The ongoing struggle between deceiver and deception detector is as alive and well in the nonhuman world as it is among human beings.

For example, mimicry is only beneficial to non-toxic butterflies if there are enough toxic ones around to ensure that attacking predators can learn that butterflies with this particular appearance are not ever tasty. Wickler (1968, p. 175) points out that older, more experienced "customers" of the cleaner fish mimics can distinguish the mimic from the model. As a result, the deception of these mimics is most likely to be successful if it is practiced on younger fish. And we noted that the elephant that pretended to pull the shower chain succeeded several times in its goal to avoid the wrath of a dominant elephant. But eventually, the dominant elephant attacked and badly injured the chain-pulling deceiver. Rüppell (1986) noted that a young

Arctic fox had driven its parent away from some food. The parent fox, in turn, gave a warning call when no apparent danger could be observed. This prompted the young fox to run away and the parent took its food. But after a few days, the young fox realized there was no danger and refused to leave its food despite the parent's warning call.

When human beings interface with the nonhuman world, the effects of nonhuman deception and perception may change dramatically. Non-poisonous snakes that mimic poisonous ones may profit from their deception when human beings are not around, but when humans are determined to eliminate poisonous snakes in an area they are not likely to look for subtle differences. Of course a burrowing owl, that nests in a hole in the ground, might scare a person with its vocalizations that imitate the rattlesnake's tail, but after the initial scare the human is not likely to kill the owl (Wickler 2013). However, the gopher snake acts and looks so much like a rattlesnake that humans often kill it even though it is harmless. There are situations where humans must learn to identify animal deception and to interact with the animals accordingly. Those who work with chimps learn that certain displays of affection may not guarantee a chimp will be friendly. Humans who fall for these ruses may be bitten or spat on (Ristau, 2014b).

Human beings can also be adept at deceiving animals. Those who work with wolves have learned that wolves sense fear (which triggers an attack) by the smoothness and coordination of movement they see, not by smell (Ginsburg, 1980). As a consequence, people who work closely with wolves have learned how to defeat the wolf's perceptual system by walking and moving purposefully and confidently no matter how much fear they actually feel.

Summary

This chapter demonstrated the omnipresence of deception in our world—from the deception and deception detection battles fought within our body by pathogens and our immune system to the complex deceptions performed by nonhuman primates with each other and with the humans who come into contact with them. If performed effectively and adapted to the circumstances, deceptive acts contribute toward an organism being selected by nature for survival; in turn, deceptive signaling is passed on genetically to offspring (Searcy & Nowicki, 2005).

Following a discussion of deception at the molecular and plant level, Rue's (1994) typology of deceptive strategies provided the framework for presenting examples of deception among insects, fish, reptiles, amphibians, birds, and mammals. These examples were classified according to their ostensible purpose for deceiving (offensive or defensive); the effects of the deception on the dupe (evasive or perversive); and the means of deception (morphology or behavior). Further detail on the way deception is enacted by nonhuman species and the processes driving their deceptive acts was based on Mitchell's (1986) work. He identified four levels of deception which increase in complexity with each level. Level I is effected mainly by appearance, level II involves the coordination of perception and action, learning characterizes deception at level III, and level IV requires planning.

The increasing skill and ability to deceive which is characteristic of Mitchell's four levels provides a useful bridge to the next chapter which will describe the increasingly complex developmental stages associated with a growing child's ability to deceive others effectively.

Things to Think About

What are some similarities and differences in human and nonhuman deception?

Can you think of any examples of morphology as a means of deception in human interaction?

Can you think of any nonhuman organisms that do not employ deception? If you answer "yes," identify the organism and explain why deception is not used. If you answer "no," explain why deception seems so pervasive.

Try to think of occasions when an animal deceived you. What happened? When did you discover the deception?

Have a group of people write down the name of any insect, fish, reptile, amphibian, or mammal *not mentioned in this chapter* on a small piece of paper. Put them all in a box and mix them up. Each person then draws one piece of paper from the box and tries to find information about any forms of deception used by the organism they drew.

References

Bolin, J.F., Maass, E., & Musselman, L.J. (2009). Pollination biology of *Hydnora africana* Thunb. (*Hydnoraceae*) in Namibia: Brood-site mimicry with insect imprisonment. *International Journal of Plant Sciences, 170,* 157–163.

Bugnyar, T., & Kotrschal, K. (2004). Leading a conspecific away from food in ravens (*Corvus corax*)? *Animal Cognition, 7,* 69–76.

Brandt, M., & Mahsberg, D. (2002). Bugs with a backpack: The function of nymphal camouflage in the West African assassin bugs *Paredocla* and *Acanthaspis* spp. *Animal Behaviour, 63,* 277–284.

Byrne, R. (1995). *The thinking ape: Evolutionary origins of intelligence.* New York: Oxford University Press.

Byrne, R.W., & Corp, N. (2004). Neocortex size predicts deception rate in primates. *Proceedings of the Royal Society B: Biological Sciences, 271,* 1693–1699.

Byrne, R., & Stokes, E. (2003). Can monkeys malinger? In P.W. Halligan, C. Bass & D.A. Oakley (Eds.), *Malingering and illness deception* (pp. 54–67). New York: Oxford University Press.

Cloudsley-Thompson, J.L. (1980). *Tooth and claw: Defensive strategies in the animal world.* London: J.M. Dent & Sons.

Damian, R.T. (1989). Molecular mimicry: Parasite evasion and host defense. In M.B.A. Oldstone (Ed.), *Molecular mimicry* (p.102). Berlin: Springer-Verlag.

Darwin, C. (1993/1859). *The origin of species by means of natural selection, or, The preservation of favored races in the struggle for life.* New York: Random House.

De Groot, A.S. et al. (2014) Immune camouflage: Relevance to vaccines and human immunology. *Human Vaccines & Immunotherapeutics, 10,* 3570–3575.

de Waal, F. (1986). Deception in the natural communication of chimpanzees. In R.W. Mitchell & N.S. Thompson (Eds.), *Deception: Perspectives on human and nonhuman deceit* (pp. 221–244). New York: State University of New York Press.

Eisner, T., Goetz, M.A., Hill, D.E., Smedley, S.R., & Meinwald, J. (1997). Firefly "femmes fatales" acquire defensive steroids (lucibufagins) from their firefly prey. *Proceedings of the National Academy of Sciences of the United States of America, 94,* 9723–9728.

Gaskett, A.C. (2011). Orchid pollination by sexual deception: Pollinator perspectives. *Biological Reviews, 86,* 33–75.

Gaskett, A.C., Winnick, C.G., & Herberstein, M.E. (2008). Orchid sexual deceit provokes ejaculation. *The American Naturalist, 171,* 206–212.

Genty, E., & Roeder, J-J. (2006). Can lemurs learn to deceive? A study in the black lemur (*Eulemur macaco*). *Journal of Experimental Psychology: Animal Behavior Processes, 32,* 196–200.

Ginsburg, B.E. (1980). The wolf-pack as a socio-genetic unit. In H. Frank (Ed). *Man and wolf: Advances, issues, and problems in captive wolf research* (pp. 401–424). Dordrecht, Netherlands: Dr. W. Junk

Goode, D. (2007). *Playing with my dog Katie: An ethnomethodological study of dog-human interaction.* West Lafayette, IN: Purdue University Press.

Goodenough, U. (1991, July–August). Deception by pathogens. *American Scientist, 79,* 344–355.

Goodall, J. (1986). *The chimpanzees of Gombe: Patterns of behavior.* Cambridge, MA: Harvard University Press.

Green, M. (2005). *Book of lies.* Kansas City, MO: Andrews McMeel Publishing.

Hare, B., Call, J., & Tomasello, M. (2006). Chimpanzees deceive a human competitor by hiding. *Cognition, 101,* 495–514.

Hoover, J.P., & Robinson, S.K. (2007). Retaliatory mafia behavior by a parasitic cowbird favors host acceptance of parasitic eggs. *Proceedings of the National Academy of Sciences, 104,* 4479–4483.

Kather, R., Drijfhout, F.P., Shemilt, S., & Martin, S.J. (2015). Evidence for passive chemical camouflage in the parasitic mite *Varroa* destructor. *Journal of chemical ecology, 41,* 178–186.

Kucharski, A.J. (2014). Immunity's illusion. *Scientific American, 311,* 80–85.

Lewis, M. (2011). Inside and outside: The relation between emotional states and expressions. *Emotion Review, 3,* 189–196.

Lloyd, J.E. (1986). Firefly communication and deception: "Oh, what a tangled web." In R.W. Mitchell & N.S. Thompson (Eds.), *Deception: Perspectives on human and nonhuman deceit* (pp. 113–128). New York: State University of New York Press.

Louwen, R. et al. (2013). A novel link between *Campylobacter jejuni* bacteriophage defence, virulence and Guillain–Barré syndrome. *European journal of clinical microbiology & infectious diseases, 32,* 207–226.

Menzel, E. (1974). A group of young chimpanzees in a one-acre field. In A.M. Schrier & F. Stollnitz (Eds.), *Behavior of nonhuman primates* (Vol. 5, pp. 83–153). New York: Academic Press.

Miles, H.L. (1986). How can I tell a lie? Apes, language, and the problem of deception. In R.W. Mitchell & N.S. Thompson (Eds.), *Deception: Perspectives on human and nonhuman deceit* (pp. 245–266). New York: State University of New York Press.

Mitchell, R.W. (1986). A framework for discussing deception. In R.W. Mitchell & N.S. Thompson (Eds.), *Deception: Perspectives on human and nonhuman deceit* (pp. 3–40). New York: State University of New York Press.

Mitchell, R.W. (1993). Animals as liars: The human face of nonhuman duplicity. In M. Lewis & C. Saarni (Eds.), *Lying and deception in everyday life* (pp. 59–89). New York: Guilford.

Morris, M.D. (1986). Large scale deceit: Deception by captive elephants. In R.W. Mitchell & N.S. Thompson (Eds.), *Deception: Perspectives on human and nonhuman deceit* (pp. 183–191). New York: State University of New York Press.

Norman, M.D., & Hochberg, F.G. (2005). The "mimic Octopus", a new octopus from the tropical Indo-West Pacific. *Molluscan Research, 25,* 57–70.

O'Hara, J.E. (1995). Henry Walter Bates—his life and contributions to biology. *Archives of Natural History, 22,* 195–219.

Osvath, M., & Karvonen, E. (2012). Spontaneous innovation for future deception in a male chimpanzee. *PloS one, 7*(5), 1–8.

Pasteur, G. (1982). A classificatory review of mimicry systems. *Annual Review of Ecology and Systematics, 13,* 169–199.

Quiatt, D. (1984). Devious intentions of monkeys and apes? In R. Harré & V. Reynolds (Eds.), *The meaning of primate signals* (pp. 9–40). Cambridge, UK: Cambridge University Press.

Ristau, C.A. (2014a). Cognitive ethology of an injury-feigning bird, the piping plover. In C.A. Ristau (Ed.), *Cognitive ethology: The minds of other animals* (pp. 91–125). New York: Psychology Press.

Ristau, C.A. (2014b). Conscious chimpanzees? A review of recent literature. In C.A. Ristau (Ed.), *Cognitive ethology: The minds of other animals* (pp. 231–250). New York: Psychology Press.

Rue, L. (1994). *By the grace of guile: The role of deception in natural history and human affairs.* Oxford: Oxford University Press.

Rüppell, V.G. (1986). A "lie" as directed message of the arctic fox (*Alopex lagopus L.*). In R.W. Mitchell & N.S. Thompson (Eds.), *Deception: Perspectives on human and nonhuman deceit* (pp. 177–181). New York: State University of New York Press.

Searcy, W.A., & Nowicki, S. (2005). *The evolution of animal communication: Reliability and deception in signaling systems.* Princeton, NJ: Princeton University Press.

Sordahl, T.A. (1988). The American avocet (*Recurvirostra americana*) as a paradigm for adult automimicry. *Evolutionary Ecology*, 2, 189.

Sullivan, E. (2001). *The concise book of lying.* New York: Farrar, Straus & Giroux.

Tanner, J.E., & Byrne, R.W. (1993). Concealing facial evidence of mood: Perspective-taking in a captive gorilla? *Primates, 34,* 451–457.

Thompson, N.S. (1986). Deception and the concept of behavioral design. In R.W. Mitchell & N.S. Thompson (Eds.), *Deception: Perspectives on human and nonhuman deceit* (pp. 53–65). New York: State University of New York Press.

Vander Meer, R.W., & Wojcik, D.P. (1982). Chemical mimicry in the *Myrmecophilous* beetle *Myrmecaphodius excavaticollis. Science, 218,* 806–808.

Wickler, W. (1968). *Mimicry in plants and animals.* New York: World University Library.

Wickler, W. (2013). Understanding mimicry—with special reference to vocal mimicry. *Ethology, 119,* 259–269.

Williams, K.S., & Gilbert, L.E. (1981). Insects as selective agents on plant vegetative morphology: Egg mimicry reduces egg laying by butterflies. *Science, 212,* 467–469.

Yoshino, T.P., & Coustau, C. (2011). Immunobiology of *Biomphalaria*-trematode interactions. In R. Toledo & B. Fried (Eds.), *Biomphalaria snails and larval trematodes* (pp. 159–189). New York: Springer.

Zohary, D., Hopf, M., & Weiss, E. (2012). *Domestication of plants in the Old World: The origin and spread of domesticated plants in Southwest Asia, Europe, and the Mediterranean Basin.* Oxford, UK: Oxford University Press.

Chapter 5

Children as Liars and Targets of Lies

It's a good thing kids are such good problem solvers. Otherwise, they might really be confused by adult messages concerning lying and deception. Early on, children are told loud and clear: "Do not lie. Lying is wrong. You will be punished if you lie." The observant child soon realizes that grown-ups sometimes engage in the very thing they are forbidding children to do. "Are adults really lying or is it something different?" they may wonder. "And if they are lying, why can't I lie?" Children who observe adults lying are more likely to lie themselves (Hays & Carver, 2014). Adding to the confusion, the child soon realizes that he or she can be punished for telling the truth as well as for lying. Nevertheless, most kids eventually figure it all out. They learn the importance of telling the truth and the necessity of having a moral compass. But they also learn that some lies are perceived as worse than others and the ability to lie in certain situations can be a valuable part of their budding social competence (Feldman, Tomasian, & Coats, 1999). Few become chronic liars (Stouthamer-Loeber, 1986). How does all this come about? In order to find out, let's begin by examining the development of the cognitive and behavioral skills which are employed during intentionally deceptive acts.

Childhood Lying: Plotting its Growth

In order to engage in the kind of behavior adults would call lies, children have to develop or master skills in five areas (Lee, 2013; Vasek, 1986).

Perspective-Taking and "Theory of Mind"

People have different needs, beliefs, attitudes, interests, and priorities. As obvious as this may seem to us as adults, we were not born knowing it. A cornerstone of Swiss developmental psychologist

> "One must have felt a real desire to exchange thoughts with others in order to discover all that a lie can involve."
>
> — J. Piaget

> "The skills which make deception possible seem also responsible for developing the more positive social skills such as empathy and compassion."
>
> — M. Vasek

> "My 9-year old is just figuring out about lying and that's a tough thing. It's hard to roll that one back. Because lying is pretty amazingly useful in life. How do you tell a kid not to use a thing that just solves every possible problem like magic?"
>
> — *Louis C.K.*

Jean Piaget's (1954) theory of cognitive development is the idea that human infants are profoundly "egocentric"—that is, unable to comprehend that someone else may have a different mental experience from their own and consequently unable to take another person's perspective. As young children develop, they not only learn that other perspectives exist, but also how to take those perspectives and use them. Children who can recognize that other people have their own minds and can thus have other perspectives are said to have developed a "theory of mind" (McHugh & Stewart, 2012). In a typical developing child, a coherent theory of mind emerges between ages 3 and 5 (although rudiments of this skill, such as following another person's gaze to understand what he or she is looking at, appear earlier). Failure to acquire a theory of mind and perspective-taking skills are the hallmark symptoms of autism, a psychological disorder that usually appears early in life (Kormaz, 2011).

Some scholars argue that a true understanding of theory of mind is unique to the human species (e.g., Penn & Povinelli, 2007). But even for adult humans, perspective-taking can be challenging. Accurate perspective-taking is hindered by the "other minds problem," which occurs because we can never know from a first-person perspective exactly how things are perceived by another person with another mind. Perspective-taking has important social implications. In both children and adults, it is often associated with greater empathy, prosocial behavior, and more favorable treatment of the person (or group) whose perspective is taken. Research consistently demonstrates that instructing people to take the perspective of another person in need leads to increased feelings of compassion and often results in offers to help the person whose perspective was taken (Malle & Hodges, 2005; Vasek, 1986). However, taking the perspective of another is also essential for someone to engage in deception. Ceci, Leichtman, and Putnick (1992) explain it this way:

> For children to engage in full-blown deception they must be able to read the listener's mind. And to read another's mind, they must be able to do two things at once. First, they must be able to conjure up an alternative reality that they can temporarily substitute for the reality they know to be authentic. (For example, they can appreciate that a sponge looks like a rock to someone viewing it from another angle.) Second, they must be able to set aside their own beliefs in the unreality of the alternative state (e.g., that it is a rock), and assume the perspective of the individual who believes this to be a reality. In short, they must be able to substitute

belief for disbelief, in accepting the stance of the other. This is also necessary for children to appreciate that their own prior mental states were false (e.g., realizing that at one time they also thought that the sponge was a rock). (p. ix)

Through perspective-taking, a liar determines that the target of a lie does not have certain information that he or she has. Perspective-taking enables liars to understand the idea of a false belief held by the target. Knowledge gained through perspective-taking is also invaluable to deceivers in determining what messages are likely to create that false belief. Some lies can become terribly complex and the liar's ability to anticipate the target's behavior is the difference between a successful and a failed lie. For example, suppose you say you were at Wanda's house and you weren't. What does the target know about Wanda? What will you say if you're asked about something you should have seen at Wanda's house? Will the target talk to Wanda?

Executive Functions

Executive functions are higher-order cognitive skills that emerge in late infancy and develop during childhood. Three of these functions—inhibitory control, working memory, and planning—are critical to deception development. Inhibitory control is the ability to suppress interfering thoughts or actions (Carlson, Moses, & Breton, 2002). To successfully mislead someone, children must not only utter false information that differs from reality but also conceal the true information it contradicts. To maintain the lie, they must inhibit thoughts and statements contrary to the lie and remember the contents of the lie, at least in the short-term. They use "working memory," a system for temporarily holding and processing information, for this purpose. Maintaining a lie also requires planning, in that liars must prepare the contents of a lie prior to uttering it in order to appear to convincing to their audience. Carlson, Moses, and Hix (1998) found that preschool children who experience difficulty with learning tasks that require a high level of inhibitory control, working memory, and planning also have difficulty with deception tasks. Clemens et al. (2010) argue that individual differences in deceptive skill are strongly related to one's ability to regulate behavior and handle the increase in cognitive load a lie creates. Thus, children's maturing executive functions seem to facilitate their successful lie-telling.

Understanding Intentionality

Lies are designed to deliberately mislead others. They are not just "mistakes." Therefore, a liar understands that his or her own behavior is intentionally designed to make the target perceive it as truthful. It is not just intentional behavior, but intentionally misleading behavior which requires perspective-taking. Acknowledging intention means acknowledging one's desire to effect certain changes in another person and the attendant responsibilities associated with those intentions. Liars must also understand that the target of their deception also may have intentions—to deceive and to detect deception.

Understanding Social Norms

Successful liars must also be aware of the specific social-cultural contexts in which lying is prohibited or permissible. For example, most societies eschew lying to conceal transgressions for personal gain, but condone "white lies" designed to spare the feelings of the person lied to. Most children over 3 understand that lying to conceal a transgression is inappropriate and they should tell the truth instead (Lyon & Dorado, 2008). However, their knowledge of this social norm doesn't strictly dictate their actual behavior. Children often report believing that lying is morally wrong, but lie anyway. In contrast, their knowledge of norms about promises does seem to affect their decisions to lie or not. Children asked to promise to tell the truth about a transgression are less likely to lie than others who are not (Evans & Lee, 2010). But they are more likely to lie in situations in which social norms direct them to refrain from being completely honest (Talwar & Lee, 2008). When deciding whether to a lie or not, children must determine the social context in which the truth or a lie is called for, as well as the specific social norm that motivates it. Failure to discriminate appropriately could lead to negative consequences.

Communication Skills

The ability to engage in the preceding cognitions associated with perspective-taking, intentionality, and social norms must work in concert with certain communication behavior in order for the deceiver to effectively lie.

One communication skill deceivers must have is a verbal repertoire from which language choices and persuasive strategies can be implemented as needed. Strategies and language choices are based on anticipated needs as well as information obtained from monitoring reactions of the target.

Deceivers also need the ability to effectively manage their own behavior—to mask or hide their true feelings and to avoid enacting any behavior that might make the target suspicious that "something just doesn't seem right"—e.g., too little or too much eye gaze, speech that is too hesitant or too rapid, too many nervous mannerisms or too little movement, or too much vocal uncertainty. Effective deceivers not only have to avoid showing some behaviors, they have to enact others. And some of these behaviors will be effective at one age and not another. A pleasant smile on a very young child, for example, may be a very effective cover for deceptive behavior, but the same behavior shown by an adult may arouse suspicion of deception.

The growing child gradually acquires each of these cognitive and behavioral skills and learns how to coordinate them for maximum effectiveness. *These are the basic skills necessary to effectively deceive others, but they are also skills which are fundamental to social competence.* A person with greater social competence is also likely to be the better liar (Feldman, Tomasian, & Coats, 1999; Lee, 2013). It is not possible to establish the exact age when children acquire certain skills because learning environments and genetic pre-wiring may vary from child to child. Nevertheless, the general developmental pattern is as follows:

Age 2–3

Observations of "deceit-like" behavior are rare prior to age two, but the following accounts of play behavior by 19 month old children have been noted. Chevalier-Skolnikoff (1986) recorded the behavior of a child who repeatedly offered his mother a toy and then laughed as he pulled it away from her when she reached for it. Ford (1996) recounts a similar experience with his own 19 month old child who repeatedly identified a picture of a zebra as a giraffe and laughed "uproariously" each time Ford would correct him.

Between the ages of two and three children will make false statements for a variety of reasons, but they have very little understanding of how their behavior affects or might affect the target of their false statement. Some false statements are simply mistakes based on a limited knowledge of the language they are learning at this time; others can be blamed on poor memory or recall. But sometimes a child's everyday reality is enriched by his or her fantasy life—e.g., "I have a rhino in my room...a real one. I do." Ceci, Leichtman, & Putnick (1992, vii–viii) tell a story about a colleague's 3 year-old child whose false statement, enhanced by fantasy, had more serious implications. The child was watching Mr. Rogers on television with his older sister while his mother worked in an adjoining room. When the child left the television to join his mother, he told her Mr. Rogers had touched his (the child's) pee-pee. At this age, some false statements are the result of wishful thinking—e.g., saying "My dad is going to take me to Disneyland" when Dad has never mentioned this possibility. But perhaps the most common form of false statements at this age involves denials of wrongdoing ("No, Billy did it.") to avoid punishment or wanting to get rewarded for doing something "good"—e.g., "I cleaned my plate, too (when that is not true)."

So, at this age none of the skills typical of adult lying ability (perspective-taking, intentionality, behavioral control) have developed much—at least with most children. Chandler, Fritz, & Hala (1989) conducted an experiment with 2 ½ year-olds and found evidence that *some* children did perform acts intended to mislead others into thinking that something false was true. A puppet hid a "treasure" in one of several containers and children were told the purpose of the game was to hide the treasure from some adults who were searching for it. Some of these children not only erased the tracks left by the puppet to the container holding the treasure, but made new tracks to an empty container. Sodian et al. (1991) also found a few children who were less than three years-old who understood the idea of creating a false belief, but even these children needed prompting and rarely anticipated the effects of their deception on the target's beliefs. Even the presence of older siblings does not seem to help a great deal in facilitating the understanding of false beliefs for 2-3 year-olds, but they can speed up such learning with children 3 ½ and older (Ruffman et al., 1998).

Age 3–6

Children develop a theory of mind and thereby acquire perspective-taking ability typically between the ages of 3 and 5. The combination of this ability and their expanding knowledge of intentionality and social norms leads children in this age range to lie with increasing frequency and skill. A number of studies support this conclusion.

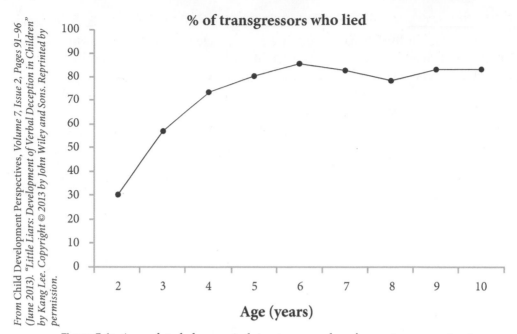

From Child Development Perspectives, Volume 7, Issue 2, Pages 91–96 (June 2013). "Little Liars: Development of Verbal Deception in Children" by Kang Lee. Copyright © 2013 by John Wiley and Sons. Reprinted by permission.

% of transgressors who lied

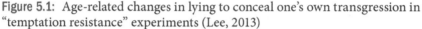

Age (years)

Figure 5.1: Age-related changes in lying to conceal one's own transgression in "temptation resistance" experiments (Lee, 2013)

One of the first forms of deception children in this age range employ is the "I didn't do it" variety, which they use to conceal violating requests and orders issued by adults ("Don't eat in the living room", "No jumping on the couch", etc.). Researchers have studied this variety in "temptation resistance" experiments in which a child is seated in a room and a toy is placed behind her. An adult experimenter instructs the child not to peek at or play with the toy for several minutes while the adult leaves the room. The child is covertly monitored while alone in the room and, when the experimenter returns, is asked whether she followed the instructions. Many children don't, allowing examination of whether they confess the transgression or lie (Lewis, 1993; Lewis, Stanger, & Sullivan, 1989). In numerous studies using this procedure conducted worldwide (reviewed in Lee, 2013), most 2-year olds confess but most 3-year olds lie, with the frequency of lying increasing through mid-childhood (see Figure 5.1).

While most children between 3 and 5 lie in this situation, they aren't especially convincing. For example, when 3-year olds lie about peeking at the toy (e.g., a Barney doll) and then are later asked by the experimenter to "guess" what the toy might be, many blurt out its name without hesitation, revealing that they both violated the instructions and lied. As they get older, children incrementally learn to avoid blatant inconsistencies. For example, a 5-year old girl who lied about peeking later said "I didn't peek at it. I touched it and it felt purple. So, I think it is Barney." Many 6-year old peekers subsequently feign complete ignorance of the toy's properties (Evans, Xu, & Lee, 2011).

Around the age of 3, children begin to tell "white lies" in situations for which social norms dictate that they not convey awkward truths. Talwar and Lee (2002) asked 3–6 year-olds to take a photograph of an adult who had a large red mark on his nose. Most children lied to this adult when he asked "Do I look okay for the photo?" but later told someone else that he did not look okay. In a similar study, children in this age range were given an undesirable present (a bar of soap) but told the giver that they liked it, even though their behavior while opening it clearly indicated disappointment (Talwar, Murphy, & Lee, 2007).

Ceci & Leichtman (1992) devised several experiments with 3 to 4 year-old children showing that they altered their messages according to perceived listener knowledge. In one study, nursery school children who believed a "loved one" might get in trouble for breaking a toy told a nursery school teacher (who was not in the room when the toy was broken) that they didn't know who broke the toy or that someone else broke it—e.g., a gremlin who flew in the window. But in a subsequent private interaction with their loved one, most of these same children said they had told the truth (that the loved one had broken the toy) to the nursery school teacher. These kids had, in fact, lied twice. Leekam (1992) says that by age 4 or 5, children "understand the effects of a false message on a listener's mind, recognizing that the listener will interpret and evaluate a statement in the light of their existing knowledge." In support of this, Sodian et al. (1991) say that by age 4 most kids have developed an understanding of false beliefs. These children have a lot to learn about how complex the other person's perspective really is and how many different ways it can be tapped, but the basic mechanism for developing this knowledge is now in place.

Despite their sometimes imperfect manifestations of it, this is also a time when we can see a child's early efforts at behavioral control to conceal a lie. In-depth analyses of videos of children's nonverbal behaviors by Talwar and Lee (2002) reveal that those in the act of telling a lie mimic the behaviors of people who tell the truth (e.g., making direct eye contact with the listener). When the situation calls for children to avert their gaze when telling the truth (because they have to ponder the answer to a question), they also deliberately avert their gaze when lying (McCarthy & Lee, 2009). By the age of 6, a child's nonverbal concealment behaviors are coordinated and natural enough to convince many adults that they are telling the truth, including their parents, teachers, social workers, police officers, and judges (Crossman & Lewis, 2006).

Age 6–9

When the young child begins spending time with other children in school, new challenges arise. The process of developing and managing new interpersonal relationships and undertaking new tasks may create new conditions for lying. Ford (1996) says some children experience what he calls "double bookkeeping"—keeping family secrets that might be embarrassing or espousing beliefs that fit one's peer group, but not one's family. In addition, many children this age are spending a lot of time playing board, card, and sports games which highlight the need for deceptive skills in order to win the game. Vasek (1986, p.288) puts it this way: "Games, then, provide a situation in which children can practice deception and its detection, learn about its functions, and become acquainted with the social implications of its use."

So during this period, children are facing a variety of conditions which may prompt them to lie and an increasing variety of situations provide ample opportunities to practice, elicit feedback, and refine their deceptive skills. The teenagers Ekman (1989) interviewed recalled that their first experience in "getting away with" a lie was when they were between age 5 and 7. Whereas some young communicators will gain confidence in their deceptive ability, others will be reminded that they still have a lot to learn as the following dialogue illustrates (Krout (1931, p. 23).

"Hello Miss Brown, my son is very ill and, I am sorry to say, cannot come to school today."

"Who is talking?" asked the teacher.

"My father," the boy answered.

This is a time when learning the norms of politeness (which may require deception) is also stressed by adult caregivers. Saarni (1984) promised an attractive toy to groups of 6, 8, and 10 year old children if they performed a particular task for her. After completing the task, the children were given a less attractive toy and their facial expressions were observed. Analysis of the expressions showed that as the child gets older, less disappointment is shown in the face. The girls in Saarni's study manifested this ability to facially mask their disappointment in the name of politeness earlier than the boys.

Age 10–12

By the end of this period, most children have developed adult-like deception skills. By about age 11 they also think about lying and truth-telling differently. Their views are in sharp contrast to five year-olds. For example, most no longer believe it is always wrong to lie and few are willing to say they've never lied (Peterson, Peterson, & Seeto, 1983). Adults, in turn, hold these pre-teens responsible for knowing what they are doing—e.g., "Don't tell me you didn't lie. You knew if you said X that I'd think Y."

This doesn't mean that these kids have nothing more to learn—only that many 10–12 year old children are able to (and do) lie without being detected. Ten year olds with more Machiavellian tendencies may be especially adroit at deception (Braginsky, 1970). Children were promised a nickel for every bitter tasting cracker they could get others to eat. The "high Mach" kids used bribery, two-sided arguments, transferral of blame to the experimenter, and lies of commission and omission. Along with their increasing verbal skills, children in this age range also show a greater sophistication in their ability to manage their nonverbal behavior as well (DePaulo & Jordan, 1982; Talwar & Crossman, 2011). But these encoding skills of 11 and 12 year old girls are likely to be superior to their male counterparts.

Age 13–18

With adult-like deception ability in place at the beginning of adolescence, teens practice their skills in an ever-expanding range of social interactions. In this period, children not only hone their skills, but also develop more sophisticated reasoning about whether and when lying serves their interests. The decision to lie or not depends in part on a consideration of whether it will assist in the attainment of a goal and at what cost. The weighting of various facts in this cost-benefit analysis becomes more complicated with age. In particular, adolescents give more thought to probabilities than younger children, considering not merely the punishment for getting caught but also the different likelihoods of getting caught in various circumstances. They also consider consequences of getting caught that extend beyond the immediate context, such as disappointment in the eyes of friends, parents, and teachers. In particular, parental disappointment is a consequence that could hinder the expansion of autonomy children crave in their teens. Thus if getting caught seems like seems like more than a remote possibility, a teen might be hesitant to risk this anticipated cost regardless of a lie's immediate benefit (Perkins & Turiel, 2007).

As the first generation to grow up immersed in an online world, teens today have opportunities to deceive via technological channels that their parents didn't have at their age. What's more, teens often exploit their parents' lack of experience and technical limitations to engage in digital deception that can be risky, rude, and sometimes illegal. In a survey of over a thousand teenagers and their parents about online behavior, about half of the teenagers admitted searching the Internet for material they believed their parents would not approve of (pornography, simulated or real violence, etc.); when asked, 86% of the parents didn't believe their children would do this. About 70% of teens overall reported hiding their online behavior from their parents. The frequency with which the young respondents reported digital deception was clearly fueled by their parents' complacency and cluelessness. Sixty-two percent of the parents reported believing their kids cannot get in serious trouble online. Only 4 in 10 parents reported using software to monitor or restrict their children's online behavior; more than half of the children of these parents claimed to know how to bypass it (McAfee, 2013).

Why Children Lie

The motivation for lying during childhood is affected by a variety of factors, including the tasks they face, the kind of relationship they have with their parents, and their own changing cognitive and physical abilities. Scholars who have addressed the question of why children lie have focused primarily on two life stages—early childhood and adolescence.

Reasons for Early Childhood Lies

There is widespread agreement that the most fundamental and common reason for lying at all ages is the desire to avoid punishment for a misdeed (DePaulo & Jordan, 1982; Vasek, 1986). Ekman (1989, p. 19) says, "This is one of the most consistent findings in scientific studies of lying."

When 21 teachers and 80 mothers were asked to identify the reasons why 4 year-olds lie, they too said "fear of punishment" was the primary reason (Stouthamer-Loeber, 1991; see Table 5.1). "Getting one's way" (obtaining something or avoiding doing something by not telling the truth) was another commonly cited reason for lying in early childhood. This study also reminds us, however, that even in early childhood there may be multiple reasons for lying and the perception of these reasons may vary depending on who is making the judgment. Teachers, for example, perceived more instances of not telling the truth to be "joking" than did mothers, but mothers were more likely than teachers to attribute the lack of truth-telling by a 4 year-old as "did not know any better."

Table 5.1   Reasons Why Four Year-Olds May Not Tell the Truth

Reasons	Percentage of Answers By Mothers	Percentage of Answers By Teachers
Fear of punishment	42.0	44.2
Did not know any better	8.0	14.9
Getting one's way	16.0	14.3
Play or fantasy	2.0	7.1
Protect self-image	12.0	5.8
Tries to please	6.0	5.8
Joking	10.0	2.6
To cause trouble	0.0	2.6
To protect someone	4.0	.7
Unclear	0.0	2.0

Although young children lie most frequently to conceal misdeeds, they also tell "prosocial" lies intended to benefit others out of politeness or altruism. Prosocial lies bring two social norms of communication into conflict—the expectations that a) speakers should be truthful and b) they should be friendly to others. To tell a prosocial lie, children must have an empathetic understanding of another's mental state and the desire to manipulate that state (e.g., Dad is embarrassed about his weight so I will tell him he looks nice). Children may be motivated to tell such a lie not only to benefit someone else but also to benefit themselves, in that it enables them to avoid an awkward interaction or be positively regarded by the person being lied to. However, a truly altruistic lie is told solely for the benefit of another and perhaps at a personal cost (e.g., taking the blame for a friend's wrongful action). Altruistic lies emerge later than polite "white lies" as children learn social norms regarding loyalty in friendship and groups (Talwar & Crossman, 2011).

Early childhood is a time when children are learning about words and body movements and how they are used to effectively communicate with those around them. When lies, deceptions, misrepresentations, and false statements take place, they can be understood as part of this process of learning what is acceptable and what isn't, what works and what doesn't. These rules are primarily learned within the confines of the child's immediate family. But family guidelines are put to the test as the child grows older, forms new relationships, and develops his or her own standards for what is appropriate and inappropriate behavior. Peer groups, teachers, and a steadily increasing appetite for autonomy provide additional contexts and reasons for lying.

The process of learning how to "make it" in school is one in which daily negotiations teach kids whether deception is useful and whether it is appropriate. Seeking praise and enhancing one's image with both teachers and peers while simultaneously avoiding punishment and hiding image-detracting information from them are central to success in school. They are also goals which often cause students to consider whether and how to deceive (Engels, Finkenauer, & van Kooten, 2006).

Reasons for Lying During Adolescence

Finding a reason to lie during adolescence is about as difficult as finding a reason to be happy when you've won the lottery. The only reason for some adolescent lies is that the adolescent just wants to see if he or she can pull it off and/or the enjoyment derived from the manipulation. But the apparent ease and frequency with which some adolescents lie may taper off as they become young adults. Even though adolescents and young adults both lie to their parents about such things as friends, dates, and money, Jensen et al. (2004) found emerging adults were less accepting of lying and reported lying less frequently than adolescents. Ekman (1989) interviewed adolescents who identified a number of different reasons for lying. Some of these reasons were basically the same as reasons given by young children—e.g., lying to avoid punishment and lying to get something that couldn't be obtained in other ways.[1] But adolescents mentioned other reasons for lying which reflected matters especially pertinent to their life stage.

Reasons Associated with Peer Group Relations

Some teenagers want to be "popular" with their peers; most just want to be accepted. The process of learning how to be accepted by one's peers presents teens with a number of situations which inevitably involve decisions about whether and/or how to tell the truth. Some common situations include: making themselves look good to others by magnifying or inventing experiences; the invention of negative stories about others in an effort to clearly distinguish oneself from those in the "out-group;" or keeping secrets for or not "ratting" on friends—even taking the blame for something they did. Ekman (1989) found many teenagers willing to lie for a friend. He posed the following situation: "Your friend broke a school tape recorder and you know he or she broke it. Your teacher asks you if you know who broke the tape recorder. Will you tell the teacher that your friend did it?" Less than a third of the teens Ekman interviewed said they would inform on their friend.

The effects of a student's "status" and peer pressure on teenage lying were aptly demonstrated in an experiment designed by Harari and McDavid (1969). Students in two junior high school classes were asked to list five people they considered worthy to represent their class at a school banquet. In one class, the researchers recruited a student who was never mentioned (low-status) and another class they selected a student who was mentioned most often (high-status). These students were then trained to enact the following behavior. When the teacher left the room, they walked to the front of the classroom, threw their gum in the wastebasket, picked up 75 cents laying on a table near the teacher's desk and put the money in their pocket while saying, "Hey, look, how about that?" as they returned to their seat. Students in each class were interviewed about whether they knew who took the 75 cents. Some students were interviewed with a fellow classmate and some were interviewed alone. No one lied to protect either the high- or low-status student when they were interviewed privately. But when they were interviewed with a fellow student, they pleaded ignorance when it came to the high-status student, but didn't mind revealing the identity of the low-status thief.

---

[1] Adolescent *malingering*, a pattern of feigning illness or inability to avoid work or responsibility, and other patterns of deception rooted in more intense psychological and/or emotional problems will be dealt with in Chapter 8.

Reasons Related to Authority Figures

People who are in charge of various aspects of an adolescent's life can expect there will be some efforts to challenge their power. Unquestioningly obeying the directives of authority figures is linked to a developmental stage adolescents believe is behind them. Secrecy and deception are commonly used by adolescents to level the playing field with authority figures. Recognizing that knowledge gives power, lies of omission ("Nobody asked so I didn't say anything.") are not unusual. It is, of course, more likely when authority figures expect teens to follow orders as if they were young children, do not reward truth-telling, hypocritically hold teenagers to standards of truth-telling they do not adhere to, and act infallible. Holt (1982, p. 254), commenting on the abuse of authority in the classroom and the effects it can have on students, said: "We present ourselves to children as if we were gods, all-knowing, all-powerful, always rational, always just, always right. This is worse than any lie we could tell about ourselves."

Reasons Associated With Growing Autonomy/Independence

During adolescence, children gain an increased sense of autonomy within the family. In the course of their teens, they typically are granted decision making responsibility for an expanding range of behaviors, including choice of dress, friends, and recreational activities. But what happens when adolescents disagree with their parents about the appropriate limits of their autonomy? In some cases, they truthfully express their difference of opinion and deal with the conflict it creates; in other cases, they lie to avoid a clash. In particular, when parents try to exert influence on an issue that young teens believe to be none of their business (e.g., a dating partner), teens may feel justified in lying to avoid what they perceive as a wrongful encroachment on their privacy (Jensen, Arnett, Feldman, & Cauffman, 2004). They may also justify lying in terms of adult social norms about deception they are learning—e.g., acting sorry when you aren't, acting like something somebody said didn't hurt when it did, etc.

What About the Parents?

Parents play an important role in determining how often their children lie, what they lie about, and the ethical framework within which lying is viewed. One way parents teach their children about lying and deception is by the way they respond to their child's deceitful and "deceit-like" behavior. Since "not telling the truth" may occur for a variety of reasons and have a variety of consequences, this underscores the need for a variety of responses. When adults vary their responses to young children according to the way the child misrepresents reality, the context in which it is done, how often it has occurred, how much harm it causes, and the apparent motive for doing it, it teaches the child what behavior is permissible and what isn't. This learning process is ongoing and adult reactions may vary considerably to the same behavior performed by a 4 year-old and a 14 year-old. Eighty mothers who recorded 1,171 instances of deception by their 4 year-olds over a period of 12 weeks varied the valence of their responses depending on how they perceived the act in question (Stouthamer-Loeber, 1991).

Table 5.2   Responding to Various Ways 4 Year-Olds Misrepresent the Truth

Behavior	Most Common Responses
	Positive/Neutral
Make-believe friend	Play along
Talking about imaginary things as if they were true	Explain reality
Plays a joke by telling untruth	Play along
	Neutral
Tells about something happening that is not true	Question
Exaggerates	Question
Boasts	No attention
	Negative/Neutral
Says he/she has done something he/she hasn't	Make finish
Denies something he/she has done	Confront/Question
Blames someone else	Confront/Question
Makes up excuses	Discourage

Parents are role models for their children and when children are regularly disappointed in their parents' behavior, receive ineffective supervision, or can't establish a warm parental bond, the probability of their lying increases (Touhey, 1973; Southamer-Loeber, 1986; Southamer-Loeber & Loeber, 1986). But the reverse is also true. Parents who perceive their adolescent children engaging in a lot of concealment and lying also seem to exhibit more withdrawal from their child. They are less accepting, less involved, less responsive, and know less about their child's activities and whereabouts (Finkenhauer, Frijns, Engels, & Kerkhof, 2005).

Needless to say, the way parents respond to lying (their own and their children's) will go a long way in determining how their kids behave. Experts say parents should consider the following guidelines:

Adapt Responses to the Life Stage of the Child

Parents should understand, for example, that the unambiguous certainty that "you should never lie" may be more palatable to younger children than older ones. Furthermore, the extent to which parents hold their children accountable for their lies will probably increase as the child learns what behavior is acceptable and what isn't. Although the way it is done may vary by age, parents may want to establish some experiences with their child early and often. For example, the extent to which an adolescent feels comfortable telling the truth to his or her parents is often the extent to which that comfort has been established throughout his or her development. It means children must have some positive experiences in which they told an unpleasant truth if parents expect that behavior to continue.

Consider the Effects of Double Standards

Some parents don't like to admit it, but others freely acknowledge the fact that they lie to their children and lie to others in front of their children while admonishing their children not to lie. One survey of several thousand parents found 59% of them saying they regularly lied to their kids (Patterson & Kim, 1991). Most parental lies are designed to ease their young child's fears, enrich their fantasy world, or control their behavior. Some appear to be told simply because the parent delights in tricking a very gullible child. A delightful collection of these parental lies (Connolley, 2004) includes the following:

- When ice cream trucks play music, it means they have run out of ice cream.
- My mom used to tell me that there was a banana factory where bananas were bent before they were sold.
- When I was younger, my parents told me that if I peed in the pool, it would rise to the top and spell out my name.

Young children may be more accepting of the fact that it's ok for parents be deceptive even if they are forbidden to do so. But as children get older, they increasingly scrutinize this disparity. Parents who say they lie to their very young children "for their own sake," may find that their children increasingly see such lies as serving the parents' needs—e.g., to maintain power and/or control over their child or to avoid discussing a difficult topic ("Daddy and I were moving some furniture around in our bedroom last night. Some of it was heavy and that was the groaning you heard"). The older a child gets, the more he or she expects to be treated like other adults—including his or her parents. When this doesn't happen, they may adopt the adult behaviors anyway.

Consider the Effects of "Struggling Visibly"

Michael Josephson of the Josephson Institute of Ethics recommends this behavior to parents. He says that all parents are bound to make mistakes and face difficult dilemmas when it comes to communicating and acting on values—like honesty. But instead of blaming others or denying a problem when problems occur, Josephson says, parents might effectively use such occasions to teach children and serve as a role model by talking about the various factors that prompted the particular deception or lie and reflecting on why it occurred and how similar situations are likely to be handled in the future.

Consider the Effects of Reciprocity

In the area of human behavior, <u>we often reap what we sow</u>. Parental honesty may encourage their children to be honest. Trust and respect may beget trust and respect. But dishonesty, suspicion, and distrust can work the same way.

Consider the Effects of Extreme Emotional Reactions

Ekman (1989) says the fear of a parent's intense anger is one of the prime reasons children lie. This doesn't mean parents can't implement punishment for lying nor does it mean they shouldn't act upset. But extreme emotional reactions to unpleasant truths may establish a level of fear that causes the child to do anything to avoid it. The child may think that the punishment for telling the truth is as great as it will be if a lie is uncovered so why not take a chance that the lie won't be discovered. The parental goal should be to understand what led to the child's lie and, if necessary, work with them on ways to change the behavior in the future.

Lie Detection

Kids as Detectors

Experimenters have devised several different procedures for eliciting lies from children. Sometimes it involves saying a bitter-tasting drink actually tastes sweet (Feldman, Jenkiins, & Popoola, 1979; Feldman & White, 1980; Feldman, Tomasian, & Coats, 1999); sometimes they are told to act like they are viewing a pleasant picture when the picture is unpleasant and vice versa (Morency & Krauss, 1982); sometimes they are asked to praise fellow students for giving what they know to be incorrect answers (Feldman, Devin-Sheeham & Allen, 1978); and sometimes children who peek at a toy they were instructed not to look at will lie about what they did (Lewis, Stanger & Sullivan, 1989; Polak & Harris, 1999). Videotapes of these deceptive behaviors, along with comparable truth-telling behavior, are then viewed by children of different ages to determine how successful they are at distinguishing honest from dishonest behavior.

Children ranging in age from 3 to 20 have been tested. It is no surprise that kids of all ages were more likely to detect lying in the youngest children. Once a child has reached 6th or 7th grade, their deception skills make detection more difficult. Even though kids can detect deception more accurately with increasing age, they are not likely to exceed the adult norm of detecting deceptive behavior of strangers at slightly better than chance accuracy (see Chapter 9). At all ages, children who are better able to put themselves in the position of the communicator being judged (role-taking) are likely to be capable of better detection. In one study, the child's detection task involved judging adults who were lying about whether they liked or disliked someone (DePaulo, Jordan, Irvine, & Laser, 1982). Groups of students from grades 6, 8, 10, 12, and college were tested. The ability to identify dishonest messages as more deceptive than honest ones did not begin to exceed chance to a significant degree until twelfth grade. In short, good deception detection may not kick in until about age 17.

As kids grow up, they also come to appreciate the fact that it may not always be desirable to accurately detect deception in others. DePaulo & Jordan (1982) found indications that even though girls are capable of detecting deception more accurately than boys, that they will sometimes refrain from reading cues that they believe senders do not want read. This occurs when liars don't do a particularly good job in covering up the behavioral affect they are trying to hide. Male and female high school students who were skilled at reading covert behavior but did not politely ignore these "leaky" behaviors were rated by their teachers as less popular and less socially sensitive.

When kids are making judgments about dishonesty, what signals do they rely on? Between the ages of 5 and 16, there is a steadily increasing tendency for children to rely on perceived inconsistencies between verbal and nonverbal behavior (Blanck & Rosenthal, 1982; Rotenberg, Simourd, & Moore, 1989). Fourth and sixth graders (but not second graders) are more likely to use indirect eye gaze and active limb movements as signs of deception (Rotenberg, 2003). Four and five year-old kids use eye gaze as a cue when someone hides something and then looks at it (Freire, Eskritt, & Lee, 2004). When interviewed about how they would know others are lying, gaze, smiling, and pitch tended to be mentioned most frequently by 2nd, 4th and 6th graders. Rotenberg (1991) found that sixth graders preferred offering a suspected liar a promise of confidentiality in order to uncover their deception whereas younger children (2nd and 4th graders) preferred the strategy of observing behavioral signs to find out if someone was lying. In general, the cues used by younger children are not elaborate or sophisticated which helps explain why they are not particularly skilled detectors.

Adults as Detectors of Kids

Most research (e.g., Feldman, Tomasian, & Coats, 1979; Feldman & White, 1980; Morency & Krauss, 1982) has found that adults are better able to detect younger than older children's lies. This could be explained by younger children's lies being particularly transparent because children only gradually acquire the cognitive and behavioral sophistication necessary to conceal through control of nonverbal behaviors. Talwar and Lee (2008) also found that children's ability to manage verbal behavior associated with successful lying in the temptation resistance situation increases with age. However, some studies have found that adults were more accurate in judging older than younger children's lies. When Newcombe and Bransgrove (2007) asked adults to rate the accuracy of two conflicting recounts of a children's story from same-aged pairs—one accurate and one inaccurate—they were more accurate in judging older pairs (i.e., 9-year-olds or adults) than younger pairs (4-year-olds). Similarly, Nysse-Carris, Bottoms, and Salerno (2011) found that lay adults and "expert" detectors (prosecutors, police officers, and clinical social workers) were more accurate in detecting lies told in a simulated "high stakes" situation (doing something that children were told could get their parents in trouble) by 6 year-olds than 3 year-olds. These researchers speculate that the older children were more cognizant of the negative consequences of lying than the younger ones, which made them more anxious and thus less able to conceal their lies.

Grady (1997) designed a study to examine the strategies parents used to find out if their adolescent children were telling the truth. While their parents were filling out some forms in one room, their children were taken to another room in which they had an opportunity to watch videotapes, read magazines, eat popcorn, work puzzles, listen to music, etc. Each parent was told to interact with their child in an effort to find out what they had been doing. Some parents were told their child might deceive them, but none of the adolescents were told to lie. Parent-child interactions lasted about ten minutes. Parents looked for ways that their child did not normally behave. They adapted strategies to what they felt would work best with their child, but the following were commonly employed: intimidation, gentle prodding ("Come on. Wasn't there anything more than that?"), contradiction ("But when I asked you what was in the room you didn't say a computer was in there."), and self-disclosure ("I remember when I was your age, I looked at some magazines my parents wouldn't have approved of when they weren't around..."). Adolescents influenced the strategies their parents used. Parents tried to make their conversation seem "normal," but short replies and the lack of conversational involvement by their children made some questioning seem more like an interrogation. When their children got upset or impatient with them, parents normally abandoned efforts at detection. Parents, without their child present, were asked to identify deception detection strategies they used as they watched a video of their interaction. Independently, their child viewed the videotape and was asked to identify deception detection strategies on the part of his or her parent. Children accurately identified about half of the strategies the parents said they used so their verbal detection strategies were fairly transparent. The disclosure strategy, however, was rarely identified as a detection strategy.

Judges, social workers, and mental health professionals are *sometimes* able to judge the veracity of children based on their experience with certain traumatic experiences like sexual abuse. When a child involved in a child custody case freely and unemotionally gives details of the abuse and occasionally uses terminology that would more likely be used by an adult, the professional may suspect that the child is repeating a story that his parent wants him or her to tell because actual incest victims are more likely to be secretive, manifest depression, and retract the allegations before restating them (Ekman, 1989). Despite a reservoir of experience and knowledge like the preceding, studies show that experts often find it difficult to distinguish true from false testimony in sex abuse cases (Ceci & Bruck, 1994; Lyon & Dorado, 2008).

So what does all this tell us about lie detection? Not surprisingly, adults and children alike are more likely to detect lies told by very young children with a gradually decreasing accuracy as the detection targets get older. Nevertheless, there are some kids whose lies are difficult to accurately detect in all age groups—including the very young. At any age, most children and adults are not particularly good at detecting deceptive behavior in face-to-face contexts—with the best accuracy rates typically between 50% and 60% (see Chapter 9). As children age, they become better liars, but they also become better detectors and use more sophisticated detection strategies. Parents who suspect their teenager of telling a lie should know that their verbal behavior is likely to reveal their suspicions and will, in turn, elicit defensive maneuvers on the part of their child.

Children Testifying in Court

In 1983, the mother of a two and a half year-old child called police to report that her son had been sodomized at the McMartin preschool in Manhattan Beach, California. As a result, police and social workers began interviewing hundreds children who were or had been enrolled in the McMartin preschool. Stories of sexual abuse and satanic rituals were commonly reported. In addition to accounts of child rape and sodomy, children reported such things as the killing of a horse, being taken on an airplane to Palm Springs, being lured into underground tunnels where day care workers dressed up like witches and flew in the air, the drinking of blood and eating of feces, and the exhumation and mutilation of bodies from a cemetery. One child said they had been regularly beaten with a ten foot long bullwhip and taken to the Episcopal church where they were slapped by a priest if they did not pray to three or four gods. Sound hard to believe? Not for the prosecutors. Seven people were charged. The seven year trial which captured the national headlines involved a series of acquittals, mistrials, and deadlocked juries. During this time Peggy McMartin Buckey and her son spent several years in jail and spent their life's savings on their defense. In 1990, all defendants were acquitted (Eberle & Eberle, 1993; Nathan & Snedeker, 1995).

The mother who made the original complaint was later determined to be a paranoid schizophrenic. Neighbors and parents who stopped by the day care facility during the day could not corroborate these bizarre happenings and the police were not able to find physical evidence (e.g., tunnels, witch costumes, horse bones, etc.) to support the allegations. This made the testimony of the children all the more important to the outcome of the case. Were these children telling the truth? If not, why? Videotapes of the initial interviews with children were revealing. In these interviews, it was not uncommon for adult interviewers to use leading questions and show children dolls with realistic genitalia ("He did touch you there, didn't he?") and coercion—e.g., praising kids who confirmed the offenses and bizarre happenings and telling those who didn't that they were "dumb." Sometimes the answers children gave to court-appointed interviewers were the result of first being "coached" (intentionally or not) in discussions with their parents. In 2005, one of the children admitted he lied in order to please the people who were questioning him (Zirpolo, 2005).

Even though the McMartin case was perhaps the most widely publicized in the United States, there were several similar cases here and abroad during the 1980s. In addition, the allegations of sexual abuse in child custody cases was increasing at this time with some reporting that between 36 and 50% were later proved to be untrue (Cramer, 1991; Ekman, M.A. M.,1989, p. 164; Green, 1986; Benedek & Schetky, 1985). Given the obvious importance of determining the truthfulness of children in situations like this, researchers have closely examined issues surrounding a child's competency to tell the truth in court and the extent to which they are subject to adult influence or "suggestion."

Children's Competency to Tell the Truth

In *Wheeler v. United States* (1895), the court determined that age, by itself, was not a good measure of whether a person is likely to tell the truth or not. Instead, competency is usually based on: 1) Can the child witness recall and describe past events? 2) Does the child witness know the difference between a truthful statement and a lie? and 3) Does the child witness understand his or her obligation to tell the truth in court? Some very young children could meet these criteria even though they often don't testify. Sometimes the competency exam is done in the courtroom and sometimes it is done by the judge in his or her chambers.

The ability to recall and describe the central facts of past events is normally not a problem for most children, even the very young. However, we also know that children typically do not report events as fully, coherently, and with as much detail as adults. If the event is stressful or associated with one's "private" parts, the reliability of children's reports can be affected in several different ways. For example, Saywitz, Goodman, Nicholas, & Moan (1991) had 36 girls between the ages of 5 and 7 given a physical exam in which their vaginal and anal areas were examined. Only eight of thirty-six 5–7 year-old girls reported it. But three girls from another group of 36 girls who were also given a physical exam without any examination of their vaginal or anal areas reported that this part of their body *was* examined.

Do children know the difference between truthful statements and lies? A number of studies provide support for the claim that by age 4 or 5 most children, but not all, are able to distinguish lies and truth (Bussey, 1992a; Bussey, 1992b). Taylor, Lussier, & Maring (2003) found most 5 year-olds capable of making the distinction between pretending and lying and Haugaard & Reppucci (1992) found most 4–5 year-olds understood that it would be a lie if their parent asked them to say something happened when it didn't or to make an inaccurate statement to protect a friend. These studies also point out that the way children conceive of a lie changes as they grow older. For example, young children are prone to see lies as deviations from what they perceive as factual reality, but beginning around age 8 or 9 the communicator's intent is increasingly used as a key distinguishing factor. Since their repertoire of experience is more limited, younger children are more likely to make accurate distinctions between lying and truth-telling if they are asked to judge examples they are familiar with. The reliability of children distinguishing mistakes and lies is likely to reach adult standards around the age of 12. It is important to remember that even adults are sometimes far from perfect in their ability to make such distinctions. Peterson, Peterson, & Seeto (1983) found half of the adults they tested labeled an exaggeration as a lie and 30% of them labeled an act of admitted guessing as a lie.

The difficulty in determining a young child's ability to distinguish between truthful statements and lies can be seen in the following dialogue excerpted from an actual competency exam. Notice how important it is to adapt one's language use to the level of the child and to clarify responses. Even though the child in this case was certified as competent to testify, it is not surprising that the defense did not agree.

Question: Let me ask you this, Linda. When you said a minute ago that you didn't know whether you would or would not tell the truth, what did you mean by that?

Answer: I don't know whether I would tell the truth or not.

Question: Would you purposely tell a lie, or make a mistake?

Answer: That's right.

Question: Which is right? That you might purposely tell a lie?

Answer: Huh uh.

Question: Or that you might make a mistake?

Answer: (Nodded head).

Question: I want to be perfectly sure what you mean. Do you mean that you would not purposely tell a lie?

Answer: No.

Question: Of course anybody can make a mistake. For instance, if you ask me what time it is and I would say 11:00 o'clock' and I would be wrong, but that wouldn't be a lie because I thought it was 11:00 o'clock. That is just a mistake. Did you mean that kind of mistake, or a deliberate mistake on purpose? That is, would it be a deliberate mistake or accidental?

Answer: Accidental.

The Court: The Court will accept her as competent.

*Excerpt from competency exam of 6 year-old girl in *Kiracofe v. Commonwealth* (1957).

There hasn't been a lot of research bearing on the issue of whether children understand their duty or obligation to tell the truth—especially in the courtroom. Viewing lying as a negative value probably precedes viewing truth-telling as a positive value. But as children age, many will come to realize that while lying isn't always bad, there are certain contexts in which truth-telling is paramount. Peterson (1991) found a majority of 6–9 year-olds thought it was worse to have a memory lapse in court than at home and worse to tell a self-protective lie in court than at home. A slightly higher percentage of undergraduate college students felt the same way.

One technique commonly used in most U.S. courts to increase truthtelling involves requiring witnesses to promise to tell the truth prior to testifying in court. Empirical studies have demonstrated that explicitly asking children to make this promise significantly decreases children's lie-telling. For example, Talwar et al. (2004) found that children between 3 and 11 who had made a promise to tell the truth were less likely to tell a lie concealing a transgression their parents had committed.

Interestingly, making children promise to tell the truth in court seems to deter lie-telling more than discussing the morality of truthtelling with a judge, as is required in moral competency examinations in U.S. courts (Evans & Lee, 2010).

Suggestibility and Children's Testimony

One reason child witnesses give false testimony is that they are coerced or misled by adults. Is it true, as some believe, that given the right conditions, an adult can get a child to agree with virtually anything he or she tells them—despite the child's recollections to the contrary? Maybe. It is true that children between the ages of three and five, as a group, are more suggestible than older children and adults. But we also know that children who are highly resistant to adult suggestions are found in all age groups. In addition, the same child may be highly suggestible in some situations and not others (Eisen et al., 1998; Doris, 1991). The following are common ways that adult interviewers exert influence over the recollections of children (Bruck & Ceci, 1999; Ceci & Bruck, 1995).

Interviewer Biases

It is not likely that the adult professionals who normally interview children in abuse cases enter the interview without any preconceptions of what happened. Children may detect these expectations and biases and allow them to enter into their memory of an event. A common way this is done is through the use of leading questions. Adults, as well as children, are subject to the effects of leading questions, but very young children are especially susceptible. Sometimes interviewers intentionally introduce new ideas and interpretations with leading questions in an effort to affect the child's memory of an event. This process, known as "coaching," is most effective when the child knows the interviewer or coach and is motivated to please him or her. For example:

> Child: "I saw Billy hit Mary."
>
> Adult Interviewer: "I know you *think* you saw Billy hitting Mary. And maybe it looked a little like a hit, but could it have been a push? Maybe Billy was just playing with Mary and you didn't see that she pushed him first and then he pushed her. Could that be what happened?"

Another way interviewers can convey their biases is by mentioning inferred traits of the people involved in an event—e.g., "Did you see the bad man hit the woman?" (Leichtman & Ceci, 1995). If the child accepts the claim that the man is generally "bad," then she might be more likely to misremember events in a way that confirms the trait ("Hitting others is the kind of thing that bad people do, so maybe I did see him hit her").

Selective Reinforcement of Information Provided

Let's assume a child is being interviewed and the interviewer suspects sexual abuse. Whenever the child mentions anything that fits the interviewer's expectations, but not with other information, the interviewer becomes attentive—encouraging the child to talk and telling the child how good they are to talk about this with the interviewer.

Peer Pressure

Young interviewees may be told that other children have already said that a particular act or event occurred. This can be a powerful force in leading the young child to an altered recollection. Principe and Ceci (2002) found that leading questions combined with either the presence of peers or a discussion of the event with peers led to inaccurate reports and the addition of information which was not experienced for these very young children.

Dolls with Realistic Genitalia

Since virtually all the dolls children play with do not have realistic genitals, this feature will draw their attention in a leading manner. While such dolls were believed to be helpful in interviews with children suspected of being sexually abused, research does not indicate that the dolls add any validity to a child's responses (Ceci & Bruck, 1993).

Garven et al. (1998) compared the more persuasive questioning techniques used by the McMartin interviewers with the use of suggestive questions alone. The McMartin approach that used peer pressure, question repetition, and selective reinforcement elicited more than three times the number of false accusations as did the suggestive question approach.

Young children are most suggestible on matters that they don't care a lot about. These may be issues or events that are unfamiliar to them, lack personal meaning for them, or pertain to details they see as peripheral or irrelevant. But some children may be more suggestible in a variety of situations—particularly those who have negative or unreliable life experiences and perceive they have little power (Bugental, Shennum, Frank, & Ekman, 2001). Scullin & Ceci (2001) developed a method to measure a child's general tendency toward suggestibility. Children are shown a ten minute video of a birthday party. In the video a fire alarm goes off, a toy gets broken, one child drops ice cream on his lap, etc. Following the video, children are asked 18 questions, some of which have false or suggestive information in them— e.g., "When Andrew broke the toy, was it an accident or did he do it on purpose?" But Andrew did not break the toy. Then the children are questioned again in the context of negative feedback about their answers to the questions. They are told they made mistakes. Four weeks later they are tested again. The extent to which children *yield* to the suggestive questions and *shift* their answers after they are told they made mistakes is the extent to which they are determined to be suggestible.

The legal system in the United States has recognized that the testimony of young children can also be altered by the presence of a perceived threat (Talwar, Lee, Bala, & Lindsay, 2004). As a result, the U.S. Supreme Court allowed child abuse victims to testify over closed-circuit television when the presence of the accused will create "serious emotional distress" (Maryland v. Craig, 1990). In 1999, the same court extended this privilege to children who *witness* a traumatic event like sexual abuse and can prove serious emotional distress will occur in the presence of the person they are accusing. In both cases, there is an opportunity for the defendant's lawyer to cross-examine the witness. These decisions were designed to protect the child witness and ensure truthful testimony, but they are also contrary to the 6th Amendment of the United States Constitution which gives the accused the right to confront those who accuse him or her of a crime. Some also believe that the use of closed-circuit testimony also tells the jury that the defendant is a person whom children fear for a good reason—because he or she is guilty. Orcutt (1998) did not find this to be true, but her experiment did not involve a defendant accused of rape or assault either.

Obtaining Accurate Child Testimony

Very young children can produce fairly accurate accounts of their experiences when they are interviewed in a non-suggestive and neutral manner. However, as we noted earlier, there are a variety of possible pitfalls associated with interviewing child witnesses. As a result, the following guidelines have been proposed (Davies, 2004; Saywitz & Geiselman, 1998).

- Establish pleasant surroundings for the child.
- Begin the interview with rapport-building small talk which is unrelated to the testimony. Tell the child that he or she knows what happened and the interviewer doesn't so the child is just being asked to tell the truth about everything he or she remembers. The child is instructed that it is ok to say, "I don't know" or "I don't understand," but the child is also asked to make a promise to tell the truth. During this phase, the interviewer may also want to demystify the legal context and allay fears associated with it.
- Begin by asking the child an open-ended question about what is remembered about the incident in question. Let them talk uninterrupted.
- Children often respond without much elaboration so questioning is the next step. Interviewers should understand that even though probing is likely to elicit more information, it may also increase the chances that the child will provide more incorrect information. Interviewers should do everything they can to avoid leading questions; to use appropriate age-adapted language; to avoid condescension, accusation, or intimidation; and to be open to more than one explanation of what happened.
- Conclude the interview on a positive note and with a brief summary of how the child's testimony is understood.

Even skilled interviewers who try to follow the preceding guidelines may sometimes find themselves using imprecise language, making incorrect assumptions, and unintentionally leading a child witness to false testimony. Consider, for example, the child in the following interview who has *not* been to his or her grandmother's house on the day in question. The interviewer's second question may be interpreted by the child as "have I *ever* been to Grandma's house?" (Vrij, 2000, p. 115).

Adult: Where have you been today?

Child: (No answer)

Adult: Did you visit Grandma perhaps, have you been to her house?

Child: (Child makes a head nod)

Adult: OK, that is nice, did you like it at grandma's place?

Child: (Child makes another head nod)

Summary

There are certain cognitive and behavioral abilities that children need in order to engage in what most adults in this culture call lying. The child must be able to understand that other people see things in different ways than they do and that they can mentally make contact with some of the other person's reality through a *theory of mind* and *perspective-taking*. Lying also requires children to have executive functions like inhibitory control so that they can conceal the truth they are trying to mislead others about. They also must understand *intentionality* and the *social norms* operating in different contexts where they might consider lying. A lie is intentionally performed to change another person's reality. In addition, children must learn that the other person has intentions, too, and may be trying to detect deception. In many contexts, social norms dictate that it is wrong to lie (e.g., lying to avoid punishment), but in others the norms encourage deception (e.g., expressing gratitude for an undesirable gift). Children must be able to distinguish between these contexts in order to weigh the costs and benefits of lying in a particular situation. They also need to have the communication skills to perform the deceptive act. This requires a linguistic repertoire, an understanding of situational norms and expectations, and the ability to manage/control their own behavior in a manner consistent with the lie being told.

Before the age of four children engage in some "deceit-like" behaviors, but most of these children do not have the necessary cognitive and behavioral skills for lying as it is understood by most adults in this culture. By four or five years-old, many children seem to have installed the basic deception program. From this point on, we see a gradual refinement of their cognitive and behavioral skills necessary for lying. Going to school provides an expanding number of relationships and opportunities for testing these skills. By the time they are 11 or 12, their skills are well-developed and lies are difficult to detect even though there is still room for considerable refinement. Lies are most easily detected with very young children, even though there are some kids who lie without being detected at all ages.

Children lie for a variety of reasons, but avoiding punishment seems to be the primary one. Dealing with popularity, status, and influence in peer groups; learning to deal with authorities; and seeking greater independence/autonomy are tasks which gain importance during adolescence and which provide additional occasions for lying and deception.

An important part of understanding the lying of children is found in the behavior of their parents. It is not unusual for parents to lie to the children they are asking to tell them the truth. Parents will sometimes argue that they lie to their children to protect them, but these lies are often performed to protect the parents themselves—to avoid having to talk about a difficult topic, to maintain power or control over their child, etc. Experts say parents need to adapt their teachings on honesty and lying to the developmental stage of the child; to be careful of asking older children to adhere to rules the parents break; to avoid pretending that they know all the right answers in front of their children, but show them how they continue to struggle to do better; to recognize that they are a model for their children and their children may behave as they do; and to make sure the punishment for children who tell the truth isn't just as severe as the punishment for lying.

The extent to which children can and will tell the truth in a court of law became a major issue after several cases involving charges of widespread sexual abuse in day care facilities in the 1980s and simultaneously increasing charges of sexual abuse in child custody cases. Even though young children do not often testify, those who do must pass a competency exam which tries to determine if the child is capable and willing to tell the truth. Children are capable of reporting the basic facts of an event, but details are often obtained through interviewing. Suggestibility through these interviews has been a major focus of social scientists. Some children are generally more suggestible than others, but suggestibility can be induced in most children through intimidation, accusation, leading questions, selective reinforcement, peer pressure, and dolls with realistic genitals.

Things to Think About

Compare human and nonhuman deception by noting similarities and differences in the four levels of deception in nonhuman deception (Chapter 4) and the developmental stages of human deception abilities in this chapter.

What could have been done to improve Linda's competency interview?

Interview one parent who has a child who is either age 4, 5, or 6; interview another parent with a child who is either age 11, 12, or 13. Neither parent should be your own. Compare their answers and indicate what you learned. Use follow-up questions as needed, but ask these basic questions: 1) Has your child ever lied to you? 2) If so, about what? If not, why not? 3) If your child has lied to you, how did you deal with it? 4) Did you ever lie to your child? 5) If so, about what? If not, explain what counts as a lie for you. 6) What is the most important thing to teach children about honesty? 7) What is the best way to teach children about honesty?

Interview one child who is either age 4, 5, or 6; interview another child who is either age 11, 12, or 13. Neither child should be a sibling. Compare their answers and indicate what you learned. You may also want to comment on your own interviewing behavior. Use follow-up questions as needed, but ask these basic questions: 1) Did you ever lie to your parents? 2) If so, about what? If not, why not? 3) Did you ever get caught in a lie to your parents? What happened? How did they react? 4) Has either of your parents ever lied to you? 5) If so, about what? If not, how do you know? 6) What is the most important thing for parents to teach their children about honesty? 7) What is the best way for parents to teach children about honesty?

References

Benedek, E., and Schetky, D. (1985). Allegations of sexual abuse in child custody cases. In E. Benedek & D. Schetky (Eds.), *Emerging issues in child psychiatry and the law* (pp. 145–156). New York: Brunner Mazel.

Blanck, P.D. & Rosenthal, R. (1982). Developing strategies for decoding "leaky" messages: On learning how and when to decode discrepant and consistent social communications. In R. S. Feldman (Ed.), *Development of nonverbal behavior in children* (pp. 203–229). New York: Springer-Verlag.

Braginsky, D.D. (1970). Machiavellianism and manipulative interpersonal behavior in children. *Journal of Experimental Social Psychology, 6*, 77–99.

Bruck, M. & Ceci, S.J. (1999). The suggestibility of children's memory. *Annual Review of Psychology, 50*, 419–439.

Bugental, D.B., Shennum, W., Frank, M., & Ekman, P. (2001). "True lies:" Children's abuse history and power attributions as influences on deception detection. In V. Manusov & J.H. Harvey (Eds.), *Attribution, communication behavior, and close relationships* (pp. 248–265). New York: Cambridge University Press.

Bussey, K. (1992a). Children's lying and truthfulness: Implications for children's testimony. In S.J. Ceci, M.D. Leichtman, and M.E. Putnick (Eds.) Cognitive and social factors in early deception (pp. 89–109). Hillsdale, N.J.: Erlbaum.

Bussey, K. (1992b). Lying and truthfulness: Children's definitions, standards, and evaluative reactions. *Child Development, 63*, 129–137.

Carlson, S.M., Moses, L.J., & Breton, C. (2002). How specific is the relationship between executive functioning and theory of mind? Contribution of inhibitory control and working memory. *Infant and Child Development, 11*, 73–92.

Carlson, S.M., Moses, L.J., & Hix, H.R. (1998). The role of inhibitory control in young children's difficulties with deception and false belief. *Child Development, 69*, 672–691.

Ceci, S.J. & Bruck, M. (1993). The suggestibility of the child witness. *Psychological Bulletin, 113*, 403–439.

Ceci, S.J. & Bruck, M. (1994). How reliable are children's statements?… It depends. *Family Relations, 43*, 255–257.

Ceci, S.J. & Bruck, M. (1995). *Jeopardy in the courtroom: A scientific analysis of children's testimony*. Washington, D.C.: American Psychological Association.

Ceci, S.J. & Leichtman, M.D. (1992). "I know that you know that I know that you broke the toy"; A brief report of recursive awareness among 3-year-olds. In S.J. Ceci, M.D. Leichtman, & M. Putnick (Eds.) *Cognitive and social factors in early deception* (pp. 1–9). Hillsdale, N.J.: Erlbaum.

Ceci, S.J., Leichtman, M.D., & Putnick, M.E. (Eds.) (1992). *Cognitive and social factors in early deception*. Hillsdale, N.J.: Erlbaum.

Chandler, M., Fritz, A.S., Hala, S. (1989). Small-scale deceit: Deception as a marker of two-, three-, and four-year olds' early theories of mind. *Child Development, 60,* 1263–1277.

Chevalier-Skolnikoff, S. (1986). An exploration of the ontogeny of deception in human beings and nonhuman primates. In R.W. Mitchell & N.S. Thompson (Eds.) *Deception perspectives on human and nonhuman deceit* (pp. 205–220). Albany, New York: SUNY Press.

Clemens, F., Granhag, P.A., Stromwall, L.A., Vrij, A., Landstrom, S., & Hjelmsater, E.R.A. (2010). Skulking around the dinosaur: Eliciting cues to children's deception via strategic disclosure of evidence. *Applied Cognitive Psychology, 24,* 925–940.

Connolley, M. (2004). *Butter comes from butterflies.* San Francisco: Chronicle Books.

Cramer, J. (March 4, 1991). Why children lie in court. *Time,* 76.

Crossman, A.M., & Lewis, M. (2006). Adults' ability to detect children's lying. *Behavioral Sciences and the Law, 24,* 703–715.

Davies, G. (2004). Coping with suggestion and deception in children's accounts. In P.A. Granhag & L.A. Strömwall (Eds.), *The detection of deception in forensic contexts* (pp. 148–171). New York: Cambridge University Press.

DePaulo, B.M. & Jordan, A. (1982). Age changes in deceiving and detecting deceit. In R.S. Feldman (Ed.) *Development of nonverbal behavior in children* (pp. 151–180). New York: Springer-Verlag.

DePaulo, B.M., Jordan, A., Irvine, A., & Laser, P.S. (1982). Age changes in the detection of deception. *Child Development, 53,* 701–709.

Doris, J. (Ed.)(1991). *The suggestibility of children's recollections.* American Psychological Association: Washington, D.C.

Eberle, P. & Eberle, S. (1993). *The abuse of innocence: The McMartin preschool trial.* Amherst, N.Y.: Prometheus Books.

Eisen, M.L., Goodman, G.S., Qin, J., Davis, S.L. (1998). Memory and suggestibility in maltreated children: New research relevant to evaluating allegations of abuse. In S.J. Lynn & K.M. McConkey (Eds.), *Truth in memory* (pp. 163–189). New York: Guilford.

Ekman, M.A.M. (1989). Kids' testimony in court: The sexual abuse crisis. In P. Ekman, Why kids lie (pp. 152–180). New York: Penguin Books.

Ekman, P. (1989). *Why kids lie: How parents can encourage truthfulness.* New York: Penguin Books.

Engels, R., Finkenauer, C., & van Kooten, D.C. (2006). Lying behavior, family functioning, and adjustment in early adolescence. *Journal of Youth and Adolescence, 35,* 949–958.

Evans, A.D., & Lee, K. (2010). Promising to tell the truth makes 8- to 16-year olds more honest. *Behavioral Sciences and the Law, 28,* 801–811.

Feldman, R.S. & Philippot, P. (1991). Children's deception skills and social competence. In K.J. Rotenberg (Ed.), *Children's interpersonal trust: Sensitivity to lying, deception, and promise violations* (pp. 80–99). New York: Springer-Verlag.

Feldman, R.S. & White, (1980). Detecting deception in children. *Journal of Communication, 30,* 121–129.

Feldman, R.S., Devin-Sheeham, L., & Allen, V.L. (1978). Nonverbal cues as indicators of verbal dissembling. *American Educational Research Journal, 15,* 217–231.

Feldman, R.S., Jenkins, S., & Popoola, O. (1979). Detection of deception in adults and children via facial expressions. *Child Development, 50,* 350–355.

Feldman, R.S., Tomasian, J.E., & Coats, E.J. (1999). Nonverbal deception abilities and adolescents' social competence: Adolescents with higher social skills are better liars. *Journal of Nonverbal Behavior, 23,* 237–249.

Finkenauer, C., Frijns, T., Engels, R.C.M.E., & Kerkhof, P. (2005). Perceiving concealment in relationships between parents and adolescents: Links with parental behavior. *Personal Relationships, 12,* 387–406.

Ford, C.V. (1996). *Lies! Lies!! Lies!!! The psychology of deceit.* Washington, D.C.: American Psychiatric Press.

Freire, A., Eskritt, M., & Lee, K. (2004). Are eyes windows to a deceiver's soul? Children's use of another's eye gaze cues in a deceptive situation. *Developmental Psychology, 40,* 1093–1104.

Garven, S., Wood, J.M., Malpass, R.S. & Shaw, J.S. (1998). More than suggestion: The effect of interviewing techniques from the McMartin Preschool case. *Journal of Applied Psychology, 83,* 347–359.

Grady, D.P. (1997). *Conversational strategies for detecting deception: An analysis of parent-adolescent child interactions.* Unpublished Ph.D. dissertation, University of Texas.

Green, A. (1986). True and false allegations of child sexual abuse in child custody disputes. *Journal of the American Academy of Child Psychiatry, 25,* 449–456.

Harari, H. & McDavid, J.W. (1969). Situational influence on moral justice: A study in finking. *Journal of Personality and Social Psychology, 11,* 240–244.

Haugaard, J.J. & Reppucci, N.D. (1992). Children and the truth. In S.J. Ceci, m.D. Leichtman, & M. Putnick (Eds.), Cognitive and social factors in early deception (pp. 29–45). Hillsdale, N.J.: Erlbaum.

Hays, C., & Carver, L.J. (2014). Follow the liar: The effects of adult lies on children's honesty. *Developmental Science, 17,* 977–983.

Holt, J.C. (1982). *How children fail.* Rev. ed. New York: Dell.

Jackson, P. (1968). *Life in classrooms.* New York: Holt, Rinehart, & Winston.

Jensen, L.A., Arnett, J.J., Feldman, S.S., and Cauffman, E.(2004). The right to do wrong: Lying to parents among adolescents and emerging adults. *Youth and Adolescence, 33,* 101–112.

Keating, C., Heltman, K.R. (1994). Dominance and deception in children and adults: Are leaders the best misleaders? *Personality and Social Psychology Bulletin, 20,* 312–321.

Keenan, J.P. (2003). *The face in the mirror: The search for the origins of consciousness.* New York: HarperCollins.

Kiracofe v. Commonwealth, 198 Va. 833 97 S. E. 2d, 14 (Va., 1957).

Korkmaz, B. (2011). Theory of mind and neurodevelopmental disorders of childhood. *Pediatric Research, 69,* 101–108.

Krout, M.H. (1931). The psychology of children's lies. *Journal of Abnormal Psychology, 26,* 1–27

LaFrenière, P.J. (1988). The ontogeny of tactical deception in humans. In R.W. Byrne & A. Whiten (Eds.), *Machiavellian intelligence: Social expertise and the evolution of intellect in monkeys, apes, and humans* (pp. 238–252). New York: Oxford University Press.

Lee, K. (2013). Little liars: Development of verbal deception in children. *Child Development Perspectives, 7,* 91–96. Leekam, S.R. (1992). Believing and deceiving: Steps to becoming a good liar. In S.J. Ceci, M.S. Leichtman, & M.E. Putnick (Eds.) *Cognitive and social factors in early deception* (pp. 47–62). Hillsdale, N.J.: Erlbaum.

Leichtman, M.D., & Ceci, S.J. (1995). The effects of stereotypes and suggestions on preschoolers' reports. *Developmental Psychology, 31,* 567–578.

Lewis, M., Stanger, C., & Sullivan, M.W. (1989). Deception in 3-year-olds. *Developmental Psychology, 25,* 439–443.

Lewis, M. (1993). The development of deception. In M. Lewis & C. Saarni (Eds.) *Lying and deception in everyday life* (pp. 90–105). New York: Guilford.

Lyon, T.D., & Dorado, J.S. (2008). Truth induction in young maltreated children: The effects of oath-taking and reassurance on true and false disclosures. *Child Abuse and Neglect, 32,* 738–748.

Maryland v. Craig, 497 U.S. 836 (1990).

McAfee. (2013). *McAfee digital deception study: Exploring the online disconnect between parents and pre-teens, teens, and young adults.* Retrieved on June 16, 2015 from http://www.mcafee.com/digital-deception.

McCarthy, A., & Lee, K. (2009). Children's knowledge of deceptive gaze cues and its relation to their actual lying behavior. *Journal of Experimental Child Psychology, 103,* 117–134.McHugh, L., & Stewart, I. (2012). *The self and perspective-taking: Contributions and applications from modern behavioral science.* Oakland, CA: New Harbinger.

Morency, N., & Krauss, R. (1982). Children's nonverbal encoding and decoding of affect. In R.S. Feldman (Ed.), Development of nonverbal behavior in children (pp. 181–202). New York: Springer-Verlag.

Nathan, D. & Snedeker, M. (1995). *Satan's silence: Ritual abuse and the making of a modern American witch hunt.* New York: Basic Books.

Nysse-Carris, K.L., Bottoms, B.L., & Salerno, J.M. (2011). Experts' and novices' abilities to detect children's high-stakes lies of omission. *Psychology, Public Policy, and Law, 17,* 76–98.

Orcutt, H. K. (1998). Detecting deception: *Factfinders' abilities to assess the truth.* Unpublished Ph.D. dissertation, SUNY-Buffalo.

Patterson, J. & Kim, P. (1991). *The day America told the truth: What people really believe about everything that really matters.* New York: Prentice Hall.

Perkins, S.A., & Turiel, E. (2007). To lie or not to lie: To whom and under what circumstances. *Child Development, 78,* 609–621.

Peterson, C.C. (1991). What is a lie? Children's use of intentions and consequences in lexical definitions and moral evaluations of lying. In K.J. Rotenberg (Ed.), *Children's interpersonal trust: Sensitivity to lying, deception, and promise violations* (pp. 5–19). New York: Springer-Verlag.

Peterson, C.C., Peterson, J. L., & Seeto, D. (1983). Developmental changes in ideas about lying. *Child Development, 54,* 1529–1535.

Piaget, J. (1954). *The construction of reality in the child.* New York: Basic Books.

Polak, A. & Harris, P.L. (1999). Deception by young children following noncompliance. *Developmental Psychology, 35,* 561–568.

Penn, D., & Povinelli, D.J. (2007). On the lack of evidence that non-human animals possess anything remotely resembling a 'theory of mind'. Philosophical Transactions of the Royal Society B: Biological Sciences, 362, 731–744.Principe, G.F. & Ceci, S.J. (2002). "I saw it with my own ears": The effects of peer conversations on preschoolers' reports of nonexperienced events. *Journal of Experimental Child Psychology*, 83, 1–25.

Rotenberg, K.J. (1991). Children's cue use and strategies for detecting deception. In K.J. Rotenberg (Ed.), *Children's interpersonal trust: Sensitivity to lying, deception, and promise violations* (pp. 43–57). New York: Springer-Verlag.

Rotenberg, K.J. (2003). Children's use of gaze and limb movement cues to infer deception. *Journal of Genetic Psychology*, 164, 175–187.

Rotenberg, K.J., Simond, L, & Moore, D. (1989). Children's use of verbal-nonverbal consistency principle to infer truth and lying. *Child Development*, 60, 309–322.

Ruffman, T., Perner, J., Naito, M., Parkin, L., & Clements, W.A. (1998). Older (but not younger) siblings facilitate false belief understanding. *Developmental Psychology*, 34, 161–174.

Saarni, C. (1984). An observational study of children's attempts to monitor their expressive behavior. *Child Development*, 55, 1504–1513.

Saywitz, K.J., & Geiselman, R.E. (1998). Interviewing the child witness. In S.J. Lynn & K.M. McConkey (Eds.), *Truth in memory* (pp. 190–223). New York: Guilford.

Saywitz, K.J., Goodman, G.S., Nicholas, E., & Moan, S.F. (1991). Children's memories of a physical exam involving genital touch: Implications for reports of child sexual abuse. *Journal of Consulting and Clinical Psychology*, 59, 682–691.

Shultz, T.R. and Cloghesy, K. (1981). Development of recursive awareness of intention. *Developmental Psychology*, 17, 465–471.

Schultz, T.R., Wells, D., & Sarda, M. (1980). Development of the ability to distinguish intended actions from mistakes, reflexes and passive movements. *The British Journal of Social and Clinical Psychology*, 19, 301–310.

Sodian, B., Taylor, C., Harris, P.L., & Perner, J. (1991). Early deception and the child's theory of mind: False trails and genuine markers. *Child Development*, 62, 468–483.

Stouthamer-Loeber, M. (1986). Lying as a problem behavior in children: A review. *Clinical Psychology Review*, 6, 267–289.

Stouthamer-Loeber, M. (1991). Young children's verbal misrepresentations of reality. In K.J. Rotenberg (Ed.), *Children's interpersonal trust: Sensitivity to lying, deception, and promise violations* (pp. 20–42). New York: Springer-Verlag.

Stouthamer-Loeber, M. & Loeber, R. (1986). Boys who lie. *Journal of Abnormal Child Psychology, 14*, 551–564.

Sullin, M.H. & Ceci, S.J. (2001). A suggestibility scale for children. *Personality and Individual Differences, 30*, 843–856.

Talwar, V., & Lee, K. (2002). Development of lying to conceal a transgression: Children's control of expressive behavior during verbal deception. *International Journal of Behavioral Development, 26*, 436–444.

Talwar, V., & Lee, K. (2008). Social and cognitive correlates of children's lying behavior. *Child Development, 79*, 866–881.Talwar, V., Lee, K., Bala, N., & Lindsay, R.C.L. (2004). Children's lie-telling to conceal a parent's transgression: Legal implications. *Law and Human Behavior, 28*, 411–435.

Taylor, M., Lussier, G.L., & Maring, B.L. (2003). The distinction between lying and pretending. *Journal of Cognition & Development, 4*, 299–323.

Touhey, J.E. (1973). Child-rearing antecedents and the emergence of Machiavellianism. *Sociometry, 36*, 194–206.

Vasek, M.E. (1986). Lying as a skill: The development of deception in children. In R.W. Mitchell & N.S. Thompson (Eds.) *Deception perspectives on human and nonhuman deceit* (pp.271–292). Albany, New York: SUNY Press.

Vrij, A. (2000). *Detecting lies and deceit: The psychology of lying and the implications for professional practice.* New York: Wiley.

Wheeler v. United States, 159 U.S. 523 (1895).

Zirpolo, K. (October 30, 2005). I'm sorry. *Los Angeles Times Magazine*, 10–13, 29.

Chapter 6

Self-Deception

Most people think they know what you mean when you say "self-deception." In fact, most people are not hesitant to admit that they have some first hand experience with it. The problem is that the experiences people call self-deception seem to include a lot of different psychological and social processes. The "essence" of self-deception is elusive (Patten, 2003). So rather than look for something that characterizes all cases of perceived self-deception, Sanford (1988) says we would do well to think of them as simply sharing a "family resemblance." Consider the similarities and differences in the following experiences:

- Rick is a college student who is taking Communication 315. He wants to be a Communication major. He made a D on the first two tests and a C minus on a short paper. He says, "The material is not hard and I understand it completely. My grades do not reflect what I know." He points out that he makes B's in "most of his classes." He is distressed his grades do not reflect his knowledge of the subject matter in this course. He believes he is smarter than other students who are getting higher grades. He also thinks his grades in Communication 315 are the result of "tricky" test questions and a professor whose lectures are boring.

- While campaigning for the Presidency, Texas Governor George W. Bush was dogged by rumors he had regularly used cocaine in his younger years and dropped out of the Air National Guard to avoid drug-testing. Bush perpetuated the rumors by persistently ducking and dodging when reporters pressed him on the issue. In his 2008 bestseller *What Happened,* former press secretary Scott McClellan recalls an evening on the campaign trail in 1999 when he asked the then-Presidential hopeful why he hadn't yet directly refuted these rumors. Bush reportedly told him he simply couldn't remember whether he had used cocaine or not. "How can that be?" McClellan writes. "How can someone simply not remember whether or nor not they used an

"I did that," says my memory. "I could not have done that," says my pride, and remains inexorable. Eventually— the memory yields."

— *Friedrich Nietzsche*

> "If deceit is fundamental to animal communication, then there must be strong selection to spot deception and this ought, in turn, to select for a degree of self-deception, rendering some facts and motives unconscious so as not to betray—by the subtle signs of self-knowledge—the deception being practiced."
>
> — Robert Trivers

illegal substance like cocaine? It didn't make a lot of sense, but Bush isn't the kind of person to flat-out lie…I felt I was witnessing Bush convincing himself to believe something that probably was not true and that deep down, he knew was not true. And his reason for doing so is fairly obvious—political convenience" (p.5). McClellan describes several subsequent episodes in the book in which he believes President Bush deceived himself to cope with unpleasant political realities stemming from the unpopularity of the Iraq War and the aftermath of Hurricane Katrina.

- Cassar and Craig (2009) asked entrepreneurs in the early stages of building start-up companies to estimate the chances that their start-ups would eventually become operating businesses. Later, the entrepreneurs whose start-ups had failed were asked to recall their estimates. Although they had actually estimated their chances of success as 80% on average, they recalled generating more pessimistic estimates, around 50%. Similarly, Biais and Weber (2009) asked investment bankers to forecast the values of several financial variables (stock and commodity prices, currency exchange rates, etc.) one week in advance. After the week had passed, the bankers recalled their predictions as being far more accurate than they really were. Surprisingly, experienced bankers were no less prone to "hindsight bias" than the novices.

- Jane Fonda recalled this instance of self-deception in her autobiography. Fonda, an academy award-winning actress, social and political activist, feminist, and mother of three, had always thought of herself as a strong, independent woman who isn't afraid to speak out against things that violate her beliefs. She did not believe a good marriage involved having group sex. To her surprise, however, she found herself actively fulfilling her first husband's desire to engage in group sex. In her words, "Sometimes there were three of us, sometimes more. Sometimes it was even I who did the soliciting. So adept was I at burying my real feelings and compartmentalizing myself that I eventually had myself convinced that I enjoyed it" (Fonda, 2005, p. 154).

- Mary and Michelle have been best friends for 20 years. Mary believes Michelle is a kind, compassionate, timid, and non-violent person who is not capable of shooting a gun, much less killing anyone. One night in a parking lot near a bar, however, she saw Michelle screaming at another woman and eventually firing a pistol that killed the woman. Despite what she saw, Mary still believes Michelle is not capable of such behavior. Mary is beginning to think it must have been somebody else she saw who looked like Michelle.

- In 2015, NBC reporter Brian Williams found himself under extreme public scrutiny for lying. A respected news anchor for decades, Williams had publicly claimed he had come under enemy fire while aboard a military helicopter in Iraq in 2003. Others on board with him challenged his account, saying the helicopter they were following had been fired on, not the one they were in. Williams eventually admitted that he "made a mistake," saying "I don't know what screwed up in my mind that caused me to conflate one aircraft with another" (Farhi, 2015).

What do these examples have in common? How are they different? What do they tell us about the needs of human beings and how their minds work? Although they don't always agree on the answers, scholars from many fields of study have tackled these and other questions about self-deception (Ames & Dissanayake, 1996; Fingarette, 1969; Lockhard & Paulhus, 1988; Martin, 1985; McLaughlin & Rorty, 1988; Mele, 2001; Trivers, 2011). Drawing on these and other resources, this chapter will seek answers to the following questions: What is self-deception? Why do we deceive ourselves? How do we deceive ourselves? and What effects accrue from self-deception?

Self, Deception, and Self-Deception

In order to better understand the act or acts of self-deception, let's examine the words used to describe the phenomenon or phenomena: *self* and *deception*.

Self

There are few things more certain to us than the sense of self. Descartes (1641/2010) famously argued that while he could doubt the existence of the world around him, he could not dismiss his first-person experience because the "I" must do the doubting. Three assumptions underlie the sense of self. First, we regard ourselves as continuous in time and space. That is, there is something that remains constant so that the "I" at work is the same person at home or on vacation, and the "I" of now is the same person I was last year and will be next year. Second, the self is unified. The world may enter our consciousness as distinct sights, sounds, smells, tastes, and tactile experiences, but they are assumed to represent a single reality that is integrated and experienced by a single self. Third, the self is an independent agent that acts in the world based on conscious choices and judgments.

As self-evident as these assumptions may seem, they unravel when scrutinized (Westerhoff, 2011). During the time that people live, they undergo significant changes in their bodies, thoughts, and emotions. Moreover, most of the things we think of as defining ourselves—skills (speaking Chinese, computer programming, legal expertise, rock climbing, etc.), social roles (daughter, mother, leader, boss, etc.), beliefs (Catholic, Democrat, environmentalist, etc.), preferences (Yankees fan, cooking enthusiast, video gamer, etc.)—are things that develop and change across time and space. Consequently, it's unclear why whatever is stable and continuous about us across the lifespan should be considered central to who we are.

The unification assumption of self is threatened by what scientists have discovered about how the brain processes physical energy. For example, physicists have established that light travels much faster than sound, but studies of human perception show that visual stimuli often take longer to process than sounds. Consequently, sights and sounds enter our senses at different speeds, and yet we perceive simultaneity between seeing someone's lips move and hearing her voice. This and many other perceptual illusions are created by the human brain to coordinate physical energy entering our senses in a disjointed fashion (Keetels & Vroomen, 2012). These illusions create an adaptive and comforting but ultimately misleading sense of perceptual unity.

The "agent" assumption is challenged by psychological research demonstrating that a conscious consideration of the reasons for making a decision sometimes happens after the decision has occurred, and thus couldn't have produced the decision in the first place (Wegner, 2003). In his studies of moral judgment, Haidt (2001, 2011) calls this the "wag the dog" illusion, equating it with a scenario in which a dog's tail is wagged and thereby makes the dog happy. When he asked people to consider moral choices while timing their responses and scanning their brain activity, they made choices quickly but produced reasons only later to justify their choices. This happened even for moral choices about bizarre situations most people never consider—Is it wrong to have sex with a dead chicken? Is it ok to defecate in a urinal? If your dog dies, would it be alright to eat it? His interview subjects all quickly decided it would be wrong to do these things, but it took them a lot longer to come up with reasons for why it would be wrong. Although his subjects maintained their choices were based on these post-hoc reasons, the evidence points to emotional responses (disgust in particular) as driving their choices, not reasons.

The idea of having a unitary self housing a vast array of thoughts, feelings, and perceptions—some of which are bound to be incompatible and inharmonious—creates a pressure for consistency which explains why certain kinds of self-deception occur. In other words, we sometimes need a mechanism like self-deception to help maintain a complicated and sometimes disorderly jumble of stimuli we call our self. As a result our self is more recognizable to us and easier to live with. The self-inconsistencies which self-deceivers wrestle with, according to Chanowitz and Langer (1985), stem from the fact that we are actually composed of many social selves—each of which seeks coherence according to the standards appropriate to its context. Our self at work, our self at school, and our self at home, for example, have separate qualities and sometimes we let them operate independently. But we also have the capacity to relate our various social selves together as sub-units or as a whole. Each of us struggles with the social and psychological demands associated with these processes.

Deception

The idea of deceiving one's self is sufficiently illogical to some people that they maintain it cannot occur. Self-deception, they argue is a paradox. You can't have one person simultaneously *know* that something is a lie and *not know* it is a lie. From this perspective, you can't be both perpetrator and victim because it requires you to be unaware of something you are aware you are doing to yourself. Those who make this argument use the diagram in Figure 6.1 to illustrate what they believe to be the absurdity and impossibility of self-deception.

Other-Deception ▶
Person **A** believes **X** is true
Person **A** tells Person **B** that **Y** is true
Person **B** believes **Y** is true and is therefore deceived by Person **A**

Self-Deception ▶
Person **A** believes **X** is true
Person **A** tells Person **A** that **Y** is true
Person **A** believes **Y** is true and is therefore deceived by Person **A**

Figure 6.1: A Common, But Limited Comparison of Other-Deception to Self-Deception

Figure 6.1 does identify one way that other-deception occurs, but it is a limited comparison because it doesn't acknowledge that other-deception can occur in a variety of ways—some of which are very analogous to the way self-deceptions occur (Nyberg, 1993). For example, sometimes people deceive others by giving support to a false belief already held by the other person; sometimes people deceive others by hiding the truth or distracting attention away from information that would lead to the truth; and sometimes people deceive others by intimating, but not actually saying, that the other person's truthful belief may be fallacious. Self-deception, too, as we will learn later, can be accomplished through similar processes—e.g., selective information searches to support preferred ideas; hiding ideas through repression or dissociation; distracting attention away from unpleasant ideas; and discounting the value of unwanted information. Similar effects may also occur in other-deception and self-deception. For example, sometimes the target of the deception is completely unaware they have been deceived; sometimes they are pretty sure they are being deceived; sometimes there is suspicion; and sometimes there is just an uneasy feeling that "something isn't right."

Self-deception does have some unique qualities and we will explore those, but it is worth noting that an expanded view of other-deception shows us that some of the processes we use to deceive others and some of the responses experienced by the targets of other-deception, can also occur as we go about deceiving our self.

Self-Deception

There are other definitions of self-deception (Gur & Sackeim, 1979; Sackheim, 1988), but the one put forth by Starek and Keating (1991, p. 146) effectively identifies the key elements:

> *"Self-deception is a motivated unawareness of conflicting knowledge in which threatening knowledge is selectively filtered from consciousness as a psychological defense, thereby reducing anxiety and inducing a positive self-bias."*

It will be a lot easier to understand self-deception if we examine further some of the key elements in this definition.

Levels of Awareness

If we were fully conscious of everything in our mind, different forms of self-deception would be difficult, if not impossible, to enact. Self-deception requires a mental environment in which thoughts can enter varying states of awareness. Thus, we may have different levels of awareness—a complete lack of awareness, a dim awareness, a level of awareness just below our fully conscious state, etc. The person giving the following account seems to be saying that she was aware of "the truth" on one level of awareness while accepting another version of "the truth" on another level:

> I did not have any voices that said, "You are not telling me the truth." I just remember sort of grabbing on to what she was saying and desperately believing that because that was what I wanted to believe….I fell for [the deceit] because I wanted to. I just didn't want the thing to happen that was going to happen. I desperately wanted to believe her and so I chose to believe her…I mean I knew the truth, I knew what I believed, I knew what I thought, and I also believed her and what she said *(Werth & Flaherty, 1986, p. 296–297)*

Awareness should be thought of as having gradations. Thoughts that are further removed from our consciousness and those that are well hidden are less accessible to us even though levels of awareness, and hence accessibility, can change. We may, for example, be highly critical of some behavior exhibited by another person while we have little awareness of the fact that we exhibit the same behavior. In time, however, we may develop an awareness that we, too, exhibit the same behavior. Self-deception and self-awareness often occur gradually (Rorty, 1996). A spouse who no longer loves her husband but finds that belief difficult to admit may continue to have sex with him; a religious person who has lost his or her faith may continue to attend church.

We live in a culture that reveres the idea that we are fully aware of everything we think and do. This belief provides a feeling of self-assurance and control. In turn, it makes us fully responsible for what we do. There's only one problem. There is a vast amount of mental activity which takes place without conscious awareness (Langer, 1978; Wegner, 2003). This ability to deal with thoughts at different levels of awareness can be quite functional. We often manage life's trials and tribulations by striving *not* to know certain things. It enables us to cope with uncertainty, anxiety, fear, confusion, and powerlessness. It facilitates self-deception.

Motivated but not Necessarily Intentional

We've established the fact that we are capable of processing stimuli at various levels of awareness and that as long as there is something we are deceiving ourselves about, we are not fully aware of it. But how do we become less aware of the things we are deceiving ourselves about? It can be done very deliberately, but more commonly it is outside of our awareness.

Intentional self-deception begins knowingly—with the purpose of convincing our self—e.g., that our bad marriage is really good. But for self-deception to occur, the belief, "my marriage is good," cannot remain at its initially high level of consciousness. Through constant repetition, social support and/or some other processes, the amount of conscious attention needed to sustain the false belief has to decrease so that the belief becomes more "automatic" and operates outside of our awareness (Bargh, 1996; Wegner & Bargh, 1998). On those occasions when self-deception has a highly intentional beginning, it is called "*brazen self-deception*" by Newman (1999).

Much self-deception, however, occurs without conscious intent. Self-deception does not require that we know we are engaging in self-deception. Sackheim (1988, p. 156) explains it this way:

> *It may well be that our success in creating and maintaining self-deception often depends on our lack of awareness of the process. Particularly when what we lie to ourselves about are issues that are highly affectively-charged and critical to our self-esteem, it is improbable that we can establish sincere conviction in the self-deceits with conscious foreknowledge of the lie. Likewise, it would be a rather exceptional circumstance if we could successfully deceive others and share with them our explicit intention to do so.*

With unintentional deception, emotion is in the driver's seat. When emotions guide our judgment, they can induce biases such as "motivated reasoning," the tendency to draw conclusions from one's experiences and other data that are emotionally preferable, regardless of their objective accuracy. In Hastorf and Cantril's (1954) classic study of this phenomenon, students from two rival colleges watched film of a football game between their schools' teams and were asked to assess the accuracy of the referees' penalty calls. Students from both schools reported the referees had assessed more unwarranted penalties against *their* team than against the rival. The emotional stake the students had in experiencing solidarity with their colleges and fellow students unconsciously motivated them to "see" different things when they watched the game film.

Motivated reasoning explains why political conservatives and liberals in the U.S. can review the same facts and yet draw radically different conclusions about issues such as climate change, income inequality, voter fraud, vaccine safety, homeland security, and even the birthplace and religion of President Barack Obama. Their deliberations about these issues tend to make the facts fit their attitudes, not vice versa. Motivated reasoning also reflects a key insight of modern neuroscience—thinking is suffused with emotion. Not only are the two difficult to separate, but our feelings come to the fore more quickly than our thoughts. Many scientists have argued that emotions evolved to promote self-protective action in the wild, prompting us to push threatening stimuli away and pull comforting ones close. Our fight-or-flight reflexes thus appear to apply to information as well as to predators.

Content

Self-deceptions are mostly about things we want to be true (but aren't). But wishful thinking alone doesn't meet the content requirements for self-deception. Self-deception requires two incongruous, contrary, or contradictory beliefs. So it is only when the evidence contrary to the wishful thinking is processed in a biased way that self-deception occurs. Strangely, however, there do seem to be times when our self-deception is about something we want to be false. Mele (2001) calls this "*twisted self-deception*" and illustrates it with the following example. An insecure, jealous husband does not want to believe his wife is having an affair. Nevertheless, when he finds small amount of unsubstantiated evidence that she is having an affair, he chooses to believe it.

The content of self-deceptions does not necessarily have to be directly about the self. For example, one can deceive oneself about the honesty of his or her stockbroker even though that deception may be indirectly related to one's investment success (or lack thereof).

Normally, self-deceptions involve beliefs and other matters which allow some latitude in determining the truth (Baumeister, 1993). It would be more difficult, for example, to deceive oneself about an automobile accident you had than to deceive yourself about who caused the accident. Some would argue that self-deceptions involving what others would consider incontrovertible facts with no "shades of gray" (like if you believed you were not involved in the automobile accident) are good candidates for therapy because they so radically violate agreed upon standards for treating reality. These beliefs can, however, be induced. In "coerced-internalized" false confessions, innocent suspects who are tired, confused, and subjected to highly suggestive interrogation techniques may eventually believe they did commit a crime and sometimes create a false memory of it in the process (Kassin, 2005; also see more on false confessions in Chapter 9). Thus, even seemingly "unquestionable facts" or events can become mentally ambiguous under the right conditions—and thereby subject to self-deception.

Self-Deception: A Social as well as a Psychological Process

Up to this point, we've focused on the mental activities involved in self-deception. But deception of one's self also involves dealing with input from other people. Sometimes it is interaction with other people that encourages a person to self-deceive. For example, person A may tell person B something he or she believes to be the truth, but person B convinces person A that it is not the truth. Person A cannot accept the idea that their original idea is not true—leading to self-deception. In a similar manner, person A might tell person B what he or she think is a lie, but person B convinces person A that the lie is really true. Person A cannot live with their newly discovered truth.

Sometimes people who are already deceiving themselves about something will present themselves to others in ways that seek confirmation for their self-deception. If they are successful, the reactions of other people help them obtain even greater psychological distance from their self-deception (Gilbert & Cooper, 1985). Self-deceivers are often so hungry for support they will eagerly embrace the slightest endorsement of their belief. Ford (1996) gives the following examples of this: 1) A wife who cannot stand the thought of her husband having an affair. She wants to preserve the marriage "because of the children" and need for financial security. She smells another woman's perfume on his clothes; finds a motel receipt for an out of town trip; and notices he is no longer interested in her sexually. Her husband says he doesn't like it, but his secretary dabs perfume on him when he isn't looking. He tells her that going to the motel and avoiding sex with her are both related to the amount of stress he faces at work. His wife accepts this explanation and feels better. 2) An administrator of a medical clinic is short-staffed and feels he can't afford to lose anyone. An alcoholic physician was reported by several staff members to tremble excessively and have a strong smell of alcohol emanating from him. The physician told the administrator that the smell was his after shave lotion. A member of physician's family told the administrator he was not an alcoholic. The administrator was relieved and sent the physician back to work.

What happens when a person's self-deception is known to their interaction partner? What if the wife who was deceiving herself about her husband's affair interacted with her best friend who knew the husband was having an affair? Sometimes the interaction partner will "play along" and support the self-deception. But sometimes they will try to expose the self-deception which is why self-deceivers are not always very anxious to raise the issue associated with their self-deception. Once the issue has been made public, the self-deceiver no long has exclusive control over it and runs the risk of having to consciously confront beliefs they wish to avoid. But even when they are confronted with their self-deception, self-deceivers are not always easily swayed. Kruger and Dunning (1999) conducted several studies of people who scored in the 12th percentile on tests of humor, grammar, and logic. They believed they were in the 62nd percentile. There are a number of different reasons why these people dramatically overestimated their abilities. One reason, relevant to our discussion of self-deception, is that these "unskilled and unaware" individuals may have received accurate feedback about their abilities but chose not to believe it. They couldn't or wouldn't take advantage of social input regarding the extent to which they lacked competence in these areas.

There is another type of social fallout associated with self-deception. Noted journalist Michael Kinsley, points out that when people avoid talking to others about the subject of a self-deception, they may also have to learn to live with the other lies this subterfuge generates:

> To work effectively, though, denial requires secrecy, and secrecy pretty much requires deception. It's simply easier to go through the day not thinking about Parkinson's disease if the people you interact with don't know you have it. This complicates the case for denial... What you do with yourself in the privacy of your head is nobody else's business. On the other hand, deceiving those around you is more troublesome....For eight years I have tried not to tell outright lies, but there have been some Clintonian evasions and prissy parsing. (Q: "You look tired. Are you O.K.?" A: "I feel fine.") And my basic intention has been to deceive. So I'm sorry about that (Kinsley, 2001, p. 73).

Self-deception may also be fostered by one's group membership. When a person *strongly* identifies with a particular group, it is integral to their self-concept. Thus, the intense identification with the values and policies one associates with "Americans," "Baptists," "Republicans," is treated like any other aspect of one's self-concept. The group label creates a filter for processing information and confirming the associated beliefs while contradictory facts are put away, ignored, or reinterpreted (Welles, 1988). Thus, when there is evidence that threatens the beliefs of a primary group, it is a threat to one's own self and self-deception becomes an option. For example, a person who believes Republicans stand for fiscal responsibility may want to deceive him or herself about the extent to which a rapidly escalating national debt during a Republican administration is a gross deviation from fiscal responsibility. A fervently patriotic American may find the reports of Americans engaged in torturing prisoners at Abu Ghraid in Iraq and Guantanamo Bay in Cuba to be sufficiently inconsistent with American values that they must be denied, repressed, or interpreted in some other way.

Interaction with a group can lead to self-deception on the part of all members of the group. Janis (1983) called this phenomenon "*groupthink*." Groupthink occurs when the group members are so intent on preserving group agreement that they fail to realistically evaluate alternative courses of action. Dissent and controversy are unwelcome. Assertions associated with group goals go unchallenged. Critical thinking is replaced by group thinking. All this is facilitated when the leader makes an early declaration of what he or she prefers. Janis points out that even when groups are confronted with feedback that their policy isn't working or is too risky, these groups tend to persist in following their original course of action. In short, the workings of the group is similar to the workings of the self-deceiving individual's mind.

Groupthink is more likely to occur within certain types of policy-making groups, within certain types of organizational structures, and within certain situational constraints (Hart, Stern, & Sundelius, 1997). It is also more likely when group members all share the same strong group identification—e.g., they are all resolutely dedicated to the same political party or religious group. Janis analyzed the group deliberations of several American foreign policy-making groups in order to discover the processes that give birth to groupthink—e.g., the escalation of the war in Korea (1950); the failed invasion of Cuba's Bay of Pigs in 1961; and the escalation of the Vietnam war from 1964–1968. The space shuttle Challenger disaster in 1986, the invasion of Iraq in 2003, and the global financial crisis of 2007–2008 also reveal the presence of groupthink and self-deception. Janis' studies revealed the three key features of groupthink (Janis, 1983, pp. 174–175):

1. The group overestimates its power and morality. It believes it is invulnerable and this leads to excessive optimism and extreme risk-taking. The group's inherent morality is never questioned.

2. The group exhibits close-mindedness. Information which challenges the group's goals and decisions are collectively discounted or rationalized. Enemy leaders are stereotyped as too evil, weak, or stupid to deal with.

3. The group exerts various kinds of pressure to insure uniformity. Individual members censor their own counter-arguments leading others to assume that silence means consent. Self-appointed "mindguards" keep opposing information from reaching the group. When a member does voice a strong counter-argument, other members make it clear that this behavior is not consistent with a loyal group member.

Self-Deception: Why Do We Do It?

People deceive themselves for a variety of reasons. Primarily self-deception serves as a way to feel better, to enhance one's abilities, and to more effectively manage the day-to-day stresses of everyday life. This is not to suggest that successful adaptation to life doesn't also involve facing and dealing with unwanted stressors and unpleasant facts. But it does mean that self-deception works effectively alongside self-confrontation and self-knowledge in coping with everyday life. Sullivan (2001, p. 180) dramatizes the point when she says:

> ...only by believing, against the evidence, that our lives have meaning and that there is hope for the future do we keep having children, or washing the windows, or spending twelve hours a day designing software that will be obsolete six months after it hits the shelves. Take away the thousand and one delusions we weave and we will be paralyzed by apathy, or run screaming for the hills, or turn to stone while staring into the unblinking void of a Godless, purposeless, blind universe...

The primary reasons for engaging in self-deception are: 1) to enhance self-esteem and protect one's self-concept; 2) to reduce cognitive dissonance; 3) to enhance deception skills; 4) to preserve physical and mental health; and 4) to enhance competitive performance. Self-deception may occur for other reasons, too, but the following will account for most instances.

To Enhance Self-Esteem and Protect One's Self-Concept

The need to think well of ourselves is strongly embedded in all of us. In fact, the ability to think of ourselves as more decent, generous, competent, smart, respected, loved, in control, etc. than we really are is probably an indispensable part of effectively negotiating everyday life (Sullivan, 2001). Very few people think of themselves as having low self-esteem or being "below average" (Baumeister, 1998). In fact, almost everyone reports being better than average across a wide range of personality characteristics. In a survey of a million high school seniors, all thought they had above average ability to get along with others and 70% thought they had better than average leadership skills. Another survey found 93% of college professors saying they were better than average at their work (Gilovich, 1991).

We often deceive ourselves about what we know or knew by using *hindsight bias* (Fischoff, 1975). When your friend tells you his girlfriend discovered a lie he had told her, it is easy for you to say, "I knew that would happen," (and to explain the reasons why you knew it would happen) when, in fact, you would have been far less certain if asked to make a prediction about what would happen before the fact. We all become a lot smarter when we know how things have turned out.

Self-deception is also used to distort the past in order to feel better about the present. Lewis (2004) says most adults derogate their past and see themselves as having undergone considerable positive change during adulthood—e.g., "I'm more stable than I used to be." In some cases these comparisons may be valid, but others may be a function of self-deception. Offer et al. (2000) studied the same people at age 14 and again at age 48. At age 48, the participants in this research tended to recall their family life and the emotional climate at age 14 as a lot more negative than they did when surveyed at age 14. Thus, we can boost our self-esteem by believing we have overcome a past which was more difficult than it actually was; by thinking more positively of our current selves than reality can confirm, and by anticipating a more positive future self than base-rate data would justify (Taylor & Brown, 1988).

Alternatively, we can distort the past by selectively recalling positive experiences and forgetting negative ones. The memory phenomenon of "nostalgia" induces a sentimentality for positive past events and periods of significance both to individuals (senior prom, the college years, "my swinging single days in New York City," "our first date," etc.) and to the public (the "Swinging" 1960s, the "Reagan Era", "when the BoSox won the World Series", etc.). Nostalgic recollections can provide existential meaning to people by reminding them of their lived experience during historic events and connections to others who share this experience (e.g., "I remember exactly where I was and who I was with when I watched the Berlin Wall come down on TV"). Routledge et al. (2011) found that people's propensity for nostalgia correlates positively with their sense of purpose in life and with their resilience in the face of existential threats. Importantly, the therapeutic power of nostalgia comes at the expense of recall accuracy. When people wax nostalgic about positive events during the "Reagan Era" (booms on Wall Street, the decline of the Soviet Union, the "return of family values"), they selectively disregard the negative ones (the Savings and Loan Scandal, the Iran-Contra Affair, the AIDS pandemic, etc.).

Curiously, using self-deception to diminish our self-esteem is also adaptive in some circumstances. It is what Hartung (1988) calls "*deceiving down*" and involves thinking less of yourself in order to match one's self-concept to a particular situational reality. Hartung offers the following example which not only illustrates why this bookkeeper deceived himself about his abilities but how he went about it.

> For example this man could be a bookkeeper who knows more about accounting than his boss knows. In order to lower his self-esteem and consequently his self-image, he might recall his school days and dwell upon a section of an accounting textbook that he never understood. Without going back to the book, he can reconstruct his conundrum, causing himself to feel the same sense of insecurity that he felt so keenly on the night before the final exam. Without being explicitly cognizant (without actually saying so to himself), he imagines that all real accountants understand that section of that textbook. If he recollects this insecurity often enough, eventually it will not need to be rehearsed. It will come to him out of context, but it will come at appropriate times. It will come when his boss insists that he use an inappropriate debiting procedure. It will come when he gets only half of the raise that he expected. It will come when someone else is complimented for work that he did. It will come when the boss's son is rude to him, and so forth. (p. 171)

To Reduce Cognitive Dissonance

Most of us want to think of ourselves as reasonable, moral, and smart. When we are confronted with information implying that we may have acted unreasonably, immorally, or stupidly, we experience discomfort. The discomfort caused by performing an action that runs counter to one's positive self-conception was referred to as "cognitive dissonance" by Festinger (1957), who developed the concept into one of social psychology's most powerful and provocative theories. According to Festinger, when we experience cognitive dissonance, we will work to reduce it just as we would to reduce hunger by eating or thirst by drinking. But unlike these other drives, the path to reducing dissonance is not so simple or obvious.

There are three basic ways we reduce dissonance. To illustrate these ways, suppose you have developed a behavioral habit that you know is unhealthy—smoking, drinking alcohol to excess, eating junk food, etc. Knowing these behaviors can harm your health and other aspects of your life will cause you dissonance as you observe yourself performing them. One way you could reduce the dissonance is by stopping the behavior altogether, but that can be difficult, especially if the habit is established or has become a biological addiction. In this case, you might opt for the second dissonance reducing strategy—justifying your behavior by changing one of the dissonant thoughts. Thus, you might justify continuing to smoke, drink, or eat junk food by questioning the scientific evidence purporting to show these things are bad for your health. But even if you are convinced the behavior really is bad for you, you can opt for the third reduction strategy of adding new thoughts about your behavior that dampen the dissonance created by existing thoughts. You might say to yourself, "Sure, smoking/drinking/junk food can be bad for my health, but it helps me cope with the stress of work and life, and so there are benefits as well as costs." Or you might put your faith in an exception to the rule: "My uncle Paul smoked liked a chimney/drank like a fish/ate like a pig for years and still lived into his 90s, so maybe I can beat the odds too."

These justifications might sound silly to health enthusiasts, which is precisely the point—people experiencing dissonance will self-deceive, sometimes in spectacular ways, to reduce it. Dieters who try but fail to lose weight may misremember themselves as being heavier when they started their diets, thereby distorting a big failure into a slight success. Executives in fossil fuel industries question the contribution of humans to climate change, despite universal agreement among climatologists that this is the case (Anderegg, Prall, Harold, & Schneider, 2010). Environmentalists who embrace the scientific evidence of humans' role in climate change deny that reducing fossil fuel consumption will slow or stall financial growth worldwide, despite a wealth of economic evidence to the contrary (Norgaard, 2010). Occasionally, dissonance-reducing self-deception can actually be helpful. For example, Taylor et al. (1992) found that men who had tested positive for HIV/AIDs but had unrealistically positive illusions about surviving the illness lived longer than those who were more "realistic." Far more often than not, though, such illusions are merely comforting in the short-term but harmful in the long-term.

Most people think of themselves as rational and certainly are capable of rational thought. However, the drive to reduce dissonance leads to thinking that is not rational but *rationalizing*. People who are in the midst of reducing dissonance get caught up in convincing themselves they are right as to induce irrational and maladaptive behavior (Aronson, 1997).

To Enhance Deception Skills

According to evolutionary theorist Robert Trivers (2011), "we hide reality from our conscious minds the better to hide it from onlookers" (p.16). That is, we engage in self-deception in part to make ourselves more adept at deceiving others. Liars who are aware of their lies are more likely to be caught. Liars who are less aware of their lies are more likely to project sincerity in their communications. When the target expresses belief in the lie, this rewards the liar and supports the utility of his or her self-deception.

Trivers (2000, 2011) argues the desire to more effectively fool our fellow human beings was the primary reason we acquired the ability to self-deceive in the first place. Essock et al. (1988) believes that humans are genetically wired to act in their own self-interests, but they find themselves having to make friends, mate, and manage resources in a society that views altruism and selflessness as an important virtue. Therefore, in order to be seen as a person who is motivated by a concern for others, one may have to engage in self-deception or order to pursue self-interests.

To Enhance Physical and Mental Health

Through self-deception a person may develop a sense of optimism and control over his or her pain or illness. The feeling of control (even though it may be an illusion) may activate certain neurochemical reactions and behaviors which, in turn, positively affect one's health. Taylor (1989) points out that the *"placebo effect"* is strong testimony to the power of unrealistic optimism in healing (see also Chapter 3). Placebos begin as lies. Patients are led to believe that some treatment (e.g., sugar pills or even fake surgery) will lead to improvement in their health. The administrator, however, expects the placebo to have little or no effect on the person's health. However, many who have been administered placebos report substantial positive effects such as reduced pain, discomfort, and even the disappearance of symptoms related to their illness.

Self-deception can affect our susceptibility to infectious diseases, for ill or good. Some "positive illusion" people tell themselves to cope with difficult circumstances (e.g., children who convince themselves their alcoholic, abusive father is a good man) require so much cognitive and emotional investment to maintain that they drain energy from immune function (von Hippel & Trivers, 2011). Conversely, religious fundamentalism, which often restricts mating or even interactions with outsiders, can help protect members of a sect from diseases carried by non-sect members. Ghobarah, Huth, and Russett (2004) cross-referenced anthropological and epidemiological analyses suggesting religions are most likely to split into rival factions in regions with the highest rates of infectious disease.

Self-deception may also be needed as one adjusts to a severe disability. An unjustified sense of optimism and control is often called for as these individuals reframe their quality of life. In what they call the *"disability paradox,"* Albrecht & Devlieger (1999) studied 150 people who had serious disabilities and found over 50% of them saying that they had an excellent or good quality of life.

To Enhance Competitive Performance

Self-deception can enhance motivation and performance during athletic competition. Starek & Keating (1991) studied highly skilled swimmers at a national competition and found that the more successful ones engaged in more self-deception. Roberto Heras, a teammate of six time Tour de France champion Lance Armstrong, said: "I think there are other riders who prepare as well as Armstrong for the Tour, but Lance knows better than anyone how to convince himself that he is stronger than the rest" (Halliburton, 2004). Whittaker-Bleuler (1988, p. 226) examined experienced and inexperienced tennis players. She concluded: "Since experienced players are better at detecting both winning and losing behavior than inexperienced players, the former may need to be more convincing when playing individuals of equivalent skill. Therefore, in order to optimize their chances of success, skilled opponents may have a greater need to self-deceive than the average player."

The 2000 Olympic Gold Medal Greco-Roman wrestling match was between American Rulon Gardner and Russian Alexander Karelin. Karelin, considered one of the greatest wrestlers in history, had not lost a match in 13 years and had won the gold Medal in Olympic Greco-Roman wrestling in 1988, 1992, and 1996. he had never lost in international competition and had not conceded a point in ten years. Although Gardner had been a national champion in his weight class, he had limited international experience and lost to Karelin in the 1997 World Championships. All the evidence pointed to another Karelin win. But Gardner had a strong belief in his ability and his preparation for the match and believed that he could win. And, in a contest now known as the "miracle on the mat," he did win—in overtime. It should be noted that in this case and others that self-deception on the part of one's opponent can also be an active ingredient in the outcome—e.g., being so certain of one's superior ability that intense preparation is precluded.

Self-Deception: How Do We Do It?

"Human self-deception is one of the most impressive software programs ever devised," Nyberg (1993, p. 81) astutely observed. Briefly, here's how it seems to work: 1) Humans have a general "confirmation bias" to seek out and interpret information that supports their prior beliefs or goals. 2) In particular, our biases toward self-enhancement and self-consistency are especially relevant to self-deception. 3) When the self is threatened with negative information—information deemed potentially harmful to the self—one or more of these biases will be implemented to deal with the threat. 4) However, if the threat persists and promises to do serious damage to the self, arousal occurs and one or more psychological defense mechanisms are activated—e.g., denial, rationalization, repression, etc. 5) The use of biased thought processes coupled with psychological defense mechanisms affect the selection, treatment, and retrieval of information about the issue in question and lead to a state of self-deception. Let's look more closely at these processes.

Confirmation Bias and Patternicity

There is an obvious difference between the way scientists and attorneys think about and use "evidence." A scientist is supposed to impartially evaluate the available research evidence to draw an unbiased conclusion about the phenomenon (physical, biological, chemical, psychological, etc.) under study. In contrast, an attorney's job is to seek out and use evidence to build a case for one side or the other in a legal dispute. By law, attorneys are not committed to an unbiased weighting of the evidence at hand; they are motivated to weigh heavily only the evidence confirming their legal position. Although professional attorneys engage in "confirmation bias" consciously and methodically in court cases, laypeople do so unwittingly when they process information in light of their beliefs and attitudes. Francis Bacon (1620/1939) described this process as follows:

> *The human understanding when it has once adopted an opinion draws all thing else to support and agree with it. And though there be a greater number and weight of instances to be found on the other side, yet these it either neglects and despises, or else by some distinction sets aside and rejects; in order that by this great and pernicious predetermination the author of its former conclusions may remain inviolate…And such is the way of all superstitions, whether in astrology, dreams, omens, divine judgments, or the like; wherein men, having a delight in such vanities, mark the event where they are fulfilled, but where they fail, although this happened much more often, neglect and pass them by (p. 36).*

Our tendency to seek out and interpret new information in a way that confirms our prior beliefs is a form of the "motivated reasoning" phenomenon described earlier in the chapter. This bias is exacerbated by human's tendency to search for meaningful patterns, or "patternicity" (Schermer, 2012). Finding meaningful patterns is of course a very good thing when there is something systematic, intentional, and/or intelligent causing the patterns to occur: hearing a radio distress signal broadcast by a sinking ship; correctly guessing the region where someone grew up based on her accent; identifying a killer based on clues left at a crime scene; etc. But people also find what they believe to be meaningful patterns in meaningless noise: the Virgin Mary on a tortilla, extraterrestrial spacecraft in fuzzy pictures of a night sky; Satanic messages in rock music played backwards; etc. Schermer argues that we make these perceptual "errors" because of their relative cost. Signal detection theorists distinguish between two basic types of perceptual errors: a Type 1 or "false positive" error, when you incorrectly see a pattern that is not really there; and a Type 2 or "false negative" error, when you don't see a pattern that really is there. In our evolutionary history, Schermer argues, Type I errors have been a lot less costly than Type 2 errors in terms of survival. For example, imagine one of our hominid ancestors was walking through unfamiliar territory and hears a rustle in the grass. If he took it to be a dangerous predator when it was really just the wind, this "false positive" error doesn't cost him more than a moment of fright. However, if he interpreted the sound as just the wind when it really had been a dangerous predator, this "false negative" error could cost him his life. Schermer argues that the combination of "false positive" patternicity and confirmation bias underlie people's proclivity to see patterns that reinforce their prior beliefs.

Self-Enhancement Bias

People have biased thought processes which help them create and maintain a favorable view of themselves (Steele, 1988). These predispositions toward self-flattery are not inevitably linked to self-deception, but they are extremely useful when self-deception is sought. These biases can be quite effective in countering and holding at bay any contrary or contradictory views of self. In a review of the relevant research in social psychology, Baumeister (1998, p. 690–691) identifies the following ways we distort data in the pursuit of a favorable view of self.

1. Dealing with Positive and Negative Feedback
   - We tend to attribute successes to our own abilities and blame our failures on external factors.
   - We tend to view evidence depicting us unfavorably as flawed while viewing positive feedback uncritically. Criticism is viewed as motivated by prejudice or other factors that discredit it.
   - We tend to spend little time processing negative information—thereby reducing the chances it is encoded into memory. On the other hand, we dwell on praise.
   - We selectively forget feedback about failure and recall feedback of a positive nature.

2. Comparing Our Self to Others
   - We tend to compare ourselves to others who will make us look good.
   - We tend to view our group membership positively while viewing "out-group" members as less worthy, less responsible for their successes, and more responsible for their misfortunes.
   - We tend to overestimate how many people have opinions similar to our own and underestimate how many people have abilities similar to our own.

3. Trait Identification
   - We tend to sort through our memory in a biased way—finding traits deemed desirable. For example, when people are led to believe that introversion is a desired trait and characteristic of success, they tend to recall instances when they were introverted; when led to believe that extroversion is related to success, people tend to remember times when they were extroverted. When people believe conflict is good for relationships, they recall a lot more conflict episodes than when they are told it is harmful to relationships.
   - We tend to think our good traits are unusual while our faults are common.
   - We tend to associate what we do as a mark of success when the standards for success are ambiguous—e.g., a sign of good parenting is "not spanking your children" if that's what you do.

Self-Consistency Bias

The self-enhancement bias is accompanied by a self-consistency bias. After all, if you think well of yourself, you'd like to maintain that state. When you feel good about yourself, stability is comforting. But sometimes we say or do something that throws into question something we believe about our self. One way we restore consistency in such situations is through *self-persuasion*—i.e., we establish and accept beliefs which will restore consistency. An example of this happened when volunteers had to go through either a mild or severe initiation to gain admission to a discussion group. The discussion group turned out to be both boring and silly. Naturally, those whose initiation was demanding had to face the fact that any sensible person would not go through that much effort to become a member of such an undesirable group. As a result, they chose to reduce their dissonance and restore belief consistency by focusing on the positive aspects of the group and persuading themselves that the group was actually more interesting than it appeared (Aronson & Mills, 1959). Tavris and Aronson (2007) make the following observations about dissonance reduction and self-justification:

> Dissonance reduction operates like a thermostat, keeping our self-esteem bubbling along on high. That is why we are usually oblivious to the self-justifications, the little lies to ourselves that prevent us from even acknowledging that we made mistakes or foolish decisions (pp. 30–31). Self-justification is not the same thing as lying or making excuses...self-justification is more powerful and more dangerous than the explicit lie. It allows people to convince themselves that what they did was the best thing they could have done... Self-justification minimizes our mistakes and bad decisions; it is also the reason everyone can see a hypocrite in action except the hypocrite (p. 4).

It should also be noted that self-persuasion is also a process that can change beliefs in order to overcome self-deception. Consider the following case involving self-denial. Students said they strongly believed AIDS was a deadly problem and that sexually active people should use condoms. But they also reported that they rarely used them. They believed everyone else was vulnerable but they weren't—or at least that's the way they behaved. In an effort to expose this self-deception and align their behavior with their publicly stated beliefs, researchers asked these college students to deliver a convincing speech about the dangers of AIDS—imploring their audience to use condoms. Speakers were also asked to speak about the situations in which they found it difficult or impossible to use condoms themselves—thereby reminding them of their own hypocrisy. The speech was videotaped and the speakers were told it was going to be shown to high school students as part of a sex education class. These speech-giving students not only purchased condoms immediately following their speech, but six months later 92% of them said they were using condoms regularly (Stone et al., 1994). The effectiveness of self-persuasion lies in the fact that the target of the persuasive message feels he or she is making a change because they want to—not because of a request from someone else.

The Role of Psychological Threat

Psychological threat plays an important role in self-deception because threat increases emotional arousal which, in turn, affects information processing. According to Paulhus & Suedfeld (1988), psychological threat and emotional arousal prompt us to reduce the complexity of our message processing to only the most salient elements—e.g., Am I going to be helped or hurt? Using an interpersonal analogy, one would not expect combatants who saw conflict as imminent to be reflecting on the complexity of the many intersecting issues involved and the multi-dimensional nature of their opponent. Instead, simple evaluative judgments like "friend/foe," "profitable/unprofitable," and "good/bad" are processed. This is likely to be the pattern when the combatants are beliefs and/or feelings and limited to a person's mind. The simple evaluative judgments tend to quickly bring the interests of the self and its need for protection to the forefront. As noted earlier, this does not necessarily mean such processing is done on a highly conscious level. When self-deception is used to protect the self, there are numerous psychological defense mechanisms available to us (Ford, 1996; Goleman, 1985; Paulhus & Suedfeld, 1988; Smith, 2004; Sullivan, 2001).

Self-Defense Mechanisms

As noted, psychological defense mechanisms for self-protection and self-deception are plentiful. However, we do not need to examine all of them to understand the way they work. Six processes will be examined: 1) denial; 2) rationalization; 3) repression; 4) dissociation; 5) projection; and 6) civilization. In daily life these processes often work in conjunction with one another with overlapping functions, so it is not always clear which process or processes are at work. By examining them separately, though, one can see the range of mental gymnastics which can be employed in the pursuit of self-deception.

Denial

Denial is the refusal to attend to something. Even though the self-deceiver may be initially conscious of the thing being denied, the ultimate goal of denial is to keep the disagreeable information out of awareness in order to enhance or protect self-esteem. This is largely accomplished by selectively giving attention to confirming data and not noticing or deemphasizing that which is disconfirming. With selective attention, unpleasant truths may be avoided all together or simply passed over quickly in order to focus more intently on other things—e.g., "Ok, maybe having sex with my intern was a mistake, but look at all the good things I've done for the American people as President. I've done this and this and this..." Sometimes we can spot the possibility of potentially threatening information and preemptively ignore it. This can be done in conversation by changing the topic or by "*willful ignorance*"—i.e., making it clear to others you do not want to know something. Without saying it directly, parents may communicate to their children that they do not want to be made aware of their sexual behavior.

Through denial one may be able to reject an unpleasant reality, but it may be obvious to others—e.g., the excessive alcohol consumption by the person who refuses to recognize it; the person who has a terminal illness and refuses to face his or her mortality; the lover who refuses to recognize the signs that her or his partner is no longer in love.

Rationalization

Rationalizing goes hand in hand with self-deception. We rationalize irrational and/or inconsistent acts, beliefs, and feelings to our self in order to justify self-deception. Often this intrapersonal justification is done at a subconscious level and the self-deceiver may not know exactly how he or she has rationalized a particular behavior unless they are forced to overtly confront it in a social context. A woman who suspected her husband of being sexually involved with someone else illustrates how excuses were used to rationalize her own belief that her husband was not engaged in this behavior:

It was funny things that just didn't, well, they seemed fishy. But when I think about it there was a part of me that didn't want to believe they seemed fishy so I wouldn't believe it...Little by little things were happening that didn't make sense, but I can remember making excuses for them myself...I didn't want to believe there was anything to find out...so I was being deceived from two angles... I was deceiving myself...I didn't sit there when it was happening saying, "I am just fooling myself." You know, I, I, as I said, I made up a lot of excuses, and really believed them...I didn't confide in anyone, too, because I was afraid of what they would tell me. I wanted to believe everything was going to be fine and I wasn't being deceived (Werth & Flaherty, 1986, p. 296).

Excuses may also be a vehicle for "making sense" out of irrational and/or inconsistent behavior when talking to others. It wouldn't be surprising if this overtly spoken message was the first time the self-deceiver had consciously justified their belief or behavior to themselves. We learn from an early age that we are better off when we can give an acceptable reason to explain why we did something—even if we really don't know why we did it. Sanford (1988) says the "thirst for rationality" is a major source of lies and he maintains that self-deception could not exist without it. When excuses are used to rationalize behavior, they are designed to minimize the fault of the actor—i.e., covering "I have acted improperly and am responsible" with "I have done nothing wrong and am not responsible." Excuses may dismiss or deny the problem, diminish the degree of harm done, or downplay one's responsibility for the problem (Snyder, 1985). The following are examples of rationalization used as a self-defense mechanism for self-deception.

- Marion Barry was Mayor of Washington, D.C. in 1990 when he was videotaped by the FBI smoking crack cocaine with a woman who was not his wife. The woman agreed to testify against him. His response was that this was all a racist plot by people out to get him.

- During the Holocaust, German physicians participated in gruesome and inhumane experiments on prisoners in concentration camps. Some viewed their work as a "duty to their country" and others saw it as "furthering scientific knowledge."

- A father is never satisfied with his son's performance and criticizes him whether he succeeds or fails. His son has bruises on his arms as a result of "roughhousing" with his father. The father tries to exert dominance and control in every aspect of his son's life. When confronted with what others perceive to be cruel and unhealthy behavior, the father says he is only doing what is necessary to prepare his son for the hardships life will throw at him. "As far as the bruises go," he said, "Well, that's just the result of playing. Guys play rough. I'm not raising a boy named Sue."

- Greg is an alcoholic. He attends weekly meetings of Alcoholics Anonymous (AA) and this makes it harder for Greg to start drinking again. But recently he stopped attending these meetings. The reason he stopped attending, he said, was because his day job at a rehabilitation center involved working with addicts all day long and he felt like another hour in the evening with addicts was more than he could handle.

Rationalization is sometimes facilitated by relationship partners. A wife, for example, may construct excuses and rationalize her husband's misdeeds, make his faults look like virtues, and downplay the importance of his shortcomings. Her behavior is based on the hypothesis that if her husband feels good about himself, the relationship will be better for her. And, indeed, Murray and Holmes (1996) found that people in satisfying relationships do exhibit these "positive illusions." What we don't know at this point is the extent to which positive illusions heaped on one partner are later used by that partner as bases for rationalizing self-deceptions.

Repression

Repression describes what happens when a person mentally blocks ideas and feelings from reaching consciousness. They are ideas and feelings that are likely to cause pain, anxiety or threat. It is a motivated amnesia or an unwillingness to recall. In Goleman's (1985, p. 117) words, it is "forgetting and forgetting we have forgotten." Traumatic events may trigger repression. For example, a rape victim may not recall information about the rape or a soldier can't recall killing people. In situations like this, an effort to retrieve the repressed information can create enough anxiety so that the accuracy of the memory may suffer a great deal.

It is not clear whether Pete Rose, arguably one of history's premier baseball players, engaged in repression or not. He did, however, maintain in numerous interviews over a period of more than 15 years, that he did not bet on baseball games involving his own team. He did admit to gambling on other sporting events and two bookies produced betting slips and other documentary evidence which indicated Rose bet on his own baseball team. Rose loved baseball and it would be understandable if he repressed the idea that he was responsible for something which tarnished the integrity of the game.

Suppression differs from repression in that it puts information or feelings away for a short time. These memories which have been set aside can then be retrieved and dealt with at a more appropriate or desirable time. One way we can suppress mental content is through a process Wegner (1989) calls "self-distraction." Self-distraction involves thinking about things that will cover and replace the things we don't want to think about—our fears, worries, secrets, or even itches. The distraction occurs because we become immersed in some activity and/or in some thoughts that blot out the unwanted ones. Many have found success in suppressing the feelings and thoughts associated with mild pain through self-distraction. For me, jogging is an activity that puts unwanted thoughts away for a time and allows me to approach them later with new clarity. While I'm jogging, there are plenty of distracting stimuli related to running and other thoughts are highly focused—shutting out everything else. Read the boxed insert below and try your own experiment in suppression.

See how you do with suppression in the activity below!!! Purple Rhino.

© Ken Benner/
Shutterstock.com

Read This and Try Not to Think of a Purple Rhino

Actually, the experiment reported here deals with a white bear instead of a purple rhino, but try not to think of a purple rhino anyway. Try to read everything in this box without thinking of a purple rhino.

People were brought into a room and seated at a table with a microphone and a hotel desk type bell. Each person was asked to spend 5 minutes saying everything that came to their mind into the microphone. Almost everyone talked nonstop about their families, plans, things in the room, what they had for lunch, etc. At the end of five minutes, each person was asked to continue talking, but not to think of a white bear. If the thought of a white bear came to mind, the person was to ring the bell. On average, people rang the bell 6 times during this 5 minute exercise—some even said white bear out loud several times.

The group's next task was to stop trying *not* to think of a white bear and, instead, to try thinking about a white bear while they talked. This time the average number of bell rings was 16 and saying white bear out loud averaged 14 times. This was more than a similar group of people who had never been asked to suppress the idea of a white bear and, from the very beginning were told to think of a white bear.

Apparently, the act of trying to suppress the idea initially made people think about it more later when they were given permission to think about it. Has this ever happened to you?

You are now free to think about a purple rhino as much as you'd like to.

See: Wegner, D. M., Schneider, D. J., Carter, S., III, & White, T. (1987). Paradoxical effects of thought suppression. *Journal of Personality and Social Psychology, 53,* 5–13.

Dissociation

This is a psychological process involving the separation and isolation of mental content—psychologically removing the links, connections, or associations to related content. We may be quite aware of the troubling behavior, belief, or emotion but not willing to acknowledge its relevance to other parts of one's self with which it is incompatible. When the associations between contrary or inconsistent content are mentally removed, it also removes the need to explain the behavior.

Jane Fonda's experience with group sex, discussed at the beginning of this chapter, is an example of dissociation. In her words, she had "compartmentalized" her group sex activity—separated it from other parts of her self which were not compatible with it. Compartmentalization was necessary in order to avoid explaining its connection to any other aspect of self or to make any changes which would bring the behavior into harmony with other parts of her self.

Projection

Projection is a self-defense mechanism that deals with unpleasant and unacknowledged realities by misattributing them to others—e.g., a manager who is unwilling to admit his own incompetence blames his failures on the fact that his employees are incompetent. A wife may accuse her husband of being disinterested in sex because her own disinterest is not compatible with her self-image as a loving and committed spouse. When the problem is not your own, there is no need to make any changes. Projection can occur in other ways as well. People may misperceive the behavior of another person and project that misperception onto themselves. For example, someone who can't face her own angry outbursts might perceive the angry outbursts of another person as a "controlled response" which makes her feel better about her own behavior.

Projection relies on our ability to selectively search for information. If we start with a preferred conclusion ("I am a good manager."), we can often find the little evidence needed to support it in a very short period of time. To reject the preferred conclusion, however, normally requires a lot of evidence and takes much longer.

In any given situation, numerous self-defense mechanisms come into play in order to sustain self-deception. Twerski (1997) says the three most common elements of what he calls *addictive thinking* (i.e., how addicts behave), are denial, rationalization, and projection. Their function is to protect the addict from intolerable awarenesses—e.g., the imagined stigma of being an addict, the fear of not being able to use drugs or alcohol again, the worry that they'll have to face and deal with certain personal and social weaknesses. However, Twerski points out that it is only after the distortions that these self-defense mechanisms cause are decreased or eliminated that the addict's recovery can begin. Multiple self-defense mechanisms can be seen in the following example as well. A mother's son has committed a horrible crime. The evidence supporting his guilt is plentiful. The mother is unable to acknowledge his guilt (denial). She believes the "crowd he hangs with" is responsible (projection). She believes she is a good mother who raised a good boy and good boys don't commit crimes like this (dissociation). She hides evidence because "it isn't relevant," and is evasive with investigators "because they are rude" (rationalization).

Civilization

In his Pulitzer-prize winning work *The Denial of Death*, anthropologist Ernest Becker (1973) argued humans are so frightened by awareness of their own mortality that they have created an elaborate and collective defense mechanism to buffer them from the fear: the notion of "civilization" or culture. He claimed a basic duality in human life exists between the physical world of objects and bodies and a symbolic world of meaning. We are able to transcend the fear of death through the noble work of "civilization" (the arts, philosophy and religion, law, government, etc.), a concept involving our symbolic halves. By focusing our attention and efforts on the "immortality project" of civilization, our symbolic selves may enjoy a sense of eternal life our physical selves cannot. This in turn gives people the feeling that their lives have meaning, a purpose, and significance in the grand scheme of things.

Although critically acclaimed, Becker's book has been controversial for many reasons, not the least of which is his claim that culture in general and religion in particular are mechanisms of mass self-deception. Moreover, Becker asserts that humans will need new "illusions" to replace these mechanisms as advances in science and engineering rob them of their capacity to distract us from death thoughts. He does not speculate about what these new illusions might be, instead recommending that people come to grips with their own mortality and thereby reduce its power to make them self-deceive.

Self-Deception: Advantages and Disadvantages

Like so many human abilities and creations, self-deception is capable of producing effects that range from great good to great harm. There are times when seeing things as they aren't can be rewarding. But when our view of reality is radically different from what our social community perceives or when we regularly refuse to cope with the problems of everyday life, self-deception becomes a liability. Even though his counsel assumes a degree of conscious control that is not often present in self-deception, Rorty (1975, p. 22) aptly captures the sought-after ideal: "What we need is not the wholesale substitution of self-knowledge for self-deception, but the gifts of timing and tact required to emphasize the right one in the appropriate place." Some of the major advantages and disadvantages of self-deception are illustrated in the following.

Mental Health vs. Mental Illness

After reviewing numerous scientific studies involving self-illusion and self-deception, Taylor and Brown (1988, p. 204) concluded that "the mentally healthy person appears to have the enviable capacity to distort reality in a direction that enhances self-esteem, maintains beliefs in personal efficacy, and promotes an optimistic view of the future." They go on to say that these illusions "appear to foster traditional criteria for mental health, including the ability to care about the self and others, the ability to be happy or contented, and the ability to engage in productive or creative work." In short, it can be a useful way to adapt and cope with everyday life. In fact, Alloy and Abramson (1979) discovered that people experiencing depression engaged in less self-deception than those who weren't depressed. Baumeister (1993 p. 178) maintains that "it may be necessary to deceive oneself in order to have a realistic chance at some of life's peak experiences...Grand ambition, romantic passion, and religious faith all require some heavy doses of faith and optimism beyond what is strictly warranted by the facts." As Vahinger (1925) noted long ago, we often act contrary to certain central realities of life—e.g., acting "as-if" we are fully in control of and/or responsible what we're doing; making plans "as-if" we were going to live forever.

On the other hand, too much self-deception or self-deception which prohibits coping with issues that demand attention are not signs of adaptive living. Not being able to face certain realities or creating a reality that impedes normal everyday living may lead to therapy or worse (Baumeister & Scher, 1988). Self-deception is often a defining characteristic of mental illness. It is an integral part of the mental life of those who engage in substance abuse and impulse control disorders like gambling, kleptomania, compulsive eating and compulsive shopping. Therapists often look for ways their client may be lying to themselves. They also try to determine how their client will react if they are forced to face the intolerable reality they have been avoiding.

Physical Well-Being vs. Physical Affliction

Self-deception is credited with overcoming pain and triggering bodily responses which assist in conquering some diseases. Unfortunately, it is also credited with facilitating serious illness and death. People sometimes ignore or dismiss symptoms of a disease because they don't want to learn that they have it. Patients sometimes fail to take medications as prescribed because they want to believe they don't need it, that they're well, or that their doctor doesn't know as much about their body as they do. Physical harm also stems from an "it can't happen to me" attitude—e.g., not wearing a helmet while riding a motorcycle or not taking steps to prevent contracting AIDS or STDs. In one study, students expressed a high degree of confidence that they could determine whether someone was lying to them about risk-related sexual behavior. Despite their confidence, the students were poor lie detectors (Swann, Silvera, & Proske, 1995).

Fooling Others vs. Fooling One's Self

Earlier we noted that one's skill at deceiving others is greatly enhanced by convincing one's self that a lie is not being told. Self-deception, then, has evolved as a support system for the many goals of lying—ranging from taking advantage of others to strengthening social bonds. But some scholars believe that the more we engage in self-deception in order to fool others, the more damage we are likely to do to ourselves (Baron, 1988; Kipp, 1985). The fallout associated with a developing ease in deceiving one's self in order to deceive others, they argue, may be a corrosion of one's sense of responsibility for one's own beliefs, a deteriorating tendency to question and scrutinize one's own beliefs, and preventing the conscious mind from processing useful information.

Performance Gain vs. Performance Loss

Sometimes performers find it advantageous to develop a belief in their abilities which is not warranted by an objective assessment. They overestimate what they can accomplish in order to develop the confidence required to do it. Sometimes, however, this type of self-deception can backfire. For example, when performers expect to accomplish feats which are too far beyond their capabilities, they fail. This failure may then lead to self-doubts about one's abilities—doubts that were not there before. In addition, performers sometimes use a public forum to boast about their talent in an effort to convince themselves as well as others. When their subsequent performance doesn't match this boasting, they become less credible to others and, equally important, to themselves.

Courageous Decisions vs. Reckless Decisions

People sometimes do extraordinary things by not calculating or miscalculating the risks involved. Some brave and courageous actions would not occur if the actor carefully calculated the risks involved. Charging an armed airplane hijacker or defending a military position against 50–1 odds instead of retreating depends on misreading reality and one's vulnerability.

But the difference between a courageous decision and a reckless decision is not always easy to see. Trivers (2000, p. 124) concluded his analysis of human disasters by saying: "There can be little doubt that self-deception makes a disproportionate contribution to human disasters, especially in the form of misguided social policies, wars, being perhaps the most costly example. This is part of the large downside to human self-deception." An analysis of the cockpit conversation prior to an airplane crash that killed 78 people in Washington, D.C. revealed what Trivers and Newton (1982) said was a clear pattern of self-deception involving denial and rationalization about instrument readings as well as other signs of danger. Wrangham (1999) says military incompetence is often the result of self-deception associated with overconfidence, ignoring or downplaying intelligence reports, and wasting manpower. In her analysis of how leaders and governments have needlessly gone to war throughout history, Tuchman (1984) says "woodenheadedness" is the source of self-deception. Woodenheadedness consists of assessing a situation in terms of preconceived fixed notions while ignoring or rejecting any contrary signs. Decisions are based on what is wished for and contrary facts can't deflect or change these wishes.

The essays in Sternberg's *Why Smart People Can Be So Stupid* (2002) remind us that intelligence does not make us immune to reckless decisions associated with self-deception. Smart people, for example, may believe so strongly in their own intelligence that they find ways to immunize or isolate themselves from "less informed" versions of the truth or surround themselves with people willing to tell them only what they want to hear. Self-inflated beliefs about one's own knowledge can also lead to feelings of invulnerability which, in turn, may lead to reckless decisions. Because there are different kinds of intelligence, a person may be smart in some areas of life and not others. President Clinton, for example, demonstrated intelligence in many of life's domains, but not when it came to relationships with certain women.

Summary

Self-deception develops in a number of different ways and involves a variety of mental processes. With an expanded view of interpersonal deception, it is possible to see similar processes at work in self-deception. If, however, one's view of interpersonal deception is limited to a conscious, intentional effort to tell someone a "truth" that you know to be false, the analogy to self-deception becomes problematic. To understand self-deception, we need to imagine information that can be housed at different levels of mental awareness and to acknowledge that human beings can deceive themselves without conscious intent—often with the help of emotions. The condition that prompts self-deception is the presence of two contrary beliefs which invite biased processing. Self-deception is a social as well as psychological process because the responses of other people can greatly affect an individual's need to self-deceive and his or her ability to maintain it. Groupthink is a process in which the nature of social deliberations of group members facilitates self-deception among them.

We engage in self-deception in order: 1) to feel better by enhancing and/or protecting our self-concept; 2) to reduce cognitive dissonance; 3) to improve our ability to persuade and deceive others; 4) to withstand pain and to generally enhance our physical and mental health; and 5) to improve our chances in winning competitive contests. Human beings tend to be biased toward self-enhancement and self-consistency so when negative information is perceived as a threat to the self, one or more of these biases are activated to deal with the threat. If the threat persists and promises to do serious harm to one's self, arousal occurs and one or more self-defense mechanism is implemented. There are many self-defense mechanisms, but denial, rationalization, repression, dissociation, and projection are commonly associated with self-deception. The very notion of "civilization" has been described as a collective defense mechanism, but this claim is controversial. Each of these mental processes can affect the selection, treatment, and retrieval of information.

The chapter concluded with an examination of several areas in which self-deception is both advantageous as well as disadvantageous—depending on how often self-deception occurs, what problems are being masked, and the extent to which the self-deception is within the bounds of what society would call "normal." Thus, self-deception can lead to mental health or mental illness, physical well-being or physical affliction, improved skill in fooling others or improved skill in fooling one's self, performance gain or performance loss, and courageous decisions or reckless decisions.

Things to Think About

In face-to-face interaction, the word "suspicious" can be used to reflect one person's doubts or uncertainty about the truthfulness of another person. Once a person becomes suspicious, his or her behavior relative to the potential liar changes—e.g., increased attentiveness, less trust, etc. If the liar perceives suspicion on the part of the target, the liar will try to counteract it. Does suspicion play a role in *self-deception*? If so, how? If not, why not?

The focus of this chapter has been primarily limited to understanding self-deception in the context of intrapersonal and interpersonal communication. Is self-deception a concept that may also be applicable to large segments of society or society as a whole? Amélie Rorty (1996, p. 82) seems to think so. Read her statement and decide whether you agree or disagree with her? Use examples to support your position. "It is virtually impossible to imagine any society that does not systematically and actively promote the self-deception of its members, particularly when the requirements of social continuity and cohesion are subtly at odds with one another...Socially induced self-deception is an instrument in the preservation of social cooperation and cohesion."

References

Albrecht, G.L. & Devlieger, P.J. (1999). The disability paradox: High quality of life against all the odds. *Social Science & Medicine, 48,* 977–988.

Alloy, L.B. & Abramson, L.Y. (1979). Judgment of contingency in depressed and nondepressed students: Sadder but wiser? *Journal of Experimental Psychology: General, 108,* 441–485.

Ames, R.T. (1996). The classical Chinese self and hypocrisy. In R.T. Ames & W. Dissanayake (Eds.), *Self and deception: A cross-cultural philosophical enquiry* (pp. 219–240). Albany, N.Y.: State University of New York Press.

Ames, R.T. & Dissanayake, W. (Eds.) (1996). *Self and deception: A cross-cultural philosophical enquiry.* Albany, N.Y.: State University of New York Press.

Anderegg, W.R.L., Prall, J.W., Harold, J., & Schneider, S.H. (2010). Expert credibility in climate change. *Proceedings of the National Academy of Sciences of the United States of America, 107,* 12107–12109.

Aronson, E. (1997). The theory of cognitive dissonance: The evolution and vicissitudes of an idea. In C. McGarty & S.A. Haslam (Eds.), *The message of social psychology: Perspective on mind in society* (pp. 20–35). Oxford, UK: Blackwell.

Aronson, E. & Mills, J. (1959). The effect of severity of initiation on liking for a group. *Journal of Abnormal and Social Psychology, 59,* 177–181.

Bargh, J.A. (1996). Automaticity in social psychology. In E.T. Higgins & A.W. Kruglanski (Eds.) *Social psychology: Handbook of basic principles* (pp. 169–183). New York: Guilford.

Baron, M. (1988). What is wrong with self-deception. In B.P. McLaughlin & A.O. Rorty (Eds.) *Perspectives on self-deception* (pp. 431–449). Berkeley, CA.: University of California Press.

Baumeister, R.F. (1993). Lying to yourself: The enigma of self-deception. In M. Lewis & C. Saarni (Eds.), *Lying and deception in everyday life* (pp. 166–183). New York: Guilford.

Baumeister, R.F. (1998). The self. In D.T. Gilbert, S.T. Fiske, & G. Lindzey (Eds.) *The handbook of social psychology.* 4th ed. Vol. 1 (pp. 680–740). New York: McGraw-Hill.

Baumeister, R.F. & Scher, S.J. (1988). Self-defeating behavior patterns among normal individuals: Review and analysis of common self-destructive tendencies. *Psychological Bulletin, 104,* 3–22.

Becker, E. (1973). *The denial of death.* New York: Free Press.

Biais, B. & Weber, M. (2009). Hindsight bias, risk perception, and investment performance. *Management Science, 55,* 1018–1029.

Cassar, G. & Craig, J. (2009). An investigation of hindsight bias in nascent venture activity. *Journal of Business Venturing, 24,* 149–164

Chanowitz, B. & Langer, E.J. (1985). Self-protection and self-inception. In M. Martin (Ed.) *Self-deception and self-understanding* (pp. 117–135). Lawrence, KS.: University Press of Kansas.

Descartes, R. (1641/2010). *Meditations on first philosophy* (7th Ed.). New York: Watchmaker Publishing.

Deutsch, E. (1996). Self-deception: A comparative study. . In R.T. Ames & W. Dissanayake (Eds.), *Self and deception: A cross-cultural philosophical enquiry* (pp. 315–326). Albany, N.Y.: State University of New York Press.

Essock, S.M., McGuire, M.T., & Hooper, B. (1988). Self-deception in social-support networks. In J.S. Lockard & D.L. Paulhus (Eds.), *Self-deception: An adaptive mechanism?* (pp. 200–211). Englewood Cliffs, N. J.: Prentice-Hall.

Farhi, P. (2015, Feb. 4). Brian Williams admits that his story of coming under fire while in Iraq was false. The Washington Post. Retrieved from http://www.washingtonpost.com /lifestyle/style/2015/02/04/.

Festinger, L. (1957). *A theory of cognitive dissonance.* Evanston, IL.: Row, Peterson.

Fingarette, H. (1969). *Self-deception.* New York: Humanities Press.

Fischoff, B. (1975). Hindsight does not equal foresight: The effect of outcome knowledge on judgement under uncertainty. *Journal of Experimental Psychology: Human Perception and Performance, 1,* 288–299.

Fonda, J. (2005). *My life so far.* New York: Random House.

Ford, C.V. (1996). *Lies! Lies!! Lies!!! The psychology of deceit.* Washington, D.C.: American Psychiatric Press.

Ghobarah, H.A., Huth, P., & Russett, B. (2004). Comparative public health: The political economy of human misery and well-being. *International Studies Quarterly, 48,* 73–94.

Gilbert, D.T. & Cooper, J. (1985). Social psychological strategies of self-deception. In M. Martin (Ed.) *Self-deception and self-understanding* (pp. 75–94). Lawrence, KS.: University Press of Kansas.

Gilovich, T. (1991). *How we know what isn't so.* New York: Macmillan.

Goleman, D. (1985). *Vital lies, simple truths: The psychology of self-deception.* New York: Simon & Shuster.

Gur, R.C., & Sackeim, H.A. (1979). Self-deception: A concept in search of a phenomenon. *Journal of Personality and Social Psychology, 37,* 147–169.

Haidt, J. (2001). The emotional dog and its rational tail: A social intuitionist approach to moral judgment. *Psychological Review, 108,* 814–834.

Haidt, J. (2011). *The righteous mind: Why good people are divided by politics and religion.* New York: Pantheon Books.

Halliburton, S. (June 27, 2004). The will to win no. 6. *Austin American Statesman,* A1, A13.

Hart, P.'t , Stern, E.K., & Sundelius, B. (Eds.),(1997). *Beyond groupthink: Political group dynamics and foreign policy-making.* Ann Arbor, MI.: University of Michigan Press.

Hartung, J. (1988). Deceiving down: Conjectures on the management of subordinate status. In J.S. Lockard & D.L. Paulhus (Eds.), *Self-deception: An adaptive mechanism?* (pp. 170–185). Englewood Cliffs, N. J.: Prentice-Hall.

Hastorf, A.H., & Cantril, H. (1954). They saw a game: A case study. *The Journal of Abnormal and Social Psychology, 49,* 129–134.

Janis, I.L. (1983). *Groupthink: Psychological studies of policy decisions and fiascoes.* 2nd Ed. Boston: Houghton Mifflin.

Kassin, S.M. (2005). On the psychology of confessions: Does innocence put innocents at risk? *American Psychologist, 60,* 215–228.

Keetels, M. & Vroomen, J. (2012). Perception of synchrony between the senses. In M.M. Murray and M.T. Wallace (Eds.), *The neural bases of multisensory processes* (pp. 147–178). London: Taylor & Francis Group. Kinsley, M. (December 17, 2001). In defense of denial. *Time,* 72–73.

Kipp, D. (1985). Self-deception, inauthenticity, and weakness of will. In M. Martin (Ed.) *Self-deception and self-understanding* (pp. 261–283). Lawrence, KS.: University Press of Kansas.

Kruger, J. & Dunning, D. (1999). Unskilled and unaware of it: How difficulties in recognizing one's own incompetence lead to inflated self-assessments. *Journal of Personality and Social Psychology, 77,* 1121–1134.

Langer, E.J. (1978). Rethinking the role of thought in social interaction. In J.H. Harvey, W. Ickes, and R.F. Kidd (Eds.), *New directions in attribution research* (pp. 35–58) vol. 2. Hillsdale, N.J.: Erlbaum.

Lewis, J.M. (2004). How much self-deception helps? *Psychiatric Times, 21,* 35–37.

Lockard, J.S. & Paulhus, D.L. (Eds.) (1988). *Self-deception: An adaptive mechanism?* Englewood Cliffs, N.J.: Prentice-Hall.

Martin, M.W. (Ed.) (1985). *Self-deception and self-understanding.* Lawrence, KS.: University Press of Kansas.

McClellan, S. (2008). *What happened: Inside the Bush White House and Washington's culture of deception.* New York: PublicAffairs.

McLaughlin, B.P. (1988). Exploring the possibility of self-deception in belief. In B.P. McLauglin & A.O. Rorty (Eds.) *Perspectives on self-deception* (pp. 29–62). Berkeley, CA.: University of California Press.

McLauglin, B.P. & Rorty, A.O. (Eds.), (1988). *Perspectives on self-deception.* Berkeley, CA.: University of California Press.

Mele, A.R. (2001). *Self-deception unmasked.* Princeton, N.J.: Princeton University Press.

Murray, S.L. & Holmes, J.G. (1996). The construction of relationship realities. In G.J.O. Fletcher & J. Fitness (Eds.), *Knowledge structures in close relationships: A social psychological approach* (pp. 91–120). Mahwah, N.J.: Erlbaum.

Newman, L.S. (1999). Motivated cognition and self-deception. *Psychological Inquiry, 10,* 59–63.Nyberg, D. (1993). *The varnished truth: Truth telling and deceiving in ordinary life.* Chicago, IL.: University of Chicago Press.

Norgaard, K.M. (2010). *Cognitive and behavioral challenges in responding to climate change.* The World Bank Development Economics and World Development Report Team.

Offer, D., Kaiz, M., Howard, K. I. , Bennett, E.S. (2000). The altering of reported experiences. *Journal of the American Academy of Child & Adolescent Psychiatry, 39,* 735–742.

Patten, D. (2003). How do we deceive ourselves? *Philosophical Psychology, 16,* 229–246.

Paulhus, , D.L., & Suedfeld, P. (1988). A dynamic complexity model of self-deception. In J.S. Lockard & D.L. Paulhus (Eds.), *Self-deception: An adaptive mechanism?* (pp. 132–145). Albany, N.Y.: State University of New York Press.

Rorty, A.O. (1975). Adaptivity and self-knowledge. *Inquiry, 18,* 22.

Rorty, A.O. (1996). User-friendly self-deception: A traveler's manual. . In R.T. Ames & W. Dissanayake (Eds.), *Self and deception: A cross-cultural philosophical enquiry* (pp. 73–89). Albany, N.Y.: State University of New York Press.

Ross, M., & Wilson, A.E. (2000). Constructing and appraising past selves. In D.L. Schacter (Ed.), *Memory, brain, and belief* (pp. 231–258). Cambridge, MA: Harvard University Press.

Routledge, C., Arndt, J., Wildschut, T., Sedikides, C., Hart, C.M., et al. (2011). The past makes the present meaningful: Nostalgia as an existential resource. *Journal of Personality and Social Psychology, 101,* 638–652.

Sackeim, H.A. (1988). Self-deception: A synthesis. In J.S. Lockard & D.L. Paulhus (Eds.), *Self-deception: An adaptive mechanism?* (pp. 146–165). Englewood Cliffs, N. J.: Prentice-Hall.

Sanford, D.H. (1988). Self-deception as rationalization. In B.P. McLaughlin & A.O. Rorty (Eds.) *Perspectives on self-deception* (pp. 157–169). Berkeley, CA.: University of California Press.

Schermer, M. (2012). *The believing brain: From ghosts and gods to politics and conspiracies—How we construct beliefs and reinforce them as truths.* New York: St. Martin's Griffin.

Smith, D.L. (2004). *Why we lie: The evolutionary roots of deception and the unconscious mind.* New York: St. Martin's Press.

Snyder, C.R. (1985). Collaborative companions: The relationship of self-deception and excuse making. In M. Martin (Ed.) *Self-deception and self-understanding* (pp. 35–51). Lawrence, KS.: University Press of Kansas.

Starek, J.E., & Keating, C.F. (1991). Self-deception and its relationship to success in competition. *Basic and Applied Social Psychology, 12,* 145–155.

Steele, C.M. (1988). The psychology of self-affirmation: Sustaining the integrity of the self. In L. Berkowitz (Ed.), *Advances in experimental psychology, vol. 21* (pp. 261–302). New York: Academic Press.

Sternberg, R.J. (Ed.), (2002). *Why smart people can be so stupid.* New Haven, CT.: Yale University Press.

Stone, J., Aronson, E., Crain, A.L., Winslow, M.P., & Fried, C.B. (1994). Inducing hypocrisy as a means of encouraging young adults to use condoms. *Personality and Social Psychology Bulletin, 20,* 116–128.

Sullivan, E. (2001). *The concise book of lying.* New York: Farrar, Straus and Giroux.

Swann, W.B., Jr., Silvera, D.H., & Proske, C.U. (1995). On "knowing your partner": Dangerous illusions in the age of AIDS? *Personal Relationships, 2,* 173–186.

Tavris, C. & Aronson, E. (2007). *Mistakes were made (but not by me): Why we justify foolish beliefs, bad decisions, and hurtful acts.* New York: Harcourt.

Taylor, S.E. (1989). *Positive illusions: Creative self-deception and the healthy mind.* New York: Basic Books.

Taylor, S.E. & Brown, J.D. (1988). Illusion and well-being: A social psychological perspective on mental health. *Psychological Bulletin, 103,* 193–210.

Taylor, S.E., Kemeny, M.E., Aspinwall, L.G., Schneider, S.G., Rodriguez, R. & Herbert, M. (1992). Optimism, coping, psychological distress, and high-risk sexual behavior among men at risk for acquired immunodeficiency syndrome (AIDS). *Journal of Personality and Social Psychology, 63,* 460–473.)

Trivers, R. (2000). The elements of a scientific theory of self-deception. *Annals of the New York Academy of Sciences, 907,* 114–131.

Trivers, R. (2011). *The folly of fools: The logic of deceit and self-deception in human life.* New York: Basic Books.

Trivers, R. & Newton, H.P. (1983, November) The crash of flight 90: Doomed by self-deception? *Science Digest,* 66–67, 111.

Tuchman, B.W. (1984). *The march of folly: From Troy to Vietnam.* New York: Knopf.

Twerski, A.J. (1997). *Addictive thinking: Understanding self-deception.* 2nd ed. Center City, MN.: Hazelden.

Vahinger, H. (1925). *The philosophy of "as-if," a system of the theoretical, practical, and religious fictions of mankind.* New York: Harcourt Brace.

Von Hippel, W., & Trivers, R. (2011). The evolution and psychology of self-deception. *Behavioral and Brain Sciences, 34,* 1–56.

Wegner, D.M. (1989). *White bears and other unwanted thoughts: Suppression, obsession, and the psychology of mental control.* New York: Penguin Books.

Wegner, D.M. (2003). *The illusion of free will.* Cambridge, MA: MIT Press.

Wegner, D.M. & Bargh, J.A. (1998). Control and automaticity in social life. In D.T. Gilbert, S.T. Fiske, & G. Lindzey (Eds.) *The handbook of social psychology.* 4th ed. Vol. 1 (pp. 446–496). New York: McGraw-Hill.

Welles, J.F. (1988). Societal roles in self-deception. In J.S. Lockard & D.L. Paulhus (Eds.), *Self-deception: An adaptive mechanism?* (pp. 54–70). Englewood Cliffs, N. J.: Prentice-Hall.

Werth, L.F. & Flaherty, J. (1986). A phenomenological approach to human deception. In R.W. Mitchell & N.S. Thompson, Eds., *Deception: Perspectives on human and nonhuman deceit* (pp. 293–311). Albany, N.Y.: State University of New York Press.

Westerhoff, J.C. (2011). *Reality: A very short introduction.* Oxford, UK: Oxford University Press.

Whittaker-Bleuler, S.A. (1988). Deception and self-deception: A dominance strategy in competitive sport. In J.S. Lockard & D.L. Paulhus (Eds.), *Self-deception: An adaptive mechanism?* (pp. 212–228). Englewood Cliffs, N. J.: Prentice-Hall.

Wrangham, R. (1999). Is military incompetence adaptive? *Evolution and Human Behavior, 20,* 3–12.

Chapter 7

Performing Lies and Deceit

Let's pretend you rubbed a magic lantern and a genie agreed to grant you a wish. Your wish was to know what behavior people exhibit when they are not telling the truth. This wish, which also happens to be the focus of this chapter, has been intensely scrutinized by scientists for the last 30 years. From this research we have learned some important things about the way liars and deceivers behave, but it has also made us realize how difficult it will be to provide a simple answer to this question—genie or not.

It should also be noted that some people do not wish to know if there are behaviors which unerringly signal deception. These people point out that our burning desire to reliably read behavioral clues of deception *in others* cools off considerably if it also means we will be unable to hide *our own* fabrications. And despite our eagerness to spot liar behavior in some instances, there are other times when we'd rather not know. Our current knowledge base should satisfy everyone. It identifies some commonly manifested liar behaviors that occur under certain circumstances, but there is no invariable list of behavior which would expose liars in all situations. In fact, there are a number of good reasons to believe that not even a genie will be able to provide us with a foolproof list of behaviors which always signal lying and deception.

Difficulties In Identifying Liar Behavior

The following reasons act as stumbling blocks when we search for observable behaviors that reliably occur during acts of lying and/or deception.

> "Never reach a final conclusion about whether a suspect is lying or not based solely on your interpretation of behavioral clues to deceit. Behavioral clues to deceit should only serve to alert you to the need for further information and investigation."
>
> — *Paul Ekman*

"Figures often beguile me, particularly when I have the arranging of them myself; in which case the remark attributed to Disraeli would often apply with justice and force: "There are three kinds of lies: lies, damned lies and statistics."

— *Mark Twain*

Determining What the Observed Behavior Really Means

The behaviors people exhibit when they are lying are not behaviors associated with lying and nothing else. Liars may manifest various nervous mannerisms, but nervous mannerisms are also a sign of anxiety—an emotion that both liars and truth tellers experience. Ekman (2000, p. 80) says, "There is no sign of deceit itself—no gesture, facial expression, or muscle twitch that in and of itself means that a person is lying. There are only clues that the person is poorly prepared and clues of emotions that don't fit the person's line." He goes on to say that many behavioral clues to deceit are signs of more than one emotion and may occur with truth tellers as well. For example, liars may sweat and swallow frequently due to fear or guilt, but truth tellers may also exhibit these behaviors if they are distressed and/or angry at being unfairly accused of lying. Some truth tellers, like some liars, are uncomfortable in social situations and, like liars, tend to take longer before responding, use indirect speech, and/or give brief replies to questions. We also need to remember that the absence of some behavior that we know liars often exhibit in certain circumstances does not necessarily mean that truth telling is taking place. The communicator may just be adept at masking certain behaviors.

Prevalent Stereotypes about How Liars Behave

Although scientific research has not identified any verbal or nonverbal behaviors unique to deception (see Chapter 9), there are nonetheless common stereotypes about liar behavior many people believe despite the lack of evidence. Several studies have found high consistency in people's stereotypes about liar behavior across different ages, professions (teachers, managers, police officers, criminals, etc.), and cultures (Castillo & Mallard, 2012; Granhag, Andersson, Stromwall, & Hartwig, 2004; Hurley, Griffin, & Stefanone, 2014; Vrij, Akehurst, & Knight, 2006). For example, a survey conducted in 63 different countries found strong cross-cultural agreement in terms of the cues people perceived as useful in distinguish deceptive from honest messages. These stereotypical cues are summarized in Figure 7.1.

If these stereotypes do not reflect the way liars really behave, how do they arise in the first place? There are several different sources for people's false beliefs about deception. First, the stereotypes reflect social norms about lying that are more prescriptive than descriptive (Bond & DePaulo, 2006). Across cultures, people are socialized to believe lying is generally the wrong thing to do and to feel shame when they do it. As a result, the cultural undesirability of lying is equated with communication behaviors perceived as undesirable or flawed (low eye contact, stuttering, nervous demeanor, inconsistent stories, etc.). Second, the stereotypes are

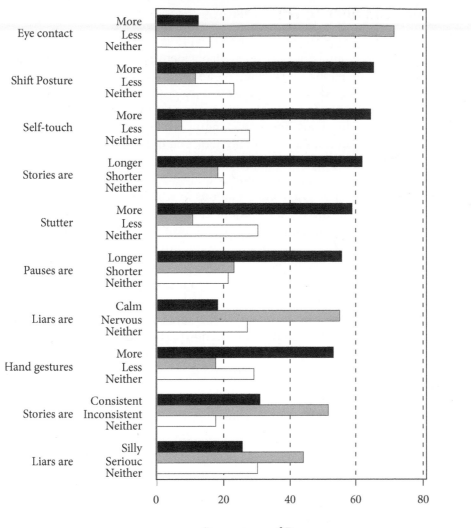

From Journal of Cross-Cultural Psychology, Volume 37, Issue 1, Pages 60–74 (January 2006). "A World of Lies" by The Global Deception Research Team. Copyright © 2006 by SAGE Publications. Reprinted by permission.

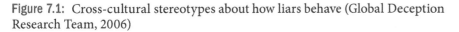

Percentage of Responses

Figure 7.1: Cross-cultural stereotypes about how liars behave (Global Deception Research Team, 2006)

communicated to us and reinforced by family members, friends, and others in our social networks, all of whom were socialized to believe these stereotypes too. Third, mass media messages about deception disseminated by popular TV shows (e.g., *Lie to Me*), news reports, and Internet commentary are permeated with these stereotypes, leading consumers to put faith in false deception clues (Hurley et al., 2014). A fourth source is confirmation bias—i.e., the human tendency to seek out and interpret new information that confirms our prior beliefs (see Chapter 6). While many people who believe stereotypes about lying behavior claim they are consistent with their past experience in successfully spotting liars (Castillo & Mallard, 2012), in all likelihood they are selectively remembering times when the stereotypes were confirmed but forgetting other times when they were disconfirmed. Confirmation bias is the chief mechanism by which stereotypes about behaviors such as lying and stereotypes about traits (age, gender, race, etc.) become entrenched in people's beliefs and attitudes (Aronson & McGlone, 2008).

Competent Liars Alter Their Behavior

In previous chapters, the point was made that lying is a survival skill. If scientists should uncover certain behaviors that reliably identify liars, this information will eventually become public knowledge. As a result, competent liars are likely to avoid the behavior in question, mask it, or create distractions so it won't be seen. Then it will no longer be a reliable sign of deceit. One example of this may have occurred with eye behavior. The long-standing, widespread, and well-known belief in the United States that "a liar will not look you in the eyes" is not a behavior *typically* manifested by liars (DePaulo et al., 2003). We also know that when people want to control their behavior, some are capable of exerting a remarkable amount of control. After polygraph examinations in which people were correctly identified as lying 88% of the time, Corcoran et al. (1978) taught people how to control their galvanic skin response and arousal level through biofeedback and relaxation training. Subsequent polygraph examinations detected lies told by these people at a rate of only 24%. With practice and/or self deception, some people are quite capable of controlling their overt behavior so it looks natural and spontaneous. Vallacher and Wegner (1985) say that people who are practiced at impressing others can coordinate numerous individual behaviors by relying on a broad goal ("I intend to make a good impression") which requires the coordination of numerous individual behaviors (smile, nod, shake hands, etc.). This removes the need to consciously attend to each separate behavior and facilitates a fluid performance.

On the other hand, the continued search for a profile of liar behavior recognizes that some human behaviors are far less subject to voluntary control than others and that these behaviors may provide clues to deception—especially with novice liars and in situations where the stakes are perceived to be high. As DePaulo et al. (2003, p. 78) says: " It is possible, for example, that people's attempts not to sound anxious would result in an even higher pitched and anxious sounding tone of voice than would have resulted if they had not deliberately tried to quiet the sounds of their insecurity." We also know that liars can't always control the many behaviors they want to control. Without practice, communicators may be as inept as a person first learning how to ride a bicycle—awkwardly trying to consciously control and coordinate a variety of individual behaviors. Long and complex messages and/or intense interrogations can make complete and undetectable control even more difficult (Wegner & Bargh, 1998). When liars are not able to effectively control their behavior, they communicate what Ekman and Friesen (1969) call leakage clues (behavior that mistakenly reveals the truth) or *deception clues* (behavior which suggests a person is lying without revealing the truth). Of course people try to exert control over their behavior for reasons other than to deceive, so deception should only become an issue when we suspect the controlled behavior is being done with the intent to deceive.

Liar Behavior May Vary as Circumstances Change

There are many aspects of the circumstances within which a person lies or deceives that may affect the kind of behavior he or she exhibits. Examples of this include: 1) the extent to which deception is expected or not; 2) the perceived consequences of deceptive success and failure; 3) the relationship and involvement of the deceiver with the target of the deception; and 4) the medium by which the liar communicates with the target.

Expectations

Situations vary with regard to whether lies are expected or not. Misleading signals given by poker or basketball players are expected and part of the game. Many people are on guard for deceptive behavior during the process of examining and purchasing a used car. On the other hand, the expectation that friends and lovers will lie to you about important things is much lower. In some situations lies are not normally expected, but when they occur it is not shocking. The point is that these different expectations have the power to influence how liars feel about their lies and how they enact them.

Consequences

Most lies we tell during the course of our daily activities do not have "major" consequences. The stakes are low. You may not even care what happens if your lie is discovered by a person who already dislikes you. But the stakes can be much higher and discovery may mean going to prison, getting a divorce, or even causing death. You would not expect to observe the same type of liar behavior when a person tells a friend that they had a nice time at their party (when they didn't) and when they tell their terrorist captors that they aren't a U.S. citizen (when they are).

Audience or Target

Who is the target of the lie? Liars may display one cluster of verbal and nonverbal behavior with people who do not know them and who have no previous interaction history with them and another cluster with those who know them better. Is there one target or many? Politicians who stretch the truth with voters have to adapt their messages and behaviors to multiple audiences (see Chapter 11). Bond et al. (2004) wanted to find out how communicators behaved when confronted with two different targets who had previously been told two different stories by the communicator. Students described how they felt about one of their teachers in front of two peers—one of whom the communicator had privately described his or her true feelings for the teacher and one of whom had been privately told the exact opposite story. In the presence of these two people who had heard very different opinions from the same person, some student communicators were instructed to tell the truth and some were not. It didn't seem to matter. In this awkward situation, the communicator seemed deceptive whether he or she was telling the truth or not. Truth tellers and liars both revealed their discomfort through equivocal, vague, and dysfluent speech.

The behavior exhibited by the target is also a factor which may influence a liar's behavior. White and Burgoon (2001) found that deceivers were less responsive than truth tellers when their interaction partner became more or less involved in the conversation. Sometimes interaction partners can inadvertently facilitate the performance of a liar—e.g., finishing his or her sentence when the liar seems to be having trouble finding the right words or attributing their partner's anxious behavior to some past event. On other occasions, though, an interaction partner can make lying (or truth telling) more difficult. For example, a liar or truth teller may change his or her behavior when a partner acts suspiciously. Sometimes the result of this changed behavior is to make speakers appear more deceptive—whether they are or not (Bond & Fahey, 1987; Burgoon et al., 1996). Different manifestations of suspicion (e.g., a furrowed brow vs. intense and persistent questioning) are also likely to elicit different responses. Needless to say, the demands for adaptation and the effects of mutual influence that occur in ongoing interactions are bound to affect the nature of a liar's behavioral profile (Buller & Burgoon, 1996).

Communication Medium

One of the most striking cultural and social changes in recent decades has been the revolution in the ways people communicate. Until the 1990s, humans were confined to communicating face to face and through letters and the traditional landline phone. Computer and smartphone use has dramatically accelerated in the last 30 years. According to a 2014 Gallup poll, texting, cellphones, and e-mail are the most commonly used non-face-to-face modes of communication; approximately 4 in 10 respondents reporting using each of these media "a lot" on the day prior to taking the survey. Use of social media came in as a close fourth. Does the communication medium people are using affect how and when they lie?

Hancock, Thom-Santelli, and Ritchie (2004) identified 3 features that can moderate the incidence of deception in different media. The first is the "distribution" of the message sender and receiver permitted by the medium in physical space. Only face-to-face communication requires close physical proximity; other media allow the sender and receiver to be distant or "distributed." The second is the "synchronicity" of the interaction—i.e., the degree to which messages are exchanged instantaneously and in real-time. Face-to-face communication is always synchronous and phone communication often is (except for the exchange of voice mail messages), but texting and e-mail are asynchronous because people read and reply to them after a time delay. The third is the "recordability" of the medium, the degree to which the interaction is automatically documented. Texting and e-mail are automatically recorded during the exchange of messages, but face-to-face and phone communication are not recorded unless the sender or receiver makes extra effort to do so. Hancock et al. hypothesized that different combinations of these features affect the frequency with which people lie in different media. Specifically, they predicted lying should occur most frequently to the extent the medium is distributed (because there are few nonverbal clues to reveal a liar's deceit) and synchronous (because most lies emerge spontaneously from conversation) but less recordable (because liar's are hesitant to leave a record of their deceit).

To test this hypothesis, Hancock et al. asked a group of college students to keep a diary of all their social communications for a week, including how often they lied. The rate of deception was calculated by dividing the number of lies by the number of social communications. On average, participants engaged in 6.11 social communications daily and lied 1.6 times per day, meaning that about 26% of the reported social communications involved a lie. The rate of reported lying by communication medium (face to face, telephone, instant messaging, and e-mail) is presented in Figure 7.2. As the researchers predicted, the highest rate of reported lying occurred on the telephone, a synchronous/distributed/less recordable medium.

Many of the lies respondents reported producing on the phone were spontaneous responses to an unexpected question, such as "Did you like the dress I wore to the party last night?" The lowest rate occurred via e-mail, an asynchronous/distributed/more recordable medium. Note, however, they also found a positive correlation between frequency of e-mail use and the lying rate in this medium (r = .43), suggesting increased experience with this communication technology increased the lying rate. No such correlation was found in the instant messaging medium, perhaps because this technology was still relatively new when the study was conducted in 2004.

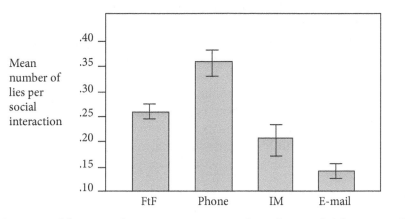

From Proceedings of CHI, 2004, Pages 129–134. "Deception and design: the impact of communication technology on lying behavior" by Hancock et al. Copyright © 2004 Association for Computing Machinery, Inc. Reprinted by permission.

Figure 7.2: Rates of deception by communication medium (Hancock, Thom-Santelli, & Ritchie, 2004)

The different rates of reported lying Hancock et al. observed in various communication media suggest people should have different expectations about the likelihood of being lied to depending on the channel by which they communicate with someone else. They also suggest specific design features of a particular medium can be used to influence lying rates. For example, if the objective in a given situation is to reduce overall deception during communication (e.g., to promote trust in financial transactions), an asynchronous and recordable medium like e-mail would be most desirable. Also, technologies supporting information about distributed communicators' physical context, such as videoconferencing, should reduce deception by reinstating some cues that would occur if the communicators were physically copresent in the same location. On the other hand, if one's goal were to facilitate deception (business fraud, espionage, etc.), a synchronous and less recordable medium like the telephone would be more desirable.

The Motivation and Motives for Lying May Affect Liar Behavior

Sometimes liars are especially concerned about "getting away with" their lie. As a result they may think a lot about how to succeed and how to fool the target. These liars are highly motivated and are determined not to get caught. For those who are socially skilled, those who are experienced liars, and those who have few qualms about lying, this heightened motivation may help them lie without emitting any obvious signs of deception. Burgoon and Floyd (2000) found that motivation sometimes enhances performance of verbal and nonverbal behavior. A strong desire to succeed may help these liars control their verbal and nonverbal behavior, but many liars experience what DePaulo et al. (1988) call a "motivational impairment"—i.e., trying very hard to manage their behavior and worrying about whether they can. As a result, they are especially likely to reveal their deception through various nonverbal signals, including facial expressions. By trying to shut down certain behaviors they think will expose them, they overcompensate and appear too rigid and inhibited. For example, a person who doesn't want to signal their deception by looking away from their interaction partner too much may end up staring at them. In this case, too much eye gaze is just as much a sign to the target that "something's not right" as too little eye gaze would be.

Liars also lie for different reasons. Any given motive for lying may be more or less troubling to the liar, easier or more difficult to accomplish, or in some other way able to affect the verbal and nonverbal behavior which accompanies it. The reasons adults lie are very similar to the reasons identified for children in Chapter 5. Most lies are told for the sole benefit of the liar, but motives are complex. There may be several reasons why a person lies and the liar may not be aware of all the reasons. A woman who lies to her husband about her affair may think her primary reason for doing so is to save their marriage and avoid hurting her husband and her child. She may let herself be only faintly aware that she is also trying to avoid the scorn of her husband and the possibility of losing her marriage, lifestyle, child, and some friends.

The main reasons adults lie are:

- *To Avoid Punishment.* High-stakes lies are often told to avoid being punished for a misdeed. Lying is especially likely to occur when the liar perceives that the punishment for telling the truth will be as great as the punishment for lying.

- *To Protect Oneself from Harm.* These lies are not designed to protect against punishment that might result from the revelation of a misdeed. Instead, they are intended to cope with situations where people anticipate or are actually threatened with harm.

- *To Obtain a Reward for Oneself.* A few of the many things people regularly try to obtain through deceit include: a job, sex, money, and a good grade in school.

- *To Protect or Help Another Person.* Lies told to help others are especially likely when the lie will also help, or at least not hurt, the liar.

- *To Win Admiration from Others.* The desire to make a positive impression on others is a common motive for lying. It may be especially strong for individuals who generally place a high value on the opinions of others or for most people in situations where the opinion of others is highly influential to the achievement of a goal.

- *To Get Out of an Awkward or Embarrassing Social Situation.* Lies are told to avoid conflict and as excuses for behavior the liar prefers to engage in. These lies are not "expected" but certainly "understood" and often viewed as benign. The target of the lie may not be interested in sanctioning the liar even if the lie is later exposed.

- *To Maintain Privacy.* Some lies are told in order to keep a part of one's personal identity from being known to others.

- *To Exercise Power Over Others.* Oppressors and the people they oppress both know the value of controlling information as a way of gaining or maintaining power. Guards and their prisoners as well as children and their parents tell lies for this reason.

- *To Fulfill Social Expectations.* These everyday lies involve politeness routines, compliments, and any other socially "authorized" lie.

- *To Have Fun.* Some lies are undertaken in the name of sport. The ones which require exposure to be enjoyed are sufficiently different than actual lying that their status as a real lie is questionable. April Fool's Day jokes and practical jokes (like feigning symptoms of a disease in front of a person who recently completed a nursing program) are examples of "put-ons" which are temporary in nature (Stebbins, 1975). But the lies told by the character Alice in the movie *Closer* did not depend on their revelation to be enjoyed. As she said, "Lying is the most fun a girl can have without taking her clothes off." The feeling of enjoyment associated with these lies can be intensified when the target is hard to fool and when the deceptive performance is known and observed by others. Facial expressions will sometimes reveal the fun these liars are having. Ekman (2000) calls such expressions "duping delight."

Although any of the aforementioned reasons might prompt adults to lie, it is important to note that none of these motives are unique to deception. For example, someone motivated to maintain her privacy could accomplish this goal through deception (e.g., giving a fake name and phone number to a stranger she met at a bar) or through honesty (e.g., telling the stranger she doesn't want to share her contact information). Thus, deception is better thought of as a potential strategy for fulfilling a motive than a desired end in itself (Levine & Kim, 2008). In general, people will not resort to deception to fulfill a motive unless the truth poses an obstacle. Levine, Kim, and Hamel (2010) asked people what they would say to others in common situations where the motive to deceive was varied by making the truth problematic or not for goal attainment. For example, participants were asked how they would respond to a dinner host who had just served a meal and then asked if they liked the food. When participants were further told to imagine they had really enjoyed the meal, they all said they would honestly report this opinion to the host. But when they imagined the food was not enjoyable, the majority (62.5%) opted for a deceptive message rather than convey a truth that might hurt the host's feelings.

The Type of Lie Told May Affect Liar Behavior

The two primary types of lies are:

- *Falsifying.* Falsification means the liar is actively trying to create a false belief within the target or support a false belief the target already believes.

- *Concealing.* Here the liar is hiding or withholding true information or feelings. Sometimes this occurs when a person decides not to provide information to a person who is known to have a false belief.

Attributions of lying and deception may also be leveled at "*misleading*" behavior, too, but as the latter part of this chapter explains, misleading behavior regularly occurs without any deceptive intent on the part of the communicator. Since the goal of creating a false belief in the target is not an inherent feature of this behavior, it is not considered a fundamental form of lying. Nevertheless, when people do feel they have been misled by such things as half-truths, indirect speech, equivocation, and distortion, they won't hesitate to label the communicator as a liar.

There appear to be some behaviors which characterize each type of lie, but none that characterize all types of lies (Buller & Burgoon, 1996; Buller et al., 1994; Ebesu & Miller, 1994). However, Frank and Ekman (2004) argue there may be behavioral consistency within certain types of lies. They found consistent facial, body, and paralinguistic behaviors with falsifications rendered in two different types of high-stakes lies. In one, the liars were giving a false opinion and in the other they were lying about taking money from a briefcase.

Lies in everyday life sometimes involve several different types. A lie may be made up of some information that is falsified, some that is misleading, and some that is concealed. In cases like this, whatever behaviors that might be associated with one type of lie would be combined in some manner. Furthermore, the behavior associated with types of lies would be expected to vary depending on whether the lie is executed spontaneously or is planned; whether the subject matter is simple or complex; whether the lie requires short or long responses; whether the lie and/or parts of the lie need to be repeated in different contexts or whether it is limited to a single performance.

Given the many ways lies can be produced, what types of lies have been studied? This is an important question because it has a direct bearing on what we claim to know about liar behavior. In their review of approximately 120 studies designed to identify liar behavior, DePaulo et al. (2003) found:

- 86% of the studies involved liars and targets who were strangers
- 84% of the studies involved students
- 57% gave no motivation to liars for telling a successful lie
- Most studies did not report on the duration of the lies, but of the 36 that did, 28 were one minute or less in duration
- Full interaction was present in only 8 studies
- About an equal number of studies involved prepared and spontaneous messages
- 60 studies involved lies about attitudes, facts, or perceptions of visual materials and 21 involved lies about transgressions.

It would seem, then, that the lie we know the most about is one involving a student who, with no motivation to succeed, tells on one occasion, a brief lie which does not deal with a transgression to a stranger in the absence of any interaction. This doesn't mean this kind of data isn't informative nor does it mean that we don't know anything about other types of lies. It just means we need to be cautious about generalizing. Too often people want to take the findings from a particular study with a particular set of conditions and draw some sweeping conclusion about lying behavior in general. And they shouldn't.

Low-Stakes Lies

Most of the lies we tell do not have serious consequences. Some are even an expected part of everyday conversation. These are called low-stakes lies because there isn't much to be gained by successfully lying and there isn't much to be lost if the lie is unsuccessful. It is true, however, that almost any lie, no matter how trivial it may seem, will offend some people. In addition, any lie which was initially treated as trivial can be transformed into a lie of great consequence when a positive relationship turns sour. Low-stakes lies are mostly told for one's personal benefit—to improve one's image, to feel better, to protect oneself from embarrassment, hurt, or disapproval, etc. We tell such lies to everyone, but more often to people we don't know all that well. These lies occur frequently. In one study, students reported lying once in every three interactions they had (DePaulo & Kashy, 1998). Low-stakes lies are also communicated via technology because it eliminates some difficulties liars feel when the target is in his or her presence. Phone contact eliminates visual contact and text messaging on cell phones, email, and computer chat rooms reduce the presence of the other to a minimum. Under these conditions, lying may be easier to enact and it may even make the liar feel less culpable for the lie (Hancock et al., 2004).

Studies that ask students to lie to a video camera by giving a false name, false biographical information, or falsely stating they saw a picture of a landscape instead of an automobile accident qualify as low-stakes lies—especially if there is no punishment and the reward of extra credit in their college course is given no matter how they perform.

The differences between behaviors of liars and truth tellers in many everyday low-stakes lies are barely discernible, if at all. They involve little stress, little emotion, and the amount of thought involved is minimal. DePaulo et al. (2003, p. 81) said, "…ordinary people are so practiced, so proficient, and so emotionally unfazed by the telling of untruths that they can be regarded as professional liars." Ekman (2000, p. 162) echoed this sentiment when he said, "Most liars can fool most people most of the time."

Low-stakes lies occur in a variety of situations. To illustrate the ubiquity of these lies, let's examine them in everyday conversation, in self-presentation, in efforts to attract a romantic partner, in flattery and ingratiation, in sports, games, magic, and in the workplace.

Everyday Conversation

Low-stakes lies infiltrate our compliments, invitations, requests, excuses, complaints, offers, and assessments (Rodriguez & Ryave, 1990). This type of lie includes the faking of orgasms to the faking of listening. To illustrate, consider the following:

- You tell someone you feel fine when you don't.
- You send an "on my way" text to a friend waiting for you at a restaurant when you are just getting out of the shower.
- You tell a political candidate you have voted when you didn't.
- You tell someone, "It's the perfect gift and I love it" when it isn't and you don't.
- You tell someone you are with, "I was *not* looking at her/him" when you were.
- You tell someone, "I'll call you tomorrow" when you have no (or only a vague) intention of doing so.
- You "like" a friend's post on Facebook when you really don't.
- You tell your date, "I never felt comfortable enough with anyone before to do what we just did" when it isn't true.
- You play the "markdown game," telling someone the thing you bought cost far less than it really did.
- You automatically say "I love you, too" when a lover or member of your family says it to you, even at times when you don't.
- You tell a group of people, "When he said that, I told really him what I thought of him," but you didn't.
- You nod and say things which lead another person to believe you agree with what they are saying, but you don't.
- You say you were studying when you were not.
- You say you were sick when you were not. As added insurance against detection, you ask someone else who knows you weren't sick to say you were.

Sometimes when people embellish their stories, their listeners consider these lies to be of little consequence and accept (sometimes even encourage) them. Tim O'Brien (1990, p. 89) illustrates this when talking about one of his buddies in his Vietnam biography: "If Rat told you, for example, that he'd slept with four girls one night, you could figure it was about a girl and a half. It wasn't a question of deceit. Just the opposite: he wanted to heat up the truth, to make it burn so hot that you would feel exactly what he felt. For Rat Kiley, I think, facts were formed by sensation, not the other way around, and when you listened to one of his stories, you'd find yourself performing rapid calculations in your head, subtracting the superlatives, figuring the square root of an absolute and then multiplying by maybe." One of our former colleagues at Purdue University was known for his tendency to embellish his stories and this prompted another professor to say the best way to listen to him was to "subtract 5000 from everything he says."

Sometime in my twenties, I started telling a story at cocktail parties and other social gatherings about how I had run the hurdles competitively in high school. I always concluded the story by saying that my career as a hurdler came to a sudden halt at one track meet when I badly injured my knee on a hurdle. None of this was true. I don't remember when I first told it, but I remember being in a group of men and women engaging in idle chit-chat. All of them had a story about some past athletic achievement. Then somebody turned to me and asked if I was an athlete in high school or college. At that moment I wanted very much to be able to say, "yes." So, without thinking a lot about it, I began with a modest statement about how I didn't play basketball, football, or tennis like others in the group. Then I added, "but I did run track." Then someone asked me what my event was. I had run the hurdles in gym class and knew a little about it so I said, "I was a hurdler." It had a novel ring and I could see I had an interested audience. Nobody questioned the veracity of my claim and it was an easy way to become an accepted member of this group of people. I didn't ever think of it as a lie. I justified it to myself by arguing that it didn't hurt anyone and there wasn't much falsehood in it. After all, I did run the hurdles in high school gym class. I just didn't run the hurdles competitively. I wasn't trying to get a job as a track coach. For about fifteen years I pulled this story out at other social gatherings when it seemed appropriate—even embellishing it a bit when I felt the need.

Then one day I thought about the relatively long life of this mythical story of mine and I decided not to tell it again. It wasn't that the story didn't have a punch. True, it wasn't the kind of story that had people on the edge of their seats, but it definitely had interest value. And I didn't dump the story because I felt like a liar either. I'm sure if I told all the people who heard the story that I was never a competitive hurdler that they wouldn't care. Most of them probably don't remember me, much less anything I said. I guess I just didn't feel the need to tell it anymore. Maybe I'm a different person now—somebody who doesn't need to be a hurdler. On the other hand, the story has become such an entrenched part of my small talk repertoire that I've had to consciously keep it from rolling off my tongue. When this happens, I usually substitute the story about how I lied about my track career, a story which seems to have more interest value than my original falsehood. The ease with which I became a competitive hurdler and the length of time I maintained that image taught me a lot about the nature of low-stakes lies and their role in self-presentation. It also made me realize how easy it is for a person who prides himself on his directness and candor in other arenas of his life to find comfort in shading the truth in informal conversation.

Self Presentation

According to DePaulo and her colleagues (1992; 2003) low-stakes lies are most productively viewed as a part of self-presentation. When we try to manage the impression we make on others, we sometimes resort to low-stakes lies to enhance that impression. Among other things, lying is used to make us look better than we really are, to hide things we consider detrimental to our image, and to shield ourselves from disapproval.

Meeting new people is often seen as an opportunity to present a new self—a person who makes more money or supervises more employees; someone who once won awards in track or bowled a perfect game; a guy who went out on a blind date with Jennifer Lawrence; a gal who did some modeling during college; etc. Feldman et al. (2002) demonstrated how self-presentation lies can be triggered and how often they occur. Students were asked to have a ten minute conversation with another student they didn't know. Some were told to make their partner think they were competent; some were told to try to make the other person like them; some weren't told anything. Overall 60% of the students said they lied. However, students who were seeking perceptions of competence and likeability lied twice as much as those who were not given any "look good" instructions. On average, there were two lies in each conversation, but the range was from 0 to 12.

Attracting a Romantic Partner

Dating is another occasion when people use low-stakes lies to present themselves in the best possible way. Deception is plentiful and frequently expected. In bars where one of the main goals is to meet other men and women, the validity of names, occupations, addresses, personality traits, income, and career skills is open to question. Both men and women deceive their dates and prospective dates, but Buss (1994) says the pool of possible partners will affect who does more deceiving. If women greatly outnumber men, then they are expected to deceive more often and vice versa.

Deception may be more prevalent during dating than in more established relationships for a variety of reasons. As potential partners are just getting to know one another and decide whether or not to pursue something more serious, the scrutiny with which they evaluate one another is particularly high. This in turn can increase the occurrence of falsifications as daters make great effort to come across as desirable and worth the relational investment (Vangelisti, 2012). Second, the dating environment may highlight people's insecurities about their attractiveness and arouse a fear of rejection, both of which may prompt daters to lie. Third, deception may also be a response to a sense of competitiveness with other daters (Toma & Hancock, 2010).

Sexual issues are a common subject for deceit. Luchetti (1999) found 20% of college students misrepresented their sexual history to their sexual partners; 33% avoided disclosing their sexual history to at least one partner. With other men, men tend to exaggerate the number of sexual partners and the specifics of their sexual activities; women tend to say they've had fewer sexual partners and experiences than they have, especially with a potential long-term male partner. Verbal and nonverbal behavior that overstates a woman's availability and desire for sex is also common.

Both men and women tell lies about possible competitors. For example, a man may tell a woman that another man is only interested in having sex with her. He, on the other hand, is more interested in her personality and the fun they have together. While this man may be sincere, the strategy he is using is also used by men to mask an intent to have sex. As Buss (1994, p. 105) notes: "While signals of commitment prove highly effective in attracting long-term mates, the simulation of commitment can be effective in attracting and seducing a woman. Men looking for casual liaisons compete by mimicking what women desire in a permanent mate."

Tooke and Camire (1991) found 88 ways that university men and women deceive each other as they try to attract a partner. Some of these included: misleading statements about their career goals; sucking in their stomachs when walking near a valued member of the opposite sex; giving the appearance of being more trusting and considerate than they actually were; and acting uninterested in having sex when it was really on their minds. Sometimes a man or woman will feign friendship with another couple in order to maintain a presence with one member of that couple. Enhancing one's physical appearance is another deceptive maneuver, practiced by both men and women, even though more attention is typically given to female endeavors in this area.

Because they play an important role in attracting a romantic partner, men are likely to exaggerate their accomplishments at work and the money they make. They may act more confident, masculine, or assertive around women than they really feel. They know the value of selling themselves as honest, vulnerable, and considerate. They may even reveal a "painful secret" that isn't painful or secret. The disclosure is designed to demonstrate his openness and trust in the woman, hoping that she will reciprocate the trust.

More and more people meet prospective dating partners online, via sites such as *OK Cupid, Match.Com, Zoosk,* and *PlentyofFish*. These sites offer powerful tools for people in their quest for a romantic partner, such as access to extensive databases of singles and the capacity to pre-screen potential dates based on demographic characteristics (age, occupation, family situation) and preferences (outdoor enthusiast, vegetarian, metalhead, etc.). However, they also provide a platform for daters to deceive before they even speak or meet prospective partners in person. Consider the information daters post about themselves in their online profiles. Toma, Hancock, and Ellison (2008) surveyed 80 people who submitted online profiles on various dating web sites. The vast majority (81%) lied about one or more of their physical attributes such as height, weight, and age. As a general rule, woman tended to lie about their weight and men lied about their height. The more a woman's actual weight was higher than average, the more she was likely to exaggerate her thinness. Similarly, men whose height was lower than average were more likely to exaggerate their height. In a follow-up study, Hancock and Toma (2009) found that about one-third of the online photographs online daters post of themselves were not representative. Overall, women's photographs appeared to be less accurate than men's photographs. Women were more likely to be older than they were portrayed in their photographs. Their photographs were also more likely to be retouched or taken from an angle that deceptively portrayed them as thinner or taller. Although people frequently distorted pictures and other information in their on-line profiles, they typically kept their alterations within believable parameters in the event they met their correspondents in subsequent face-to-face meetings.

The magnitude of deception in on-line profiles Hancock and his colleagues observed should not come as a big surprise. An on-line profile is the equivalent of a first date. Anyone who has been on a first date will remember putting their best foot forward. Women dress with great contemplation and take extra time to put on their makeup. Men ensure their clothes are color-coordinated and wrinkle-free. Conversations are rehearsed before any words were exchanged. Behavioral quirks are carefully camouflaged with polite talk and impeccable manners. These extra steps are taken to make a first impression that is more favorable than it is accurate.

Flattery and Ingratiation

Low-stakes lies are also used as false praise. We sometimes give compliments we don't think are deserved in order to make the target feel good which, in turn, may make them feel obligated to help the complimenter in the future. Jones (1964) calls this a "subversive masquerade." Despite the fact that it is widely understood that people do this, ingratiation strategies (especially giving undeserved compliments and appearing to agree with another person's opinion) can be very effective (Gordon, 1994). We like people who appear to like us; we like people who seem to agree with us; we like people who say they see good things in our behavior; and we like people who ask our opinion and advice. These acts are usually initiated by the liar, but occasionally the target will provide the setup—e.g., "Do you think I'm smart?" If the truth is likely to hurt, deception may be called for as a response to this question. It may even be expected. Fundamentally, the goals of the ingratiator are to: 1) locate a target who can provide benefits; 2) identify what the target needs/wants to hear; and 3) determine ways to satisfy the target's wants/needs in a way that will be believed and that increases the probabilities that future benefits will ensue from the target.

Some of the issues in play for the effective performance of deceptive compliments and opinion agreement are identified by Stengel (2000) and Jones (1964).

- Consider the benefits of praising someone behind their back. If your positive comments eventually reach the target, your intent to obligate the target to you is less likely to be perceived. In other words, avoid the perception that your compliment is given because you want some benefit in return. Make the compliment one that addresses a characteristic of the target that cuts across situations.

- Ingratiation is especially difficult with people who have authority over the complimenter because his or her motives are immediately in question. In such cases, subtlety is the order of the day. Compliment or agree with a supervisor while simultaneously communicating a lack of dependence on him or her. In other words, the message is that the ingratiator's behavior is being performed without any desire for any benefits in return. Oddly enough, even if the ingratiator's motive for complimenting or opinion agreement is crystal clear to the target, it may still have the desired effect.

- Don't make a habit of *always* agreeing with the target. Pick issues that are important to the target and issues where your true opinion will be difficult to verify. Allow the target to see you disagree with others. Show some initial resistance to the target's opinion, then follow this with agreement. When possible, anticipate the target's opinion and state it as your opinion before he or she does.

Sports and Games

To effectively play and win various sporting activities and games, deceptive skills are required (Mawby & Mitchell, 1986). Basketball players use their eyes and shifting body positions to provide misleading information to the person guarding them about their direction of movement, where they will pass the ball, and whether they intend to shoot. A boxer's left hook may only be effective if his or her opponent is defending against an expected right jab. Offensive linemen in football mislead their opponents about the direction of a running play by the way they block. A pass receiver in football may run the same route at the same speed several times in order to establish an expected routine for the pass defender. Then the receiver will exploit the defender's expectations by changing his speed and running a different route.

Whether it is football, boxing, chess, or poker, winning often depends on misleading one's opponent. As long as it remains within the rules of the game, this type of deception is tolerated and expected. The stakes are low when acts of deception are revealed in games played for enjoyment. But the stakes can be high for professional athletes who may lose their livelihood if their ability to deceive is ineffective. Does game-playing deceit transfer to everyday life? Obviously the game of life and games played for sport are different in many ways. But there may be some lessons that transfer—e.g., learning to anticipate a person's reaction to a deceptive maneuver, learning various ways to mask one's real intentions, learning the importance of preparation and practice for effective execution of deception, learning the value of setting up a deceptive move by preceding it with truthful behavior, learning not to overuse any particular type of deception, etc. Deception in the context of sporting events, like deception in everyday life, has to be adapted to the circumstances. A basketball player who fakes a shot fifty feet from the basket is not likely to fool many opponents and a player who uses the same deceptive maneuver over and over is not likely to enjoy much success. In sporting events, like everyday life, deceivers learn to develop deceptive maneuvers by violating what others believe is expected or normative.

Athletic deceivers not only learn how to deceive their opponents, but also to detect when their opponents are attempting to deceive them. Sebanz and Shiffrar (2009) asked notive and experienced basketball players to view videos of other players preparing to perform deceptive moves (faking a pass or a jump shot) against an opponent. The videos ended right before the deceptive moves were executed. Participants were shown these videos along with others in which players were preparing to make real passes or jump shots and were asked to distinguish between fake and real attempts. Expert players performed somewhat better than novices (60% vs. 54%) in detecting fake moves from the videos. Sebanz and Shiffrar speculated that the experts likely drew on their own experience in performing the fake moves to distinguish true from fake moves made by other players.

Like many card games, deception is critical to the success of poker players. Good players know that other players are closely watching their behavior in order to determine whether they have a strong hand or not. Poker is usually played for money so every player is looking for "tells" (short for telegraph), which are unintended verbal and/or nonverbal signals which may indicate the quality of another player's cards, the player's intention to bet, and whether the bet will be large or small (Caro, 2000). Accurate detection of such information can give a player a huge advantage.

Therefore, like liars in other contexts, poker players try to mask their feelings and intentions. A common way of masking their behavior is to "neutralize" emotions. This is frequently done through the use of an unchanging neutral facial expression, minimal hand and posture movement, and no verbal behavior. When poker players try to maintain the same static facial expression when playing a strong hand or a weak hand, this is called a "poker face." Some players even wear sunglasses to keep other players from observing any dilation of their pupils which might occur when they are dealt a strong hand.

Instead of masking, some poker players try to confuse or mislead their opponents. Confusion occurs when players deliberately change moods—sometimes engaging in relaxed chatter and a happy facial expression when they have a poor hand and sometimes when they have a good hand; being quiet and deliberate with a good hand on one occasion and performing the same behavior with a poor hand on another occasion (Hayano, 1980). Poker players also use misleading signals. For example, a player may set a trap with a false tell—e.g., pressing one's lips tightly together every time he or she is "bluffing" (pretending to have better cards than he or she does). Later, when there is a lot of money at stake and he or she has a good hand, the player presses his or her lips together. The other players think he or she has a weak hand and they continue to bet more money because they think they can beat the bluffer. New and inexperienced poker players are not good deceivers. They straighten their posture and look attentive when they have good cards; they are quick to grasp their chips to bet when they have good cards and slow to grasp them when they have bad cards. Sometimes novice poker players, like novice liars, will "oversell" their lie—e.g., dramatizing the weakness or strength of their cards to such an extent that it is not believable.

Magic

Magicians are expected to be deceitful, so their performance necessitates the mastery of various deceptive maneuvers. The targets of this deceit, not unlike some targets of everyday deceit, may experience conflicting feelings—i.e., both wanting and not wanting to know the details of the deceptive act. It is not unlike the feeling we may have when someone says, "This was great. We'll have to have lunch together again sometime." On the one hand we suspect this is not the truth and we'd like to find out how the person really feels; on the other hand, we want to enjoy the positive feelings that accompany an acceptance of the comment at face value.

Magician Peter the Adequate (http://www.peterthe adequate.com) freely admits that he is a professional deceiver. From his comments, it is not hard to see how some of the same skills he uses as an entertainer are also used by deceivers in everyday life.

- "I rely on audience assumptions about how they think things work and how a trick is done."
- "Misdirection is the key. Audiences follow movement, gaze direction, things that are higher, and things that are closer. Misdirection can be accomplished with props, speech, hands, or an assistant."
- "I give the audience reasons to believe what I want them to believe."
- "I convince myself the ball is in my hand (when it isn't)."
- "I practice so often I can often think five or six steps ahead."
- "I tell the audience some truths with some lies."

The Fitzkee Trilogy is a series of three books detailing the activities of magicians. In one of those books, Fitzkee (1945) provides some tips for deception which complement those made by Peter the Adequate: 1) Repetition of apparently the same action will eventually become monotonous and commonplace. When that occurs, it ceases to attract close attention and clears the way for the magician to engage in secret maneuvers. 2) The control of one's voice, especially during the time of the deception, is necessary for success of the trick. Hesitations, slower speech, stammering, and pitch change are all signals to the audience that something is happening that they need to attend to. 3) Provide the audience with familiar things and let them assume they know what you are dealing with. 4) Do not explain what should be obvious. It leads to suspicion. If you cut the bottom out of a tomato can and show the cylinder to the audience, they will assume it is like other tomato cans and is empty. If you say it is empty, they may wonder if it is.

The Workplace

According to Shulman (2007), lying and deception are part of the infrastructure of most places of work. Despite being a part of the everyday reality at most places of work, the consequences for much of the deception that takes place there is not usually serious (i.e., low-stakes)—e.g., politeness rituals enacted with rude customers; professing adherence to an official set of rules but behaving in ways that are at odds with them; falsely complimenting a person who can help you get ahead; telling a supervisor only what you believe they want to hear; pretending to have accomplished more than you have; etc. Of course, given the right circumstances, these and other forms of deception can become high-stakes lies, but cheating customers, fraudulently acquiring or spending money, hiding flaws in products, covering up evidence in order to maintain harmony within the work group, etc. are more likely candidates for high-stakes lies. In some cases, deception may even be considered part of a company's product. This might occur when a public relations firm intentionally misleads the public or some other audience about its client.

High-Stakes Lies

Some of the lies human beings tell to each other are likely to have strong negative consequences if they are uncovered. If they aren't uncovered, the liar's gain may also be considerable. These are called high-stakes lies. Because the stakes are high, researchers believe the liar's overt behavior is likely to manifest the cognitive and emotional strain which often accompanies such lies.

Cognitive and Emotional Processes

A person who is afraid of the consequences of his or her lie is expected to manifest emotional signs of fear, apprehension, or general arousal. Apprehension is also thought to be high when the target of the lie is perceived as difficult to fool, when the target is suspicious, and when the liar has had little practice at lying. Other emotional signs of deceit might be associated with a liar's guilt, anger, or even happiness ("duping delight"). It is presumed that liars who try to cover up these emotions will show affective states which are inappropriate for the demands of a particular situation (Ekman, 2001). Cognitive signs of lying are based on the presumption that high-stakes lies are complex and liars are unable to control their behavior—causing, for example, inconsistencies in their story and hesitations in telling it. Attempts to control behavior while engaging in important lies may produce behavior which seems too rehearsed or too awkward (Zuckerman et al., 1981). The underlying belief regarding these signs of deception based on cognitive difficulty and inappropriate emotions is that they will distinguish liars from truth tellers when the stakes are high. In order to determine the validity of this assumption, researchers had to find ways to compare high-stakes liars with truth tellers in a controlled laboratory where it could be effectively studied. How do they do this?

Generating High-Stakes Lies for Research

Even though these studies are not plentiful, several different methods have been used to successfully generate high-stakes lies under controlled conditions. Horvath and his colleagues (1973; 1994) compared the interrogations of actual criminal suspects who subsequently had been determined to be telling truths or telling lies. Other researchers have involved people in stealing, false opinion, and cheating situations. These formats created conditions which made the cognitive and emotional demands of the participants similar to those they would experience in a real criminal investigation. A study by Frank and Ekman (2004) illustrates the stealing and opinion formats. In both conditions, there was a reward for a successful deception and punishment for an unsuccessful one. Like truth tellers in actual criminal investigations, the truth tellers in this experiment faced the same reward/punishment structure established for the liars. In the stealing format, a person is left alone in a room with $50. Some were given the choice of whether to take the money or not and others were instructed to take it. All participants knew they would be interrogated later about this act. If a person took the $50 and convinced the interrogator that he (all participants in this study were men) did not take it, he could keep the $50. If he took the money, denied it, and the interrogator judged him to be lying, he would forfeit the $50 plus a $10 participant fee. Thieves who were caught lying also expected they would have to sit on a cold metal chair in a small room and "endure anywhere from 10–40 randomly sequenced, 110 dB startling blasts of white noise over the course of an hour." None of the participants actually received this disciplinary action, although they were exposed to a demonstration of it. If a person told the truth and the interrogator judged them to be telling the truth, they received a $10 bonus on top of their $10 participant fee. If truth tellers were judged to be lying, they received no participant fee, no bonus money, and expected they would have to endure an hour with periodic bursts of loud, irritating noise. In the opinion format, participants were given a list of social issues like, "Should convicted cold-blooded murderers be executed?" Then they are asked to indicate how strongly they agreed or disagreed with each issue. The issue a person felt most strongly about was the issue he was expected to support, either truthfully or falsely. The reward-punishment system for the opinion-giving scenario was the same as for the theft scenario.

The general framework for the cheating format is as follows (Exline et al., 1970; Shulman, 1973). Two people are brought into a laboratory, seated next to each other and told they are in a decision-making experiment. One of them is a confederate who is working with the experimenter, but the other person doesn't know this. The experimenter gives them a piece of paper with thousands of randomly placed black dots on it and they are asked to decide within five minutes how many dots are on the page. Accurately counting the dots is not possible. They are told that the pair guessing the closest will win $50. Soon, the experimenter is called out of the room for "an important phone call." As soon as the experimenter leaves the room, the experimenter's confederate starts looking around and points out that he thinks the experimenter has the answer to their problem on his or her desk. The confederate tries to get the other person to accompany him to the experimenter's desk to find out the answer. If the naïve participant does not go, the confederate looks at the answer and reports back that the number of dots is 16,798. The confederate then suggests they put down 16,700 in an effort to win the $50 and proceeds to do so whether the other person agrees or not. The experimenter returns and tells the pair that their time is up and that he or she now wants to interview each of them about their decision-making process. The pair is first interviewed together and then individually. When interviewed together, the majority do not confess; when interviewed alone, the majority do confess. The interrogation strategy is to gradually increase the pressure on the interviewee. First, the experimenter asks how they arrived at their answer. Vague replies follow. The experimenter then says "there must be something else you did because "the chances of guessing as close as you did are 1 in 10 million." Finally, the experimenter says the interview is over, but adds that the university requires that a statement be read to all students reminding them that experiments are governed by the same honor code as classrooms. Cheating during any university activity will be dealt with severely. The students are debriefed and their behavior, which is videotaped, is then compared to those who were not involved in cheating (truth tellers) while working on the dots problem.

The Behavior of Liars

Given the expectation that liars are trying to control any behavior that might reveal their deception, the early attempts to isolate liar behavior looked closely at nonverbal behavior. It was assumed that liars knew how to control their verbal behavior, but nonverbal behavior was not as much under the liar's conscious control. Polygraphs, and more recent attempts to study the brain activity of liars, are also based on the belief that there are some aspects of the liar's behavior that he or she cannot control. But the more we learned about nonverbal behavior, particularly those behaviors that get regular social commentary and feedback, the more we realized that some nonverbal behavior is far more controllable than we originally believed. Researchers also discovered that even physiological responses measured by the polygraph can be altered by a liar in order to avoid detection. On the other hand, we have also learned that some verbal behavior is not as well-controlled as we thought. In addition, some subtle nonverbal behaviors are typically outside of the liar's control. False smiles, micro-momentary and poorly timed facial expressions are examples of this (Ekman, 2000). We also know that liars don't always control behavior that is within their control. Thus, the profile of liar behavior may not be limited to a few hard to control behaviors. Instead, it is likely to be a combination of verbal, vocal, nonverbal, and physiological signals which, as a group, tend to be associated with lying.

Several scholars have summarized the research that distinguishes verbal, vocal, and nonverbal behavior of liars from truth tellers (Knapp & Comadena, 1979; Zuckerman et al., 1981; Vrij, 2000). These research summaries examined all types of lying (except pathological) in an effort to look for common features. Knapp et al. (1974) predicted that deceivers would manifest verbal and nonverbal behaviors which signaled uncertainty, vagueness, nervousness, reticence, dependence on others, and negative affect. Behaviors in those categories have been repeatedly found in research. The most recent and comprehensive summary of this research was a meta-analysis conducted by DePaulo et al. (2003). She and her colleagues examined 120 separate studies and 158 different behaviors. Liars lied for various reasons and under varied conditions. Their four conclusions, listed below, are based on the most common findings and provide general guidelines and expectations. They do not address the fact that some liars have their own idiosyncratic behaviors (e.g., audible swallowing) that occur when they are telling a lie and not when they are telling the truth. It should also be reiterated that these are behaviors that distinguish liars from truth tellers (a comparison), not just liar behavior per se. Given certain circumstances and skills, a liar may manifest all, some, or none of these features.

1. Liars are less forthcoming than truth-tellers. They respond less (shorter responses; less elaboration); they seem to be holding back; they speak at a slower rate; and they take longer before responding. When liars have time to plan their lie, this difference in response latency tends to decrease.

2. Liars tell stories that are less plausible. Their stories make less sense. They contain more discrepancies; the stories are less engaging (have more word and phrase repetitions); liar behavior is less immediate (more indirect, fewer self-references); more uncertain; less fluent (more hesitations, errors, pauses); and less active (fewer gestures). Liars, unlike truth tellers, also seem to want their stories to be without error. They make fewer spontaneous corrections during the telling of their stories and they are less likely to admit they can't remember something.

3. Liars make a more negative impression. Overall they seem less cooperative; make negative statements; use more words denoting anger and fear; use offensive language; complain; smile less; and seem more defensive.

4. Liars are more tense. They have higher pitch, fidget more, and their pupils are dilated for longer periods.

Even though many of the studies supporting the preceding findings have quantified the frequency and duration of multiple cues (40% of the studies observed ten or more behaviors), we still have a lot to learn about the organization and coordination of these behaviors when they do occur.

Lying in Close Relationships

Compared to relationships with strangers and acquaintances, close relationships create a context and expectations for lying which are likely to alter liar behavior dramatically. To begin, we tell fewer lies to those we identify as close relationship partners. But lies that violate the basic understandings of a close relationship are likely to be explosive (DePaulo & Kashy, 1998). What are those things that make liar behavior different in close relationships (Knapp, 2005)?

- In a close relationship, you interact and expect to influence your partner frequently. Each partner learns how the other behaves when telling the truth and how they act when telling lies of individual and relationship support. When a partner in a close relationship lies about something detrimental to the relationship, it will be in the context of a partner who may be very sensitive to non-normative behavior.

  Close relationship partners establish rules about how the partners should and should not act in a given context. Roloff and Miller (2006) characterize these rules as "prescriptions that, if obeyed, should reduce the destructive nature of interpersonal conflicts" (p.105). Among these prescriptions are idealized rules about communication that portray honesty as desirable at any cost and deception as unacceptable and malignant. However, when examined through the lens of a relationship, it may not be obvious to either partner when he or she has broken a "rule" about truthtelling or deception. Thus, although the partners may agree that lying is wrong, they may enact and detect lies in very different ways. While one partner may adopt a stance requiring "full and complete" disclosure in the relationship, the other may believe only "important information" needs to be disclosed, perhaps in the interest of tact or avoiding conflict. Paradoxically, sometimes not disclosing something to the other partner is interpreted by that partner as deception, and thereby can create an explosive conflict (Roggensack & Sillars, 2014).

- Each person in a close relationship is aware of the vulnerabilities of their partner and is expected to recognize and respect them. Thus, many lies in close relationships are designed to help one's partner—making them feel good, building up their self-esteem, turning their faults into virtues, constructing excuses for misdeeds, and selectively concealing negative feelings. Each partner trusts the other to tell all the truth that is important to the health and welfare of the relationship. Neither partner is expected to harm or take unfair advantage of the other.

- Relationship partners are emotionally invested in their relationship and expect it to continue. The continuing nature of these relationships means that the subject of a lie may have a long life. Some piece of the story that doesn't fit the liar's earlier portrayal may come up months or years later and need explanation.

- Close relationship partners are a team. As such, they will co-construct some lies. Barnes (1994) says that sometimes one partner in a close relationship knows that the other partner is lying, but pretends not to—thereby engaging in what he calls *connivance*. There may also be denial by one partner that the other is not part of the team—e.g., "He lies to others, but not to me." A close relationship team may also *collaborate* in their lies. This can be done by literally asking one's partner not to reveal certain information or the pair may agree to lie to a third party. The idea that partners to a close relationship are a team also means that when they lie to make their partner feel good, it is also likely to serve them well. When a liar's partner feels good, the liar may also feel good.

Is It Lying? Introducing the Blood Relatives

Language, for better or worse, gives us a lot of options for communicating. We can be clear or ambiguous, direct or indirect, precise or general, or accurate or inexact without intending to lie or mislead. The veterinarian may want to show sensitivity to your loss by saying your cat was "put down" instead of "killed;" a politician may fear that specific public revelations about a plan may seriously hinder his or her ability to effectively negotiate privately, so he or she is vague; an engineer may use language with the public that only other engineers understand because that's the way he or she is accustomed to talking. In addition, sometimes we use language that appears to be evasive when we are trying not to be evasive. When someone asks you if you are going to Bob's party, you may respond, "Bob and I are best friends" which is intended as a "yes." But since it is also an ambiguous yes, the speaker can always deny he said he was going to the party if he decides not to go. Linguistic contingencies are plentiful in our everyday speech. When someone says, "I intend to get to the bottom of this," the implication is that he or she will try hard to determine what happened. However, all that was actually said was that the person *intended* to "get to the bottom of this"—not that he or she will. Nor does the statement say how hard the person will try to "get to the bottom of this."

Since linguistic constructions that leave room for interpretation are so much a part of our non-deceptive everyday interaction, the question of deception is often not an issue. In fact, every time we try to persuade someone or effectively communicate with them, we make language choices designed to achieve the certain desired results with a target. Nevertheless, there are occasions when ambiguous, indirect, imprecise, inexact, and confusing words are perceived by audiences as deceptive. Why? Because everyone knows how language *can* be used to misrepresent ideas. They've had experiences (as sender and receiver) with distortion, exaggeration, overstatement, minimization, and other linguistic manipulations. When attributions of deception are made, the audience or target perceives important consequences associated with the message; they also have reasons to believe the message was consciously and intentionally designed to mislead or create a false belief. When people are on the receiving end of what they believe to be deceptive messages of this type, they know it will be hard to prove. Falsehoods can be revealed by finding contrary factual evidence. But the proof that misleading messages are deliberate often hinges on interpretations of language use and the establishment of a motive to mislead. Because this form of deception is able to accomplish goals that a liar might wish to achieve, but do it in a way that makes it harder to classify as a lie, Herzog (1973, p. 15) predicted that its use will steadily increase:

> America will be the first civilization to eliminate lies. Soon, in America, the lie will be superfluous, unnecessary, and will be buried. The lie is not vanishing because it is being killed off, like some hapless species of wildlife. It is not disappearing because it

was legislated out of existence, like a noxious fume, or because it has atrophied from lack of use. Clearly, lies cannot be regarded as victims of higher morality. The lie is a casualty of progress…The new device that is making the lie obsolete can be called the Fake Factor, or for those who require still more trenchant terminology, the B. S. Factor….this factor causes a subtle skewing of sense, a distortion of meaning, without ever become an actual lie.

There are many linguistic constructions that might receive attributions of deception, but we will discuss six of them: equivocation, contextomy, paltering, spin, bullshit, and doublespeak. Unlike lies, each of these acts can be performed without the intent to create a false reality in the target. However, it is not unusual for people to use them to create a false reality. As a result, deception is sometimes attributed to these acts even when that is not the speaker's intent.

Equivocation

Some messages that are perceived as evasive, indirect or ambiguous result from what Bavelas et al. (1990) call an avoidance-avoidance conflict. In other words, a person finds him or herself in a situation where they don't want to tell the truth but they don't want to lie either. Both may elicit negative reactions, so they equivocate. For example, let's assume a husband has found some old letters that reveal his wife had an affair several years ago. After reading the letters, he says to his wife: "You must have really loved him." The wife knows the content of the letters so she wants to avoid saying no because she knows the husband will then point to various sentences which offer testimony to the contrary. On the other hand, she wants to avoid saying yes because she knows how much that would hurt her husband and she wants their relationship to remain intact. She chooses instead to equivocate by saying, "I hardly knew him." The implication is that no matter what the letters say, the only kind of love the husband should find threatening would

DOONESBURY © 2004 G.B. Trudeau. Reprinted with permission of UNIVERSAL UCLICK. All rights reserved.

be one that involved knowing the other person well and this was not the case. The husband may realize he didn't get a direct answer to his question which gives him the option of charging his wife with an evasive answer. But he may also be secretly happy he didn't get a straightforward, unequivocal response.

In other cases, however, equivocation can result in charges of deceptive intent. For example, let's assume a person has been charged with a DWI and is asked by a police officer if he or she was convicted of driving under the influence of alcohol within the last year and the response is, "I still have my driver's license." The driver doesn't want to admit to a previous DWI conviction nor does he or she want to lie to the police officer. In this case, however, the response is more likely to be perceived as deliberately misleading.

Contextomy

"Contextomy" refers to the act of altering the meaning of another person's belief by cutting away the context surrounding a specific quotation attributed to that person. Most of the time we don't expect people to accurately quote others in conversation and we are often willing to overlook contextomies when everyone is aware of their existence—e.g., quotes from critics in movie advertisements. We all know that these ads often select a word or phrase from a reviewer's comments which makes it appear that the critic is endorsing the movie. For example a movie ad may read: "Jocko Trumble says, 'Tom Hanks gives a brilliant performance.'" The few people who check out Trumble's actual review will read, "The only redeeming part of this entire movie, and it is less than a minute in length, is when Tom Hanks gives a brilliant performance as a garbage man."

In other situations, contexomy has serious consequences and attributions of intentionally deceptive behavior are more likely. In the 2006 Senate race in Missouri, television ads sponsored by Republican Senator Jim Talent criticized his opponent Claire McCaskill by featuring quotes like "spreading untruths," "clearly violated ethical standards" with the name of the *Kansas City Star* newspaper below the quotes. Even though the *Star* ran stories that included these words, they were the words of McCaskill's opponents, not those of the Star's editors or reporters. The implication that the *Star* endorsed or made these statements wasn't true. In another ad, Talent's campaign accurately quoted a 2004 *St. Louis Post-Dispatch* article about McCaskill which said she "used this office (state auditor) transparently for political gain." What the ad didn't say was that the quote was taken from an otherwise positive endorsement of McCaskill by the *Dispatch* which said she was a "promising and dynamic leader" (FactCheck.org, "Talent for Deception, October 21, 2006).

McGlone (2005) gives two politically motivated examples. In one case a single sentence from Martin Luther King's famous "I Have a Dream" speech was used to support the contention that King was against affirmative action. In the other case, a quote from a book written by former Vice President Al Gore was used by his opponents to show that he was willing to sacrifice the health and welfare of people in order to save the Pacific Yew tree. The entire quote from Gore's book is presented below, but the quote that was widely circulated to brand Gore's stance is underlined and in italics. Do you think the section in italics accurately represents Gore's position?

Most of the [tree] species unique to the rain forests are in immi-nent danger, partly because there is no one to speak up for them. In contrast, consider the recent controversy over the yew tree, a temperate forest species, one variety of which now grows only in the Pacific Northwest. The Pacific Yew can be cut down and processed to produce a potent chemical, Taxol, which offers some promise of curing certain forms of lung, breast, and ovarian cancer in patients who would otherwise quickly die. It seems an easy choice—sac-rifice the tree for a human life—until one learns that three trees must be destroyed for each patient treated, *that only specimens more than a hundred years old contain the potent chemical, and that there are very few of these Yews remaining on earth. Suddenly we must confront some very tough questions. How important are the medical needs of future generations? Are those of us alive today entitled to cut down all of those trees to extend the lives of a few of us, even if it means that this unique form of life will disappear forever, thus making it impossible to save human lives in the future (Gore, 1992, p. 119)?*

Paltering

As contextomy illustrates, a statement need not be false to be deceptive. "Paltering" refers to the use of accurate statements with the intention of conveying an inaccu-rate impression (Schauer & Zeckhauser, 2013). Unlike a lie of commission, palter-ing only involves truthful statements; and unlike a lie of omission, it entails actively misleading a target rather than merely omitting relevant information. Advertisers wishing to draw consumers' attention to the contents of an envelope sometimes put a government warning about tampering with the mail on the outside of the envelope while also omitting a return address, thus purposefully creating the false impression the envelope contains an official letter from a government agency. Some Ph.Ds may make restaurant or hotel reservations using the title "Dr.," hoping in the process to lead the establishment to believe they are (typically wealthy) phy-sicians rather than (middle-income) academics. The Internal Revenue service is alleged to deliberately select the period immediately preceding the April 15th tax-filing deadline as the time to initiate tax-fraud investigations and send out press releases about audit practices; as a result, taxpayers believe the probability of audits and criminal prosecution is higher than it really is (Pender, 2015). Politicians routinely present extreme and unrepresentative examples of social problems—e.g., Linda Taylor, the woman Ronald Reagan decried for collecting excessive public assistance and became known as the "welfare queen"—with the intent of leading voters into making erroneous generalizations (in reality, welfare fraud is relatively rare and unprofitable; Levin, 2013).

Rogers et al. (2014) investigated corporate executives' attitudes toward paltering in business negotiations. A sample of executives was presented with the following scenario:

"Sometimes during negotiations people say things that are factually true but create an impression in their counterparty that is false. This is called 'paltering.' Imagine that over the last 10 years your

sales have grown consistently and that next year you expect sales to be flat. In order to convey the impression that sales will continue to grow, you might palter by saying 'over the last 10 years our sales have grown consistently' and not highlight your expectation that sales this coming year will be flat."

After reading this definition and example of paltering, the executives were then asked about their paltering habits during business negotiations and their attitudes toward this behavior. A majority of executives reported paltering in some or most of their negotiations (66%), whereas only 34% said they had done so in only a few or none of their negotiations. Moreover, 80% said they perceived their paltering as "acceptable and honest" communication. However, a follow-up study indicated that the targets of paltering in negotiations generally perceive it as the ethical equivalent of making an intentionally false statements. These findings suggest paltering is an especially pernicious form of deception because, unlike lies of commission and omission, it allows the deceiver to preserve an honest self-image. As a result, palterers may be more inclined to deceive using truthful but misleading statements rather than falsifications or contextomies.

Spin

The origin of the term "spin" has been linked to a baseball pitch. When the pitcher spins the ball as it is pitched, it curves, making it hard for the batter to accurately see and hit. Putting a spin on a story simply means that the communicator finds a way to make it look like something it isn't; to redirect a target's attention to a particular part of the story or interpreting the story in a way that is favorable to the communicator goal. The communicator's goal is to redirect the target's thinking in a way that is favorable to his or her point of view (Jackson & Jamieson, 2007). At its best, spin: 1) looks like it is addressing an issue directly, but it isn't; 2) cannot be factually disproved; and 3) uses language that allows interpretation so that the spinner can deny lying. The spinner is a person who is predisposed to a particular point of view and perceives several possible interpretations of the information in question, so his or her spin on the story is not perceived as lying. The use of half-truths and refocusing techniques are two common ways to spin.

Half-truths

A few examples should adequately explain the use of half-truths. In the 2004 U.S. presidential campaign, Bush said that Kerry voted for higher taxes on social security benefits. This was true, but the statement implied that Kerry was a person who did not have the concerns of older Americans at heart. This was not true. The money from increased taxes on social security benefits was intended to provide additional financial support for Medicare, a program for older Americans. Bush also failed to mention that he had not proposed repealing the tax increase on social security benefits in any of his own tax cut bills.

In 1996, President Clinton said he had put 100,000 new police officers on American's streets. He had signed a bill authorizing 100,000 new police officers, but at the time of his statement, only about 40,000 were funded and only about 21,000 of them were actually on duty.

In order to make light of those who wanted to regulate automobile emissions, an opponent commented: "The vegetation in your backyard gives off as many hydro-carbons as the law permits in your car." It is true that that the vegetable and auto emissions are comparable. What was not said, however, was that automobile emissions include carcinogens which are a cause of cancer.

President Bush's election victory in 2004 was considered a mandate by his supporters because, they argued, he got more votes than were ever cast in a U.S. presidential election. Kerry's supporters were quick to point out that this was true for their candidate as well.

Refocusing and Redirecting

Spin can also be accomplished by refocusing and redirecting. President Bush justified the invasion of Iraq because he claimed they had weapons of mass destruction. When no weapons of mass destruction were found, the war was later justified on the grounds that "we have removed a terrible despot in Saddam Hussein and brought democracy to Iraq."

Refocusing and redirecting also occurs when people are asked questions they don't want to answer. When asked, "Are we going through a depression?" the target of the question may appear to be restating the question, but in reality he or she states another question—e.g., "As I understand your question, you are really asking about the present state of the business cycle. Business income in this country has never been higher..." (Washburne, 1969).

Statistics can also be used to refocus and redirect thinking (Holmes, 1990; Huff, 1954). Schweitzer (1979, p. 2) said, "You can describe a 1% return on sales as a ten-million dollar profit; a 15% return on investment; an increase in profits of 40% (compared to the preceding four-year-period); or a decrease of 60% from last year, and prove any one of them by statistical manipulation." Notice how easy it is to argue that robberies involving a weapon have increased either 5% or 100% from the following data.

	2014	2015
All Robberies	400	400
Robberies With Weapons	20	40

One person might argue that, "There has been a small increase of 5% in robberies with weapons. In 2014 it was 5% of all robberies and in 2015 it was 10% of all robberies." Another person might say, "There has been a tremendous increase of 100% in robberies with weapons. In 2014 there were 20 and in 2015 that figure doubled to 40."

Bullshit

Liars are very concerned about the possible impact of a target learning the truth. As a result, they make a special effort to hide it or guide targets away from it. Bullshitters, on the other hand, have little regard for the truth. It doesn't concern them. Frankfurt (2005, p. 55) put it this way, "It is impossible to lie unless you think you know the truth. Producing bullshit requires no such conviction." From this perspective, bullshitters may say things that are accurate or inaccurate, but accuracy is not the issue for them. They are not trying to hide the truth. Instead, they are hiding their lack of concern for the truth. Bullshitters are not concerned with where they find information or whether it is true as long as it supports their overall purpose. Others may sometimes accuse them of lying when they make false statements, but reactions to bullshit are often benign. People who participate in "bull sessions" typically suspend their concern for factual accuracy as well as their certainty that the speaker really believes what he or she is saying.

Frankfurt (2005, pp. 16–18) provides the following example to illustrate bullshit. A Fourth of July orator is rambling on about such things as "our great and blessed country, whose Founding Fathers under divine guidance created a new beginning for mankind." The orator believes what he or she is saying and is not concerned about whether his or her audience agrees that the country is blessed and great, whether the Founding Fathers had divine guidance, or whether they created a new beginning for mankind. Instead, Frankfurt argues, the statements are more likely designed to convey an impression of the speaker as a patriot, a person who cares deeply about the origin, mission, and distinction of his or her country, a person who is religious, etc.

Bullshitting is widely practiced (Penny, 2005). Frankfurt (2005, p. 63) tells us why:

> Bullshit is unavoidable whenever circumstances require someone to talk without knowing what he is talking about. Thus the production of bullshit is stimulated whenever a person's obligations or opportunities to speak about some topic exceed his knowledge of the facts that are relevant to that topic. This discrepancy is common in public life, where people are frequently impelled—whether by their own propensities or by the demands of others—to speak extensively about matters of which they are to some degree ignorant.

Larson's (2006, p. 65) view of bullshit differs from Frankfurt's. He argues that bullshit often does hide or mask the truth, but it is done in such a way that it isn't a direct contradiction of something that others subscribe to as truth. When President Bush said, "Freedom is on the march in Iraq," Larson saw this as an effort to avoid mentioning specific problems that need to be addressed. He elaborates by saying:

> Who needs evidence when circumlocutory claims act like evidence: when fundamentalists preach obedience to morality because it's the literal word of God; when Enron uses legalese to fake loans to itself and then record the loan's interest as income; …Such pretenses are not indifferent to the truth; they are the truth. Moreover, they are the truths of technological savvy that McLuhan warned us of, a kind of bewitching misrepresentation.

Doublespeak

The term doublespeak has been around since the 1950s but it was popularized by an annual doublespeak award given by the National Council of Teachers of

English and in the works of Lutz (1981; 1996; 1999). Lutz uses the term to describe a broad spectrum of language use which he believes are deliberate misrepresentations of reality. He believes the words are incongruous with reality. The more disturbing ones, he believes, are used by people in positions of power to mislead others for their own purposes. He fears that if doublespeak is not exposed, it will structure the way we construe and experience reality. Rosen's (2003) observations concerning the labels given to programs in the Bush administration are compatible with Lutz' definition of doublespeak. Rosen says that the so-called "healthy forests" program allows increased logging of protected wilderness; that the "clear skies" program permits greater industrial pollution; and the new "opt in" feature of the head start program is simply a way of telling the states that they will now share a greater portion of the costs of the program.

As noted earlier, language used to make things seem better, easier, or more complicated than they really are can be used for good or ill (or somewhere in between). Many of the same forms of doublespeak which we sometimes detest and consider deceptive are used in daily intercourse without a lot of concern for anyone's intention to deceive. Our reactions are more likely rooted in our expectations, attitudes, and values than in the language form itself. Unless there is a clear factual and/ or tangible referent, words and phrases that don't fit *our* view of reality are more likely to be seen as a deceptive distortion of reality. But tangible referents are subject to interpretation as well. It is possible that the same behavior could be seen as either the work of "terrorists" or the work of "freedom fighters," depending on whose side you're on.

Although the distinctions between them are not always sharp, Lutz illustrates doublespeak by discussing four ways in which language is used:

- *Euphemisms.* These are constructions which try to cover up what might otherwise be a painful reality. Lutz is particularly concerned about euphemisms used to soften painful realities he believes the public should face. One example is the use of the term "incontinent ordinance" to refer to military bombs and artillery shells that kill civilian noncombatants. He also points out that the subject of the book you are currently reading, lying and deception, is often discussed by people in ways that make it seem less onerous—e.g., "strategic manipulation", "reality augmentation," "disinformation," "gave false impression," "made an incomplete statement," "made an inoperative statement," "misspoke," or "counterfactual proposition."

- *Jargon.* This is specialized language which people in a particular trade or profession use, but when it is used with the general public or people in another trade or profession, it can be confusing or misleading. For example, a crack in a metal support beam might be described as a "discontinuity," or a tax increase as "revenue enhancement."

- *Bureaucratese.* Lutz also calls this "gobbledegook." It is a way of confusing a target audience with technical terms, jargon, long sentences, and the like—i.e., the proverbial "word salad." Lutz (1989, pp. 5–6) gives the following example. During the investigation of the 1986 Challenger space shuttle explosion, Jesse Moore, NASA's associate administrator, was asked if the performance of the shuttle program had improved with each launch or if it had remained the same. His answer was: "I think our performance in terms of liftoff performance and in terms of the orbital performance, we knew more about the envelope we were operating under, and we have been pretty accurately staying in that. And so I would say the performance has not by design drastically improved. I think we have been able to characterize the performance more as a function of our launch experience as opposed to it improving as a function of time."

- *Inflated Language.* This is language used to make things seem better than they really are—to "puff" them up, make them seem impressive, make them seem more important. When the job title of a car mechanic is changed to an "automotive internist," most people don't care and the mechanic is happy. But when Chrysler Corporation "initiates a career alternative enhancement program" which really means they are laying off 5000 workers, people are more likely to be concerned about a cover up.

Summary

The possibility that we might be able to tell when a person is lying by simply observing certain tell-tale behaviors has been a matter of great interest to laymen and scientists alike. There are, however, a number of reasons why an unerring profile of liar behavior may not be possible. For example, behaviors signal things like anxiety or anger, not lying per se. Truth tellers also experience anxiety and anger. Furthermore, when the behavior of liars is made public, competent liars will try to behave differently. In addition, liars do not behave the same way all the time. The extent to which lies are expected, the perceived consequences of being discovered, the liar's relationship with the target, the liar's motives for lying, desire to succeed, and whether the lie involves falsification, concealment, misleading, or some combination of these, will all affect the kind of behavior the liar manifests.

Low-stakes lies do not have serious consequences and, in some situations, are expected as part of daily interaction. Behavioral differences between liars telling low-stakes lies and truth tellers are extremely difficult to perceive. Several low-stakes lies are told daily by most people. They are often told to strangers and acquaintances, but they are also a staple for the maintenance of close relationships. Low-stakes lies are triggered when people want to present themselves in a positive way, when trying to impress and attract a romantic partner, when flattering or ingratiating oneself to others, in various sporting activities, and when performing magic.

When serious consequences are associated with the telling of a lie, it is considered a high- stakes lie. Sometimes the high-stakes liar also perceives a substantial reward if the lie is not discovered. Researchers believe that we are more likely to develop a behavioral profile of high-stakes liars because they are likely experiencing more intense emotions and cognitive difficulties.

An analysis of more than a hundred studies comparing the behavior of liars and truth tellers, found specific behaviors supporting the following conclusions: 1) liars are less forthcoming than truth-tellers; 2) liars tell stories that are less plausible;

3) liars make a more negative impression; and 4) liars are more tense. Liars in close relationships are likely to behave differently. They tell lies to support and protect their partner; they know their partner is likely to spot behavior that deviates from their normal patterns; they know the story associated with a lie can come up at any time during the length of the relationship; and they actively collaborate and conspire with their partner on some lies.

The chapter concluded with a discussion of six acts which can be performed with the intention to create a false reality in the target (lying), but they are also acts which can and are often performed without deceptive intentions. When persons or groups perceive harm associated with these acts, they are likely to characterize them as intentionally deceptive. We discussed six of these acts: equivocation, contextomy, paltering, spin, bullshit, and doublespeak.

Things to Think About

Identify the circumstances when each of the following exchanges would: a) be accepted as a legitimate response without any concern for deceptive intent; b) create suspicion as to why the question was answered in that fashion; and c) definitely be considered deliberately evasive with deceptive intent.

1. Have you ever used illegal drugs?

    I don't use illegal drugs.

2. Have you seen Mark Knapp?

    I can't say that I have.

What is the difference between saying a particular behavior is a "behavior of liars" and saying a particular behavior is a "behavior of liars when compared to truth tellers?"

Do you think most people's attitude toward bullshit is more benign than toward lying? Why? Frankfurt (2005, p. 61) says "…bullshit is a greater enemy of truth than lies are" because the bullshitter is not concerned with the truth and the liar is." Do you agree?

Find and record at least one example of all the "blood relatives" of lying (equivocation, contextomy, paltering, spin, bullshit, and doublespeak) that have been communicated by the political party *you support*. Analyze them in terms of their intent and consequences. Pair yourself up with another person who supports a different political party. If you do not identify with a political party, find another person like yourself and flip a coin to see who does research on the Republicans and who examines the Democrats. When you are finished, compare your findings with your partner. How difficult was this? Why? Does your partner agree with your analysis of the intent and consequences for each example?

References

Albert, E.M. (1972). Culture patterning of speech behavior in Burundi. In J.J. Gumperz and D. Hymes (Eds.), *Directions in sociolinguistics: The ethnography of communication* (pp. 72–105). New York: Holt, Rinehart & Winston.

Aronson, J., & McGlone, M.S. (2008). Social identity and stereotype threat. In T. Nelson (Ed.), *Handbook of stereotyping and discrimination* (pp. 153–178). New York: Psychology Press.

Barnes, J.A. (1994). *A pack of lies: Towards a sociology of lying.* New York: Cambridge University Press.

Bavelas, J.B., Black, A., Chovil, N. & Mullett, J. (1990). *Equivocal communication.* Newbury Park, CA: Sage.

Bond, C.F., Jr., & DePaulo, B.M. (2006). Accuracy of deception judgments. *Personality and Social Psychology Review, 10,* 214–234.

Bond, C.F., Jr. & Fahey, W.E. (1987). False suspicion and the misperception of deceit. *British Journal of Social Psychology, 26,* 41–46.

Bond, C.F., Jr., Thomas, B.J., & Paulson, R.M. (2004). Maintaining lies: The multiple-audience problem. *Journal of Experimental Social Psychology, 40,* 29–40.

Bowers, J.W., Elliott, N.D., & Desmond, R.J. (1977). Exploiting pragmatic rules: Devious messages. *Human Communication Research, 3,* 235–242.

Buller, D.B. & Burgoon, J.K. (1996). Interpersonal deception theory. *Communication Theory, 6,* 203–242.

Buller, D.B., Burgoon, J.K., Buslig, A.S., & Roiger, J.F. (1994). Interpersonal deception VIII. Further analysis of nonverbal and verbal correlates of equivocation from the Bavelas et al. (1990) research. *Journal of Language and Social Psychology, 13,* 396–417.

Buller, D.B., Burgoon, J.K., Buslig, A.S., & Roiger, J.F. (1996). Testing interpersonal deception theory: The language of interpersonal deception. *Communication Theory, 6,* 268–289.

Buller, D.B., Burgoon, J.K., White, C.H., & Ebesu, A.S. (1994). Interpersonal deception VII. Behavioral profiles of falsification, equivocation, and concealment. *Journal of Language and Social Psychology, 13,* 366–395.

Burgoon, J.K., & Floyd, K. (2000). Testing for the motivation impairment effect during deceptive and truthful interaction. *Western journal of Communication 64,* 243–267.

Burgoon, J.K., Buller, D.B., Ebesu, A.S., White, C.H., & Rockwell, P.A. (1996). Testing interpersonal deception theory: Effects of suspicion on communication behaviors and perceptions. *Communication Theory, 6,* 243–267.

Burgoon, J.K., Buller, D.B., Guerrero, L.K., Afifi, W.A., & Feldman, C.M. (1996). Interpersonal deception: XII. Information management dimensions underlying deceptive and truthful messages. *Communication Monographs, 63,* 50–69.

Buss, D.M. (1994). *The evolution of desire: Strategies of human mating.* New York: Basic Books.

Caro, M. (2003). *Caro's book of poker tells: The psychology and body language of poker.* New York: Cardoza Publishing.

Castillo, P.A., & Mallard, D. (2012). Preventing cross-cultural bias in deception judgments: The role of expectancies about nonverbal behavior. *Journal of Cross-Cultural Psychology, 43,* 967–978.

Corcoran, J.F.T., Lewis, M. D., & Garver, R. B. (1978). Biofeedback—conditioned galvanic skin response and hypnotic suppression of arousal: A pilot study of their relation to deception. *Journal of Forensic Sciences, 23,* 155–162.

DePaulo, B.M. (1992). Nonverbal behavior and self-presentation. *Psychological Bulletin,* 111, 203–243.

DePaulo, B.M., & Kashy, D.A. (1998). Everyday lies in close and casual relationships. *Journal of Personality and Social Psychology, 74,* 63–79.

DePaulo, B.M., & Kirkendol, S.E. (1989). The motivational impairment effect in the communication of deception. In J. Yuille (Ed.), *Credibility assessment* (pp. 51–70). Belgium: Kluwer.

DePaulo, B.M., Lindsay, J.J., Malone, B.E., Muhlenbruck, L., Charlton, K., & Cooper, H. (2003). Cues to deception. *Psychological Bulletin,* 129, 74–118.

Ebesu, A.S. & Miller, M.D. (1994). Verbal and nonverbal behaviors as a function of deception type. *Journal of Language and Social Psychology,* 13, 418–442.

Ekman, P. (2001). *Telling lies.* New York: Norton.

Ekman, P. & Friesen, W.V. (1969). Nonverbl leakage and clues to deception. *Psychiatry, 32,* 88–106.

Ekman, P., O=Sullivan, M., & Frank, M.G. (1999). A few can catch a liar. *Psychological Science, 10,* 263–266.

Exline, R.V., Thibaut, J., Hickey, C.B., & Gumpert, P. (1970). Visual interaction in relation to Machiavellianism and an unethical act. In P. Christie & F. Geis (Eds.), *Studies in Machiavellianism.* New York: Academic Press.

Feeley, T.H., & deTurck, M.A. (1998). The behavioral correlates of sanctioned and unsanctioned deceptive communication. *Journal of Nonverbal Behavior, 22,* 189–204.

Feldman, R.S., Forrest, J.A., & Happ, B.R. (2002). Self-presentation and verbal deception: Do self-presenters lie more? *Basic and Applied Social Psychology, 24,* 163–170.

Fitzkee, D. (1945). *Magic by misdirection.* San Rafael, CA.: Saint Raphael House.

Frank, M.G. and Ekman, P. (2004). Appearing truthful generalizes across different deception situations. *Journal of Personality and Social Psychology, 86,* 486–495.

Frankfurt, H.G. (2005). *On bullshit.* Princeton, NJ: Princeton University Press.

Galasiski, D. (2000). *The language of deception: A discourse analytical study.* Thousand Oaks, CA: Sage.

Global Deception Research Team. (2006). A world of lies. *Journal of Cross-Cultural Psychology, 37,* 60–74.

Gordon, R. (1994). Impact of ingratiation on judgments and evaluations: A meta-analytic investigation. *Journal of Personality and Social Psychology, 71,* 54–70.

Gore, A. (1992). *Earth in the balance.* New York: Houghton Mifflin.

Granhag, P. A., Andersson, L.O., Strömwall, L.A., & Hartwig, M. (2004). Imprisoned knowledge: Criminals beliefs about deception. *Legal and Criminological Psychology, 9,* 103–119.

Hancock, J.T., Thom-Santelli, J., & Ritchie, T. (2004). Deception and design: The impact of communication technology on lying behavior. *Proceedings of CHI 2004,* 24–29. Hancock, J. & Toma, C. (2009). Putting your best face forward: The accuracy of online dating photographs. *Journal of Communication, 59,* 367–386.

Hayano, D.M. (1980). Communicative competency among poker players. *Journal of Communication, 30,* 113–120.

Herzog, A. (1973). *The b.s. factor: The theory and technique of faking it in America.* New York: Penguin Books.

Holmes, C.B. (1990). *The honest truth about lying with statistics.* Springfield, IL: Charles C. Thomas.

Horvath, F.S. (1973). Verbal and nonverbal clues to truth and deception during polygraph examinations. *Journal of Police Science and Administration, 1,* 1138–152.

Horvath, F.S., Jayne, B., & Buckley, J. (1994). Differentiation of truthful and deceptive criminal suspects in behavior analysis interviews. *Journal of Forensic Sciences, 39,* 793–807.

Huff, D. (1954). *How to lie with statistics.* New York: Norton.

Hurley, C.M., Griffin, D.J., & Stefanone, M.A. (2014). Who told you that? Uncovering the source of believed cues to deception. *International Journal of Psychological Studies, 6,* 19–32.

Jackson, B. & Jamieson, K.H. (2007). *UnSpun: Finding facts in a world of disinformation.* New York: Random House.

Jones, E.E. (1964). *Ingratiation: A social psychological analysis.* New York: Appleton-Century-Crofts.

Keyes, R. (2004). The post truth era: Dishonesty and deception in contemporary life. New York: St. Martin's Press.

Knapp, M.L. (2006) Lying and deception in close relationships. In A.L. Vangelisti and D. Perlman, eds., *Cambridge handbook of personal relationships.* New York: Cambridge University Press.

Knapp, M.L. & Comadena, M.E. (1979). Telling it like it isn't: A review of theory and research on deceptive communications. *Human Communication Research, 5,* 270–285.

Knapp, M.L., Hart, R.P., & Dennis, H.S. (1974). An exploration of deception as a communication construct. *Human Communication Research, 1,* 15–29.

Larson, T. (August/September, 2006). On bovine excrement. *Free Inquiry, 26,* 64–65.

Levin, J. (2013, December 19). The welfare queen. *Slate.com.* http://www.slate.com/articles/news_and_politics/history/2013/12/

Levine, T.R., & Kim, R.K. (2008). Some considerations for a new theory of deceptive communication. In M.S. McGlone & M.L. Knapp (Eds.), *The interplay of truth and deception* (pp. 16–34). New York: Routledge.

Levine, T.R., Kim, R.K., & Hamel, L.M. (2010). People lie for a reason: Three experiments documenting the principle of veracity. *Communication Research Reports, 27,* 271–285.

Luchetti, A.E. (1999). Deception in disclosing one's sexual history: Safe-sex avoidance or ignorance? *Communication Quarterly, 47,* 300–314.

Lutz, W. (1989). *Doublespeak.* New York Harper & Row.

Lutz, W. (1999). *Doublespeak defined: Cut through the bull**** and get the point.* New York: HarperCollins.

Lutz, W. (1996). *The new doublespeak: Why no one knows what anyone's saying anymore.* New York: HarperCollins.

Mawby, R. and Mitchell, R.W. (1986). Feints and ruses: An analysis of deception in sports. In R.W. Mitchell and N.S. Thompson (Eds.), *Deception: Perspectives on human and nonhuman deceit* (pp. 313–322). Albany, NY: State University of New York Press.

McGlone, M.S. (2005). Quoted out of context: Contextomy and its consequences. *Journal of Communication, 55,* 330–346.

McGlone, M.S., & Baryshevtsev, M. (2015). Deception by quotation. In J. Meibauer (Ed.), *The Oxford handbook of deception* (pp. 220–233). Oxford, UK: Oxford University Press.

Metts, S. (1989). An exploratory investigation of deception in close relationships. *Journal of Social and personal relationships, 6,* 159–179.

Nyberg, D. (1993). *The varnished truth. Truth telling and deceiving in ordinary life.* Chicago: University of Chicago Press.

O'Brien, T. (1990). *The things they carried.* New York: Broadway Books.

Ng, S.H. & Bradac, J.J. (1993). *Power in language: Verbal communication and social influence.* Newbury Park, CA: Sage.

Pender, K. (2015, April 15). IRS income tax audit chances are slim, except for these people. *San Francisco Chronicle.* http://www.sfchronicle.com/business/networth/article/.

Penny, L. (2005). *Your call is important to us: The truth about bullshit.* New York: Crown.

Rodriguez, N., & Ryave, A. (1990). Telling lies in everyday life: Motivational and organizational consequences of sequential preferences. *Qualitative Sociology, 13,* 195–210.

Rogers, T., Zeckhauser, R., Gino, F., Schweitzer, M., & Norton, M. (2014). *Artful paltering: The risks and rewards of using truthful statements to mislead others.* Faculty Research Working Paper Series, John F. Kennedy School of Government, Harvard University.

Roggensack, K.E., & Sillars, A. (2014). Agreement and understanding about honesty and deception rules in romantic relationships. *Journal of Personal and Social Relationships, 31,* 178–199.

Roloff, M.E., & Miller, C.W. (2006). Social cognition approaches to understanding interpersonal conflict and communication. In J.G. Oetzel & S. Ting-Toomey (Eds.), *The SAGE handbook of conflict communication: Integrating theory, research, and practice* (pp. 97–128). Thousand Oaks, CA: Sage. Rosen, R. (July 14, 2003). Bush doublespeak. *San Francisco Chronicle,* p. B7.

Schauer, F., & Zeckhauser, R. (2009). Paltering. In B. Harrington (Ed.), *Deception: From ancient empires to internet dating* (pp. 38–54). Stanford, CA: Stanford University Press.

Schweitzer, S.C. (1979). *Winning with deception and bluff.* Englewood Cliffs, NJ: Prentice-Hall.

Sebanz, N., & Shiffrar, M. (2009). Detecting deception in a bluffing body: The role of expertise. *Psychonomic Bulletin & Review, 16,* 170–175.

Shulman, D. (2007). *From hire to liar: The role of deception in the workplace.* Ithaca, N.Y.: Cornell University Press.

Shulman, G.M. (1973). *An experimental study of the effects of receiver sex, communicator sex, and warning on the ability of receivers to detect deceptive communicators.* Unpublished master's thesis, Purdue University.

Stebbins, R.A. (1975). Putting people on: Deception of our fellow-man in everyday life. *Sociology and Social Research, 69,* 189–200.

Stengel, R. (2000). (*You're too kind*) *A brief history of flattery.* New York: Simon & Shuster.

Toma, C.L., & Hancock, J.T. (2010). Lying for love in the modern age. In M.S. McGlone & M.L. Knapp (Eds.), *The interplay of truth and deception* (pp. 149–163). New York: Routledge.

Toma, C.L., Hancock, J.T., & Ellison, N. (2008). Separating fact from fiction: An examination of deceptive self-presentation in online dating profiles. *Personality and Social Psychology Bulletin, 34,* 1023–1036. Tooke, J., & Camire, L. (1991). *Patterns of deception in intersexual and intrasexual mating strategies. Ethology and Sociobiology, 12,* 345–364.

Vallacher, R.R., & Wegner, D.M. (1985). *A theory of action identification.* Hillsdale, NJ: Erlbaum.

Vangelisti, A. (2012). Interpersonal processes in romantic relationships. In M.L. Knapp & J.A. Daly (Eds.), *The SAGE handbook of interpersonal communication* (pp. 597–631). Thousand Oaks, CA: SAGE.

Vrij, A. (2000). *Detecting lies and deceit.* Chichester, England: Wiley.

Vrij, A., Akehurst, L., & Knight, S. (2006). Police officers', social workers', teachers', and the general public's beliefs about deception in children, adolescents and adults. *Legal and Criminological Psychology, 11,* 297–312.

Washburne, C. (1969). Retortmanship: How to avoid answering questions. *ETC: A Review of General Semantics, 26,* 69–75.

Wegner, D.M. & Bargh, J.A. (1998). Control and automaticity in social life. In D.T. Gilbert, S.T. Fiske, & G. Lindzey (Eds.), *The handbook of social psychology.* 4th ed. Vol. 1 (pp. 446–496). New York: McGraw-Hill.

White, C.H. & Burgoon, J.K. (2001). Adaptation and communicative design: Patterns of interaction in truthful and deceptive conversations. *Human Communication Research, 27,* 9–37.

Zuckerman, M., DePaulo, B.M., & Rosenthal, R. (1981). Verbal and nonverbal communication of deception. In L. Berkowitz, ed., *Advances in experimental social psychology* (Vol. 14, pp. 1–59). New York: Academic Press.

Chapter 8

Specialists in Lying and Deception

Everyone lies at some point in their lives, but some people lie more than others. In a large survey of adults in the U.S., Serota, Levine, and Boster (2010) found that while the average number of lies per day reported by respondents was between 1 and 2 (1.65), the majority reported telling few or no lies and just a small subset reported telling many. In a follow-up survey in the U.K., Serota and Levine (2015) examined the characteristics of "prolific liars," defined as people who reported lying 5 times or more per day (289 of 2,980 respondents, about 10% of the sample), in contrast to a majority of respondents who reported lying about twice per day. Compared to typical low-frequency liars, prolific liars tended to be younger and were more likely to be male, work in technical occupations, and have higher occupational status (managers or supervisors). They reported telling about 6 times as many "little white lies" (e.g., saying you like a gift you really don't) per day as typical liars, and almost 20 times as many "big lies" (e.g., saying "I love you" to someone you don't). They reported lying to their relationship partners and children more than typical liars, although curiously were somewhat less likely to report lying to their mothers. Not surprisingly, prolific liars were also more likely to experience serious negative consequences of lying. They were much more likely than typical liars to say they had been dumped by a relational partner (19.7% vs. 5.2%) or fired from work (13.1% vs. 1.5%) for lying. While prolific liars reported telling more lies to more people and suffering more negative consequences than typical liars, they did not express stronger feelings of guilt or remorse for their deceit. Based on the numerous and often substantial differences between the groups, Serota and Levine (2015) recommend that researchers treat prolific liars as a distinct population from typical low-frequency liars.

Prolific liars "specialize" in deception. What does it take to qualify as a specialist? To a large extent, the answer is practice, practice, practice. Lying specialists lie repeatedly and habitually. As a result, most are skilled liars. Lying is an indelible part of their

> "Fraud is the homage that force pays to reason."
>
> — *Charles Curtis*

> "In today's financial regulatory environment, it's virtually impossible to violate the rules. It's also impossible for a violation to go undetected for a considerable period of time."
>
> — *Bernie Madoff*

life style. The distinction between a lie and the truth is often less important to them than saying whatever is necessary to accomplish a desired goal. Lies are so commonplace that specialists may even tell lies when they aren't necessary. People addicted to drugs and/or alcohol is a good example. Addicts initially use lies to deny or minimize their usage, to cover up problems linked to their usage, or to create situations which would facilitate their usage. But as Twerski (1997, p. 63) says: "…sooner or later it [lying] takes on a life of its own. The addict manipulates just to manipulate and lies just to lie, even though there may be nothing to gain. Manipulation and lying, instead of being a means to an end, actually become ends in themselves." In addition to addicts, lying specialists appear in a variety of roles such as: imposters, con-artists, identity thieves, people with a haunting secret (e.g., being abused as child; or being a sex offender), people who alter the history of their past accomplishments and activities (imposeurs), and people who perpetrate a hoax.

Lying specialists manifest their behavior in a variety of ways. Some lie while remaining in a single role (e.g., a father trying to make himself look good to his children); some perform multiple roles (e.g., an art dealer who is also a spy; a husband who has several wives; a teacher who impersonates a prison guard). Sometimes these different roles are enacted simultaneously; sometimes sequentially. Some of these liars develop other specialized skills (e.g., printing knowledge for forging currency and documents or medical knowledge for treating illnesses and doing surgery). Their goals may be to swindle others, to help others, to make themselves look and feel good, or to enjoy the deceptive performance itself. Some of these liars specialize in a particular content area (e.g., military service) while others use a broad knowledge base in order to be successful.

Despite the many ways lying specialists manifest themselves, there are some characteristics which seem to be widely shared. Aside from those with certain personality disorders, lying specialists are likely to be socially adept—familiar with situational/behavioral norms and expectations, able to anticipate the reactions of others, and able to adapt accordingly for the manipulation of their targets. They are often outwardly self-confident and willing to take risks. Adhering to ethical and moral standards is secondary (or non-existent) to getting what they want.

The general public seems to have a mixed reaction to some of these lying specialists. On the one hand, they are resented and condemned for their disregard of truthfulness. Those who use lying to swindle others are sent to prison. Targets of lying specialists are not likely to have any kind words for them. On the other hand, the public is often intrigued, even captivated by certain charming scoundrels who specialize in lying. As long as we aren't involved with lying specialists, we may find a certain fascination with their brazen disregard for the truth and how they manage to carry out their duplicitous lives. We may be interested and curious about why they weren't uncovered sooner. People who treat lying like most people treat truth-telling are an oddity. And oddities draw our attention. Sometimes we even admire the ingenuity, effort, audacity, and skill of these super liars without approving of what they do. It is not unlike the admiration we have for the deceit of a skilled magician. The big difference, of course, is that we give permission to magicians to fool us; lying specialists do not seek our consent.

To further understand these specialists in lying and deception, this chapter examines: 1) psychological disorders in which lying is a prominent feature; 2) imposeurs; 3) imposters; 4) con artists; and 5) hoaxers. These categories enable us to talk about various types of lying specialists, but the behavior of any given liar may encompass several of these categories—e.g., an imposter may be a con artist with a particular personality disorder.

Psychological Disorders

The German physician Anton Delbruck (1891) is credited with being the first to describe the concept of "pathological lying" in patient case studies. He observed that some of his patients told lies so abnormal and disproportionate as to deserve a special psychiatric category he described as *pseudologia fantastica*. To date, however, there is no consensus among mental health professionals about the definition of pathological lying, although there is general agreement about its core elements (Dike, Baranoski, & Griffith, 2005). Pathological lying is characterized by a long (perhaps lifelong) history of frequent and repeated lying for which no apparent psychological motive or external benefit can be discerned. Although ordinary lies are goal-directed and intended to obtain an external benefit or avoid punishment, pathological lies appear to be without purpose. In some cases, they may even be self-incriminating or damaging, which makes the behavior even more puzzling. Dike (2008) offers the following case vignette:

> "Mr A was desperate. He was about to lose yet another job, not because he was at risk for being fired, but because his lying behavior had finally boxed him into a corner. He had lied repeatedly to his colleagues, telling them that he had an incurable disease and was receiving palliative treatment. Initially, his coworkers treated him with sensitivity and concern, but as the weeks wore on, the scrutiny of his colleagues became increasingly pointed. He had to tell more and more outrageous lies to cover his tracks and justify having a terminal illness. Finally, when the heat became too unbearable, he suddenly stopped going to work. On the face of it, it would seem Mr A told these lies to gain the sympathy of his colleagues, but the consequences of his lying, in terms of emotional distress and potential loss of job, far outweighed any perceived gain. Mr A had lost several other jobs in the past because of his lying, and he was becoming frustrated. Family members reported that he often told blatant lies, and even when confronted, and proved wrong, he still swore they were true. Mr A finally sought psychiatric help after concluding that he could not stop himself from lying."

Mr. A's pattern of behavior is familiar to psychotherapists—excessive lying, easily determined to be false, mostly unhelpful to the liar in any apparent way, and sometimes harmful to the liar, yet told repeatedly over time. Even prominent and successful individuals engage in this pattern. For example, California Superior Court Judge Patrick Couwenberg was removed from office not only for lying in his official capacity (claiming to have academic degrees and military experience he clearly did not have) but also for lying under oath to a commission investigating his behavior. A psychiatric expert witness diagnosed him with *pseudologia fantastica* and suggested the judge needed treatment. Why such a successful individual would repeatedly tell lies that could damage his credibility and put him in trouble with the law or other administrative bodies is baffling. Was his lying behavior completely within his control, or was there something different about his pattern of lies?

Some forensic psychiatrists believe pathological lying may someday be classified as a separate and distinct psychological disorder (Hausman, 2003), but it is currently treated as a symptom of other disorders. Anyone may engage in habitual lying for a brief period of time or in conjunction with a particular life event. But lying in conjunction with a "personality disorder" means it is an enduring pattern of maladaptive behavior exhibited in a wide variety of situations. People with personality disorders deviate considerably from cultural expectations regarding interpersonal functioning, thinking, and impulse control. Lenzenweger, Lane, Loranger, and Kessler (2007) estimated that about 9% of the people in the USA suffer from some kind of personality disorder. The DSM-5 (Diagnostic and Statistical Manual of Mental Disorders Edition 5, 2013) identifies compulsive lying as a central characteristic of five personality disorders: antisocial, borderline, narcissistic, histrionic and obsessive-compulsive. Diagnosis is often based on a person having some, but not necessarily all of the traits associated with a particular personality disorder. Thus, any two people with the disorder may not have exactly the same characteristics.

Antisocial Personality Disorder (Sociopathy and Psychopathy)

People diagnosed with this disorder have little, if any, regard for the needs of others. There is no remorse when they hurt others; no love when others are kind. They are almost devoid of empathy, emotional sensitivity, and ethical standards. Other people are useful only to the extent that they play a role in serving and gratifying the needs of the person with the antisocial personality disorder. When others are not serving the needs of this person, he or she is likely to get frustrated, irritable, and aggressive. These personalities want what they want when they want it. As a result, people with this personality disorder are often in conflict with authorities over unlawful behavior. Their relationships at home and at work are unstable, frequently changing, and filled with self-serving manipulations and cheating. However, they can be very persuasive, even charming, in efforts to establish such relationships (Forward, 1999).

The DSM-5 lists "sociopathy" and "psychopathy" as subtypes of anti-social personality disorder. Some mental health professionals use the terms interchangeably, but others argue there are important and significant distinctions between the types (e.g., Pemment, 2013). According to their perspective, sociopaths tend to be nervous and prone to emotional outbursts, including fits of rage. They also tend to be uneducated, living on the edge of society, and unable to hold down a steady job for very long. While they have difficulty forming attachments with individuals, they may form attachment to groups with an anti-social orientation (street gangs, white supremacist collectives such as KKK or Stormfront, etc.). When they commit crimes, they are typically spontaneous, haphazard, and disorganized. In contrast, psychopaths often have disarming or charming personalities; while they too find it difficult to form emotional attachments to individuals, they find it easy to gain their trust, which they then use for manipulation. Psychopaths are often well-educated and hold steady jobs. Some are so good at manipulation that they have families and other long-term relationships without those around them ever suspecting their true malignant nature. When they commit crimes, they tend to plan them out in a calm, cool, and meticulous manner. Many notorious and prolific serial killers such as Ted Bundy, Jeffrey Dahmer, John Wayne Gacy, and Dennis Rader have been diagnosed by forensic psychiatrists as psychopaths (Martens, 2014).

Lying is an addiction for both sociopaths and psychopaths. Lies are told frequently, effortlessly, and without much guilt or anxiety. They may even find it difficult to understand why others value truth, especially when it hurts to tell it. Because they practice lying so often, they can confront even the most challenging confrontations to their credibility with considerable aplomb. On occasion they will admit to a lie or promise to change their behavior, but normally this is a tactic to establish trust for a future lie (Cleckley, 1982).

People with an antisocial personality disorder are overwhelmingly male.

Borderline Personality Disorder

Sudden, sometimes intense, mood swings are characteristic of the borderline personality disorder. A rational and efficient worker may, for no apparent reason, become unreasonable and irresponsible; an understanding and committed lover may become angry, close-minded, and absent. Their behavior is hard to predict. These mood swings are often linked to the person's idealization of a job or person which leads to euphoric feelings but also creates unrealistically high expectations. In time, there will be anxiety, frustration, and/or rejection associated with the object of idealization. This leads to disappointment of major proportions and anger. Anger may be directed at self as well as at others and lead to self-destructive behavior in the form of self-mutilation, abuse of alcohol/drugs, or spending money excessively. Impulse control is a problem for the person with a borderline personality.

In addition to the lying that may be associated with various self-destructive behaviors, people with this disorder often use lies as a weapon to get even with people for not living up to expectations or for disappointments they are believed to have created. Spreading false rumors or filing a fraudulent lawsuit are ways people can use to "get even" with those who shattered their dreams.

People with a borderline personality disorder are overwhelmingly female.

Narcissistic Personality Disorder

People with narcissistic personality disorder are pathologically preoccupied with themselves. They exaggerate their achievements and expect this portrayal to be accepted by others. They require an excessive amount of admiration, but have relatively little empathy for those who might provide the veneration they desire. They view themselves as "special" and entitled to special treatment. Ironically, an outwardly self-confident, even arrogant, behavior may mask a low sense of self-esteem.

Lies, exaggerations, and half-truths are used by people with this disorder to support the grandiose personae they have created. This may occur in self-presentations or in the exploitation of others for his or her own needs. In order to maintain the brilliant, skilled, attractive, and immeasurably successful self they have created, narcissists are also skilled at self-deception. Unless they deceive themselves, the narcissists aren't able to function very well.

Not surprisingly, people with this disorder often seek and achieve positions of power and prestige. Rijsenbilt and Commandeur (2013) report evidence indicating an overrepresentation of narcissistic personalities among corporate CEOs who have been prosecuted for financial fraud. Although never formally diagnosed, several psychiatrists have suggested that former investment advisor Bernie Madoff, currently serving a life sentence for perpetrating the largest Ponzi scheme in history, has this disorder. Dr. Gerald Bryant of the Forensic Psychology Group claimed Madoff's ability to conceal fraud on such a massive scale was driven in part by a narcissistic belief that no matter what he did, he was so much smarter than everyone else he would never get caught. That it took so long for the Securities and Exchange Commission to catch on to Madoff's scheme simply reinforced this belief. "Authorities looked at Madoff a number of times and didn't do anything," Bryant observed, "so his crimes became substantiated in his mind. He most likely felt no remorse over what he had done" (International Business Times, 2011). Paulhus (2014) characterized Madoff as possessing a "dark personality" common to many white-collar criminals that combines malignant narcissism with Machiavellianism (see Chapter 3).

Males are slightly more likely than females to have a narcissistic personality disorder.

Histrionic Personality Disorder

The word "histrionic" is associated with excessively dramatic and emotion-laden behavior, like that of an actor. These affectations are designed to call attention to themselves. The speech of a person with this disorder may be theatrical; their appearance and dress may be flamboyant. They are not comfortable for long if they aren't the center of attention. Like all the preceding personality disorders, people with a histrionic personality disorder are self-centered and demanding, but unlike the sociopaths, they are not violent. These individuals try to build their self-esteem by calling attention to themselves, using flattery to get others to meet their needs, engaging in sexually seductive behavior, responding positively to suggestions by others, and not dwelling on frustrations and unpleasantries.

People with this disorder tell lies in order to garner and hold attention and to offset feelings of threat and rejection. A person with a histrionic personality disorder might, for example, spontaneously make up a story for his or her co-workers that he or she was nearly run over by a gypsy riding a bicycle while returning from lunch. It is the kind of story sure to draw a crowd. And, like the narcissist, a person who depends on being the center of attention to boost his or her self-esteem is dependent on proficient self-deception.

Women are more likely to have a histrionic personality disorder than men.

Obsessive-Compulsive Personality Disorder

An obsessive-compulsive personality disorder is characterized by a preoccupation with orderliness, rules, matters of right and wrong, and interpersonal control at the expense of flexibility, openness, and efficiency. The things that occupy this person's attention often keep them from seeing the "big picture." Because emotions are held in check, personal relationships may lack the kind of closeness that free-flowing feelings may provide. This person's obsession with perfection may deter success in some occupations and facilitate it in others. However, the amount of time and effort dedicated to work may be at the expense of leisure time activities and friendship maintenance.

Compared to the lies told by those with other personality disorders, those told by the obsessive-compulsives seem pretty benign. Their lies are primarily designed to maintain secrets and protect their independence.

Men are twice as likely to have an obsessive-compulsive personality disorder as women.

What Do These Personality Disoders Have in Common?

Each personality disorder is different, but some characteristics are shared by several of them. For example, many people diagnosed with these personality disorders tell a lot of undetected lies and become confident, skilled liars. Their ability to deceive themselves and the negligible amount of guilt or anxiety they feel about lying facilitates their ability to deceive others. They are extremely self-oriented and use lies to get what they want, including a boost to their typically low self-esteem. Their low self-esteem may be the result of growing up in a dysfunctional family environment. Absent or neglectful parents, family members who engage in physical abuse, and family members with a drug and/or alcohol addiction are not uncommon in the lives of these people. They are not likely to get the love and attention they need as children. And as adults they tend to avoid emotional ties and close relationships because it makes the lying and exploitation a lot easier. If all this reminds you of Machiavellianism (discussed in Chapter 3), you see the same connections that McHoskey et al. (1998) saw. They maintain that psychopathy and Machiavellianism are essentially the same personality construct.

Factitious Disorders

Lying is also a key symptom of "factitious disorders," in which people deliberately act as if they are physically or mentally ill when they are not. Unlike people who feign illness to acquire drugs or avoid punishment (known as "malingerers" and described in the next section), those with a factitious disorder behave this way because of an inner need to be seen as ill or injured, not to achieve an external benefit. Factitious disorders are frequently comorbid with (i.e., they co-occur with) personality disorders. There are three factitious disorders generally recognized by mental health professionals: Ganser Syndrome, Munchausen's Syndrome, and Munchausen's Syndrome by Proxy.

Ganser Syndrome, sometimes called "prison psychosis," is a factitious disorder first observed in prisoners following solitary confinement. People with this syndrome exhibit short-term episodes of bizarre behavior resembling schizophrenia. Symptoms include confusion, repeated mimicking of vocalizations (echolalia) and movements (echopraxia) of other people, and bizarre conversational interaction. Absurd answers are offered for simple questions: *Q: How many legs does a dog have? A: 10. Q: What is the day of the week after Monday? A: Friday.* The disorder is extremely rare – only 94 diagnosed cases ever, of which about 3 in 4 have been male. Approximately 1 in 3 diagnosed with the syndrome has had a prior history of mental illness. In approximately half the cases has the person developed comorbid mental illnesses (depression, Tourette's syndrome, etc.) during the factitious episode, but in less than 10% did mental illness persist after the episode. The vast majority of Ganser sufferers (76%) exhibit no recollection of their symptoms after the episode. What appears to be common to almost all Ganser cases is an individual faced with stress whose ability to cope is compromised by chronic personal problems (alcohol abuse, drug use, etc.) and situational pressures, such as losing a job or being incarcerated (Mendis & Hodgson, 2012).

Munchausen's syndrome was named after Baron von Munchausen, an 18th Century German Cavalry officer who was well known for exaggerating his adventures. People with this syndrome deliberately create or exaggerate illness symptoms in several ways. In some cases, they simply claim to have symptoms they don't have (e.g., "I have blood in my urine"). In others, they alter lab tests (e.g., adding blood to a urine sample) to make it look as if they are sick. In still others, they intentionally hurt themselves to create the symptoms (e.g., consuming a household cleaning product to induce blood in urine). In one documented case, a patient was admitted to over 400 hospitals (Boyd, 2014). Munchausen Syndrome patients are routinely examined by physicians, so in order to be successful in their deception they need to have an extensive knowledge of the diseases they are faking. Those who carry on their pretense even when they are not being scrutinized by a physician may also enhance their chances of deceiving others. But doctors may become suspicious when the patient reports symptoms that sound too much like descriptions in medical textbooks. A severe personality disorder is often at the heart of this syndrome, but there can be other driving forces. Ford (1996) identified three possibilities: 1) A person who feels vulnerable and incompetent in other areas of life may feel clever, skillful, and powerful by fooling physicians and nurses. 2) For a person who needs a clear and well-defined identity, a "sick person", particularly one with a serious disease, satisfies that need while simultaneously generating attention and feelings of self-importance. 3) A person with an excessive and/or unmet need to be cared for and nurtured may also find satisfaction in being treated for a false disease

Munchausen's Syndrome by Proxy (MSBP) is an often misdiagnosed form of child abuse in which people induce symptoms of a disease in their own children (usually preverbal) and then give false reports to medical caregivers (Talbot, 2004). The vast majority (95%) of people diagnosed with MSBP are women. British pediatrician Roy Meadow (1977) was the first to identify MSBP cases. In one, a six year old girl's mother put her own blood in her child's urine sample to make her appear ill. The child saw sixteen doctors, was admitted to the hospital twelve times, catheterized, x-rayed, and given eight different types of antibiotics. Several methods used by MSBP patients to inflict factitious illness in children have been documented, including poisoning, drawing blood to induce anemia, rubbing dirt into wounds to cause infection, and choking to the point of asphyxiation (Criddle, 2010). Once the abused child is hospitalized, the perpetrator gets the attention she has been seeking. She will pretend to be grief-stricken by what has happened to the child she loves and the physician and hospital staff provide a wealth of comfort and support. On occasion, MSBP occurs with adults. For example, a nurse may induce cardiac arrest in a patient to enjoy the exhilaration and excitement derived from being a member of the medical team seeking to remedy the problem.

Imposeurs

Imposeurs are people who retain most of their own personal identity, but fabricate key elements such as experiences they never had, skills they never learned, degrees they didn't earn, jobs they never had, and awards they never received(Keyes, 2004). These falsehoods may be written and/or oral; biographical or experiential; they may involve forged documents or misleading props. They may be done with self-ish or altruistic motives, but may also reflect the imposeur's "deepest yearnings and feelings of inadequacy" (Keyes, 2004, p. 71). Like other skilled liars, the best imposeurs mix lies with related truths—e.g., "I was in the Army (true) where I flew helicopters (can fly a helicopter, but did not fly one in the Army) in Iraq (false)." Another lie may be implicit in this statement if the person was not an Army offi-cer since helicopter pilots are officers. Even though the deceptive ability of impo-seurs is sometimes formidable, they are amateurs when compared with imposters. That's why they are classified separately even though the nature of their behavior is similar.

Imposeurs probably occupy all domains of human life, but a representative illus-tration of their behavior can be seen in stories about relationships, the military, illness, and crime.

Relationship Stories

One of our sisters-in-law worked with a man who constantly linked his own iden-tity with famous people. He claimed, for example, that his uncle was rocket pioneer Werner von Braun; that he and his family had dinner with President Eisenhower on several occasions; that J.C. Penny used to hold him on his knee when he was a child and give him nickels; that his aunt was the movie actress Deanna Durbin; and that he partied with poet Alan Ginsburg and actress Tallulah Bankhead. His stories made him an interesting and entertaining co-worker, but as the list of famous people in his past grew longer, his credibility grew weaker.

Wolff (1979/1990) tells the story of his father whose ordinary life, burdened by debts and wrongdoings, fashioned the life he wanted with lies. He wanted to be a father who was admired and respected, a father a son could look up to. He bought stylish clothes, added "II" (sometimes "III") after his name, and recounted his fic-tional days at Yale and his membership in Yale's exclusive Skull and Bones frater-nity. In this make-believe life he served in the Office of Strategic Services (OSS), America's first intelligence agency. He professed to be an aeronautical engineer, but not of Jewish heritage (which he was). About his father, Wolff (1979/1990) said: "He would not make peace with his actualities, and so he was the author of his own circumstances, and indifferent to the consequences of this nervy program...I once believed that he was most naturally a fictioneer" (p. 9, 10).

Identities are also invented in order to control and/or defraud a romantic relationship partner (Campbell, 2000). A man, for example, may say he is from a wealthy family or makes a lot of money in order to develop a relationship with a wealthy woman. He may try to increase the credibility of his claims by renting or borrowing an expensive car. A person who falsely claims to have an MBA in accounting or investment banking may be setting the stage for taking charge of his or her partner's money. In addition to greed, fabricated stories in close relationships can also be used to control and create dependence—e.g., "I'm a doctor so you come to me when you have any questions about health matters."

Sometimes couples work together to make up or embellish aspects of their relationship history to impress friends, draw public attention, and even reap financial gain. A notorious example is Herman and Roma Rosenblat's (2009) memoir "Angel at the Fence." The book purports to tell how the couple met and later married under poignant circumstances. According to the story, they met in 1944, when he was a young Jewish man imprisoned in the infamous Buchenwald concentration camp in Nazi Germany and she (also Jewish) was posing as a Christian with her family at a nearby farm. Rosenblat claimed she had tossed him apples and passed other food to him through an electrified camp fence for several months, until he was transferred to another location. He did not see her again until the war was over and the two had moved with their families to the United States. As the story went, they met in 1957 on a blind date in Coney Island, New York, discovered their "shared past," and married shortly thereafter. A few days before the book was to be released, Oprah Winfrey invited the couple to appear on her TV program and tell "the single greatest love story I have heard in 22 years of doing this show." Fueled in part by the public attention generated by the Rosenblats appearance on her show, the film rights of their story were purchased by a major movie studio for $25 million weeks before the book was to be published.

The media coverage also drew attention to their story from several Holocaust scholars. Historian Kenneth Walzer, who was familiar with the physical layout of the Buchenwald camp, publicly challenged the story on the grounds that it would have been impossible for civilians or prisoners to approach the perimeter fence without being detected by SS guards. Walzer also determined that although Roma and her family did pose as Christians in the German countryside, in 1944 they resided in a town over 200 miles away from Buchenwald. Several survivors who were in the camp at the same time as Herman were later interviewed and none could recall him ever mentioning a girl throwing apples over the fence (Sherman, 2008). Family members of the couple, including their own children, also raised questions about the memoir's accuracy. In light of these questions, the publisher canceled the book's release and demanded the Rosenblats return a six-figure advance. The couple publicly admitted the story was invented several days later.

Military Stories

There are always people who claim military experiences and medals who never served in the military. They do it for one or more of the following reasons: to make their résumé look better, to make their life seem more significant, even heroic; to gain respect and self-esteem; to savor being associated with others who are admired; to provide documentation for a fantasy or wished-for life; or to make them feel like they have accomplished something important for their country. It is also common for some who have served in the military to fabricate their rank, where they served, what they did, and/or what medals they earned.

Richard Spencer served six years in the U.S. Navy and was discharged after he was convicted of forgery (Sylvester, 2000). Later he claimed to have been the captain of the USS Enterprise and eventually promoted himself to Rear Admiral. He gave himself the Congressional Medal of Honor, the Silver Star, and the Distinguished Service Medal—all of which he wore on the admiral's uniform he purchased at a military salvage store. He gave speeches to local Rotary Clubs in which he recounted his life as a Navy SEAL and prisoner of war in Vietnam. None of this was true. During divorce proceedings, he sent his wife a letter with a forged Navy seal he scanned from a library book. Then he convinced a petty officer at a local naval recruiting office to deliver the letter to her by pretending to be his aide.

For 15 years, Edward Dailey went to extraordinary lengths to create his make-believe military life (Moss, 2000). He served in the Korean War, but spent all of his time well behind the front lines as a clerk and mechanic. After the war he forged documents praising himself for commanding his troops under fire, bravely rescuing a fellow soldier, and spending time as a prisoner of war. These imaginary actions served as the basis for forging Silver Star and Distinguished Service Cross citations. When a fire destroyed some Army records, veterans were asked to provide the lost information. This prompted Dailey to forge his name and photo on an original photo of soldiers in a regiment that had seen a lot of combat during the Korean War. By the time his sham was uncovered, he had convinced several men in that regiment that he had actually served in combat with them. He attended reunions and inserted himself into stories of the regiment. He did this by finding out things about soldier B when talking to soldier A. Then he would use the information obtained from A to show B he knew him and describe things they did together. Dailey had one soldier believing that he had rescued him after he was knocked unconscious. When questions were raised about this 7th Cavalry regiment's participation in the killing of civilians at the Korean village of No Gun Ri, Dailey admitted he was there. Second Lieutenant Robert Gray said, "Everyone assumed he was there. No one questioned it. He wove such a damn web."

A spate of military imposeurs in the 2000s prompted the U.S. Congress to pass the Stolen Valor Act of 2013. This law makes it a crime for someone to falsely claim having received any of a series of military decorations or awards including the Purple Heart, Silver Star, and Medal of Honor. The penalty for violating this law is a fine of up to $100,000 and up to a year in prison (Yarnell, 2013).

Some people falsely report combat experiences without claiming to have won awards or even having served in the military. For example, Brian Williams lost his post as anchor and managing editor of the NBC Nightly News for falsely claiming he had been aboard a military helicopter in Iraq in 2003 that drew enemy fire. In truth, he was riding in an aircraft behind the helicopter that had been fired upon. Further investigation revealed this was not only time Williams misrepresented his experience in war zones (Fahri, 2015). He also falsely claimed to have flown into Bagdad with the Navy Seals (who do not "embed" journalists), to have been present at the Brandenburg Gate the night the Berlin Wall fell in 1989 and in Cairo's Tahrir Square during the "Arab Spring" protests of 2011 (Bancoff, 2015). After Fox News host Bill O'Reilly publicly criticized Williams for these deceptions, it came to light that O'Reilly had fabricated stories of his own about being fired upon while covering the 1982 Falklands War in Argentina and being assaulted by protestors during the 1992 Los Angeles riots (Corn and Shulman, 2015). However, O'Reilly was not fired for his fabrications. In fact, the negative coverage created a huge ratings boost for his show from viewers convinced that the challenges to his recollections were just liberal propaganda. Many reporters who called for Williams to be fired did not recommend ousting O'Reilly on the grounds that he isn't a "journalist" in a strict sense. "It's ridiculous to compare Bill O'Reilly to Brian Williams," according to *Washington Post* reporter Sally Quinn. "O'Reilly is an entertainer and everything he does is totally subjective, including his memories" (Chariton, 2015).

Illness Stories

Unlike people with factitious disorders like Munchausen's Syndrome, *malingerers* feign illness symptoms for an external incentive—e.g., compensation from an insurance company, obtaining desired drugs, avoiding work, putting off an exam, dodging military service, or evading criminal prosecution. Malingerers invent pain, sickness, and injury that never existed, but they may also report symptoms related to an illness long after recovery should have occurred. Some forms of malingering are considered less serious than others—e.g., feigning illness in order to avoid sex or a social commitment. But malingering may also be costly (e.g., people falsely reporting they are too sick to work) and/or illegal (e.g., scams designed to defraud insurance companies). Because malingering can have serious social consequences, considerable effort has been put into effective methods of detection (Hall & Poirier, 2001; Halligan, Bass, & Oakley, 2003; McCann, 1998; Rogers, 1988). Sometimes malingerers can be extremely effective liars, especially when there is much to gain and they have time to prepare their story. Sometimes they benefit from the fact that most observers have a hard time distinguishing between real and faked expressions of pain (Craig & Hill, 2003). But faking mental illness to professionals is far more difficult, even when the malingerer has knowledge of the symptoms and behavior associated with a particular mental illness (Kropp & Rogers, 1993; Resnick & Knoll, 2005). The verbal behavior of malingerers may offer clues to deception—e.g., reporting obvious symptoms of an illness, but ignoring subtle ones that should also be present; or reporting too many symptoms, some of which are not likely to co-occur (Young, 2014). Nevertheless, some malingerers succeed in fooling psychiatrists. For example, Mafia boss Vincent "The Chin" Gigante deceived some of the most respected forensic psychiatrists for years by malingering schizophrenia—wearing a bathrobe out in public, muttering about voices in his head, slobbering while recounting frightening hallucinations, and engaging in other bizarre behaviors. A Harvard psychiatrist, 5 former presidents of the American Academy for Psychiatry and Law, and even the forensic expert who created the standard test for psychiatric malingering all judged him as incompetent to stand trial at some point. Ultimately, he admitted to maintaining his charade from 1990 to 1997 during evaluations of his competency to stand trial for racketeering (Newman, 2003).

Crime Stories

Victims of crimes are not always victims. Some people go to great lengths to stage a crime to make it look like they are the victim. This is known as the *crying wolf phenomenon*. In 2004, a University of Wisconsin honors student was found tied up near a marsh in Madison, Wisconsin. She told police she'd been held captive at knife point by her abductor for four days. In 2003, a woman in Washington falsely reported she had been raped in a park while her 5-year old daughter played nearby. That same year a New York girl made up a story about being punched in the face by a man with a swastika tattoo after she refused to get into his car (Parmer, 2004). At first, the stories these people tell are very credible. Initial attention is naturally focused on the perpetrator identified by the victim. In addition, many of those who "cry wolf" are often people who have no criminal record and no apparent reason for lying (O'Sullivan, 2003). Some confess when facts do not support their story. The Wisconsin student's deception was revealed when detectives watched a store surveillance tape showing the girl purchasing the rope and knife she said her abductor used to hold her captive.

Why do they do it? It appears to be the result of an intense desire for attention, sympathy, love, caring, and/or help. They believe that by becoming the victim of a serious crime their boyfriend, parents, or some other person close to them will no longer ignore and neglect them.

Others who fake crimes are also seeking attention, but it is attention for a cause. For example, a faculty member at a California college was believed to have slashed tires, smashed a car's windshield and spray-painted it with racial slurs prior to giving a speech against campus hate crimes. A Mexican-American student at Northwestern University filed two false reports of hate crimes purportedly directed at his heritage in order to call attention to race relations on campus (Parmer, 2004). Sometimes crime fakers are aided and abetted by reporters with an agenda. In 2015, *Rolling Stone* reporter Sabrina Rubin Erdely published a widely-read article describing a horrific sexual assault of a University of Virginia freshman female in a fraternity house and how the school mishandled the incident. For several days after it was published, the article served a noble purpose: It sparked a national conversation about sexual violence on college campuses and the indifference with which campus administrators respond to these brutal crimes. However, an investigation by the Charlottesville Police found "no basis to conclude that any assault happened in the fraternity house" and "no substantive basis to support the account alleged in the *Rolling Stone* article" (Robinson & Stolberg, 2015). It eventually came to light that not only did the alleged victim fabricate several characters and crucial episodes in the story, but author Erdely never even attempted to contact the fraternity members she had accused of perpetrating the assault. A review by the Columbia School of Journalism concluded Erdely had "failed to engage in basic, even routine journalistic practice" (Somaiya, 2015). *Rolling Stone* eventually retracted the article and Erdely publicly apologized, although her apology did not mention the fraternity members who were accused. Despite the public outcry and a lawsuit filed by UVA against the magazine, Erdely is still on its writing staff.

Imposters

There is a phenomenon known as *imposter's syndrome*, but it is very different than the behavior of people we call imposters. People who experience imposter's syndrome feel like they are imposters, but they aren't. Instead, they are high achieving individuals who see themselves as frauds. They believe that their accomplishments have been obtained because they are physically attractive, because they are likeable, because they are lucky, or any reason other than their own talents. In fact, they often have a low self-concept and worry that someone will reveal the sham they've been carrying on. Film and television actor, Michael J. Fox, is a winner of numerous awards (Emmys, Golden Globes, People Choice) but he wrote this in his 2002 autobiography:

> *Perhaps because my success was so sudden and outsized, I had the feeling that I was getting away with something…I couldn't help feeling there was something inauthentic about the whole thing—if not the situation itself, then at least my position in it. Perhaps there was something you could do to be worthy of all this—the money, the attention, the indulgence—but had I met the criteria? And so in time I began to feel like an imposter. It's almost as if I expected someone, at any moment, to kick in my door and tell me the charade had gone as far as it was going to go.*

Actual imposters are also worried about whether they are fooling others, but it has nothing to do with an ill-gotten persona. It is because they have enacted a false persona designed to fool others and they worry that it will be exposed. The behavior of an imposter is normally far more complex than that of an imposeur. Imposters engage in longer, more elaborate deceptions. They assume different names and different identities. Deception for an imposter is a part of a lifestyle. The good ones are confident, quick learners, skilled communicators, and people who know how to effectively enact the roles they choose to play. As noted in the following cases of famous imposters, there may be many reasons behind their imposture—e.g., the need to live a life other than the one they have; the need to obtain something they want; the need to prove something to themselves or someone else; or the need to gather information about an enemy.

Ferdinand Waldo "Fred" Demara, Jr.

Demara was one of, if not the, most successful imposters of the 20th Century (Crichton, 1959). A Hollywood version of his extraordinary life appeared in the movie, "The Great Imposter" (1961). He did not graduate from high school, but managed to pose as a Ph.D. in Psychology. He worked as a teacher, deputy sheriff, college dean, monk, civil engineer, assistant warden in a Texas prison, and a biologist involved in cancer research. He deserted the U.S. Army and joined the U.S. Navy. He later deserted the U.S. military and joined the Canadian Navy where he impersonated a physician. He reportedly performed the tasks associated with each role quite well and his surgical skill was featured in newspaper articles. He spent time in prison, but he did not seem to be driven by the desire to take advantage of people for his personal financial gain. In fact, he liked helping people. But there was a drive for identity and he seemed to enjoy the experience and challenge of living lives other than the one he had.

In each of the impostures he performed, Demara established his credentials with faked or stolen documents. He kept his impostures within the areas he had experienced—the Catholic Church, the military, educational institutions, and prisons. On the job, he sought ways to fulfill others' needs. He fostered feelings of affinity toward him and through self-deception, showed complete confidence in his ability to perform his job. He was able to learn things quickly and pulled an infected tooth from his ship's Captain after reading about the procedure the night before.

David Pecard

David Pecard had at least eight different names and posed as a lawyer, police officer, soldier, and emergency room technician (CBS News, 48 Hours, 2002). He enlisted and deserted the Army at least seven different times under seven different identities. He conducted investigations for the FBI and arrested a wanted con man. As a lawyer, he obtained the early release of an inmate. But he also was also charged with sexual abuse and conning a couple out of $7,500. One of the detectives who arrested him said, "He's got that air about him, that you will buy whatever he's selling." This was never truer than when Pecard prepared briefs and argued convincingly in court that the charges against him should be dismissed.

Like Demara, Pecard knew the value of learning. He took courses in medicine and law and learned Chinese and Korean. If he needed credentials he didn't have, he forged them. To get a new social security number, he argued that he had been out of the country his entire life doing missionary work. "Doors can be opened if you know how to open them. I am a chameleon. I adapt. It's what I've been my whole life," Pecard said.

Escaping from an unhappy home life, he developed his first new identity at age seven. When he was turned down for a paper route, he went to an office that managed a different route of the same paper, gave them a different name and age, and was hired. When he was fourteen, he posed as an eighteen year old to enlist in the Army. The Army discharged him when they learned his actual age, but a few months later he managed to enlist in the Army again, using a different name. He explained his multiple impostures by saying, "When I reach a point where I can no longer safely be that person, then I have one focus. I must survive and I must create a new person."

Frank Abagnale

Abagnale was another remarkably gifted imposter whose exploits also led to the Hollywood film, "Catch Me If You Can" (2002). He masqueraded as an airline pilot, pediatrician, hospital administrator, and lawyer (Abagnale, 1980). He wrote about 2.5 million dollars worth of bad checks served time in prison in France, Sweden, and the United States. He was smart enough to pass bar exams and to convince the United States government to cut his prison time from twelve years to five. He did that by convincing law enforcement agencies that his knowledge and experience would greatly assist them in catching swindlers and preventing fraud.

Running away from an unhappy home life at sixteen, Abagnale learned various dishonest ways to survive. He needed to be older in order to get work so he changed the date on his driver's license. He needed money so he put his checking account number on bank deposit slips in a bank. When people filled them out and turned them in, the money went to his account. He used his father's credit card to buy four tires for his car. Then he told the seller that he would sell them back to him for half of what he just paid as long as it was in cash. For two years he impersonated an airline pilot so he could catch a free ride to places all over the world. He would stay in hotels where airline crews stayed and where the airlines picked up the bill. In order to carry off this imposture, he convinced an airline representative that dry cleaners had lost his uniform and he needed a new one. He was also able to get a fake identity card made by posing as a person wanting to do business with the company that made airline identity cards.

Gerald Barnes

Barnes was a notorious imposter but he differs from the aforementioned imposters in several important ways (Fernandez, 2001; Fitzgerald, 2001). Rather than assume a variety of identities, Barnes stuck with his impersonation of a physician. He used the same set of phony physician documents to reestablish his career after each of his five arrests. Although he did work at community clinics, his primary goal was to lead a life that only wealth can bring. Toward that end, he bilked businesses, insurance companies, and Medicare for approximately five million dollars. Unlike Demara, Barnes was never recognized for his medical knowledge or skill. It is reported that one of his patients died while many others were misdiagnosed.

Gerald Barnbaum, aka Gerald Barnes, always loved acting and appeared in plays during and after college. Those who knew him said he was particularly skilled at picking up another person's mannerisms and mimicking them. During one of his arrests, he convincingly faked a heart attack and was hospitalized. He was granted a degree in Pharmacy from the University of Illinois, but he really wanted to be a physician. He read medical texts, enrolled in continuing education courses for physicians, and worked as an assistant to some doctors from India who had recently arrived in the United States. He obtained a job as a physician with a false résumé because no one checked any of the claims on the résumé. He saw a chance to get a permanent identity when he found out there was another California physician named Gerald Barnes. He told the California Medical Board that he was Gerald Barnes and that his diploma and license had been lost in a fire. Copies of these documents were sent to him and he used them throughout his life as an imposter.

Frederic Bourdin

Frederic Bourdin was a serial imposter nicknamed "The Chameleon" by the American press. Unlike those reviewed earlier, Bourdin rarely pretended to have an occupation he wasn't qualified for. In fact, during the height of his impersonating career he never admitted he was of legal working age. Born and raised in France, Bourdin first drew the attention of the FBI in 1998, after a tip from a private investigator hired by the TV tabloid show *Hard Copy*. The P.I. had been hired to investigate the extraordinary story of Nicholas Barclay. At the age of 13, Barclay was reported missing by his family in San Antonio and had not been seen nor heard from in 3 years. In 1997, the family received a phone call from a youth shelter in Spain from someone claiming to be Nicholas. The caller explained that he had been kidnapped in the U.S. and then sold into a child prostitution ring in Europe. During his captivity, so he claimed, the kidnappers had injected his eyes with a chemical and did not allow him to speak English, thereby transforming the brown-eyed boy with a Texas accent into the blue-eyed, French-accented adolescent he had become. He convinced the family he was Nicholas and was flown to Texas, where he lived with them for several months.

The hired P.I. did not find this story credible, however. After examining several old photos of Nicholas, he became convinced the person living with the Barclay family was not their son and notified the authorities. The FBI obtained a court order to take the young man's fingerprints and DNA, which were identified as belonging to 28-year old Bourdin, not the 16-year old missing boy he claimed to be. He had nothing to do with Nicholas Barclay's disappearance, but had learned of the boy's identity and disappearance by calling the National Center for Missing and Exploited Children in Virginia from the youth shelter in Spain. In 1998, Bourdin pleaded guilty to passport fraud and perjury and was imprisoned for 6 years in the U.S. After completing his sentence and returning to Europe, he continued to impersonate abused and abandoned adolescents, insinuating himself into youth shelters, orphanages, foster homes, and hospitals in 14 different countries over a 2-year period. When he was captured again in northern France, the authorities launched an investigation to determine why a 30-year old man would pose as a teenage orphan. They found no evidence to suggest a sexual or financial motives. "In my twenty years on the job, I've never seen a case like it," prosecutor Eric Maurel said. "Usually people con for money. His profit seems to have been purely emotional" (Grann, 2008, p. 71). Bourdin has apparently ended his career as an imposter and now lives with his wife and 4 children in Le Mans, France. Bourdin's exploits have been the subject of a fictionalized film (*The Chameleon*, 2010) and a documentary (*The Imposter*, 2012).

Spies

Some spies maintain their personal identity and secretly collect and pass classified information to another group or country. For example, FBI agent Robert Hanssen and CIA agent Aldrich Ames passed secret documents and the names of Russian citizens who were spying for the U.S. to the Russian KGB. Even though this type of spy is required to act like someone they are not, spies who infiltrate and assume the role of the enemy are imposters who face special challenges. FBI agent Joe Pistone, who assumed the name of Donnie Brascoe and infiltrated the New York Mafia for six years is a good example of this type of spy (Pistone, 1987).

The first objective for spies who want to be accepted as a member of an enemy group is to gain entrance. This must be done slowly and without any hint that this is the goal. Whether it is the Mafia or an intelligence unit of the enemy, outsiders are viewed with suspicion and mistrust. Brascoe, an Italian-American, hung around restaurants and bars frequented by members of the mob. He cut his hair and dressed like they did; he used their language; he showed respect to family members; and avoided conversations that didn't involve him. Like them, he adopted a way of interacting which demanded respect, showed indignation toward personal questions, and a willingness to settle disagreements by fighting. But unlike other imposters who assume the mannerisms and identity of their adopted group, the scrutiny and wariness of infiltrators like Brascoe is much more intense, as are the penalties for exposure. He said he tried not to tell many lies to avoid the possibility of inconsistent information raising suspicion. He said he'd been raised in an orphanage that burned down so his early history could not be checked. He also carried the phone number of an FBI agent who would portray a criminal and vouch for his competence as a jewel thief.

Unlike other imposters, Donnie Brascoe periodically interrupted his imposture to become Joe Pistone again with his wife and children. In addition, Brascoe was not afforded the luxury of becoming all that he could become within his Mafia role. The credibility of his later testimony against these wiseguys could not be tainted by criminal activity that was not staged in cooperation with the FBI.

Spies need to gain the trust of their enemy and this can be done by providing them with seemingly important information. Normally this information is approved by the spy's boss and is not as valuable as it looks. Sometimes spies turn into double agents, employed by both parties. This may be the most difficult game of deception and one with considerable risk.

Female Imposters

Even though the imposters noted thus far have all been male, imposture is not exclusively a male activity. There have been women disguised as men in the military, one of whom achieved the rank of Lieutenant Colonel in the Civil War (Hall, 1993) and there have been women imposters and con artists (DeGrave, 1995).

Women imposters and spies face all the same challenges as men, but when women assume the role of a male imposter they face the additional challenges of looking and acting like a man as well as the role they are trying to portray. During the middle ages it was not unusual for a woman in a small village to try to escape a dismal future by posing as a male, leaving the village, and enjoying the benefits of a male dominated culture. One such person may have been a woman who eventually became Pope, although scholars disagree on the authenticity of this story (Boreau, 2001; Stanford, 1999). The truth of Loreta Janeta Velazquez' (1876/1972) autobiography is also disputed, but she claims to have raised a battalion of men and fought at the U. S. Civil War's first battle of Bull Run, at Shiloh, and at Fort Donelson as Lieutenant Harry T. Buford. Later, as a female, she became a spy for the Confederacy in Washington, D. C.

In the editor's introduction to Velazquez' memoir, he says she was adept at dressing like a man and imitating male behavior. She had to frequent saloons and be able to walk, drink, smoke, spit, swear, and tell bawdy stories like a man. The editor of her book said she was an entertaining conversationalist with a "fund of racy anecdotes."

Figure 8.1: Picture of Loreta Janeta Valazquez as Harry T. Buford (left) and as Loreta Janeta Valazquez

Copyright © University Library, The University of North Carolina at Chapel Hill. Reprinted by permission

Sarah Edmonds spent two years disguised as a male book salesman before she joined a military regiment during the Civil War. She was a medical orderly and a mail courier, but her own claim that she was also a spy is disputed. After the war she returned to her female identity, married, and became the only woman to receive a soldier's pension for her Civil War service (Gansler, 2005).

Norah Vincent spent a year and a half masquerading as a man (Ned) in order to find out how men behaved and what their life was like (Vincent, 2007). She hired a voice coach; had a makeup artist alter her face and hair; gained weight and lifted weights to add muscle; and wore a "packable softie" to imitate a male's genitals. As a male, she participated with an all-male bowling team and a men's therapy group, went to a strip clubs, dated women, and worked as a male salesman. She had this to say about portraying a man:

> In the end, the biggest surprise in Ned was how powerfully psychological he turned out to be. The key to his success was not in his clothing or his beard or anything else physical that I did to make him seem real. It was in my mental projection of him, a projection that became over time undetectable even to me. People didn't see him with their eyes. They saw him in their mind's eye. They saw what I wanted them to see, at least at first, while I still had control over the image. Then later they saw what they expected to see and what I had become without knowing it: the mind-set of Ned (p. 282).

Figure 8.2: Picture of Norah (left) and Norah as Ned (right)

Identity Thieves

Although many of the imposeurs and imposters reviewed earlier could be described as "identity thieves," the term is typically used to describe criminals who use someone else's personally identifying information (name, social security number, credit card number, etc.) to commit fraud and other crimes. The term was coined in 1964, but did not enter common parlance until the 1990s with the advent of the Internet, the principal medium through which identity theft now occurs. Identity theft can both facilitate and be facilitated by other crimes. For example, possessing other people's social security numbers without their permission can make it possible to commit crimes such as bank fraud and espionage, and in turn crimes like robbery and burglary may result in the misappropriation of social security numbers. Identity theft victimizes both the people whose identifying information is stolen as well the various third parties defrauded (government, banks, insurance providers, etc.).

Identity theft became a federal crime in the U.S. in 1998 when Congress passed the Identity Theft Assumption Deterrence Act. The subsequent Identity Theft Penalty Enhancement Act established harsher penalties for thieves who use stolen credentials to commit another federal crime (e.g., Medicare fraud). Identity theft has been the most commonly reported consumer fraud complaint to the Federal Trade Commission since 2004. In 2013, about 12.6 million Americans were victims (most had credit card numbers stolen) and on average incurred $365 in direct costs as well as many hours spent filing reports and restoring their credit (Finklea, 2014).

Identity theft is a rapidly evolving criminal threat, with new forms developing on a regular basis. Six of the most common forms are described on the following pages.

Financial Identity Theft

Financial identity theft occurs when someone steals another person's personally identifiable information and commits a crime that results in financial injury to the victim. Information can include the name, bank account number, credit card numbers, social security number, and other personal financial data. It is the most common form of identity theft, accounting for approximately 28% of all cases (Federal Trade Commission, 2013). Once thieves have accessed victims' information, they have the tools necessary to counterfeit checks or ATM cards and wipe out accounts, open utility, cable, or cellular accounts in the victim's name, apply for car loans or mortgages, claim their tax refunds from the IRS, file for bankruptcy, and other activities, all potentially resulting in vast debts and destroyed credit.

Criminal Identity Theft

When criminals falsely identify themselves to police as other people at the point of arrest, they have committed "criminal identity theft" (Newman & McNally, 2005). In some cases, criminals have previously obtained state-issued identity documents using credentials stolen from others, or have simply presented fake IDs. When this subterfuge works, charges may be placed under the victim's name, getting the criminal off the hook. Victims might only learn of such incidents by chance—e.g., discovering a driver's license is suspended when stopped for a minor traffic violation, or through a background check performed by a potential employer.

It can be difficult for the victims of criminal identity theft to clear their records. The steps required can differ dramatically depending on the jurisdiction in which the crime occurred and whether the true identity of the criminal can be determined. Victims might need to locate the original arresting officers and prove their own identity by some reliable means such as fingerprinting or DNA testing. Obtaining an expungement of court records may also be required. Authorities might permanently maintain the victim's name as an alias for the criminal's true identity in their criminal records databases. Another problem victims of criminal identity theft often encounter is that various data aggregators may still have the incorrect criminal records in their databases even after court and police records are corrected. Thus it is possible that a future background check will return the incorrect criminal records. This is just one example of the kinds of impact that may continue to affect the victims of identity theft for months or even years after the crime, on top of the psychological trauma that being 'cloned' typically creates.

Medical Identity Theft

Medical identity theft occurs when someone seeks medical care under the identity of another person. In addition to risks of financial harm common to all forms of identity theft, the thief's medical history may be added to the victim's medical records. Inaccurate information in the victim's records is difficult to correct and may affect future insurability or cause doctors relying on the misinformation to deliver inappropriate medical care (Finklea, 2014).

Child Identity Theft

Child identity theft occurs when a minor's identity is used by another person for the impostor's personal gain (Power, 2011). The impostor can be a family member, a friend, or even a stranger who targets children. Children's social security numbers are valued because they do not have any other credentials associated with them. Thieves can establish lines of credit, obtain driver's licenses, or even buy a house using a child's identity. This fraud can go undetected for years, as most children and their parents do not discover the problem until they apply for a driver's license or a job. Child identity theft is one fastest growing forms of identity theft (FTC, 2013).

Synthetic Identity Theft

An increasingly prevalent new form of identity theft is *synthetic identity theft,* in which identities are completely or partially fabricated. The most common technique involves combining a real social security number with a name and birthdate other than the ones associated with the number. Synthetic identity theft is difficult to track because it often doesn't show up on the credit reports of any of the individuals whose credentials were grafted into the synthetic identity, but instead may appear as an entirely new person to a credit rating agency. Synthetic identity theft primarily harms the creditors who unwittingly grant the fraudsters credit. Individual victims can be affected if their names become confused with the synthetic identities.

Synthetic identity fraud first made major headlines in 2007 when two hackers were convicted for managing approximately 500 fake personas in 200 residences in 14 states (Conkey, 2007). In 2013, 18 people were prosecuted for running a $200 million credit card scam that created 7,000 new identities. These stories are clear examples of how synthetic identity fraud is growing as an area of concern. Synthetic identities are used to obtain financial services, medical benefits, insurance and rental housing, among other things. Additionally, organized crime and terrorist groups are realizing the benefits that the anonymity of synthetic identities can bring to their operations (IBM Analytics, 2015). Because children do not have public database records, their social security numbers are ideal for creating synthetic identities (Power, 2011).

Cons and Con Artists

Scams or cons are designed to take the target's money without a weapon. This is made possible because the con appeals to the target's needs. The need for quick and easy money is common, but targets may be conned because of their need to find a romantic partner, to grieve for a deceased loved one, to increase their sexual prowess, to improve their appearance, to catch a thief, or any number of other needs the con artist promises to fulfill. There are many well- known con artists (Larson, 1966; Nash, 1976; Weil & Brannon, 1948/2004) and many types of cons.

There are cons that take place quickly and those that develop over time and involve several contacts, people, and locations. Cons focus on sales, investments, psychic readings, faith healings, gambling, romance, lottery or inheritance winnings, and many other topics. Each con has a distinct strategy but cons often include the following strategies (Faron, 1998; Hankiss, 1980; Langenderfer & Shimp, 2001; Maurer, 1940/1999).

Running a Con: The Fundamentals

1. Select a vulnerable victim or "mark." Sometimes visual cues prompt selection, but marks may also self-select by answering an advertisement, phone call, or email. Those who are most vulnerable are those who have little knowledge and/or experience with the subject of the con.

2. Make the "bait" for the con seem "authentic"—i.e., linked to reliable sources, a happenstance occurrence, etc. At this point, the main goal for the con artist is to gain the victim's confidence and to set the stage for working together. This can be facilitated with verbal behavior which establishes a positive feeling by the mark for the swindler.

3. Build on needs of the mark. At this point, the mark is told how he or she can make a lot of money, can be the recipient of a miracle cure; can win a valuable prize, etc. without any risk. It is usually a story that sounds too good to be true (and it is), but it is tempting to the mark because it taps into a powerful need. Often, the story will have some true information that accompanies the scam to make it more convincing. Doubts of the mark are anticipated and talked about.

4. Provide a "convincer." For many cons, the belief that the probabilities are overwhelmingly in the mark's favor is enough of a "convincer." But sometimes the mark is given a strong reason to believe the con artist when he or she is given a small amount of what is promised—e.g., a mark who is shown how easy and quickly he or she can get a large payoff from a small amount of money. Other cons steer the mark to a "neutral" person who is actually part of the con. This person may be a bystander, a reference for the con's identity, an expert, or any "outsider" who testifies to the legitimacy of the scam.

5. Extort money from the mark. Payment normally precedes the promised rewards. Sometimes payment is made on the spot, but if it is determined the mark has more to give, the extortion may take place over a longer period of time. But no matter how long the con takes, there is always a sense of urgency for the mark to act immediately or the promised rewards may no longer be attainable. Any further consultation by the mark with anyone else is prohibited by the con artist.

6. The con is completed. This may necessitate a trick or swap. Like a magician, the con artist uses distraction and misdirection, keeping the mark's focus on the rewards to be gained.

7. Blowing off the mark. This may involve both physical separation and reasons for the mark to keep quiet. Marks who are trying to obtain money in a manner they know is dishonest have a clear reason to keep quiet, but other victims may not report a scam because they feel embarrassed or mistakenly fear they are culpable in some way.

Types of Cons

The following types of cons, while far from being comprehensive, illustrate various ways cons take place.

The Big Con

Three members of the Irish Travelers, a group known nationwide for home repair scams, expected a multi-million dollar payoff for a con staged at a Disney World hotel (Faron, 1998). Here's how it worked. A woman had sex with a friend, then checked into a Disney hotel room. Her brother, dressed in a Dracula costume, made sure he was seen hanging around. He even told some of the housekeeping staff that he had left his hotel key in his room and wanted them to let him in. They didn't, but they remembered him. Later his sister let him into her room. He tied her up with duct tape and beat her with his fists and a club. The blood, bruises, semen, and the woman's ability to act like a rape victim convinced the police she had been raped. Disney wanted to avoid the bad publicity this crime might generate if the suit went to court, so they were ready to settle with the woman for three million dollars. But the victim's sister was greedy. She wanted a bigger share than her brother and sister had promised her. When it was not forthcoming, she told police about the scam.

Internet Scams

The U.S. State Department estimates that internet scams cost people hundreds of millions of dollars each year. With the internet, the bait for the con can reach millions of people and if only a small percentage of these recipients are conned, the financial profit can be substantial.

One popular example in recent years is called the "Nigerian Letter Scam." The Federal Trade Commission received more than 55,000 complaints about this scam in 2005 (Zuckoff, 2006). The basic strategy of the con has been around since the 1920's when it was called the "Spanish Prisoner" and appeals were made via letters and later with fax machines. Here's how it works.

Recipients receive an email message from a person who claims to be in possession of a large sum of money (e.g., 25 million dollars). The letter goes on to say that this money has to be moved to another country or it will be lost. The person with the "fortune" says he or she has heard that the recipient of the email has a fine reputation and since his or her need to deposit the money in an American bank is so great, he or she is willing to give the recipient 25% of the money for assisting in the money transfer. If the mark agrees to help, they are likely to lose money rather than gain it. Sometimes they are asked to pre-pay money for a tax, a bribe, shipping and handling fees, or some other cost involved in the transfer of funds (which never occurs). Sometimes the mark is asked to provide his or her bank account number which is used to fleece them; sometimes the mark is asked to cash forged checks and forward the money to a bank in another country; and sometimes the victim actually travels to Nigeria to complete the deal and is robbed at the airport.

New types of online scams are created on a regular basis. The following are several types that have become prevalent in recent years (Federal Bureau of Intelligence, 2014):

- "Phishing" emails are designed to look like they come from a financial institution or a shopping web site. At first glance, the logo, graphics, and wording looks authentic. If you don't have an account with *eBay* or *Barclay's Bank*, you may think a mistake has been made and ignore the request. But sooner or later an email will arrive with a name and logo of a company with which you do business. The email indicates that the security on your account may have been compromised and fraud may have occurred. In order to reestablish your account and safeguard it you need to click on the site provided and input your personal account information, social security number, and passwords again. If you don't, your account will be cancelled. The site provided, of course, is the con artist's site, not the company you do business with.

- Millions of Americans are using dating sites, social network sites like Facebook, and chat rooms to meet potential romantic partners. While many forge successful relationships, scammers also use these sites to meet potential victims. They create fake profiles to build online relationships and eventually convince people to send money in the name of love. Some even make wedding plans before disappearing with the money. An online love interest who asks for money is almost certainly a scam artist.

- In an advance payment credit scam, you receive an e-mail with the "good" news that you've been "pre-qualified" to get a low-interest loan or credit card, or to repair your bad credit even though banks have turned you down. To take advantage of the offer, you have to ante up a processing fee of several hundred dollars. A "pre-qualified" offer simply means you've been selected to apply for a credit card or loan. You still have to complete an application and you can still be turned down. If you paid a fee in advance for the promise of a loan or credit card, you've been hustled. You might get a list of lenders, but there's unlikely to be any loan and the person you've paid has taken your money.

- In a recent twist, scam artists are using the phone to break into your computer. They call claiming to be computer techs associated with well-known companies like *Microsoft*. They say that they've detected viruses or other malware on your computer to trick you into giving them remote access or paying for software you don't need. These scammers take advantage of your reasonable concerns about viruses and other threats. They know that computer users have heard time and again that it's important to install security software. But the purpose behind their elaborate scheme isn't to protect your computer; it's to make money. Scammers have been peddling bogus security software for years. They set up fake websites, offer free "security" scans, and send alarming messages to try to convince you that your computer is infected. Then, they try to sell you software to fix the problem. At best, the software is worthless or available elsewhere for free. At worst, it could be malware—i.e., software designed to give criminals access to your computer and your personal information.

- Work-at-home scams begin with an email ad promising a steady income for home-based work, typically in medical claims processing, online searching, international shipping, rebate processing, envelope-stuffing, or assembling crafts and other items. The ads use variations on these themes: "Be your own boss," "Earn thousands of dollars working at home," etc. What the ads don't say is that you will have to spend your own money to fulfill the terms of the assignment—placing newspaper ads, making copies of documents, and buying supplies, software, or equipment to do the job. They probably also won't say you will be paid for all the hours you put in, either. It's hard to find a promoter of home-based businesses who will pay you for all the time and money you spend, and who accepts your work as up to their "standards of quality."

Street Cons

Street cons vary, but many involve "finding" things on the street—a diamond ring or a package full of money. In the "Indian Head Penny" scam, a mark and a con both come upon a bag of Indian head pennies in a place with high pedestrian traffic. The bag has a phone number on it. The con artist convinces the mark to call the number. The call is answered by the "owner" (also part of the con) who says he will pay a thousand dollars for the return of his coin collection. Then the con artist who discovered the collection with the mark says he is willing to let the mark have most of the reward because he has to go to another appointment. He will settle for $250 now and let the mark make a $750 profit when he collects the reward. If the mark agrees, he will soon find out that the address given by the so-called owner of the coin collection does not exist and the phone number is no longer in service (Faron, 1998).

With "Three Card Monte," one con shows three cards to bystanders and bets $20 that he can turn the cards over and move them so quickly that a person will not be able to select a specific card from among the three. The mark watches as bystanders win more often than they lose so he or she makes a bet. What the mark doesn't know is that the bystanders are part of the con and eventually he or she will lose much more than he or she wins. In the "Block Hustle," a mark is shown some brand new television sets and other electronic equipment on the back of a truck. The mark is told he or she only has to pay about a quarter of what the retail price would be. The mark may suspect they are stolen, but can't pass up such a good deal. The mark pays and a box with a "television" label is put in his or her car. The mark discovers later that there is no TV in the box and the cons are nowhere to be found (Faron, 1998).

Faith-Healers

Pat Robertson, Oral Roberts, Peter Popoff, Ernest Angley, W. V. Grant, and Leroy Jenkins are among other evangelical preachers who have practiced faith-healing. They claim the ability to repair broken bones and eradicate tumors simply by touching the patient and invoking God's name. There are no doubt some people who may experience some temporary pain suppression brought on by temporal lobe epilepsy or the release of endorphins during a heightened emotional state (Hines, 2003). But independent records of people who have experienced long-term healing from faith healers do not exist. In addition, faith-healers engaging in fraud are commonly exposed (Randi, 1989). Sometimes the people who are healed are working with the faith-healer. People who don't need to be in a wheelchair can miraculously walk; "blind" people who still have some visual acuity can miraculously see. One man, who also posed as a woman, was healed by four different healers in six different cities of six different diseases under four different names. Some of the scams performed by faith-healers are similar to those done by magicians. W. V. Grant's "leg stretching miracle" is an old carnival trick. Peter Popoff wore a receiver in his ear and his wife transmitted information to him about people and their illness. These people had previously filled out cards with this information and Popoff pretended to have divinely obtained this information. Unlike the faith-healers who use such tricks, magicians admit they are doing tricks rather than enacting spiritual powers. As a result, their audiences are likely to fill their pockets with far less money.

Sales and Investments

Sales and investment scams are the bread and butter of con artists. The most notorious con artists are exceptionally persuasive and able to sell virtually anything—even things that don't exist and things they don't own. Arthur Furguson sold the Admiral Nelson statue in London's Trafalgar Square, complete with fountains, to an American businessman. He later tried to sell the Statue of Liberty. Victor Lustig twice sold the Eiffel Tower as scrap iron and conned gangster Al Capone (Larson, 1966). Oscar Hartzell made hundreds of thousands of dollars from investors eager to help him establish his claim to the supposedly lucrative Sir Francis Drake estate. Drake died in 1596 (Rayner, 2002). During the 1920s and 1930s, "Dr." John Brinkley convinced many American men to have goat glands implanted in their testicles to restore their sexual prowess. At the height of his popularity, he was doing fifty of these operations a month (Lee, 2002; Marinacci, 1997a). Charles Ponzi made millions of dollars through a "pyramid scheme." Investors were told they could double the amount of their investment in ninety days. Investors flocked to Ponzi and as long as he kept getting new investors, he could pay earlier investors. Eventually, he was audited and arrested (Dunn, 1975). In 2008, Bernie Madoff was sentenced to 150 years in prison for running the biggest pyramid scheme in U.S. history. A well-respected financier, Madoff convinced thousands of investors to hand over their savings, falsely promising consistent profits in return. He conned investors out of almost $65 billion and went undetected for decades. Few of his victims have regained any of their substantial losses.

Joseph R. "Yellow Kid" Weil, according to Marinacci (1997b), is "arguably the greatest con man in American history." He devised numerous phony deals, some with props and several "helpers"—not unlike the cons portrayed in the 1973 movie, "The Sting." One of Weil's favorite scams involved horses. He got himself admitted to the American Turf Association and purchased several horses. Then he spread the word that he was secretly training a fast horse named Black Fonso. At the same time, he told gamblers, he was racing a slow horse with the same name and similar features. When the time was right, he said he'd switch horses, bet heavily on a horse that was probably at 100–1 odds to win and reap the winnings. Marks were taken to his secret training track and shown a magnificent horse that ran a fast time. What they weren't told was that this horse only ran fast in the morning and that the fast and the slow Black Fonso were one and the same. On the day when the race was supposed to be fixed, the marks gave thousands of dollars to Weil which he was supposed to bet on Black Fonso to win. Weil kept the money and Black Fonso lost (Weil and Brannon, 1948/2004; Marinacci, 1997b).

Psychics and Paranormal Phenomena

Psychics claim abilities which require a sixth sense—e.g., the ability to read people's minds, to move objects without touching them, to predict the future, to levitate, and to communicate with the dead. Despite the lack of scientific evidence for these amazing powers and the exposure of many psychics as frauds (Randi, 1982), 73% of all Americans continue to believe in the paranormal (Musella, 2005). 41% believe in ESP; 37% in haunted houses; 32% in ghosts; 31% in telepathy; 26% in clairvoyance; 25% in astrology; 21% believe in communication with the dead; 21% in witches; 20% in reincarnation; and 9% in channeling spiritual entities. Given these statistics, it is not surprising that psychics continue to flourish. Some probably believe they have these powers, but many know they are just playing out a scam.

Psychic surgery is a process which purportedly involves no cutting, pain, or scars. The psychic simply reaches into a person's body and removes a tumor or some other diseased material. To an untrained observer, it looks shockingly real. But instead, it is more like a magician's trick. Blood is concealed in a false finger. The patient's skin is folded in such a way that the psychic's hand appears to be going into the body when it is actually grabbing some hidden chicken entrails which are then displayed as the patient's diseased material.

Wiseman (1997) says psychic frauds employ a variety of strategies. Initially, they do everything they can to show that they are unwilling, unable, and/or have no reason to engage in fraudulent behavior. Saying they don't accept payment for their services, for example, is one way to buttress their credibility. The believability of the psychic fraud's performance is certainly enhanced when it is linked to something the mark wants very much to believe—e.g., that a recently deceased spouse can be contacted. Psychics typically say they are not in complete control of their amazing powers so it is hard to know what will happen. This means anything that happens can be interpreted as the psychic and the mark see fit. Like magicians, psychics learn to do tricks when the mark's attention is relaxed or diverted. They are most effective when they are in charge of establishing the conditions for their performance—e.g., "No video cameras. They send out bad electronic vibes." or "Darkness is essential." In séances, people may be asked to hold hands so they are less likely to touch a wire or an accomplice. Psychic frauds must also be prepared to explain things that seem to have logical explanations—e.g., "I couldn't do that alone," or "I'm not strong enough to do that," or "I can't talk like that."

Who Gets Scammed and Why?

As Faron (1998) points out, *any of us can be conned, given the right circumstances.* Still, there are some people who are more likely to fall victim to a scam than others. Some of the most common include:

- People who are socially isolated are likely to be less familiar with signs typically associated with scams and less familiar with the way scams are conducted.

- People who have important needs to satisfy and little hope of doing so are also vulnerable. They are ready to believe anything—e.g., the cancer patient who desperately wants to believe in the power of a faith healer; the lonely, dateless person who believes a con artist is actually a person who will provide romantic companionship. In general, people under time pressure to make important choices may be more easily manipulated by hustlers (Stajano & Wilson, 2011).

- People who have a strong visceral response to the subject of the scam. Visceral responses can override a rational decision-making process. Common visceral responses activated by con artists include fear, greed, and sexual desire. The overwhelming urge to quickly satisfy these needs is why cons often require the mark to respond immediately (Langenderfer & Shimp, 2001). Some people even have a feeling they may be entering into a scam, but the promised payoff is so attractive to them that they end up participating anyway.

- People who strongly believe they can't be conned because they are too smart and/or too knowledgeable. Sometimes these "smart" people rely too heavily on stereotypes and general probabilities which con artists use to their advantage. In addition, people who think they can't be conned may not feel the necessity to check out things they "know" are true which, of course, is exactly what the con artist wants.

- People who, without questioning, easily attribute expertise to others and defer to their judgment—even when others don't. This is not the same as being trustful [see "What Do You Know About Trustful People?" below]

What Do You Know About Trustful People?

1. **T F** Trustful people are more gullible than mistrustful people.
2. **T F** Trustful people are less perceptive of what others are really feeling than mistrustful people.
3. **T F** People with poor opinions of themselves are less trustful than people with a good opinion of themselves.
4. **T F** Stupid people are trustful; smart people are mistrustful.
5. **T F** Trustful people rely on others to direct their lives for them; mistrustful people rely on themselves.
6. **T F** Trustful people are more trustworthy than mistrustful people.
7. **T F** Trustful people are less anxious, suffer less psychological distress, and have generally better health than mistrustful people.
8. **T F** Trustful people are liked by others far more than mistrustful people.

Answers at the end of the chapter.

Hoaxes

Like cons, hoaxes are designed to fool people. But hoaxes are usually designed for large audiences and the payoff is less likely to be financial. People create hoaxes to make a point, to gain notoriety for an idea, to further their reputation and career, or simply because they enjoy playing practical jokes. The revelation of numerous hoaxes associated with a particular phenomenon does not extinguish belief in the phenomenon—e.g., Bigfoot, UFOs, and crop circles. And it is certainly true that, despite the hoaxes, we may someday discover a real Bigfoot, a spaceship from another planet, or aliens who communicate with us by making crop circles. When hoaxes are repeatedly revealed, however, we should become more skeptical.

Hoaxes are a common cultural activity (Kominsky, 1970; *U.S. News & World Report*, 2002). There are so many hoaxes on the internet that several web sites are exclusively dedicated to checking the factuality of information, rumors, and urban legends. These include: http://snopes.com/ ; http://www.truthorfiction.com/ ; and http://www.hoaxbusters.org. Another site devoted to debunking myths and promoting a scientific approach to inexplicable phenomena is: http://skeptic.com. Some noteworthy hoaxes include the following:

Aliens

Many humans believe Earth has been visited by beings from other places in the solar system. Three commonly claimed sources of evidence for this include: crop circles, a film of an alien autopsy, and the sighting of unidentified flying objects (UFOs). Some people honestly believe they have been abducted and analyzed by aliens even though hypnopompic and hypnagogic hallucinations, mental states between sleep and wakefulness, may be an important factor in explaining this experience (Shermer, 1997/2002; Hines, 2003).

In the 1970s, huge circles and later complex geometric figures were found impressed on fields of wheat, barley, and other crops in southern England (see Figure 8.3). Because some of these circles were surrounded by four smaller circles, it was easy for some to assume these were impressions made by the landing pods of alien space-ships. Later, as the designs became more complex, they were interpreted by some to be the way aliens chose to communicate with us. By the 1990s there were thousands of these crop circles in several countries. In 1991, two Englishmen admitted they had been making crop circles for 15 years. They explained how they did it with planks and ropes. This inspired other hoaxers. Physicist Eltjo Haselhoff (2001) admits that humans could have made even the most complex designs, but he argues that certain characteristics of the grain found in some crop circles cannot be the result of the methods currently revealed by hoaxers. So there is still more to learn.

© Jason Hawkes/Corbis

Figure 8.3: Photo of a crop circle

In 1995, Fox TV aired a film which purportedly showed a 1947 autopsy of an alien who was found in the wreckage of a UFO in Rosswell, New Mexico. The data to support the authenticity of the film was weak, at best. The wreckage housing the alien was never confirmed as an alien spaceship; the story of how the film was acquired was not consistent; the entire original film was not analyzed by Eastman Kodak for authenticity; security marks on the film disappeared after they were labeled as phony by military experts; and special effects analysts said the film was flawed in some important ways. Then, in 2006, British hoaxers confessed that the film was shot in England using 48 year old film. The "alien" was filled with sheep brains and chicken entrails (Horne, 2006).

Hoaxers have admitted the creation of visual phenomena that others have labeled as UFO sightings and many UFO photos have been faked. Some UFO sightings have simply been natural phenomena which were unfamiliar to the observer (Sagan, 1996). There are, of course, some visual phenomena which have yet to be explained, but observers who label them UFOs are subject to the many problems associated with eyewitness observations (see Chapter 2). Consequently, we need more than eyewitness testimony alone to conclude that alien spaceships have visited our planet.

Figure 8.4: Metallic scraps, The Roswell Daily Record and the feet of an alien body lie on an autopsy table in the UFO museum. Roughly 1000 people a day visit the UFO museum in Roswell, NM. On July 5, 1947, Mac Brazel found metallic scraps at Foster Ranchlands and by July 8th the Roswell Army Air Field reported finding a flying saucer.

Media

Joey Scaggs has been hoaxing the media for years (http://www.joeyskaggs.com/). His goal is to manufacture a story that he knows TV stations and newspapers will relish and often broadcast or publish without checking its validity. His hoaxes are designed to remind the media how vulnerable they are to false and misleading stories. He creates plausible stories he knows reporters will want to report. In addition to stories of general appeal, Scaggs says the media will predictably look for certain kinds of stories on Thanksgiving, anniversaries of disasters, etc. so he gives them what they want. After the story runs, he tells them it is a hoax. Generally, however, news organizations are not interested in reminding their readers and viewers that they fell for a hoax because they failed to check it out. Compared to the hoax, retractions get little if any publicity.

In one prank, Scaggs pretended to have invented a computer that would objectively analyze famous court cases using software made up of laws and expert legal opinions. He said his computer had analyzed the O.J. Simpson trial and found him guilty. Reporters salivated and they interviewed Dr. Joseph Bonuso (Scaggs), who explained what his computer could do without ever having to demonstrate it—which, of course, he couldn't. In 1992 he pretended to be a roving priest riding around at the Democratic national convention with a tricycle-mounted "portafess" (confessional booth) on the back. He gave multiple interviews to the press and only later did someone decide to check his priestly credentials. He got the press to bite on a story that he had established a "cathouse for dogs"—a place where people could take their dog to obtain sexual gratification without any worries of pregnancy occurring. He was responsible for false stories about impoverished artists living in water towers in Manhattan, a "fat squad" that followed dieters around to make sure they didn't go off their diet, and a cure for baldness that involved scalps from cadavers.

Religion

Miracles are integral to some religious beliefs so it is not surprising that some hoaxers try to create their own miracles—e.g., a statue that cries real tears or bleeds real blood. Italian chemist, Luigi Garlaschelli, is one of a group of scientists who has weighed in on the shroud of Turin, a cloth which purportedly covered Jesus after his crucifixion. Even though scientific tests have shown that the fabric is from the 14th century, some argued that the tests were inaccurate. Since the shroud was purportedly wrapped around the body and face, Garlaschelli reasoned that the facial image on the shroud should be distorted, like a Mercator map projection. It wasn't. To prove his point, Garlaschelli covered one of his students in paint and asked him to lie on a slab. Then he covered him with a shroud. When it was removed, the facial image was distorted, not in perfect proportion like the shroud of Turin (Williams, 2005).

Science and Medicine

Scientists are in the business of testing and retesting claims, so one might reasonably assume this would not be fertile ground for hoaxers. *Au contraire*. Park (2000) recounts numerous scientific hoaxes. In 2005, a South Korean scientist claimed to have cloned human cells and gained international celebrity. Subsequently, an investigation found the data for his claim to be fabricated. Four widely publicized scientific hoaxes include: Piltdown Man, Bigfoot, the "Sokol hoax," and the MMR vaccine controversy.

In 1912, paleontologists in England believed they had found the "missing link" between humans and apes, but it wasn't until about 1950 that the hoax began to unravel (Russell, 2003). The hoaxer, still unknown, assembled an ape jaw and a woman's skull, remodeled the teeth, and stained them to make them look ancient. Even though later discoveries were at odds with the large brain cavity of Piltdown Man, skeptics were often ignored because there was such a strong desire to believe that an important find had been made. Eventually, chemical tests showed the bones weren't as old as originally thought and that the cranium and jaw were not the same age.

Prankster Rant Mullens had been carving large feet out of wood and leaving footprints in the woods of northern California since 1930. But it wasn't until 1958 that similar oversized footprints made by Ray Wallace, a neighbor of Mullens, gained international notoriety and firmly established the reputation of a creature unknown to science. This large, ape-like primate who walks on two feet is known as Bigfoot. Sasquatch was the name given to a similar animal reportedly seen by Native Americans. Since the "discovery" of the Wallace footprints, which he admitted he made, Bigfoot sightings continue to be reported and Bigfoot hunters continue their search. In 1967 Roger Patterson reportedly shot a film of Bigfoot which has been carefully scrutinized by experts (Daegling, 2004). These analyses have not established the film's authenticity nor have they proven it to be a hoax.

Physicist Alan Sokol was apparently fed up with the articles published in *Social Text* (and other academic journals) that denied the existence of objective realities and supported the idea that reality is socially constructed. Sokol felt that the value, methods, and findings of science were under fire. He believed this kind of theorizing wasn't going to help people develop an anti-AIDS treatment or a solution to global warming. He believed it is important to be able to distinguish true and false ideas in both the sciences and humanities. Instead of writing an article which directly stated his misgivings with these ideas, he undertook a hoax which he hoped would expose the lack of critical standards for judging the ideas he opposed. He wanted to find out how much scientific rigor was associated with the process of publishing in *Social Text*. He believed that an article which favored the views of the social constructionists could be published even though it was full of bogus claims—claims which Sokal said any math or physics student would immediately realize were bogus. The article was accepted by the editors of *Social Text* without being examined by knowledgeable experts who would have readily identified the invalid claims made by Sokal. After the editors of *Social Text* published his article, Sokal published an article in *Lingua Franca* which exposed his hoax (Editors of *Lingua Franca*, 2000).

In 1998, a team of British medical researchers led by physician Andrew Wakefield published an article in the respected medical journal *The Lancet*. The researchers described a set of endoscopy and biopsy findings they characterized as evidence for a novel syndrome linking children's development of autism with receiving the MMR (measles, mumps, and rubella) vaccine. At a pre-publication press conference, Wakefield recommended parents forego the combined MMR in favor of single-disease vaccines in light of the findings. His recommendation was widely reported, causing vaccination rates in the UK and Ireland to drop sharply, which in turn was followed by an increase in measles and mumps cases in these countries, several of which resulted in deaths and permanent injury. Investigative journalists later discovered that Wakefield and colleagues had published the article without declaring multiple conflicts of interests, including their financial stake in a pharmaceutical company developing new single-disease vaccines to compete with the MMR. An independent scientific panel reviewed the research reported in the article and concluded Wakefield and his team had fabricated evidence supporting the MMR—autism link while discarding other evidence showing no link. *The Lancet* eventually retracted the article and Wakefield was found guilty by the British General Medical Council of professional misconduct serious enough to strip him of his license to practice medicine. The scientific consensus continues to be that no evidence links MMR to the development of autism in children and the vaccine's benefits greatly outweigh its risks. In a review of the controversy and disease epidemic caused by Wakefield's actions, Flaherty (2011) describe the episode as "the most damaging medical hoax of the last 100 years" (p. 1303).

Hoax Protection

Like scams, we are all subject to believing in hoaxes. But there are some things we can do to minimize the risk.

- *Pay attention to your beliefs.* On any particular issue, why do you believe the way you do? (see Chapter 2 on the ways people come to the truth) Can you admit your biases? Are you willing to? Are there incentives for you to believe certain things (MacDougall, 1958)? What are those things you want desperately to be true? What do you believe can never be any different? People often go through life without a lot of thought about questions like this. Instead, they focus on the weird, irrational, and biased beliefs *of others*. Once a belief is established, people commonly read and listen to information and people who support that belief and ignore the substance of the opposition. This is particularly true when the belief is strongly endorsed and the pressure of peers to hold the belief is high (Knowles & Linn, 2004). Contrary to expectations, exposure to contrary beliefs does not necessarily weaken one's belief; it can strengthen it. If you do not examine the nature of your beliefs, much less question them, you are especially vulnerable to hoaxes that seem to support your beliefs and more likely to falsely label a counter-belief phenomena as a hoax.

- *Get in the habit of checking the veracity of information and the reliability of information sources.* Sometimes valid information is difficult, if not impossible, to find. Sometimes we depend on sources like the press, the internet, or our friends to validate information for us and they report unverified claims and superstitions (MacDougall, 1983). Despite these problems, an investigative mind-set is a barrier to imposters, hoaxers, and cons who depend on your belief that they do not need to be checked out. Some scams, for example, may be checked on http://www.fraudaid.com/ If checking is hampered in significant ways, it may be prudent to withhold judgment or participation until such checking can be accomplished.

- *Know the difference between science and pseudoscience* (Kida, 2006; Sagan, 1996; Shermer, 1997/2002; Shermer, 2001). Science is dedicated to confirming or not confirming hypotheses about phenomena that can be tested. These tests are conducted under conditions which are as unbiased as possible. Subsequent testing by others is expected. Scientists make mistakes, biases sometimes affect their results, and their conclusions may be limited by current knowledge and methods of measurement. But the nature of science is to admit these problems, try to correct them, and continue testing in the pursuit of valid findings. On the other hand, hoaxes often rely on pseudoscience for their claims. People who make a claim based on pseudoscience are not likely to seek systematic, unbiased, and independent testing of their claim.

  Some of the more common characteristics of pseudoscientific claims include: 1) the use of scientific-sounding terms like "resonant vibrations" without any indication of what they mean and how they can be measured; 2) the exclusive use of anecdotal observations which cannot be verified in other ways to prove the validity of a claim; 3) the use of "mysterious forces" or "special powers" to explain the unlikely co-occurrence of two events, or for that matter, any phenomenon; and 4) rationalizing or not reporting negative findings and/or failures.

- ***Resist the temptation to explain everything.*** Learn to live in a world where there is much to learn and much we don't know about both natural phenomena and magic tricks. There is nothing wrong with suspending judgment until further data is available. Instead of remaining in a state of "limbo" relative to some phenomenon, many people like to immediately settle on an explanation. This may be a productive strategy on some occasions, but it also sets up the *confirmation bias* and makes it harder to objectively weigh new information that does not agree with the initial explanation (Nickerson, 1998). For example, when people experience phenomena that seems inexplicable based on what they know, they may immediately choose to understand it as something spiritual, demonic, or the result of alien beings. Later, when the phenomenon is explained in terms of science, nature, or very human tendencies, it can be very difficult to change the more mystical initial belief. It may be especially difficult if Shermer (2000) is correct in maintaining that human beings are inclined toward "magical thinking."

Summary

Lying specialists lie a lot and are generally quite skilled at it. They can be identified by examining various manifestations of their behavior. For example there are five personality disorders associated with pathological liars: antisocial, borderline, narcissistic, histrionic, and obsessive-compulsive. Most of these personality disorders are associated with people who are very self-oriented, come from dysfunctional families, and didn't get needed love and attention as children. As adults, they use lies to exploit others to get what they want, including a boost in self-esteem.

Imposeurs are people who enhance certain aspects of their personal identity but usually do not try to change their entire identity. They may claim jobs, military experiences, awards, sports experiences, wealth, and relationships they never had. People with factitious disorders such as Munchausen's Syndrome simulate a disease they don't have. When parents do the same thing with their children it is known as Munchausen's Syndrome by Proxy. Both are designed to get attention. When people fake an illness to get a tangible reward, it is known as malingering. Some people seek attention by claiming to be a victim of a crime when they aren't or pretending to be a victim of a crime in order to make a point.

When people have "imposters syndrome" they feel like their success is ill-gained and that they don't have the talent other's think they have. This is very different than an imposter who assumes a false persona or identity. Famous imposters reviewed in this chapter include Ferdinand Demara, Jr., David Pecard, Frank Abagnale, Gerald Barnes, Frederic Bourdin, and spies who infiltrated an enemy organization. Most of the notorious imposters have been men, but there are some well-known examples of women spies. In the age of the Internet, imposters are proliferating through the practice of stealing people's personally identifiable information such as social security numbers and bank account passwords. "Identity thieves" use this information to impersonate the people they rob from in order to make purchases, take out loans, receive medical care, and apply for passports.

Con artists are also specialists in lying. They try to take a mark's money with nothing more than their communicative skills. Familiar cons occur on the internet and the street; by faith-healers and psychics; and often involve buying or investing in something. The "big con" is a more elaborate scam involving several people, places, and props. Anyone can be conned, but the socially isolated and gullible are especially at risk. People who feel that the promised payoff of the con will satisfy strongly felt needs are also people who are easily conned. Trusting people do not seem to be more gullible than mistrustful people and they are likely to have a more satisfying life.

Cons are often directed at a single mark, but hoaxes tend to fool large numbers of people. The payoff for a con is monetary but that is not usually the case with hoaxes. Well-known hoaxes have involved aliens, the media, religious icons, and science. As with cons, anyone can be the victim of a hoax, but this risk can be lessened by analyzing one's own beliefs, learning to check the veracity of information, knowing the difference between science and pseudoscience, and learning to be comfortable without knowing why some phenomena occur.

Things to Think About

What kind of scam would you be most vulnerable to because of your expectations, needs, and beliefs? Indicate who would perpetrate the scam and how it would develop.

Indicate whether you do or do not believe alien spaceships have visited out planet. Then develop a persuasive speech, based on research, *supporting the view you do not currently hold.*

Design what you believe would be a successful hoax. Indicate how it would occur and what you expect to happen.

Answers to the Trustful People Test

1. **F**; 2. **F**; 3. **T**; 4. **F**; 5. **F**; 6. **T**; 7. **T**; 8. **T**.

For additional readings on trust, see: Holmes, J.G. (1991). Trust and the appraisal process in close relationships. In W.H. Jones and D. Perlman, eds. *Advances in Personal relationships.* (Vol. 2, pp. 57–104). London: Jessica Kingsley; Johnson-George, C. & Swap, W. (1982). Measurement of specific interpersonal trust: Construction and validation of a scale to assess trust in a specific order. *Journal of Personality and Social Psychology, 43,* 1306–1317; Rempel, J.K., Holmes, J.G., & Zanna, M.P. (1985). Trust in close relationships. *Journal of Personality and Social Psychology, 49,* 95–112; Rotter, J.B. (1971). Generalized expectancies for interpersonal trust. *American Psychologist, 26,* 443–452; Rotter, J.B. (1980). Interpersonal trust, trustworthiness and gullibility. *American Psychologist, 35,*1–7; Sabatelli, R.M., Buck, R., & Dreyer, A. (1982). Locus of control, interpersonal trust, and nonverbal communication accuracy. *Journal of Personality and Social Psychology, 44,* 399–401;

References

Abagnale, F. (1980). *Catch me if you can*. New York: Gosset & Dunlap.

Bankoff, C. (2015). Brian Williams might have also lied about Navy SEALs, the Pope, and the Berlin Wall. New York Magazine. http://nymag.com/daily/intelligencer/2015/02/ williams-might-have-also-lied-about-seals.html.

Boreau, A. (2001). *The myth of Pope Joan* (trans. L. G. Cochrane). Chicago: University of Chicago Press.

Boyd, A. (2014). Cutaneous Munchausen syndrome: Clinical and histopathologic features. *Journal of Cutaneous Pathology*, 41, 333–336.

Campbell, S. (2000). *Romantic deception: The six signs he's lying*. Holbrook, Mass.: Adams Media Corp.

CBS News, 48 Hours. (June 5, 2002). The imposter. Retrieved January 11, 2006 from http://www.cbsnews.com/stories/1999/11/10/48hours/main55788.shtml and The imposter's early years. Retrieved January 11, 2006 from http://www.cbsnews.com/stories/1999/11/10/48hours/main54256.shtml.

Chariton, J. (2015). Bill O'Reilly vs. Brian Williams: Why the media is treating them differently. *The Wrap*. http://www.thewrap.com/bill-oreilly-vs-brian-williams-a-tale-of-two-media-responses/

Cleckley, H. (1982). *The mask of sanity* (5th ed.). St. Louis, MO: Mosby.

Conkey, C. (2007). The borrower who never was: Synthetic identity fraud hits credit bureaus, Banks. *The Wall Street Journal*. http://www.wsj.com/articles/SB119362045526074445.

Corn, D., & Schulman, D. (2015, February 15). Bill O'Reilly has his own Brian Williams problem. *Mother Jones*. http://www.motherjones.com/politics/2015/02/bill-oreilly-brian-williams-falklands-war.

Craig, K.D., & Hill, M. (2003). Misrepresentation of pain and facial expression. In P.W. Halligan, C. Bass, & D.A. Oakley (Eds.) *Malingering and illness deception* (pp. 326–347). New York: Oxford University Press.

Crichton, R. (1959). *The great imposter*. New York: Random House.

Criddle, L. (2010). Monsters in the closet: Munchausen syndrome by proxy. *Critical Care Nurse*, 30, 46–56.

Daegling, D.J. (2004). *Bigfoot exposed: An anthropologist examines America's enduring legend*. New York: AltaMira Press.

DeGrave, K. (1995). *Swindler, spy, rebel: The confidence woman in nineteenth-century America*. Columbia: University of Missouri Press.

Delbruck, A. (1891). Die pathologische Luge und die psychisch abnormen Schwinder: Eine Untersuchung uber den allmahlichen Uebergang eines normalen psychologischen Vorgangs in ein pathologisches Symptom, fur Aerzte und Juristen. Stuttgart.

Diagnostic and statistical manual of mental disorders / Edition 5: (2013). Washington, D. C.: American Psychiatric Association.

Dike, C. (2008). Pathological lying: Symptom or disease? *Psychiatric Times*. http://www.psychiatrictimes.com/articles/pathological-lying-symptom-or-disease.

Dike, C., Baranoski, M., & Griffith, E. (2005). Pathological lying revisited. *The Journal of the American Academy of Psychiatry and the Law, 54*, 342–349.

Dunn, D.H. (1975). *Ponzi: Boston swindler*. New York: McGraw-Hill.

Erdely, S.R. (2014). *A rape on campus: A brutal assault and struggle for justice at UVA*. Rolling Stone. http://web.archive.org/web/20141120205928/ http://www.rollingstone.com/culture/features/a-rape-on-campus-20141119.

Farhi, P. (2015, February 4). Brian Williams admits that his story of coming under fire while in Iraq was false. *The Washington Post*. http://www.washingtonpost.com/lifestyle/style /2015/02/04/.

Faron, F. (1998). *Rip-off: A writer's guide to crimes of deception*. Cincinnati, OH.: Writer's Digest Books.

Federal Bureau of Intelligence. (2014). *Internet Crime Complaint Center Annual Report*. https://www.fbi.gov/news/news_blog/2014-ic3-annual-report.

Federal Trade Commission. (2013). *Guide for assisting identity theft victims*. http://ftc.gov/idtheftresources.

Fernandez, E. (February 18, 2001). Bizarre medical masquerade: Determined con man steals Stockton doctor's identity for 20 years. *San Francisco Chronicle*, A1.

Finklea, K. (2014). *Identity theft: Trends and issues*. Washington, DC: Congressional Research Service.

Fitzgerald, R. (November, 2001). The impostor. *Reader's Digest*, 62–71.

Flaherty, D.K. (2011). The vaccine-autism connection: A public health crisis caused by unethical medical practices and fraudulent science. *Annals of Pharmacotherapy, 45*, 1302–1304.

Ford, C.V. (1996). *Lies! Lies!! Lies!!! The psychology of deceit*. Washington, D. C.: American Psychiatric Press.

Ford, C.V., King, B.H., Hollender, M.H. (1988). Lies and liars: Psychiatric aspects of prevarication. *American Journal of Psychiatry, 145*, 554–562.

Forward, S. (1999). *When your lover is a liar*. New York: HarperCollins.

Fox, M.J. (2002). *Lucky man: A memoir*. New York: Hyperion.

Gansler, L.L. (2005). *The mysterious private Thompson: The double life of Sarah Emma Edmonds, Civil War soldier*. New York: Free Press.

Grann, D. (2008). The chameleon: The many lives of Frederic Bourdin. *The New Yorker, 84* (24), 66–79.

Hall, R. (1993). *Patriots in disguise: Women warriors of the Civil War*. New York: Paragon House.

Hall, H.V., & Poirier, J.G. (2001). *Detecting malingering and deception: Forensic distortion analysis*. 2nd ed. Boca raton, FL.: CRC Press.

Halligan, P.W., Bass, C., & Oakley, D.A. (Eds.) (2003). *Malingering and illness deception*. New York: Oxford University Press.

Hamrick, S.J. (2004). *Deceiving the deceivers: Kim Philby, Donald Maclean, & Guy Burgess*. New Haven, CT.: Yale University Press

Hankiss, A. (1980). Games con men play: The semiosis of deceptive interaction. *Journal of Communication, 30*, 104–112.

Haselhoff, E.H. (2001). *The deepening complexity of crop circles: Scientific research and urban legends*. Berkeley, CA.: Frog, Ltd.

Hausman, K. (January 3, 2003). Does pathological lying warrant inclusion in the DSM? *Psychiatric News, 38*, 24.

Hines, T. (2003). *Pseudoscience and the paranormal*. 2nd Ed. Amherst, NY: Prometheus Books.

Horne, M. (April 16, 2006). Max Headroom creator made Roswell alien. *The Sunday Times, Britian* (http://www.timesonline.co.uk/article/0,,2087-2136617,00.html).

IBM Analytics (2015). *Synthetic identity fraud: Can I borrow your SSN?* Armonk, NY: IBM Corporation.

International Business Times (2011, February 4). Psychiatrist reveals how to spot another Bernie Madoff. http://www.ibtimes.com/psychiatrist-reveals-how-spot-another-bernie-madoff-263601.

Keyes, R. (2004). *The post-truth era: Dishonesty and deception in contemporary life*. New York: St. Martin's Press.

Kida, T. (2006). *Don't believe everything you think: The 6 basic mistakes we make in thinking*. Amherst, N.Y.: Prometheus Books.

Kominsky, M. (1970). *The hoaxers: Plain liars, fancy liars, and damned liars*. Boston: Branden Press.

Kropp, P.R. & Rogers, R. (1993). Understanding malingering: Motivation, method, and detection. In M. Lewis & C. Saarni, *Lying and deception in everyday life* (pp. 201–216). New York: Guilford.

Langenderfer, J. & Shimp, T.A. (2001). Consumer vulnerability to scams, swindles, and fraud: A new theory of visceral influences on persuasion. *Psychology & Marketing, 18*, 763–783.

Larsen, E. (1966). *The deceivers: Lives of great imposters.* New York: Roy Publishers.

Lenzenweger, M.F., Lane, M.C., Loranger, M.S., & Kessler, R.C. (2013). DSM-IV personality disorders in the National Comorbidity Survey Replication. *Biological Psychiatry, 62*, 553–564.

Lee, R.A. (2002). *The careers of John R. Brinkley.* Lexington, KY: University of Kentucky Press.

Marinacci, M. (1997a). Dr. John Brinkley (1885–1941): Getting America's goat. Retrieved 1-17-06. http://pw2.netcom.com/~mikalm/brinkley.htm

Marinacci, M. (1997b). Joseph Weil (1875?–1976): The yellow kid. Retrieved 1-17-06. http://pw1.netcom.com/~mikalm/weil.htm.

Martens, W.H.J. (2014). The hidden suffering of the psychopath. *Psychiatric Times.* http://www.psychiatrictimes.com/psychotic-affective-disorders/hidden-suffering-psychopath/.

Meadow, R. (1977). Munchausen syndrome by proxy: The hinterland of child abuse. *The Lancet, 2*, 343–345.

Maurer, D.W. (1940/1999). *The big con: The story of the confidence man.* New York: Anchor Books.

McCann, J.T. (1998). *Malingering and deception in adolescents: Assessing credibility in clinical and forensic settings.* Washington, D. C.: American Psychological Association.

MacDougall, C.D. (1958). *Hoaxes.* New York: Dover.

MacDougall, C.D. (1983). *Superstition and the press.* Buffalo, N.Y.: Prometheus Books.

McHoskey, J.W., Worzel, W. & Szyarto, C. (1998). Machiavellianism and psychopathy. *Journal of Personality and Social Psychology, 74*, 192–210.

Mendis, S., & Hodgson, R.E. (2012). Ganser syndrome: Examining the aetiological debate through a systematic case report review. *European Journal of Psychiatry, 26*, 96–106.

Moss, M. (June 1, 2000). A soldier's lie. *Austin American Statesman*, A2.

Musella, D.P. (September/October, 2005). Gallup poll shows that Americans' belief in the paranormal persists. *Skeptical Inquirer, 29*, 5.

Nash, J.R. (1976). *Hustlers and con men: An anecdotal history of the confidence man and his games.* New York: Evans.

Newman, A. (2003, April 13). Analyze this: Vincent Gigante, not crazy after all these years. *New York Times.* http://www.nytimes.com/2003/04/13/weekinreview/.

Newman, G.R., & McNally, M.M. (2005). *Identity theft literature review: Report for the National Institute of Justice Focus Group.* Washington, DC: U.S. Department of Justice.

Nickerson, R.S. (1998). Confirmation bias: A ubiquitous phenomenon in many guises. *Review of General Psychology, 2,* 175–220.

O'Sullivan, M. (2003). The fundamental attribution error in detecting deception: The boy-who-cried-wolf effect. *Personality and Social Psychology Bulletin, 29,* 1316–1327.

Paulhus, D.L. (2014). Toward a taxonomy of dark personalities. *Current Directions in Psychological Science, 23,* 421–426.

Park, R. (2000). *Voodoo science: The road from foolishness to fraud.* New York: Oxford University Press.

Parmar, N. (August, 2004). Crying wolf. *Psychology Today, 37,* 13–14.

Pemment, J. (2013). Psychopathy versus sociopathy: Why the distinction has become crucial. *Aggression and Violent Behavior, 18,* 458–461.

Pistone, J.D. (1987). *Donnie Brascoe: My undercover life in the Mafia.* New York: Penguin.

Power, R. (2011). *Child identity theft.* CyLab Technical Report, Carnegie Mellon University.

Randi, J. (1995). *An encyclopedia of claims, frauds, and hoaxes of the occult and supernatural.* New York: St. Martin's Press.

Randi, J. (1989). *The faith healers.* Amherst, N.Y.: Prometheus Books.

Randi, J. (1982). *Flim-flam!: Psychics, ESP, unicorns, and other delusions.* Amherst, N.Y.: Prometheus Books.

Rayner, R. (2002). *Drake's fortune: The fabulous true story of the world's greatest confidence artist.* New York: Doubleday.

Resnick, P.J., & Knoll, J. (2005). Faking it: How to detect malingered psychosis. *Current Psychiatry, 4* (11), 13–25.

Rijsenbilt, A., & Commandeur, H. (2013). Narcissus enters the courtroom: CEO narcissism and fraud. *Journal of Business Ethics, 117,* 413–429.

Robinson, O., & Stolberg, S. (2015, March 23). Police find no evidence of rape at UVA fraternity. *New York Times.* http://www.nytimes.com/2015/03/24/us/police-to-release-results-of-uva-rape-inquiry.html.

Rogers, R. (Ed.) (1988). *Clinical assessment of malingering and deception.* New York: Guilford.

Rosenblat, H. (2009). *Angel at the fence.* New York: Berkely Books (canceled before publication).

Russell, M. (2003). *Piltdown man: The secret life of Charles Dawson & the world's greatest archaeological hoax.* Gloucestershire, England: Tempus.

Serota, K.B., Levine, T.R., & Boster, F.J. (2010). The prevalence of lying in America: Three studies of self-reported lies. *Human Communication Research, 36,* 2–25.

Serota, K.B., & Levine, T.R. (2015). A few prolific liars: Variation in the prevalence of lying. *Journal of Language and Social Psychology, 34,* 138–157.

Sherman, G. (2008, December 26). The greatest love story ever sold. *The New Republic.* http://www.newrepublic.com/article/books-and-arts/the-greatest-love-story-ever-sold.

Shermer, M. (2001). Baloney detection. *Scientific American, 285,* 36.

Shermer, M. (2000). *How we believe: Science, skepticism, and the search for god.* 2nd ed. New York: Henry Holt.

Shermer, M. (1997/2002). *Why people believe weird things: Pseudoscience, superstition, and other confusions of our time.* New York: Henry Holt.

Somaiya, R. (2015, April 2015). Rolling Stone article on rape at University of Virginia failed all basics, report says. *New York Times.* http://www.nytimes.com/2015/04/06/business/ media/rolling-stone-retracts-article-on-rape-at-university-of-virginia.html.

Editors of *Lingua Franca.* (2000). *The Sokal hoax: The sham that shook the academy.* Lincoln, NE: University of Nebraska Press.

Stajano, F., & Wilson, P. (2011). Understanding scam victims: Seven principles for systems security. *Communications of the ACM, 54,* 70–75.

Stanford, P. (1999). *The legend of Pope Joan: In search of the truth.* New York: Henry Holt & Co.

Sullivan, E. (2001). *The concise book of lying.* New York: Farrar, Straus and Giroux.

Sylvester, R. (October 22, 2000). Admiral impersonator who wore phony medals gets prison sentence. *Austin American Statesman,* A22.

Talbot, M. (August 9, 2004). The bad mother. *The New Yorker, 80,* 63–75.

Twerski, A.J. (1997). *Addictive thinking.* (2nd ed.) Center City, MN: Hazelden.

U. S. News & World Report (August26–September 2, 2002). The art of the hoax, 30–79.

Velazquez, L.J. (1876/1972). *The woman in battle: A narrative of exploits, adventures, and travels of Madame Loreta Janeta Velazquez.* New York: Arno Press.

Vincent, N. (2007). *Self-made man: One woman's journey into manhood and back again.* New York: Viking.

Weil, J.R. & Brannon, W. T. (1948/2004). *Con man: A master swindler's own story.* New York: Broadway Books.

Williams, D. (November 13, 2005). In Italy, chemist scrutinizes science of religious miracles. *Austin American Statesman*, A16.

Wiseman, R. (1997). *Deception and self-deception: Investigating psychics.* Amherst, New York: Prometheus Books.

Wolff, G. (1979/1990). *The duke of deception: Memories of my father.* New York: Vintage Books.

Yarnell, E.C. (2013). Medals of dishonor? Military, free speech, and the Stolen Valor Act. *Veterans Law Review*, 5, 56–135.

Young, G. (2014). *Malingering, feigning, and response bias in psychiatric/psychological injury: Implications for practice and court.* Dordrecht, Netherlands: Springer-Verlag.

Zuckoff, M. (May 15, 2006). The perfect mark: How a Massachusetts psychotherapist fell for a Nigerian e-mail scam. *The New Yorker*, 82, 36–42.

Part III Lie Detection

How do people determine whether a person is lying or not? How accurate are these methods? Who are the most accurate lie detectors? The following chapters focus on these questions. Chapter 9 deals with lie detection as it is observed in both everyday encounters and police interrogations. Chapter 10 looks at drugs and devices used to assist lie detectors. These include polygraphs, brain scans, truth serums, voice analyzers, and the like.

Chapter 9: Unassisted Lie Detection
Chapter 10: Assisted Lie Detection

Chapter 9

Unassisted Lie Detection

As long as there have been liars, there have been lie detectors. Throughout most of human history, these lie detectors had to rely on strategies that did not involve machines designed to identify liar behavior. Crude machines used to torture suspected liars have been used for centuries, but the purpose of these machines is more to inflict pain and elicit confessions than to identify liar behavior *per se*. Unassisted lie detection, then, relies solely on a *detector's skill* in questioning the suspect, observing the suspect's behavior, gathering lie-relevant information, and making a decision about the suspect's veracity. Even though efforts to build an unerring lie detection machine are as frenzied as ever (see Chapter 10), unassisted lie detection is likely to be the method people most often use for a long time to come. How do people go about detecting lies without the assistance of drugs or machines?

Ways People Detect Lies

In everyday life, people don't usually rely on a single approach as they go about trying to determine whether somebody is lying or did lie to them. Instead, they usually use two or more of the following four methods identified by Park et al. (2002b). And unlike many lie detection experiments which require immediate lie detection decisions, lie detection in everyday life sometimes takes place over days, weeks, or months.

Obtaining Information from Others

Consider this not-so-hypothetical example. Jill tells her teacher that she was ill and couldn't take an exam. The teacher allows Jill to take a makeup exam and she makes an A. Rachel, who lives in the dorm with Jill, knows she lied about being sick. In addition, Rachel took the exam on the day it was given even though she felt

> "If you can't lie no better than that, you might as well tell the truth."
>
> — *Delbert McClinton & Gary Nicholson*
> Lie No Better

> "Tell me the truth. Please stop me from guessing."
>
> — *Doug Sahm*
> Tell Me the Truth

sick. She got a C and isn't happy about Jill getting an A so she tells the teacher that she knows Jill lied about being sick. As a result, the teacher questions Jill and looks for other evidence that will confirm or deny her illness claim.

Whistleblowers, like Rachel, provide information that often triggers a lie detection investigation. They are usually members of an organization who report on misconduct in their organization for the purpose of serving the public good. Lies are normally associated with the reported misconduct (Alford, 2001; Glazer & Glazer, 1989; *Time,* 2002/2003). For example, Jeffrey Wigand exposed executives in his own tobacco company who lied about what they knew about their product, Cynthia Cooper of Worldcom and Sherron Watkins of Enron unmasked fraudulent accounting practices which misled investors and the public, Coleen Rowley of the FBI went public with the information that her office reported information on an al Qaeda terrorist prior to 9/11 and her superiors were slow to take action on it, and Edward Snowden exposed the secret surveillance practices of the NSA to the public. Even though the general public may think of whistleblowers as heroic guardians of the truth, they typically get little support from their fellow employees. They know the whistleblower is going to be targeted by the organization's power structure and they don't want to be in the line of fire. Besides, they are reluctant to join an effort to ruin the reputation of the company responsible for their paycheck. It is not unlike a group of people standing idly by while a person gets mugged (Latané & Darley, 1970). The costs for the whistleblower are often high. Many lose their jobs; some lose their house and have to file bankruptcy. Snowden had to seek asylum in other countries to evade prosecution. Employees of intelligence-gathering agencies are required by law to report wrongdoing to their own agency, which is often the target of their complaint. In so doing, they risk losing their security clearance and transfer to a menial job (Carr, 2005). Other companies may be reluctant to hire a person who views the value of truth telling over company loyalty. Laws exist to protect whistleblowers, but they are generally ineffective and many whistleblowers say they would be reluctant to do it again. But they also report they felt a strong obligation to speak out and that losing their job was secondary to doing what they felt was right.

In both of the preceding examples, earnest lie detection began after a third party provided information, but sometimes information from others is deliberately sought in order to verify a suspected lie.

Finding Physical Evidence

Lie detectors, like detectives, sometimes find physical evidence that counters information they've been told. The lipstick on a man's collar seems contrary to his denial of any contact with females during the day; a woman may claim there has been no contact between her and her ex-boyfriend, but phone records suggest otherwise; a half empty bottle of vodka found in a person's backpack raises doubts about the owner's claim to have stopped drinking. Finding physical evidence which seems to expose a lie does not always guarantee that it will. Sometimes apparently incriminating evidence can be reasonably explained. Until such explanations are forthcoming, however, it will surely increase suspicion and form the basis for further information gathering by the lie detector.

Receiving a Confession

The participants in the Park et al. (2002b) study said that lies are also uncovered when liars confess. Some confessions are the result of confronting the liar with information, evidence, and questions. Unsolicited confessions also occur. For example, a romantic partner who has repeatedly lied about being an executive with a large company decides one day to admit to his partner that he is a postal clerk. Is lie detection a part of this process? In one sense, no. But the lie detector may have indirectly facilitated the confession by helping to create a relationship where truth was valued, where guilt was emphasized, where understanding was expected, etc. Confessions may also occur inadvertently. A liar may forget the story he or she told months earlier and accidentally tell what really happened during a casual conversation. One of the people in the Park et al. study reported that his roommate had denied drinking his milk. Later, he overheard his roommate talking on the phone and saying, "My roommate actually believed me about the milk." As noted later in this chapter, all three of these confession types are also found in police work as well.

Behavioral Observation and Listening

Lie detection processes often involve decisions about the suspected liar's verbal and nonverbal behavior. As Vrij (2008) suggests, lying can be more cognitively complex than truth telling and this results in increased strain on memory. As a result liars may reveal verbal and nonverbal behaviors which betray their message. Observers might respond to specific details—e.g., "He wouldn't look at me after I asked him that question," or "I knew people who worked there had to have a badge so when she said she didn't need one, I knew she didn't work there." Observers may also detect verbal inconsistencies that suggest deception.

Having knowledge about facts relevant to the lie or familiarity with a particular context will aid in detecting lies. Also, taking what is said and fact checking the information will significantly increase the possibility of catching a liar. Blair, Levine, and Shaw (2010) call this process *content in context*. The accessibility of the Internet and the vast amount of information people post to their own social media profiles makes information gathering for corroborating a story easy to do. Expert knowledge (e.g., a detective familiar with the type of crime), possessing factual information relevant to the lie, and having general familiarity allow one to ask questions that are diagnostically strategic and context sensitive (Levine, Blair, & Clare, 2014). Avoiding broad, scripted, and irrelevant questions increases lie detection accuracy.

According to Feeley and Young (1998), global judgments are by far the most frequent way of determining deceptive behavior—e.g., "His account just didn't seem plausible," or "She acted funny; something wasn't right." A metaanalytic study by DePaulo et al. (2003) found that liars can be detected via some global judgments such as the liar's vocal and verbal involvement, and cooperation and ambivalence. Also, relying on unconscious processes rather than traditional truth-lie judgment dichotomies may more accurately reflect how suspicion and lies are detected (ten Brinke, Stimson, & Carney, 2014). However, according to Bond, Levine, and Hartwig (2015) the majority of *indirect measures* (e.g., ambivalence) are inferior to direct judgments of veracity.

The process of examining another person's behavior for clues to deception is the most popular method used by researchers to determine how accurate we are in detecting deception. In addition, most of this research focuses on judgments of truth or deception by people who are not in dialogue with the person being judged. However, in everyday conversation, and in police interviews, behavioral cues are normally assessed by a person who is interacting with the person being judged.

Can We Accurately Detect Lies by Observing Behavior?

Some writers make the process of unassisted lie detection seem very easy. Lieberman (1998, p. 65), for example, provides the readers of his book with "a series of questions which virtually guarantees that you will know (a) if you're being lied to and (b) what the truth is if it's not obvious from the lie." The results of research on the ability of human beings to detect lies told by other human beings tell a different story.

The way researchers typically study lie detection skills is to ask people to view a number of relatively short video clips of a stranger speaking to a video camera. These strangers tell the truth in half the videos and lie in the other half. The job of the detector is to judge accurately which people are telling the truth and which ones are lying. The strangers may be addressing their opinion on a controversial topic, whether they like or dislike a person, whether they have just viewed a pleasant or emotionally disturbing video, or whether they have or have not just taken some money from an adjoining room.

So detectors do not enter the testing situation suspicion-free. They know they will be exposed to some people who are lying. After seeing somebody they don't know talk for perhaps a minute, they are expected to make a judgment about that person's veracity. In some experiments, the deception detector is provided with either positive (monetary) or negative (restriction to a small, dark room for several hours with periodic blasts of loud noise) incentives to do well, but external motivation is not always provided in these experiments. Believing that detectors are more accurate at detecting high-stakes lies, some experiments induce people to lie or tell the truth about actual cheating and stealing they've participated in (see Chapter 7), but this is not typical. In addition to liar and lie detector motivation, critics point out that lie detection in everyday life is not usually limited to a single, brief exposure and that detectors have an opportunity to interact with the person they are observing. There are, of course, occasions when non-interactive observations of veracity are made—e.g., jurors viewing witnesses, law enforcement officers viewing suspects while another officer interrogates them, or observing a sales person interacting with another client while you are waiting. In addition, Malone and DePaulo (2001) point out that the typical way of studying lie detection has many features that we all face in everyday situations—e.g., the lies are of little consequence, not well planned, often involve feelings, and because the liars are not especially worried about getting caught, they exhibit relatively little discomfort that might otherwise be associated with lies involving higher stakes.

Ways of Measuring Accuracy

As noted above, lie detectors are shown an equal number of people who are honest and dishonest. Accuracy is most often expressed as the percentage of correct judgments. If a person correctly identified twelve of twenty communicators (ten truth tellers and ten liars), this person's lie detection accuracy would be 60%. Measuring accuracy in this way forces observers to make an unqualified decision regarding truth or deception.

But our decisions about whether a person is lying aren't always unambiguous. We may be thinking, "Something makes me think this person is lying, but I'm not entirely sure." In fact, DePaulo and Morris (2002) found that a person's ambivalence was a better way of distinguishing lies and truths than the actual lie/truth judgments. They found lies were far more ambivalent for judges than truths. Of course, intuitive judgments are also subject to bias and inaccuracy (Myers, 2002), but listening to judges talk out loud as they go about deciding on lie/truth judgments may provide valuable information that the final lie/truth judgment does not. A seven-point rating scale in which a seven indicates complete assurance that the person being judged is deceptive would also allow judges to show how certain they are about their decision. Rating scales are not frequently used to measure lie detection accuracy, but they are informative when perceptual gradations involved in decision making are important.

Accuracy scores do not reflect a person's ability to identify the specific nature of the truth that a deceiver is withholding or covering up or what Ekman (2001) calls leakage. Accuracy scores are only concerned with judgments of deception, not leakage—e.g., "I think this person is not telling everything he knows, but I'm not sure what it is he's hiding." However, some lie detection efforts are especially focused on leakage. With those suspected of malingering, there is less emphasis on confirming the presence of deception and more emphasis on whether the way a particular illness is faked is consistent with what is known about that illness (Rogers, 1988).

Lie Detection Accuracy: Nonprofessionals

Now that we know how observational lie detection is measured, we can answer the central question: how accurate are we? Vrij (2008) reviewed 39 studies and found an accuracy rate of 57%; Malone and DePaulo (2001) analyzed more than 100 studies with the average detection rate at 54%; DePaulo and Morris (2005) examined 253 samples, involving mostly students as lie detectors, with an average accurate rate of 53%. The inescapable conclusion is that untrained observers are able to detect deception at rates that slightly exceed chance. If you flipped a coin or randomly guessed on each trial you would be competitive with those who based their judgments on what they perceived as truth telling and deceptive behavior.

Are groups more accurate lie detectors than individuals? Individual perceptions of truth tellers and liars have been compared with the collective decisions of groups. Frank et al. (2004) found that small groups containing six people were statistically more accurate than individuals in their judgments of deceptions, but not truthful statements. The accuracy rate of the individuals and small groups in another study found accuracy scores that slightly exceeded chance which echo the findings of the extant literature on lie detection (Park et al., 2002a). The detection rate for people rating those who do not share the same culture, language, or degree of literacy is no worse than the rate for those who do share these characteristics (Bond & Atoum, 2000; Bond & Rao, 2004).

Lie Detection Accuracy: Professionals

The accuracy rates of professionals—police officers, customs officers, federal polygraphers, robbery investigators, judges, lawyers, and psychiatrists are generally no better than that of the laypersons—within the 45–60% accuracy range (Ekman and O'Sullivan, 1991; Vrij, 2008).

There are, of course, some individuals in these studies of laypersons and professionals who are far more accurate than their peers. These skilled detectors will be discussed later in the chapter. There is something more troubling, however, for those who wish our lie detection skills exceeded the slightly better than chance levels reported in most studies. Due to the "veracity effect," most people's accuracy in detecting lies *per se* may actually be worse than 50%.

The "Veracity Effect"

A lie detector's accuracy score is typically derived from the number of accurate identifications of both truth tellers and liars. However, human observers tend to perceive more messages as truthful (truth bias) than deceptive which results in a greater accuracy for truthful messages and a lower accuracy for deceptive ones. Levine et al. (1999) called this the "veracity effect." When half the speakers being judged are telling the truth and half are liars, the truthful speakers are typically identified about 67% of the time, but our ability to identify the liars accurately is more likely around 34–37% (Levine et al., 2006; Park et al., 2002a). In situations and relationships where the rate of truth telling is high and there is no reason to suspect lies, our ability to detect lies accurately sinks even lower.

The truth bias, which negatively affects our ability to detect lies, is a result of both social and cognitive processes. Socially we assume people will normally tell us the truth which leads us to perceive many more truths than lies. We get in the habit of generously treating messages that sound strange as truthful until more specific information is obtained. It's an efficient and friendly way to proceed. In addition, the experiments conducted by Gilbert and his colleagues (1990; 1993) remind us that incoming messages are initially, if only for a split second, accepted or represented in our mind as true *prior* to a rational analysis of their veracity. The truth bias, according to DePaulo (1994, p. 83), can be summed up this way: "...the empirical fact is that most people seem to believe most of what they hear most of the time." Because of the nature of their work or their social environment, however, some people may behave very differently. Instead of being biased toward the truth, they have a lie bias.

Lie Bias Effects

Prison is a place where residents are exposed to a lot of lies and get timely feedback on their accuracy in detecting them. The ability to detect lies accurately is a crucial part of adapting to this environment. It is not surprising, then, to find that prisoners have a lie bias. They are substantially more accurate than chance in detecting lies, but below 50% in detecting truths—the reverse of the veracity effect (Bond et al., 2005; Hartwig et al., 2004).

A lie bias does not automatically mean lies will be detected more accurately. Without timely feedback on one's ability to detect lies, a lie bias can impede detection accuracy in the same way a truth bias does. Experienced law enforcement officers who were trained in observational lie detection also showed a lie bias and assumed too often that a suspect was lying (Meissner & Kassin, 2002). Elaad (2003) found that police interrogators often overestimated their ability to detect lies. In a situation where the expectation for lies is high, combined with detectors who are confident they are good at detecting lies, there is likely to be a bias toward perceiving lies. If these interrogators do *not* receive timely information about the accuracy or inaccuracy of their lie judgments, we would *not* expect their lie detection ability to be high.

Lie Detection Accuracy in Close Relationships

As noted earlier, studies of lie detection accuracy are largely based on the behavior of people unknown to the judges. Is lie detection accuracy helped or hindered when the person being judged is a close relationship partner? It can help or hinder (Knapp, 2006).

Sometimes relationship closeness facilitates accurate lie detection. For various reasons, a close relationship partner may lie in transparent ways. With high stakes lies, behavioral signs of guilt or fear may overshadow any attempts at concealment. The lack of practice with serious lies may also negatively affect performance. There may even be a subconscious desire to be caught. In addition, the detector is well aware of the liar's baseline behavior and is sensitive to any unusual changes in that behavior. Thus, we would expect a person who is suspicious of deception would be more accurate when judging a close relationship partner than a stranger (Stiff et al., 1992).

However, there are forces working against lie detection accuracy. Lie detectors in close relationships know the problematic nature of suspicion. When a detector reveals her suspicious behavior, it has the potential to reduce trust and closeness so she may not want to act on her suspicion. In other words, lie detection may take a back seat to relationship maintenance even when lies are suspected. Furthermore, the liar is just as familiar with the target's behavior as the target is of the liar's. Therefore, inaccurate lie detection in close relationships may be due to the strategic reading and use of the target's behavior by the liar. About half the time, for example, the adolescents in Grady's (1997) study (discussed in Chapter 5) were able to identify strategies their parents used to detect their deception. The truth bias is even stronger in close relationships than it is in the general population, so serious lies are completely unexpected and detection is not even an issue. Low-stakes lies which support the close relationship partner and the relationship are expected, but, again, detection is not an issue.

Why Aren't We More Accurate?

It would not be practical to list all the factors that could restrict the accurate identification of another person's deceptive behavior. There are too many of them. However, the following list is long enough to make it easy to understand why we aren't more accurate while simultaneously engendering admiration for those few whose lie detection skills are high.

Biases and Stereotypes

One of the most common problems associated with human lie detection is a disparity between what people think liars look like and how they act and how they really look and act (Strömwall et al., 2004). Kaufmann et al. (2003) found perceptions of credibility strongly influenced by social stereotypes regarding "appropriate" emotional expressions. Studies show that people who subscribe to popular stereotypes like "liars won't look at you" or "liars fidget a lot" are not likely to be good lie detectors (Feeley & Young, 1998; Vrij & Mann, 2001). Lie detectors who believe they are observing a liar are likely to see behaviors they associate with liars even though they aren't manifested by the speaker (Levine, Asada, & Park, 2006). Since liars are also familiar with common beliefs about liar behavior (e.g., fewer other-directed gazes), it is not surprising when liars don't manifest this behavior. Nevertheless, people maintain these beliefs because they think back to a time when a liar they knew did look away or fidget a lot and ignore all the other occasions when the liars they experienced did not manifest these characteristics. This is known as a *confirmation bias* (Nickerson, 1998).

The *Othello error* occurs when a lie detector interprets any behavioral sign as indicative of lying and not something else. A person's anger and/or nervousness, for example, might be the result of being accused of lying rather than signs of lying (Ekman, 2001).

People also have beliefs about what liars and truth tellers look like (Yamagishi et al., 2003; Zebrowitz et al., 1996). But a person who is perceived to have an honest face (babyfacedness, large eyes, facial symmetry, attractive) is not always going to be honest. The perceptual problem occurs because once we perceive someone as an honest or dishonest person, we are more likely to perceive their behavior in line with that perception. A negative or positive bias toward people from a given culture or ethnic group can work the same way.

Stereotypes and biases are also linked to a common observational error called *the Brokaw hazard* (Ekman, 2001). The Brokaw hazard occurs when the lie detector fails to acknowledge that a particular manifested behavior may just be that particular person's way of communicating and not a sign of deception. Good detectors try to base their judgments on changes in behavior rather than the presence of a particular type of behavior—e.g., changes in hesitant speech rather than on hesitant speech *per se*.

Lie detectors also seem to believe that aberrant or "weird" behavior (e.g., periodically raising one's voice without an apparent reason, occasional eye movements which follow a nonexistent flying insect, or doing intermittent stretching exercises with one's arms and legs) means a person is more likely to be dishonest (Levine et al., 2000; Bond et al., 1992).

Overlooking or Incorrectly Using Behavioral Cues

Lie detection accuracy is also affected by the ways lie detectors approach the behavioral cues manifested by the liar. As Ekman (1996) pointed out, parents not only don't teach their children what cues liars use, they often teach them to ignore them in order to facilitate effective social relations. As a result poor detectors: 1) often base their judgment of deception on a single nonverbal cue even though they understand there may be many relevant cues, and 2) overlook or minimize nonverbal cues and pay undue attention to verbal cues when judging deceptive messages (O'Sullivan, 2003). Ekman (2001, p. 165) also cautions, "…the absence of a sign of deceit is not evidence of truth."

Making Judgments While Participation in Dialogue

Although deception detection experiments do not usually involve dialogue between the detector and the suspected liar, it is a common condition in everyday lie detection. Several factors detract from accurate lie detection during interaction (Burgoon, Buller & Floyd, 2001; Dunbar et al., 2003). First, the behavior being observed by the lie detector is not independent of his or her own behavior. What is being observed, then, is the process of mutual influence—not an uncontaminated performance by a liar. Second, the process of questioning or probing in order to detect deception seems to have a generally positive effect on perceptions of the target's honesty, but does not increase lie detection accuracy (Levine & McCornack, 2001). Surprisingly, this "probing effect" also occurs with prisoners who enter the encounter with a lie bias (Bond et al., 2004). Third, conversations require each interactant to pay attention to what is verbalized, making it more difficult to focus solely on nonverbal behavior. In addition, the verbal behavior is likely to be a mixture of truths, half truths, and falsehoods (unlike a typical lie detection experiment) which may also make unambiguous perceptions of lying difficult. Fourth, lie detection experiments that involve viewing a videotape allow the observer to maintain a constant eye gaze with an unobstructed frontal view of the suspect's face and body. Politeness norms and movements which occur in conversations mean behavioral observations are often gleaned from short glances and some body features will be perceptually more accessible than others. Finally, lie detectors in conversations do not usually obtain immediate feedback to validate or deny their inferences about deception—feedback which is necessary in order to improve one's detection accuracy.

Characteristics/Behavior of the Liar

Some characteristics of liars also inhibit accurate lie detection. For example, the communication styles of Machiavellian and extroverted personalities make their lies harder to detect (Vrij, 2008). The demeanor of skilled liars or those with little concern for the truth may resemble the behaviors of trustworthy and honest individuals. Also, truth tellers who portray idiosyncratic or nervous behaviors can raise suspicion. Levine et al. (2011) discuss how manipulating sender demeanor in deception judgment tasks drives accuracy scores. That is, there are those who look like liars, and others who come off as honest—regardless of facts associated with their assertions. These performances play an important role in how they are judged by others.

Characteristics/Behavior of the Detector

Despite the fact that lying and lie detection have been important features in human development over the past five or six million years, the ability to detect lies with a high degree of accuracy has not become a selected, hard-wired trait (Ekman, 1996). Those with poor memories or who do a poor job of monitoring their own behavior are likely to be even less skilled.

Learning lie detection skills is also problematic. Instead of learning to look for lying clues in a person's demeanor, we learn to politely ignore suspicious behavior, to be cautious about accusing someone of lying, and to rely on non-observational types of information to validate another's lying behavior. Sometimes we ignore deception clues because we want to be misled. In short, the motivation to detect lies accurately is often constrained. Most of us seem to know that, despite the costs, trust enriches life more than suspicion does. Sometimes there are costs for people who are skilled at detecting subtle signs of covert behavior. The skills necessary to be an effective lie detector negatively affected students' popularity and social sensitivity ratings as well as their relationship satisfaction (DePaulo & Jordan, 1982).

Passive Observation vs. Active Questioning

A majority of the studies concerned with human lie detection accuracy report on the findings taken from experiments and lie detection tasks which rely on passive observers who: are not interacting with the source, are not themselves asking any questions, and who are relying on verbal and nonverbal responses to scripted contextual questions (e.g., why didn't you steal the check?). This is not usually how determinations of veracity happen in everyday life. Interestingly, observing a suspect being questioned can lead to enhanced source believability or a *probing effect* (Levine & McCornack, 2001). But in law enforcement interviews questions are not overly scripted—as they often are in research studies—and there is prior knowledge or evidence which can be used to develop questioning relative to the lie. Any answers provided throughout the interview can be used in strategic follow-up questions. This type of *active questioning* reflects the methods of skilled lie catchers. Simply interacting and probing a source may result in lie detection accuracies that reflect those of passive observation studies (e.g., slightly above chance; Levine & McCornack, 2001). But the *strategic use of evidence* and prompting for diagnostically useful information can lead to high judgment scores in experts and laypersons (Levine et al., 2014). Levine (2015) summarizes the findings of studies which examine a variety of active questioning methods and shows that accuracy rates range from 69–100%.

Professional Lie Detectors

Some of the preceding factors that detract from the accurate lie detection in the general public also affect professionals who are involved with lie detection as part of their work. For example, police training manuals sometimes provide misleading information about behavioral cues exhibited by liars—e.g., liars don't look at you, liars make unnatural posture changes, liars engage in nervous self-manipulations, liars place their hands over their mouth when speaking, etc. (Inbau et al., 2001). As a result, police officers have as many incorrect beliefs about deceptive behavior as do laypersons (Strömwall, Granhag, & Hartwig, 2004). In one study, those who were trained to use the invalid cues found in police manuals actually performed worse than those who had received no training (Kassin and Fong, 1999). Studies that examine the skills of professionals often do not allow them to interact with those being judged—therefore, they are unable to question subjects as they would in their line of work. In studies where professionals are allowed to interview subjects without being constrained by a script, accuracy rates can be exceptionally high—in one case an expert was able to achieve 100% (Levine et al., 2014).

The accuracy of professionals can be compromised because police interrogations are interactive and officers may pay less attention to nonverbal cues and more to verbal behavior. The motivation for police officers to detect any deception behavior is sometimes less important than obtaining evidence for a conviction. Biases and invalid stereotypes applied to suspects in police interviews can be especially dangerous because the presence of such cues may cause the investigators to focus all their energy on getting a confession from this person whom they think is lying. If they are mistaken, they may not find out until after a trial which may take months or years. Feedback delayed this long is not likely to be part of a worthwhile learning experience. Sometimes the belief that a truth teller is lying is so strong and so much time and energy has been invested in this belief by an officer that any information to the contrary, no matter when it is received, will not be treated as a learning experience.

As a result of confronting many more liars than truth tellers in their line of work, police officers typically overestimate their ability to detect lies (Elaad, 2003). Experience with liars is certainly an important part of learning to detect lies, but a comparable number of experiences with truth tellers, which they often don't have, is needed as a basis for comparison.

Highly Skilled Lie Detectors

Not everyone is an average or below average lie detector. Some people are highly skilled. Who are these people and what is their secret for successful lie detection?

Some preliminary answers to these questions occurred when Ekman and O'Sullivan (1991) tested the lie detection ability of several different professional groups and they noticed that the 34 secret service officers' accuracy rate of 65% exceeded that of all the other groups. More than half of these secret service officers scored 70% or above. The researchers attributed their success to several factors: 1) detecting truthful and deceptive intent is central to their job in the secret service and they are trained accordingly; 2) they learn to focus on nonverbal signals which might identify individuals who intend to harm the people they are protecting; 3) the importance of their job makes them highly motivated observers and they get plenty of practice on the job; and 4) they also need to keep an open mind about a person's guilt and innocence which puts any tendency toward a truth or lie bias in check.

Subsequent studies showed that highly skilled lie detectors weren't limited to secret service officers. Some clinical psychologists and law enforcement officers also showed exceptional skill at lie detection. They had several things in common: 1) a high motivation to improve their skill in deception detection; 2) experience with liars on the job; 3) judged by others who knew them to be skillful lie detectors; 4) closely examined nonverbal behavior, but did not rely on stereotypes of a liar's nonverbal behavior; 5) noted less-obvious verbal behavior involving ambiguous and contradictory statements; and 6) able to detect subtle facial cues involved in the hiding of strong emotional reactions (Ekman, O'Sullivan & Frank, 1999; Vrij & Mann, 2001; Vrij & Mann, 2005). The ability to perceive subtle facial signals of people lying about their emotions was also a skill found in a group of brain-injured people with severe deficits in their ability to understanding spoken sentences (aphasics). Their ability to detect emotions associated with lies was significantly better than people without any language impairment (Etcoff, et al., 2000).

Wizards

With the preceding studies providing clear evidence that some people are highly skilled lie detectors, O'Sullivan and Ekman set out to find the best of the best or what they called the wizards (O'Sullivan & Ekman, 2004; O'Sullivan, 2005). They tested more than 12,000 people on three different types of lies: lies about feelings, lies about opinions, and lies about committing a crime. The 14 people who scored 80% or better on each of these tests were identified as lie-detection wizards. Another group of 15 *almost* wizards scored 90% on one type of lie and 80% or better on one of the other two types of lies. The wizards came from different occupational groups: therapists, law enforcement officers, judges, arbitrators, and artists. Virtually all were between 40 and 60 years of age. They tended to be introverts, but paid attention to their own behavior. Overall, they tended to understand that not all liars act the same way and they paid attention to both language and nonverbal communication. As with much of the lie deception research, there are critiques to the research on wizards. Bond and Uysal (2007) explain that the findings on wizards may be due to statistical chance. A metaanalyic study by Bond and DePaulo (2008) found that liar credibility is the most important factor driving accuracy differences among judges—these authors claim this was an artifact driving results in the studies on wizards.

Training

Is it possible to train people to be significantly better lie detectors? Probably, but we don't currently have enough data to know exactly how effective training can be. Some training programs have increased accuracy rates dramatically (deTurck et al., 1990; Frank & Feeley, 2003), but Vrij (2008) says the average rate of trained observers is 57% and the average rate for untrained observers is 54%. Few training programs achieve accuracy rates as high as 65%. However, relying on training methods which match judges' background and professional experience (Hurley et al., 2014; Shaw et al., 2013) or familiarity with the lie situation (Reinhard et al., 2011) is important in obtaining higher accuracy results. Also, Blair, Levine, and Vasquez (2015) provided judges with multiple opportunities to engage in a deception-detection task over a six-week time period. They showed increases in accuracy rates from 69 to 89%. But, changing the context of the task from a cheating scenario to a mock robbery resulted in lowered accuracy scores. This further supports the notion that, while training does increase accuracy of deception detection, lie detection training in one context may not generalize to another context.

Like a number of other training programs, Levine et al. (2005) briefly trained people to look for certain nonverbal cues and compared the accuracy of those groups with groups that received no training. Consistent with previous training studies, this type of training results in very modest improvements in lie-detection accuracy. But the work of Levine and his colleagues also raises the possibility that these modest improvements might not be due to the training *per se* as much as to the content of the training because the training encourages more acute observation. Their experiments found, for example, that people trained to look for bogus nonverbal cues (unrelated to lying behavior) were significantly more accurate lie detectors than people who received no training and only slightly less accurate than those who were trained to look for nonverbal behavior typically associated with liars.

As previously mentioned, a major reason for the modest results associated with lie detection training has to do with the nature of the training itself (Bull, 2004; Frank & Feeley, 2003). Successful training programs need to be developed in accord with what we have learned from experts and effective detectors. For example, 1) trainees need to be motivated to succeed and to see the relevance of the training to their personal and/or career goals; 2) trainees must be willing to give up old biases and stereotypes about liar behavior; 3) training materials need to focus on a variety of different truth tellers and liars; 4) the stakes for the liars should be moderate to high; 5) trainees need to get immediate feedback on their performance and plenty of individual attention from the trainer; 6) trainees need to have plenty of time to practice; 7) trainees should be encouraged to talk about their lie/truth decisions so trainers can use this information to guide future performance; 8) trainees should be taught the value of attending to both nonverbal and verbal behavior; and 9) trainees should be exposed to different models of lie detection. For example, a model that emphasizes skill in perceiving what Ekman and Friesen (1978) call micromomentary facial expressions (less than half a second in length); or a model, based on research, that focuses on learning what behaviors or patterns of behavior typically distinguish liars and truth tellers. This approach might involve a specific behavior like the presence of "distancing" words (fewer self-references) or something general like any behavior that doesn't seem to fit the situation or the speaker's baseline behavior. Also, as we have seen from the recent research by Levine (2015), lie-detection training that focuses on the use of content in context and active/diagnostic questioning can substantially increase accuracy rates in deception detection.

Police and Military Interrogations

When lie detection is part of your job, the process assumes special characteristics which are not present in everyday lie detection. We will explore those characteristics in the context of police and military interrogations in this section.

Pre-Interrogation Interview

Interrogators usually proceed with the assumption that the suspect is guilty and their job is to persuade the interviewee to confess. Police interrogations, however, may be preceded by a pre-interrogation interview in which the extent to which the interviewee is guilty or innocent is sought through information gathering. If interviewers do not find reasons to believe in the interviewee's guilt, the person is sent home; if they suspect the interviewee is involved in the crime, a more intense interrogation occurs. People are subjected to pre-interrogation interviews for a variety of reasons—e.g., an informant implicates them in the crime, they are related to the victim, or simply a detective's hunch. The two major problems with many pre-interrogation interviews involve: 1) Interviewers frequently do not enter these interviews with a pure fact-finding mindset. Too often the fact-finding is done with the belief that the interviewee had something to do with the crime; 2) This mindset is too often accompanied by poor police training about behaviors associated with deception and a tendency by police officers to be overconfident about their ability to detect deception based on behavioral observation. As a result, interrogators may confidently perceive deceptive behavior at this stage when it isn't there—e.g., thinking a person shouldn't be as nervous as he or she appears (Elaad, 2003; Kassin, 2005).

If a person is perceived to be deceptive in the pre-interrogation interview or identified as a suspect prior to any interview, they are told: 1) they do not have to talk to the officers, but if they do, their statements can be used as evidence against them; and 2) they are told they can obtain legal counsel. However, these Miranda rights (Miranda v. Arizona, 1966) can be voluntarily waived and the interrogators can begin a more aggressive interrogation. About 80% of the time, suspects will waive their Miranda rights and submit to an interrogation. Sometimes police will make suspects think that things will turn out better for them if they agree to answer questions without delay. Thinking they have nothing to fear, 81% of the people who are innocent waive their right to silence and counsel. This is true for only 36% of those who are guilty (Kassin & Gudjonsson, 2004).

Interrogating a Suspect

Interrogators tend to conduct interrogations as if the suspect were guilty. Sometimes this triggers a self-fulfilling prophecy—i.e., acting as if a person is guilty causes them to act in ways that make them seem guilty which confirms the original assumption. The presumption of guilt can be a powerful factor in blinding an interrogator to information that casts doubt on the suspect's guilt. For example when an innocent person falsely confesses to a crime, he or she may get key facts wrong and they go unnoticed by the interrogator, even something as obvious as saying a victim who was known to have been shot once was shot multiple times.

Interrogations involve isolation, confrontation, and other strategies designed to elicit a confession. The basic paradigm is to break down the suspect's defenses and then build trust with the interrogator (Kassin, 1997; 2005; Kassin & Gudjonnson, 2004; Sargant, 1957/1997). Bruce Boardman, who was an interrogator with the Austin, Texas police department, told us that police interrogators need to consider the following:

- If possible, enter the interrogation with information about the suspect. At key points the interrogator can reveal this information—e.g., "Jerry, I realize you couldn't ask your brother for money because he passed away last year." This tells the suspect that you know some things and it makes him or her wonder what else you know.

- The goal or goals of the interrogation should be clear in the interrogator's mind. Not all questions will be directly related to these goals, but it is important to know what you want the questioning to produce.

- Start with easy questions. The first goal is to get the suspect used to talking.

- The lives that many suspects lead involve little recognition of their humanity. Sometimes interrogators can capitalize on this and obtain the information they desire by treating them in a compassionate manner.

- Make lying an issue. Tell the suspect that truth telling will make the interview go smoothly, but if you catch him or her lying about a small thing, you know they'll lie about bigger things and that won't be good.

- Use your own style. Trying to imitate somebody else's style or playing a role is less comfortable and less effective than using a pattern you are familiar with.

- Different crimes may require different approaches. Burglars may not feel much guilt for their crime. After all, they reason, other people have more than I do so what's wrong with distributing the wealth? With this kind of crime, an interrogator may have to make the suspect believe that burglary is a serious crime. On the other hand, when a sex crime is involved, the guilt may be so overwhelming for the suspect that the interrogator needs to play down the terrible nature of the crime in order to get the suspect to talk— e.g., "I can understand how a person who was subjected to as much child abuse as you were could do something like this. Under those same conditions, any of us might have done this."

- Eliminate distractions in the interrogation room. Have the suspect face you with a blank wall behind you. Sometimes another officer is in the room. Sometimes it may be necessary to invade the suspect's personal space as part of the effort to break down his or her defenses.

- When the suspect begins to talk about the crime, do not interrupt. You can always go back and flesh out details.

Interrogation Strategies

There are numerous strategies used by interrogators to uncover lies and encourage a suspect to confess. Kalbfleisch (1994) has detailed thirty-eight different strategies, but most of them can be distilled into the following three:

- *Intimidation.* Intimidation is used to break down the suspect's defenses. It can be done in several different ways. Attacking the person and what they say is one way—e.g., "Don't lie to me, scum!" Intimidation can also be accomplished by pointing out inconsistencies in a suspect's story and challenging the suspect to explain them. If the suspect omits or distorts any information, no matter how small, this can be used to charge him or her with lying about other things. After talking loudly to the suspect for a time, interrogators can also intimidate a suspect by suddenly staring at them in silence after a suspect's response. Sometimes interrogators will put pressure on a suspect by telling him or her that they are exhibiting deceptive behavior—e.g., "You're sweating," or "When I asked you about X you sure did take a long time to answer. Why was that?"

- *Persuasive appeals.* Interrogators also use various persuasive appeals to get suspects to tell the truth or confess to a crime. The following four appeals are common: 1) A friendly approach is sometimes effective. The interrogator may express empathy ("I know what you're going through and it must be painful"), the desire to help ("I'm concerned about you; confess and let me help you"), or praise ("I believe deep down you're a good guy; the kind of guy who wants to do the right thing"). 2) Sometimes the interrogator stresses the futility of resisting—e.g., "Don't make a bad situation worse. We're going to find out what happened with you or without you so why keep fighting it?" 3) Making truth telling and/or confessing sound like a way to relieve the suspect's discomfort is another common appeal—e.g., "Believe me, confession is good for the soul. You'll feel better about yourself and you'll help your family get closure." The familiar "good cop/bad cop" routine is another method designed to give the suspect a way of relieving the discomfort created by the bad cop by confessing to the good cop. 4) Sometimes interrogators try to minimize the severity of the crime in order to gain a confession. This can be done by telling the suspect that he or she was overwhelmed by circumstances (drugs, alcohol, peer pressure) and that others have done much worse. An interrogator may even hint that what happened might have been an accident.

- *Lies and deception.* Interrogators may say they have an eyewitness or a fingerprint when they don't; they may tell one of several suspects that he or she is the only one who is denying involvement in the crime when that isn't true; or they may test a suspect's truthfulness by distorting information in a question—e.g., Knowing that Mr. Jones had a broken leg, the interrogator may say, "You told us you saw Mr. Jones last week. Did he still have the cast on his arm at that time?

The twelve most common strategies actually used in videotaped police interrogations by three police departments in California are presented in Table 9.1.

Table 9.1   Frequently Observed Interrogation Strategies

1. Appeal to suspect's self-interest (88%)
2. Confront the suspect with existing evidence of guilt (85%)
3. Undermine the suspect's confidence in his or her denials (43%)
4. Identify contradictions in the suspect's alibi or story (42%)
5. Ask specific "behavioral analysis" interview questions (40%)
6. Appeal to the importance of cooperation (37%)
7. Offer moral justifications and face-saving excuses (34%)
8. Confront the suspect with false evidence of guilt (30%)
9. Praise or flatter the suspect (30%)
10. Appeal to the detective's expertise and authority (29%)
11. Appeal to the suspect's conscience (23%)
12. Minimize the moral seriousness of the offense (22%)

Source: Leo, 1996.

Deceptive Strategies

Several strategies uncovered by Kalbfleisch (1994) and Leo (1996) indicate the use of deception by the interrogator in order to uncover a suspect's deception or elicit a confession. Is this fair? In general, the courts have said yes (Frazier v. Cupp, 1969) except under conditions when the trickery and deceit would "shock the conscience of the community" or "make an innocent person confess." Police manuals, according to Shuy (1998), advise against making promises or threats, but permit flattery, rough talk, trickery, accusations, and lies. So it would be illegal for a police interrogator to say, "Confess or we'll make it hard on your family. You wouldn't want cocaine found in your son's car would you?" It would, however, be legal for an interrogator to tell a suspect that he or she has certain evidence when it does not exist—e.g., "We have your fingerprints on the murder weapon" or "The person you were with that night said you did it." Another permissible lie would be to say that several different investigators have been working on this case and they have all concluded that the suspect is guilty. Interrogators may also falsely tell a male rape suspect that the victim was a prostitute with the expectation that the suspect will confess to what he now thinks is a lesser crime (Barker & Carter, 1990).

Other less obtrusive, but equally deceptive, information-gathering methods can be used to supplement the interrogation process. For example, the Israeli General Security Services has reportedly promised prisoners their freedom if they are able to obtain specific information from another prisoner that can be validated. In another instance, several listening devices are planted in such a way that they are likely to be discovered by the prisoners while others that would record their conversations remain well hidden (Bowden, 2003). Also, omitting to mention what authorities already know is a useful tactic. Granhag et al. (2013) show how techniques such as the *strategic use of evidence,* framing, and incremental disclosures about facts are advantageous to the interrogation process.

Torture?

Torture is not something we hear much about in police interrogations and the United States has agreed to abide by the Geneva Convention which prohibits torturing prisoners of war.

Nevertheless, there were numerous reports of military prisoners at American bases in Abu Graib, Iraq; Guantanamo Bay, Cuba; and Bagram Airfield in Afghanistan who were tortured from 2001 to 2005. During this time President Bush repeatedly said, "I will never order torture," but he also said that he did not believe prisoners identified as "terrorists" were covered under international treaties banning torture. Vice President Cheney also said the United States does not engage in torture, but he actively sought an exemption from the ban on torture for the CIA. After photos of abuses at Abu Graib were made public, the CIA suspended the following methods: pretending to suffocate prisoners, putting them in stress positions for extended periods of time, bombarding them with intermittent light and noise, depriving them of sleep, withholding pain medication, using dogs to induce fear, and making them think they were being interrogated in a country that authorized torture.

What constitutes torture? Not everyone agrees. Extreme interrogation methods use physical, social, and psychological methods to break down the resistance of prisoners, make them feel they are no longer in control of their environment, instill fear, and then promise to help them out of their despair if they cooperate. Some believe these objectives can be achieved with "moderate physical pressure" which they do not consider "severe" enough to be torture. Those who subscribe to this "torture lite" regimen would not include the following as torture: sleep deprivation; isolation from human contact; questioning for 20 hours straight; exposure to extreme heat or cold; the use of drugs to cause confusion; rough treatment in the form of slapping, shoving, or shaking; and forcing a prisoner to stand or sit in uncomfortable positions for long periods of time. On the other hand, few disagree that such things as pulling out fingernails, maiming, burning, and sending electric shocks to a person's genitals constitute torture.

The important question, of course, is whether torture, no matter what methods are included, gets a person to tell the truth or confess. Police and military interrogation experts do not think torture is always the best way to elicit truthful information. During World War II, the Nazis arrived at the same conclusion. Under torture, people will confess to anything and say whatever their captors want to hear, it is also a process that can have detrimental effects on the people doing it, and it provides a justification for one's enemy to also use torture. According to Bowden (2003), no law can be sufficiently nuanced to cover all situations in which torture might be appropriate. So he believes we should agree to ban torture, recognizing that our military interrogators are likely to engage in behavior that could be labeled torture in certain selected cases. Subsequently, a court will consider the circumstances and determine whether such methods were called for or not.

Interrogation, like any communication process, requires audience adaptation. The same method will not be effective with every suspect. Hacker (1976) makes this point when he identifies three types of terrorists: criminals, crusaders, and crazies. Crusaders, he observes, are less likely to respond to threats or promises of better treatment, but they may talk a great deal as a result of some flattery.

Confessions

A confession is a powerful form of evidence. For a jury, the presence of a confession is likely to overshadow other strong evidence of a person's innocence.

Why Do People Confess?

People make confessions for a variety of reasons (Kassin & Gudjonsson, 2004). Gudjonsson and Sigurdsson (1999) found confessions attributable to three sources. By far the most influential is the perceived *weight of the evidence* against the suspect. If the suspect is convinced that it is powerful, he or she is more likely to perceive the futility in professing innocence. They call the second factor *external pressure*. External pressure comes from interrogation techniques and a suspect's fear of what the police might do if he or she doesn't confess. The third factor involves *internal pressure*. Internal pressure refers to guilt and other emotions experienced by the suspect and the extent to which these feelings can be alleviated by a confession. Internal pressure is illustrated in the first three examples below, whereas external pressure is exemplified by the last two examples.

- *Seeking notoriety.* There are always some people who voluntarily confess to crimes they did not commit. When there is a lot of publicity about the case, there are even more people willing to admit they committed the crime. Unmet needs for recognition or acceptance are behind some of these confessions; others may be related to some pathological need for self-punishment.

- *Individual personalities and dispositions.* The interrogation process is designed to persuade the suspect to confess and some people are more compliant and suggestible than others. This includes both guilty and innocent suspects. Their suggestibility is exacerbated by such things as sleep deprivation and isolation (Gudjonsson, 2003). Naïveté, anxiety, and diminished mental abilities may also make a person prone to confess. On the other hand, highly dogmatic people with strong beliefs may resist confessing for a long time. Confessions may also be difficult to obtain from people with few emotional attachments.

- *Trying to protect someone else.* Sometimes people who share the guilt with others will protect them by making a confession that excludes them. But an innocent person may also try to protect a person he or she thinks (or knows) is guilty by confessing to a crime.

- *Confusion and misunderstanding.* The process of being physically restrained and interrogated can be a chaotic process, calling for rapid decisions about a variety of unfamiliar matters. These are not ideal conditions for rational decision making. In addition to facing a confusing and possibly unfamiliar situation, suspects are sometimes confronted with trickery and deceit by interrogators. Confused and anxious suspects may hear an interrogator say, "If you confess, we'll be done with you and you can get out of here." In the heat of the moment, the suspect may mistakenly think this means he or she can go home instead of to jail. When an interrogator falsely makes a suspect believe there is evidence that he or she committed the crime, both guilty and innocent people may confess. An innocent person may seriously question their own memory. Kassin and Gudjonsson (2004) tell of a 14-year-old boy who was falsely told that his hair was found in his dead sister's hand, that her blood was in his bedroom, and that he failed a polygraph exam. The boy thought he had a split personality and confessed to the crime.

- *Seeking relief.* People also confess because they are looking for a way to deal with a physically and mentally exhausting situation. A feeling of isolation and hopelessness brought on by the interrogation process can trigger confessions from both guilty and not guilty suspects. The innocent suspect realizes that repeated denials are not providing the desired relief so confession begins to look like a way to cope with the situation. When interrogators make a suspect believe that there is plenty of evidence to convict, an innocent suspect may think: "Even though I didn't do it, nobody will believe me so I might as well make a deal by confessing." Sometimes interrogators facilitate confessions by suggesting that confession will lead to more leniency. If the evidence against them is strong and there is, in fact, some leniency in exchange for a confession, suspects at the top of an organizational hierarchy are likely to jump at the chance rather than endure the strain of further interrogation.

False Confessions

Federal and local law enforcement agencies conduct their interrogations by relying on the structure of the *Reid technique* (Inbau et al., 2001) or the *behavioral analysis interview*. Using these methods interrogators rely on confrontations of guilt. Sympathy, crafting messages that morally justify the crime or explain how motives could justify one's actions, and rapport building are also used to instill a value in truth telling during the interrogation. These interrogation techniques may solicit false confessions because they are confrontational, potentially coercive, and highly suggestive (Kassin et al., 2010). Wright et al. (2015) found that the suggestive power of these interrogation techniques can lead witnesses to corroborate false allegations.

Confessing to something they did not do is not something most people think they would do. However, it has happened to enough innocent people to make us wonder whether there are conditions that would cause all of us to do the same thing. People have confessed to murdering a person who was still alive and to crimes that occurred when there was strong evidence that they were nowhere near the scene of the crime when it was committed. With the advent of DNA testing, a number of convictions based on false confessions have been uncovered. Between 1971 and 2002 there have been 125 proven false confessions, 81% of them for murder (Kassin & Gudjonsson, 2004). A study of wrongful convictions for violent crimes in Illinois from 1989 to 2010 found 33 cases that involved false confessions (Anyaso, 2011).

Under the right conditions, almost anyone might make a false confession. Some people do it because they are sensation seekers, but the most vulnerable seem to be: 1) teenagers, 2) people who are easily persuaded, 3) people who reach a point where they think it is futile to declare their innocence any longer, 4) people who are afraid or have a low tolerance for confrontation and conflict, and 5) people with mental disabilities.

One of the most famous false confession cases involved five males between the ages of 14 and 16 who confessed to the rape and brutal assault of a woman jogger in New York City's Central Park in 1989 (Kassin & Gujonsson, 2004). The woman was unable to identify her attacker or attackers so the confessions were extremely influential in convicting the boys and sending them to jail. There was no physical evidence that linked any of the boys to the crime. Thirteen years later another man admitted that he alone raped the woman and his DNA linked him to the crime. Why did the boys confess? They initially denied the attack, but after many hours of being interrogated separately, each boy confessed. In theory, a true confession would contain information that the perpetrator alone would know. But sometimes interrogators, intentionally or not, provide information about the crime that suspects incorporate into their confession. There were many discrepancies in the boys' stories, but these were discounted when enough other details were consistent with the crime. One of the boys initially tried to confess by saying the woman's head injuries were caused by punching. Later, when he was asked: "Don't you remember somebody using a brick or stone?" he said the injuries were caused by a rock. Still later he indicated a brick was used. One boy said he remembered cutting the victim's clothes off with knife, but there were no knife cuts on the clothing. Two boys were taken to the park and each one pointed in a different direction when asked where the crime took place. One boy said the victim wore blue shorts and a t-shirt. She was actually wearing long black tights and a long-sleeve jersey. Before his confession, another boy was taken to the crime scene and shown photos of the victim, making it difficult to know what he gleaned from this information and what he knew prior to that. Four of the suspects spent about seven years in prison and the fifth man was imprisoned for approximately 13 years. In 2014 the city agreed on a $14 million settlement with the five men for their wrongful incarcerations, but continued to avoid blame for wrongdoing in the case (Weiser, 2014).

Another well known false confession case involved a 1997 murder of a woman in Norfolk, Virginia (Bennett, 2005). This case begins with one sailor who said he was at home in bed with his wife when the crime occurred. The wife's account was not taken before she died of cancer three months later. During his interrogation, he was falsely told that the police had an eyewitness who saw him leave the victim's apartment. He took a polygraph test and was falsely told that he failed it. He began to question his own memory and was told that, unless he confessed, he'd face the death penalty. After 13 hours of interrogation, the sailor confessed. But his DNA was not a match so the police proceeded on the assumption that he did not act alone. A friend of his who was described as "slow" and easily persuadable due to a previous head injury was then interrogated. His defense was that he was on duty—a claim that was not checked. After hours of questioning, the second sailor also confessed, but his DNA was not a match. This led to an interrogation of a third and fourth sailor, each of whom confessed, even though their DNA did not match that at the crime scene. In 1999 a convicted rapist admitted that he alone had committed the crime and his DNA was a match. However, after his initial confession he changed his story to include the other sailors. Later he said his inclusion of the other sailors was at the request of the police. In 2006, the case of Derek Tice, the fourth sailor convicted, was overturned because police continued to interrogate him after he invoked his Miranda right to remain silent and his lawyer did not object to the admission of his subsequent confession as evidence in court.

Reducing the Number of False Confessions

There are a number of changes in the way interrogations are conducted which could reduce the number of false confessions (Kassin & Gudjonsson, 2004). Most interrogations are between 2 to 4 hours, but false confessions often take much longer, averaging 16.2 hours. This suggests that the physical and psychological toll associated with very long interrogations is high enough to lead to false confessions. The tactic of presenting false evidence and lying to the suspect substantially increases the number of false confessions and should be minimized. Some European law enforcement agencies do not permit this tactic. In addition, outright promises of leniency or implied leniency (e.g., telling the suspect that his crime was an accident or morally justified and that a jury will be lenient with him if he confesses) also cause innocent people to confess and courts will now reject confessions in which leniency was directly stated.

Video and/or audio recording of the interrogation process is also a way of reducing false confessions. At the same time it reduces the number of appeals, charges of misconduct, and increases the number of guilty pleas. Recording frees the interrogator from taking notes and provides an opportunity to view the video again in order to listen and watch carefully certain selected segments. Recorded interrogations can be beneficial for everyone involved—suspects, lawyers, juries, police officers, and judges. Over 20 states require recording during interrogations and in 2014 the U.S. Department of Justice required all of its federal agencies to record interrogations. However, many of these prescriptions to require recording do not specify between audio and video formats. Great Britain and some states such as Minnesota, Maine, Alaska, and Illinois require video recording of interrogations in capital cases and the police forces in some large U.S. cities also video record. One area of controversy has to do with when the taping should begin—at the beginning of the interrogation or when the confession begins. If the confession is the only thing recorded, this will not cut down on charges of coercion during the interrogation (Peres & Pallasch, 1998). When the interrogation is video recorded, researchers also say that the video should focus on both the interrogator and the suspect because observers (juries) tend to underestimate the amount of pressure exerted by the interrogator when the camera focuses entirely on the suspect (Lassiter et al., 1992).

Very young children are especially susceptible to interrogation techniques designed to elicit a confession and this has prompted new ways of dealing with such situations. Children younger than 13 who are charged with murder or sex crimes must be represented by a lawyer during interrogation and a parent or guardian is required for felony cases. California enacted a statute in 2013 requiring interrogations of juveniles in homicide investigations to be video recorded.

Summary

People use a variety of ways to find out if someone is deceiving them. One common method is to observe the target's nonverbal behavior and to listen to what he or she says. Research tells us that most people aren't particularly skilled at distinguishing liars and truth tellers by observing their behavior, with the majority scoring slightly better than chance would predict (53–57%). Since judgments are normally affected by the truth bias, people typically identify truth tellers at a much higher rate (67–68%) than liars (37–44%). In addition to the truth bias, there are many other reasons associated with our cognitions and perceptual processes that contribute to our lack of skill in identifying liars by their behavior. Research is showing us that relying on what sources say in context increases lie-detection accuracy. For those people who engage in lie detection as part of their job, the accuracy rates are somewhat higher, but they, too, are plagued by problems that inhibit high rates of detection. Training may be able to improve a person's lie detection skills, but we won't know how much impact training has until further studies are conducted. There may be some people whose lie-detection skills are extremely high. These "wizards" are at least 80% accurate in judging three different types of lies.

Unassisted lie detection in police and military interrogations differs markedly from everyday lie detection. These interrogations often employ methods to break down a suspect's defenses followed by efforts to build trust. Questioning strategies typically involve intimidation, persuasive appeals, as well as lying and deception. Research shows that active questioning and the strategic use of information during interrogations significantly increases accuracy rates during deception detection. Legally, interrogators are allowed to tell suspects that they have evidence against them that they do not have. Although the United States maintains it does not torture military detainees, there is evidence that it has occurred in recent years even though experts say it can elicit a lot of invalid information.

For police and military interrogators the observation of deceitful behavior is only important as it relates to a confession of guilt. As a result, an overly zealous interrogator can induce an innocent person to confess to a crime he or she didn't commit. Guilty or innocent, people confess because they think the weight of evidence is against them, because the interrogation strategies have been persuasive, and/or because the suspect has certain personal characteristics and/or agendas that lead him or her to confess. False confessions can be reduced by not allowing interrogators to tell suspects they have evidence that they do not have, by eliminating marathon interrogation sessions, and by video recording both interrogator and suspect.

Things to Think About

Try to list a few situations where someone lied to you about something meaningful. How did you discover the truth? Did you know they were lying to you at the time? How? Determine the ways you discovered the truth and cite information discussed in this chapter.

Do you believe there are any circumstances in which torturing a suspect in order to get him or her to tell the truth would be justified? What about lying to a suspect? If yes, what are those circumstances? If no, why not?

Do you think there are any conditions under which you would confess to a crime you did not commit? If you answered no, why not? If you answered yes, what are the conditions?

Would you like to be a wizard? Why or why not? How accurate would you like to be in identifying liars by observing their nonverbal and verbal behavior? Why? How accurate would you like most people to be? Why? [Use a 1–100% scale for your answers, with 100% being completely accurate all the time.]

References

Alford, C.F. (2001). *Whistleblowers: Broken lives and organizational power.* Ithaca, NY: Cornell University Press.

Anyaso, H.H. (2011). The high cost of wrongful convictions in Illinois. Dollars wasted, lives lost & ruined, justice run amok: A landmark investigation. Northwestern University: http://www.northwestern.edu/newscenter/stories/2011/06/wrongful-conviction-cost.html Retrieved July 11, 2015.

Barker, T., & Carter, D. (1990). "Fluffing up the evidence and covering your ass": Some conceptual notes on police lying. *Deviant Behavior, 11,* 61–73.

Bennett, B. (2005, December 12). True confessions? *Time Magazine,* p. 45–46.

Blair, J.P., Levine, T.R., & Shaw, A.S. (2010). Content in context improves deception detection accuracy. *Human Communication Research, 36,* 423–442.

Blair, J.P., Levine, T.R., & Vasquez, B.E. (2015). Producing deception detection expertise. *Policing: An International Journal of Police Strategies & Management, 38,* 71–85.

Bond, C.F., Jr., & Atoum, A.O. (2000). International deception. *Personality and Social Psychology Bulletin, 26,* 385–395.

Bond, C.F., Jr., & DePaulo, B.M. (2008). Individual differences in judging deception: Accuracy and bias, *Psychological Bulletin, 134,* 477–492.

Bond, C.F., Jr., Levine, T.R., & Hartwig, M. (2015). New findings in nonverbal lie detection. In P.A. Granhag, A. Vrij, & B. Verschuere (Eds.), *Detection deception: Current challenges and cognitive approaches.* (pp. 37–58). Hoboken, NJ: Wiley & Sons.

Bond, C.F., Jr., Omar, A., Pitre, U., & Lashley, B.R. (1992). Fishy-looking liars: Deception judgment from expectancy violation. *Journal of Personality and Social Psychology, 63,* 969–977.

Bond, C.F., Jr., & Uysal, A. (2007), On lie detection wizards. *Law and Human Behavior, 31,* 109–115.

Bond, C.F., Jr., & Rao, S.R. (2004). Lies travel: Mendacity in a mobile world. In P.A. Granhag & L.A. Strömwall (Eds.), *The detection of deception in forensic contexts* (pp. 127–147). New York: Cambridge University Press.

Bond, G.D., Malloy, D.M., Thompson, L.A., Arias, E.A., & Nunn, S.N. (2004). Post-probe decision making in a prison context. *Communication Monographs, 71,* 269–285.

Bond, G.D., Malloy, D.M., Arias, E.A., Nunn, S.N., & Thompson, L.A. (2005). Lie-based decision making in prison. *Communication Reports, 18,* 9–19.

Bowden, M. (2003, October). The dark art of interrogation. *Atlantic Monthly, 292,* 51–76.

Burgoon, J.K., Buller, D.B., & Floyd, K. (2001). Does participation affect deception success? A test of the interactivity principle. *Human Communication Research, 27,* 503–534.

Carr, R. (2005, December 11). In federal job: Blow whistle, get boot. *Austin American Statesman,* A1, A6.

DePaulo, B.M. (1994). Spotting lies: Can humans learn to do better? *Current Directions in Psychological Science, 3,* 83–86.

DePaulo, B.M., & Jordan, A. (1982). Age changes in deceiving and detecting deceit. In R.S. Feldman (Ed.), *Development of nonverbal behavior in children* (pp. 151–180). New York: Springer-Verlag.

DePaulo, B.M., Lindsay, J.J., Malone, B.E., Muhlenbruck, L., Charlton, K., & Cooper, H. (2003). Cues to deception. *Psychological Bulletin, 129,* 74–118.

DePaulo, B.M., & Morris, W.L. (2004). Discerning lies from truths: Behavioural cues to deception and the indirect pathway of intuition. In P.A. Granhag & L.A. Strömwall, (Eds.), *The detection of deception in forensic contexts* (pp. 15–40). New York: Cambridge University Press.

deTurck, M.A., Harzlak, J.J., Bodhorn, D.J., & Texter, L.A. (1990). The effects of training social perceivers to detect deception from behavioral cues. *Communication Quarterly, 38,* 1–11.

Dunbar, N.E., Ramirez, A. Jr., & Burgoon, J. K. (2003). The effects of participation on the ability to judge deceit. *Communication Reports, 16,* 23–33.

Ekman, P. (1996). *Why don't we catch liars? Social Research, 63,* 801–817.

Ekman, P. (2001). *Telling lies: Clues to deceit in the marketplace, politics, and marriage.* New York: Norton.

Ekman, P., & Friesen, W.V. (1978). *Facial action coding system (FACS): A technique for the measurement of facial movement.* Palo Alto, CA: Consulting Psychologists Press.

Ekman, P., & O'Sullivan, M. (1991). Who can catch a liar? *American Psychologist, 46*, 913–920.

Ekman, P., O'Sullivan, M., & Frank, M.G. (1999). A few can catch a liar. *Psychological Science, 10*, 263–266.

Elaad, E. (2003). Effects of feedback on the overestimated capacity to detect lies and the underestimated ability to tell lies. *Applied Cognitive Psychology, 17*, 349–363.

Etcoff, N.L., Ekman, P., Magee, J.J., & Frank, M.G. (2000). Lie detection and language comprehension. *Nature, 405*, 139.

Feeley, T.H., & Young, M.J. (1998). Humans as lie detectors: Some more second thoughts. *Communication Quarterly, 46*, 109–126.

Frank, M.G., & Feeley, T.H. (2003). To catch a liar: Challenges for research in lie detection training. *Journal of Applied Communication Research, 31*, 58–75.

Frank, M.G., Feeley, T.H., Paolantonio, N., & Servoss, T.J. (2004). Individual and small group accuracy in judging truthful and deceptive communication. *Group Decision and Negotiation, 13*, 45–59.

Frazier v. Cupp, 394 U. S. 731 (1969)

Gilbert, D.T., Krull, D.S., & Malone, P.S. (1990). Unbelieving the unbelievable: Some problems in the rejection of false information. *Journal of Personality and Social Psychology, 59*, 601–613.

Gilbert, D.T., Tafarodi, R.W., & Malone, P.S. (1993). You can't not believe everything you read. *Journal of Personality and Social Psychology, 65*, 221–233.

Glazer, M.P., & Glazer, P.M. (1989). *The whistleblowers.* New York: Basic Books.

Grady, D.P. (1997). *Conversational strategies for detecting deception: An analysis of parent-adolescent child interactions.* Unpublished Ph.D. dissertation, University of Texas.

Granhag, P.A., Strömwall, L.A., Willén, R.M., & Hartwig, M. (2013). Eliciting cues to deception by tactical disclosure of evidence: The first test of the Evidence Framing Matrix. *Legal and Criminological Psychology, 18*, 341–355.

Gudjonsson, G.H. (2003). *The psychology of interrogations and conversions: A handbook.* New York: Wiley.

Gudjonsson, G.H., & Sigurdsson, J.F. (1999). The Gudjonsson Confession Questionnaire-Revised (GCQ-R): Factor structure and its relationship with personality. *Personality and Individual Differences, 27*, 953–968.

Hacker, F. (1976). *Crusaders, criminals, crazies: Terror and terrorism in our time.* New York: Norton.

Hartwig, M., Granhag, P.A., Strömwall, L.A., & Andersson, L.O. (2004). Suspicious minds: Criminals' ability to detect deception. *Psychology, Crime & Law, 10,* 83–95.

Hurley, C.M., Anker, A.E., Frank, M.G., Matsumoto, D., & Hwang, H.C. (2014). Background factors predicting accuracy and improvement in micro expression recognition. *Motivation and Emotion, 38,* 700–714.

Inbau, F.E., Reid, J.E., Buckley, J.P., & Jayne, B.P. (2001). *Criminal interrogation and confessions* (4th ed.). Gaithersburg, MD: Aspen.

Kassin, S.M. (1997). The psychology of confession evidence. *American Psychologist, 52,* 221–233.

Kassin, S.M. (2005). On the psychology of confessions: Does innocence put innocents at risk? *American Psychologist, 60,* 215–228.

Kassin, S.M., Drizin, S.A., Grisso, T., Gudjonsson, G.H., Leo, R.A., & Redlich, A.D. (2010). Police-induced confessions: Risk factors and recommendations. *Law and Human Behavior, 34,* 3–38.

Kassin, S.M., & Fong, C.T. (1999). 'I'm innocent!': Effects of training on judgments of truth and deception in the interrogation room. *Law and Human behavior, 23,* 499–516.

Kassin, S.M., & Gudjonsson, G.H. (2004). The psychology of confessions: A review of the literature and issues. *Psychological Science in the Public Interest, 5,* 33–67.

Kalbfleisch, P.J. (1994). The language of detecting deceit. *Journal of Language and Social Psychology, 13,* 493–520.

Kaufmann, G., Drevland, G.C.B., Wessel, E., Goverskeid, G., & Magnussen, S. (2003). The importance of being earnest: Displayed emotions and witness credibility. *Applied Cognitive Psychology, 17,* 21–34.

Knapp, M.L. (2006). Lying and deception in close relationships. In A.L. Vangelisti & D. Perlman (Eds.), *Cambridge handbook of personal relationships* (pp. 517–532). New York: Cambridge University Press.

Lassiter, G.D., Slaw, R.D., Briggs, M.A., & Scanlan, C.R. (1992). The potential for bias in videotaped confessions. *Journal of Applied Social Psychology, 22,* 1838–1851.

Latané, B., & Darley, J.M. (1970). *The unresponsive bystander: Why doesn't he help?* Englewood Cliffs, NJ: Prentice Hall.

Leo, R.A. (1996). Inside the interrogation room. *The Journal of Criminal Law and Criminology, 86,* 266–303.

Levine, T.R. (2015). New and improved accuracy findings in deception detection research. *Current Opinion in Psychology, 6,* 1–5.

Levine, T.R., Blair, J.P., & Clare, D.D. (2014). Diagnostic utility: experimental demonstrations and replications of powerful question effects in high-stakes deception detection. *Human Communication Research, 40,* 262–289.

Levine, T.R., & McCornack, S.A. (2001). Behavioral adaptation, confidence and heuristic-based explanations of the probing effect. *Human Communication Research, 27,* 471–502.

Levine, T., Asada, K.J.K, & Park, H.S. (2006). The lying chicken and the gaze avoidant egg: Eye contact, deception, and causal order. *Southern Communication Journal, 71,* 401–411.

Levine, T.R., Park, H.S., & McCornack, S.A. (1999). Accuracy in detecting truths and lies: Documenting the "veracity effect." *Communication Monographs, 66,* 125–144.

Levine, T.R., Kim, R.K., Park, H.S., & Hughes, M. (2006). Deception detection accuracy is a predictable linear function of message veracity base-rate: A formal test of Park and Levine's probability model. *Communication Monographs, 73,* 243–260.

Levine, T.R., Feeley, T.H., McCornack, S.A., Hughes, M., & Harms, C.M. (2005). Testing the effects of nonverbal behavior training on accuracy in deception detection with the inclusion of a bogus training control group. *Western Journal of Communication, 69,* 203–217.

Levine, T.R., Anders, L.N., Banas, J., Baum, K.L., Endo, K., Hu, A.D.S., & Wong, N.C.H. (2000). Norms, expectations, and deception: A norm violation model of veracity judgments. *Communication Monographs, 67,* 123–137.

Levine, T.R., Serota, K.B., Shulman, J., Clare, D.D., Park, H.S., Shaw, A.S., … Lee, J.H. (2011). Sender demeanor: Individual differences in sender believability have a powerful impact on deception detection judgments. *Human Communication Research, 37,* 377–403.

Lieberman, D.J. (1998). *Never be lied to again.* New York: St. Martin's Press.

Malone, B.E., & DePaulo, B.M. (2001). Measuring sensitivity to deception. In J.A. Hall & F.J. Bernieri (Eds.), *Interpersonal sensitivity: Theory and measurement* (pp.103–124). Mahwah, NJ: Erlbaum.

Meissner, C.A., & Kassin, S.M. (2002). "He's guilty!": Investigator bias in judgments of truth and deception. *Law and Human Behavior, 26,* 469–480.

Miranda v. Arizona, 384 U. S. 336 (1966).

Myers, D.G. (2002). *Intuition: Its powers and perils.* New Haven, CT: Yale University Press.

Nickerson, R.S. (1998). Confirmation bias: A ubiquitous phenomenon in many guises. *Review of General Psychology, 2,* 175–220.

O'Sullivan, M. (2003). The fundamental attribution error in detecting deception: The boy-who-cried-wolf effect. *Personality and Social Psychology Bulletin, 29,* 1316–1327.

O'Sullivan, M. (2005). Emotional intelligence and deception detection: Why most people can't "read" others, but a few can. In R.E. Riggio & R.S. Feldman (Eds.), *Applications of nonverbal communication* (pp. 215–253). Mahwah, NJ: Erlbaum.

O'Sullivan, M. & Ekman, P. (2004). The wizards of deception detection. In P.A. Granhag & L.A. Strömwall (Eds.), *The detection of deception in forensic contexts* (pp. 269–286). New York: Cambridge University Press.

Park, H.S., Levine, T.R., Harms, C.M., & Ferrara, M.H. (2002a). Group and individual accuracy in deception detection. *Communication Research Reports, 19,* 99–106.

Park, H.S., Levine, T.R., McCornack, S.A., Morrison, K., & Ferrara, M. (2002b). How people really detect lies. *Communication Monographs, 69,* 144–157.

Peres, J., & Pallasch, A.M. (1998, August 20). Confession debate: To tape or not? *Chicago Tribune.*

Reinhard, M.A., Sporer, S.L., Scharmach, M., & Marksteiner, T. (2011). Listening, not watching: situational familiarity and the ability to detect deception. *Journal of Personality and Social Psychology, 101,* 467–484.

Rogers, R. (Ed.) (1988). *Clinical assessment of malingering and deception.* New York: Guilford.

Sargant, W. (1957/1997). *Battle for the mind: A physiology of conversion and brain-washing.* Cambridge, MA: ISHK.

Shaw, J., Porter, S., & ten Brinke, L. (2013). Catching liars: Training mental health and legal professionals to detect high-stakes lies. *The Journal of Forensic Psychiatry & Psychology, 24,* 145–159.

Shuy, R.W. (1998). *The language of confession, interrogation, and deception.* Thousand Oaks, CA: Sage.

Stiff, J.B., Kim, H.J., & Ramesh, C.N. (1992). Truth biases and aroused suspicion in relational deception. *Communication Research, 19,* 326–345.

Strömwall, L.A., Granhag, P.A., & Hartwig, M. (2004). Practitioners' beliefs about deception. In P.A. Granhag & L.A. Strömwall (Eds.), *The detection of deception in forensic contexts* (pp. 229–250). New York: Cambridge University Press.

ten Brinke, L., Stimson, D., & Carney, D.R. (2014). Some evidence for unconscious lie detection. *Psychological Science, 25,* 1098–1105.

Time (2002, December 30/2003, January 6). The whistleblowers: Cynthia Cooper of Worldcom, Coleen Rowley of the FBI, Sherron Watkins of Enron, pp. 30–60.

Vrij, A. (2008). *Detecting lies and deceit: The psychology of lying and the implications for professional practice* (2nd ed.). Cheshire, UK: Wiley.

Vrij, A. (2004). Guidelines to catch a liar. In P.A. Granhag & L.A. Strömwall (Eds.), *The detection of deception in forensic contexts* (pp. 287–314). New York: Cambridge University Press.

Vrij, A., & Mann, S. (2001). Telling and detecting lies in a high-stake situation: The case of a convicted murderer. *Applied Cognitive Psychology, 15,* 187–203.

Vrij, A., & Mann, S. (2005). Police use of nonverbal behavior as indicators of deception. In R.E. Riggio & R.S. Feldman (Eds.), *Applications of nonverbal communication* (pp. 63–94) Mahwah, NJ: Lawrence Erlbaum Associates, Inc.

Vrij, A., Edward, K., Roberts, K.P., & Bull, R. (2000). Detecting deceit via analysis of verbal and nonverbal behavior. *Journal of Nonverbal Behavior, 24,* 239–263.

Weiser, B. (2014, September 5). Settlement is approved in Central Park jogger case, but New York deflects blame. *New York Times*: http://www.nytimes.com/2014/09/06/nyregion/41-million-settlement-for-5-convicted-in-jogger-case-is-approved.html Retrieved July 11, 2015.

Wright, D.S., Nash, R.A., & Wade, K.A. (2015). Encouraging eyewitnesses to falsely corroborate allegations: Effects of rapport-building and incriminating evidence. *Psychology, Crime & Law, 21,* 1–13.

Yamagishi, T., Tanida, S., Mashima, R., Shimoma, E., & Kanazawa, S. (2003). You can judge a book by its cover: Evidence that cheaters may look different from cooperators. *Evolution and Human Behavior, 24,* 290–301.

Zebrowitz, L.A., Voinescu, L., & Collins, M.A. (1996). "Wide-eyed" and "crooked-faced": Determinants of perceived and real honesty across the life span. *Personality and Social Psychology Bulletin, 22,* 1258–1269.

Chapter 10

Assisted Lie Detection

Picture the following scene. A criminal suspect sits in a police interrogation room with a metal colander on his head. Yes, a colander—the bowl with holes in it that most people use to drain cooked pasta or wash lettuce for salads. Wires run from the colander to a nearby copying machine. The suspect is told this is a lie-detection machine. The police interrogators have already placed on the copying machine a piece of paper with the words, "He's lying" written on it. When the suspect gives an answer the interrogators don't believe, they press the copy button and the machine prints out the message that the suspect is lying. Convinced that the machine is able to detect his lies, the suspect confesses.

This story first surfaced in 1977 in the *Philadelphia Inquirer* and was attributed to "a small police department in the county." But no police department in Pennsylvania or anywhere else has ever admitted using this colander-as-lie-detector strategy. Nevertheless, the story won't die. It has been widely circulated for many years on the Internet and reprinted in such places as the *Wall Street Journal, Playboy,* and Ann Landers' column. It was also depicted in an episode of the television series *Homicide* (Mikkelson, 2011). Jimmy Kimmel uses a variation of this faux lie-detector machine on children in several skits called *Lie Detective*. He uses a colander equipped with lights, buzzing sounds, and other props to aid in his interrogation of children. He asks the children awkward questions, waits for their polite response, and then activates the sounds and lights on the colander. He then suggests what he thinks is the correct (better) answer and encourages the children to admit to things like peeing in the pool or cussing. The fascination with the urban legend of the colander lie detector lies in the apparent stupidity of the criminal who believed that this "machine" could actually tell if he was lying. But how "stupid" was he? If the "machine" was made to look and act in a way that was credible to most people, would their behavior differ all that much?

> "I don't know anything about polygraphs, and I don't know how accurate they are, but I know they'll scare the hell out of people."
>
> — President Richard Nixon

> "The polygraph works if most people who take the test think it will."
>
> — Paul Ekman

> "[W]e have enough evidence to say that an innocent person has nearly a 50/50 chance of failing a lie detector test, odds that are much worse than in Russian roulette."
>
> — *David Lykken*

An FBI agent who had previously worked as a police officer told us of an interrogation he had conducted as a cop. He used a guise similar to the colander trick on a suspect to a murder. To elicit a confession the suspect was told that a new technology had been used to extract the last thing the victim saw before being murdered. The ruse explained that the police had a computer that could tap into the victim's brain and retrieve images from the last moments of his life. The suspect was led to believe that the results from tapping into the victim's brain revealed images of the suspect as he enacted the murder. Believing the police had these *hard facts* the suspect confessed to the crime.

Studies using various types of "bogus pipeline" procedures tell us that our faith in machines can affect the truthfulness of our answers. People who are convinced that a sophisticated-looking machine or some new technology can detect their true attitudes toward some issue are less likely to distort their attitudes toward that issue when "connected" to the machine (Roese & Jamieson, 1993). When women believed their responses to a question about the number of sexual partners they had would be read by the experimenter, the average number of sexual partners reported was 2.6; the average number of sexual partners reported by a similar group of women who believed their responses were being monitored by a machine that detected lies was 4.4. Questions about exposure to hardcore and softcore erotica and masturbation followed a similar pattern (Alexander & Fisher, 2003).

Our Faith in Machines as Lie Detectors

This chapter focuses on "assisted" lie detection and, in addition to drugs and questionnaires, the assist also comes from machines. Many law enforcement and military organizations are continually seeking a never-fail machine to detect lies. Paul Ekman found this out following the 9/11 tragedy in New York City. Ekman knows as much about liar behavior and how to accurately observe that behavior as anyone in the world. He has trained members of the FBI, Secret Service, police units, and military intelligence on the observation of liar verbal and nonverbal behavior. But when he inquired how he might help the CIA, Department of Defense, and other federal agencies one representative told him, "I can't support anything unless it ends in a machine doing it" (Henig, 2006).

The fervent search for a machine that will invariably expose those liars who have or intend to do us harm is understandable. At the same time, we should carefully consider what we wish for—in case we get it. As Henig (2006) puts it:

> *[W]e might find ourselves with instruments that can detect deception not only as an antiterrorism device but also in situations that have little to do with national security: job interviews, tax audits, classrooms, boardrooms, courtrooms, bedrooms...Worse than living in a world plagued by uncertainty, in which we can never know for sure who is lying to whom, might be to live in a world plagued by its opposite: certainty about where the lies are, thus forcing us to tell one another nothing but the truth (p. 57).*

Has there ever been an infallible lie-detection machine? No. Will there be? Some experts believe the odds are against it despite extraordinary amounts of money and effort directed toward its development. Part of the problem is that we give machines more credit than they are due. We are often quick to acknowledge human frailties in lie detection, but slow to acknowledge similar problems with lie-detection machines. Some of the problematic assumptions about machines that gird our faith in them include: 1) the belief that machines are so reliable they will always perform the same way; 2) the belief that machines act independently of any biases or frailties human beings might have—forgetting that humans build them, operate them, and interpret their output; 3) the belief that machines are capable of performing without error—i.e., they are 100% accurate; 4) the belief that a machine will somehow eliminate the inevitable ambiguities involved in any perceptual event; 5) the belief that machines can detect bodily functions that can't be controlled or manipulated by human beings; and 6) the belief that a machine can detect lies rather than certain physiological and neurophysiological behavior which may or may not be linked to lying.

The ability of a machine to satisfy our need for an infallible and unambiguous lie detector is a major focus for this chapter. We will examine machines that monitor heartbeats and stomach chemistry, brain activity, microtremors in the voice, skin conductance, respiratory activity, blood pressure, and face/body heat. In addition, we will examine other ways of "assisting" lie detection such as the use of drugs, hypnosis, paper and pencil tests, and computer analyses of facial expressions and verbal behavior. We begin with what is probably the best known "lie detector" machine: the polygraph.

The Polygraph

To begin, we should point out that even though a polygraph is often called a lie detector, it does not detect lies. It detects physiological changes in a person's body which are the result of cognition, arousal, anxiety, and/or stress. These changes are then *interpreted* by the polygraph examiner as being deceptive, truthful, or inconclusive. Interpretation of the examinee's responses is necessary because no one has ever identified a distinctive physiological response that is always characteristic of liars and never characteristic of truth tellers. As a result, the responses to a polygraph exam may be subject to different interpretations. Government agencies often have more than one examiner who will review the results from the output of a polygraph exam, and some agencies have a centralized center where all results are sent for a final analysis.

The Evolution of a Machine

In the late 19th and early 20th centuries, European physiologists and psychologists were exploring possible connections between physiological responses and lying. In 1915, William Marston, a Harvard psychologist who later created the comic book character Wonder Woman, said his work showed a link between systolic blood pressure readings and lying. The prototype for today's polygraph, however, was developed in 1921 by John Larson and Leonarde Keeler. This machine measured several physiological responses and was portable. Keeler opened the first private polygraph business. By 1988 there were over thirty accredited polygraph schools (Lykken, 1998). In 2015, according to the American Polygraph Association's website, they are the largest international professional polygraph association in the world with approximately 2,800 members from more than 25 countries.

Who Administers and Takes Polygraph Exams?

The United States is more enamored with the polygraph than any other country on the planet. A small number of countries use the polygraph in conjunction with criminal cases. For example, it wasn't until 2014 that the United Kingdom created a law that required the use of the polygraph for screening high-risk sex offenders. Police agencies in the UK have only been using the test since 2013, but it cannot be required and is only administered voluntarily with the consent of a suspect or detainee (Marshall & Thomas, 2015). It is much more prevalent and has a variety of uses in the United States—e.g., employee security screening, employment selection, pre-probation release of sex offenders and periodic tests thereafter, suspected malingering, on the job sexual harassment charges, corporate theft, contested divorces, and accusations of child abuse and rape. In one case, polygraph exams were used to determine whether high school students had violated a school rule forbidding attendance at parties that served alcohol (Hughes, 2001). Polygraphs play a big role in who becomes a law enforcement officer, who has access to our most powerful weapons, and who can be entrusted with our most closely guarded secrets. The national concern for security and widespread publicity about corporate scandals, student cheating, financial scams, leaks about government secrets, and whistleblowing have created a climate in which the polygraph (and future devices) are likely to thrive.

Even though the administration of the polygraph in criminal cases gets the most publicity, more exams are given to employees and prospective employees. In the 1980s employers' use of the polygraph to screen prospective employees was so widespread that President Reagan signed the Employee Polygraph Protection Act in 1988. This act prohibits private corporations from using polygraphs to screen employees, but there are exceptions. People applying for positions with federal, state, and local governments are frequently asked to take a polygraph exam; exams may also be given to certain non-governmental employees who are engaged in work that is related to national security, a security service firm (e.g., armored car firms), or pharmaceutical manufacturers, distributors, and sellers. Employees who are suspected of theft in the workplace are not protected by the Employee Polygraph Protection Act of 1988 (Barnhorn & Pegram, 2011).

The common feature among those employees who can be asked to take a polygraph exam is their exposure to information, products, and services which affect the safety of many people. While high government officials believe this is an appropriate use of the polygraph, they may not think it applies to them. In 1985, President Reagan believed information was being leaked by one or more of his cabinet members. He ordered polygraph tests, but George Shultz, his Secretary of State, refused to take one and threatened to resign. He said, "Management through fear and intimidation is not the way to promote honesty and protect security" (Kelley, 2004). While there is disagreement about the accuracy of polygraph exams used in criminal cases, there is far less controversy about the problematic nature of using polygraphs to select employees, to generate a pool of employee suspects as in a jewelry store theft, or in employee screening. As Furedy and Heslegrave (1991, p. 162) put it: "Contrary to popular opinion, it is not possible to classify people as being, in general, more or less honest, but only with respect to specific situations."

Can Polygraph Results Be Entered as Evidence in Court?

In general, the results of polygraph tests are not admissible as evidence in U.S. courts. However, polygraph test results can be entered as evidence in New Mexico courts and courts in a number of other states will accept polygraph results if both the prosecution and defense have agreed to it (Kelley, 2004). To further illustrate the difficulty in giving a simple answer to this question, five of the eleven U.S. Circuit Courts leave the matter up to the trial judges. For now, anyway, the Supreme Court does not support the results of polygraph tests as evidence. As one of eight Supreme Court justices who voted to uphold the military's ban on admitting polygraph evidence in court-martial cases, Justice Thomas said, "there is simply no way to know in a particular case whether a polygraph examiner's conclusion is accurate, because certain doubts and uncertainties plague even the best polygraph exams" (*United States v. Scheffer*, 1998).

The polygraph can have powerful effects even if it is not admitted into court as evidence. For example, it can be used to induce confessions. When a suspect is told that he or she has failed a polygraph test and subsequently interrogated, 30–40% of the suspects confess (Lykken, 1998). For a person who strongly believes in the accuracy of the polygraph, a failing result may make them think they are repressing information about their guilt. Some, under such conditions, have made false confessions. Even refusing to take a polygraph exam can increase the chances that a person will be a suspect or, at a minimum, perceived as someone who has something to hide. Sometimes people who are being screened for security purposes will be given a polygraph exam periodically. These people have to pass multiple polygraph exams and no matter how many times they pass, one failure will have an adverse effect on their job. Without any formal charges being made, an innocent person's career can be ruined if he or she fails a polygraph exam. The case of career FBI agent Mark Mullah shows how this can happen. After failing a polygraph test, he was subjected to a surprise search of his home at night. All of his financial records were examined, and his personal notes and correspondence were analyzed. No charges were ever filed but his career with the FBI was essentially over because the suspicion surrounding him would not disappear (Zelicoff, 2002).

How Does the Polygraph Work?

Most polygraphs measure three types of physiological responses. Pneumatic tubes are placed around the examinee's chest and stomach; these tubes measure the depth and rate of breathing. An inflated blood pressure cuff wrapped around the examinee's bicep gives an approximate mean of systolic and diastolic blood pressure. A clip containing metal electrodes is attached to the examinee's fingers which measures the skin's electrical resistance. Increased stress causes the hand to sweat, thereby causing electrical resistance to decrease. Changes in these physiological responses in reaction to the examiner's questions are printed out on graph paper or stored in a computer. Some exams also include the use of a movement pad that is placed on the chair where examinees sit. The device measures general movements that might interfere with testing data such as the use of countermeasures by examinees (see American Polygraph Association-FAQ, 2015).

The examiner tries to minimize any distractions that may influence the examinee's reactions. As a result, the examiner is often positioned behind the examinee and the examinee is told to maintain a steady position and give only yes or no answers. Needless to say, effective polygraph exams require examinees who are cooperative and believe in the polygraph's ability to detect their lies.

Procedures Followed in Polygraph Exams

Most polygraph exams last from 60 to 90 minutes. Before the physiological monitors are attached to the examinee, the examiner talks with the examinee about the exam. During this phase, the examiner tries to build rapport and talks about the questions that will be asked. Discussing the questions is designed to prevent any ambiguity the examinee might have about what the question means. But a critical part of this initial discussion is devoted to convincing the examinee that the polygraph will unerringly detect the examinee's lies. For the exam to be effective, innocent people must think, "I am not going to lie so I'm confident the machine will show I'm telling the truth." Guilty people must think, "Uh oh. I don't think I'm going to be able to lie without this machine picking it up." The examiner can cite research findings and talk about his or her vast experience with an air of confidence in order to enhance the examinee's belief in the accuracy of the polygraph exam. But it is not unusual for an examiner to demonstrate the machine's infallibility by asking the examinee to lie about which playing card he or she selected. Even though the examiner might be able to identify a change in bodily tension when the examinee is shown his or her card and denies it, an examiner may want to eliminate any risk by using a marked or specially constructed deck of cards. Ironically, then, deception is used to convince a person that a machine can detect deception. Since information about the polygraph's fallibility is increasingly available, it is likely to be increasingly difficult to convince examinees that they are invariably accurate. One method of questionable effectiveness is for those scheduling polygraphs to warn examinees to avoid searching the Internet or not to discuss with others how to beat the polygraph.

Polygraph exams are used for several different purposes. Each purpose necessitates a different type of question which can affect the accuracy of the polygraph. For example, a criminal suspect can be asked a very specific question which clearly differentiates truthful and deceptive respondents ("Did you take the blue topaz necklace from the display case?"). The questions asked to employees for security screening purposes are typically broader and the criteria for "passing" and "failing" on any given question are not as clear cut ("Have you ever revealed classified information to an unauthorized person?"). When polygraphs are used for employee selection, the examiner must make inferences about whether truthful answers about a person's past ("Have you used marijuana at all in the last three years?") have any bearing on whether the applicant for an FBI job will become an enemy spy or whether arousal during a "no" response to this type of question means this person should not be hired.

The two primary approaches to questioning are called the Control Question Test and the Guilty Knowledge Test.

Control Question Test

Polygraph exams initially used two types of questions—relevant ("Did you murder Alex de Grate?") and irrelevant ("Is the temperature below freezing in this room?"). It was assumed that the murderer would show a great deal more physiological arousal in response to the relevant question than to the irrelevant question. The problem, of course, was that some innocent people also showed a strong response to the relevant question if they knew Mr. de Grate, if they had an emotional reaction to murders involving knives, or if they were worried about being falsely accused and going to jail.

The "solution" to this was the development of "control" questions. The control questions, created by the examiner, are designed to elicit a level of arousal in innocent examinees that will be higher than their arousal to relevant questions. For example, both truth tellers and liars may deny that they ever took something that wasn't theirs before they were twenty years old. But the truth tellers who believe the machine can unerringly detect lies may be worried that this will be perceived as a lie—which they want to avoid. The examiner has emphasized the need to tell the truth, but added that too many admissions of inappropriate behavior also will be a concern. Subsequently, when asked a relevant question about the crime, it is assumed that the arousal of truth tellers will be lower than it was on the control question because they are certain they are telling the truth about their lack of involvement in the crime. On the other hand, it is assumed that the arousal of liars to the relevant questions will exceed their response to the control questions.

Polygraph exams using the control question technique typically ask three types of questions: neutral, control, and relevant. The questions are asked in sequence several times as illustrated in Table 10.1.

Some modifications of the Control Question Test exist. For example, in the directed lie test examinees are told to lie to each control question (Honts, 1994; Raskin et al., 1989). The goal is to try to make sure the examinee is not telling the truth on the control questions, but Lykken (1998) says this does little to improve the test. In the positive control test, examinees are told to answer a relevant question truthfully one time and deceptively the next—assuming that the greater arousal will occur with the lie. But Lykken (1998) points out that a rape victim might have similar levels of arousal for truthful and deceptive answers to "Did X use threats and force you to have intercourse with him?"

Table 10.1   A Control Question Test Sequence

Neutral 1:	Do you live in the USA?
Control 1:	During the first 20 years of your life, did you ever take something that did not belong to you?
Relevant 1:	Did you take that camera?
Neutral 2:	Is your name Alicia?
Control 2:	Prior to 1987, did you ever do something dishonest or illegal?
Relevant 2:	Did you take that camera from the desk?
Neutral 3:	Were you born in the month of November?
Control 3:	Before the age of 21 did you ever lie to get out of trouble or to cause a problem for someone else?
Relevant 3:	Did you participate in any way in the theft of that camera?

(Adapted from Vrij, 2001, p. 176)

It is no surprise that the assumptions associated with the control question approach have been challenged. People don't always react in predictable ways. A memory triggered by a word or phrase in a relevant question may heighten the arousal of an innocent person and make them look guilty. In addition, the success of these polygraph exams is highly dependent on the skills of the examiner. The examiner must be able to convince the examinee that his or her lies will be detected. The examiner must also be able to construct relevant questions that will elicit the responses liars and truth tellers are expected to give. In the question, "Did you pass the counterfeit money?" both liars and truth tellers can truthfully answer "yes." But it is likely that a "no" answer to the question, "Did you know the money you passed was counterfeit?" is not a true answer for both guilty and innocent examinees. Questions also need to be adapted to the person being tested—e.g., "Have you ever told a lie to avoid getting into trouble?" might be a useful control question for some examinees, but not a person with a long criminal record. A polygraph exam is not a standardized test so the influence of the examiner can be profound.

Guilty Knowledge Test

The Guilty Knowledge Test is a polygraph exam based on the assumption that the perpetrator of a crime will know things about the crime that innocent suspects will not. For example, assume a person had been killed with a knife. Four knives are shown, one at a time, and the suspect is asked if the knife displayed is the one used in the killing. The suspect is instructed to say "no" each time, but the assumption is that the killer will show more physiological arousal when the knife used in the killing is shown. The arousal for innocent suspects should be similar for all the knives (Lykken, 1998). All questions are in a multiple choice form with each alternative having an equal likelihood of being chosen. It is best if the examiner does not know which alternative is associated with the crime so that bias is not interjected into the way the questions are asked. A preliminary polygraph exam with people who are known to be innocent of the crime will provide guidance on the equality of the alternatives and the extent to which any of the alternatives may create arousal for an innocent person.

For criminal cases, the Guilty Knowledge Test has advantages over the Control Question Test, but it is not without its own problems. For example, a guilty person may not be aware of certain, seemingly obvious, aspects of the crime scene. The perpetrator may not have perceptions and memories expected of him or her. On the other hand, an innocent person may have knowledge of the crime scene but not be the person who committed the crime. Guilty knowledge tests are not always easy to construct because they depend on using information known only to the guilty person and, in many cases, the details of a crime are widely publicized in the media.

Interpreting Polygraphs

There is no standard method of interpreting polygraphs and no standardized rules for determining the magnitude of arousal on each channel that clearly indicates a lie. In short, there is no typical "lie response." Some operators look at the general response trends and form a judgment; others will assign numerical values to differences in responses to control and relevant questions. Cutoff points for "inconclusive" tests are often arbitrary. Many examiners score their own tests and are therefore subject to any biases associated with their view of the suspect—e.g., the knowledge that this person is a sex offender, the knowledge that the person is law enforcement's prime suspect, or the examinee's sullen facial expression. *Forensic confirmation biases* (Kassin, Dror, & Kukucka, 2013) or *tunnel vision* (Findley & Scott, 2006) may lead to interpretation errors. Honts (1994) said that computer scoring is as good as human examiners, but still only about 70% accurate in classifying liars and truth tellers correctly.

Several cases vividly point out how polygraph interpretations can vary dramatically. Floyd "Buzz" Fay failed a polygraph exam and served two and a half years of a life sentence for a murder he did not commit. From his jail cell he sent the results of his polygraph exam to several polygraph experts. One said the charts indicated Fay was truthful and two others said the results should be interpreted as inconclusive (Kleinmuntz & Szucko, 1984a). Dr. Wen Ho Lee worked in nuclear-weapon development at the Los Alamos National Laboratory and was suspected of espionage. He took a polygraph and was told he passed. Later, an FBI polygraph examiner looked at the same data and concluded Lee had lied. Kleinmuntz and Szucko (1984b) examined the accuracy of six polygraph examiners who had similar experiences and who had taken the same polygraph training course. False positive error rates (identifying truth tellers as liars) varied between 18 and 50%; false negative rates (identifying liars as truth tellers) between 18 and 36%.

How Accurate Is the Polygraph?

There is no simple answer to this question. Part of the problem is that there are different types of polygraph exams (Control Question Test, Guilty Knowledge Test) that are given for different purposes (employee selection, employee screening, criminal investigations). Nevertheless, claims are made for the overall accuracy of the polygraph exam and those claims vary dramatically. Not surprisingly, people who make their living giving polygraphs and law enforcement agencies that are trying to preserve the credibility of the polygraph often claim accuracy rates above 85%. Independent researchers often put the accuracy rate well below 80%. Saxe (1994) says the best controlled studies have error rates between 25% and 75%. Vrij (2000) also maintains that the error rates of both the Control Question Test and the Guilty Knowledge Test are substantial. Suffice to say, if you were innocent and failing a polygraph exam would send you to jail or ruin your career, you'd want a lot more assurance of the machine's accuracy than can now be given. Scientists serving on the Committee to Review the Scientific Evidence on the Polygraph (2003) reported:

> [W]e conclude that in populations of examinees such as those represented in the polygraph research literature, untrained in counter-measures, specific-incident polygraph tests can discriminate lying from truth telling at rates well above chance, though well below perfection (p.4).

The difficulty in being more precise about the polygraph's accuracy is compounded by the dearth of studies that provide trustworthy data. Laboratory studies often lack the realism associated with actual polygraph exams and studies based on actual polygraph exams often lack important controls—e.g., knowing what "ground truth" is (confessions? court decisions?), maintaining consistent procedures, etc. How should "inconclusive" results affect the accuracy rate? Some reports simply ignore them.

When polygraphs are inaccurate, they may identify truth tellers as liars (false positives) or they may identify liars as truth tellers (false negatives). For those who say, "I have nothing to hide so I wouldn't mind taking a polygraph test," they should know that false positives are the most common mistake. Iacono and Patrick (1988) report a study in which 87% of the guilty test takers were correctly identified, but only 56% of the innocents. Lykken (1998, p. 277) goes so far as to say, "an innocent suspect has nearly a 50:50 chance of failing a Control Question Test administered under adversarial circumstances…" Test takers who are especially anxious aren't necessarily anxious on every question; sometimes they are the most anxious on just the relevant questions. While the error rate on false negatives is lower, the effects can still be powerful. The infamous Green River serial killer murdered at least 48 women between 1982 and 2002. As a suspect in 1984, he took and passed a polygraph (Harden, 2003).

Most experts agree that the accuracy rate for polygraph screening exams that use the Control Question Test is lower than exams given in criminal cases that use the Guilty Knowledge Test. Unlike the questions used in criminal cases, screening exams employ broad questions that cover a number of different areas. The polygraph has been notoriously bad at catching spies. Double agents like Aldrich Ames, Karl Koecher, Larry Wu-Tai Chin, and Ana Belen Montes passed several polygraph exams. In addition, innocent and trustworthy employees have had their careers ruined by false positive results on a polygraph screening exam. From the data they examined, the Committee to Review the Scientific Evidence on the

Polygraph (2003) calculated that if 10,000 polygraphs were given to a population that included 10 spies, almost 1,600 innocent people would fail the test and 2 spies would pass it. The Committee's report concludes:

> Its [the polygraph] accuracy in distinguishing actual or potential security violators from innocent test takers is insufficient to justify reliance on its use in employee security screening in federal agencies (p.6).

For some, actual accuracy is less important than perceived accuracy. When perceived accuracy is high, the polygraph becomes more of a deterrent. To illustrate this, Saxe (1991) reports the following experiment. He and his colleagues gave students the option of taking money from a drawer. They were told they could keep it if they passed a polygraph exam. One group was told that a new type of computer polygraph was being tested and there was some doubt about its accuracy. In a rigged demonstration of the machine's effectiveness, it failed to detect a lie. Another group was told the new computer polygraph was virtually infallible and a rigged demonstration successfully demonstrated this. Most of the students who had taken the money and believed the machine was infallibly accurate were identified as guilty, along with some innocent students. None of the students who took the money and did not believe in the polygraph's accuracy were identified but some of the innocent students were misidentified as guilty. In 1983 a study by the Congressional Office of Technology Assessment concluded: "It appears the NSA [National Security Agency] (and possibly the CIA) use the polygraph not to determine deception or truthfulness *per se*, but as a technique of interrogation to encourage admissions" (Kelley, 2004, p. 20).

Can the Polygraph Be "Beat"?

A guilty person who wants to appear innocent on a polygraph exam using control questions would try to increase his or her arousal on the control questions, hoping it would be greater than his or her arousal on the relevant questions. Common ways of doing this are biting one's tongue or pressing one's toes into the floor (or on a tack hidden in a shoe) on the appropriate question. Waid et al. (1981) found the tranquilizer meprobamate to be effective in reducing arousal to relevant questions, but there is not a strong body of research on the effectiveness of drugs and/or alcohol in beating a polygraph exam. Drugs that alter memory or one's sense of responsibility for a crime are likely to be the most effective. Some people may have the ability to alter their arousal levels by cognitively evoking emotional images or doing math problems but this has not been carefully studied. There may be people who can beat polygraphs because they convince themselves they are not lying or don't care if they are lying, but we know very little about this.

Several studies do indicate that, with training, half or more of the examinees who employ countermeasures can beat the polygraph (Honts & Hodes, 1982; Honts, Raskin & Kircher, 1983; Honts et al., 1994; Honts et al., 1996). While in prison, Floyd "Buzz" Fay learned how the control question polygraph test worked and trained 27 self-confessed convicts for 15–20 minutes resulting in 23 of the 27 being able to fool the polygraph (Kleinmuntz & Szucko, 1984; Lykken, 1998; Sullivan,

2001). In another case, liars who were accurately identified 80% of the time were given either biofeedback or relaxation training. With an increased ability to control their bodily responses, the accuracy of the polygraphs was reduced to about 20% (Corcoran, 1978). However, training people to beat the polygraph using countermeasures has gained the attention of federal prosecutors. In 2013 an Indiana man was sentenced to eight months in prison for obstructing justice—he was teaching people countermeasures for their polygraph exams. A retired Oklahoma City police officer pleaded guilty in 2015 for running the website polygraph.com which provided instructional materials, DVDs, and personal training on how to beat federal polygraph exams. He faces heavy fines and up to 20 years in prison.

In response to countermeasures which remain readily available at sites like anti-polygraph.org or wikihow.com, some polygraphers rely on counter countermeasures. Some of these counter countermeasures involve observation, asking examinees to remove their shoes so they cannot use a tack under their toe to inflict pain, and some rely on movement detection devices.

Good for You, but Not Good for Me

In 1963 and again in 1974 Congressional committees recommended against the widespread use of polygraph exams. Sam Ervin, a U.S. senator from North Carolina, spoke against the polygraph during the 1974 committee and referred to the polygraph as *twentieth-century witchcraft* (Lykken, 1998). The 2003 Committee to Review the Scientific Evidence on the Polygraph simply reinforced the polygraph's shortcomings identified by the earlier committees. Members of Congress know about these shortcomings and do not want to take a polygraph exam. In an effort to find a security leak associated with 9/11, Congress called on the FBI. But when the FBI requested some members of Congress take a polygraph exam, they refused. Senator Shelby said, "I don't know who among us would take a lie-detector test. First of all, they're not even admissible in court, and second of all, the leadership [of both parties] have told us not to do that" (Zelicoff, 2002, p. A23). Nevertheless, in 1999 Senator Shelby was instrumental in gaining approval for the administration of a polygraph exam to 15,000 scientists in an effort to uncover any spies who had been leaking information to China about nuclear weapons—despite the polygraph's dismal record in identifying spies and Shelby's own aversion to the machine.

As long as people crave a way of detecting lies and believe there is a machine capable of doing so, the machine becomes a powerful force in society (Adler, 2007). The polygraph has hung around as long as it has, despite all of its flaws, because we seem to want a lie detector machine desperately and newer techniques such as functional magnetic resonance imaging (fMRI) have not gained widespread acceptance to replace it—but, as we will discuss below, efforts are in place.

The Measurement of Stress as an Indicator of Lying

The polygraph is anchored to the assumption that liars will reveal themselves through physiological arousal. Several other efforts to build a lie detector are based on the dubious assumption that all liars experience stress. As a result, devices measuring stress in the voice, eyes, stomach, and mouth have been linked to lie detection.

Stress in the Voice

The Psychological Stress Evaluator (PSE) first appeared in the 1970s. It was supposed to measure microtremors in the human voice that occur during times of stress. It was also marketed as a lie detector, presumably based on the assumption that liars will exhibit stress. During the next thirty-five years, the device changed its name to Voice Stress Analyzer (VSA) or Computer Voice Stress Analyzer but little else differed. Some companies have marketed a *new* product called Layered Voice Analysis (LVA) and claim that it works independent of previous VSA processes. Nemesysco is a company that advertises LVA on their website. It clearly states that LVA is not a voice stress technology and that it can detect "brain activity traces" using the voice as a medium (in any language); they proclaim the tool also relies on algorithms to extract over 120 emotional parameters that can be reduced to 9 basic emotion categories.

Mass media often reiterate manufacturers' claims of 99% accuracy for devices that detect stress and deception in the voice. They repeat claims that these devices can accurately analyze voices heard over the telephone or on audio recordings, and that they are used among the law enforcement community. In 1999, a Texas state representative introduced a bill (which failed) that would have allowed licensed officers to use computerized voice stress analyzers in criminal investigations. With the concern for screening airline passengers following 9/11, a form of the VSA that could fit into the eyeglasses of security personnel was marketed.

The fact that these lie and/or stress detectors have been around so long doesn't mean that they have been endorsed by the scientific community. On the contrary, numerous experiments cited by Hollien (1990) show that neither the PSE nor VSA adequately measure vocal microtremors, much less the variations in microtremors associated with different levels of stress. The most that can be said is that it can *sometimes* detect high stress levels. As for detecting deception, researchers conclude that voice stress analysis is about as accurate as flipping a coin (Hollien, 1990; Horvath, 1982). Damphouse's (2008) study conducted for the Department of Justice on VSA and LVA programs used over 300 recent arrestees who were randomly interviewing at a county jail about their drug usage. Urine tests were conducted post interviews to determine ground truth regarding their recent drug use. On average the two programs were 15% accurate in detecting lies and about 91% accurate in determining those who were nondeceptive. However, neither program was able to weed out lies with much confidence and the overall accuracy rates were reported as 50% in determining deception about recent drug use. One study on LVA used blind samples and provided the outputs of truth tellers and liars minus the voice recordings so that examiners could not use voices in their analyses (Harnsberger, Hollien, Martin, & Hollien, 2009). The outputs were provided to two instructors from the manufacturer of the LVA and two scientists trained by the manufacturer. Accuracy rates were between 42 and 56% and false positive rates (inaccurately judging a truth as a lie) were even higher—between 40 and 65%.

Our own experience with voice stress analysis occurred when the first author bought a version called Truster. Dr. Knapp tried to show his students how it worked by having liars and truth tellers speak into the unit's microphone. Any intruding sound seemed to affect the results and often led to an inconclusive reading—e.g., "might be lying" or "might be telling the truth." This was also true as the speaker varied his or her distance from the microphone or changed his or her voice volume. Needless to say, it is hard to imagine how such a device could ever reliably measure microtremors in telephone voices as is advertised. In fact, Hollien (1990, p. 281) points out that the microtremors purportedly measured have a much lower frequency range than a telephone will pick up. Smart phone apps are being developed to detect stress in the voice during real-life situations (Lu et al., 2012), but these programs are not yet designed to detect deception. Although programs on phones are likely to adopt VSA technology to provide users with decisions about others' veracity, these programs will also face many of the shortcomings mentioned previously.

Stress in the Eyes

A thermal-imaging camera can measure how much heat is emitted by various parts of the body at a distance of ten or twelve feet. During a stressful fight/flight response, the blood flows to a region just inside each eye and the temperature in that region increases. Assuming all liars suddenly feel the need to run away when lying and that no other cognitive, emotional, or physical activity (real or imagined) increases the temperature around the eyes, the Department of Defense conducted a study of the thermal-imaging camera's ability to detect lies (Pavlidis et al., 2002). Twenty soldiers at Fort Jackson, South Carolina were tested in a simulated theft scenario which asked liars to stab a mannequin and rob it of $20. Six of the eight liars (75%) and eleven of the twelve truth-tellers (92%) were accurately identified. A traditional polygraph exam was also given to these soldiers and 75% of the liars and 67% of the truth tellers were accurately classified. The researchers concluded that more research is needed, but that the results of thermal-imaging are comparable to those of the polygraph. Given what we know about the polygraph, this is not a strong endorsement.

Stress in the Stomach

A team of gastroenterologists tested the idea that the gastrointestinal tract is sensitive to mental stress associated with lying (Pasricha, Sallam, Chen, & Pasricha, 2008). Stomach and heart measurements were taken of 16 liars and truth tellers who participated in a guilty task test using a deck of playing cards. Their heart and stomach activity was measured during the task using an EGG (electrogastrogram) and an EKG (electrocardiogram). The EGG was affected by lying, showing a significant decrease in the normal gastric slow waves. The heart rate of both liars and truth tellers increased significantly by participating in the task, but did not differ from one another. The researchers believe the EGG should be added to the standard polygraph in order to improve polygraph accuracy, and the medical school where the study was conducted has filed a patent for the use of the "gut-brain" relationship for lie detection.

Stress in the Mouth

If the preceding efforts don't offer enough proof that security agencies are willing to explore any and every avenue for that elusive key to identifying liars, Henig (2006) indicates the Department of Defense is supporting research on a "sniffer" test that measures stress hormones on one's breath. Some research on deception has relied on saliva samples to detect levels of the hormone cortisol caused by the stress associated with lying (ten Brinke, Stimson, & Carney, 2014).

The preceding attempts to measure stress to detect lies are all based on the assumption that deceiving others invokes stress. While this is true in some instances, not all lies increase stress. Furthermore, some liars don't show physiological stress in situations where we would expect it to occur.

Scanning the Brain for Lies

Since 9/11 and the war on terrorism a lot of money and effort have been directed toward new lie-detection machines. Brain scans are based on the assumption that the brain will reveal a different pattern of activity during lying and truth telling. One approach to mapping the brain uses an electroencephalograph and has often been referred to as "brain fingerprinting." The examinee wears a headband with electronic sensors that register his or her neurological responses (electrical activity) to words and images flashed on a screen. Like the polygraph's Guilty Knowledge Test, brain fingerprinting is based on the belief that certain words and images will produce very different brain activity within the perpetrator of a crime than in an innocent suspect. A brain wave called a P300 indicates a person has recognized something familiar (Farwell & Donchin, 1991).

The peer-reviewed scientific research on brain fingerprinting is minimal and critics have pointed out numerous problems with the procedure. Farwell and Donchin's original study (1991) claimed a 100% accuracy rate for classifying liars and truth tellers, but 12.5% of those tested were classified as "inconclusive" (meaning it wasn't clear if they were lying or telling the truth). Rosenfeld et al. (2004) were able to teach people how to reduce the rate of identifying guilty suspects from 82% to 18% using simple countermeasures. Rosenfeld also claims that a replication of Farwell and Donchin's original study detected concealed information at only 48% (Feder, 2001). Hu, Hegeman, Landry, and Rosenfeld (2012) were able to overcome examinees' use of countermeasures by increasing the number of irrelevant stimuli in the test. They report detection rates from 71 to 92% using this method. In another study, reminding examinees that the veracity of their messages was scanned via brainwaves and giving them occasional reminders enhanced test sensitivity (Rosenfeld, Hu, & Pederson, 2012). However, federal law enforcement agencies point out that brain fingerprinting is not an effective method for screening purposes and that its validity is heavily dependent on the examiner's skill in selecting the probe questions from information about the crime (U.S. Accounting Office, 2001). For example, an innocent person may be familiar with certain aspects of the crime and not be the perpetrator; similarly, the perpetrator of the crime may not remember the color of his murder victim's dress. All of life's experiences are not stored in memory forever or with the same accessibility. Drugs, alcohol, brain damage, and anxiety while perpetrating the crime can all affect the likelihood of detecting guilty knowledge.

Scientists and companies in the private sector are also using another brain mapping technique called functional magnetic resonance imaging (fMRI) to distinguish liars from truth tellers. A person lies flat on his or her back in a tubular machine (weighing up to ten tons) with his or her head immobilized. These machines are also very expensive—some costing as much as $3 million (Talbot, 2007). Yes and no answers are made with a response mechanism attached to the fingers. Bodily movement may negatively affect the scan and the presence of any metal in the body such as a medical implant or metal fragments in the eye will render a subject untestable. The machine measures blood flow to activated areas of the brain during lying and truth telling. A number of studies, ranging in accuracy from 77% to 90%, have found specific regions of the brain that are activated during deception (Ganis et al., 2003; Kozel et al., 2004a; Kozel et al., 2004b; Langleben et al., 2002; Lee et al., 2002; Phan et al., 2005; and Spence et al., 2001). Private companies such as *No Lie MRI* and *Cephos Corporation* were started in 2006 and promote the technology for legal, employment, and national security screenings; they promote the technology's accuracy rating at 90%. Different types of lies sometimes reveal more regions of activation, but most studies find brain activation during lying in the anterior cingulate cortex (3 inches behind the middle of the forehead) and the prefrontal cortex (a few inches inside the skull near the left ear). These brain areas are activated during a wide range of other mental functions as well, but their association with response inhibition and higher-order decision making suggests how they might be associated with a lie response. Nancy Kanwisher, a cognitive scientist at M.I.T., doesn't think the current brain-mapping for lies is very specific. She says, "Saying 'You have activation in the anterior cingulate' is like saying, 'You have activation in Massachusetts'" (cited by Talbot, 2007, p. 61).

Researchers readily admit that there is much to learn about using fMRI for the purposes of deception detection. The legal system has also recognized issues surrounding the use of fMRI in courtrooms and although attempts have been made, U.S. courtrooms do not allow results from these tests as evidence (Rusconi & Mitchener-Nissen, 2013). There may be several unique neural pathways for different types of lies. For example, patterns of brain activity may be different for half-truths, denials, and exaggerations. Patterns for lies that include some truth may be different than those that are strictly lies. Kosslyn believes there are differences between spontaneous and well-rehearsed lies (Henig, 2006), Lee et al. (2002) focused on feigned memory impairment, and Phan et al. (2005) examined lies involving increased anxiety. In addition, we need to know more about the responses of different types of individuals, especially those who do not show the expected pattern (Ganis et al., 2003). Ultimately the machine should be able to unfailingly distinguish truth tellers from liars when their motivations and reactions are consistent with a real, high-stakes situation. We know relatively little about the effectiveness of countermeasures, but one study found altered breathing, delayed responses, and mentally imaging a specific place to be ineffective (Kozel et al., 2005). However, a more recent study showed it was quite simple to train participants in fMRI-specific countermeasures that would lower accuracy rates (Ganis, Rosenfeld, Meixner, Kievit, & Schendan, 2011). Examinees who are non-compliant (e.g., delaying responses or moving their head) can also be problematic for the test. Kosslyn emphasized the work that needs to be done when he said:

> Searching for a 'lie zone' of the brain as a counterterrorism strategy is like trying to get to the moon by climbing a tree. It feels as if you're getting somewhere because you're moving higher and higher. But then you get to the top of the tree and there's nowhere else to go, and the moon is still hundreds of thousands of miles away. Better to have stayed on the ground and really figured out the problem before setting off on a path that looks like progress but is really nothing more than motion. Better, in this case, to discover what deception looks like in the brain by breaking it down into progressively smaller elements, no matter how artificial the setup and how tedious the process, before introducing a lie-detection device that doesn't really get you where you want to go (Henig, 2006).

Despite the theoretical, ethical, legal, procedural, and accuracy problems, the fMRI has often received unbounded praise from media sources. A CNBC report described it as a "sure-fire way to identify a liar." Just the words, "brain scans indicate…" are enough to make many people believe what would otherwise be labeled a "bad explanation" (Talbot citing Weisberg, p. 58). The apparently unquenchable desire to discover a machine that will identify lies means there will be huge market for such a product. As a result, companies are eager to administer fMRIs in the pursuit of uncovering deceptive behavior (Ritter, 2006). The website brainsontrial.com provides an extensive look into fMRI technology for use in deception detection.

Do Truth Serums Make People Tell the Truth?

Movies and television shows have frequently shown a prisoner who is injected with sodium pentothal or sodium amytal and whose secrets subsequently come flowing out. It is true that sodium pentothal and sodium amytal may induce a state of relaxation and/or drowsiness, it is true that a person may lose some inhibitions and talk more, but it does not follow that people in this state will then tell the truth and nothing but the truth. In a case involving a confession to a murder obtained after a police physician administered a so-called truth serum, the U.S. Supreme Court ruled that the conviction was unconstitutional (Townsend v. Sain, 1963). A 1956 federal appeals court made little distinction between alcohol intoxication and truth serums, saying:

> The intravenous injection of a drug by a physician in a hospital may appear more scientific than the drinking of large amounts of bourbon in a tavern, but the end result displayed in the subject's speech may be no more reliable (Lindsey v. United States, 1956).

A stronger dose of sodium pentothal is commonly used as a sedative, an anesthetic during surgery, and it is the first of three drugs administered to those facing execution by lethal injection. The use of barbiturates to elicit repressed and suppressed information from patients has long been used in psychotherapy, but does not provide a sure-fire way of dealing with suspected malingering (Rogers & Wettstein, 1988). In fact, these so-called truth serums also make a patient more susceptible to suggestion so psychiatrists sometimes inadvertently bias the feelings and/or memories the patient reveals. Furthermore, these drugs can lead a person to confuse truth and illusion (Sullivan, 2001) so it is no surprise that some state courts treat confessions and testimony induced by these truth serum drugs as inadmissible. Some researchers are finding that oxytocin, a hormone also used as a drug, may increase honesty and cooperation (Arueti et al., 2013). But, as we have seen with other truth serums, it is not likely to be used in real applications or allowed in legal proceedings.

Integrity Tests: Paper Lie Detectors?

Each year millions of integrity tests, also known as honesty tests, are given to people—primarily as a pre-employment screening procedure. The tests are designed to reduce the effects of illegal (theft) and counterproductive (absenteeism) behavior in the workplace. Some tests focus on the identification of certain personality characteristics—e.g., hostility, dependability, conscientiousness, and trouble with authority. Other tests focus specifically on an applicant's attitudes toward honesty and previous involvement with theft and other counterproductive work behavior. These tests, then, are not really designed to detect lies; they are designed to detect honesty.

Even though the socially desirable answer to questions like those in *Testing Your Honesty* (see boxed insert below) may seem obvious, the creators of the test normally have ways to offset the "faking good" response (Miner & Capps, 1996). Prelac (2004) has developed his own method of determining truthful subjective data in situations where there is no measure of objective truth, but integrity tests typically use other methods. Sometimes special scales are constructed from data derived by asking people to answer questions according to what they think is the desired response, sometimes items with a high degree of social desirability are eliminated or given less weight in scoring, and sometimes the consistency or inconsistency associated with several items will indicate a "faking good" response. When the test taker is suspected of "faking good," this will invalidate his or her test. Honesty and integrity tests are not typically concerned with people who might be "too honest," but the whistleblower phenomenon raises this possibility.

The question of whether honesty tests actually measure honesty has been controversial (O'Bannon et al., 1989; Ones et al., 1993; Sackett et al., 1989; U.S. Congress, 1990). In a perfect world, the employee's honest and dishonest behavior on the job would be compared with his or her test score in order to determine the validity of the test. But, as is readily obvious, the honesty criterion is not easy to establish. For example: 1) the data from a person who would have been honest on the job may not be included because he or she was denied employment due to an honest admission of stealing something as a child; 2) a lot of dishonest (and honest) employee behavior is unknown to the employer; 3) a person may be treated as a dishonest employee for lying about something trivial, but that same person might be honest about a matter with serious consequences. An examination of the results of 300 studies using integrity tests used meta-analytic procedures to synthesize the findings of over 130 of them. The study found that the validity of integrity tests is low for job and training performance, counterproductive work behaviors, and turnover (Iddekinge, Roth, Raymark, & Odle-Dusseau, 2012). The extent to which a self-reported attitude will predict behavior is always subject to special conditions arising in an unforeseen context. Almost everyone believes they are generally honest and will honestly report that as they answer items on an honesty test. But it does not necessarily follow that their behavior in an actual situation, even one similar to an item on the test, will mirror their response to the test item.

Nevertheless, a number of studies report positive correlations between honesty test results and 1) counterproductive workplace behavior (e.g., job turnover, absenteeism); and 2) supervisor ratings of employees. Critics argue that too many of the studies supporting the validity of these tests were conducted by people associated with the development of the tests.

Honesty tests, like other methods of assisted deception detection, are subject to a certain amount of error. These tests will eliminate some people with integrity who would have been upstanding employees and support the hiring of others who turn out to be thieves. Many agree that honesty tests should not be the sole basis for an employment decision, but that they are likely to be a screening measure that is as good, if not better, than the alternatives—e.g., references, a background check, a drug test, or an integrity-focused interview.

Answer the following questions with a yes or no. They are the kind of questions you might be asked on a pre-employment integrity test.*

1. Do you believe a person who writes a check for which he or she knows there is no money in the bank should be refused a job in which honesty is important?

2. Do you believe a worker who takes money from the place where he or she works should go to jail?

3. Do you think a person should be fired by a company if it is found that he or she helped the employees cheat the company out of overtime once in a while?

4. If you found $100 that was lost by a bank truck on the street yesterday, would you turn the money over to the bank, even though you knew for sure that there was no reward?

5. On the 20th of each month, an old employee took company money to pay his mortgage. On the 30th of each month, payday, he paid it back. After 15 years, the man was finally seen by his boss putting the money back. No shortage was found, but his boss fired him anyway. Do you think the boss did right?

6. Do you think that the way a company is run is more responsible for employee theft than the attitudes and tendencies of employees themselves?

*These are sample items adapted from the Reid Report's "Integrity Attitude Scale."
John E. Reid & Associates, Inc., 250 Wacker Dr., Suite 1100, Chicago, IL 60606.

Assisted Analyses of Verbal Clues to Deception

In everyday interaction, people can listen for verbal clues to deception, but computers provide a way of rapidly analyzing units of varying sizes in the speech of a suspected liar. What language patterns do these methods attribute to liars and how accurate are they?

Pennebaker and his colleagues (2007) developed a computer program that searches 2,300 words and word stems, each of which can be put in several different categories—e.g., the word "cried" could be classified as "sadness," "negative emotion," "overall affect," and a "past tense verb." Their system, *Linguistic Inquiry and Word Count (LIWC)*, has identified the following linguistic features as occurring significantly more among liars than truth tellers: fewer first person singular pronouns (I, me, my); more negative emotion words; and fewer "exclusive" words—i.e., prepositions and conjunctions such as "but," "except," "without," and "exclude" that are used by the speaker to distinguish one thing from another (Pennebaker, 2011).

Statement Validity Analysis (SVA) was originally developed as a way of testing the veracity of testimony by child witnesses and victims in cases of sexual abuse

(Undeutsch, 1982). Courts in several European countries allow the results of SVA to be introduced as evidence. SVA involves three steps: a structured interview with the target, an analysis of the verbal content contained in a transcript of the initial interview, and an interpretation of the content analysis using a standard set of questions (Köhnken, 2004). The problems associated with SVA are plentiful. The content analysis is dependent on a single person and laboratory studies show SVA is inaccurate 25–35% of the time (Vrij, 2000). Bull (2004) said that attempts to train police and social workers on how to perform the content analysis were problematic.

Another approach is called the *Scientific Content Analysis (SCAN)* (Sapir, 1987). This system for deception detection is based on assumptions about the nature of truthful statements versus untruthful statements. Individual differences in personality, gender, and culture are not taken into consideration (Shearer, 1999). McClish (2008) developed his own method of *Statement Analysis (SA)* by combining information from methods like SCAN with what he intuitively derived from his own experience at the U.S. Marshall's Service Training Academy. His website, statementanalysis.com, features a program built into the domain where users can upload a text statement and receive an analysis of deception—there is a minimal subscription for this service.

Reality Monitoring (RM) is a method of analyzing language use that is based on the belief that true memories are encoded differently than created ones (Johnson & Raye, 1981; Sporer, 2004). True memories are believed to contain more representations attributed to the senses and more contextual information—e.g., remembered feelings and precise story details. Vrij (2015) cites various studies that show RM is able to identify liars from 63 to 72% of the time. Overall, he claims the tool obtains about 70% accuracy. It is not really used by practitioners, and cannot be used under all conditions.

In an effort to test several of the preceding methods, Porter and Yuille (1996) conducted an experiment. They told some university students to steal money from a folder in a professor's office while others were given permission to retrieve the same folder (without the money in it) from the same office. In a subsequent interview, some students were told to confess the truth, others were told to create a truthful alibi, still others were told to mix some true statements with some lies, and the last group was told to invent a completely false alibi. All of the students were given a small monetary payment to increase their motivation. Each student was interrogated with the same structured interview and their responses were transcribed for analysis. The verbal behavior on the transcript was analyzed with SVA, RM, Lexical Diversity (type-token ratio), and Sapir's SCAN. Only 3 of 18 language features showed any significant differences between liars and truth tellers. These three, all from SVA, identify the verbal behavior of truth tellers as containing *more details,* being *twice as coherent,* and having more *admissions of memory loss.*

Using computer programs and other linguistic analysis tools to examine various kinds of verbal behavior does provide a quicker and more systematic way of analyzing a complex data set, but as we have seen with all of the mechanisms in this chapter, achieving a very high rate of distinguishing liars from truth tellers is difficult. Reliably detecting veracity using certain patterns of verbal behavior and lexical patterns will require more research and further advances in technology.

Computer-Assisted Analyses of Facial Clues to Deception

Feelings are reflected in facial expressions so when liars want to mask their true feelings, they display a deceptive expression. However, the facial expression (or some part of it) reflecting the liar's true feelings may "leak" and appear in a fleeting facial microexpression. These microexpressions are often missed by untrained human observers (Ekman, 2001), but with training or video records, these expressions can be identified. The Facial Affect Coding System (FACS) enables researchers to code virtually any facial movement (Ekman, 1978).

FACS is being used in conjunction with computers that read videotaped faces in order to identify the type of facial expression, its intensity, and the onset/offset time (Bartlett et al., 1999; Cohen et al., 1999). The computer-assisted analysis of facial expressions is faster and more accurate than human observers. Bartlett, Littlewort, Frank, and Lee (2014) found that trained human observers were 55% accurate in discriminating between actual and faked facial expressions of pain; the computer was 85% accurate on the same task. But as discussed in the previous chapter, liars' faces may not always be the best place to look for lies. All of us get a lot of social feedback on our faces and this facilitates a proficiency at facial deception. Practiced liars or those with a high level of motivation to succeed in a deception may show exceptional skills. In addition, the face may be a good place to look for some kinds of deception and not others. For example, Ekman, Friesen, and O'Sullivan (1997) had nurses tell an interviewer they were watching a pleasant film when, in fact, the film vividly portrayed amputations and burns. In this study, the researchers specifically focused on the extent to which nurses (who were highly motivated based on their career ambitions) manifested their true feelings in the way they smiled. Only about half of the nurses who were lying about the film they were watching were correctly identified. But a subsequent laboratory study involving lies about a theft or about political beliefs accurately classified 80% of both liars and truth tellers relying on FACS to measure microexpressions (Frank & Ekman, 1997). Context, motivation, and the type of lie being told (e.g., false smiles versus opinion lies) all seem to influence the degree to which the face may betray liars.

Automated Computer Programs and Avatars

Recently, researchers at the University of Arizona began testing the Automated Virtual Agent for Truth Assessments in Real-Time (AVATAR) with U.S. Customs and Border Protection. The machine has a screen which displays an animated talking face asking yes or no questions to travelers crossing the border who have been pre-screened. The system monitors vocalics, eye movement, pupil dilation, and facial expressions and analyzes these cues to make a determination of veracity. Although published research is lacking on the success of this type of system, the researchers claim that the system reached up to 90% accuracy during its development in the lab (Border Patrol Kiosk, 2012). Burgoon, Schuetzler, and Wilson (2014) examined how computer programs are able to examine patterns or global trends in nonverbal cues during deception. The presence of rigidity in the body during concealed knowledge tests is also being examined with computer kiosks that interact with humans (Twyman, Elkins, Burgoon, & Nunamaker, 2014).

As more of our communication continues to take place via the Internet and through social media, deception detection via computer-mediated channels becomes increasingly important. Scientists are creating tools to detect fake Facebook profiles (Saini, 2012), spam product reviews (Ott, Cardie, & Hancock, 2012), and fake tweets (Gupta & Kumaraguru, 2013). Even research communities are seeking out computer-assisted tools to detect researchers who submit publications containing faked data (Konnikova, 2015).

Some basic questions remain when dealing with automated computer-assisted deception detection: Are the correct cues being measured? Is the measurement process effective and appropriate to the situation? Is the accuracy in identifying lies high enough to warrant further research with the system? Also, we must recognize that there may be effects of avatar-human interactions that we do not yet understand. For example, some people may not like talking to a non-human during an interview containing suspicious questioning. Although people are often enamored with the idea of finding a sure-fire way to detect lies, and the use of new technologies in everyday communication is becoming very common, the combination of some of the factors mentioned here may lead to frivolous pursuits.

Summary

This chapter, like the preceding one, focused on lie detection. The central question addressed in this chapter is whether machines, drugs, questionnaires, or computers provide accurate lie detection. The inescapable conclusion is that all known methods of lie detection are fallible and subject to substantial error rates, often 25% or more.

The polygraph is known as a lie-detection machine, but all it really detects are changes in a person's physiological arousal, measured by breathing, blood pressure, and skin conductance. It is the interpretation of these changes that occur in response to certain questions that determines whether a lie is believed to have occurred or not. Due to the possibility of different interpretations given to the same data, and a sufficiently high error rate (often more than 25%), polygraphs results are not admissible as evidence in most court cases. The polygraph is least accurate when it is used to screen employees and more accurate when testing a suspect's knowledge of a crime. The most common polygraph error is identifying truth tellers as liars. Several studies indicate examinees can artificially alter their arousal in order to create a false polygraph reading. Despite numerous problems associated with the use of polygraphs as lie detectors, they are still widely used by law enforcement agencies.

Functional magnetic resonance imaging (fMRI) is an attempt to show which areas of the brain are activated when people lie. Some regions of the brain are stimulated for certain types of lies, but there may be more than one "lie response." Law enforcement and security agencies are hopeful that brain mapping will replace the polygraph as a more accurate method of detecting lies. Currently, the procedure is too expensive and faces too many limitations to experience widespread usage.

Mechanisms that show little likelihood of replacing the polygraph include those based on the assumption that liars will always manifest stress. Measuring stress in the voice, eyes, stomach, and the mouth are all ways that have been explored in the quest to find a better lie detector. Truth serums do not detect lies or truth. They make a person less inhibited and more talkative, but can't guarantee truth telling. Integrity questionnaires are designed to measure the honesty of prospective employees. Their validity is poor and often difficult to measure and their questions are strongly affected by social desirability. This chapter also discusses attempts to use computers to analyze the verbal and facial behavior of liars and truth tellers in an effort to identify distinguishing characteristics. This chapter closes by visiting initial explorations toward using computers that can interact with humans to catch lies and by touching on attempts to detect deception via online and social media communication.

So far our belief that machines will provide us with an infallible lie detector is unwarranted. We have examined physiological, psychological, and neurological data associated with liars and have yet to uncover a clearly identifiable lie response—a pattern that occurs every time a person lies. Given the different types of lies, individual differences, and the inevitable use of countermeasures, the future identification of a lie response is doubtful. As a consequence, we will have to treat lie detection like we treat other predictions about human behavior—in terms of probabilities and as only one piece of information relative to the likelihood that a person has lied. It is especially important that the public is aware of the potential for error and invasion of privacy associated with any so-called lie detector marketed to the general public. We too often think about how machines can serve us and too little about how we end up serving machines.

Things to Think About

Why do you think it is so hard to develop a machine that will identify liars and truth tellers with a high degree of accuracy? In your answer, consider the nature of language, the nature of lies, and the nature of human beings.

Do you think the fascination with machines as lie detectors is peculiar to our own cultural history and values?

You are an inventor and you have just designed the perfect lie detector instrument. What does it look like and what is it capable of doing?

You have just been approached by a person who has invented the perfect lie detection instrument. It can be held in one's hand, it is 100% accurate, and it can detect lies at 100 feet. The inventor wants to begin manufacturing and selling these devices to anyone who will buy them. They are fairly expensive, but most people can afford one. You have the power to decide whether this product is marketed or destroyed. Make a list of the advantages and disadvantages you foresee and decide whether to approve it or not.

Do the Internet and social media make it easier or more difficult to catch lies? If there were ways to ensure that everyone could detect deception via social media do you think people would continue to use these channels as a way to interact? Or might social media usage fall out of favor?

References

Adler, K. (2007). *The lie detectors: The history of an American obsession.* New York: Free Press.

Alexander, M.G., & Fisher, T.D. (2003). Truth and consequences: Using the bogus pipeline to examine sex differences in self-reported sexuality. *Journal of Sex Research, 40,* 27–35.

American Polygraph Association, frequently asked questions (2015). Retrieved from http://www.polygraph.org/section/resources/frequently-asked-questions

Arueti, M., Perach-Barzilay, N., Tsoory, M.M., Berger, B., Getter, N., & Shamay-Tsoory, S.G. (2013). When two become one: the role of oxytocin in interpersonal coordination and cooperation. *Journal of Cognitive Neuroscience, 25,* 1418–1427.

Barnhorn, D., & Pegram, J.E. (2011). Speak the truth and tell no lies: An update for the Employee Polygraph Protection Act. *Hofstra Labor and Employment Law Journal, 29,* 141–187.

Bartlett, M.S., Hager, J.C., Ekman, P., & Sejnowski, T.J. (1999). Measuring facial expressions by computer image analysis. *Psychophysiology, 36,* 253–263.

Border Patrol Kiosk Detects Liars. (2012). *Emergency Management.* Retrieved at http://www.emergencymgmt.com/safety/Border-Patrol-Kiosk-Detects-Liars.html

Bull, R. (2004). Training to detect deception from behavioural cues: attempts and problems. In P.A. Granhag & L.A. Strömwall, (Eds.), *The detection of deception in forensic contexts* (pp. 251–268). New York: Cambridge University Press.

Burgoon, J.K., Schuetzler, R., & Wilson, D.W. (2015). Kinesic patterning in deceptive and truthful interactions. *Journal of Nonverbal Behavior, 39,* 1–24.

Cohen, J.F., Zlochower, A.J., Lien, J.J., & Kanade, T. (1999). Automated face analysis by feature point tracking has high concurrent validity with manual FACS coding. *Psychophysiology, 36,* 35–43.

Committee to Review the Scientific Evidence on the Polygraph, Board on Behavioral, Cognitive, and Sensory Sciences, and Committee on National Statistics, Division of Behavioral and Social Sciences and Education, National Research Council of the National Academies. (2003). *The polygraph and lie detection.* Washington, DC: The National Academies Press.

Corcoran, J.F.T., Lewis, M.D., & Garver, R.B. (1978). Biofeedback—conditioned galvanic skin response and hypnotic suppression of arousal: A pilot study of their relation to deception. *Journal of Forensic Sciences, 23,* 155–162.

Damphousse, K.R. (2008). Voice stress analysis: Only 15 percent of lies about drug use detected in field test. *National Institute of Justice Journal, 259,* 8–12.

Ekman, P. (2001). *Telling lies: Clues to deceit in the marketplace, politics, and marriage.* New York: Norton.

Ekman, P., & Friesen, W.V. (1978). *Facial action coding system: A technique for the measurement of facial movement.* Palo Alto, CA: Consulting Psychologists Press.

Ekman, P., Friesen, W.V., & O'Sullivan, M. (1997). Smiles when lying. In P. Ekman & E. Rosenberg (Eds.), *What the face reveals* (pp. 201–216). New York: Oxford University Press.

Farwell, L.A., & Donchin, E. (1991). The truth will out: Interrogative polygraphy ("lie detection") with event-related brain potentials. *Psychophysiology, 28,* 531–547.

Feder, B.J. (2001, October 9). Truth and justice, by the blip of a brain wave. *New York Times,* p. D3.

Findley, K.A., & Scott, M.S. (2006). The multiple dimensions of tunnel vision in criminal cases. *Wisconsin Law Review, 2,* 291–397.

Frank, M.G., & Ekman, P. (1997). The ability to detect deceit generalizes across different types of high stake lies. *Journal of Personality and Social Psychology, 72,* 1429–1439.

Furedy, J.J., & Heslegrave, R.J. (1991). The forensic use of the polygraph: A psychophysiological analysis of current trends and future prospects. In J.R. Jennings, P.K. Ackles, & M.G.H. Coles (Eds.), *Advances in psychophysiology,* Vol. 4 (pp. 157–189). London: Jessica Kingsley.

Ganis, G., Kosslyn, S.M., Stose, S., Thompson, W.L., & Yurgelun-Todd, D.A. (2003). Neural correlates of different types of deception: An fMRI investigation. *Cerebral Cortex, 13,* 830–836.

Ganis, G., Rosenfeld, J.P., Meixner, J., Kievit, R.A., & Schendan, H.E. (2011). Lying in the scanner: Covert countermeasures disrupt deception detection by functional magnetic resonance imaging. *Neuroimage, 55,* 312–319.

Gupta, A., Lamba, H., & Kumaraguru, P. (2013). $1.00 per rt# bostonmarathon# prayforboston: Analyzing fake content on Twitter. In *eCrime Researchers Summit* (pp. 1–12). IEEE.

Harden, B. (2003, November 6). Killer of 48 women makes deal to avoid death penalty. *Austin American Statesman,* pp. Al, 9.

Harnsberger, J.D., Hollien, H., Martin, C.A., & Hollien, K.A. (2009). Stress and deception in speech: Evaluating layered voice analysis. *Journal of Forensic Sciences, 54,* 642–650.

Henig, R.M. (2006, February 5). Looking for the lie. *New York Times Magazine,* Section 6, pp. 47–57.

Hibler, N.S., & Scheflin, A.W. (2012). Maximizing the usefulness of hypnosis in forensic investigative settings. *American Journal of Clinical Hypnosis, 55,* 32–55.

Hollien, H. (1990). *The Acoustics of crime: The new science of forensic phonetics.* New York: Plenum.

Honts, C.R. (1994). Psychophysiological detection of deception. *Current Directions in Psychological Science, 3,* 77–82.

Honts, C.R., & Hodes, R.L. (1982). The effect of multiple physical countermeasures on the detection of deception. *Psychophysiology, 19,* 564–565.

Honts, C.R., Raskin, D.C., & Kircher, J.C. (1983). Detection of deception: Effectiveness of physical countermeasures under high motivation conditions. *Psychophysiology, 20,* 446–447.

Honts, C.R., Raskin, D.C., & Kircher, J.C. (1994). Mental and physical countermeasures reduce the accuracy of polygraph tests. *Journal of Applied Psychology, 79,* 252–259.

Honts, C.R., Devitt, M.K., Winbush, M., & Kircher, J.C. (1996). Mental and physical countermeasures reduce the accuracy of the concealed knowledge test. *Psychophysiology, 33,* 84–92.

Horvath, F. (1982). Detecting deception: The promise and reality of voice stress analysis. *Journal of Forensic Sciences, 27,* 340–352.

Hu, X., Hegeman, D., Landry, E., & Rosenfeld, J.P. (2012). Increasing the number of irrelevant stimuli increases ability to detect countermeasures to the P300-based complex trial protocol for concealed information detection. *Psychophysiology, 49,* 85–95.

Hughes, J. (2001, November 5). Illinois high school uses lie detectors to get to the bottom of a drinking scandal. Associated Press.

Iacono, W.G., & Patrick, C.J. (1988). Assessing deception: Polygraph techniques. In Rogers, R. (Ed.), *Clinical assessment of malingering and deception* (pp. 205–233). New York: Guilford.

Johnson, M.K., & Raye, C.L. (1981). Reality monitoring. *Psychological Bulletin, 88,* 67–85.

Kassin, S.M., Dror, I.E., & Kukucka, J. (2013). The forensic confirmation bias: Problems, perspectives, and proposed solutions. *Journal of Applied Research in Memory and Cognition, 2,* 42–52.

Kelly, J. (2004). The truth about the lie detector. *Invention and Technology, 19,* 14–20.

Kleinmuntz, B., & Szucko, J.J. (1984a). Lie detection in ancient and modern times: A call for contemporary scientific study. *American Psychologist, 39,* 766–776.

Kleinmuntz, B., & Szucko, J.J. (1984b). A field study of the fallibility of polygraphic lie detection. *Nature, 308,* 449–450.

Köhnken, G. (2004). Statement validity analysis and the 'detection of the truth.' In P. A. Granhag & L.A. Strömwall (Eds.), *The detection of deception in forensic contexts* (pp. 41–63). New York: Cambridge University Press.

Konnikova, M. (2015, May 22). How a gay-marriage study went wrong. *The New Yorker.* Retrieved from http://www.newyorker.com/science/maria-konnikova/how-a-gay-marriage-study-went-wrong.

Kozel, F.A., Johnson, K.A., Mu, Q., Grenesko, E.L., Laken, S.J., & George, M.S. (2005). Detecting deception using functional magnetic resonance imaging. *Biological Psychiatry, 58,* 605–613.

Kozel, F.A., Padgett, T.M., & George, M.S. (2004b). A replication of the neural correlates of deception. *Behavioral Neuroscience, 118,* 852–856.

Kozel, F.A., Revell, L.J., Lorberbaum, J.P., Shastri, A., Elhai, J.D., Horner, M.D., Smith, A., Nahas, Z., Bohning, D.E., & George, M.S. (2004a). A pilot study of functional magnetic resonance imaging brain correlates of deception in healthy young men. *Journal of Neuropsychiatry and Clinical Neurosciences, 16,* 295–305.

Langleben, D.D., Schroeder, L., Maldjian, J.A., Gur, R.C., McDonald, S., Rangland, J.D., O'Brien, C.P., & Childress, A.R. (2002). Brain activity during simulated deception: An event-related functional magnetic resonance study. *NeuroImage, 15,* 727–732.

Lee, T.M.C., Liu, H.L., Tan, L.H., Chan, C.C.H., Mahankali, S., Feng, C.M., Hou, J., Fox, P.T., & Gao, J.H. (2002). Lie detection by functional magnetic resonance imaging. *Human Brain Mapping, 15,* 157–164.

Lindsey v. United States, 237 F .2nd 893, 896 (9th Cir. 1956).

Lu, H., et al. (2012). StressSense: Detecting stress in unconstrained acoustic environments using smartphones. *In Proceedings of the 2012 ACM conference on ubiquitous computing,* 351–360.

Lykken, D.T. (1998). *A tremor in the blood: Uses and abuses of the lie detector.* New York: Plenum.

Marshall, D., & Thomas, T. (2015). Polygraphs and sex offenders: The truth is out there. *Probation Journal, 62,* 128–139.

McClish, M. (2008). *I know you are lying* (7th ed.). Winterville, NC: PoliceEmployment.com.

Mikkelson, B. (2011). Next case on the court colander. Retrieved from http://www.snopes.com/legal/colander.asp

Miner, J.B., & Capps, M.N. (1996). *How honesty testing works.* Westport, CT.: Quorum.

O'Bannon, R.M., Goldinger, L., & Appleby, G.S. (1989). *Honesty and integrity testing: A practical guide.* Atlanta, GA: Applied Information Resources.

Ones, D.S., Viswesvaran, C., & Schmidt, F.L. (1993). Comprehensive meta-analysis of integrity test validities: Findings and implications for personnel selection and theories of job performance. *Journal of Applied Psychology, 78,* 679–703.

Ott, M., Cardie, C., & Hancock, J. (2012). Estimating the prevalence of deception in online review communities. *In Proceedings of the 21st international conference on World Wide Web* (pp. 201–210). ACM.

Pasricha, T., Sallam, H., Chen, J., & Pasricha, P.J. (2008). The moment of truth: stress, lying and the GI tract. *Expert Review, Gastroenterol Hepatol, 2,* 291–293.

Pavlidis, I., Eberhardt, N.L., & Levine, J. (2002). Human behavior: Seeing through the face of deception. *Nature, 415,* 35.

Pennebaker, J.W. (2011). *The secret life of pronouns: What our words say about us.* New York: Bloomsbury Press.

Pennebaker, J.W., Booth, R.J., & Francis, M.E. (2007). Linguistic Inquiry and Word Count (LIWC 2001). Austin, Texas: Liwc.net.

Phan, K.L., Magalhaes, A., Ziemlewicz, T.J., Fitzgerald, D.A., Green, C., & Smith, W. (2005). Neural correlates of telling lies: A functional magnetic resonance imaging study at 4 Tesla. *Academic Radiology, 12,* 164–172.

Porter, S., & Yuille, J.C. (1996). The language of deceit: An investigation of the verbal clues to deception in the interrogation context. *Law and Human Behavior, 20,* 443–457.

Prelec, D. (2004). A Bayesian truth serum for subjective data. *Science, 306,* 462–466.

Raskin, D.C., Kircher, J.C., Horowitz, W.W., & Honts, C.R. (1989). Recent laboratory and field research on polygraph techniques. In J.C. Yuille (Ed.), *Credibility assessment* (pp. 1–24). Dordrecht: Kluwer Academic Publishers.

Ritter, M. (January 29, 2006). Brain scans may be used as lie detectors. *Associated Press.*

Roese, N.J., & Jamieson, D.W. (1993). Twenty years of bogus pipeline research: A critical review and meta-analysis. *Psychological Bulletin, 114,* 363–375.

Rogers, R., & Wettstein, R.M. (1988). Drug-assisted interviews to detect malingering and deception. In Rogers, R. (Ed.), *Clinical assessment of malingering and deception* (pp. 105–204). New York: Guilford.

Rosenfeld, J.P., Hu, X., & Pederson, K. (2012). Deception awareness improves P300-based deception detection in concealed information tests. *International Journal of Psychophysiology, 86,* 114–121.

Rosenfeld, J.P., Soskins, M., Bosh, G., & Ryan, A. (2004). Simple, effective countermeasures to P300-based tests of detection of concealed information. *Psychophysiology, 41,* 205–219.

Rusconi, E., & Mitchener-Nissen, T. (2013). Prospects of functional magnetic resonance imaging as lie detector. *Frontiers in Human Neuroscience, 7.*

Sackett, P.R., Burris, L.R., & Callahan, C. (1989). Integrity testing for personnel selection: An update. *Personnel Psychology, 42,* 491–529.

Saini, H.K. (2012). Detecting fake Facebook profiles. *CSI Communications, 24.*

Sapir, A. (1987). *The LSI course on scientific content analysis* (SCAN). Phoenix, AZ: Laboratory for Scientific Interrogation.

Saxe, L. (1994). Detection of deception: Polygraph and integrity tests. *Current Directions in Psychological Science, 3,* 69–73.

Shearer, R.A. (1999). Statement analysis: SCAN or scam? *Skeptical Inquirer, 23,* 40–43.

Spence, S.A., Farrow, T.F., Herford, A.E., Wilkinson, I.D., Zheng, Y., & Woodruff, P. W. (2001). Behavioral and functional anatomical correlates of deception in humans. *Neuroreport, 12,* 2849–2853.

Sporer, L.S. (2004). Reality monitoring and detection of deception. In P.A. Granhag & L.A. Strömwall (Eds.), *The detection of deception in forensic contexts* (pp. 64–102). New York: Cambridge University Press.

Sullivan, E. (2001). *The concise book of lying.* New York: Farrar, Straus & Giroux.

Talbot, M. (2007, July 2) Duped. *The New Yorker,* 52–61.

ten Brinke, L., Stimson, D., & Carney, D.R. (2014). Some evidence for unconscious lie detection. *Psychological Science, 25,* 1098–1105.

Townsend v. Sain, 327 U.S. 293 (U.S. Supreme Court, 1963).

Twyman, N.W., Elkins, A.C., Burgoon, J.K., & Nunamaker, J.F. (2014). A rigidity detection system for automated credibility assessment. *Journal of Management Information Systems, 31,* 173–202.

Undeutsch, U. (1982). Statement reality analysis. In A. Trankell (Ed.), *Reconstructing the past: The role of psychologists in criminal trials* (pp. 27–56). Deventer, The Netherlands: Kluwer.

United States v. Scheffer, 523 US 303 (1998).

U.S. Congress, Office of Technology Assessment. (1990). *The use of integrity tests for pre-employment screening* (OTA-SET-442). Washington, DC: U.S. Government Printing Office.

U.S. General Accounting Office (2001). *Investigative techniques federal agency views on the potential application of "brain fingerprinting".* Washington, DC: U.S. Government Printing Office.

Van Iddekinge, C.H., Roth, P.L., Raymark, P.H., & Odle-Dusseau, H.N. (2012). The criterion-related validity of integrity tests: An updated meta-analysis. *Journal of Applied Psychology, 97,* 499–530.

Vrij, A. (2000). *Detecting lies and deceit: The psychology of lying and the implications for professional practice.* New York: Wiley.

Vrij, A. (2015). Verbal lie detection tools: Statement Validity Analysis, Reality Monitoring and Scientific Content Analysis. In P.A. Granhag, A. Vrij, B. Verschuere (Eds.), *Detecting deception: Current challenges and cognitive approaches* (pp. 3–36). West Sussex, UK: Wiley & Sons.

Waid, W.M., Orne, E.C., Cook, M.R., & Orne, M.T. (1981). Meprobamate reduces accuracy of physiological detection of deception. *Science, 212,* 71–73.

Willing, R. (2003, November 5). The truth lies in technology. *USA Today,* pp. D1–2.

Zelicoff, A.P. (2002, August 9). Polygraph hypocrisy. *Washington Post,* p. A23.

Part IV

Lying and Deception for the Masses

The context for lying and deception in these final three chapters of the book is the public arena. Chapter 11 focuses primarily on spoken messages delivered by political leaders to mass audiences and addresses the differences between public and face-to-face lies. How much honesty do people really want from their leaders and how much deception are they willing to tolerate? In Chapter 12 we turn our attention to written messages that reach the masses, examining lying and deception by journalists, historians, and others. Chapter 13 is devoted to the deceptive nature of visual messages seen by the public and delivered over the Internet, via social media, and in movies, television shows, advertising, and the news.

Chapter 11

Speaking to the Public: Lies and Political Leadership

The preceding chapters have portrayed lying and deception largely within the context of interpersonal communication. But falsehoods and fabrications also take place on a grander scale, involving groups, organizations, communities, and nations. The following chapters, then, take a look at mendacity for the masses. Understanding the nature of fabrications that take place between political leaders and the American public is the primary focus of this chapter.

Public lies are not an entirely distinct species. They have some characteristics in common with interpersonal lies. For example, the reasons for lying are not all that different even though the language may be—e.g., "I didn't tell you in order to protect our marriage" vs. "Withholding that information from the public is in the interest of national security." Self deception is another quality found in both interpersonal and public acts of deception. The need for makers of a failed public policy to convince themselves that their policy is sound is not all that different from what a spouse may do in response to a failing marriage. The types of lies in both public and interpersonal spheres range from relatively unimportant (low stakes) to serious (high stakes). Messages designed for public consumption, like those targeted at a specific other person, may also use linguistic constructions that leave the question of intentional deceit ambiguous. We identified these as the blood relatives of deception in Chapter 7. The mutual influence of liar and target is also a feature that interpersonal and public lies share. By the expectations they espouse and their response to deceptive messages, the public exerts an influence on the construction of messages directed its way by leaders; similarly, leaders influence public responses by the way they choose to publicly communicate.

"The political arena is second only to warfare as a domain where lies are expected, do in fact occur, and to a substantial extent are tolerated."

— J. A. Barnes

"Political language...is designed to make lies sound truthful and murder respectable, and to give an appearance of solidity to pure wind."

— George Orwell

"To know how to disguise is the knowledge of kings."

— *Cardinal Richelieu*

Despite these and other similarities with the manifestation of deception in interpersonal contexts, public lies are also distinguished by certain characteristics that comprise its unique identity.

Special Characteristics of Public Lies

The special nature of public lies can be understood by examining a few distinguishing features: 1) the target audience; 2) information control; 3) message distribution and responsibility; and 4) detection responsibility.

Adapting to Multiple Audiences

The target of public lies sounds like a single entity, *the* public, but *the* public is comprised of many audiences, each with its own needs and goals. In a democracy, a leader needs as many votes from each of these audiences as possible in order to be elected—and stay elected. How does a person, whose own beliefs are bound to be at odds with some of the audiences whose support he or she needs, communicate in order to gain widespread support? One approach is to invoke abstract national and/or cultural ideals to which virtually every audience subscribes. But this does not address any specific issues of interest and each audience eventually wants to know what the prospective leader will do for them—specifically. Some audiences hire lobbyists whose job is to persuade politicians that in order to serve their own interests, they will need to serve the interests of the audience they represent. Inevitably, groups with incompatible interests seek favor from the same politician. At the same time, however, it is important that the politician's positions are consistent as reported in the media.

In an effort to gain the votes of audiences with contrary views, the temptation may be great for a leader to act as if he or she supports goals and positions that he or she does not. Put another way, deception can be a useful mechanism for mobilizing various sources of power needed by the politician. But Rue (1994, p. 215) cautions that the process of building social coherence [the confluence of interests] through deception "… is achievable only within certain optimal limits of deception. That is, if there is too little or too much of it, then the social order will break down."

Information Control

The perpetrators of public lies are likely to have a lot more access to and control over information relevant to the fabrication than do the public targets of their lies. Leaders realize that their ability to create and access information is a crucial factor in maintaining power. Sometimes pertinent information can be made even less accessible to the public when a deceiver classifies it for national security reasons. In addition, individuals and/or groups loyal to the public liar may receive and use relevant information (true or false) that is not provided to other public groups.

Public lies may also be shaped and structured in elaborate ways, using a variety of resources at the command of the leader. The goal is to influence when an issue is discussed and how the public should think about it. When he was a presidential candidate, Richard Nixon was televised while he pretended to be taking phone calls from the public.

> *In reality he was giving carefully rehearsed answers to questions prepared by his staff. When a voter asked a question on the telephone, Nixon's staff simply reworded it in the form of a prepared question, attributed the question to the voter, and allowed Nixon to recite his prepared answer. And Nixon and his supporters continued to stage such events throughout his presidency (Pratkanis & Aronson, 2000, p. 140).*

Access and control of information also allows presidents to falsely report or interpret events so that they fit a predetermined policy. During the presidential campaign of 1964, Lyndon Johnson repeatedly stated that he would not escalate the war in Vietnam by bombing North Vietnam even though the Pentagon Papers later revealed that plans for bombing were being discussed while he was making these public assurances. Johnson's opponent for the presidency labeled his position on bombing as "soft" and Johnson was eager to counter that perception. The Tonkin Gulf incident provided that opportunity. On August 2nd, 1964 three North Vietnamese PT boats closed rapidly on two U.S. destroyers in the Tonkin Gulf. One of the destroyers fired first and one machine gun bullet from the PT boats struck one destroyer. No one was injured. Two nights later on August 4th, a sonar operator reported a "continuous torpedo attack" resulting in the destroyers firing for four hours at nothing. This series of events was interpreted by Johnson and his Secretary of Defense, Robert McNamara, as a vicious attack on American troops and justification for escalating the war by bombing North Vietnam. Wise (1973, p. 28) says:

> *The public... had to rely entirely on Lyndon Johnson and Robert McNamara for their news of the incident...In short, in the crucial field of national security, the government controls almost all the important channels of information. And where government controls the channels of information, there is a greater possibility that information will be distorted. In the foreign policy area, therefore, the potential for government lying is high.*

Almost 40 years after the Tonkin Gulf incident, retired Secretary McNamara confirmed Wise's point by finally admitting what many journalists and critics of the Johnson administration had expected all along. In an interview for the documentary *The Fog of War* (Morris, 2003), he acknowledged the alleged August 4th attack on U.S. destroyers never happened. With Johnson's approval, McNamara fabricated the story as a pretense for escalating the war against North Vietnam.

Two of the primary justifications George W. Bush gave the American public for the invasion of Iraq in 2003 were that: 1) Iraq had weapons of mass destruction and planned to use them against the U.S.; and 2) Iraq was working with the terrorist organization Al Qaeda. The evidence supporting these claims was severely lacking and some key information known to Bush that countered his claims was not revealed by Bush to the American public. A key Iraqi defector reported the destruction of Iraq's weapons of mass destruction and inspectors from the United Nations were unable to locate any. Bush said that a report from the International Atomic Energy Agency proved Iraq was developing nuclear weapons, but the chief spokesman for the IAEA said, "There's never been a report like that issued from this agency" (Rampton & Stauber, 2003, p.87). The IAEA also countered Bush's claim that aluminum tubes purchased by Iraq were suited to enrich uranium for nuclear weapons. In addition, the unmanned aircraft for delivery of these weapons were not capable, as Bush claimed, of reaching the U.S. And the documents Bush cited as "proving" that Iraq was attempting to buy 500 tons of uranium from Niger were previously identified as fake by the CIA, IAEA, and a team of forensic experts. The Iraq-Al Qaeda connection was primarily based on a claim that one of the 9/11 hijackers had met with an Iraqi in the Czech Republic. After an extensive investigation, the FBI determined that the hijacker was in Virginia at the time of the supposed meeting. After a Czech investigation, the president of the Czech Republic told President Bush the story was false, but it continued to circulate unchecked in the U.S. media and the words Iraq and Al Qaeda were repeatedly linked in messages from the Bush administration to the public. In short, the Bush administration possessed information that was contrary to their primary claims for going to war with Iraq, but they did not accept it and selectively controlled the information output to the American public.

Barack Obama surged from his status as an idealistic but inexperienced first-term Illinois senator to winning the Presidency by promising a new era of "hope and change." This slogan was aimed specifically at the outgoing Bush administration, whose credibility with the American public deteriorated after revelations about the false pretenses for the invasion of Iraq, its botched response to Hurricane Katrina, and its reluctance to police Wall Street, which fueled the 2008 economic meltdown. During the course of his first presidential campaign, Obama pledged among other things to comprehensively reform America's healthcare system, in a way that would "bend the cost curve downward" while expanding insurance coverage to all Americans. When Republican opponents countered that federal control of the health insurance market would create higher costs and push millions of Americans out of their current plans, Obama reassured voters that "if you like your plan, you can keep your plan." He continued to make this promise repeatedly after being elected, through the legislative fight to pass the Affordable Care Act of 2010, and during the 2012 campaign when Republican rival Mitt Romney warned voters that insurers might have to cancel many plans. Obama's promise was exposed as false in 2013, when insurers canceled millions of individual-market health insurance policies to replace them with ACA-compliant plans. Although some in the administration argued Obama's promise was based on "incomplete data" (resembling the "faulty intelligence" excuse Bush claimed as the impetus for invading Iraq), it came to light that officials from the Department of Health and Human Services had provided the president with a report in 2010 explicitly stating it was unlikely his promise could be kept. White House officials reportedly put the "sensitive" report on "lockdown" until after the 2012 election (Griffin & Frates, 2013).

Leaders may have legitimate reasons for not revealing certain sources of information, but saying their sources are classified or "sensitive" is also a strategy used by leaders who do not want their claims to be closely scrutinized. So, as Wise (1973, p. 345) points out, "One of the most damaging aspects of government lying is that even if the truth later emerges, it seldom does so in time to influence public opinion or public policy."

Message Distribution and Responsibility

Presidents and other leaders in today's world do not have to deliver their own deceptive messages. They have plenty of team members and supporters who assume this responsibility—sometimes with and sometimes without explicit instructions from their leader. This is why a leader's accountability for deception is often difficult to prove. The following exchange before a U.S. Senate investigating committee shows how John Poindexter, President Reagan's National Security Advisor, wanted to communicate in such a way that his boss could always deny knowing that the U.S. was selling arms to an enemy (Iran) and giving the money from the sales to a guerilla group in Nicaragua (Barnes, 1994, p. 112).

> Poindexter: I made a very deliberate decision not to ask the President so that I could insulate him from the decision and provide some future deniability for the President if it ever leaked out.

> Question: And when you say "deniability", are you saying that your decision was not to tell the President so that he would be able to deny that he knew of it?

> Poindexter: That's correct.

This process is called *plausible deniability* (Walton, 1996).

Normally, the President provides a general framework for his or her policies and goals to close associates. But even if this message is explicit, the president's accountability for it may be protected by the many people involved in carrying out his or her instructions. The actions on behalf of the president by cabinet members, other government agencies, public relations firms, and political supporters often buffer his or her responsibility for deceptive intent. Nevertheless, deception does occur when government sources try to manipulate information that is disseminated to the public. This can occur in a variety of ways but usually involves attempts to influence news reports. Three common strategies are: 1)event staging, 2) pseudo-events, and 3) planting prepackaged and unidentified news reports with the news media.

Staged Events

Both major political parties have created props, planted audience questions, scripted the President's behavior, and in other ways staged press releases and other political events to ensure they cast an impression of a President who is positive, confident, and in control. But in 2005, a satellite television feed accidentally captured these preparations for a reportedly spontaneous "give and take" video-conference President Bush scheduled with American troops in Iraq. It was billed as a chance for the President to hear directly from the troops and White House reporters were summoned to witness the event. The participating soldiers were hand picked and coached for 45 minutes prior to the interaction on what questions the President would ask, what answers they should give, and how best to express their answers. Even with the preparation, there were awkward moments when the answers didn't match the questions. At first, the existence of any rehearsal was denied by the White House and Pentagon. Later a White House spokesman said the briefing was done in order to make the soldiers feel at ease.

Pseudo-Events

A "pseudo-event" is an event that occurs solely for the purpose of generating media and public attention. The term was coined by historian Daniel Boorstin (1992) to describe a tactic perfected by Edward Bernays, who founded the field of public relations and also happened to be a nephew of psychoanalysis pioneer Sigmund Freud. A crucial element of Bernays' strategy was to create pseudo-events which on their surface appeared to have a purpose different from their true goal. For example, consider a famous pseudo-event Bernays created in 1929 during the Easter Parade in New York City. A group of well-dressed women led by Bertha Hunt started a scandal by walking into a crowded Fifth Avenue during the height of the parade and lighting up cigarettes. At the time, smoking tobacco was chiefly a habit for men in the United States. Women who smoked were stigmatized as being "of low character" and occasionally arrested for engaging in what most people thought should be a strictly male activity (Segrave, 2005). Bernays informed several newspapers in advance that this "protest act" was going to happen, saying the women were smoking in a public place to display their "liberation" from outdated sexist mores. And that's how the press covered it—the *New York Times* ran a story about it titled "Group of Girls Puff at Cigarettes as a Gesture of Freedom" (Tye, 1998). Coverage of what came to be known as the "Torches of Freedom March" quickly spread to newspapers across the country. In truth, the women were not smoking in public as a protest. Bertha Hunt (Bernays' secretary) and several of her friends had been paid to do it by George Washington Hill, President of the American Tobacco Company. Hill was an opportunist, not a feminist. "If I can crack the women's market, it will be like opening a new gold mine right in our front yard," he told Bernays (Brandt, 2009, p. 82). Public attention to the "march" made Hill's wish come true—women's use of tobacco in public increased dramatically across the country. The impact of this pseudo-event on women's smoking stems in part from its masquerade as something other than an ad campaign; previous campaigns that explicitly encouraged women to buy cigarettes had failed miserably (Segrave, 2005).

This tactic has been used by several presidential administrations to manage public relations. The aforementioned second Tonkin Gulf attack on U.S. ships claimed by the Johnson Administration could be counted as a pseudo-event, although technically there was no "event" in the first place. A more canonical but equally deceptive example occurred during the George H.W. Bush Administration in 1990. A 15-year old Kuwaiti girl identified only as Nayirah appeared before the "Congressional Human Rights Caucus" in Washington, DC to describe war atrocities she witnessed when her country was invaded months earlier by Iraqi troops led by President Saddam Hussein. Her oral testimony lasted only 4 minutes, but received extensive news coverage that shocked the American public. Nayirah claimed to have been present when Iraqi soldiers forced their way into a hospital in Kuwaiti City and burst into the nursery where she worked as a volunteer. She reported watching in horror as the soldiers "took the babies out of incubators, took the incubators, and left the children to die on the cold floor. It was horrifying." President Bush quoted Nayirah's testimony numerous times in the weeks that followed as he made a case to the American public for why the U.S. should intervene. Public sentiment toward getting involved in the "crisis in the Persian Gulf" was initially quite negative, but Americans gradually came to accept Bush's case, thanks in part to Nayirah's heart-wrenching testimony. But 2 years after the U.S. entered the mercifully brief "Gulf War," it came to light that Nayirah's account was a complete fabrication. She had not observed soldiers entering the hospital, nor had she ever volunteered in the hospital, nor was she even in Kuwait during the Iraqi occupation. At the time, she was attending a private boarding school in Maryland, a privilege she enjoyed as the daughter of the Kuwaiti Ambassador to the U.S. And despite its official sounding title, the "caucus" she testified before was not technically a government-sponsored event, but a publicity stunt created by the PR firm Hill & Knowlton with funding from the Kuwaiti government and quiet encouragement from the Bush Administration (MacArthur, 1992).

Prepackaged News

In 1983, Jamieson and Campbell made an observation that might easily have been made yesterday: "There is considerable evidence of the power of government to manipulate press coverage. Government agencies spend huge sums of money to disseminate their messages through the mass media" (p. 103). This can be done through news "leaks" or newspaper editorials, but an increasingly popular method is the video news release (VNR). These professionally produced video segments are designed to present a particular point of view while appearing to be just another tv news story produced by a tv network or local station.

> *"Thank you, Bush. Thank you, U.S.A.," a jubilant Iraqi-American told a camera crew in Kansas City for a segment about reaction to the fall of Bagdad. A second report told of "another success" in the Bush administration's "drive to strengthen aviation security"; the reporter called it "one of the most remarkable campaigns in aviation history." A third segment, broadcast in January, described the administration's determination to open markets for American farmers. To a viewer, each report looked like any other 90-second segment on the local news. In fact, the federal government produced all three. The report from Kansas City was made by the State Department. The "reporter" covering airport safety was actually a public relations professional working under a false name for the transportation Security Administration. The farming segment was done by the Agriculture Department's office of communications (Barstow & Stein, 2005).*

VNRs frequently feature scripted questions in interviews with senior administration officials who give rehearsed answers. The reporters behave as they do in any other news story. When television stations insert these prepackaged government news stories into their newscasts, they save the time and cost of developing a story to fill that time. They may be produced by public relations firms hired by federal agencies even though some federal agencies produce their own. Thousands of VNRs are distributed and many are broadcast—some without acknowledgement of the government's role in their production (Barstow & Stein, 2005; Nelson & Park, 2014). When the source is not identified, the producers of VNRs hold the local stations responsible for deceiving the public.

Despite the fact that many messages from leaders emanate from sources other than their own mouth, presidential candidates and presidents do speak directly to the public on occasion—e.g., presidential debates, press conferences, and formal televised speeches. But rehearsals and scripting of behavior are very much at play in these appearances, so the behaviors typically associated with liars in more spontaneous contexts (see Chapter 7) may not be useful indicators of deception. When leaders have such a high degree of control over the dissemination and delivery of their messages, the methods of deception detection need to be adapted accordingly.

Detection Responsibility

When a leader communicates a deceptive message to the public, he or she has the advantage of special access to and control over information relevant to the issue. In addition, the question of whether the leader initiated the deceptive message can be hidden in a complex network of people and organizations who distribute the message. However, the sheer number of possible lie detectors representing the public interest can offset these advantages. Broadcast and print reporters, bloggers, whistleblowers, and special interest organizations are some of those who take on the responsibility for detecting deceptive public messages. The Annenberg School of Communication at the University of Pennsylvania maintains FactCheck, a system that monitors the factual accuracy of claims made by politicians in tv ads, debates, speeches, interviews, and news releases. PR Watch, a project of the Center for Media and Democracy, specifically focuses on deceptive and misleading public relations campaigns. The quantity and diversity of these lie detectors means that there may be differing views on what is deceptive, the seriousness of the deception, and the source of the deception. But it is the public participation in and discussion of these issues that enables consensus if it is to be.

One thing is clear. The public is responsible for detecting lies directed its way. Some states have laws against political lying, but they are ineffective because: 1) they often conflict with the First Amendment right to free speech; 2) they require proof the lie was done knowingly and with malice; and 3) they often cannot be enforced quickly enough in political campaigns to offset any damaging effects the lie may have had. Ohio Governor Bob Taft was found guilty of violating Ohio's law against making false statements by a bipartisan elections commission. He received a letter of reprimand and went on to become governor (Jackson, 2004).

In 1997, voters in the state of Washington were asked to consider implementing physician-assisted suicide. Opponents of the initiative distributed a leaflet that said, in part, that this proposal would "let doctors end patients' lives without benefit of safeguards" and a person with "no special qualifications" could terminate a life, including "your eye doctor." The State brought suit against the opponents of initiative 119, saying they had violated a state law against making false statements in political advertising. In a 5–4 vote, the Washington State Supreme Court argued that the responsibility for determining the truth or falsity of political speech did not rest with the State, but with the people. In their words:

> The very purpose of the First Amendment is to foreclose public authority from assuming a guardianship of the public mind...In this field every person must be his own watchman for truth, because the forefathers did not trust any government to separate the true from the false for us...In political campaigns the grossest misstatements, deceptions, and defamations are immune from legal sanction unless they violate private rights—that is, unless individuals are defamed...It assumes the people of this state are too ignorant or disinterested to investigate, learn, and determine for themselves the truth or falsity in political debate, and it is the proper role of the government itself to fill the void. This assumption is especially flawed in cases like this where the truth of the assertion may be readily tested against the text of the initiative (State of Washing v. 119 Vote No! Comm, 1998).

To What Extent Does the Public Want Honesty from Their Political Leaders?

The answer to this question is more complicated than one might think. On one hand, the American public does not maintain a high level of trust in the truthfulness of political and governmental leaders. The public is aware of many lies perpetrated by elected officials. As a result, the public regularly calls for its leaders and prospective leaders to exhibit greater honesty. At the same time, however, many don't expect leaders will ever exhibit the high level of honesty often called for. There may be an undercurrent of understanding that a certain amount and kind of deception is a necessary part of a leader's behavior. In addition, it is clear that the public doesn't always want to hear the truth. On several occasions, they have cast their presidential votes for the candidate they felt was more dishonest and voted against candidates who were explicitly forthright. And given the quantity of leader behavior that is or might be deceptive, leaders are held accountable for relatively few falsehoods and punished for even fewer. In short, the public says they want more honesty from their leaders, but they don't expect or want them to be totally honest.

Diminishing Trust and the Demand for Truth

Even though all U.S. presidents have probably lied to the American public, Bok (1978, p. 142) believes that in 1960 when President Eisenhower lied about sending planes to spy on the Soviet Union, "it was one of the crucial turning points in the spiraling loss of confidence by U.S. citizens in the word of their leaders." Shortly thereafter, lies told to the American public about the conduct of the Vietnam War were revealed in the Pentagon Papers and President Nixon resigned after it was discovered he authorized and lied about a burglary of the Democratic Party's national headquarters. As a result, Bok (1978, p. xviii) cites a 1975/76 Cambridge Survey Research poll of adult Americans that found 69% agreeing that "over the last ten years, this country's leaders have consistently lied to the people."

The passage of time has done little to change the public trust in its leaders. An October, 1992 Time/CNN poll found 63% of the respondents saying they had little confidence that government leaders talk straight and 75% believed there was less honesty in government in 1992 than there was in 1982. Nearly 40% said neither of the 1992 candidates for President (Bush and Clinton) usually told the truth. Gallup polls conducted over the last 40 years show a scalloped but overall consistent decline in American's trust of all three branches of the federal government (see Figure 11.1).

Figures represent the percentage with a "great deal" or "fair amount" of trust in the branch.

Copyright © 2013 Gallup, Inc. All rights reserved. The content is used with permission; however, Gallup retains all rights of republication.

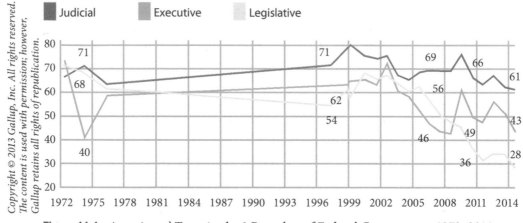

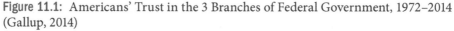

Figure 11.1: Americans' Trust in the 3 Branches of Federal Government, 1972–2014 (Gallup, 2014)

A familiar charge by public deception detectors is that presidential candidates do not keep their campaign promises after they are elected. However, Fishel (1985) examined concrete promises by Presidents Kennedy, Johnson, Nixon, Carter, and Reagan and found serious, good faith efforts to keep roughly two-thirds of their promises. A study of Clinton's promises comes to the same conclusion (Jamieson, 2000, p. 33, 249). The problem, of course, is that there is little or no effort devoted to about 33% of their promises and some important promises are not kept despite a president's best efforts to do so. Furthermore, the public is not likely to remember many promises that are kept when one or more of special significance are not— e.g., keeping the country out of war, ending a war, reducing the deficit, balancing the budget, providing adequate medical care, etc. People may not remember the promises Barack Obama has kept, but many will remember losing health insurance plans they liked after he said "if you like your plan, you can keep your plan."

The Consequences of Distrust

The negative fallout from this distrust is cynicism and a sense of helplessness within the public. Voters may find it hard to punish a candidate for deceptive behavior when both candidates appear to be deceptive. Some don't vote; others express their cynicism in banter like this: "How can you tell when a politician is lying?" "When the politician opens his or her mouth." The public's sense of futility in the face of lying leaders was ironically captured nicely by President Nixon, who reportedly had no compunction about lying to anyone—the press, the public, or his closest staff members (Gergen, 2000; Reeves, 2001):

> *...when information which properly belongs to the public is systematically withheld by those in power, the people soon become ignorant of their own affairs, distrustful of those who manage them, and—eventually—incapable of determining their own destinies (Wise, 1973, p. 339).*

A healthy society could not exist if no one ever trusted what politicians say. But a certain level of distrust may actually be functional in a democratic society. Barnes (1994, p. 33) put it this way:

> *Luckily in a democracy no-one can believe everything said by all politicians, for what one politician says is likely to be contradicted by another. Thus one argument in favour of democracy is that it prompts us to treat all statements by politicians with caution (p. 33). The combined requirements of success in conflict and leadership put a premium on the exercise of deceit, a premium whose existence is recognized, luckily by many but unfortunately not all, of the intended dupes. This recognition provides at least a partial curb on the chances for successful deception. How great a curbing effect it has varies with the openness of the society concerned (p. 35).*

Wariness, however, is usually not sufficient and it is usually accompanied by a public outcry for greater honesty. In 1987, 72% of those polled said the President should *never* lie to the American pubic and 59% said he or she should *never* lie to a foreign government (*U.S. News & World Report*). Not as many of today's savvy citizens are likely to subscribe to these extremes, but they still demand leaders with a greater sense of integrity and honesty. Or do they?

Tell Us the Truth, but Tell Us What We Want to Hear Too

Many political analysts agree that presidential candidate Walter Mondale made a mistake that severely damaged his campaign when he said he might have to increase taxes in order to deal with the growing national debt. Former Governor of California Gray Davis was roundly criticized as an alarmist by the citizens of his state when he said there was credible evidence that terrorists were planning to bomb certain bridges and nothing happened. Political truth tellers don't always fare well (Garcia, 2004; Keller, 2001). The public does not often respond favorably to a leader who dwells too long on the complexity of an issue; admits to being conflicted about his or her position; or confesses to being puzzled about how to solve a problem. Garrett and Penny (1998, p. 8) attribute this to the fact that "absolutism sells" so politicians seek to make complex issues deceptively simple and identify solutions as bipolar—either good or bad.

> *Absolutism is behind the good and evil caricatures that dominate American political debate. Special-interest groups spawn the absolute images that define our political debate. The politicians they*

influence parrot their absolutism, often leaving mainstream voters with a set of two equally unattractive options...Politicians and special interests make it easy for the media to tell complicated stories in a simple, melodramatic fashion. Almost every political issue that rises to national consciousness ends up being summarized as a matter of white hats fighting black hats."

Leaders who receive public support are not only expected to have answers, they should have feel-good answers. When the public responds in this way, it is sure to play an influential role in any deceptive, inconsistent, or ambiguous messages from their leaders. Boorstin (1992, p. 5) leaves little doubt about the role the public plays in structuring the messages it receives: "By harboring, nourishing, and ever enlarging our extravagant expectations we create the demand for the illusions with which we deceive ourselves. And which we pay others to make to deceive us." "Barnum's great discovery," Boorstin adds, "was not how easy it was to deceive the public, but rather how much the public enjoyed being deceived"(p. 209).

Does the Public Favor Dishonesty?

A month prior to the 1988 Presidential election and again in 1992, voters were asked by pollsters to rate the candidates' honesty on a scale of 1–10 with 10 being the most honest. In both years, the candidate who rated highest lost the election. In 1988, Bush won with a 6.4 rating while Dukakis had 6.9; in 1992, Clinton won with a 5.8 rating with Perot at 6.7 and Bush at 6.2. In 1996, 58% of those polled rated Dole having the most honesty and integrity, but Clinton was elected even though only 40% said he had the most honesty and integrity (Louis Harris Poll, 1988; Princeton Survey Research, 1992; and Gallup Poll, 1996). How can we explain the public's call for honest leaders with their election of candidates who are rated less honest?

The answer given by some political consultants is that likeability trumps perceptions of dishonesty. When politicians tell the public what they want to hear, make them feel comfortable, and demonstrate control of the situation, they become more likeable. Bailey (1988) says effective leaders engender a public trust that is based on something more akin to the kind of love you might have for a family member coupled with certain heroic virtues like courage, endurance, and a vision for the future. Once this kind of relationship has been achieved, it tends to diminish the desire for the close scrutiny and accounting of leader behavior. This might help to explain this comment made by Jonathan Chait (2006) of the *New Republic*. After noting several instances of deceptive behavior by Senator John McCain, he explained his preference for McCain as President: "I think McCain has a genuine desire to transform his party and his country, and he's willing to say things he doesn't agree with in order to be able to do it."

There may even be an unspoken public awareness that getting things done and effectively communicating are not always characteristic of the person who can always be counted on to be honest. Honesty, then, is a vital part of leadership, but leadership encompasses a great deal more than honesty alone.

Occasionally, public officials are held accountable for their lies—in court or at the ballot box. But the public typically does not hold leaders accountable for much of their deceptive behavior. This is particularly true when the leader is popular and the lives of the voting public are reasonably happy. But Jamieson (2000) points out that this is a perilous stance to take. Tolerance for deceptive discourse, she observes, makes the public a partner to the leader's deception, diminishes the value of the voter, and sets an inappropriate standard for those who govern.

Lying and Deception: The Leader's Perspective

Given the public's repeated call for honest political leaders, it is no surprise that politicians respond by saying they will be honest. Richard Nixon, one of our most deceptive Presidents, told Republican delegates in 1968, "Truth will become the hallmark of the Nixon administration." Following Nixon's Watergate scandal, President Carter told voters he would never lie to the American public. U.S. Senator John McCain dubbed his 2000 bid for the Republican presidential nomination "The Straight Talk Express." President Reagan frequently told a story about his confessing to a personal foul that referees missed in a high school football game to illustrate how telling the truth had been firmly instilled in him. However, the story was not true (Pfiffner, 2004, p. 30). If a leader believes that truth is a commodity that only one person can possess, this necessitates characterizing one's opponents as falling short in this area—charging that they distort information, change their position on an issue, etc.

Deception Plays a Role in the Political Process

Even as politicians trumpet their commitment to truth telling, they know that deception is also a part of the leader's communicative repertoire. In 2000, Senator McCain's "straight talk express" derailed in South Carolina when he lied about his true feelings concerning the flying of the Confederate flag over South Carolina's Capitol. The cause, he later said, was to keep from losing the South Carolina primary. Gearing up for a run at the Republican presidential nomination in 2008, McCain cultivates a friendship with televangelist Jerry Falwell whom he called an "evil influence on the Republican Party" a few short years ago. He also praises President Bush's leadership on the war on terror even though he has previously criticized many of Bush's decisions associated with it.

Politicians must make themselves and their accomplishments look good while undermining their opponents; members of their own party may require support they don't deserve; members of the opposition party may have to be cajoled in order to pass legislation; diverse groups of contributors and voters may want promises of future support; etc. Each of these circumstances may create difficult choices and deception is not an uncommon response. As Garrett and Penny

(1998, p. 2) observed: "If speaking the truth means losing the battle, political calculations often call for a lie." Rue (1994, p. 246) believes some deception is an integral part of the political process:

> It may be true, as Lincoln observed, that leaders cannot survive by deceit alone, but it is equally true that if social coherence is to be maintained, then leaders must fool some of the people some of the time...They have the impossible task of building and maintaining confluences of interests among diverse groups of diverse individuals. I am only arguing that they cannot succeed without deceit...If democracy were truly inconsistent with deception, then how does it come to pass, one wonders, that election campaigns are dominated by it? It comes to pass because the political system rewards it.

Leaders Are Likely to Be Skilled Deceivers

If politicians do decide to respond to certain situations with deceptive messages, they are likely to do so with considerable skill. This is particularly true for those at the top of the political food chain. They have the most experience. Deception is one manifestation of the many ways successful people manipulate their social environment. Being an effective communicator requires manipulation and may require deception in order to achieve a wide range of goals, including the establishment of reciprocal alliances, moving up in an organizational hierarchy, and acquiring resources (Buss et al., 1987, p. 1219). Deception, like truth telling (as I noted in Chapter 1), is a way of accomplishing things.

Keating and Heltman (1994) offered some direct support for the belief that male leaders can be good deceivers if they choose to be. First, males were videotaped lying and telling the truth about their opinion of a distasteful drink. The degree to which each man was thought to be acting truthfully was rated without hearing the words they spoke. Later, the men participated in a group decision-making project without an appointed leader. The men who emerged as leaders in the decision-making groups were also the men whose deceptive messages were rated as most truthful. This pattern was also observed with children, but not adult females.

The Political Downside of Deception

Even though political leaders may become skilled deceivers who learn to use lies to accomplish worthwhile (and not so worthwhile) goals, they always run the risk of suffering the negative consequences that can accompany this behavior. Negative consequences may take many different forms as Cliffe et al. (2000, p. 37–38, 41) point out:

> Political deceits are often counterproductive. Even when they are genuinely employed as a tactic to further a good end, they may rebound and have detrimental effects once they are discovered and brought to light. They may cause further lies to be necessary and lead to retaliation by opponents. Equally damaging is the cynicism, disrespect and distrust of politicians once deceptions are uncovered...Secrecy and deception offend against a citizens' right to know, which gives substance to the notion of democratic accountability,

and which is a condition for effective participation and a means of ensuring that government actions represent the interests of their citizens. Secrecy and lies break the conditions on which political power is checked and controlled.

Presidential lies are often judged by the consequences that accrue from them. Positive consequences stemming from a policy that involved lies by a president may render the lies less consequential; negative consequences, however, are likely to magnify the outrage over the lies. Alterman (2004), however, cites several cases in which presidential lies to Congress and the American public about matters of war and peace seemed to have had minor consequences in the short term, but had major negative consequences for American policies in the long run—e.g., how Roosevelt's lies about agreements he made with Stalin at the Yalta conference set in motion more than four decades of a "cold war" with the Soviet Union.

Negative consequences may also take the form of voter disapproval or the disintegration of the deceiver's character. The risk to the deceiver's character is greater as deception becomes a less conscious and habitual response. When lying becomes an easy response and any sanctions associated with it are far from the deceiver's mind, deception may lose the strategic value it may have had. The deceiver has put aside the public's right to know and thinks he or she is the best judge of what the public needs. The goal of serving others takes a permanent back seat to the deceiver's own political desires. And the deceiver's reality becomes distorted by a belief in his or her own lies, which may lead to a sense of invulnerability and righteousness. Bok (1978, p. 173) addresses the issue in this way:

> *As political leaders become accustomed to making such excuses, they grow insensitive to fairness and to veracity. Some come to believe that any lie can be told so long as they can convince themselves that people will be better off in the long run. From there, it is a short step to the conclusion that, even if people will not be better off from a particular lie, they will benefit by all maneuvers to keep the right people in office.*

The Blood Relatives of Deception Pay Another Visit

Without information bearing on a speaker's intention to deceive, we run the risk of attributing deceptive intent to those who have none. For example, Ekman (2000) points out that a broken promise is not a lie unless the promise-maker did not intend to keep it; a false account may occur because the speaker believed it to be true or was unaware of contrary information; an exaggeration may not have been intended to be taken literally. At the same time, however, there are some linguistic and message constructions that seem more likely to stir within us the possibility of deception.

In Chapter 7 we introduced the concept of deception's blood relatives. The idea is that there are some ways of constructing messages that increase the possibility that people will make attributions of deception—without any knowledge of the speaker's intent. Deceivers use these constructions, but they are also constructions that occur in everyday speech without any intention to mislead (Bavelas et al., 1990).

Imprecision, ambiguity, and indirectness are but a few examples. Without proof of deceptive intent, then, the most that can be said is that these messages sometimes accentuate a close kinship to deception. Because these constructions are closely associated with deception, the presence of any contextual indicators of deception (e.g., the situation calls for it or rewards it) will quickly lead to an attribution of deception. Deception's blood relatives, according to Rue (1994, p. 246), comprise a useful part of the political leader's communicative repertoire.

> *There are many honest and truthful ways to elicit positive responses from voters, but it has long been recognized that they are less effective than deceptive means. Exaggeration, distortion, quoting out of context, innuendo, false promises, pandering, scare tactics, and flat-out-lies have become the standard fare of political campaigns.*

The Blood Relatives' DNA

The way political speakers treat language, facts, and sources helps us understand why the blood relatives of deception bear such a close resemblance to deception itself. These constructions also help a speaker who is so inclined to deflect intent, responsibility, and previous knowledge.

Language

There are many ways to use language to deceive while simultaneously providing a reasonable defense against those who say deception has occurred. Some of these include: a) implying something but not asserting it; b) using abstract terminology to create ambiguity rather than clarity; c) being imprecise rather than precise; and d) addressing an issue indirectly rather than directly.

For example, a politician may *imply* action, if not policy, by saying: "Our cars should get better gas mileage and we should not be dependent on oil. We need to use more ethanol." On the other hand, no action or policy was asserted so the intent to mislead can be denied. When a politician knows his or her message will be heard by multiple audiences, he or she may use *abstract and/or coded terminology* like "family values" to communicate with supporters while denying that there was any intent to mislead other audiences (Fleming et al., 1990). Euphemisms are a way of *avoiding precise language* without admitting any intent to mislead—e.g., President Reagan's use of the phrase "tax reform" instead of "tax increase." Luntz (2007), a pollster for the Republican Party, advises candidates on the positive and negative power of certain words. He would have recommended "tax simplification" instead of "tax reform." To be positive, he advises, use "electronic intercepts" instead of "wiretapping;" "opportunity scholarships" instead of "vouchers;" "exploring for energy" instead of "digging for oil." "Prosperity" can be counted on to deliver a positive reaction, whereas labeling an opponent as a product of "Washington" is likely to produce a less positive one. *Indirect speech* may be tangential ("Did you smoke marijuana?" "I never broke the laws of my country.") or a non-sequitur ("How do you explain Bush's low approval ratings in the polls?" "Remember, these are only snapshots in time."). While these responses may be considered evasive and not the response preferred, labeling them as lies will be difficult to prove. Deceivers pay close attention to language and those who wish to expose them must listen carefully. When a politician says, "I have authorized more new law enforcement officers to ensure the safety of our citizens than the previous two administrations combined" a listener would do well to focus on the word "authorized." There is no indication whether this authorization was approved and authorization does not have anything to do with making citizens safe.

Facts

Attention to potentially deceptive messages may also be linked to the way a speaker uses facts. Attributions of half truths occur when listeners are aware of *pertinent omissions* and think they should have been included. Marro (1985) gives this example: "Question: Has the Assistant Secretary of State been invited to China? Answer: No. (Meaning: He will go to China as an adviser to the vice president. It is the vice president who has been invited. Therefore, I am not lying. Rationale: I have to say this because protocol requires that the Chinese must publicly extend the invitation.)" In some instances, the speaker can argue that the omission was not pertinent or that he or she was unaware of the information. When a speaker does intend to mislead his audience, it is safer if the audience is unaware of the omission—e.g., a politician who accuses his opponent of proposing 2.2 trillion dollars in new spending without also saying that his or her own proposal contains 2.5 trillion in new spending.

The use of *inaccurate facts* is often the basis for accusing a person of a deliberately misleading message. But the speaker may respond by saying he or she was only repeating information they were given or that it was what he or she believed to be true at the time it was said. Cannon (2007), for example, argues that President George W. Bush believed he told the truth and that any statements he made that turned out to be false were made with the belief that they were true. Critics, however, point out that his initial lack of diligence in seeking out and weighing a diversity of facts bearing on a decision and his subsequent refusal to admit factual errors can turn attributions of "mistakes" into "deception" and "self-deception."

Unique interpretations of facts may also be a part of the deceiver's communicative bag of tricks. His or her defense is that the interpretation is not deliberately deceptive, and merely his or her own perception. But efforts to mislead can be transparent if they run counter to popular belief and/or other known facts. President Clinton's special interpretations were viewed within the situational demands for lying and other factual information. He denied having an "affair" with Monica Lewinsky because he felt the term affair implied romance and that was not the case; he also denied having a "sexual relationship" with Lewinsky because he said he believed this phrase meant "intercourse," which was not part of their relationship. It was equally hard for Jim Oberweis in the 2006 Illinois GOP gubernatorial campaign to defend his interpretations when he ran ads with selected news stories written about his opponent but changed the headlines to reflect negatively on his opponent (FactCheck, 2006). Political candidates are notorious for interpreting the same data in very different ways. For example, in the 2004 Presidential campaign, Bush said Kerry voted over 350 times for higher taxes on the American people during his twenty year Senate career. The Bush campaign included votes Kerry cast to leave taxes unchanged (when Republicans proposed cuts) and also votes he cast in favor of tax cuts proposed by Democrats that Bush aides viewed as watered down (FactCheck, 2004).

Inconsistent statements legitimately occur when politicians face circumstances that alter their views. But incongruent position and policy statements may also be used deceptively. This can occur when audience support is sought by telling them what they want to hear, not what the politician believes. Thus, politicians often consider their own inconsistency as a modification of their position or a reversal, but their opponent's inconsistencies are "waffling," "indecisiveness," and "flip-flopping." If their language is carefully crafted or the inconsistency not well publicized, a politician may be able to argue that the seemingly inconsistent message is not inconsistent at all. If the inconsistency was not recorded, the politician may say he or she doesn't even remember having made the statement.

Finally, deceivers sometimes use *irrelevant facts* to bolster the case for their political position or to attack others. Consider the compelling and factual story of Sarah McKinley told by gun rights advocate Gayle Trotter during a U.S. Senate hearing on gun violence in 2013:

> *Home alone with her baby, Sarah McKinley called 911 when two violent intruders began to break down her front door. Before police could arrive and while Ms. McKinley was still on the phone with 911, these violent intruders broke down her door. One of the men had a foot-long hunting knife. As the intruders force their way into her home, Ms. McKinley fired her weapon, fatally wounding one of the violent attackers. The other fled.*

Trotter told this story to support her case for why senators should vote against renewing the U.S. Assault Weapons Ban of 1994, which had expired in 2004. Efforts to renew the ban began shortly after the 2012 tragedy at Sandy Hook Elementary School in Newtown, Connecticut, when Adam Lanza murdered 20 young students and 6 adult staff members with an assault weapon before turning it on himself (Barron, 2012). Trotter's purpose in relating the story was clear—guns may be used to harm innocent people, but innocent people can also use them to defend themselves when police are slow to respond to a call for help. However, the Remington 870 Express 12-gauge shotgun Ms. McKinley used to fend off her attackers did not count as an assault weapon under the proposed legislation and thus would not have been banned by it (Weiner, 2013). As an informed and experienced gun rights advocate, it is very hard to believe Trotter was not aware of this; it is more plausible that she intended to create a misleading impression with a frightening but irrelevant narrative.

Sources

Speakers have ways of deflecting accountability for their own statements by attributing what they say to other sources. Sometimes the speaker claims that the source of information must remain *anonymous* for fear of retribution or because the information has implications for national security—e.g., "a 'highly placed' source in X country revealed that…" Sometimes sources are identified in an effort to state the politician's position without taking full responsibility for it—e.g., "The think tank, Completely Unbiased, Inc. said my opponent's positions represent a danger to our democratic system."

Presidential Lies

Jody Powell, President Jimmy Carter's press secretary, said that the government has the right and sometimes an obligation to lie to the American public in "certain circumstances." This is not a new idea. More than 2300 years ago, Plato described what he called "the noble lie." These were lies told by government leaders for their perception of the public good—to maintain order and keep society functioning in a productive manner (Jowett, 1982). The fact that U.S. Presidents and other government officials have lied to the American people throughout the nation's history is hardly debatable (Polman, 2003). But whether these lies can be justified by "certain circumstances" is debatable. Pfiffner (1999; 2004) identified five common types of presidential lies which vary in the amount of damage they are likely to do to society. Only one type of lie is justified by the circumstances.

Justified Lies

Most people believe our leaders are justified in lying to our country's enemies, particularly in a time of war. In World War II the U. S. Army had a special unit whose primary duty was to deceive and trick the enemy (Gerard, 2002). However, not everyone is equally approving of lies to an enemy that also requires deceiving the American public. So when a President lies to his or her own citizens, the criterion for acceptability is directly linked to whether it was necessary in order to protect American lives.

An example of a justified lie was when President Carter told reporters in 1980 that a military mission to save 52 American hostages held in Iran would definitely fail and was not being planned. In fact, a military rescue plan had been in effect for several months. By telling the truth, Carter would have jeopardized the mission and the lives of those involved.

Minor Lies

It is difficult to understand why presidents tell some lies. They are lies about matters that have little or no relevance to their ability to govern and give them no apparent political advantage. Since some people suspect minor lies lead to major lies, telling minor lies have the potential to be damaging to the politician. But, as noted in Chapter 7 with "Knapp's Confession," lies in casual conversation don't always have a very logical raison d'etre.

President Johnson repeatedly told the story about how his great grandfather had died at the Alamo. Later, when the story was challenged, he said it was a slip of the tongue and that his great grandfather had actually died at the battle of San Jacinto. Historian Doris Kearns found no evidence of this either.

President Reagan claimed to have photographed Nazi death camps at the end of World War II. But he never left California during World War II even though he did have and show films of death camps.

President Kennedy claimed he had completed a speed reading course and could read 1200 words per minute. This assertion was especially curious since he was able to read about 700–800 words per minute, which is twice as fast as most people.

Lies to Prevent Embarrassment and Preserve Political Viability

These lies are commonly expected from political figures. They are not justified, but they are generally not as serious as lies that cover up important facts or policies. This type of lie is clearly motivated by the self-interest of the politician despite their belief that such lies are necessary in order to gain or maintain a position from which they could help the American people.

President Kennedy lied about having Addison's disease and his physicians also lied about it. For Kennedy, this was a painful and debilitating disease that required painkillers for his back, steroids, anti-spasmodics for colitis, antibiotics for urinary tract infections, and others medicines. Kennedy feared public knowledge of this would ruin his chance to become and serve as President.

Vice President Ford discussed the possible resignation and pardon of President Nixon with White House Chief of Staff Alexander Haig in 1974. Ford admitted meeting with Haig but lied about the subjects discussed at the meeting.

President George W. Bush didn't disclose his 1976 arrest and conviction for driving under the influence of alcohol until growing evidence forced him to in the closing days of the 2000 presidential campaign.

President Obama has spoken candidly about his struggles with smoking, but claimed to have kicked the habit entirely when he began his first term in 2008. Nevertheless, several sources have disputed this claim, most notably Dr. Jeffrey Kuhlman, his assigned White House physician (Altman & Zeleny, 2010).

Lies to Cover Up or Omit Important Facts

Presidents sometimes lie about events that have a major impact on the American people—facts they have a right to know. These lies represent a serious breach of trust and represent the kind of lies that impugn the government's credibility and debase the democratic system.

President Eisenhower's 1960 denial that America was sending U-2 spy planes over the Soviet Union is often cited as the beginning of an era in which the public's trust in the truthfulness of public officials began to erode. Although Eisenhower did not want anything to jeopardize the signing of a nuclear test ban treaty with the Soviet Union, he was sending spy planes over their territory. The Soviets knew about the spy planes, but Congress and the American public did not. When the Soviet Union said they had shot one down, Eisenhower said this would be impossible since we weren't engaged in spying on the Soviet Union. Then the Soviets showed photos of the plane's wreckage and the pilot who had safely ejected.

In 1962, President Kennedy said there were no American troops engaged in combat in Vietnam. He did not say that American pilots were flying helicopters for South Vietnamese combatants.

President Nixon repeatedly lied when he said he had nothing to do with the burglary of the Democratic National Committee headquarters in the Watergate office complex. At one point he told the CIA to tell the FBI to stop their investigation because it would reveal a CIA covert operation. His role in this burglary and cover up was a criminal act and led to his impeachment and resignation.

Vice President George H. W. Bush said he was "out of the loop" on discussions involving the selling of arms to Iran (considered an enemy) for hostages. He claimed he had no foreknowledge of this plan and must have been deliberately excluded from these meetings to protect him. However, testimony by his Secretary of State and Secretary of Defense pointed out that he was at several meetings in which they objected to the plan and Bush supported it (Walsh, 1994).

According to the evidence gathered by Woodward (2006), the George W. Bush administration repeatedly avoided telling the truth about the war in Iraq to the American public, Congress, and themselves.

Lies of Policy Deception

The most serious lies, according to Pfiffner (2004), occur when the President says the government is following one policy when, in fact, they are following another. This, he argues, is an abuse of power and negates the role of the people in the governing process.

During the presidential campaign of 1964, President Johnson said he would not send American "boys" to Vietnam to fight battles that Vietnamese "boys" should be fighting. Nevertheless, he continued to send American troops to Vietnam and withheld information about the extent to which our troops were involved in the fighting. He thought that negative information about the war would be detrimental to his "great society" domestic programs so he continued to present optimistic views of the war despite military reports to the contrary. To Congress, he understated the cost of the war and the true number of troops requested by his generals. As the war continued, his military commanders learned that Johnson only wanted to hear good news, which further distorted the information about the war.

The bombing of Cambodia in 1969 involved falsified reports and lies. President Nixon sent a message to the ambassador to South Vietnam indicating that there would be no more bombing in Cambodia. But he told his military commanders to continue the bombing. He told them to say they were only providing support to the South Vietnamese soldiers. North Vietnam, South Vietnam, and Cambodia knew of the bombing, but Congress and the American public did not.

The policy of the United States during the mid-1980s was to make no concessions to terrorists for the return of hostages. Iran wanted weapons for the release of American hostages held in Lebanon. In addition, Congress voted to shut off funds for the support Contra rebels in Nicaragua and President Reagan signed it. Despite these policies, arms were sold to Iran and the money for these weapons was diverted to the Contras. At different points in the investigation, Reagan said he didn't approve these transactions, that he couldn't remember whether he approved these transactions, and that he did approve these transactions.

In 2013, former National Security Agency contractor Edward Snowden began leaking classified material documenting the immense powers the NSA possesses to surveil Americans' telephone and electronic communications. For years, the intelligence agency swept up the telephone data of virtually every American and maintained the ability to spy on virtually anyone's internet activity with a keystroke. These revelations contradicted the testimony of James Clapper, the Director of National Intelligence who months earlier had told Congress the NSA did not collect information "in bulk" on American citizens. He later apologized with the Orwellian excuse that his blatant lie was the "least untruthful" answer he could think of (Kessler, 2013). The Obama administration and several members of Congress then went on the defensive, consistently telling the American people the NSA surveillance programs were legal, constitutional, and checked by thorough congressional oversight. But then new documents leaked by Snowden contradicted these claims. These documents revealed that members of Congress who are supposed to be able to provide oversight were systematically denied basic information about surveillance capabilities by the NSA. They also revealed that in 2011, a secret ruling from the Foreign Intelligence Surveillance Court found significant parts of the NSA's domestic spying activities to be in violation of the Fourth Amendment to the U.S. Constitution prohibiting unreasonable searches and seizures. Sources within the intelligence community (unnamed, of course) have said President Obama was made aware of the ruling as soon as it was rendered by the court, but took no action to remedy the problem (Ackerman, 2015).

Maintaining Public Vigilance

How can the public be alert to the deceptive behavior of political leaders? Given the leader's skill with language, their control of information, and their various options for disseminating information, public lie detection is a formidable task. The press, bloggers, and various concerned organizations are likely to continue investigating the factual accuracy of statements by these leaders. But citizens also need to practice critical listening skills. Listening closely to what a political leader says and how it is said will not automatically reveal the deceivers and the truth tellers. It may, however, cause a listener to suspend his or her judgment about the truthfulness of a speaker's remarks until further information can be obtained. If enough listeners from different political parties demand more responsible rhetoric, it has a better chance of happening. The following questions represent only a few of the standards that listeners could employ to address concerns about deception.

- *Does the speaker cite an accessible source for his or her claim?* When an accessible source is cited, it can be checked. When sources are unidentified or inaccessible to others, the credibility of the claim rests entirely on the credibility of the speaker.

- *Does the speaker compare his or her own efforts to those of his or her opponent?* When speakers criticize something their opponents have done, listeners will profit by hearing how the speaker's own behavior compares with his or her opponent's. This gives the listener more tangible information to check out, serves as a preventative measure for selective omissions, and tends to reduce an "attack only" form of discourse.

- *Does the speaker provide sufficient detail and contextual information?* Like interpersonal deception, lies to the public are often short on specifics. Details not only provide more things to check, but show the speaker's desire to fully inform the listener. Ambiguity and high level abstractions may be called for on occasion, but they also increase the zone of the unknown.

- *Does the speaker address the issue or question directly?* There may be good reasons for a speaker to evade or ignore an issue. When listeners are unaware of these reasons, however, they are likely to wonder if the speaker has something to hide.

- *Is the speaker responsible for what he or she says?* When speakers attribute information or claims they make to others, without formally acknowledging it as their position, they also set the stage for negating responsibility for the claim at a later time. Listeners have a right to know what the speaker is willing to be accountable for.

- *Does the speaker show an understanding of a complex world and an appreciation for the limitations of certainty?* Political leaders need to convince listeners that they know what they are doing while simultaneously acknowledging the probabilistic nature of the issues we all face. The likelihood of future deception increases when leaders are extremely absolute or extremely conditional in their behavior.

- *Does the speaker develop an argument?* Claims alone do not show the way a person thinks. However, the development of an argument gives a listener a chance to understand and evaluate the speaker's reasoning, how different ideas were brought together, and how he or she developed their attitudes and opinions.

Jamieson (2000, p. 56) says that a citizen's judgment is facilitated when candidates are unambiguous, fair, consistent, accurate, unbiased, and tell the full story. She summarizes her position and mine this way:

> *The likelihood that the public will be misled is minimized if the competing views are available and tested by advocates, audiences, and the press, if all sides engage in warranted argument, and if they accept responsibility for defending their own claims and the claims others offer on their behalf. This concept sounds idealistic, but unless a certain critical degree of substantive interchange is preserved among candidates, the people, and the media that control their encounters, the possibility of a critical information deficit will exist.*

Summary

Public lies have some special characteristics. They have to be adapted to multiple audiences. The deceiver has a great deal more control over the relevant information than the target. Associates of the deceiver often deliver his or her message, making responsibility for the deception elusive. The responsibility for detecting public deception is clearly up to the nation's press, its citizens, and special interest groups.

The public typically calls for more honesty from its political leaders, but they also want them to say what they want to hear. This means leaders and prospective leaders respond by saying they will be honest and forthright with the public, but deceptive behavior often occurs. In this sense, then, the public's mixed message to political leaders makes them a party to the deception. Since the mid-20th Century, the public trust in American political leaders has waned considerably. Many citizens have a cynical view of truth telling as practiced by politicians, and expect them to deceive. Curiously, however, many political lies go unpunished and sometimes voters even choose to vote for the politician they believe is the least honest.

Leaders are good communicators and can be skilled deceivers if they choose to be. They understand that there are many opportunities for deception in the life of a politician. Ironically, many see deception as a way to remain politically viable. Although some deception of the public by political leaders may be necessary, their deceptive behavior can and does have negative consequences as well—for the deceiver, the public, and the democratic process.

Proof of political lies requires evidence of the speaker's intention to deceive. This is often very difficult to obtain—especially since the same language can be used to tell the truth and a lie. The blood relatives of deception are messages that have features that commonly elicit suspicion or attributions of deception—e.g., ambiguity, lack of detail, indirectness, etc. The skillful use of language, facts, and sources allows a leader to be deceptive while simultaneously allowing him or her to deny it. Nevertheless, enough evidence for presidential lies exists to identify various types according to their degree of acceptability. Public lies about governmental policies are the most egregious, but lies about matters of national security can be justified.

The chapter concluded with some guidelines for listening critically to messages of political leaders—not with the intent of invariably highlighting deceptive behavior, but as a way of remaining alert to the possibility of deception.

Things to Think About

Do you think the public is in any way accountable for lies told by political leaders? If not, why not? If so, in what ways and to what extent? Use specific examples.

This chapter focused on deceptive behavior by political leaders directed toward the general public. Select another leader category—e.g., religious, business, scientific, legal, labor, volunteers—and compare it to the material in this chapter. Discuss similarities and differences.

In the 1960 presidential debates, Kennedy proposed supporting U.S. intervention in Cuba by supporting the anti-Castro exiles. He claimed that the exiles were receiving no support from the administration. Vice President Nixon, his opponent, knew exiles were being trained for a possible invasion of Cuba, but felt he could not reveal this. So he chose to attack Kennedy's proposal as reckless and irresponsible—exactly the opposite of what he believed. Was this lie justified? If not, why? If so, on what grounds? Name any other ways you think Nixon could have handled this situation.

References

Ackerman, S. (2015, June 9). Obama lawyers asked secret court to ignore public court's decision on spying. http://www.theguardian.com/world/2015/jun/09/obama-fisa-court-surveillance-phone-records.

Alterman, E. (2004). *When presidents lie: A history of official deception and its consequences.* New York: Viking.

Altman, L.K., & Zeleny, J. (2010, February 28). Obama passes checkup but still struggles with smoking habit. *New York Times.* http://www.nytimes.com/2010/03/01/us/politics/ 01obama.html

Bailey, F.G. (1988). *Humbuggery and manipulation: The art of leadership.* Ithaca, N.Y.: Cornell University Press.

Barnes, J.A. (1994). *A pack of lies.* New York: Cambridge University Press.

Barron, J. (2012, December 12). Nation reels after gunman massacres 20 children at school in Connecticut. *New York Times.* http://www.nytimes.com/2012/12/15/nyregion/shooting-reported-at-connecticut-elementary-school/.

Barstow, D. & Stein, R. (March 13, 2005). The message machine: How the government makes news; Under Bush, a new age of prepackaged television news. *New York Times,* Section 1, 1.

Bavelas, J.B., Black, A., Chovil, N., & Mullett, J. (1990). *Equivocal communication.* Newbury Park, CA: Sage.

Bok, S. (1978). *Lying: Moral choice in public and private life.* New York: Pantheon Books.

Boorstin, D.J. (1992). *The image: A guide to pseudo-events in America.* New York: Vintage Books.

Brandt, A. (2009). *The cigarette century.* New York: Perseus.

Buss, D.M., Gomes, M., Higgins, D.S. & Lauterbach, K. (1987). Tactics of manipulation. *Journal of Personality and Social Psychology, 52,* 1219–1229.

Cannon, C.M. (Jan/Feb, 2007). Untruth and consequences. *Atlantic, 299,* 56–61.

Chait, J. (April 30, 2006). McCain's a weasel, but he's my weasel. *Austin American Statesman,* H3.

Cliffe, L., Ramsay, M. & Bartlett, D. (2000). *The politics of lying: Implications for democracy.* New York: St. Martin's Press.

Ekman, P. (2001). *Telling lies: Clues to deceit in the marketplace, politics, and marriage.* New York: Norton.

FactCheck.org Document (March 23, 2004). Bush accuses Kerry of 350 votes for "higher taxes" higher than what?

FactCheck.org Document (March 3, 2006). Faking news in the Illinois governor race.

Fishel, J. (1985). *Presidents and promises: From campaign pledge to presidential performance.* Washington, D. C.: CQ Press.

Fleming, J.H., Darley, J.M., Hilton, j.L. & Kojetin, B.A. (1990). Multiple audience problem: A strategic communication perspective on social perception. *Journal of Personality and Social Psychology, 58,* 593–609.

Gallup Poll for CNN/*USA Today,* June 18–19, 1996.

Garcia, A. Jr. (September 4, 2004). We demand the truth, then punish the politicians who speak it. *Austin American Statesman,* A19.

Garrett, M. & Penny, T.J. (1998). The fifteen biggest lies in politics. New York: St. Martin's Press.

Gerard, P. (2002). Secret soldiers: The story of World War II's heroic army of deception. New York: Dutton.

Gergen, D.R. (2000). *Eyewitness to power.* New York: Simon & Shuster.

Griffin, D., & Frates, C. (2013, October 30). Sources: White House told insurance execs to keep quiet on Obamacare. *CNN Politics.* http://www.cnn.com/2013/10/30/politics/obamacare-white-house-pressure/.

Jackson, B. (June 3, 2004). False ads: There ought to be a law! Or—maybe not. FactCheck.org Special Report. Retrieved May 18, 2006 from: http://factcheck.org/SpecialReports188.html

Jamieson, K.H. (2000). *Everything you think you know about politics…and why you're wrong.* New York: Basic Books.

Jamieson, K.H. & Campbell, K.K. (1983). *The interplay of influence.* Belmont, CA: Wadsworth.

Jowett, B. (trans., 1982). *Plato's Republic.* New York: Modern Library.

Keating, C.F. & Heltman, K.R. (1994). Dominance and deception in children and adults: Are leaders the best misleaders? *Personality and Social Psychology Bulletin, 20,* 312–321.

Keller, J. (November 18, 2001). It's true: We can't handle the truth. *Austin American Statesman,* L8.

Kessler, G. (2013, June 12). Clapper's least untruthful statement to the Senate. *Washington Post.* http://www.washingtonpost.com/blogs/fact-checker/post/james-clappers-least-untruthful-statement-to-the-senate/2013/06/12/.Louis Harris Poll, October 18–November 4, 1988.

Luntz, F. (2007). *Words that work: Its not what you say, it's what people hear.* New York: Hyperion.

MacArthur, J. (1992, January 6). Remember Nayirah, witness for Kuwait? *New York Times.* http://www.nytimes.com/1992/01/06/opinion/.

Marro, A. (March/April, 1985). When the government tells lies. *Columbia Journalism Review, 23,* 29–41.

Morris, E. (2003). *The fog of war.* New York: Sony Pictures Classics.

Nelson, M.R., & Park, J. (2014). Publicity as covert marketing? The role of persuasion knowledge and ethical perceptions on belies and credibility in a video news release story. *Journal of Business Ethics.* doi: 10.1007/s10551-014-2227-3.

Pfiffner, J.P. (2004). *The character factor: How we judge America's presidents.* College Station, TX: Texas A & M Press.

Pfiffner, J.P. (1999). The contemporary presidency: Presidential lies. *Presidential Studies Quarterly, 29,* 903–917.

Polman, D. (June 29, 2003). To tell the truth. *Austin American Statesman,* H1, H5.

Pratkanis, A. & Aronson, E. (2001). *Age of propaganda: The everyday use and abuse of persuasion.* New York: W. H. Freeman.

Princeton Survey Research, October 20–November 2, 1992.

Rampton, S. & Stauber, J. (2003). *Weapons of mass deception.* New York: Jeremy P. Tarcher/Penguin.

Reeves. R. (2001). *President Nixon: Alone in the White House.* New York: Simon & Shuster.

Rue, L.D. (1994). *By the grace of guile.* New York: Oxford University Press.

Segraves, K. (2005). *Women and smoking in America, 1880–1950.* New York: McFarland & Co.

Sun, L.H., & Somashekhar, S. (2013, October 29). Obama accused of breaking promise to consumers as health plans cancel policies. *Washington Post.* http://www.washingtonpost.com/national/health-science/obama-accused-of-breaking-promise-to-consumers-as-health-plans-cancel-policies/2013/10/29/.

State of Washington v. 119 Vote No! Comm., 135 Wn. 2d 618, 1998

U.S. News & World Report (February 23, 1987) p. 54.

Tye, L. (1998). *The father of Spin: Edward L. Bernays and the birth of public relations.* New York: Henry Holt and Co.

Walsh, L.E. (1994). *Iran-Contra: The final report.* New York: Three Rivers Press.

Walton, D. (1996). Plausible deniability and evasion of burden of proof. *Argumentation, 10,* 47–58.

Weiner, R. (2013, January 30). Gayle Trotter: Guns make women safer. *Washington Post.* http://www.washingtonpost.com/blogs/post-politics/wp/2013/01/30/gayle-trotter-guns-make-women-safer/.

Wise, D. (1973). *The politics of lying: Government deception, secrecy, and power.* New York: Random House.

Woodward, B. (2006). *State of denial.* New York: Simon & Shuster.

Chapter 12

Deceptive Writing in the Public Arena

Deceptive writing is a phenomenon that occurs in a variety of venues common to daily life. This chapter examines four of these arenas. The first two concern authors writing about *other people and events*: 1) gathering and reporting the news, and 2) writing history. In the other two variants, the subject of the deceptive writing is *the author*: 3) writing memoirs, and 4) résumé writing. Each of these has gained more than a little notoriety in recent years as a fairly consistent source of distortion, misinformation, and misrepresentation.

Gathering and Reporting the News

The framers of the U.S. Constitution knew it was important to have a press that was not controlled or operated by any branch of government. In fact, the First Amendment to the Constitution places freedom of the press on par with such bedrock rights as freedom of speech and religious liberty. The founders believed that those who control information control people's decisions (and thus their lives). Those who gather and report information, therefore, should be as independent of the government as possible. This vision of a free press is one that allows the gathering and reporting of information without the kind of censorship and manipulation characteristic of totalitarian societies. A free press can provide opportunities for the voicing of various perspectives, no matter how unpopular. A free press can also assume responsibility for uncovering vital information that would otherwise remain hidden from a public that has a right to know (e.g., Watergate in the 1970s and NSA wiretapping in the 2010s). In short, an independent press is the agent of a free citizenry—serving as a source of reliable information, a forum for discussion, and a defense against demagoguery.

> "History is the version of past events that people have decided to agree upon."
>
> — *Napoleon Bonaparte*

Despite this noble design, the reality is more complicated. While the public continues to maintain belief in the important role of a free press in American society, it is also a source of persistent criticism in opinion polls. A Pew Research Center poll conducted in 2013 found 68% of respondents (of all political stripes and demographic backgrounds) agreeing that the press does a good job of preventing leaders from "doing things that shouldn't be done," a double-digit increase from two years earlier. Aside from this "watchdog" role, however, Americans tend to view other core functions of the press with much greater skepticism. In the same 2013 survey, 67% of Americans felt that news organizations were inaccurate in their reporting (up from about 50% in 2001). Elsewhere in the 2013 data, clear majorities denigrated the press for being uncaring, politically biased, too focused on unimportant stories, and unduly influenced by power. The Gallup organization summed up the overall attitudinal trend this way: "Americans' trust in mass media has generally been edging downward from higher levels in the late 1990s and the early 2000s" (McCarthy, 2014).

There are, no doubt, many reasons for this erosion of public trust. One possibility is that the decay is structural in nature, paralleling the overall decline in reliance on traditional news sources in favor of social media sites and other digital sources (Rupp, 2014). Yet Gallup has found little confidence in news sources of any kind, old or new, regardless of platform. Faith in traditional newspapers stands at 22%, news from the Internet at 19%, and television news at 18%. Of the 16 American institutions Gallup asked the public to evaluate, only Congress ranked lower (Newport, 2015).

In the end, the simplest explanation for the causes of this ongoing decline may be the numerous high-profile examples of deceptive journalism that continue to plague the industry. Journalists who make up, plagiarize, or exaggerate the stories they report are not numerous when compared to the total number of reporters or the total number of stories. But when deception occurs a great deal of public attention ensues and the impact on a news organization's credibility can be devastating, potentially calling into question the veracity of all its reporting, be it past, present, or future. No caliber of organization seems immune to this phenomenon, nor does the experience level of the journalist appear to have much of a bearing on the practice. The examples of such lapses are too numerous to list in their entirety, but the following are representative.

Deceptive News

- 1981—*Washington Post* reporter Janet Cooke was fired and had to return a Pulitzer Prize for a story about an eight-year-old heroin addict who didn't exist. He was, she said, a composite of many young addicts she had uncovered.
- 1998—Veteran reporter for the *Boston Globe*, Mike Barnicle, was fired for writing a story that could not be verified about two cancer patients who became friends. He also published George Carlin jokes without acknowledging the comedian. Patricia Smith, also with the *Boston Globe*, was fired when she admitted occasionally making up a colorful quote when she felt it would make a better story. She said the basic ideas in her stories were honest

even though the characters were sometimes fictional. This was also the year Stephen Glass, who wrote for the *New Republic*, admitted he made up all or parts of dozens of stories. He even made fake documents that were designed to provide verification of his stories.

- 1999—A reporter for the Owensboro Kentucky *Messenger-Inquirer* fabricated five columns about her life-and-death struggle with cancer when, in fact, she had AIDS.

- 2000—Three interns at the *San Jose Mercury News* were suspended for plagiarizing and using unverified quotes and sources. A political reporter at the *Sacramento Bee* admitted to fabricating and plagiarizing stories.

- 2003—Over the course of four years, in 36 of 73 stories, reporter Jayson Blair of the *New York Times* plagiarized, invented quotes, and lied about his reporting location. Another *Times* reporter, Rick Bragg, was suspended and later quit after it was discovered that he used the work of researchers, interns, and strangers in his own stories and did not give them credit.

- 2004—Veteran reporter Jack Kelly of *USA Today* and his editor resigned in response to revelations of fabricated stories and other deceptive behavior. Kelly reportedly asked his friends to act like they were the sources of information for certain stories and wrote scripts for them to follow.

- 2008—Lobbyist Vicki Iseman sued the *New York Times* for libel after the prestigious "paper of record" published a tabloid-like article on its front page in February 2008. The article intimated that she and then-presidential candidate John McCain had an affair in the late 1990s (Orey, 2009). Other news organizations publicly excoriated the *Times* for publishing a piece that was little more than hearsay (Kinsley, 2008). A year after the article was published, Iseman dropped her lawsuit. In exchange, the *Times* agreed to publish a retraction of sorts, in which its editors stated that the newspaper "did not intend to conclude … that Ms. Iseman had engaged in a romantic affair with Senator McCain or an unethical relationship" (Kurtz, 2009).

- 2012—Despite an already successful career as a monologist and cultural critic, Mike Daisey decided to fabricate key elements of his 2010 performance "The Agony and the Ecstasy of Steve Jobs," which purported to describe horrific working conditions at Apple factories in China. But it wasn't until excerpts of the monologue were aired to the scrutiny of a wider audience on public radio's *This American Life* in January of 2012 that things began to unravel. Initially insisting that they had spent weeks fact-checking Daisey's chilling details (such as gun-toting factory guards and the use of underaged workers), *This American Life* retracted the story two months later (Isherwood, 2012).

- 2014—*Rolling Stone* was forced to admit that their trust in reporter Sabrina Rudin Erdely was "misplaced" after key details of her article "A Rape on Campus" were called into question by *The Washington Post* (Shapiro, 2014). Erdely's original story purported to describe the brutal gang rape of a female student at a fraternity house on the campus of the University of Virginia. Perhaps to its credit, *Rolling Stone* ultimately asked the dean of the Columbia School of Journalism for an independent investigation of the failure. His formal report was published by the magazine in April 2015, along with a full and formal retraction of the rape story (Coronel et al, 2015).

- 2015—Ending his reign as television's most popular news anchor, *NBC Nightly News'* Brian Williams was suspended for several months and then permanently removed when it came to light that he had repeatedly said, in his own words, "things that weren't true" (Calamur, 2015). When recounting details of his experiences as an embedded journalist during the Iraq War, Williams maintained over the years that he had been in a helicopter that was hit by enemy fire (Bauder, 2015). In a testament to the perhaps-unintentional but ever-growing journalistic power of social media, it was a simple Facebook comment by a veteran who was present during Williams' Iraq tour that proved to be the latter's undoing. In early February 2015, *NBC Nightly News* showed Williams taking a soldier to a New York Rangers game. At the event, the announcer told the crowd that the veteran, Sergeant Major Tim Terpak "was responsible for the safety of Brian Williams and his NBC News team after their Chinook helicopter was hit and crippled by enemy fire." When NBC posted this footage on Facebook, Lance Reynolds, a crew member from the actual helicopter struck in Iraq that day (which was not Williams') felt compelled to comment. "Sorry dude," he wrote. "I don't remember you being on my aircraft." With that, the proverbial floodgates opened and other service members present at the Iraq incident joined in repudiating Mr. Williams' version of events (Somaiya, 2015). Williams' initial apologies online and on-air did little to silence his critics. He admitted he knew it was the helicopter in front of him that had been hit, but that "constant viewing of the video showing us inspecting the impact area" and "the fog of memory over 12 years" made him "conflate" the two vehicles (Tritten, 2015). "This was a bungled attempt by me to thank one special veteran," he added (Mahler et al, 2015). It didn't help matters that two years earlier Williams had regaled David Letterman with an unhesitatingly clear, vivid, and detailed description of the events he would later attribute to a faulty memory.

- 2015—Having been accused by *Mother Jones* magazine of multiple instances of journalistic deception, Fox News personality Bill O'Reilly seems to be made of Teflon. Unlike Williams, the far more serious accusations against O'Reilly don't appear to stick—despite evidence that directly contradicts his statements (Rothkopf, 2015). Among other things, he is accused of exaggerating his record as a war correspondent and fabricating certain aspects of his assignments—for example, trips to Northern Ireland and the Falklands that never happened (Corn & Schulman, 2015). To date, O'Reilly has yet to admit any wrongdoing, casting aspersions on his accusers instead (Waldman, 2015).

Deceptive News Gathering

Sometimes reporters believe it is necessary to use deception in order to report a story truthfully. For example, a reporter may pretend not to be a reporter or lie about the real point of the story being developed. Some news organizations prohibit their reporters from misrepresenting themselves and many journalists point out that they would not like someone doing it to them. Nevertheless, the use of

By permission Steve Kelley and Creators Syndicate, Inc.

deception to get a story was established long ago. In 1887, Nellie Bly of the *New York World* got herself admitted to the New York City Women's Lunatic Asylum in order to expose the horrible practices occurring within its walls.

Undercover journalism continues today and in some instances is considered prize-worthy. About 22% of the journalists in one survey said that pretending to be somebody else to get a story may be justified (Weaver and Wilhoit, 1996). The most common justifications are linked to: 1) the belief that the reporters are merely lying to bad people who are doing harmful things and, 2) the inability to get the information using non-deceptive methods. Undercover segments by television reporters also tend to get good audience ratings, but this is not likely to be used as a justification for deceptive news gathering.

Since the 1960s, television news has presented numerous reports in which reporters gathered information using hidden cameras. They have exposed car repair scams, physical abuse in orphanages and nursing homes, discriminatory behavior toward African-American customers and job applicants, and more. In 1992, ABC News reporters used hidden cameras to expose unsanitary food handling procedures at the Food Lion grocery chain. Food Lion sued ABC and a national dialogue about the ethics of deceptive news gathering ensued. Following the statement that journalistic deception is generally wrong, the Poynter Institute, a school specifically devoted to journalism, said it may be justified if it meets the following criteria:

1. The story is of profound importance and vital to the public interest—e.g., when great harm is being done to people.
2. All other alternatives to get the story have been exhausted.

3. The reporter and employer are willing to reveal publicly how the deception was used to get the story and the reasons for it.

4. The reporter and employer are willing to provide the time, funding, and resources in order to pursue the story fully.

5. The harm prevented as a result of the story outweighs any harm caused by acts of deception.

6. Prior to the deception, the reporter and employer should thoroughly discuss and weigh the short and long range consequences of their deception, its impact on journalistic credibility, their motivations, the deceptive act relative to their editorial mission, and the legal implications of the action.

Guidelines like these encourage reflection and discussion, but still allow considerable latitude in decision making. For example, what is of "profound importance" to one news organization may not be to another. The harm prevented versus the harm done is also a judgment that may garner widely different views. As a response to Food Lion's charges that ABC had inaccurately presented information by the way they edited the 45 hours of undercover videotape, a seventh guideline has been suggested (Davidson, 1998; Meyer, 1997):

7. The whole data set gathered by the reporter(s) must be available for examination as a check on accuracy and any misleading ideas resulting from the editing process.

Attributions of Deception

In the preceding examples of reporters who deliberately falsified stories and lied to gain access to information, the intent to deceive is pretty clear. However, there are numerous characteristics and practices associated with the gathering, writing, and presenting of the news that serve as a lightning rod for accusations of deception within the news media—whether deceptive intent is involved or not. The story may be accurately perceived as misleading, distorted, incomplete, or biased, but deceptive intent may not be involved. Deceptive or not, the following factors may be *perceived* as deceptive and negatively impact the credibility of the news media.

Poor Journalism

Journalistic errors are highly visible. When reporting errors occur, some people are bound to see this occurrence as a deliberate attempt to mislead the public, a sign that journalists can't be trusted, a sign that the news media outlet making the error can't be trusted, or all of the above. But journalists, like everyone else, don't always do their job perfectly—a necessary and sufficient condition for deception. One problem that can occur is the reliance on limited or biased sources of information. A reporter may rely too often on the same people for information (Lee & Solomon, 1990). Deception is also highlighted when local TV news stations run a video news release (VNR) and the public relations firm or government agency which produced it is not identified. When the true identity of the VNR's producers is revealed by sources other than the TV station responsible for it, it raises the specter of intentional deception (even though unidentified VNRs may be run for other reasons).

On September 11, 2002, WHBQ, the Fox affiliate in Memphis, marked the anniversary of the 9/11 attacks with an uplifting report on how assistance from the United States was helping to liberate the women of Afghanistan.

Tish Clark, a reporter for WHBQ, described how Afghan women, once barred from schools and jobs, were at last emerging from their burkas, taking up jobs as seamstresses and bakers, sending daughters off to new schools, receiving decent medical care for the first time, and even participating in a fledgling democracy. Her segment included an interview with an Afghan teacher who recounted how the Taliban only allowed boys to attend school. An Afghan doctor described how the Taliban refused to let male physicians treat women.

In short, Ms. Clark's report seemed to corroborate, however modestly, a central argument of the Bush foreign policy, that forceful American intervention abroad was spreading freedom, improving lives, and winning friends.

What the people of Memphis were not told, though, was that the interviews used by WHBQ were actually conducted by State Department contractors. The contractors also selected the quotes used from those interviews and shot the video that went with the narration. They also wrote the narration, much of which Ms. Clark repeated with only minor changes.

As it happens, the viewers of WHBQ were not the only ones in the dark.

Ms. Clark, now Tish Clark Dunning, said in an interview that she, too, had no idea the report originated at the State Department. "If that's true, I'm very shocked that anyone would false report on anything like that," she said...

*Excerpted from: Barstow and Stein, 2005.

Helen Thomas (2006), a White House correspondent for more than forty years, believes the White House press corps does not adequately keep the public informed when they assume information put out by the administration is the complete story. Boehlert (2006) and Rich (2006) believe the same could be said about the press in general. The press often dismissed the need to develop stories based on evidence that President Bush knowingly misled the nation in making the case to go to war in Iraq. They argued that the public was well aware that Bush made false claims about Saddam Hussein's link to Al Qaeda and the presence of weapons of mass destruction in Iraq. A July 2006 Harris poll, however, revealed that 50% of the Americans polled believed that Iraq had weapons of mass destruction and 64% believed that Saddam had a strong connection to Al Qaeda. Critics of the press point to such findings as a sign that the press abdicated its responsibility to keep American citizens accurately informed.

The need to verify information is at the heart of good reporting. When a quote or story is printed and/or broadcast and it turns out to be false, attributions of deception are likely to be forthcoming even though there may not have been any intent to deceive. In May 2005, *Newsweek* said that a forthcoming military report would attest to the fact that American interrogators had flushed a copy of the Koran down a toilet to unnerve detainees. A reliable, but anonymous, government source was cited. After a number of people died in Muslim riots in several cities around the world, *Newsweek* said their source would not stand by the original report so they were retracting the story. Even though their government source would not verify the report, detainees released from Guantanamo Bay had been complaining about copies of the Koran being thrown in the toilet for two years (Seelye & Lewis, 2005). Far less serious, but also unverified, was the story that women with blonde hair would be extinct within 200 years. CBS, ABC, CNN, and numerous other news media reported the article without checking with the World Health Organization, the supposed source of the information. In 2002, the story was traced to a German women's magazine that cited the work of a nonexistent anthropologist at the WHO. The false story, however, continued to circulate into 2006.

News stories are inevitably incomplete, but when information deemed critical and highly relevant to the story is omitted, the question of deceptive intent may be raised. In October 2002, Pribble et al. (2006) analyzed 1,799 health news stories and found 75% of them did not include an interview with a health professional or have specific recommendations on how to prevent or ameliorate a medical condition. Only 12% noted the prevalence of a disease, which is important in assessing risk. The West Nile Virus was the second most frequently reported topic even though only about 1% of the American TV audience faced the possibility of contracting it. When stories about new drugs omit potentially harmful side effects or fail to examine possible ties between drug researchers and drug companies, the public may understandably feel deceived.

When a journalist's "faulty thinking" (Cohen, 1997) occurs in conjunction with a strongly held bias of a reader or viewer, it is no longer a very human trait we all indulge in. For example, stating that the economy has been strong since this president took office implies the president's policies are a cause of the strong economy when, in fact, that relationship may be spurious. Perhaps the economy was stronger before this president took office. Weaver (1994) considers it faulty thinking when journalists fail to treat newsmakers as impression managers. He refers to this source-reporter relationship as a "culture of lying":

> *The central fact about the interaction between news media and the people they cover is that* the people being covered know the media are watching and behave accordingly. *As a result, the actions the media cover as news aren't spontaneous events but self-conscious efforts to create favorable impressions. For their part* the news media are aware that newsmakers are performing, but they nonetheless treat newsmakers' fabrications as authentic actions, *covering or ignoring these performances as they see fit (p. 6).… We encounter the culture of lying in the contrived statements of government and corporate officials trying to look good on the nightly news. We encounter it in a union leader's complacent advocacy of an action that will benefit his members in the short term but endanger their jobs and harm the U.S. economy in the long term. We see it in phony claims of danger to national security made by businesses seeking protection from foreign firms making better products at lower prices (p. 13).*

Employer Constraints

Newspapers, magazines, and television news are part of a money-making business. Can a free press corps devoted to reporting truthfully and accurately coexist effectively within an organization whose primary goal is to make a financial profit? The reporter's target audience, advertisers, and parent company all have vested interests in the content of their reporting. Auletta (2003, p. xii) put it this way: "I worry about the owners of journalistic properties making business decisions that harm journalism…As a reporter, I've learned it's the nature of corporate executives to extol the virtues of synergy, profit margins, the stock price, cost cutting, extending the brand, demographics, ratings, and getting on the team. Journalists rarely share these concerns…" One cost-cutting measure that has affected some news organizations is a reduction in the number of fact-checkers. This is a business decision with potentially direct consequences on the accuracy of reporting (Featherstone, 1997). In 1984 there were fifty companies in the United States with controlling interests in the news media. In 2005 there were six. People associated with these companies and the companies themselves are often active in shaping the events that become news. Lee and Solomon (1990, p. xiv) ask the obvious question about reporters who work for these companies, "Will they bite the hand that feeds them?" Thomas (2006) points out that "the hand that feeds them" may extend beyond the corporation itself because some aspects of the corporation's business may be dependent on maintaining a positive relationship with certain highly placed people in the U.S. government or possibly the government of another country.

This doesn't necessarily mean a reporter's story will be censored or that he or she will be told what to write. But some influence is inevitable. In order to make money, stories have to be timely and interesting, but corporate concerns may make certain stories less of a priority. The news may be inextricably linked to their employer's other products—e.g., the TV newscaster who has to say, "Up next: the hottest *Survivor* finale parties! Plus the rest of the news!" The ownership may also influence the way news is presented. For example, some believe news should be easy to understand and full of familiar images with minimal space and time given to the complexities and uncertainties that often accompany life's stories. The fear that a competitor will print or air a story first can affect both the depth of a report and the source verification process. News bureaus also engage in copycat reporting in an effort to match their competitors. This process can lead to distortion. After one story about President Ford being "accident prone" occurred, reporters looked for other instances of this behavior. After several more stories, Ford's image as a "bumbler" was secure (Cohen, 1997). Any time a person is characterized by repeatedly emphasizing one aspect of his or her behavior, distortion is a legitimate complaint.

Competition can also lead to problems. If one newspaper gets a quote wrong, it is likely to be repeated many times by competing news services before it is corrected. Tate (1984) illustrates the absurdity of copycat reporting in the story of an early 20th century reporter who was asked why so many stories of shipwrecks featured a cat that survived. The reporter said: "One of those wrecked ships carried a cat, and the crew went back to save it. I made the cat the feature of my story, while other reporters failed to mention the cat, and were called down by their city editors for being beaten. The next time there was a shipwreck there was no cat; but the other ship news reporters did not wish to take chances, and put the cat in. I wrote a true report, leaving out the cat, and then I was severely chided for being beaten. Now when there is a shipwreck all of us always put in a cat."

Producing the Story

Various decisions about how much space to devote to a story, where to position the story relative to other stories, and the reporter's choice of words are all potential sources of perceived or actual deception. Even the decision about what stories should be reported is one that affects the public's perception of how accurately reality is being presented. For example, an editor may not want to do a story detailing malnutrition, homelessness, disease, and abuse occurring among thousands of children in a foreign country. The story is depressing, costly, and difficult to obtain. During the late 1930s and early 1940s, American newspapers, including the *New York Times* (owned by Jews of German descent) consciously ignored or downplayed the mass murders that were taking place in Nazi Germany (Leff, 2005; Lipstadt, 1986). But the heroic struggle to retrieve a single child who fell down a well in the United States may be a headline story for a week.

"Hyping" a story can also distort reality. National news stories are frequently the driving force behind a local story on the same issue. This is a practice that runs the risk of magnifying the importance of the story or the frequency of the event being reported. Shark attacks on human beings are rare and the frequency remains fairly constant, but in the absence of other headline-grabbing stories, a few prominent and fear-provoking stories can make shark attacks seem like an epidemic. In 2002, news stories about child abductions were plentiful even though the number of child abductions by strangers had been between three and five thousand per year since the 1980s (Gándara, 2002; Kirn, 2002). Crime reporting, says Penny (2005), "has more than doubled since the eighties, even though the overall crime rate has steadily declined." Based on stories in the press, the American Automobile Association issued a publication saying road rage was increasing. The press then cited the AAA report as the source of information that road rage was a national problem.

Reporter Biases

Reporters, like every other human being, are subject to their own personal, perceptual, and memory biases that can influence actual or perceived distortions in their stories. Attitudinal biases encompass such things as political party preference and stereotypes about certain groups. A reporter may, for example, interview more people with attitudes known to be similar to his or her own than people whose opinions are different. Some journalists believe that the most influential bias is not political, but professional—that is, the bias toward getting a provocative or sensational story that will build their reputations as skilled reporters.

Observational biases include all the difficulties experienced by eyewitnesses—missing parts of the story that *are* there while seeing other parts that aren't (see Chapter 2). Sometimes reporters will start with an idea of how a story will develop and then find information that confirms it (Nickerson, 1998). The strong belief, for example, that obesity in young children is a major problem may cause a reporter to miss key evidence to the contrary.

Two boys in Boston were playing basketball when one of them was attacked by a rabid Rottweiler. Thinking quickly, the other boy ripped a board off a nearby fence and wedged it into the dog's collar and twisted it, breaking the dog's neck.

A newspaper reporter from the *Boston Times* witnessed the incident and rushed over to interview the boy. The reporter began entering data into his laptop, beginning with the headline: "Brave Young Celtics Fan Saves Friend from Jaws of Vicious Animal."

"But I'm not a Celtics fan," the boy said. "Sorry," replied the reporter.

"Hitting the delete key, the reporter began again, "Kennedy Fan Rescues Friend from Horrific Dog Attack." "But I'm not a Kennedy fan either," noted the boy.

"We're in Boston," said the reporter, "and I assumed everybody here is either a fan of the Celtics or a Kennedy. What team or person do you like?"

"I'm a Houston Rockets fan and I really like George W. Bush," the boy proudly responded.

Hitting the delete key, the reporter typed a new headline: "Arrogant Little Conservative Bastard Kills Beloved Family Pet."

*This story is fiction.

Biases of News Consumers

Sometimes it doesn't matter how hard journalists try to present the news in an unbiased and balanced manner. Highly partisan readers and viewers on both sides of an issue are not likely to want or to perceive any news as "fair" unless it unequivocally favors their point of view. When the other side of the issue in question is presented, it is, by definition, a sign of bias in their minds. Even news consumers whose views on an issue are not extreme are likely to have a similar reaction if they are convinced the media is biased (Giner-Sorolla & Chaiken, 1994). Research by Vallone et al. (1985) and Perloff (1989) confirm this "hostile media" phenomenon. Vallone and his colleagues recruited 144 pro-Israeli and pro-Arab observers who were shown six American news clips from the 1982 Israeli war with Lebanese Arab militants. Both were certain the coverage was heavily biased in favor of the other side. The pro-Arab viewers heard 42 references that painted Israel in a positive light while the pro-Israeli viewers heard only 16; the pro-Israeli viewers heard 57 references that painted Israel in a negative light and the pro-Arab viewers heard only 26. For highly partisan viewers, whether they represent a country or a political party, the mainstream news media is often perceived as hostile. The cognitive road from hostile to deceptive may not be a long one.

Is Objectivity the Antidote?

Beginning in the 1920s the idea of objectivity began to grow roots in American journalism. It was an idea designed to temper a reporter's subjectivity and bias which, in turn, was expected to broaden the consumer base for the news organizations (Schudson, 1990; 2001; Kaplan, 2002).

But there has never been widespread agreement on exactly what objective journalism means. Normally, it implies one, several, or all of the following: fairness, balance, truth, and accuracy. Martin (1997) identifies three common interpretations of the term: 1) being nonpartisan by not advocating a position on a controversial issue, 2) maintaining value neutrality by stating facts without making value judgments, and 3) not distorting facts and understanding. Many journalists think of objectivity as a way of describing their method of reporting rather than a personal trait. It is something one should always strive for—knowing that it can never be fully actualized. Truthful reporting, then, is viewed as a process. Kovach and Rosensteil (2001) say journalistic truth is like scientific and historical truth. They call it *functional truth*—the best truth at the time, but subject to further investigation and change. It is more, they say, than the accuracy of a single story.

What processes will contribute toward greater objectivity in a reporter's work? Schudson (1990, p. 4), drawing on principles associated with the scientific method, suggests the following: 1) stories and statements can be subjected to independent observation and verification; 2) reporters and employers should be personally committed to public interest journalism and minimizing bias; reporters should be forthright about their biases and methods, admit mistakes, and be honest about what they know and don't know; 3) reporters should submit their work to a process of intersubjective consensus involving editors, sources, and others; and 4) a skeptical mindset for both reporters and editors should be maintained. It is important to point out, however, that in everyday practice, the guidelines for being "objective" can be complex.

For example, the idea of trying to avoid value judgments may be a worthy aspiration in many cases, but even value neutrality can be viewed as a value statement. Furthermore, writing in a value-free manner is deceptive if the story is based on information solely from sources the reporter knew were biased (Kovach & Rosensteil, 2001). Even if value neutrality could be achieved, it might not always be in the public's best interest. Edward R. Murrow was the kind of reporter others are told to emulate, but much of his reputation as a journalist is linked to advocacy, not neutrality—e.g., his critical exposure of Senator Joseph McCarthy's demagoguery and his appeals on behalf of America's migrant farm workers. In contrast to the calls for objectivity in the 1930s, MacDougall (1972, p. vi) said reporters needed to "…crusade more and should be interpretative to explain why bad situations exist." William Randolph Hearst and Joseph Pulitzer claimed they were advocating for the public interest when they exaggerated atrocities in Cuba that led to the Spanish-American War. Hearst also worked with the U.S. government to enact legislation against marijuana by exaggerating its harmful effects. The problem with advocacy, of course, is that the line between advocating for personal interests or causes and advocating for the public interest is not always clear.

A reporter's personal value judgments can be troublesome even when they are not part of his or her official reports. *Wall Street Journal* reporter Farnaz Fassihi practiced value neutrality in her official reports from Iraq, but her personal email to forty of her friends was filled with value judgments that were contrary to the positive images of the war maintained by the president and his administration. It wasn't long before her email was widely circulated on the Internet. Her reporting on Iraq was terminated because her biases, although originally expressed privately, had become part of her public record as a reporter (Read, 2004).

Another fundamental precept of objective reporting is to "stick to the facts." But what facts? Every happening can be reported with different facts, thereby creating a situation in which a factually accurate story may be perceived by some people as hiding the truth. Furthermore, different types of facts may be considered news in one generation and not in another. In the 1950s, sports reporter Bud Collins told his editor at the *Boston Herald* about some heated exchanges he had had with one of baseball's greatest players, Ted Williams. His editor told him that the readers of the *Herald* weren't interested in his problems with ballplayers—only what happened in the game (Bianchi, 2002). Today, it would not be surprising to find the facts associated with a game taking a back seat to facts associated with a ballplayer's temper tantrum.

But reporters at a sporting event might also avoid seeking facts about a "streaker" or people demonstrating for a cause because doing so would only give them the publicity they seek. In that case, people who attended the game and people who read or heard about it from the press would have experienced a different set of facts. Correcting factual inaccuracy may also be put aside when related facts are plentiful and important. Jamieson and Waldman (2002) tell the story about how the Bush Administration told reporters that Osama Bin Laden admitted on a videotape that some of the 9/11 hijackers did not even know they were on a suicide mission. This was reported, but reporters who later saw the videotaped basis for this "fact" found Bin Laden saying that not all the hijackers knew the details of the operation, but they did know they were on a "martyrdom operation." But other 9/11 stories superseded the need for "setting the record straight" on this one.

Sometimes facts need a journalist's interpretation to make sense of them. For example, a reporter may need to supplement the fact that the Giants won a game by pointing out that the win was likely to be a psychological relief for the team since it ended a fourteen-game losing streak. Interpreting the facts is a necessary part of the reporter's job and not inconsistent with an objective approach. But journalistic interpretation, unlike that of fiction writers, is constrained. McLeese (1998) contends that the pressure on journalists to write stories that are as interesting as fiction can lead to an abuse of factual interpretation, as was the case with Patricia Smith at the *Boston Globe* described earlier. In McLeese's words:

> ...the lines distinguishing fact from fiction, let alone fact from truth, have become increasingly blurred. The most ambitious feature stories are expected to emulate the best short stories—with the same sharply etched characterization, psychological motivation, evocative description, narrative momentum and moral purpose.

Even though journalists are more constrained than novelists in how they report a story, Vietnam veteran and novelist Tim O'Brien (1990, pp. 179–180) maintains that "story-truth" can be truer than what he calls "happening-truth." He explains it this way:

> I want you to know that story-truth is truer sometimes than happening-truth. Here is the happening-truth. I was once a soldier. There were many bodies, real bodies with real faces, but I was young then and I was afraid to look. And now, twenty years later, I'm left with faceless responsibility and faceless grief. Here is the story-truth. He was a slim, dead, almost dainty young man of about twenty. He lay in the center of a red clay trail near the village of My Khe. His jaw was in his throat. His one eye was shut, the other eye was a star shaped hole. I killed him.

"Balanced" reporting is another guideline often associated with objectivity. The process of seeking both sides of a controversial issue will presumably offset any tendency to slant the news toward one point of view. However, some issues have many slightly different points of view. Do all these need to be represented? Does balance mean that all points of view should be given equal weight or credibility? A reporter may try to be fair and balanced with regard to the facts of a story, but this may also mean that not all the people who provided information to the reporter will play an equal role in the story. Most scientists, for example, believe the planet is experiencing global warming, but some don't. Would a reporter be rewarded for his or her objectivity and reporting in the public interest by allowing both points of view to contribute equally to the story?

While it may be productive to aspire to objectivity, most reporters are savvy enough to realize they can never fully achieve it. Despite their best efforts, they will occasionally produce inaccurate and/or unintentionally deceptive news reports. Sometimes the perception of deceptive and/or biased news reports has less to do with a reporter's behavior and more to do with the nature of the news consumer's knowledge and attitudes. So the credibility of the news is partly dependent on reporters' commitment to serving the public interest and partly on the public's understanding and acceptance of the various constraints under which the news is produced and perceived.

Writing History

News journalists write about current events; historians write about news events that took place in the past. Both are reporters so it is not surprising that their plight is similar when it comes to matters of truthfulness and deception.

Historical events, like current events, are happenings that can be reported in different ways. Some aspects of an event are selected for telling and others are not. The past "as it actually happened" is subject to revision and reinterpretation. Santayana (1905–06/1998, p. 397) put it this way: "History is always written wrong, and so always needs to be rewritten." But, as Popper (1950, p. 450) said, "this does not mean, of course, that all interpretations are of equal merit. First, there are always interpretations which are not really in keeping with the accepted records; secondly, there are some which need a number of more or less plausible auxiliary hypotheses if they are to escape falsification by the records; next, there are some that are unable to connect a number of facts which another interpretation can connect, and in so far 'explain.'" Shermer and Grobman (2000) believe the best interpretations of history use a method they call "historical science." Among other things, this method involves peer review; strives for objectivity in an effort to control bias and/or forthrightly acknowledges biases; couches claims in terms of probabilities and the likelihood of error; and builds arguments on the convergence of multiple forms of evidence—e.g., written documents, eyewitness testimony, photographs, physical evidence, etc.

Deception and the Writing of History

A number of well-known and respected American historians have admitted plagiarizing material and publishing inaccurate quotes (Italie, 2002). In one case, Steven Ambrose, World War II historian and author of *Band of Brothers*, referenced material taken from other sources with footnotes, but failed to indicate that the material was a verbatim account. Sometimes authors are intentionally deceptive—fully aware that they are using the words of others as their own or making up facts to make an historical event more vivid or interesting. Producing intentionally false historical accounts may be motivated by money, political or religious biases, or a desire to enhance one's reputation as a historian. Deception of a less intentional sort may occur when an author is careless or inaccurate in labeling notes taken from other sources. Over time, these notes can be viewed by the author as his or her own words.

Many believed British historian David Irving was unfairly rewriting history when he claimed that the gas chambers at Auschwitz did not exist and that no Jew was gassed there during World War II. He said that documents do not show Hitler was out to annihilate the Jews or that he issued orders to that effect. In general, he was denying that the Holocaust ever existed. The denial of the Holocaust had been espoused by individuals and in books since World War II, but because Irving had written a number of historical accounts of World War II, Sherman and Grobman (2000, p. 49) say he was "arguably the most historically sophisticated of the deniers." After historian Deborah Lipstadt published her book, *Denying the Holocaust: The Growing Assault on Truth and Memory*, Irving sued her for libel. In 2000, a British court denied his charge and made him pay $3.1 million in costs Lipstadt had incurred. In 2006, he was sentenced to three years in an Austrian prison because Austrian law prohibits anyone from denying or diminishing the reality of the Holocaust. Irving broke this law by what he said in two speeches given to Austrian audiences in 1989.

Factors Leading to Distortion and Deception

Like the process of producing the news, historical accounts are subject to possible distortion during the information gathering, analyzing, and/or writing phases. There are historians who make mistakes because they don't do their job well, there are historical accounts that are influenced by the wishes of publishers and community groups that constrain and/or change them, there are historians whose writing style and choice of words seem to slant the interpretation of an event, and there are personal biases through which historians and public audiences view past events. Each of these factors could be part of an intentionally deceptive act or simply one that is perceived that way. Historians are not always aware of the biases that may lead them to produce an inaccurate historical account. But even when history writers freely acknowledge their biases, they seldom link their biases to an *intentional* desire to produce an inaccurate historical account. The following factors are some common sources of distortion and inaccuracy in the writing of history. (Lowen,1995; 1999; Ayres, 2000; Ravitch, 2003).

Creating Heroes and Glorifying the Past

Keyes (2004, p. 49) points out that America, like other cultures, has its heroes, legends, and stirring quotes, but he goes on to say: "A striking number of America's historical legends are apocryphal in whole or in part. Many of our most stirring quotations—'Give me liberty or give me death,' 'No taxation without representation,' 'I have not yet begun to fight!'—were never uttered in the form they're remembered, at the time they were supposed to have been said, or by the person who was supposed to have said them." Sometimes the history we learn is about people and events that fulfill the images we wish for, a history of "wartless stereotypes," a "Disney version" of history (Lowen, 1995). Historians and community leaders who prefer this type of history are happy to repeat old myths. Accuracy is less of an issue than the maintenance of unblemished and inspiring tales. They are not interested in revealing any imperfect or repugnant aspects for fear the person or event in question will no longer be considered worthy. This may occur, but a person's status as a role model might also be enhanced by the knowledge that he or she experienced frailties common to all human beings and still achieved great things. Students of history may also learn some important lessons from a history presented with all its imperfections. Consider the following:

- Columbus is credited with discovering America. A holiday is named in his honor. Historians use his name as a way of dividing historical epochs (e.g., pre-Columbian). But many Europeans and Africans reached different parts of North America long before Columbus and Columbus' ships did not reach what is now the United States. There is little evidence that Columbus or his crew believed the world was flat. Columbus wanted to find gold and, when he didn't, he returned to Spain with 500 of the nearly 5,000 slaves he would eventually transport to Europe. In 1499 he did find gold on Haiti and brutally forced the native Arawaks to mine it for him (Loewen, 1995).

- George Washington is called the "father of our country." He was America's first president and his face adorns the one-dollar bill and Mount Rushmore. Early in his life he was a slave owner. He is remembered as a great military general, but his career included some important military defeats—enough so the Continental Congress considered firing him more than once. He was not eager to go to war with the British and argued against separation from

Great Britain in the Virginia House of Commons (Ayres, 2000). Fleming (2005) says the winter Washington spent at Valley Forge with his troops was not severe, as is often reported, but relatively mild. The story that Washington told his father he had chopped down a cherry tree because he could not tell a lie is a lie. A biographer made it up in order to enhance Washington's image (Weems, 1806).

- Abraham Lincoln is often said to be America's greatest president. His face is on the five-dollar bill and rises six stories high on Mt. Rushmore. He is well known for signing the Emancipation Proclamation and freeing America's slaves. At the same time, Bennett (2000) says he liked "darky" jokes, habitually used the "N" word, and supported the Fugitive Slave Act which compelled the return of escaped slaves to their owners. In debates he emphasized whites should remain in a "superior" position to blacks and that blacks should not have the right to vote, serve on juries, marry whites, or hold public office. As president, he opposed the spread of slavery, but in 1862 he wrote to the **New York Times** that if he could save the Union without freeing any slave, he would do it (Lind, 2005). Pfiffner (2004) points out that good politicians work within the political realities they face and that Lincoln could not have been elected president and subsequently been in a position to sign the Emancipation Proclamation if he had positioned himself as an abolitionist.

- Helen Keller is known for her extraordinary achievements in the face of her disabilities. She was blind and deaf but learned to read and write. She couldn't speak, but later learned to speak in a whisper. She graduated from college, wrote many books, and received a Pulitzer Prize for her autobiography. She helped found the ACLU, supported the NAACP, and led suffrage marches. She was also a radical socialist who supported the communist revolution in Russia.

- Woodrow Wilson was the governor of New Jersey and president of the United States. He played a primary role in the founding of the League of Nations, an international organization dedicated to avoiding war. He prohibited child labor, established the Federal Trade Commission, and limited railroad workers to eight-hour work days. But he also sent more American troops to fight in Latin America than at any other time in our country's history. He was a racist who would not appoint African Americans to political offices and vetoed a racial equality clause in the League of Nations.

- The Puritans are often thought of as dreary, pleasure-hating people. Calling a person "Puritanical" implies they have a stern, rigid morality, believe in self-control and hard work, and consider pleasure as wrong or unnecessary. But Norton (2002) says Puritans liked to drink, play games, and enjoyed sex. She says they often wore colorful outfits and consumed large quantities of beer, rum, ale, and alcoholic cider.

Larger than life heroes and villains are a vital part of any society's history. Learning how their images were created and how those images evolve and change over time is an act of truth-seeking.

1. **T F** The Plymouth colony was the first European settlement in what is now the United States of America.

2. **T F** Only 35 of the 102 people aboard the *Mayflower* were Pilgrims.

3. **T F** The modern tradition of the Thanksgiving celebration was not introduced until 1863—242 years after the first Pilgrim celebration.

4. **T F** The Pilgrims were not introduced into the modern Thanksgiving celebration until the 1890s—nearly 40 years after it became an annual celebration in the United States.

5. **T F** Squanto, a Native American from the Plymouth region, was sold into slavery and taken to Spain; he escaped and made his way from Spain to England and eventually caught a ship back to the Plymouth colony.

6. **T F** The reason for the Thanksgiving celebration of 1621 was to give thanks for surviving the first harsh winter.

*Answers at the end of the chapter.

Political Biases

Both right-wing and left-wing political groups have tried to influence the content of public school history textbooks. Each group wants to make the writing of history comport with their values.

In one case, the Texas Board of Education stated that the history textbook *Out of Many, A History of the American People* could not be used in Texas because it contained information about prostitution that was inappropriate for high school students (Associated Press, 2002). In a section of the book called "Cowboys and Prostitutes," the book says that 50,000 women west of the Mississippi worked as prostitutes during the second half of the 19th century. It went on to say: "In cattle towns, many women worked as prostitutes. Like most cowboys, most prostitutes were unmarried and in their teens and 20s. Often fed up with underpaid jobs in dressmaking or domestic service, they found few alternatives to prostitution in cattle towns." The Texas Board of Education thought this was an unflattering depiction of the West, an exaggeration of the practice of prostitution, an implication that all cowboys went to prostitutes, and a failure to acknowledge that prostitution was not limited to the area west of the Mississippi. Underlying the desire to exclude scandalous or morally offensive behavior from high school textbooks, Ravitch (2003) believes, is the worry by some adults that textbook content will have a powerful influence on a student's values and behavior. Some teachers, of course, can only wish that were the case.

According to Ravitch (2003), it is the influence of political pressure groups that has led to a portrayal in '90s-era world history books of all civilizations as equally advanced and equally humane. She points out that this "cultural equivalence" is not likely to help students understand why some civilizations flourished and others didn't, why some populations seem forever trapped in poverty, and why democracy and human rights are important in multiethnic and multireligious societies.

Religious Biases

Different translations of the Bible sometimes tell different stories. This may be due to different judgments/biases made by the authors, translators, or religious groups who want a text consistent with their beliefs. Sometimes changes are made to reflect current linguistic and/or political preferences as in the changing of "sons of God" to "children of God." The *New International Version* of the Bible provides a footnoted alternative for the translation of "Red Sea" as "sea of reeds" or marshy area. This translation would open up the possibility that the Red Sea did not have to be miraculously parted for people to pass through as is common in the Exodus story. Those who find this problematic may prefer to use the *King James Version* that omits this alternative translation (Avalos, 2006).

People who believe that the Bible is an accurate historical account of what actually happened can simply believe that the authors were infallible reporters so no corroborating evidence is necessary. Others, however, seek archeological evidence to verify Biblical accounts (Laughlin, 2000). Archeologists have been searching for evidence to support the story of Exodus for nearly a century and now believe that there is no conclusive evidence that the Israelites were ever in Egypt, were enslaved, wandered in the desert for years, or conquered the land of Canaan under Joshua's leadership (Watanabe, 2001). Finkelstein and Silberman (2001) say Exodus was written 600 years after it supposedly happened and was likely intended as a political manifesto to unite Israelites against rival Egyptians. But for some Jews and Christians the historical truth is less important than the powerful effect of a story about freedom. Carol Meyers, a professor of religion at Duke University, says the writers of the Bible did not set out to write history using the same standards for accuracy and truth that we apply today. "People who try to find scientific explanations for the splitting of the Red Sea are missing the boat in understanding how ancient literature often mixed mythic ideas with historical recollections," she said. "That wasn't considered lying or deceit; it was a way to get ideas across" (Watanabe, 2001).

Publisher Constraints

Publishers are interested in historical accuracy, but the strength of this commitment may waver when the choice is between accuracy and sales. All high schools in Texas use the same history textbook; the same is true of California. Thus, if a publisher's book is adopted in one or both states it is a major source of income. As a result, they want very much to please the textbook decision-making boards in large-market states like these. Companies have admitted that they are well aware that state education boards can dictate content and this can lead to changes they (and the authors) think are erroneous in order to appease some board members (Bahadur, 2001; Editorial, 2002; Ravitch, 2003).

Accuracy may also compete for priority as publishers attend to other things that will sell their books. For example, a high school textbook that is less accurate historically may sell better due to "packaging"—e.g., an attractive cover, plenty of graphs, cartoons, color photos, etc. Textbook publishers also tend to copy the formats of competing books that have sold well. In some cases, that means an inaccurate or superficial treatment of some historical event is repeated or that coverage of certain events is repeatedly ignored.

Writing Decisions

Attributions of deception and/or distortion in high school American history textbooks may also emanate from the author's language and writing style. Among other things, this may involve the extent of coverage given to a historical event, the extent to which the event is shown to be interdependent with other events, the certainty with which information is presented, and the use of words that communicate a positive or negative affect.

Loewen (1995) says authors of high school history texts too often try to write in a way that will not offend anyone. One illustration of how difficult the achievement of this goal might be is found in the offense taken by some feminist groups to the phrase, "founding fathers" (Ravitch, 2003). In the process of trying to produce a history book that doesn't offend anyone, writers may produce a history that is not only less accurate, but one that students find uninteresting, superficial, and at odds with the goal of creating a citizenry knowledgeable about their country's past.

The information in these texts that is relevant to any particular event is too often gleaned from familiar sources, including competing textbooks. Without a skeptical stance or a desire to look for a new perspective, the standard stories are repeated over and over. We learn, for example, about evolution in the context of Charles Darwin and fail to learn that Alfred Russell Wallace is considered to be the "co-discoverer" of the theory of natural selection (Shermer, 2002); we learn that Charles Lindbergh was the first to fly solo across the Atlantic Ocean, but fail to learn that 80 others had made the flight before him (Ayres, 2000); we are told that an engineer who worked for RCA invented television when, in fact, it was a teenage Idaho farm boy named Philo T. Farnsworth (Schatzkin, 2002); we learn that Edison invented the electrical current, but not that Nikola Tesla developed the alternating electrical current (AC) that powers our homes and businesses and that it was also Tesla, not Marconi, who invented radio (Cheney, 2001); we are led to believe that Betsy Ross sewed the first American flag, but fail to learn that this claim, made by her grandson, cannot be supported by other evidence (Ayres, 2000); and we learn that the Wright brothers were the first to engage an airplane in sustained flight, but do not learn about the others who may have flown an airplane before the Wright brothers (Biggs, 2003; Ayres, 2000; Shulman, 2002).

Writing Memoirs

In theory, a memoir or autobiography is a written account of thoughts, emotions, people, and events that the author actually experienced. It is one person's truth—the author's. But Mencken (1924, p. 270) says: "Honest autobiography is…a contradiction in terms." Any given event experienced by the memoirist may also be experienced by others and they may not perceive it the same way. Unlike journalists, however, memoirists are not always obligated to account for different perspectives in their story. Given the imperfect nature of memory, some discrepancies with the memories and perceptions of others are expected and viewed as natural. Many authors, some well known, believe memoirs should be considered creative literature and released from a factual standard. However, some of today's memoirs by public figures will be the basis of future historical accounts and the extent to which they are valid is an important issue. The public is often willing to overlook some exaggerations and, on occasion, grant plenty of dramatic license. This is particularly true when the memoir is especially well written, the author is not a public figure, or the story depicts something the public has a strong desire to believe—e.g., a child's experiences in World War II concentration camps or a drug addict's road to ruin followed by his rehabilitation.

When a memoir is based on a person's life experiences, but the author creatively blends in fictional elements in order to make a good story, it can be labeled as such. In 1968, Exley called his book, *A Fan's Notes*, a "fictional memoir." After Frey's *A Million Little Pieces* was widely criticized for its inaccuracies, subsequent editions carried a disclaimer. When disclaimers accompany memoirs, they typically mention one or more of the following: that the time sequence of events has been altered, that composite characters have been created, that names have been changed, and/or that other details have been made up. Stephen Glass, the journalist who admitted faking dozens of stories when he worked for *The New Republic*, took no chances with his memoir, *The Fabulist*. Even though the book is about a character named Stephen Glass who experiences the same journalistic rise and fall that the author did, the book is labeled fiction.

Fiction can infiltrate memoirs in many ways—none of which, Goodman (2006) believes, is good for public consumption: "The morphing of truth and fiction promotes a world in which facts are 'subjective' and reality 'flexible.' It feeds an indifference to honesty and a belief that every truth is up for grabs. At its most extreme it lends credibility—street cred—to such frauds as the Holocaust denial." Some memoirs are intentionally deceptive and, like news reports and the writing of history, some are either unintentionally deceptive or perceived as deceptive when they aren't.

Deceptive Memoirs

The purported Holocaust memoir, *Fragments: Memories of a Wartime Childhood*, by Wilkomirski won the National Jewish Book Award. But when so many facts alluded to in the memoir could not be verified, it was determined to be a completely fraudulent account that qualified more as a novel than a memoir (Maechler, 2001).

More commonly, the deceptiveness in memoirs is limited to a specific event or events that the author may have exaggerated or changed in order to make a more interesting or dramatic story. Rigoberta Menchú, who won the Nobel Peace Prize in 1992, authored an autobiography about Mayan peasants and the horrors of war in Guatemala. Stoll's (1999) research, however, indicates that certain events in the book could not have happened as they were portrayed and others could not have been recalled from the author's memory. *A Million Little Pieces*, a memoir about the author's drug addition and recovery, became a best seller. When some of the facts in the book were disputed, the author acknowledged that his life and the book were not a perfect match (Martelle & Collins, 2006).

When memoirs focus on growing up with dysfunctional family members, it is not surprising if charges of deception are made against the author by members of the family. Some of Helget's family members and neighbors flatly deny some of the events recounted in her widely praised *A Summer of Ordinary Ways*. Members of Augusten Burroughs' family sued him over his memoir, *Running With Scissors*.

Factors Leading to Distortion and Deception

Memoirs, like other forms of public writing we've addressed in this chapter, are affected by various factors that either lead to deception or produce an account that is perceived as slanted or deceptive. The following are common:

Poor Memory

Memoirists depend on their personal recall of events and remembered happenings are not always accurate. Readers recognize the imperfect nature of memory and often grant memoirists a certain margin of error in recall. This is not the case, however, when documentary evidence can be produced that is contrary to the facts recalled by the memoirist. This was the case with Reich's 1997 memoir, *Locked in the Cabinet*, an account of his tenure as a member of President Clinton's cabinet.

Subjective Perceptions

In Helget's *The Summer of Ordinary Ways*, she says she saw her father kill a cow with a pitchfork when she was a child. Her father says this never happened, but admits she may have seen him trying to move an already dead cow with a pitchfork (Tevlin & Williams, 2005). Memoirists don't always perceive things the way others do, particularly as children. Although counter-perceptions expressed by numerous people may cast doubt on the truthfulness of a memoir, memoirists' perceptions are normally accepted as an inherent part of writing one.

Advocacy

When memoirs are written with the goal of advocating for a cause, the desire to be persuasive may supersede the desire to adhere to actual events in one's life story. *I, Rigoberta Menchú* mixed fact and fiction in an effort to call the world's attention to the tragic happenings in Guatemala. Some of the happenings that Menchú made up may actually have occurred, but they were not drawn from her experience. Some have described this work as a "biomythography"—meaning that a life story is supplemented with fictional material in order to portray a "greater truth." The cause in *Fragments* is the Holocaust—depicted from a child's perspective. It is a stirring and often believable account. But it is fiction. The author of *A Million Little Pieces* wanted to inspire others to help those addicted to drugs and give hope to addicts in the recovery. A completely true account of the author's life may also have been a best seller, but the author may have felt that his story needed a more persuasive punch in certain places.

In similar fashion, Peggy Seltzer, a white suburbanite educated at private schools, justified writing *Love and Consequences* (2008) in literary blackface—posing as biracial gang member Margaret B. Jones and writing in her own form of Ebonics—because she was "giving a voice to people who people don't listen to" (Listverse,

2010). Before being exposed, early reviewers had been overwhelmingly positive. But, says writer David Mills, "all they know about the black world is what they've read in other media," referring not only to Seltzer but also to the mostly white, mostly middle and upper class editors who approved the manuscript in the first place. Her publisher recalled the book, offering refunds to anyone who had already purchased a copy (Bates, 2008).

Making a Better Story

As noted earlier, the public often allows a memoirist a certain amount of embellishment. In fact, if they write a terrific story, some readers may not care how much of it is untrue. For example, one Amazon.com reviewer of *The Summer of Ordinary Ways* said: "Who among us hasn't been absolutely certain about the way an event transpired, only to be unequivocally told that's not how it happened? And if there is some fiction or wishful thinking thrown into this story, well—life isn't often very exciting, and I bet you can't show me ANY memoir that is without embellishment…If I were to later find out that this entire book was in fact a novel and not a work of non-fiction, I wouldn't appreciate it any less—it is that well-written." In the front matter of Judith Blunt's memoir, *Breaking Clean*, she says, "I want to acknowledge those who might choose a different version of the story than the one I tell…I've long since made my peace with the variety of fiction we call truth."

Publisher's Needs

Most publishers are primarily concerned about signing memoirs that will sell well. They don't want to get sued, but they also know people expect memoirs may not be entirely accurate. Because of possible lawsuits, accuracy may become more of an issue for memoirs by public figures. Unlike newspapers and magazines, however, many book publishers do not have fact checkers.

Writing Résumés

Résumés are not technically "written for the public," but they may be viewed by a wide spectrum of employers, recruiters, search committees, human resources department employees, etc. If the résumé belongs to a public figure, it is scrutinized by an even larger audience. To what extent do people include deceptive information on their résumés? In one study 473 out of 1,100 résumés contained one or more significant inaccuracies (Koeppel, 2006). The hundreds of firms that now do résumé checking operate on the assumption that about 25% will have some major misrepresentation in them.

Deceptive Résumés

The most frequent résumé lies deal with education, with unearned college degrees topping the list. Fraudulent medical degrees and medical board certifications are not unusual. Keyes (2004, p. 65) says that an investigation by the General Accounting Office (now the Government Accountability Office) found 28 senior federal employees with bogus college degrees. Other common résumé lies include: place of birth; dates of previous employment; descriptions of previous jobs; inflated salary figures of previously held jobs; and false references.

SARGENT © 2002 Austin American-Statesman. Reprinted with permission of UNIVERSAL UCLICK. All rights reserved.

Putting false information on résumés is not limited to any particular industry, gender, job, or salary level. Executives from Oracle, Lotus Development Corp., Radio Shack, Bausch & Lomb, Veritas Software, and the U. S. Olympic Committee have done it. A former athletic director at Dartmouth University and a former Poet Laureate of California also did it (Cullen, 2006; Keyes, 2004). In 1979, Marilee Jones misrepresented her college degrees when she applied for a job at the Massachusetts Institute of Technology. Eventually, she co-authored an important book about college admissions and became the dean of admissions at M.I.T. But she never changed her false résumé and was asked to resign in 2007 when the fabrications were uncovered. It is not without irony to note that her well-received book on the college admissions process urged students not to try to be perfect.

The web site, fakeresume.com, even gives advice on how to be more strategic in putting false information on one's résumé—e.g., rent your own post office box as an address for references or use your friends to act as references; don't leave gaps in employment history and if you do, attribute it to a tragic death in the family; order or make fake degrees and transcripts; and have a ready and believable story to tell about anything you fake.

Factors Leading to Distorted and Deceptive Résumés

Some people believe the act of putting false information on their résumés is so widespread that they would be foolish and non-competitive if they didn't do it. Some rationalize that the lies are not going to hurt anyone; others reason that they aren't telling much of a lie when they say they have a college degree and they are only six credits short. Because they are only a few credits short of the degree and they've had enough courses to feel like a college-educated person, they give themselves the degree. From the employer's perspective, it is this faulty reasoning process—resulting in the decision to lie—that makes this person an undesirable employee. The employer reasons that the deceiver has set a precedent and may decide to use some version of this same reasoning process once he or she is on the job. A false résumé may make the preparer feel better about him or herself, but when employers discover such information they think less of the person.

The line between a résumé that emphasizes a person's strengths and a résumé that is deceptive about a person's strengths is not hard to see. There's a big difference between a college student who lies about her grade point average and one who honestly reports that she had a 3.2 grade point average in her major, biology—but omits the fact that her overall grade point average was 2.6. If the question of her overall GPA arises in a job interview, she can be forthright about it and provide any reasons to explain why it is lower.

The negative impact of a deceptive résumé is sometimes years in the making. Bill Richardson, former governor of New Mexico, said he was drafted to play pro baseball by the Kansas City Athletics when he was a young man. Thirty-eight years later he admitted this information was not correct (Smith, 2005). Successful football coach George O'Leary left false information on his résumé for years, but it was only after he was hired to coach at Notre Dame that these facts were checked and he was fired after a week on the job. Keyes (2004, p. 67) uses O'Leary's situation to address the question of why an old résumé lie is so important when the perpetrator has repeatedly demonstrated successful performance on the job. He says: "... many wondered if this punishment fit the crime. The phony athletic achievements and spurious master's degree he claimed were merely youthful indiscretions, they said. O'Leary's successful decades as a high school and college football coach more than compensated. That left an important question unanswered, however: What happened to the truthful job applicants who competed with O'Leary for the many jobs he'd won on the basis of phony credentials? This question must be posed to anyone who uses an embellished résumé to win a position."

Summary

News reports, historical accounts, memoirs, and résumés are all documents written for public consumption. Some writers in each venue have deliberately fabricated information in these documents. In addition, there are factors associated with the production of each document which can influence unintentionally deceptive writing and truthful accounts that others perceived as deceptive.

Acts of intentionally deceptive news writing are not frequent, but they have a profoundly adverse effect on the credibility of news organizations. In addition, reporters sometimes use deception to gain access to information and must contend with various factors that may influence actual or perceived slanting of the news. Some sources of news bias emanate from the reporter's methods of news gathering and the way he or she writes the story. The reporter's employer is another potential source of news bias. But sometimes the perception of biased news is rooted in the biases of the news consumers—e.g., the perceptions of a particular news event by those who have a highly partisan view about that event, known as the "hostile media effect." Although some news organizations are content to be known by their biases, most try to reduce sources of bias and perceived bias by adopting methods to ensure greater objectivity and emphasizing their commitment to producing news in the public's interest.

There are many similarities in the writing of history and the writing of news. Each deals with an evolving truth, each has experienced intentionally deceptive writers, and each has to cope with a variety of factors that may inject bias into its writing. The writing of history may be influenced not only by a writer's own needs and biases, but also by the preferences of his or her publisher. Sometimes political and/ or religious groups also try to influence the way history is written.

Even though memoirists also face factors that can lead to slanting and bias in their writing, these authors often receive less sanctioning for inaccuracies and biases. Embellishment and dramatic license are often tolerated, but when the author is a public figure and/or documentary evidence is found that refutes the author's account, the author is held accountable. Although memoirs are usually thought of as personal truths, they are sometimes written with the intent of being a more general truth.

Résumé writers try to emphasize their strengths, but they are not encouraged to lie. Nevertheless, firms that check résumés report that about 25% of the time people provide inaccurate information about some significant aspect of their background and experience. These résumé lies are primarily about the person's education, but lies about previous employment and salary are also common.

Answers to the Thanksgiving Test

1. **F** There were many settlements in the area that is now the United States prior to 1620, but the Plymouth colony was not a quest for gold or an attempt to claim land for a foreign government. Instead, there were individuals and families seeking religious freedom—an appealing way to begin the history of America. It is often necessary, however, to sanitize this "feel good" beginning—downplaying or omitting unpleasantries like the settlers' treatment of Native Americans which involved killing and enslaving them, stealing their crops, spreading disease among them, and robbing their graves (Loewen, 1995; Philbrick, 2006).

2. **T**

3. **T**

4. **T**

5. **T** Normally Squanto is depicted as a Native American who learned English from fishermen and taught the Pilgrims how to plant corn and other crops, helping them survive the winter. Some, but not all, historians believe there is evidence that Squanto was captured as a young boy and taken to England. After working for a British captain for nine years, the captain helped him return to America. Historians do agree that in 1614 he was sold as a slave and taken to Spain. Against all odds, he escaped and made his way to England. In 1617 he made it back to Newfoundland, but had to return to England again in order to catch a ship to Cape Cod in 1619. On his return, he found his entire village had been decimated by disease. Given the situation, it is not surprising to find Squanto working closely with the settlers (Loewen,1995).

6. **F** The Thanksgiving feast of 1621 was most likely a traditional English celebration of a successful harvest.

Things to Think About

This chapter dealt with the writing of news, history, memoirs, and résumés. Select another venue in which there is writing for the public—e.g., science. As an initial reference, see: Park, R. L. (2000). *Voodoo science: The road from foolishness to fraud*. New York: Oxford. Identify any known acts of deception (e.g., the cloning experiments reported by Hwang Woo-Suk from South Korea) and the factors that may lead to perceived or actual deception in scientific writing.

Cut out and sort into two piles several newspaper articles that you think are: 1) deceptive and/or greatly distorted/slanted and 2) several that you think exhibit little distortion/slanting. Mix up the two piles and have another person read the articles and sort them into the same two piles. Discuss why you agree and/or why you disagree with the way the other person sorted the articles.

Identify passages in this chapter you think are deceptive and/or distorted/slanted. List the reasons for your perceptions. Ask others if they agree with you.

References

Associated Press (2002, July 8). Education board's decision draws fire from co-author. *Austin American Statesman*.

Avalos, H. (2006, February/March). Twisting scripture. *Free Inquiry, 26*, 38–44.

Ayres, T. (2000). *That's not my American history book: A compilation of little-known events and forgotten heroes*. Dallas, TX: Taylor Trade Publishing.

Bahadur, G. (2001, November 10). Board accepts book with changes. *Austin American Statesman*, pp. B1, 5.

Barstow, D., & Stein, R. (2005, March 13). The message machine: How the government makes news; Under Bush, a new age of prepackaged television news. *New York Times*, Section 1, 1.

Bates, K.G. (2008, March 21). Writers respond to a 'faux memoir' of gang life. *National Public Radio*. Retrieved from http://www.npr.org/.

Bauder, D. (2015, June 19). Williams loses 'Nightly News' anchor job. *Austin American Statesman*, p. A4.

Bennett Jr., L. (2000). *Forced into glory: Abraham Lincoln's white dream*. Chicago: Johnson Publishing Co.

Bianchi, M. (2002, July 10). Dysfunctional stars are nothing new. *Austin American Statesman*, p. D2.

Blunt, J. (2002). *Breaking clean*. New York: Knopf.

Boehlert, E. (2006). *Lapdogs: How the press rolled over for Bush*. New York: Free Press.

Borden, S.L., & Pritchard, M. (1997). News sources and deception. In E.D. Cohen & D. Elliott (Eds.), *Journalism ethics: A reference handbook.* (pp. 102–106). Santa Barbara, CA: ABC-CLIO.

Briggs, J. E. (2003, May 31). Wrong about the Wright brothers? *Austin American Statesman*, p. A1, 22.

Burroughs, A.X. (2002). *Running with scissors.* New York: Picador.

Calamur, K. (2015, June 18). It's official: Brian Williams out as 'NBC Nightly News' anchor. *National Public Radio.* Retrieved from http://www.npr.org/.

Cheney, M. (2001). *Tesla: Man out of time.* New York: Touchstone.

Cohen, E.D. (1997). Forms of news bias. In E.D. Cohen & D. Elliott (Eds.), *Contemporary ethical issues* (pp. 58–64). Santa Barbara, CA: ABC-CLIO.

Corn, D., & Schulman, D. (2015, February 19). Bill O'Reilly has his own Brian Williams problem. *Mother Jones.* Retrieved from http://www.motherjones.com/.

Coronel, S., Coll, S., & Kravitz, D. (2015, April 5). Rolling Stone and UVA: The Columbia University Graduate School of Journalism Report. *Rolling Stone.* Retrieved from http://www.rollingstone.com/.

Cullen, L.T. (2006, May 1). Getting wise to lies. *Time*, p. 59.

Davidson, S. (1998, November/December). Food lyin' and other Buttafuocos. *IRE Journal, 21*, 6–10.

Davis, T.W. (2004). *Shifting sands: The rise and fall of Biblical archaeology.* New York: Oxford University Press.

Editorial. (2002, November 28). Member made right call in voting against textbooks. *Austin American Statesman.*

Featherstone, L. (1997, July/August). Chucking the checkers. *Columbia Journalism Review, 36*, 12–13.

Finklestein, I., & Silberman, N. A. (2001). *The Bible unearthed: Archaeology's new vision of ancient Israel and the origin of its sacred texts.* New York: Free Press.

Fleming, T. (2005). Myth and truth at Valley Forge. *American History, 40*, 42–50.

Frey, J. (2003). *A million little pieces.* New York: Doubleday.

Gándara, R. (2002, August 17). Despite all the headlines, abductions by strangers are rare. *Austin American Statesman*, p. D3.

Giner-Sorolla, R., & Chaiken, S. (1994). The causes of hostile media judgments. *Journal of Experimental Social Psychology, 30*, 165–180.

Glaberson, W. (2000, July 25). Portrait of a hero under fire is redrawn. *Austin American Statesman*, pp. A1, 7.

Glass, S. (2003). *The fabulist: A novel*. New York: Simon & Schuster.

Goodman, E. (2006, January 20). Fuzzing the line between fact and fiction. *Austin American Statesman*, p. A11.

Goodnough, A. (2006, September 9). U.S. paid journalists for Cuban coverage. *Austin American Statesman*, p. A15.

Grossman, L.K. (1997, March/April). To err is human, to admit it divine. (media's failure to admit errors). *Columbia Journalism Review*, *35*, 16–17.

Guttenplan, D.D. (2000, February). The Holocaust on trial. *The Atlantic Monthly*, 45–48, 50–53, 56–66.

Helget, N.L. (2005). *The summer of ordinary ways: A memoir*. St. Paul: Borealis Books.

Isherwood, C. (2012, March 18). Speaking less than truth to power. *The New York Times*. Retrieved from http://www.nytimes.com/.

Italie, H. (2002, January 24). Slips, accusations bedevil several popular historians. *Austin American Statesman*, pp. A1, 12.

Jamieson, K.H., & Waldman, P. (2002). *The press effect: politicians, journalists, and the stories that shape the political world*. New York: Oxford University Press.

Kaplan, R.L. (2002). *Politics and the American press: The rise of objectivity, 1865–1920*. New York: Cambridge University Press.

Keyes, R. (2004). *The post-truth era: Dishonesty and deception in everyday life*. New York: St. Martin's Press.

Kirn, W. (2002, August 26). Invasion of the baby snatchers. *Time Magazine*, p. 38.

Kinsley, M. (2008, February 25). McCain and the Times: The real questions. Retrieved from http:/www.slate.com.

Koeppel, D. (2006, April 23). Fudging the facts on a résumé is common, and also a big risk. *New York Times*.

Kovach, B. & Rosenstiel, T. (2001). *The elements of journalism: What news-people should know and the public should expect*. New York: Crown.

Kurtz, H. (2009, February 20). Lobbyist Vicki Iseman settles libel suit over N.Y. Times story linking her to McCain. *The Washington Post*. Retrieved from http://www.washingtonpost.com/.

LaBrecque, R. (1997, March/April). Touch of the poet: *The Boston Globe's* Patricia Smith is a lightning rod. *Columbia Journalism Review*, *35*, 15.

Laughlin, J.C.H. (2000). *Archaeology and the Bible*. New York: Routledge.

Lee, M.A., & Solomon, N. (1990). *Unreliable sources: A guide to detecting bias in the news media*. New York: Lyle Stuart.

Leff, L. (2005). *Buried by the Times: The Holocaust and America's most important newspaper*. New York: Cambridge University Press.

Lind, M. (2005). *What Lincoln believed: The values and convictions of America's greatest president*. New York: Doubleday.

Lipstadt, D.E. (1986). *Beyond belief: The American press and the coming of the Holocaust, 1933–1945*. New York: Free Press.

Lipstadt, D.E. (1993). *Denying the Holocaust: The growing assault on truth and memory*. New York: Free Press.

Listverse. (2010, March 6). Top 10 infamous fake memoirs. Retrieved from http://www.listverse.com/.

Loewen, J.W. (1999). *Lies across America: What our historic sites get wrong*. New York: The New Press.

Loewen, J.W. (1995). *Lies my teacher told me: Everything your American history textbook got wrong*. New York: The New Press.

MacDougall, C.D. (1972). *Interpretative reporting*. 8th ed. New York: Macmillan.

Maechler, S. (2001). *The Wilkomirski affair: A study in biographical truth*. New York: Random House.

Mahler, J., Somaiya, R., & Steel, E. (2015, February 5). With an apology, Brian Williams digs himself in deeper with copter tale. *The New York Times*. Retrieved from http://www.nytimes.com/.

Martelle, S., & Collins, S. (2006, January 11). Memoir might need reshelving under 'hoax.' *Austin American Statesman*, pp. A1, 12.

Martin, M. (1997). Objectivity and news bias. In E.D. Cohen & D. Elliott (Eds.), *Journalism ethics: A reference handbook* (pp. 54–57). Santa Barbara, CA: ABC-CLIO.

Mazzetti, M., & Daragahi, B. (2005, November 30). The conflict in Iraq: US military covertly pays to run stories in Iraqi press. *Los Angeles Times*, p. Part A, p. 1.

McCarthy, J. (2014, September 17). Trust in mass media returns to all-time low. Retrieved from http://www.gallup.com.

McLeese, D. (1998, June 23). When truth gets tweaked by journalists. *Austin American Statesman*.

Menchú, R. (1984). *I, Rigoberta Menchú: An Indian woman in Guatamala*. London: Verso.

Mencken, H.L. (1924). *Prejudices* (fourth series). New York: Knopf.

Meyer, P. (1997, February 17). Food Lion case shows that cameras, indeed, can lie. *USA Today*, p. 15A.

Newport, F. (2015, February 11). Brian Williams situation plays out in context of already low trust in mass media. Retrieved from http://www.gallup.com.

Nickerson, R.S. (1998). Confirmation bias: A ubiquitous phenomenon in many guises. *Review of General Psychology*, 2, 175–220.

Norton, M.B. (2002). *In the devil's snare: The Salem witchcraft crisis of 1672*. New York: Knopf.

O'Brien, T. (1990). *The things they carried*. New York: Broadway Books.

Orey, M. (2009, January 5). The lobbyist v. the New York Times. *Business-Week Online*. Retrieved from http://www.ebscohost.com. Accession number 36005845.

Paterno, S. (1997, May). The lying game. *American Journalism Review*, *19*, 40–45.

PennyPerloff, R.M. (1989). Ego-involvement and the third person effect of televised news coverage. *Communication research*, 16, 236–262.

Pew Research Center (2013, August 8). Amid criticism, support for media's 'watchdog role' stands out. Retrieved from http://www.people-press.org/.

Pfiffner, J.P. (2004). *The character factor: How we judge America's presidents*. College Station, TX: Texas A&M Press.

Philbrick, N. (2006). *Mayflower: A story of courage, community, and war*. New York: Viking.

Popper, K.R. (1950). *The open society and its enemies*. Princeton, N.J.: Princeton University Press.

Pribble, J.M., Goldstein, K.M., Fowler, E.F., Greenberg, M.J., Noel, S.K., & Howell, J.D. (2006). Medical news for the public to use? What's on local tv news. *The American Journal of Managed Care, 12*, 170–176.

Ravitch, D. (2003). *The language police: How pressure groups restrict what students learn*. New York: Knopf.

Read, R. (2004, October 3). Reporters feelings on Iraq highlights perils of e-mail. *The Oregonian*, Northwest Section, p. A13.

Reich, R.L (1997). *Locked in the cabinet*. New York: Knopf.

Rich, F. (2006). *The greatest story ever sold: The decline and fall of truth from 9/11 to Katrina*. New York: Penguin Press.

Rothkopf, J. (2015, March 2). Fox News finally stops pretending the Bill O'Reilly scandal is a liberal conspiracy. *Salon.* Retrieved from http://www.salon.com/.

Rupp, K.L. (2014, September 19). Confidence lost. *U.S. News & World Report.* Retrieved from http://www.usnews.com.

Santayana, G. (1905–06/1998). *The life of reason.* Amherst, NY: Prometheus Books.

Schatzkin, P. (2002). *The boy who invented television: A story of inspiration, persistence, and quiet passion.* Burtonsville, MD: TeamComBooks.

Schudson, M. (1990). *Origins of the ideal of objectivity in the professions.* New York: Garland.

Schudson, M. (2001). The objectivity norm in American journalism. *Journalism, 2,* 149–170.

Seelye, K., & Lewis, N.A. (2005, May 17). Newsweek says it is retracting Koran report. *New York Times,* p. A 1.

Shapiro, T.R. (2014, December 5). Key elements of Rolling Stone's U-Va. gang rape allegations in doubt. *The Washington Post.* Retrieved from http://www.washingtonpost.com/.

Shaw, D. (1991, January/February). Profiles of deception: How the news media are deceiving the American people. *Columbia Journalism Review, 29,* 55–58.

Shermer, M. (2002). *In Darwin's shadow: The life and science of Alfred Russell Wallace: A biographical study on the psychology of history.* New York: Oxford University Press.

Shermer, M., & Grobman, A. (2000). *Denying history: Who says the Holocaust never happened and why do they say it?* Berkeley, CA: University of California Press.

Shulman, S. (2002). *Unlocking the sky: Glenn Hammond Curtiss and the race to invent the airplane.* New York: HarperCollins.

Smith, T. (2005, November 24). Billy ball: One-time prospect acknowledges draft info wrong. *Albuquerque Journal.*

Somaiya, R. (2015, February 4). Brian Williams admits he wasn't on copter shot down in Iraq. *The New York Times.* Retrieved from http://www.nytimes.com/.

Stoll, D. (1999). *Rigoberta Menchú and the story of all poor Guatemalans.* Boulder, CO: Westview Press.

Tevlin, J., & Williams, S.T. (December 15, 2005). Dark and stormy memoir creates family rift; A Minnesota writer is lauded—and accused of betraying the truth. *Minneapolis Star Tribune*, p. 1A.

Thomas, H. (2006). *Watchdogs of democracy? The waning Washington press corps and how it has failed the public.* New York: Simon & Shuster.

Tritten. T. (2015, February 4). NBC's Brian Williams recants Iraq story after soldiers protest. *Stars & Stripes.* Retrieved from http://www.stripes.com/.

Vallone, R.P., Ross, L., & Lepper, M.R. (1985) The hostile media phenomenon: Biased perception and perceptions of media bias in coverage of the Beirut massacre. *Journal of Personality and Social Psychology*, 1985, 49, 577–585.

Waldman, P. (2015, February 24). The Bill O'Reilly scandal, made simple. *The Washington Post.* Retrieved from http://www.washingtonpost.com/.

Watanabe, T. (2001, April 22). Faiths defend Exodus story as science offers new history. *Austin American Statesman*, pp. H1, 5.

Weaver, P.H. (1994). *News and the culture of lying.* New York: Free Press.

Weaver, D.H. & Wilhoit, G. C. (1996). *The American journalist in the 1990s.* Mahwah, N.J.: Erlbaum.

Weems, M.L. (1806/1968). *The life of George Washington.* 5th ed. Augusta, GA: Geo. P. Randolph.

Wilkomirski, B. (1996). *Fragments: Memories of a wartime childhood.* New York: Schocken.

Chapter 13

Visual Deception in the Public Sphere

This visual image by surrealist painter René Magritte challenges our perception of reality, but we know it is a painting and we don't usually expect paintings to be faithful re-creations of the reality we perceive with our eyes. We expect artists to challenge the way we usually see things. We do, however, expect other types of visual images to be credible images of our perceived reality. The extent to which these expectations are warranted and the extent to which they are met is the focus of this chapter.

Every day we are confronted with a tremendous amount of information contained in mediated visual images. We have the ability to record, send, and receive visual images instantly at any time and place with our cell phones. Visual images are so much a part of our society that Lester (2006, p. 415) says they help to define it: "We live in a blitz of mediated images. Pictures fill our newspapers, magazines, books, clothing, billboards, TV screens, and computer monitors as never before in the history of mass communications. We are becoming a visually mediated society. For many, understanding the world is being accomplished, not by reading words, but by reading images."

Museum Boijmans Van Beuningen, Rotterdam/Studio Tromp, Rotterdam

These images affect what we buy and what we think we know about our world; they play a central role in many professions, including medicine, teaching, religion, politics, and entertainment. Some countries sell more novels that resemble comic books than those that rely solely on words. Commercial advertising often relies on the premise, "you have to see this to believe it." Whether it is an illustration of how much moisture two different types of paper towels will absorb or a person's face before and after the use of an acne cream, the viewer is expected to believe in the effectiveness of the product because, "I saw it with my own eyes." As

Messaris (1997, p. 135) observes, "…photography supplies crucial documentation without which an ad can lose much of its power to convince the viewer…the use of photographs implicitly reassures the prospective customer that what she or he is seeing is a truthful representation of the real thing."

We even prefer ultrasounds, information about the body that is obtained from sound waves, to be presented in a visual manner. Sturken and Cartwright (2001, p. 300) contend: "It is because there exists a cultural preference for the visual that ultrasound's display capabilities have been adapted to conform to the visual conventions of the photograph and not to the standard of, say, the graph or the numerical record." The modern 3D and live video (4D) ultrasounds which allow parents to see their baby in the womb as if they were looking at the fetus with their own eyes is a popular option (Figure 13.1).

The advent and rapid growth of technology and the Internet allows people to post and distribute visual images rapidly and with ease. A 2015 Pew Research Center study reported that 89% of U.S. adults self-identify as Internet users and in 2014 they found that nearly two-thirds of Americans are smartphone owners. Trends of usage are remarkable, for example, in 2005 about 8% of adults used social networking sites while in 2014 approximately 74% of adults were using online networking. In 2001, Rumbough found 37% of college students used the Internet to meet new people, but only 11% posted a picture. Students without photos admitted

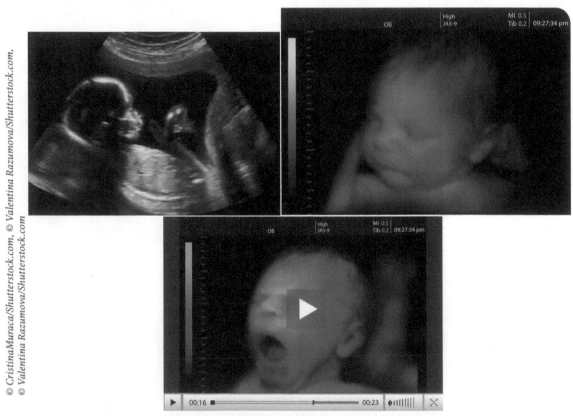

© CristinaMuraca/Shutterstock.com, © Valentina Razumova/Shutterstock.com, © Valentina Razumova/Shutterstock.com

Figure 13.1: Visual images from ultrasound technologies; Traditional (top left), 3D (top right), and live video/4D (bottom)

to lies about their identity, age, weight, and gender. Current norms for online communication generally encourage users to provide a photograph of themselves—but as Hancock and Guillory (2015) point out, people use various techniques to engage in *positive self-presentation* when posting images. Online daters who are less attractive tend to rely on deception to compensate both in the images they post and in self-descriptions (Toma & Hancock, 2010). Sites like Facebook and phone apps like Snapchat now rely heavily on video sharing, but the ease and accessibility of capturing videos allows sharing videos that portray a specific message or show the user in a positive way. As discussed in Chapter 7, deception via the Internet is more complicated than posting a fake or favorable picture, but instead occurs across many dimensions and is complex.

The Credibility of Visual Images

Why do these mediated visual images play such dominant role in our society? To a large extent, the development of a visual culture is the result of two strong, widespread, but fallacious, beliefs. One belief is that our eyes see things as they "really" are—that our eyes will not deceive us. Underlying this belief is that if we can't trust our eyes to see the world as it really is, our very survival as a species is threatened. It is worth noting, however, that visual perception by our species has always been subject to cognitive and emotional sources of distortion. The second belief is that cameras are able to capture reality; people often fail to recognize that a photo (even when unaltered) can only tell part of the story.

Myth #1: We See Things As They Really Are

Even though our eyes are subject to some of the same distortions that affect cameras (e.g., lighting and viewing location), we don't view our world like a camera. Unlike cameras, our eyes are connected to our brain. As a result, what we see is affected by other sensory and cognitive processes—each of which has the power to distort what we see. Memories, expectations, biases, and heightened emotions may all affect our visual perceptions. Sometimes we see what we expect to see; sometimes we see things that aren't even there. It has been said that we don't see things as *they* are; we see things as *we* are. Barry (1997, p. 15) puts it this way:

> ...they [eyes] are our main source of information about the world, sending more data more quickly to the nervous system than any other sense. Yet what our eyes register is not a picture of reality as it is. Rather our brains combine information from our eyes with data from our other senses, synthesize it, and draw on our past experience to give us a workable image of our world...The visual world, then, is an interpretation of reality but not reality itself. It is an image created in the brain, formed by an integration of immediate multi-sensory information, prior experience, and cultural learning. In short, it is a mental map, but it is not the territory...What we refer to as "reality" is really a maplike mental image, the end product of a process that begins with light refraction in the environment and ends in the intricate and complex dynamics of the mind.

Myth #2: Cameras See Things As They Really Are

The erroneous belief that our eyes are capable of capturing an unbiased image of reality is compounded by a belief that an unbiased imprint of reality is captured by cameras and other mechanical devices designed to record matter in our environment—i.e., a record of what a person would see with his or her eyes. Since the reality portrayed in moving pictures (videos, movies) is usually perceived as even more like the reality experienced by the eyes, its truth value is likely to be even stronger than photographs. Barry (1997, pp. 150–51) points out that those who believe camera images don't lie are ignoring all the possible human interventions that may affect the nature of the image:

> *Because we tend to believe the photograph as an accurate portrayal of reality, we also tend to read the external effects of lighting, lens, angle, framing, editing, and cropping as internal attributes of the subject. This tendency to project photographic treatment as a property of the subject is clearly one of the most dangerous aspects of the "seeing is believing" attitude, because it projects onto the subject a seeming "reality" that has no basis in fact.*

Magic tricks rely on people's belief that they are seeing things as they really are in much the same way photographic hoaxes rely on viewers' belief that photos don't lie. In fact, soon after the photographic process was developed in the 1830s, people began experimenting with ways to alter and fake images in photos (Brugioni, 1999; Kobre, 1995; Lester, 1988). In the 1860s, "spirit photographers" would pre-expose a part of a negative plate with an image of a client's deceased loved one and then use the same plate to photograph the client. This was sufficient evidence for many to believe that the spirits of their relatives were hovering around them. They had to believe that their eyes are unable to see the spirits of the dead, but this feat could be accomplished by this relatively new process of photography. Doctored photos of Germany's Kaiser Wilhelm supposedly cutting off the hands of babies were used as propaganda in World War I. Stalin's communist Russia was notorious for editing photos (King, 1997). Faking photos in American political campaigns occurred as early as 1928.

One of the most noted cases of photographic faking involved author Sir Arthur Conan Doyle, creator of the shrewd and unusually insightful detective, Sherlock Holmes. Doyle, himself, wasn't nearly as astute as his character, Holmes. He found several photos in which fairies appeared to be completely credible. This was consistent with his prior belief in spirits and other supernatural phenomena. The photos were taken in 1917 by two girls in Cottingley, England. They were trying to convince the father of one of the girls that fairies really did exist. So they cut out pictures of fairies in a children's book and used hat pins to position them for the photos (see Figure 13.2). Eventually, the photos were touted as evidence of the supernatural by groups with such beliefs. When the internationally known Doyle certified the photos as authentic, the girls refused to admit their hoax. It wasn't until 1982 that the *British Journal of Photography* exposed the fake and later the two women confessed to their hoax. One significant observation was that the moving wings of the fairies were not blurred like the moving water in the waterfall. What Doyle and others saw in this photo was what they wanted to see. They were also willing to believe that a photograph could capture what they couldn't see with their own eyes.

The knowledge that an occasional trickster or an ethically challenged person faked a photograph has not been sufficient to discredit significantly the validity of photographs for the public at large for over 180 years. Faking visual images was considered infrequent and largely the work of people with technical skills in photography. Some fakes were perceived as entertaining and some "retouching" was considered appropriate when lighting and other problems altered the desired reality. At the same time, however, attention was given to the possibility that faked photos might have a profound and negative impact in some situations. In these cases, says Barry (1997, p. 151), faked photos appear "truly sinister, particularly when associated with areas where truth is considered sacrosanct, as in justice, science, and journalism. When these areas are corrupted, the whole superstructure of the society is threatened." Even during the very early days of photography, corroborating evidence or testimony to the authenticity of some photos was required—e.g., in the important prisoner abuse trial of Confederate captain and commander of Andersonville Prison, Henry Wirz, in 1865 (Goldberg, 1991).

Figure 13.2: The Cottingley fairies

Seeing and Believing in the Digital Age

A number of things changed when visual images were digitized and computer programs developed that could almost seamlessly alter any aspect of those images. Since the introduction of the Photoshop software in 1989, almost anyone with a computer and access to the software has been able to alter recorded visual images. Currently, free software is accessible online for editing photos and videos. It has made it so that everyone can edit visual images. Messaris (1997) predicts that advertising will increasingly give target audiences the ability to manipulate various aspects of ads. In this way, social media allows consumers to interact with one another, manipulate advertising content, and avoid traditional company-to-consumer ads (Mangold & Faulds, 2009). Audiences are also changing the visual content of movies. The so-called "phantom-edit" of *Star Wars Episode 1, the Phantom Menace* was considered by many to be an improvement over the original, but many other attempts to edit the film were not (Robey, 2002; Wille, 2014). The "phantom editor" was later revealed to be Mike Nichols, a professional film editor. However, (actual) fan editing was popularized by the "Purist Edit" done to make *The Lord of the Rings: The Two Towers* more closely follow the original book by J. R. R. Tolkien. A company named CleanFlicks took it upon themselves to edit movies to favor the religious values of their Utah-based family customers. However, in 2006 a federal judge ruled that their practices were in violation of U.S. copyright laws (Mason, 2009).

Those who work with digital visual images can also create realistic images that have no referent in reality. Deceased persons and extinct species can be "brought back to life." Musicians and performing artists frequently rely on holograms to entertain crowds by bringing deceased rappers such as Tupac Shakur or Biggie Smalls onto stage. The musician/artist Kanye West has used holograms of himself during concerts. Movies such as *Jurassic World*, the *Harry Potter* film series, and *Transformers* blur the boundaries between computer-generated imagery and the behavior of live, human actors. The movie *Fast and Furious 7* relied on multiple virtual techniques to complete the movie after actor Paul Walker died before the filming was complete. Making life-like and believable virtual actors is not easy. Human hair and skin are difficult to create on computers, but modern animation techniques are making this increasingly possible (see Figure 13.3). Being able to coordinate different body parts and adjust them to cultural, regional, and ethnic differences is another major hurdle. And lighting effects too often seem unnatural on virtual characters. Today, we are finding it increasingly difficult to distinguish actual living actors. In the future, we are likely to face more digital clones of actual movie stars and even virtual movie stars for whom there is no "actual." (Hufstutter, 2002; Taub, 2003).

Copyright © 2014 by Chris Jones. Reprinted by permission.

Figure 13.3: "Mr. Head," computer generated character, chrisj.com.au for video

As a result of the widespread access to digital editing equipment, advances in the creation of virtual realities, and sharing via the Internet, many believe visual images are losing their credibility. Social media sites like Twitter aid in the prevalence of deceptive image sharing. After Hurricane Sandy in 2012 researchers used an automated system to detect over 10,000 unique tweets containing fake images (e.g., sharks swimming down the street; Gupta, Lamba, Kumaraguru, & Joshi, 2013). Mitchell (1992, p. 223) put it this way: "…because they [digital images] are so easily distributed, copied, transformed, and recombined, they can readily be appropriated (or misappropriated) and put to uses for which they were not originally intended. Thus they can be used to yield new forms of understanding, but they can also disturb and disorient by blurring comfortable boundaries and by encouraging transgression of rules on which we have come to rely." Sturken and Cartwright (2001, pp. 20–21) are only a bit more circumspect when they say: "Digital imaging thus can be said to have partially eroded the public's trust in the truth-value of photography and the camera image as evidence." As a result of the current skepticism directed at the credibility of visual images, we would expect a heightened vigilance in examining the nature of these images.

But that doesn't appear to have happened. Curiously, visual images do not seem to be experiencing the widespread skepticism that critics believed would follow naturally from the knowledge that recorded images could be so frequently and easily altered. The belief that a photo was absolute proof of an event was thought to be no longer valid once Photoshop came on the scene.

> *What attorney would risk introducing an 8-by-10 print as evidence of a murder scene if jury members knew how to rotate bodies and paintbox skin tones on their home computers? So far, nothing of the sort has happened; indeed, quite the reverse. Despite the shame visited this summer [2006] upon photojournalists for their "fauxtography" in Lebanon—darkening skies, adding smoke and fire to scenes of battle—evidence produced by cameras has never been so prevalent or taken for granted (Woodward, 2006).*

Woodward goes on to say that the belief that photographs still tell the real story of an event has not faltered in people's minds, and some photographers themselves have the greatest faith in the accuracy of photographs.

Why do visual images tend to retain their credibility when we know they can be so easily manipulated? Perhaps the relationship of visual images to deception is similar to that of words to deception. Despite the widespread knowledge that words can be used to manipulate narratives, numerous studies show that we still maintain a *truth bias* for verbal behavior. We expect people to tell us the truth unless we have reason to believe otherwise. The truth bias applied to visual materials would suggest that most people believe most of what they see most of the time. Perhaps our affinity for visual truth is like that of verbal truth in that it is preferable to the alternatives—widespread distrust, suspicion, paranoia, and ultimately a dysfunctional society.

But a bias toward truthful images does not mean people are (or should be) naïve about deceptive images. Prestigious journals like *Science* or the *Journal of Cell Biology* have developed guidelines for photos that accompany any scientific paper they receive. While the occurrence of fraudulent photos of cells and other scientific data is extremely rare, the effects could be extremely powerful. Scientists are working on algorithms to detect added background features, rotations, changes in illumination, etc. in these visual images (Wade, 2006).

For everyday citizens, understanding how visual images are faked and being vigilant for harmful fakes is part of being an effective consumer of visual information. Sometimes this may mean visiting the website Snopes.com to check out the validity of a visual image that seems suspicious, but more often we have to rely on our knowledge of how people deceive others visually. Barry (1997) calls this ability "visual intelligence" and Messaris (1994) calls it "visual literacy." Like spoken deception, visual deception can be accomplished in many ways—e.g., through omissions, additions, half-truths, material presented out of context, etc. Some visual deception, like some verbal deception, is judged dangerous and harmful while others are not. And just as we give a magician permission to deceive us, we may sometimes seek entertainment in faked visual images. So, our perception of deception in visual images varies, just like it does with verbal behavior. And, as we noted in Chapter 1, these varying perspectives of deception depend on each person's perceptions of the situation, the intent of the image-maker, and the perceived effects of the image.

Manipulating Recorded Visual Images

What techniques are used to fake recorded visual images? There are about as many ways to deceive via recorded visual images as there are with words, but the most common ways to fake visual images are the following: 1) setting the scene prior to the recording so that it communicates a particular message, 2) using the camera or other recording device in ways that make the recording communicate the desired message, 3) modifying the recorded image so that it tells the story desired by the image-maker, and 4) falsely labeling the recorded image (Barry, 1997; Brugioni, 1999; Dondis, 1973; Messaris, 1994, 1997; Mitchell, 1992).

Setting the Scene

Like theatrical performances, visual images can be staged with the use of props, costumes, and actors. The photographer or producer may also tell the people being recorded where and how to position themselves and how to act—e.g., "speak with less fluency so it seems more realistic." Amateur photographers also do this when they look for the most desirable background for a shot or tell people to smile. Having people smile or "say cheese" was not always a standard part of photography in the United States and it is still not practiced in every country throughout the world. To sell more cameras, the Eastman Kodak company began an advertising campaign that started in 1893 and lasted for decades (Kotchemidova, 2010). The goal was to show how personal photography could be fun so all the images of people being photographed in these ads looked happy and were smiling. By the 1940s the idea that smiling was an expected part of having your photo taken was firmly entrenched in America's culture (Kotchemidova, 2006).

To the extent that a person provides the expected smile for a photographer when his or her mood is not a happy one means the image is potentially deceptive. Over time the person enacting the faked smile may forget it was faked and family members may have always pretended that the photo was taken on a day when everyone was happy. It is rare that the intent of these common visual pretenses in family photos and videos is to fool or persuade the public. But staging an enthusiastic audience response to a political candidate's speech that did not occur and using it in a campaign video is. So is a so-called "reality" TV show that uses actors who pretend to be actual police officers making arrests of actual criminals without making this information known to the viewer.

Due to the uncooperative nature of wild animals, nature filmmakers may also resort to staging certain events—e.g., putting a male and female dung beetle close together to increase the possibility of filming their mating. Sometimes the expense of sending a film crew to a remote location is offset by creating the life and death drama of a particular animal using computers or moving prey into a more convenient location to speed up the process. Marty Stouffer, known for his stoic sounding voice overs and eloquent portrayals of animals on his show *Wild America*, used techniques including tying down a rabbit with fishing string so a raccoon could catch it, moving larvae from their natural resting place so fish would eat them, and using fences to keep (sometimes farm-raised) wildlife in the shot (Palmer, 2010). After several allegations of unethical behavior and lawsuits PBS canceled the show. But staging hard-to-film natural behavior is certainly a more acceptable deception than staging an animal's behavior that would not normally occur—e.g., provoking fights between animals that would otherwise avoid each other or provoking animals to attack and then showing how they are shot in "self defense" (Bousé, 2003). The most infamous case of staging was when filmmakers photographed some Artic rodents called lemmings for the documentary *White Wilderness* in 1958. A Disney film crew photographed a few dozen lemmings outside of their native habitat, put them on a snow-covered turntable, filmed them from various angles to create the illusion of a mass migration, and transported them to a cliff where they herded them off and into a river (Douglas, 1992; Maltin, 1984; Poundstone, 1986). This "evidence" of lemmings committing mass suicide became so much a part of American folklore that the term "lemming-like" has been used to refer to people who engage in self-destructive behavior. The idea that lemmings deliberately commit mass suicide by periodically jumping off cliffs is pure fiction, but millions of Americans believed the staged and visually recorded account—including your authors. Many still believe it.

Staging a shot in photography is not a new practice. Walt Whitman, one of America's most influential poets, also participated in the staging of a well-known photograph (Figure 13.4). Whitman, in an effort to show his synergy with nature, had his studio portrait taken with a cardboard butterfly wired to his index finger. He swore the butterfly was real, but he didn't explain why the butterfly was in the studio or why it was flying around in weather that required Whitman to wear a heavy cardigan jacket. Another way to stage a recorded image is to place certain objects in the background or foreground that will enhance or detract from the main image—e.g., a war hero photographed with his country's flag in the background.

Courtesy of the Library of Congress

Figure 13.4: Whitman with butterfly, 1877

Staging an individual photo seems like child's play when compared to the belief that the entire 1969 Apollo 11 space mission to the Moon was staged somewhere in the Nevada desert. This belief gained momentum soon after the astronauts returned (Kasing, 1976), but 32 years later the Fox television program, *Conspiracy Theory: Did We Land on the Moon?* gave new life to the belief that there was a massive cover-up. Staging, conspiracy theorists argued, was evident from discrepancies in the photographs purportedly taken by astronauts on the Moon. For example, the sky behind a photographed astronaut was black and no stars were showing. Plait (2002) and others point out that the daytime sun was shining directly on the white suit of the astronaut and additional light was being reflected from the Moon's surface. Thus, a very short exposure time was set on the camera. A longer exposure time would have revealed the stars, but overexposed everything else in the photo. Conspiracy theorists also believe that staging is evident in the shadows shown in the photos. For example, they argue that without air to diffuse the light and with the Sun as the only source of light, the shadows should be black and they aren't. Scientists point out that there were other sources of light, but not soundstage lighting. The Moon's surface and the astronauts' suits were the other sources of light (Plait, 2002).

There are many other issues raised by those who believe the Moon-landing was staged, and, like the preceding, they are all linked to an interpretation of photographs by Apollo 11 astronauts. We don't have to examine every one of these issues in order to appreciate: 1) how both sides of this controversy believe that photographs reveal the truth, 2) how standards for judging photographic accuracy in one environment may or may not apply to another, and 3) how perceptions of photographs can be so strongly influenced by attitudes that even the opinions of professional photographers and scientists will not change them.

Ways of Recording the Visual Image

Schwartz (2003, p. 30) points out that a photographer is always making decisions about how to record a visual image that will affect what it portrays:

> *Decisions regarding the equipment and supplies used—cameras, lenses, film stocks, developers, photo papers—shape the nature of the images produced. Darkroom procedures such as cropping, burning, and dodging provide emphasis and focus viewers' attention. Photographers employ their knowledge of the medium when they choose among the array of alternatives available—the way different lenses depict space, the selective focus that controlling depth of field offers, the rendition of light and shadow resulting from the use of natural or artificial light. The photographer decides where to stand (kneel or climb), how to address the subject, how to frame it, and when to release the shutter.*

Thus, different types of information are represented when different ways of recording a visual image are employed. Color photographs provide hues that black and white photos do not. Symbolically, black and white photography may also communicate a temporal dimension—i.e., the past. Three-dimensional visual images provide information that is not contained in two-dimensional images. The point is that it is possible to distort and deceive viewers by using a method of recording that does not accurately represent the image in question. As Mitchell (1992, p. 221) says:

> *…image-production processes make certain representational commitments: they record certain kinds of things and not others, and they record some kinds of things more completely and accurately than others…Different medical-imaging techniques—CT, ultrasound, PET, MRI, and so on—are committed to acquiring different types of data about bony and soft tissue diseases and physiological activities, and so are used for different diagnostic purposes.*

Once the type of image-recording is selected, the image-maker must decide what to shoot. Out of all the possible images to record, which should be selected? Sometimes individual shots will accurately represent the reality they capture, but inaccurately reflect the "big picture." For example, video footage of soldiers defeating an enemy in a given location may not be representative of the fact that the enemy is winning most of the battles; scenes of a horrible massacre of innocent people by one group of people may discredit the normally constructive behavior of others from the same group. A politician who has been touring a poverty-stricken section of town for several hours and seriously contemplating the obvious problems momentarily smiles in response to a humorous comment made by his host and a photographer shoots his smiling face with urban blight as the backdrop—making the politician look insensitive to the obvious problems and inaccurately representing 99.5% of his or her behavior in this situation. Abraham (2003) shows how stereotypes of African Americans can be perpetuated with visual images that show them primarily in conjunction with stories of violence, poverty, and drugs. Visual stereotyping, he says, can be particularly insidious because it doesn't proclaim itself openly. When reporters use hidden cameras, they may seek out only those images that verify their expectations and ignore contrary images. In drone strikes targeted at militants and leaders of the Taliban and Al Qaeda, pictures are often shown of the unmanned aircraft and a head shot of the leader who has been killed. The American government releases these images in an effort to appeal to the use of precision bombing and reduced civilian casualties. But reports reveal that between 2004 and 2011 drones killed approximately 2,900 civilians. It has taken up to eight drone strikes to kill a militant target and eight to fifteen civilians die for every militant killed (Benjamin, 2013). Photos of the aftermath of drone attacks are generally not shown to the public.

After selecting the image-making device and the image to be recorded, the image-maker chooses the kind of shot that will best communicate the desired message. Camera shots are like words in the sense that each type of shot has a multi-meaning potential and context plays a crucial role in determining its meaning. For example, the greater the distance from an object of attention, the less attention it is likely to get. Too many other stimuli occupy the frame. But a scene from Alfred Hitchcock's film *North by Northwest* illustrates how attention can be maintained with a long shot. The hero is hiding in a balcony above a room that contains the heroine and some villains who plan to murder her. He tries to warn her with a message on a book of matches that he drops into the room. Normally, close-ups of the matchbook and/or the heroine's face would be used to draw the viewer's attention, but instead, the shot is taken from the hero's perspective far above. This point of view gives the viewer a sense of involvement with an apprehensive hero without decreasing his or her attention to or anticipation about the distant book of matches.

Still photography, video, and film share the ability to alter meanings through the use of distance, focus, point of view, color, lighting, balance, angle, density, contrast, and a host of other features. But unlike still photographs, films and videos can move with a moving target and make an uninterrupted visual record. The resulting array of possible shots would fill a sizeable dictionary although the purpose of most shots is to elicit varying degrees of attention and emotion (Langford, 1998; 2000; Messaris, 1994; 1997; Monaco, 2000). To illustrate a few of the ways different meanings can be accomplished with different camera shots, consider the following.

Location of the Shot

Cameras are often used to capture what would be a viewer's normal way of seeing something. But since things can be seen from many angles and in many different ways, the photographer decides what "natural viewing" will be like. People who take "selfies" (with stick or without) have to decide what viewing angle will provide the image they are seeking to communicate. A person photographed from below may appear taller and more powerful or of higher status. This effect is especially effective if the viewer already perceives or desires the person to be an object of respect and/or authority. Animals like alligators and snakes are routinely photographed using camera angles to make them appear as if they are of record-breaking size and then the photos are circulated on the Internet. When a camera records a still or moving image from the shoulder area of person A, the viewer sees the rest of the frame just like person A and through this first-person perspective feels a sense of involvement with A. In the following example, the camera effectively captured a person's performance by ignoring it. In the 1935 film *Ruggles of Red Gap*, actor Charles Laughton was supposed to recite the Gettysburg Address. The Director, Edward Dymytryk, shot the scene with a camera directly on Laughton more than 40 times and wasn't happy with the effect. Then he decided to turn the camera on the audience while Laughton spoke. Test audiences laughed at Laughton's recitation while facing the camera, but praised his speech when the audience was the focus. The audience shot was used in the movie and Laughton's performance was considered so well done that he was frequently asked to deliver the speech at celebrations of Lincoln's birthday (Dymytryk, 1984).

Focusing and Close-Ups

The word "focus" may refer to the clarity with which a shot is taken or to the tight framing of the shot's target. "Soft" focus can be used to create a more ambiguous or even romantic mood while a sharp focus is associated with clarity. Close-ups are used to signal greater intimacy, involvement, and/or more importance while distant shots commonly provide the context and set the scene for future close-up shots. Close-ups make things stand out and, when something or someone is noticeable, it is also perceived to have influence in that situation. When a camera focuses on one person in a two-person conversation, the person in focus is more likely to be perceived as a causal agent. When the camera focuses solely on a person making a confession to a crime, mock jurors are more likely to judge the confession voluntary and perceive the suspect as guilty than if both suspect and interrogator were videotaped (Lassiter, 2002).

Length of Shot

With video and film, the duration of camera shots may also have meaning. Rapid shifting of shots within the same scene may signal that things are moving quickly, but rapid shot changes between two different scenes may suggest that the two scenes are taking place at the same time and that there may be some future connection between the two. When the duration of a shot is longer, it may create anticipation for what comes next or the lack of activity if the shot is held too long. Since we typically don't look at any one thing for a long period of time, long camera shots also have the potential to make viewers uneasy.

Clarity of Shot

Indistinct images may mean less importance and cause your eyes to focus on something else. Indistinct shots of Bigfoot and the Loch Ness Monster can add or detract from believability because they prohibit close scrutiny and perpetuate the myth. Fuzzy images allow the viewer to read into the photo whatever he or she wants. Blurry shots may also be used to indicate speed when something is stationary.

Needless to say, the way a person operates a camera determines the reality recorded by that image-maker. But the reality of these images can be subjected to further changes after it is recorded.

Modifying the Recorded Image

Once the image is recorded, it can be modified in many ways, including, but not limited to, the following: 1) rearranging, 2) retouching, 3) inserting, and 4) deleting.

Rearranging

Rearranging takes the visual subjects in a photo, film, or video and rearranges or repositions them in order to tell a different and/or more dramatic story. Figure 13.5 shows how the level of involvement and secrecy can be altered by repositioning the bodies of the participants. Figure 13.5 is our effort to duplicate the same series of photos containing former President George H.W. Bush and former British Prime Minister Margaret Thatcher which can be found on p. 218 of Mitchell's *The Reconfigured Eye* even though we were unable to get permission to reprint it for this volume. Continuity where continuity doesn't exist can also be accomplished with video images. For example, parades and golf matches would be much less interesting to the viewer if they were presented in real time and space. Instead, shots taken at different times and/or places become part of a coherent narrative. In interviews and debates, the "reaction shots" are not always expressions that immediately followed the previous comment.

One of the most infamous examples of repositioning occurred in 1982 when editors at the *National Geographic Magazine* digitally moved two Egyptian pyramids closer together in order to look better on the magazine cover. Given the magazine's reputation for producing "true" images of nature, the minor adjustment of the pyramids' proximity to one another was viewed by many as scandalous.

Photo rearrangement is also used to make politicians look foolish. In 2012, a photo circulated showing Mitt Romney and the Fischer family posing for a picture backstage in front of the U.S. flag. The woman's shirt displayed the R logo for his campaign and the shirts of the children spelled out the rest of his last name. A quick digital rearrangement of the M and O on two of the children's shirts changed the arrangement from Romney to his logo followed by the word money (see http://goo.gl/T87MRa). In 2001, Senator Tom Daschle saluted the flag, like his fellow

Figure 13.5: The effects of rearranging proximity and position

Courtesy of Mary Lieb

Courtesy of Mary Lieb

Figure 13.6: The pledge of allegiance with a rearranged arm

senators, by placing his right arm over his heart, but someone edited the photo by portraying Daschle covering his heart with his left hand. Figure 13.6 shows our attempt to duplicate the photo because we were not allowed to reprint it here (see also http://snopes.com/photos/politics/daschle.asp).

Retouching

Retouching is usually done to make the visual image look more pristine or to alter perceptions of attractiveness. Among other changes, it is not unusual for visual images of movie and television personalities, models, public figures, and people appearing in advertisements to have their skin tone altered, the thickness of their eyebrows or hips reduced, their wrinkles, stray hairs, and skin blemishes removed, their teeth and eyes whitened, and their pupils, breasts, and buttocks enlarged. In 2015, Kim Kardashian attempted to "break the Internet" with a photo shoot showing her nude rear-end published online in *Paper* magazine. The public did respond to the photos, but a lot of attention was given to the blatant retouching of her back, waist, and buttocks. There is no shortage of videos and photos showing "before and after" of women being retouched via programs like Photoshop (Figure 13.7). In 2014, a Utah school was accused of removing items from female students' yearbook photos such as visible tattoos and nose rings. They also added sleeves and undershirts when students lacked them. The following year, a high school senior attending a private school took to the website Reddit to communicate dismay at administrators for (re)issuing student IDs which contained face thinning, skin smoothing, skin and lip recoloring, and eyebrow recoloring and shaping. Watch the video at https://goo.gl/O2y0Dh to see how drastically Photoshop can change a person's appearance.

Photos of criminals and others who have been missing for years can be retouched in order to show what changes time has likely brought about. In June 1994, O. J. Simpson's photo appeared on both *Time* and *Newsweek* magazines. *Time's* photo was darkened (see http://hoaxes.org/photo_database/image/darkened _mug_shot). Time said it was done for dramatic effect, but it was viewed by many readers as an attempt to make Simpson appear more sinister. Retouching is also done with nature scenes—e.g., when an editor wants greener grass or a "cleaner"

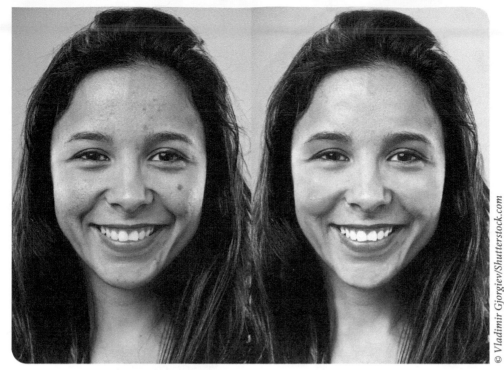

Figure 13.7: Photoshopped image of a woman

© Vladimir Gjorgiev/Shutterstock.com

image of the planet Venus. In the 2005 movie *March of the Penguins*, the snow in the area where the birds congregated was covered by defecation—but the film-makers edited it to white ice and snow to keep with the majestic portrayal given throughout the film.

Inserting

Sometimes photos, or parts of photos, are inserted into another photo or content from two separate photos are combined to make an entirely new visual image. This process has been used to put long deceased family members into a current family photo. In an official photo taken at the 1999 wedding of England's Prince Edward, his nephew, Prince William, did not smile. No problem. William's smiling face in another photo was digitally inserted in the official photo and all was well in the royal household. As mentioned previously in this chapter, movies often insert living actors into films with deceased people or insert deceased actors into new films. Since movies are designed to be entertaining, the intent of these insertions is rarely considered deceptive. But attributions of deception for other public manipulations of visual images are more likely—even though the originator of the insertion considered it a humorous act rather than a deceptive one. For example, the 1989 cover of *TV Guide* placed Oprah Winfrey's head on the body of movie actress Ann-Margaret. See Figure 13.8 for an example of this. And circulating images with the heads of female celebrities on the naked bodies of other females is apparently so common it requires special websites with the purpose of identifying the fakes. The so-called "last photo of a tourist taken from the observation deck of the World Trade Center" (see http://www.truthorfiction.com/lastpic/) was supposedly produced from a camera found in the rubble after terrorists flew planes

Left: © Alliance; middle: © Iakov Filimonov; both from Shutterstock.com

Figure 13.8: Head and body switch

into the twin WTC towers on September 11, 2001. It is believed to have originated with a Hungarian named Peter who sent it to his friends and who, subsequently, sent it to their friends and it eventually circulated around the world. A great many people believed it was an authentic photo, but those who analyzed the photo noted such things as: 1) "Peter" hardly seems dressed appropriately since the weather that day in New York was warm and sunny; 2) Only one of the planes striking the towers approached from the northern direction shown in the photo and the north tower had no outdoor observation deck; 3) Even if it did have an observation deck, it would not have been open to tourists at the time it was struck; 4) The only American Airlines plane to strike the WTC was a Boeing 767, not the Boeing 757 in the photo. Once the hoax was exposed, he became a meme and photos showing "Peter" at the Hindenburg disaster in 1937 and riding in President Kennedy's car just prior to his assassination were circulating on the Internet.

The University of Wisconsin became more diverse by inserting the face of an African American student into a brochure photo showing a group of football fans. A lawsuit brought by the student edited into the photo resulted in a $10 million settlement to be used for recruitment of minority students and diversity initiatives. Diversifying universities (in photography) is widespread. See Figure 13.9 for an example. Pippert, Essenburg, and Matchett (2013) analyzed over 10,000 photos from 165 institutions of higher education in the United States and found that the majority of schools portray diversity to prospective students that differs significantly from the actual student population.

© Monkey Business Images/Shutterstock.com

Figure 13.9: Institutions have altered photos intended for use on promotional materials in an effort to appear more diverse

In 2003 Brian Walski used his computer to combine two photographs he captured moments apart of a British soldier directing Iraqi civilians to take cover during combat (see www.youtube.com/watch?v=CwWOYDd1H-8). But when a reader of the *Los Angeles Times* noticed that the front-page photo was altered Walski was dismissed from the staff. Apparently, Walski preferrred the blending of two photographs better than any one of them and he didn't feel like it significantly changed the story of the event. But, the *LA Times* and other newspapers depend on policies for altered photographs which maintain their credibility as sources of news. When photos are altered for any reason, it raises questions about the extent to which other information might be altered to tell a better story. So it is understandable why they decided to fire him.

Even though harm may have accrued from some of the preceding examples, the originators are likely to claim that harm was not the intent of their visual manipulation. There are, however, other examples of insertions which were created explicitly for the purpose of hurting others. In fact, given the right software and the right photos, a person can be shown in an intimate embrace at a motel with someone he or she doesn't even know. Senator John Warner's 1996 campaign featured a television ad that depicted his opponent, Mark Warner, shaking hands with former Governor Wilder in the company of President Clinton. Both Wilder and Clinton were unpopular with many Virginia voters. But the image of Mark Warner's face was superimposed on the body of Senator Charles Robb who had actually been photographed two years earlier shaking hands with Wilder. The Kerry-Fonda photo (see http://www.snopes.com/photos/politics/kerry2.asp) was widely circulated on the Internet during John Kerry's 2004 presidential campaign in an effort to depict him as "soft" on dealing with terrorists. A photo of Jane Fonda taken in 1972 was inserted into a 1971 photo of Kerry. The two were not appearing together as the photo indicates (Light, 2004; Hafner, 2004).

Deleting

Visual images can also be altered by taking something away from the original—a person, an object, a sound, etc. Cherished photos of yourself that also happen to have hated in-laws or an ex-spouse in them can be preserved without the presence

John Filo/Getty Images

Figure 13.10: Original photo by John Filo of Kent State Massacre—before deletion of fence post

of the offending parties. All prisoners in the New York State prison system are required to have their photograph taken when they are clean shaven. But Rabbi Shlomo Helbrans, who was sentenced to four to twelve years for kidnapping, requested an exemption under religious grounds. Eventually, the case was settled by sending the Rabbi's bearded photo to a company that digitally eliminated the beard.

In Stalin's Russia, the deletion of personal and political rivals from photos was a common practice (King, 1997), but it has been done by other political leaders including Hitler and China's Mao Zedong. The hope was that these deletions would permanently alter the historical record of the country. Benito Mussolini had a horse handler removed from a photo where he was posing with a sword in the air while on horseback so that he looked more heroic. The Pulitzer Prize-winning photo of the Kent State Massacre by John Filo shows a woman screaming over a body lying face down in the street. A fence post was awkwardly positioned behind her head so it was deleted before being published in multiple magazines (Figure 13.10).

Labeling the Recorded Image

Labeling a visual image requires little effort since the visual image itself is left intact. Mislabeling for deceptive purposes can be a relatively straightforward and uncomplicated act. For example, the "Surgeon's Photo" of a toy submarine with a model of a serpent's head attached received the label of the Loch Ness Monster. Only after 60 years was this intentional lie revealed. In 2015, a local Fox affiliate in Memphis posted a photo on its social media page showing a massive urban fire. The comment read "Baltimore in flames," but the photo was from a fire in Venezuela the previous year—the photo spread rapidly before someone recognized it was not Baltimore. The station quickly removed the photo and posted an apology.

With the rapid speed of the Internet and social media sites pictures often become viral quickly. In 2014, Abdel Aziz Al-Atibi posted a photo he took of his young nephew and two piles of rocks he constructed to resemble shallow graves. The Internet took over and the photo was quickly (mis)labeled as an image of an orphaned child from Syria lying near shallow graves of his parents who were killed in war. When the artist realized his photo was construed as a real photo he released shots of his happy nephew from the photo shoot (see http://hoaxes.org/photo_database/ image/orphaned_syrian_boy_sleeping_between_his_parents_graves).

Internet memes often rely on labeling to create the relevant meaning intended for recipients of a visual image. Memes generally use a photo that has become popular on the web, a photo of a celebrity, or an image of some other type of entertaining element and rely on different labels to vary the context of the photo.

Sometimes the content of the visual image is not disputed, but it is labeled in a deceptive way by the message accompanying the image. For example, email scams often use the actual logos of legitimate banks in order to deceive their victims.

In 1988, a political opponent of Massachusetts Governor Dukakis showed a sign warning of radioactive contamination and charged Dukakis with polluting Boston harbor. The sign was accurate and was near water, but its location was actually near the Boston Navy Yard, a facility under the jurisdiction of the federal government. In 1999 Fox television showed an archaeologist uncovering various artifacts in an Egyptian tomb as if he didn't know what it was he might find. Actually, one of the tombs was discovered in the 1800s and the archaeologist had discovered another tomb a month before the broadcast. The archaeologist and crew knew everything that would be "found" before the show began. Wise (1990) says ABC News broadcast an unlabeled simulation of an actor resembling accused American spy Felix Bloch handing over a briefcase to another man in the context of a story about the Bloch spy case. Many viewers believed they were seeing an actual transaction between a spy and a Soviet agent. In 2009, a video of Barack Obama's trip to Russia circulated with a description about how Russian officials snubbed him. With the help of deceptive labeling the video created the impression that the Russians refused to shake the president's hand. However, in the video Obama was introducing a Russian politician to U.S. officials. Watching the video with the proper information alters the interpretation entirely. Sometimes deceivers rely on viewers to provide the desired label of the visual image based on its perceived content. For example, a photo of a brutal dictator who is smiling and playing with his grandchild may, for some, provide evidence that he is not the brutal dictator others make him out to be. When the larger context of a photo is cut away (cropping) so that only the facial expressions and/or behavior of the remaining person's image can be seen, the attributions made about the person may be very different than those evoked when the subject is seen in the original context.

Mislabeling isn't always intentional, although sometimes it is difficult to tell. For example, is the following deceptive labeling or just a poor job of reporting? An Associated Press photo in 2000 showed a man with a bloodied head and an Israeli policeman standing behind him. The policeman in the photo was labeled as the

By permission Michael Ramirez and Creators Syndicate, Inc.

attacker of the Palestinian. Actually, the "Palestinian" was a Jewish-American student who was being rescued by the policeman from a mob of Palestinian rioters.

Another possible source of misleading labeling occurs when a visual image is labeled solely according to its genre—e.g., movie, documentary, advertisement, news, science, art, etc. The viewer must then assume whatever degree of truthfulness or fiction he or she associates with the genre. However, truth and fiction are increasingly melded together in each genre. In other words, the genre labels are less effective than they used to be in delineating whether a viewer is seeing truth or fiction.

A television infomercial may be accurately labeled, but the interview or talk show format "may be able to endow the events that occur in them with an aura of authenticity" (Messaris, 1997, p. 143). A television program devoted to an alien autopsy or questioning whether the United States actually landed men on the moon may begin with the necessary disclaimer, but viewers who do not see the beginning of the show may find the content credible. In the 1991 movie *JFK*, new and fictional material was seamlessly blended into some old, grainy, black and white film from the 1960s. Since movies are made for the viewers' entertainment, they are generally considered fictional, but the segment in *JFK* combined grainy, black and white footage of the actual Kennedy assassination with similar looking fictional footage. The intent was to make this segment of the film look authentic and support the theme developed in the rest of the movie which was in color. A television miniseries about the events leading up to the September 11, 2001 terrorist attack on the World Trade Center was based on interviews and documents from the September 11 Commission's report. It was presented in the style of a documentary. But the show itself contained fictional scenes, composite characters and dialogue, as well as time compression. Former Secretary of State Madeline Albright and former National Security Advisor Sandy Berger argued that they were portrayed in fictional and defamatory ways. The problem here is the attempt to make a recent factual occurrence into a dramatic production. The TV audience, not to mention the central characters who were being portrayed, had their own view of how these events actually unfolded, but strict adherence to these perceptions may not have provided the drama and entertainment the show's producers were trying to achieve. While the overall framework for the show was true, some of the scenes within it were not. Some movies exemplify similar issues. When films claim to be telling a "true" story (e.g., *A Beautiful Mind*), the amount and kind of dramatization is bound to raise questions about what can be believed and what can't. "Mockumentaries" or mock documentaries are found in movies and on television. They are presented as if they were factual—using unscripted scenes and actual file footage to bolster the pretense of reality even though their fictional nature is sometimes revealed through comedy and satire. One mockumentary, *Death of a President* (2006), superimposes President George W. Bush's face on an actor's body and develops a story around his assassination in October 2007. Despite the fact that the movie is clearly fiction, the reality it portrays has been too forbidding for most distributors and theaters to offer it to their clients.

The label "reality television" seems to imply that the viewer will get a glimpse of people acting in natural, spontaneous, and unscripted ways. From this perspective, reality television isn't all that real, but many viewers disregard the label and watch these shows as if they were called "dramatic stories television." This perspective acknowledges that the participants on reality TV are often coached to say things that will make a good story or their behavior is edited for the same purpose. Staged scenes, reenactments, and edited dialogue are commonplace. On *The Dating Experiment* a female participant did not like a suitor that the producers wanted her to like. So they interviewed her and asked her about her favorite celebrity. She said she really loved Adam Sandler. For the show, Sandler's name was edited out, and the male suitor's name was inserted. When a couple on *Joe Millionaire* went for a walk behind some trees, the following statement that the woman had made earlier in the day in a completely different context was dubbed in: "It's better if we're lying down" (Poniewozik, 2006). In 1999, actors rented a house in Idaho and masqueraded as deranged new homeowners who mud wrestled in their front yard and covered the rest of the yard with 52 pink flamingos. This was to be part of a hidden camera special called *World's Nastiest Neighbors* (Lowry, 1999). A colleague of ours was a participant on a reality TV show, *Elimidate*, when he was in college. He told us some lies may even begin before participants are selected. In order to be selected, prospective participants make up stories to make themselves look like an energetic, outgoing, and slightly outrageous person who has the potential to generate a good story line. Once the show starts, participants are coached on how to produce conflict and action by confronting and challenging the other participants. The producers even helped select the participants' clothes for the images they wanted to portray. They even told our colleague which girls should be eliminated and which ones should be selected. Reality shows have evolved to take on other (sometimes inappropriate) elements of deception in their plots. For example, *Undercover Boss* has the CEO of a company act as a normal customer or entry-level worker to interact with the employees in their organization. A few other guises used for "reality" entertainment were a millionaire on a dating show who was really a construction worker, or a dating show where the male participants were (unknowingly) competing to court a transgender female.

Spotting Fake Visual Images

There will always be experts who are able to use far more sophisticated techniques than the average citizen to determine faked visual images. Brugioni (1999), for example, discusses vanishing point analysis, date-time-shadow sun angle analysis, computers that search for discrepancy lines or pixel anomalies, identifying marks on the film paper, and many others. Digital photos can be masked with an invisible watermark to detect alterations of the image. These digital watermarks are useful because the watermark cannot be seen without a known algorithm. If a watermarked image is altered it can be detected via programs that rely on statistical schemes (Ohkita, Yoshida, Kitamura, & Fujiwara, 2009). Although some manufacturers sell digital cameras with watermarking capabilities, the technology has not gained wide acceptance (Meerwald & Uhl, 2009). Researchers are developing software that anyone can use on their own computer to detect manipulated images (Sutardja, Ramadan, & Zhao, 2015). There are websites like Snopes.com that citizens often rely on for identifying true and false visual images. The Google image search platform (image.google.com) not only allows users to search for photos by terms, but also has a reverse image search tool where a link to a photo or image file can be used. The search engine provides web results of websites containing the exact or similar images which provides a quick way to find out if a photo might have been altered. For fun you can upload a photo of yourself and Google will find images of people who look similar to you! In addition to these resources, however, there are things each citizen can do to increase his or her skill in assessing the validity of visual images.

First, Be Alert to the Possibility of Deceptive Visual Images

Most of the visual images citizens view are not intentionally manipulated, but the availability of inexpensive software that makes the altering of digital images easy should make consumers of visual images wary. If a particular visual image is worth the time to question, the first area of concern should be the source of the image. Is the image-maker identified? Is there any reason to question the motives of the source relative to this image, whether it is identified or not?

Second, Examine the Visual Image

You don't have to be an expert in the detection of visual manipulation in order to look for some obvious signs of deception. Look for various kinds of inconsistencies.

Sometimes inconsistencies are derived from one's knowledge of how things normally work. For example, someone sent me a photo of a person carrying the metal frame of an automobile on the front of his bicycle. I wondered why the front tire wasn't depressed? I also wondered why the weight on the front didn't cause the rear of the bike to rise up? A tipoff that the photo of Senator Daschle (replicated in Figure 13.6) was faked was the knowledge that male suit coats have their buttons on the right hand side so the left side of the coat would be on top when it is buttoned. But the Daschle photo showed the opposite pattern of overlap. If you see a photo of a submarine's missile supposedly coming out of the water and there are no ripples in the water, you know something is very wrong. If something is supposed to be in motion and it is a completely clear, unblurred image, you have reason to be suspicious. If the weather is warm and the person in the photo has on winter clothes, this may be a sign that the image has been doctored.

Inconsistencies may also be found within the visual image itself. If the background is not consistent, it may mean something has been inserted; if the focus of images nearest to the camera and those furthest from the camera is similar, this may be a sign of tampering. The obvious differences in lighting and shadows between the students at the football game and the student whose head was inserted into the photo used in the University of Wisconsin brochure is a primary clue to this type of deception. Computer-generated images sometimes stand out because they are very clear, with well-defined edges. Skilled fakers may also do some smudging to cover their tracks. In 2015, the National Rifle Association used the addition of a bright sun glare to try to cover up their editing tracks. They posted a photo on their website showing a diverse group of citizens at a pro-gun rally. Others on the web pointed out it was an altered stock photo. The original photo did not show the people holding pro-NRA signage, and the addition of the glare was an obvious attempt to cover up evidence of editing.

Third, Don't Hesitate to Use Qualifiers When Talking About the Authenticity of Visual Images

Most of us have developed a sense of caution about what other people tell us. When we suspect they may not be telling us the truth, we are reluctant to accept it unequivocally. We say things like, "Well, he said he wasn't the one who did it, but I sure wouldn't be surprised to find out he did do it." Visual images sometimes deserve the same kind of healthy skepticism and caution. You might, for example, say: "I know what it looked like in the video, but videos and photos can be altered. Let's find out if the video is authentic first." Then do a little homework to see if you can find information about whether the image was altered.

Summary

We live in a society that fills our experience with the content of mediated visual images. Visual images exert a strong influence on what we know and believe about our world. Normally, people believe these images are credible. There is a visual truth bias. The belief that our eyes and our cameras see things as they "really are" is a strongly held belief by many—despite the widespread knowledge that our eyes can deceive us, that recorded visual images can be faked, and that the doctoring of visual images is increasingly accomplished with considerable expertise by everyday citizens.

The doctoring of visual images has a long history. Photographs were faked soon after photography was invented. But the digital revolution has made it possible to manipulate visual images almost seamlessly, place deceased people in motion pictures, and create computer-generated beings that are increasingly looking and behaving like live human beings. Our visual world is rapidly and dramatically changing and that requires each citizen to increase his or her visual intelligence. Some doctored visual images are funny or inconsequential, the equivalent of a white lie, but others can be catastrophic when they throw into question serious matters in science, law, religion, journalism, etc.

Some of the many ways visual images can be manipulated were identified in this chapter. They included: 1) setting or staging a scene in order to convey a particular message; 2) using a camera in ways that promote a particular message—e.g., the length, angle, and clarity of the shot and/or the distance and location of the camera; 3) modifying the visual image after it is recorded—e.g., rearranging, retouching, inserting, and/or deleting the content; and 4) labeling the recorded image in ways that lead to the desired interpretation.

The chapter concluded with some specific recommendations for citizens as they process and experience mediated visual images. Without compromising our visual truth bias, we also need to be alert to the possibility that a visual image has been tampered with. We also need to learn some basic ways to scan a visual image for possible detection and use resources that make it their business to detect fake visual images. The way we talk about visual images should also be subject to the same kind of qualifiers that we use with the verbal behavior we process.

Things to Think About

There seems to be a "truth bias" for both verbal behavior and mediated visual images. There are also deceptive visual images that could be classified as "low-stakes" and "high-stakes" lies, just like verbal behavior was classified in Chapter 7. Can you identify other similarities in the production and detection of deceptive visual images that are similar to spoken and written deception?

Why do you think people tend to trust visual images as authentic (truth bias) when they know it is so easy to alter these images?

Find a publicly distributed visual image. Go to a website like memegenerator.net or use an app on your phone to add a label. What did you do to make your (mis) labeling more believable? How might others' views of the photo be biased by reading the label instead of concentrating on the photo?

Take a photo and make two versions of it. In one version put a truthful label and in the other put a deceptive label. Show it to your friends and family and see if they can detect the deceptively labeled photo. Why were they good or bad at this task?

References

Abraham, L. (2003). Media stereotypes of African Americans. In P.M. Lester & S.D. Ross (Eds.), *Images that injure.* 2nd Ed. (pp. 87–92). Westport, CT: Praeger.

Barry, A.M.S. (1997). *Visual intelligence: Perception, image, and manipulation in visual communication.* Albany, New York: SUNY Press.

Benjamin, M. (2013). *Drone warfare: Killing by remote control.* New York: Verso.

Bousé, D. (2003). Computer-generated images: Wildlife and natural history films. In L. Gross, J.S. Katz & J. Ruby (Eds.), *Image ethics in the digital age* (pp. 217–245). Minneapolis, MN: University of Minnesota Press.

Brugioni, D.A. (1999). *Photo fakery.* Dulles, VA: Brassey's.

Dondis, D.A. (1973). *A primer of visual literacy.* Cambridge, MA: MIT Press.

Douglas, S. (1992, February 21). Scientists demolish lemming legends. *The Vancouver Sun,* p. D2.

Dymytryk, E. (1984). *On film editing: An introduction to the art of film construction.* Boston: Focal Press.

Goldberg, V. (1991). *The power of photography: How photographs changed our lives.* New York: Abbeville Press.

Gross, L., Katz, J.S., & Ruby, J. (Eds.) (2003). *Image ethics in the digital age.* Minneapolis, MN: University of Minnesota Press.

Hafner, K. (2004, March 11). The camera never lies, but the software can. *New York Times.*

Hancock, J. T., & Guillory, J. (2015). Deception with technology. In S.S. Sundar (Ed.), *The handbook of the psychology of communication technology* (pp. 270–288) Malden, MA: John Wiley & Sons.

Huffstutter, P.J. (2002, December 16). Lights! Camera! Virtual action! *Austin American Statesman,* pp. D1, 4.

Kasing, B. (1976). *We never went to the Moon.* Pomeroy, WA: Health Research Books.

King, D. (1997). *The commissar vanishes: The falsification of photographs and art in Stalin's Russia.* New York: Metropolitan.

Kobre, K. (1995). The long tradition of doctoring photos. *Visual Communication Quarterly, 2,* 14–15.

Kotchemidova, C. (2006). Why we say "cheese": Producing the smile in snapshot photography. *Critical Studies in Media Communication, 22,* 2–25.

Kotchemidova, C. (2010). Emotion culture and cognitive constructions of reality. *Communication Quarterly, 58,* 207–234.

Lam, B. (2004, November). Don't hate me because I'm digital. *Wired Magazine, 12,* 11.

Langford, M. (2000). *Basic photography.* 7th ed. Boston: Focal Press.

Langford, M. (1998). *Advanced photography.* 6th ed. Boston: Focal Press.

Lassiter, G.D. (2002). Illusory causation in the courtroom. *Current Directions in Psychological Science, 11,* 204–208.

Lester, P.M. (1988). Faking images in photojournalism. *Media Development, 1,* 41–42.

Lester, P.M. (2006). *Visual communication: Images with messages.* Belmont, CA: Wadsworth.

Light, K. (2004, February 28). Fonda, Kerry and photo fakery. *Washington Post,* p. A21.

Lowry, B. (1999, May 16). "Inside Edition" vs. Fox: When reality attacks! *Austin American Statesman,* pp. E6–7.

Maltin, L. (1984). *The Disney films.* New York: Crown.

Mangold, W.G., & Faulds, D.J. (2009). Social media: The new hybrid element of the promotion mix. *Business horizons, 52,* 357–365.

Mason, M. (2009). *The pirate's dilemma: How youth culture is reinventing capitalism.* New York: Simon & Schuster.

Meerwald, P., & Uhl, A. (2009). Watermarking of raw digital images in camera firmware: embedding and detection. In T. Wada, F. Huang, & S. Lin (Eds.), *Advances in image and video technology* (pp. 340–348). Berlin: Springer.

Messaris, P. (1994). *Visual literacy: Image, mind, and reality.* Boulder, CO: Westview.

Messaris, P. (1997). *Visual persuasion: The role of images in advertising.* Thousand Oaks, CA: Sage.

Mitchell, W.J. (1992). *The reconfigured eye: Visual truth in the post-photographic era.* Cambridge, MA: MIT Press.

Monaco, J. (2000). *How to read a film.* New York: Oxford University Press.

Ohkita, K., Yoshida, M., Kitamura, I., & Fujiwara, T. (2009). Improving capability of locating tampered pixels of statistical fragile watermarking. In A. Ho, Y. Shi, H. Kim, & M. Barni (Eds.), *Digital Watermarking* (pp. 279–293). Berlin: Springer.

Palmer, C. (2010). *Shooting in the wild: An insider's account of making movies in the animal kingdom.* San Francisco: Sierra Club Books.

Plait, P.C. (2002). *Bad astronomy: Misconceptions and misuses revealed, from astrology to the Moon landing "hoax."* New York: Wiley & Sons.

Pippert, T.D., Essenburg, L.J., & Matchett, E.J. (2013). We've got minorities, yes we do: visual representations of racial and ethnic diversity in college recruitment materials. *Journal of Marketing for Higher Education, 23,* 258–282.

Poniewozik, J. (2006, February 6). How reality tv fakes it. *Time Magazine, 167,* 60–62.

Poundstone, W. (1986). *Bigger secrets.* Boston: Houghton Mifflin.

Robey, T. (2002, January 26). The birth of a new film phenomenon—the amateur cut. *The Daily Telegraph,* Retrieved January 18, 2004 from LexisNexis Academic: http://web.lexis-nexis.com

Rumbough, T. (2001). The development and maintenance of interpersonal relationships through computer-mediated communication. *Communication Research Reports, 18,* 223–229.

Schwartz, D. (2003). Professional oversight: Policing the credibility of photojournalism. In L. Gross, J. S. Katz & J. Ruby (Eds.), *Image ethics in the digital age* (pp. 27–51). Minneapolis, MN: University of Minnesota Press.

Sturken, M., & Cartwright, L. (2001). *Practices of looking: An introduction to visual culture.* New York: Oxford University Press.

Sutardja, A., Ramadan, O., & Zhao, Y. (2015). *Forensic methods for detecting image manipulation - copy move* (Technical Report No. UCB/EECS-2015-84). University of California at Berkeley.

Taub, E.A. (2003, September 4). It's tricky, grafting Brando's sneer to Bogart's shrug. *New York Times* p. G8.

Toma, C.L., & Hancock, J.T. (2010). Looks and lies: The role of physical attractiveness in online dating self-presentation and deception. *Communication Research, 37,* 335–351.

Wade, N. (2006, January 24). It may look authentic; here's how to tell it isn't. *New York Times.*

Wille, J. (2014). Fan edits and the legacy of The Phantom Edit. *Transformative Works and Cultures, 17.* http://dx.doi.org/10.3983/twc.2014.0575.

Wise, D. (1990, May 13). The Felix Bloch affair. *New York Times Magazine,* 42.

Woodward, R.B. (2006, September 19). One 9/11 picture, thousands of words: Rorschach of meanings. *Wall Street Journal,* p. D6.

What Does It All Mean?

We wrote this book because we believe deception and truth telling are central to the understanding and effective execution of human interaction. Therefore, learning about the issues associated with deception and truth telling should better equip citizens to evaluate the integrity of messages directed at them and to create messages with these standards in mind. But books mean different things to different people and the "take home points" aren't always what the author intended. Readers of this book, like the readers of any book, will mentally sort through the many impressions they've had along the way and settle on a few that seem to be personally useful in making sense of the book. We can only hope that some of the following ideas will be considered during that process:

- *Deception is a form of communication that is represented in the behavior of all living organisms on Earth.* It is often critical to the survival of a species. It has been a part of human behavior for millions of years. It is part of our communicative repertoire and it can be a useful or disastrous strategy for achieving our goals. Since we perceive that most of our deceptive messages serve useful purposes, there is no reason to believe people will ever stop being deceptive. But there is also no reason to believe that the continued presence of deception in our social world, no matter how harmful it may appear, will lead our society to ruin. That's because the detectors of lies are constantly working on ever more accurate and effective ways to detect, prohibit, and punish those whose lies are not sanctioned. Still, false accusations of deception will continue to be a part of our social world due to the imperfect nature of lie-detection methods. One of the most effective deterrents to harmful lies may be a citizenry that understands the complex nature of deception and has thought about ways to cope with it. Nevertheless, we can expect some liars will continue to alter their behavior in ever more subtle ways to avoid detection. This is not surprising since it is the same process used by other species to maintain their survival. Most people, however, will tell the truth as they perceive it, most of the time. And despite the vulnerabilities associated with the truth bias, people realize they profit more by assuming that most messages they process are truthful.

- *Lying, deception, and truth are complex phenomena and not always easy to understand.* Each is communicated symbolically and symbols like language and/or visual images can be manipulated in seemingly endless ways. But there are still plenty of popular books, magazines, and tabloids that offer articles bent on simplifying the phenomena. They print articles on the "five easy ways to identify lies" or prescribe honesty in relationships as if everyone had the same referent for the term. Deception and truth are uncomplicated for those who like to neatly divide their experiences. For them, honesty is good; deception is bad. The fact that genres like memoirs and documentaries can no longer be counted on to be entirely truthful and truthful events are sometimes blended into fictitious accounts is frustrating for those with this either-or perspective. Sometimes heated arguments in which behavior is summarily categorized as honest or deceptive can take on a more rational tone if the discussion focuses more on specific aspects of the transaction like the context, relationship, and intent of the communicators. It is difficult for people who understand deception and truth telling as clearly distinct points on either end of a continuum to appreciate the paradoxical nature that sometimes characterizes the way we deal with these issues. For example, people who describe themselves as honest even though they freely admit they sometimes lie; people who say they do not like dishonest politicians, friends, or spouses but continue to support them in the face of their dishonesty; people who say they value honesty above all else, but not if it means being disloyal; or people who are well aware of the complexity, subtlety, and uncertainty associated with acts of deception and honesty, but act as if there were no such contingencies when talking to their children or someone they dislike, or they are trying to mobilize a mass of people during a crisis.

- *The sheer amount of information and the diversity of information sources available today make the ability to identify reliable information especially important.* Good decisions require reliable information and the identification of reliable information requires knowledge and vigilance. According to testing by the Educational Testing Service, only 52% of 6,300 high school seniors and college freshmen were able to judge accurately the objectivity of a website (Katz, 2007). Using the Internet is not the same as using it wisely. Despite our tendency to trust much of the information we encounter, skilled consumers of information are also aware of techniques used by con artists and message anomalies that create suspicion. Citizens should be fully aware of the "warning signs of trickery" and ways to cope with today's "spin doctors" detailed by Jackson and Jamieson (2007). They should also know other sources like Snopes.com and FactCheck.org that can help them identify reliable information.

- *Attending to and evaluating deception and honesty in the messages others send can increase one's sensitivity to such issues associated with their own messages.* Unfortunately, this sensitivity does not always lead to the production of messages that meet the standards we apply to others. Some will always prefer the irresponsible ease of a "do as I say, not as I do" philosophy. Compounding the difficulty in creating responsible messages is the fact that effective communication strategies (eliciting the desired audience response) and deceptive communication strategies are not always easy to distinguish. What is public relations spin or an effective marketing strategy to one person may be deceptive manipulation to another. However, conscientious communicators who are knowledgeable about lying and deception and concerned about what is right and wrong are likely to grapple with these issues in a more productive way. Of course, knowledge of anything can be used for good or ill so some may choose to use their knowledge to manipulate others for their own gain.

Learning the truth about deception may be a long journey. Reading this book is but one step in what can be a lifetime of learning. It will involve learning from others and from your own communication successes and failures. You may feel very certain about your understanding of deception and truth telling at one point in time and very uncertain at another. Nevertheless, journeys involving continued learning are inherently rewarding, if not always pleasant.

References

Katz, I.R. (2007). ETS research finds college students fall short in demonstrating ICT literacy: National policy council to create national standards. *College & Reference Libraries News, 68*, 35–37.

Jackson, B., & Jamieson, K.H. (2007). *UnSpun: Finding facts in a world of disinformation.* New York: Random House.

Author Index

Subject Index

Political honesty, public demand
  of, 321–325
    absolutism, 323–324
    consequences of distrust, 322–323
    diminishing trust, 321–322
    tolerance for deception, 324–325
    See also presidential lies; public lies
Polls, 22, 32, 42, 321–322, 342
Polygraphs, 29, 166, 281–290
    accuracy of, 287–289
    administration of, 282–283
    beating using countermeasures,
      289–290
    evolution of, 282
    interpretation of, 287
    procedures followed, 284–287
        Control Question Test, 284–286
        Guilty Knowledge Test, 286–287
    results as evidence, 283
    working of, 284
Ponzi scheme, 208
Popoff, Peter, 228–229
Poynter Institute, 345–346
PR Watch, 320
Prepackaged news, 319–320
Presidential lies, 331–334
    justified lies, 331
    lies to cover up, 332–333
    lies of policy deception, 333–334
    lies to prevent embarrassment, 332
    minor lies, 331
    See also political honesty, public
      demand of; public lies
Prince, The, 51
Prison psychosis, 209–210
Probing effect, 257, 258
Projection, 151
Prolific liars, 203–205
Prosaically lies, 106
Pseudo-events, 318–319
Pseudologia fantastica, 205–206
Psychic phenomena, 230
Psychic surgery, 230

Psychological disorders, 205–210
    common characteristics, 209
    See also individual disorders
Psychological Stress Evaluator
  (PSE), 291
Psychopathy, 206–207
Public lies
    adapting to multiple audiences, 314
    blood relatives of deception,
      327–330
    detection responsibility, 320–321
    downside of deception, 326–327
    information control, 314–317
    message distribution, 317–320
        prepackaged news, 319–320
        pseudo-events, 318–319
        public vigilance, 334–335
        staged events, 317–318
    requirement of deception, 326
    role of deception in political dis-
      course, 325–326
    See also political honesty, public
      demand of; presidential lies
"Purist Edid", 379
"Pyramid scheme", 229

R

Rabies virus, 74
Rader, Dennis, 207
"Radical" honesty, 33, 45
    justifications for, 45–49
Raising Kids with Character (2006), 64
Rationalization, 141, 147–149, 151
Reagan, 317
Reality Monitoring (RM), 299
Reality television, 394
Reasons for lying, 170–171
"Reciprocal altruism", 3–4
Recklessness, 154
Redirecting 191
Reid technique, 268

Relationship stories, 211–212
Repression, 149–150
Resume writing, 363–365
    deceptive, 363–364
    factors leading to, 364–365
Rhinovirus, 75
Roberts, Oral, 228–229
Robertson, Pat, 228–229
Rolling Stone, 215
Romance, 176–178
Romney, Mitt, 316, 387
Roosevelt (President), 54
Rose, Pete, 149
Rowling, J.K., 19

S

Sales and investments scams, 229–230
San Blas Kuna, 5
Scams, 22–23
Schizophrenia, 210, 214
*Scientific Content Analysis
  (SCAN)*, 299
Scruton, Roger, 19
Selective lies, 59
Self, meaning of, 131–132
Self-consistency bias, 145–146
Self-deception, 60
    advantages and disadvantages
      of, 152–154
    content requirements of, 135–138
    examples of, 129–131
    intentional, 134–135
    levels of awareness, 134
    meaning of deception, 132–133
    meaning of self, 131–132
    and other-deception, 132–133
    reasons for, 138–143
        to enhance deception skills,
          141–142
        to enhance physical and mental
          health, 142–143

to enhance self-esteem, 138–140

to reduce cognitive dissonance, 140–141

unintentional, 134–135

workings of, 143–152

confirmation bias and patternicity, 143–144

psychological threat, 146–147

self-consistency bias, 145–146

self-defense mechanisms, 147–152

self-enhancement bias, 144–145

Self-denial, 146

Self-distraction, 149

Self-enhancement bias, 144–145

Self-esteem, 138–140

Self-justification, 146

Self-persuasion, 145–146

Self-presentation, positive, 377

Self-preservation, 176

Sexual abuse, of children, 31

Sexual affairs, 54

Sign language, in apes, 89–90

Simpson, O.J., 388

Situation, perceptions of, 12–13

Snakes, 83

Snopes.com, 381, 395

Snowden, Edward, 60–61, 250, 333–334

Social media, 22–23, 105

variations in behavior of liars, 168–169

Social norms, understanding, 100

"Social proof", 23

Social skills, and deceit, 8,

Sociopathy, 206–207

Sodium amytal, 295–296

Sodium pentothal, 295–296

Sokol, Alan, 235

Solomon (Robert), 3

Spanish Prisoner, 226

Spencer, Richard, 213

Spies, 219–220

Spin, 190–191

half-truths, 190–191

redirecting 191

"Spirit photographers", 378

Sports, 179–180

Staged events, 317–318

Star Wars Episode 1, the Phantom Menace, 379

Statement Validity Analysis (SVA), 298–299

Steven, Colbert, 20

Stolen Valor Act (2013), 213

Stomach, as stress indicator, 292–293

Stormfront, 206

Street cons, 228

Stress, as an indicator of lying, 291–293

in eyes, 292

in mouth, 293

in stomach, 292–293

in voice, 291–292

Students, 42–43, 44

Subversive masquerade, 178

Surveillance programs, 60–61

Surveys, 172

contradictions, 44

on occupation and honesty, 22

lying amongst students, 42–43, 44

See also experiments

Surveys, 321–322

on deceit, 6–7, 8, 172

Synthetic identity theft, 224

T

Taft, Bob, 320

Theory of cognitive development, 98

"Theory of mind", 98, 101

Thermal imaging, 292

Tiger swallowtail butterfly, 78–79

Torture, 266

Tourette's syndrome, 210

Trickery, 88

Truster, 292

"Truth bias", 23

Truth serum, 295–296

Truth

based on feelings, 20–21

based on observation, 25–31

and characteristics of observer, 26–28

conditions of observation, 28–29

"constant", 32

devices used, 29

memory, 29–31

based on reasoning, 23–25

incorrect inferences, 24–25

based on what we are told, 21–23

and certainty, 19, 31–32

defined, 19

telling of, 32–34

circumspection in, 33–34

validity of, 34–35, 44

Trypanosome virus, 75

Tunnel vision, 287

Twitter, 23, 380

U

"Unenlightened disease", 43

Unintentional self-deception, 134–135

Unique interpretations, 329

Unwinding, The, 7

USA PATRIOT Act, 61

V

Velazquez, Loreta Janeta, 220–221

Venus fly trap, 76

Veracity effect, 254

"Veracity principle", 50

Verbal clues to deception, assisted analyses of, 298–299

"Verbal overshadowing", 29

Video news release (VNR), 319–320, 346